A History of Market Perfoi

This exciting new volume examines the development of market performance from antiquity until the beginning of the twentieth century.

Efficient market structures are agreed by most economists to serve as evidence of economic prosperity, and to be prerequisites for further economic growth. However, this is the first study to examine market performance as a whole, over such a large time period. Presenting a hitherto unknown and inaccessible corpus of data from ancient Babylonia, this international set of contributors are for the first time able to offer an in-depth study of market performance over a period of 2,500 years.

The contributions focus on the market of staple crops, as they were crucial goods in these societies. Over this entire period, all papers provide a similar conceptual and methodological framework resting on a common definition of market performance combined with qualitative and quantitative analyses resting on new and improved price data. In this way, the book is able to combine analysis of the Babylonian period with similar work on the Roman, early and late medieval and early modern period.

Bringing together input from Assyriologists, historians specializing in ancient history, economic historians and economists, this volume will be crucial reading for all those with an interest in ancient history, economic history and economics.

R.J. van der Spek is Professor of Ancient Mediterranean and West Asian History at VU University, Amsterdam.

Bas van Leeuwen is Senior Researcher at Warwick University, UK, and a Post-doctoral Researcher at VU University, Amsterdam and Utrecht University, the Netherlands.

Jan Luiten van Zanden is Faculty Professor of Global Economic History at Utrecht University, the Netherlands.

Routledge Explorations in Economic History
Edited by Lars Magnusson, Uppsala University, Sweden

A History of Market Performance

From Ancient Babylonia
to the modern world

**Edited by R.J. van der Spek,
Bas van Leeuwen and
Jan Luiten van Zanden**

Routledge
Taylor & Francis Group

LONDON AND NEW YORK

First published 2015 by Routledge

2 Park Square, Milton Park, Abingdon, Oxfordshire OX14 4RN
52 Vanderbilt Avenue, New York, NY 10017

Routledge is an imprint of the Taylor & Francis Group, an informa business

First issued in paperback 2019

British Library Cataloguing in Publication Data
A catalogue record for this book is available from the British Library

Library of Congress Cataloging-in-Publication Data
A catalogue record for this book has been requested

ISBN: 978-0-415-63544-8 (hbk)
ISBN: 978-0-367-86730-0 (pbk)

Typeset in Times New Roman
by Sunrise Setting Ltd, Paignton, UK

Contents

Figures

Tables

Preface

The Babylonian market project

This book is the synthesis of a research project 'On the efficiency of markets in pre-industrial societies: the case of Babylonia.' The project was provoked by the fact that since 1996 a huge dataset of several thousand commodity prices from ancient Iraq has become available and accessible, derived from Babylonian cuneiform texts, in particular the Babylonian astronomical diaries. These documents not only contain the notation of celestial phenomena, but also notes on historical events on earth, the level of the Euphrates and a detailed registration of prices of food and wool. With this dataset it became possible to carry out statistical and econometric research and to stretch out the history of price formation, market efficiency and market performance to the first millennium BC.

The project, started in 2007, was funded by the Netherlands Organization for Scientific Research (NWO) and directed by Bert van der Spek at Vrije Universiteit (VU University), Amsterdam in cooperation with Jan Luiten van Zanden (University of Utrecht and the International Institute for Social History in Amsterdam). Postdoctoral researcher Bas van Leeuwen applied modern econometric theory to the evidence of the price formation and two PhD students, Joost Huijs and Reinhard Pirngruber, studied the impact of empire on the development of prices in Hellenistic and Parthian Babylonia, using the evidence of prices and historical events described in the astronomical diaries.

On 19–21 May 2011 an 'Academy Colloquium', funded by the Royal Netherlands Academy of Arts and Sciences (KNAW), was held in the 'Trippenhuis', the headquarters of the KNAW in Amsterdam, in which scholars specializing in Ancient Babylonian and Mediterranean history cooperated with economic historians of later periods and specialists in econometrics and statistics. The participants from very different fields of research indeed (Assyriology, ancient history, economic history from the Middle Ages to the modern world, econometric theory) found the meeting very special and inspiring. One of the specialists in mediaeval economic history was delighted that he for once represented the 'later' periods, instead of always being connected with the earliest times.

The present volume is in a way the result of this conference, though contributors to this book do not exactly match the participants of the colloquium. Another result of this conference is a special issue (57/2, 2014) of the *Journal of the Economic and Social History of the Orient*, edited by Bas van Bavel (University of Utrecht), on 'Emerging and declining markets for land, labour and capital: Iraq from c. 700 BC to c. 1100 AD' (with contributions by Michael Jursa on the Neo-Babylonian and Persian empires, Bert van der Spek on Hellenistic and Parthian Babylonia, Khodadad Rezakhani Michael Morony on the Sasanian empire and Bas van Bavel, Michele Campopiano and Jessica Dijkman on early Islamic Iraq).

A file containing the Babylonian prices is uploaded on the website of the International Institute for Social History (IISH) (www.iisg.nl/hpw/babylon.php) and also on the website of the 'Early Economies Hub' of the *Centre for Global Economic History* in Utrecht (www.cgeh.nl/early-economies-hub). For our own research we constructed a dataset of daily prices between c. 480 and 61 BC and converted it into a monthly dataset for the period 560–60 BC, adding the data from the studies of Vargyas (2001) and Jursa (2010); hence we compiled data covering half a millennium of price history in ancient Iraq. The monthly dataset is appended at the end of this book.

The project was embedded in various other projects concerning economic history and the history of prices. The idea to include the Babylonian price data in a more general history of prices was suggested by Jan Luiten van Zanden, who had started to collect a database of prices and wages on the website of the IISH, www.iisg.nl/hpw/. The Babylonian database was uploaded to this site in 2005 and has also become part of 'Clio-Infra' (www.clio-infra.eu/), the large-scale project on the collection and making available of historical data for academic purposes. Part of this project was a conference, 'Towards a Global History of Prices and Wages', which convened in Utrecht on 19–21 August 2004.

Bert van der Spek
Bas van Leeuwen
Jan Luiten van Zanden

Acknowledgements

This research project was funded by the Netherlands Organization for Scientific Research (€500,000) and the Royal Netherlands Academy of Arts and Sciences (KNAW) (EUR 20,000).

We profited greatly from cooperation with the so-called START project, funded by the Austrian Research Fund (FWF), 'Economic History of Babylonia in the First Millennium BC', conducted by Michael Jursa in Vienna between 2002 and 2009. There has been an enduring cooperation of both research groups with Sitta von Reden (Freiburg) and Dominic Rathbone (London) for the study of comparative price history in the Ancient Mediterranean. Bert van der Spek participates in the research group 'Impact of Empire' of the National Research School in Classical Studies in the Netherlands (OIKOS).

This project has been a prime example of international and interdisciplinary research and we thank all contributors for their endeavours to make this successful.

1 An introduction

Markets from Ancient Babylonia to the modern world

R.J. van der Spek, Bas van Leeuwen and Jan Luiten van Zanden

Introduction

Markets are fundamental institutions of modern society, and have since Adam Smith's *Wealth of Nations*, published in 1776, been held responsible for static efficiency resulting from specialization (e.g. McMillan 2002) as well as for dynamic efficiency caused by innovation (e.g. Baumol 2002). This importance of markets for economic development has led one author (Studer 2008: 395) to argue that 'most economists and economic historians would agree that efficient market structures are both evidence of economic sophistication and prosperity as well as prerequisites for further economic growth'. Markets appear very early in recorded history (see the various contributions on the Babylonian economy in this volume), have obviously evolved over time, and have come to dominate many forms of social and economic interaction in recent times. Yet what is missing is a broad overview of the way in which markets changed in the very long run; in particular, there is hardly any relevant literature trying to compare 'early' forms of market exchange, as they came into existence during antiquity, with markets that functioned during the 'modern' period (from the late Middle Ages to the present).

This volume sets out to ask these questions: how did markets perform and how were they embedded in social and political institutions?

Although there is a broad agreement that markets are important for social and economic development, it is difficult to determine exactly what markets are. Even though the study of markets has gained more attention since the accompanying study of economic institutions and structures necessary for economic growth have been pushed further and further back in time, its definition still often depends on scientific field and/or scholarly tradition. Perhaps the best example is the debate between formalist and substantivist approaches to ancient economic history, which has hindered a role for economic historians working on the ancient world in more recent debates about the working of markets. The substantivist stance, advocated by Polanyi (1944, 1957 and 1968), holds that ancient economy cannot be studied with standard modern economic principles such as the working of the market, the profit-maximizing and want-satisfying logic and rationality of the *homo oeconomicus*, as the formalist economic view demands. Economy was embedded in social rules, customs, status, reciprocity, rather than in the hard rules of the market economy with prices set by the law of supply and demand.

Thanks to the influential book of Moses Finley, *The Ancient Economy* (1973), research on the ancient world has long been dominated by the substantivist approach. Therefore, although the Finleyan theory was not always shared, the basically non-quantitative Finleyan research methodology was almost universally applied in ancient history. This led to a divide between economic history and ancient history, the former largely applying economic theory and quantifiable analyses and the latter focusing on social and descriptive history. Moreover, it prevented the possibility of analysing ancient markets by modern economic theoretical and quantitative methods, as those markets were not supposed to be a 'market economy' (see for example Renger 1994, 2005).

Historians of antiquity searched for a way to escape the substantivist–formalist debate by developing new 'modes of production'. That is, they searched for a way to describe modes of exchange without calling it a market. We may refer to concepts such as the 'tributary mode of production' (Briant 1982), the 'bazaar economy' (Bang 2008) and the 'commercialization model', as advocated by Jursa (2010: 783ff and Chapter 5, this volume), borrowed from Hatcher and Bailey (2001: 121). Actually the older concept of the Marxist 'Asiatic mode of production' and Polanyi's 'marketless economy' still lurk behind many of these studies. Nowadays the insight is growing that the opposition between the 'primitivist' and the 'modernist' approach obscures the fact that neither ancient nor modern man is always fully acting as *homo oeconomicus* and that the formalist approach of the ancient economy may lead to the conclusion that in some respects it was primitive and in other aspects remarkably modern.[1]

A practical impediment to a formalist approach of ancient economies is the lack of quantifiable data, which has prevented a thorough statistical analysis. It is therefore no surprise that, from a quantitative point of view, the discussion on the efficiency of markets largely focuses on the period from the late Middle Ages onwards when data start to become more abundant. Yet ancient historians increasingly acknowledge the necessity of quantification. The editors of *The Cambridge Economic History of the Greco-Roman World* expressly declare that their book 'improves on substantivist approaches by providing crude statistics on economic performance', and 'goes beyond both sides in the old primitivist–modernist debate by developing general theoretical models of ancient economic behavior and putting them in a global, comparative context' (Scheidel *et al.* 2007: 11–12). Conferences have recently been organized on just this theme (Bowman and Wilson 2009; De Callataÿ and Wilson, forthcoming). Quantification obviously does not only concern prices, but also counting graves, settlements, issued coins, shipwrecks and so forth.

One of the features of this debate was that it was based on a rather narrow interpretation of a market economy; illustrative is Polanyi's (1944: 68) definition of the 'market economy' as 'an economic system controlled, regulated, and directed by markets alone; order in the production and distribution of goods is entrusted to this self-regulating mechanism'. Such a 'pure' system, however, has never existed in historical reality; the view that markets are always embedded in and regulated by social and political institutions has gained strength as a result of the rise of New Institutional Economics (North 1990). This led to a much broader definition of markets which can be applied in all periods of time and all regions and had been used in other disciplines, most notably economics and economic history of the medieval and modern worlds. This broader interpretation is defined by Gravelle and Rees (1992: 3) in their book *Microeconomics* as: 'a market exists whenever two or more individuals are prepared to enter into an exchange transaction, regardless of time or place'. As such this fits in with definitions that were in vogue in other disciplines.

Of course, this still means that one has to properly determine the factors that influence market performance in each region and time period. That this is no small task may be shown by the discussion on markets in early modern England. North and Thomas (1973) as well as Landes (1969) have argued that the lowering of transaction costs and increased private economic activity led to increased market performance, while authors such as Masschaele (1993), Britnell and Campbell (1995) and Clark (2004) argued that markets in the medieval period already performed remarkably well; consequently change in market performance did not occur in the early modern period.

One of the main conclusions of the 'Academy Colloquium' in Amsterdam (see Preface) and thus tenet of this volume is that the broad definition of markets as used in new institutional economics, as outlined above, is well suited for the societies studied here. Hence, in this volume we take as point of departure the concept that certain principles of markets, such as the law of demand and supply, are probably valid in all times, but that the actual functioning of markets – their 'performance' – is strongly affected by the society they are part of.

Market performance and market efficiency

The aim of this volume is to study market performance. How do we define this concept? So far we have talked about the 'performance' of markets as if this concept is self-evident. This is not true, however. Many studies refer to 'market integration', 'market efficiency' or similar concepts when discussing what we will call in this volume market performance. For its use in this volume, market performance may be defined as the capability of markets to adapt to exogenous shocks. Let us explain this with an example. In a perfectly working market an external shock due to, for example, a failed harvest will lead to rising prices, which will trigger trade, the sale of grains from storage houses, etc. Hence, even though prices will increase to some extent, the increase in the price of food will be mitigated by economic adaptations, and the degree to which this will occur will be related to the quality of the institutional (and geographical) framework. Low transaction costs due to, for example, favourable trading routes or a well-organized trading system, will mean that large compensating trade movements will occur, reducing the net impact of the harvest failure on prices. Hence in some regions markets will show much higher price rises than in other regions and/or time periods.

This definition of market performance makes it logical to use the theoretical observation, most clearly explained by Persson (1999), that price volatility tells us something about how markets are performing. As argued before, the lower price volatility is, the better markets can adapt to unexpected shocks and, consequently, the better they perform.

The next obvious question to ask is what factors determine how well markets perform. An answer given in much of the literature (e.g. Persson 1999; Jacks 2005) is trade. After all, if one region suffers from a failed harvest, it can import grain from other regions. Other than transportation and transaction costs, prices should become equal in the exporting and importing regions and price changes become smoothed ('the law of one price'). In early economies especially, trade was probably a major factor of market performance. Yet, even though it was a major factor, it was by no means the only one, as plenty of studies covering such diverse periods and locations as China in 100 BC to medieval England have shown (e.g. Swann 1950; Boserup 1965; Elvin 1973). Foldvari and Van Leeuwen (2011) distinguished, besides trade, three other 'proximate' (i.e. having a direct effect on price volatility) causes of market performance: storage, consumption diversification and technological development.

Besides trade, the second most important factor is storage or, as it can also be seen, intertemporal risk reduction. After all, people may store in years of plenty and consume when prices start increasing and thereby smooth price development. However, the degree to which storage affected prices is subject to debate, as in many of the western countries little evidence of extensive storage is found (e.g. McCloskey and Nash 1984; Van Leeuwen et al., 2011). For non-western countries such as China considerable evidence for grain storing is found (e.g. Swann 1950; Will and Bin 1991), but even there it is doubtful whether it had a big effect on price volatility and market performance as such, given the frequent occurrence of famines.

The basic idea behind the third factor identified by Foldvari and Van Leeuwen (2011), consumption diversification, is simple: the higher incomes are, the easier it is for people to switch between different types of foodstuffs, as they are not bound to eat only the cheapest products. A diversified economy will therefore be less vulnerable to exogenous shocks.

Finally, technological development may be mentioned as a fourth proximate cause of increases in market performance. After all, if technological advances generate higher agricultural output per capita, a drop in output is less likely to immediately lead to dire circumstances and, hence, to massive price fluctuations.

Together, the factors described above may be considered *proximate* causes of market performance. They are called proximate causes since they not only directly affect market performance, they can be considered *to be* market performance. Thus we defined a decrease in price volatility caused by these factors to be market performance. In order to gain some insight into what moves market performance over time, it is therefore important to analyse the role of the *ultimate* causes that have an effect on market performance via the proximate causes, as well. One obvious example is geography. After all, a mountain range itself does not have a direct effect on price volatility, but if a country is separated from other countries by a mountain range this will reduce trade and increase transportation costs. Another ultimate factor is the existence and effects of institutions (North 1990; cf. Coase 1998). This concerns private institutions defined by trading rules (e.g. Greif 1989), property rights, or politics, as governments may remove the threat of robbers, create roads, take care of storage, create reliable means of exchange (silver, money), or offer help in case of abnormal market conditions.

The case of Babylonia

The nature of the evidence

This book has a strong focus on ancient Babylonia. This is because for the first time we can analyse market performance all the way back to the sixth century BC owing not only to a now-prevailing broader view of the definition of markets (a change of paradigm) but also, and in particular, to the vast amount of data now available from this region that allows quantitative research. The documents in question, written in cuneiform script on clay tablets that have the advantage of being fire-resistant so that many have survived, come from the period of the Neo-Babylonian empire (612–539 BC), the Persian or Achaemenid empire (539–331 BC), the empires of Alexander the Great and the Seleucids (331–141 BC) and the Parthian or Arsacid empire (141–61 BC, i.e. until the end of the relevant period served by cuneiform documentation). Tens of thousands of documents from this region and period survived, administrative and legal documents that provide a unique insight into the Babylonian economy and allows quantitative, statistical and econometric research which is hardly possible anywhere else before the later Middle Ages (perhaps with the exception of Ptolemaic and Roman Egypt). It enables us to stretch out the long-term history of market performance by c. 1,500 years. The seminal study by Jursa (2010) on the Babylonian economy is obligatory literature for economic historians.

The most stunning part of the evidence is the detailed recording of thousands of prices of food and wool. This evidence comes from a surprising source: the meticulous work of Babylonian scholars who in a quite modern way collected evidence and made databanks. The collection which interests us here is that of the so-called astronomical diaries. These astronomical diaries are a dataset for research in the field of divination, a type of scholarship for which Babylonia was well known (praised as well as condemned) in antiquity. They contain a notation of celestial phenomena followed (in an increasing degree over time) by information on other (ominous) events that were supposed to be related to the position of the planets, such as strokes of lightning, the direction of the wind, monstrous births, the level of the Euphrates, temple robberies, famines, human and crop diseases, but also deeds of kings (such as visits to Babylon and concomitant visits to temples, and military campaigns), important events in Babylon and the level of the prices of six commodities, including barley, dates (staple crops) and wool.

The basic purpose of Babylonian scholarship was to find out regularities in the relations between the position of the planets and other factors. In one field they were very successful: after centuries of scientific research the Babylonian astronomers were able to predict the constellation of the planets and the stars, and lunar and solar eclipses. They were possibly less successful in another field: they hoped that if there was regularity in celestial phenomena, they might one day also find regularities in other phenomena which seemed irregular but may not be so, such as the death of kings, the level of the Euphrates and the volatility of prices. It would give them a real grip on the future. They thought that studying omens and phenomena on earth and in the sky in a coordinated approach would help them, as they believed that signs in heaven paralleled those on earth.[2] The fact that these data (including data on market prices) were recorded at all thus means they were considered unpredictable, and they form an excellent source of data for the analysis of the efficiency of markets.

These astronomical diaries have become accessible to a wider readership by the publication of the tablets in three volumes in a transcription and translation by the late Abraham Sachs and by Hermann Hunger (Sachs and Hunger 1988, 1989 and 1996). The prices have been collected in Slotsky (1997) and Vargyas (2001) (but cf. Van der Spek and Mandemakers 2003) and by the VU University Amsterdam research team (see Preface).

Recently a new corpus of texts has been published: documents containing just series of prices, without astronomical observations or other information (Slotsky and Wallenfels 2009). They seem to be the outcome of a real interest in prices: the ancient compilers of these lists seem to have had a real scientific interest in the development of prices. One tablet (no. 7), for instance, collects month VIII (harvest month) prices for the Seleucid years[3] SEB 178–185 (134–127 BC), but others (e.g. no. 8) try to give a complete overview of all months in the period SEB 185–190. While the astronomical diaries give the exchange value of 1 shekel of silver, these texts often have 2 shekels as point of reference and on two occasions it is even 1 mina of silver (60 shekels). Where we can compare the prices in these texts with those in the astronomical diaries it is striking that the list prices confirm those in the diaries; sometimes exactly, sometimes one document gives the average prices of a month while the diary has more detailed information (beginning, middle and end of the month). As in the diaries, the prices in the lists become more and more detailed as they pertain to smaller and smaller parts of the month (days or cluster of days). The data contained in the price lists have enhanced our knowledge considerably.

Money and prices in the astronomical diaries

What we call prices are as a matter of fact not prices, but notations of the purchasing power of the shekel (a weight measure of c. 8.33 grams of silver, roughly 2 Greek drachmas) in relation to five basic foodstuffs: barley, dates, *kasû* (variously translated as mustard or cuscuta (dodder), used as spice for the preparation of date beer[4]), watercress (some translators have cardamom[5]) and sesame (all in litres[6]) and wool (in *minas* (pounds)). Instead of today's practice of giving, say, the price of a hectolitre of, say, barley in shekels, the Babylonians reported how much one could buy for 1 shekel. The full formula is as follows: 'That month: the exchange value of barley (was): *n* litres, dates: *n* litres, cuscuta: *n* litres, cress: *n* litres, sesame: *n* litres, wool: *n* pounds, for 1 shekel of (refined) silver, (that was given in the land[7])'. Most often the formula was abbreviated to: 'That month: the exchange value was: barley: *n* litres, dates: *n* litres; etc.' Very often the time scale was more precise: 'The month: the exchange value was: barley, beginning of the month: *x* litres, middle of the month: *y* litres, end of the month: *z* litres; dates etc.' In the Parthian period the prices are often presented per (cluster of) days! Twice there were even different prices for the morning and the afternoon. Sometimes there is reference to scarcity, as e.g. in Diary-324B 12': '[That month (II, c. May 325 BC)] the sale of barley and the sale of everything else was interrupted in the streets of Babylon until the fifth; (the exchange value of) barley: 9 litres, on the sixth and seventh: 24[+ litres . . . .]; in the middle of the month, barley: 36 litres; at the end of the month: 48 litres; dates, in the middle of the month 36 litres, at the end of the month 42 litres; etc.' These prices exhibit hardship and extreme high prices in the time of Alexander the Great. The supply of food fell to (nearly) zero until the fifth of the month; conditions improved somewhat on the sixth day, possibly owing to the arrival of a new harvest. The fact that wheat is missing may be surprising. It is caused by the gradual salinization of the soil due to millennia of irrigation. Barley is more salt-resistant and so it became the staple crop (Jacobsen and Adams 1958; Jacobsen 1982; but cf. the reservations expressed by Powell (1985)).

Thus the texts give what I now call, on the advice of Dominic Rathbone, '*exchange values*'. The Babylonian word (*mahīru*, written ideographically KI.LAM) is derived from the verb *mahāru*, 'to receive', and is used for 'market', 'purchase', 'merchandise', and the like. Often the word is translated as 'price', and in some cases it is correct, and in a certain sense it is also correct in our texts: it is the price of silver, or better the purchasing power of silver, namely what one can buy for 1 shekel of silver.

It is really important to convert exchange values into prices, as not doing this leads to grave errors, as is shown by the studies of Slotsky (1997) and Vargyas (2001). To mention one example: the average of the exchange values converted into a price is not the same as an average price.[8]

In this volume, we converted exchange values in our tables into normal prices expressed in grams of silver per 1,000 litres of barley, sesame, cress, cuscuta, dates, and per pound of wool.[9] It is a fortunate coincidence that the Babylonian litre (*qû* or *qa*, written ideographically SÌLA) more or less conforms to the modern litre (it was perhaps slightly less) and that corresponding to our metrical system the Babylonian cubit is 50 cm and the Babylonian pound (*manû*, MA.NA) is 500 grams (Powell 1990: 508–10). In the present volume grain prices are mostly measured in grams of silver per hectolitre (in Babylonia, the ancient Mediterranean and Medieval England (see Chapters 2, 3, 9, 10, 16, 18, 19 and 20)). We are well aware of the difficulties of this approach (e.g. in respect to debasements and the trust in official coinage, irrespective of debasements; see the observations by Mayhew, Chapter 16, this volume), so that some authors reckon with the nominal prices in the region and period under research, or do both. So Jursa (Chapter 5) and

Hackl and Pirngruber (Chapter 6) work principally with shekels per *kurru*, occasionally converted into grams of silver per 1,000 litres; in the chapters on China (Chapters 12, 13 and 17) prices are given in silver *taels*; sometimes both measures were used.

The shekel was the basic monetary unit in Babylonia for millennia. *Coinage* was of recent date in Babylonia. It existed in the Achaemenid empire, but then the use of coinage was largely restricted to the western part of the empire. The introduction of coinage in Mesopotamia, effectively only in the Hellenistic period, was different from the introduction of coinage in Greece. In Greece the introduction of money and coinage went hand in hand and was the same process; in Mesopotamia the introduction of coinage was only a paragraph in the history of money.

Exclusive use of coinage, based mainly on the Attic standard, was abruptly introduced by Alexander the Great. The metrical unit was the drachma (weighing c. 4.31 grams); the didrachm (8.62 grams) more or less equalled the shekel; the 4 drachma piece, the tetradrachm, weighing 17.25 grams, also called *statēr*, was a kind of standard unit. The astronomical diaries continued to reckon in shekels throughout their history (until 61 BC), but administrative documents right from Alexander's reign use the formula 'x shekels of silver in staters of Alexander' and, under later kings, in staters of the reigning king. Sometimes specific coins are mentioned, such as the 'elephant staters' and the 'lion staters' (see Duyrat, this volume, Chapter 14, n. 61). Some texts add: 'according to the counting (*manûtu*) of Babylon' (possibly referring to the exchange rate between shekels and drachmas; see for more information Doty 1979: 69ff; Van der Spek 1981: 218f; 2005; 1998: 211, 246–7; Stolper 1993: 22–3). It is difficult to be sure if coins were always weighed (that is what the texts suggest), but it seems as though a rule of thumb emerged that 1 shekel equalled 2 drachmas. This may especially be the case in respect to the lighter staters struck in Babylon in the early Hellenistic period (cf. Duyrat, Chapter 14) and in the Parthian period (see Van der Spek, Foldvari and Van Leeuwen, this volume, Chapter 19).

The Babylonian calendar

The diaries report their data per month according to the Babylonian calendar. This was a lunar calendar, which consisted of twelve lunar months of 29 or 30 days, with the occasional intercalation of an extra month after months VI or XII in order to keep up with the solar year: seven intercalations in a period of 19 years. The system worked very well, but it must be kept in mind that the Babylonian months moved backwards a whole month in the solar year within three years before the situation was redressed by the insertion of an intercalated month. Consequently, the first month of the Babylonian year, Nisan, could start between Julian March 24 and April 23; in one year April could roughly correspond with month XII, in another year with month I. Therefore, for the purposes of this volume, we converted all Babylonian months into Julian months.

The editors of the diaries have numbered the diaries corresponding to the Babylonian years before common era according to astronomical usage, which means that diary no. –330 corresponds to 331 BC. That is, the Babylonian year –330 runs from April 13 331 to April 2 330 BC.[10] In their edition different tablets concerning the same year are marked with A, B, C etc.

A preview of Babylonian prices

In this volume we shall discuss the Babylonian evidence in more detail. A glance at the evidence reveals the high volatility of the Babylonian prices. Figure 1.1 shows the range between the highest and lowest prices per decade in the Hellenistic period, our best documented period. If we take this into account, one must conclude that the integration of the food market of Babylonia with the rest of the world was poor. Even in the rather stable period of Babylonian history, i.e. from 300 to 141 BC, prices of 1,000 litres of barley fluctuated from 2.56 shekels to 41.67 shekels, i.e. the highest price is more than sixteenfold of the lowest price. More detail on this issue will be available in Van der Spek, forthcoming.

The fact that grain prices were so volatile must be attributed to the fact that importing grain to (or exporting it from) Mesopotamia was difficult. Mesopotamia had deserts and steppes on its western borders and the Zagros Mountains in the east. Potential markets in Syria (to be reached upstream on the Euphrates) were practically out of reach, the more so as barley was an inferior product in relation to wheat (cf. Jursa 2010: 76, 209, 293). Interregional trade, within Babylonia, was relatively straightforward as a result of the tight canal network (Jursa 2010: 62–152; Jursa, Chapter 5, this volume). But in most cases the entire region had to cope with the same climatic conditions. Famines were bound to hit the whole of Babylonia, which allowed limited price variations (Kleber 2012).

The trade in wool is another story. The volatility of its prices is less distinct, certainly due to the higher elasticity of demand, but probably also owing to export possibilities. There had been a demand for Babylonian textiles in the Near East ever since the twentieth century BC and from as far away as Rome in the time of the republic and the empire (see Chapter 2). For the other trade goods information is thin. We know more about imports than exports. Imported products were wood, metal and silver (Graslin-Thomé 2009). So there must have been export goods as well, but we simply do not have much information about them.

The structure of this book

The book is subdivided into five sections which represent different aspects of the research: *Methodology*; *Market performance in Babylonia and the Mediterranean in antiquity*; *Market performance from the Middle Ages to the nineteenth century AD*; *Markets and Money*; *Long-term patterns*. The book is then rounded off with some *Concluding remarks*.

Methodology

First of all Peter Foldvari and Bas van Leeuwen (Chapter 2) explain the main concepts of this book: market performance and market efficiency. Lennart

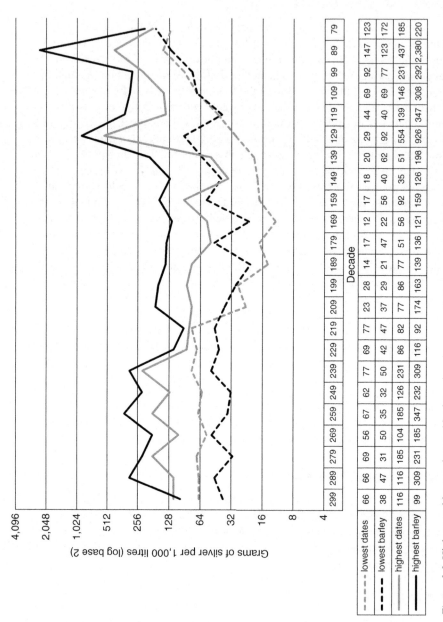

	299	289	279	269	259	249	239	229	219	209	199	189	179	169	159	149	139	129	119	109	99	89	79
lowest dates	66	66	69	56	67	62	77	69	77	23	28	14	17	12	17	18	20	29	44	69	92	147	123
lowest barley	38	47	31	50	35	32	50	42	47	37	29	21	47	22	56	40	62	92	40	69	77	123	172
highest dates	116	116	185	104	185	126	231	86	82	77	86	77	51	56	92	35	51	554	139	146	231	437	185
highest barley	99	309	231	185	347	232	309	116	92	174	163	139	136	121	159	126	198	926	347	308	292	2,380	220

Figure 1.1 Highest and lowest date and barley prices in grams of silver per 1,000 litres (log base 2 scale) per decade (299 = 299–290 BC).

Hoogerheide and Siem-Jan Koopman (Chapter 3) subject the Babylonian evidence to a statistical and econometric analysis in order to cope with the problem of how to handle historical time series with many missing data. They suggest a model to overcome the problems and make some suggestions for the relation and interaction of the price trends, especially as regards barley and dates. Karl Gunnar Persson (Chapter 4), whose book on the grain markets of Europe, discussed above, was the theoretical point of departure of this project, expounds on the welfare effects of a market that is performing well.

Market performance in Babylonia and the Mediterranean in antiquity

Michael Jursa (Chapter 5) gives a broad insight into market performance and market integration in Babylonia in the 'long sixth century' BC – the period of the Neo-Babylonian and the early Achaemenid empires – in all respects a period of economic expansion. Johannes Hackl and Reinhard Pirngruber (Chapter 6) discuss commodity prices in the later Achaemenid and early Hellenistic period, a period in which Babylonia experienced the disadvantage of losing the position of being the core of an empire and the coming of Alexander the Great, which led to the introduction of coinage and the minting of the vast Persian treasury (5,000 tonnes of silver value). In Chapter 7 Joost Huijs, Reinhard Pirngruber and Bas van Leeuwen examine the development of the prices of barley and dates in the later Hellenistic and early Parthian period, and try to explain the impact of climate and war on it. In Chapter 8 Sitta von Reden and Dominic Rathbone collect and study the price data from Ptolemaic Egypt, Delos and Athens (SvR) and the Roman empire (DR) and conclude that the Mediterranean gradually developed, as a result of the impact of the Roman empire, from a conglomerate of regional markets in the Hellenistic period to a connected market. Eltjo Buringh and Maarten Bosker (Chapter 9) study how the Roman empire and especially the Roman army was crucial to the emergence and flourishing of the market economy. After the demise of Roman military power in late antiquity the market immediately vanished, only to return in the later Middle Ages in often different regions and under different circumstances. This bring us to the Middle Ages.

Market performance from the Middle Ages to the nineteenth century AD

This section presents two case studies on Western Europe and two on China. Victoria Bateman (Chapter 10) discusses price volatility and markets in late medieval and early modern Europe, embedded in a general discussion of market performance in general and in relation to ancient Babylonia in particular. Liam Kennedy and Peter Solar (Chapter 11) turn to markets and price fluctuations in England and Ireland, AD 1785–1913, with special attention to market integration and the dual crop agriculture (grain and potatoes) in Ireland. Liu Guanglin (Chapter 12) explores market integration in Song China (AD 960–1279), while Carol Shiue (Chapter 13) goes on to relate the organization and scope of grain markets in Qing China (AD 1644–1911).

Markets and money

Prices are not only determined by supply and demand of the marketed goods, but also by the amount of money in circulation. It is fascinating to note how silver played the role of means of exchange from the third millennium BC in Mesopotamia until the end of the nineteenth century AD in the whole world. Even today the price of silver is an indicator of the performance of the economy. This state of affairs makes comparisons over time possible. Understanding the possible effects of monetary expansions and contractions in historic societies is often difficult because of limited opportunities to quantify the amount of silver in circulation. Problems are exacerbated by coinage debasements and the fact that silver is, apart from being a means of exchange, also a commodity. Intervention of the state is in this field is unavoidable and it is clear that the introduction of new silver into circulation, or a silver drain for whatever reason out of the country, has a deep impact on prices and exchanges. It is not a coincidence that monetary policy is a major issue in the debate on how to combat an economic crisis. In most of the historical periods government intervention had no economic objective at all (in most cases money was brought into circulation in order to pay armies), but the consequences were no less far-reaching.

In this section we tackle these issues in the Near East from the sixth to first centuries BC (Frédérique Duyrat, Chapter 14), in the north-western fringes of the Roman empire (Joris Aarts, Chapter 15), in medieval and early modern England (Nick Mayhew, Chapter 16) and in China in the long nineteenth century AD (Peng Kaixiang, Chapter 17). Of course, money plays its role also in the other chapters. In the article by Eltjo Buringh and Maarten Bosker (Chapter 9) the circulation of money is a major parameter, and Aarts' study in Chapter 15 shows how at a local level the picture can diverge from the general pattern, simply by an earlier withdrawal of Roman troops. Michael Jursa discusses how silver (even in very small amounts) became the major means of exchange in sixth-century BC Babylonia and this view is corroborated here in Frédérique Duyrat's contribution. Bert van der Spek, Peter Foldvari and Bas van Leeuwen (Chapter 19) discuss the role of silver in comparison to other periods, societies and regions.

Long-term patterns and concluding remarks

The final chapters try to go a step further, beyond region and periods of time, by discussing a number of the foregoing issues over time. The first problem to be tackled is the role of storage as means of mitigating price fluctuations and thereby increasing market performance (Foldvari and Van Leeuwen, Chapter 18). The second contribution (Bert van der Spek, Peter Foldvari and Bas van Leeuwen, Chapter 19) concerns the role of silver in market exchanges and the quantification of money in circulation in historical periods. It presents a model which allows us to estimate relative changes of money in circulation over time. Finally, Bas van Leeuwen, Peter Foldvari and Jan Luiten van Zanden (Chapter 20) give an overview of long-run patterns in market performance and the genesis of the market economy in the Near East and Europe from Nebuchadnezzar to Napoleon (560 BC to AD

1800). They measure market efficiency (not changing much over time) and market performance (trend mainly upwards, as a result of improved transport possibilities and improving institutions).

In the final chapter the editors of the volume (Bert van der Spek, Bas van Leeuwen en Jan Luiten van Zanden, Chapter 21) try to draw some general conclusions with an outlook to the twentieth century AD.

Notes

1 The irony of the debate is that Polanyi (1957) took exactly the highly interesting corpus of twentieth-century BC cuneiform documents belonging to the Assyrian community in Kaniš (Kültepe – South East Turkey) as the basis for his argument for a marketless economy in the Near East, but the corpus on closer scrutiny reveals on the contrary a remarkable feeling for market relations, price setting, and profit-maximizing behaviour (cf. Veenhof 1972; Dercksen 1996).

2 The best study on Mesopotamian scholarship in this field is Rochberg (2004).

3 From 311 BC a real era is used: the Seleucid era (SE). According to the Babylonian calendar (SEB) it started Nisan (April) 311 BC, but in the Macedonian Calendar (SEM) the new year, and hence the era, started with Dios (October) 312 BC. The Babylonian and Macedonian calendars are both lunar and the Macedonians took over the Babylonian intercalation system.

4 Stol 1994; Slotsky 1997: 32.

5 Stol 1983–4; Slotsky 1997: 34. Cf. Chicago Assyrian Dictionary s.v. *sahlû*.

6 The capacity of the Babylonian litre (SÌLA/*qû* or *qa* (a fossilized accusative)) is subject to debate. In modern literature the capacity is computed as being 0.946 or 0.842 litres. Slotsky (1997) uses both measures on one page (p. 46, one in the text, one in Table 1). For the *mina* Slotsky also uses a double standard: 453.60 grams in the text, c. 505 grams in Table 1. Fortunately, Marvin Powell, an expert in ancient metrology, has suggested in view of the uncertainties to stick to 1 litre for a *qa*, 500 grams for a mina (thus $1/60^{th}$ mina = 8.333 grams for a shekel) and 50 cm for a cubit, since these measures are related to each other (just as in our modern metric system), and give a fair measure of accuracy and avoid errors: obviously wise advice indeed (Powell 1984, 33, 41–2, 46). Consequently, Slotsky's Table 1 should be discarded. One *qa* is 1 litre, 1 *kur* is 180 litres. See also Powell 1990: 503–4.

7 Cf. Slotsky 1997: 12. It is not quite clear to me what this formulaic phrase, added on occasion, means: it refers either to the exchange value, 'that was given in the land', i.e. the price that was paid in the land (but I do not think that the astronomers would argue that the prices were valid in all of Babylonia), or it refers to the silver 'that was given in the land', i.e. to the silver that circulated as currency in Babylonia.

8 More on this in Van der Spek and Mandemakers (2003); Van der Spek www.iisg. nl/hpw/babylon.php

9 Actually our tables contain everything: dates according to the Babylonian and the Julian calendar, recordings of litres per shekel, prices in shekels and in grams of silver per 1,000 litres and per tonne (with the conversion rate of 1 litre barley = 0.62 kg and 1 litre of dates = 0.75 kg).

10 The Babylonian calendar is conveniently converted into the Julian calendar by Parker and Dubberstein (1956) and Chris Bennett (www.tyndalehouse.com/egypt/ ptolemies/chron/babylonian/chron_bab_cal.htm); minor corrections are given by Sachs and Hunger (1988). One would perhaps expect us to use the Gregorian calendar, but it is a well-established practice among historians of astronomy to use the Julian calendar. For our purposes (e.g. studying seasonality) it does not matter very much. In 384 BC

the equinoxes took place on 26 March and 27 September, in 65 BC on 23 March and 25 September, not far away from the Gregorian norm of c. 20/1 March and 22/3 September.

Bibliography

Baker, H. D. and Jursa, M., eds. Forthcoming. *Documentary Sources in Ancient Near Eastern and Greco-Roman History: Methodology and Practice*, Oxford: Oxbow Books.

Bang, P. F. 2008. *The Roman Bazaar*, Cambridge: Cambridge University Press.

Baumol, W. J. 2002. *The Free-Market Innovation Machine, Analyzing the Growth Miracle of Capitalism*, Princeton: Princeton University Press.

Boserup, E. 1965. *The Conditions of Agricultural Growth, the Economics of Agrarian Change under Population Pressure*, London: Allen & Unwin.

Bowman, A. and Wilson, A., eds. 2009. *Quantifying the Roman Economy. Methods and Problems*, Oxford: Oxford University Press.

Briant, P. 1982. 'Produktivkräfte: Staat und tributäre Produktionsweise im Achämenidenreich', in *Produktivkräfte und Gesellschaftsformationen in vorkapitalistischer Zeit*, edited by J. Hermann and I. Sellnow, Berlin: Akademie Verlag: 351–72.

Britnell, R. H. and Campbell, B. M. S., eds. 1995. *A Commercialising Economy: England, 1086 to c.1300*, 1st edition, Manchester: Manchester University Press.

Clark, G. 2004. 'The Price History of English Agriculture, 1209–1914', *Research in Economic History*, 22: 41–124.

Coase, Ronald. 1998. 'The New Institutional Economics', *American Economic Review*, 88: 72–4.

De Callataÿ, F. and Wilson, A., eds. Forthcoming. *Long-term Quantification in Ancient History*, forthcoming.

Dercksen, J. G. 1996. *The Old Assyrian Copper Trade in Anatolia*, Istanbul: Nederlands Historisch-Archaeologisch Instituut.

Doty, L. T. 1979. 'The Archive of the Nanâ-iddin Family from Uruk', *Journal of Cuneiform Studies*, 30: 65–90.

Elvin, M. 1973. *The Pattern of the Chinese Past*, Stanford: Stanford University Press.

Finley, M. 1973. *The Ancient Economy*, Berkeley: University of California Press.

Flynn, D. O. and Giráldez, A., eds. 1997. *Metals and Moneys in an Emerging Global Economy*, Aldershot: Variorum.

Foldvari, P. and Van Leeuwen, B. 2011. 'What Can Price Volatility Tell Us about Market Related Institutions? Conditional Heteroscedasticity in Historical Commodity Price Series', *Cliometrica*, 5: 165–86.

Foldvari, P., Van Leeuwen, B. and Van Zanden, J. L. 2011. 'Long-run Patterns in Market Performance and the Genesis of the Market Economy. Markets around the Mediterranean from Nebuchadnezzar to Napoleon (580 BC and 1800 AD)', CEPR discussion paper No. 8521, August 2011.

Graslin-Thomé, L. 2009. *Les échanges à longue distance en Mésopotamie au Ier millénaire. Une approche économique*, Paris: De Boccard.

Gravelle, H. and Rees, R. 1992. *Microeconomics*, 2nd edition, London: Longman.

Greif, A. 1989. 'Reputation and Coalitions in Medieval Trade: Evidence on the Maghribi Traders', *Journal of Economic History*, 49: 857–82.

Hatcher, J. and Bailey, M. 2001. *Modelling the Middle Ages. The History & Theory of England's Economic Development*, Oxford: Oxford University Press.

Jacks, D. 2005. 'Intra- and International Commodity Market Integration in the Atlantic Economy', *Explorations in Economic History*, 42: 381–413.

Jacobsen, Th. 1982. *Salinity and Irrigation Agriculture in Antiquity. Diyala Basin Archaeological Project: Report on Essential Results, 1957–58*, Malibu CA: Undena Publications.

Jacobsen, Th. and Adams, R. M. 1958. 'Salt and Silt in Ancient Mesopotamian Agriculture', *Science*, 21: 1251–8.

Jursa, M. 2010. *Aspects of the Economic History of Babylonia in the First Millennium BC: Economic Geography, Economic Mentalities, Agriculture, the Use of Money and the Problem of Economic Growth.* With contributions by J. Hackl, B. Jankovic, K. Kleber, E. E. Payne, C. Waerzeggers and M. Weszeli, Münster: Ugarit-Verlag.

Kleber, K. 2012. 'Famine in Babylonia. A Microhistorical Approach to an Agricultural Crisis in 528–526 BC', *Zeitschrift für Assyriologie*, 102: 219–44.

Landes, D. S. 1969. *The Unbound Prometheus, Technological Change and Industrial Development in Western Europe from 1750 to the Present*, Cambridge: Cambridge University Press.

Masschaele, J. 1993. 'Transport Costs in Medieval England', *Economic History Review*, 46: 266–79.

McCloskey, D. N. and Nash, J. 1984. 'Corn at Interest: the Extent and Cost of Grain Storage in Medieval England', *American Economic Review*, 74: 174–87.

McMillan, J. 2002. *Reinventing the Bazaar. A Natural History of Markets*, New York: W. W. Norton.

North, Douglass C. 1990. *Institutions, Institutional Change and Economic Performance*, Cambridge: Cambridge University Press.

North, D. C. and Thomas, R. P. 1973. *The Rise of the Western World, a New Economic History*, Cambridge: Cambridge University Press.

Parker, R.A. and Dubberstein W.H. 1956. *Babylonian Chronology 626 B.C.–A.D. 75*, Providence, Rhode Island: Brown University Press.

Persson, K. G. 1999. *Grain Markets in Europe 1500–1900. Integration and Deregulation*, Cambridge: Cambridge University Press.

Polanyi, K. 1944. *The Great Transformation*, Boston: Beacon Press.

—— 1957. 'Marketless Trading in Hammurabi's Time', in *Trade and Market in the Early Empires. Economies in History and Theory*, edited by K. Polanyi, C. M. Arensberg and H. W. Pearson, Glencoe, Ill: The Free Press & The Falcon's Wing Press: 12–26.

—— 1968. *Primitive, Archaic, and Modern Economies. Essays of Karl Polanyi*, edited by George Dalton, Garden City, New York: Doubleday & Co.

—— 1977. *The Livelihood of Man*, edited by H. W. Pearson, New York: Academic Press.

Polanyi, K., Arensberg, C. M. and Pearson, H. W., eds. 1957. *Trade and Market in the Early Empires. Economies in History and Theory*, Glencoe, Ill: The Free Press & The Falcon's Wing Press.

Powell, M.A. 1984. 'Late Babylonian Surface Mensuration. A Contribution to the History of Babylonian Agriculture and Arithmetic', *Archiv für Orientforschung* 31: 32–66.

—— 1985. 'Salt, Seed, and Yields in Sumerian Agriculture. A Critique of the Theory of Progressive Salinization', *Zeitschrift für Assyriologie*, 75: 7–38.

—— 1990. 'Maße und Gewichte' ('Measures and Weights' – article written in English), *Reallexikon der Assyriologie*, 7: 457–517.

Renger, J. 1994. 'On Economic Structures in Ancient Mesopotamia', *Orientalia*, 63: 157–208.

—— 2005. 'K. Polanyi and the Economy of Ancient Mesopotamia', in *Autour de Polanyi: vocabulaires, théories et modalités des echanges*, edited by Ph. Clancier, F. Joannès, P. Rouillard and A. Tenu, Paris: De Boccard: 45–65.

Rochberg, F. 2004. *The Heavenly Writing*, Cambridge: Cambridge University Press.

Sachs, A. and Hunger, H. 1988. *Astronomical Diaries and Related Texts from Babylonia*. Volume 1: *Diaries from 652–262 BC*, Vienna: Verlag der österreichischen Akademie der Wissenschaften.

—— 1989. *Astronomical Diaries and Related Texts from Babylonia*. Volume 2: *Diaries from 261–165 BC*, Vienna: Verlag der österreichischen Akademie der Wissenschaften.

—— 1996. *Astronomical Diaries and Related Texts from Babylonia*. Volume 3: *Diaries from 164–61 BC*, Vienna: Verlag der österreichischen Akademie der Wissenschaften.

Scheidel, W., Morris, I, and Saller, R., eds. 2007. *The Cambridge Economic History of the Greco-Roman World*, Cambridge: Cambridge University Press.

Slotsky, A. L. 1997. *The Bourse of Babylon. Market Quotations in the Astronomical Diaries of Babylonia*, Bethesda MD: CDL Press.

Slotsky, A. L. and Wallenfels, R. 2009. *Tallies and Trends. The Late Babylonian Commodity Price Lists*, Bethesda MD: CDL Press.

Stol, M. 1983–4. 'Cress and its Mustard', *Jaarbericht Ex Oriente Lux*, 28: 24–32.

—— 1994. 'Beer in Neo-Babylonian Times', in *Drinking in Ancient Societies. History and Culture of Drinks in the Ancient Near East*, edited By L. Milano, Padua: Sargon SRL: 155–183.

Stolper, M. W. 1993. *Late Achaemenid, Early Macedonian, and Early Seleucid Records of Deposit and Related Texts*, Napoli: Istituto Universitario Orientale.

Studer, R. 2008. 'India and the Great Divergence: Assessing the Efficiency of Grain Markets in Eighteenth- and Nineteenth-century India', *Journal of Economic History*, 68: 393–437.

Swann, N. 1950. *Food and Money in Ancient China: the Earliest Economic History of China to AD 25. Han Shu 24 with related texts, Han Shu 91 and Shih-Chi 129*, Princeton: Princeton University Press.

Van der Spek, R. J. 1981. 'Review of: H. Kreissig, *Wirtschaft und Gesellschaft im Seleukidenreich* (Berlin: Akademie Verlag 1978)', *Bibliotheca Orientalis*, 38: 212–19.

—— 1998. 'Cuneiform Documents on Parthian History: The Raḥimesu Archive. Materials for the study of the standard of living', in *Das Partherreich und seine Zeugnisse. The Arsacid Empire: Sources and Documentation. Beiträge des internationalen Colloquiums, Eutin (27–30 Juni 1996)*, edited by J. Wiesehöfer, Stuttgart: Franz Steiner Verlag: 205–58.

—— 2005. *Commodity Prices from Babylon (385–61 BC)*, available online www.iisg.nl/hpw/babylon.php (accessed 13 May 2014).

—— Forthcoming. 'The Volatility of Prices of Barley and Dates in Babylon in the Third and Second Centuries BC', in H. D. Baker and M. Jursa, eds, forthcoming.

Van der Spek, R. J. and Mandemakers, C. A. 2003. 'Sense and Nonsense in the Statistical Approach of Babylonian Prices', *Bibliotheca Orientalis*, 60: 521–37.

Van Leeuwen, B., Foldvari, P. and Pirngruber, R. 2011. 'Markets in Pre-industrial Societies: Storage in Hellenistic Babylonia in the Medieval English Mirror', *Journal of Global History*, 6: 169–93.

Vargyas, P. 2001. *A History of Babylonian Prices in the First Millennium BC. 1. Prices of the Basic Commodities*, Heidelberg: Heidelberger Orientverlag.

Veenhof, K. R. 1972. *Aspects of Old Assyrian Trade and its Terminology*, Leiden: E. J. Brill.

Wang, Helen. 2004. *Money on the Silk Road: The Evidence from Eastern Central Asia to c. AD 800*, London: The British Museum Press.

Will, P.-É. and Bin Wong, R. 1991. *Nourish the people: the State Civilian Granary System in China, 1650–1850*, Ann Arbor: The University of Michigan Center for Chinese Studies.

Part I
Methodology

2 Market performance in early economies

Concepts and empirics, with an application to Babylon

Peter Foldvari and Bas van Leeuwen

Introduction

From the 1900s onwards, economic historians tended to view economic development as 'modern' during and after the Industrial Revolution and as largely Malthusian before. The differences between the two kinds of societies can be defined in several ways. The demographic difference is probably the most apparent: in a traditional society both fertility and mortality are supposedly related to per capita income, while modernization gradually changes this relationship. Another way of defining the difference is to look at markets. The difference in the distributional mechanisms of these societies has been subject of a debate for about five decades now. Modernists believe that markets played an important role even in the ancient societies, while primitivists, among whom Finley (1973), following Polanyi (1968), is the most prominent, believe that it is a mistake to project market mechanisms of our days back into the past. In their view we should rather look on the ancient economies as mainly consisting of small economic units engaged in sustenance agriculture (Andreau 2002, 33–49; see also Van der Spek *et al.*, Chapter 1, this volume).[1]

However, even if the primacy of the market has been restored, it remains still unclear what exactly are the main characteristics of a market and what drives its change over time (Feinman and Garraty 2010). The main definition of markets is based on the efficient market hypothesis. However, the question remains as to how useful such a concept is, since the hypothesis of efficient markets, as introduced by Fama (1970), is about the degree that available information is incorporated into the prices, making it impossible for individuals to gain excessive profits at a relatively low risk using all publicly available information about the past.

Current research into the economic history and especially the price history of pre-modern economies is therefore rarely concerned about market efficiency. Instead the main focus is on price volatility, its welfare implications and the different ways in which a market may react to unexpected events. Even though the two concepts are not completely separable, long-term changes in price volatility, occurring either through storage, market integration by trade, or the introduction of better institutions, should rather be labelled as 'market performance'. This concept has been defined by Foldvari and Van Leeuwen (2011) as the ability of markets to cope with shocks, that is, the effect of unexpected events. Exploring long-term changes in market performance requires specific statistical techniques, and sometimes the departure from traditional measures of volatility that are designed for stationary time series.

In the next sections we discuss market efficiency and market performance from ancient Babylonia until the Industrial Revolution. A formal discussion of both concepts as well as their interrelatedness follows. We then present an analysis of market efficiency and market performance in Babylon, and go on to discuss the relation between both concepts over time. We end with a brief conclusion.

Market efficiency versus market performance

One of the fundamental problems in these discussions is how the working of markets is defined. Lie (1997: 342) described them as the 'hollow core at the heart of economics', while even those economic theories that do refer to the working of markets are often badly aligned with other social sciences (Dilley 1996).

A clear example is the so-called market efficiency hypothesis (Fama 1970). Basically, this theory argues that markets are efficient as long as a person is unable to predict next year's prices and, hence, is unable to make a profit with this information. Even though several kinds of information can be available (from private sources, government sources, etc.), most studies focus on the temporal relation of prices (i.e. price changes over time), because people very rarely have access to other kinds of inside information.

When the information people have only exists from past prices, this is called 'weak market efficiency' (as against strong market efficiency, when people have alternative sources of information at their disposal). With this type of information, in order for people to be unable to predict future prices, next year's prices must on average not deviate from this year's prices. Or, more formally,

$$\ln p_t = \gamma \ln p_{t-1} + \varepsilon_t, \quad \text{where} \quad \varepsilon_t \sim \text{iid}(0, \sigma_\varepsilon^2). \tag{2.1}$$

If $\gamma = 1$, this implies that the best guess for next year's price is this year's price. This is the method employed by, for example, Temin (2002). It can also be tested in a more formal way by applying a unit root test. In that case we test whether a high price this year means a lower price next year and vice versa, i.e. whether the time series is stationary. This is tested in the following manner:

$$\ln \Delta p_t = \beta \ln p_{t-1} + \varepsilon_t, \tag{2.2}$$

where $\beta = \gamma - 1$. The null hypothesis is one of stationarity (or random walk), which is fulfilled if β is not statistically different from 0, i.e. $\gamma = 1$.

This method was employed for Babylon by Temin (2002), followed by Romero *et al.* (2010). Using the abundantly available price data for the period 472–62 BC, he estimated the predictability and seasonality of prices. Based on a first-order autoregressive model, he concludes that the data are either random walk or very close to it. If the Babylonian prices do indeed prove to be random walk processes, then we can conclude that agents were not able to systematically predict the change of prices (and achieve a profit by doing so) based on prices of the past (i.e. $\gamma = 1$), which fulfils the condition of the weak form of the efficient market hypothesis.

However, market efficiency only captures one factor of market operations, i.e. information flows. It is not even certain that information flows are better in the seventeenth century AD compared to the fourth century BC. This all depends on flows of information available to buyers and sellers which are difficult to quantify. One might, for example, assume that the introduction of new goods as well as colonial trade might have disrupted the information on prices within a country. Therefore, in historical analysis the concept of market performance is given more focus. This concept has been defined by Foldvari and Van Leeuwen (2011) as the ability of markets to cope with shocks, that is, the effect of unexpected events.[2] Factors that enhance a market's capability to deal with such shocks are trade (which makes it possible to reduce shortages by imports of foodstuffs), storage (intertemporal risk reduction by storing food from the previous harvest), technology (increasing output and making production less vulnerable to, for example, natural disasters), consumption diversification (diversification of consumption means that people have the possibility to consume other foodstuffs when one harvest fails), institutions (e.g. government actions can reduce risks by applying appropriate policy measures), and monetary shocks (increases/decreases in the money supply may change the relative prices of products and, hence, the demand for certain products).

As outlined above, the way to quantify the market's reaction to shocks in the long run depends on unexpected price volatility. To analyse this, many studies have used the coefficient of variance (CV, i.e. standard deviation divided by the mean). The basic idea is that the more volatile markets are (i.e. the higher the CV), the less they are able to deal with shocks and, consequently, the less effective are the factors that dampen those shocks (trade, storage, technology, consumption, institutions and monetary developments). However, the problem with the CV is that it captures the effects of both expected and unexpected price shocks. For example, one can imagine that the annual price volatility of a one-crop society is bigger than that of a multiple-crop society, since in the former just one harvest failure can already cause famine. However, whether a country is a one- or two-crop society depends on its agricultural structure and therefore can be predicted. Also, increases and decreases in price level, for example caused by inflation, may influence the CV (since it uses an unconditional mean). To filter out these country, region and structure specific effects, Foldvari and Van Leeuwen (2011) suggest analysing the residual variance (or conditional variance) instead of the variance of the price series themselves. This basically means modelling the prices first and then further analysing only that part of the variation that was random and unexpected.

In the next section we empirically outline the concepts of market efficiency and market performance for Babylon. Subsequently we present a direct theoretical and empirical comparison of the two concepts.

Market performance and market efficiency in Babylon

The data

Market efficiency and market performance are thus the two leading, but also different, concepts to describe the working of markets. The question is how they are related. However, before addressing that question, we first have to analyse these concepts for one of the earliest societies for which enough data are available: Babylonia (i.e. Slotsky 1997; Vargyas 2001; Slotsky and Wallenfels 2009; Jursa 2010; Van der Spek 2005 and forthcoming; Appendix, this volume).

The first period for which we are able to make a full set of calculations of market efficiency and market performance is for Babylon c. 400–50 BC, where we have an abundant set of price data from the so-called astronomical diaries (ADs). In these diaries the position of the stars and planets was recorded together with a plethora of earthly phenomena that were supposedly influenced by them (see Chapter 1, this volume). Fortunately for research, some of the factors that were supposedly influenced by the position of the stars included the prices of barley, dates, cuscuta,[3] watercress, sesame and wool.

Before being able to address the issue of market efficiency and market performance, we first have to look at the reliability of prices. The first question is whether these prices were indeed 'market prices', rather than prices set by the government or other institutions. However, the mere fact that they were recorded in the ADs suggests that they were unpredictable and, therefore, market prices (Van der Spek and Mandemakers 2003: 528–30; Chapter 1, this volume). Furthermore, we find the other AD observations to be quite accurate, increasing our confidence in the price data.

More worrisome, though, is the large number of missing observations in the price data. If we estimate the total duration of the diaries to be about 600 years, the implied survival rate is just 5.5 per cent. Fortunately, there is a quite large literature on the statistical consequences and treatment of missing data (Allison 2001; Little and Rubin 2002; McKnight *et al.*, 2007). Based on this literature, one may conclude that, even though there are numerous methods to cope with the problem, the options are quite limited. First of all, it is necessary to establish whether the data are missing completely at random (MCAR), missing at random (MAR) or missing not at random (MNAR). The first concept means that the probability that an observation is missing is independent of the value of the variable and of any other variables. In our case this means that the 'missingness' of the price data are independent of both the level of prices as well as from all other possible variables (such as wars, climate, seasonality, etc.). For the data to be MAR, the probability that an observation is missing should not be related to other variables we use in an analysis. For example, if we look at the relation between climate and prices, the

Table 2.1 Results from the runs-test (Babylonian prices)

	Barley	Cress	Dates	Cuscuta	Sesame	Wool
Number of missing observations	3,557	3,733	3,603	3,764	3,704	3,757
Number of available observations	535	359	489	328	388	335
p-value of the test[a]	0.000	0.000	0.000	0.000	0.000	0.000

Note:
[a] The null hypothesis is that the series are not serially correlated.

missingness of prices should not be related to climate. This is less restrictive than MCAR, since the assumption that the missingness is independent of all variables is dropped.

If missingness is MCAR, 'listwise deletion' (simply deleting the missing observations) will not lead to a bias. The same applies if the data are MAR. However, if missingness is not at random (MNAR), it becomes necessary to use more sophisticated techniques – such as imputation techniques (filling in the missing values) – to work with the data, and model the missingness of the data itself.

In order to test the missingness in the Babylonian data, we performed a Wald-Wolfowitz or runs-test.[4] As the test results suggest in Table 2.1, we must reject the idea that the missingness of the data are completely random: it seems that the tablets containing the data survived in groups as indicated by the serial correlation. In other words: a tablet is more likely to have survived if the previous tablet also survived. This is partly because consecutive periods with prices can be found on one tablet. However, such a relationship may also have existed if the tablets from successive periods were stored close to each other, because in the event of a disaster, the observations for successive periods were more likely to perish. A simple linear probability model (LPM) confirms this finding: for all our series we find that the probability of the availability of an observation is increased by 50 to 60 per cent if the previous period's observation was not missing either. A similar finding can be obtained from Little's MCAR (Little 1988) test. We carried out this test on our series to find out if we can reject the null hypothesis that they are MCAR. The test statistic is 294.664, and the 1 per cent critical value of the chi-square distribution with 175 degrees of freedom is 221.438. Hence we can confirm with high probability that Babylonian data are not MCAR.

Unfortunately, the MAR hypothesis is basically non-testable. The only way to solve this issue is to perform regressions of the missingness of the data on the variables of interest. We did so and found that the missingness was uncorrelated with wars, politics, climate, seasons, river level, etc. This, combined with the probability that most of the AD were found at random by illegal excavations, suggests that we can use these data to draw reliable conclusions. Finally, as we will see, using different kinds of techniques (including imputation) results in basically the same coefficients, suggesting that the data are MAR and can thus be used in economic analyses.

Market efficiency

How can we use these data to estimate the degree of market efficiency? As previously pointed out, the weak form of market efficiency basically means that the autoregressive (AR)-coefficient is equal to 1 (see also Equation (2.3)) and prices are thus random walks. With unit root tests we formally test if the logarithms of the price series are random walk processes. Since they usually have a trend, we assume that they are random walk processes, generally described for product i as:

$$\ln p_{i,t} = \ln p_{i,t-1} + \varepsilon_{i,t} \quad \text{with} \quad \varepsilon_t \sim \text{iid}(0, \sigma_\varepsilon^2), \tag{2.3}$$

where we assume that the error-term ε is a white noise process, independently and identically distributed with zero mean. An important property of random walk series is that their change is completely random, as can be seen if we take the first difference of Equation (2.3):

$$\Delta \ln p_{i,t} = \varepsilon_{i,t}. \tag{2.4}$$

We apply two types of formal tests: the Dickey-Fuller (D-F) test and the KPSS test (Kwiatkowski *et al.*, 1992). Because we have a lot of missing observations, we do not include lags of the dependent variable in the D-F test (that would make it an Augmented D-F test). The KPSS test and the D-F test have different null hypotheses (D-F – non-stationarity, KPSS – stationarity), so their simultaneous use can be advantageous. Therefore, we use both methods.

The D-F and the KPSS tests indicate that the all price series are I(1), i.e. they are random walk processes (see Tables 2.2 and 2.3). From an economic point of view, this means that no agents could have possibly predicted changes in prices, and the rational expectation regarding prices is the primitive expectation, that is, that prices do not change from one period to the other. Using the expectation operator this can be expressed as follows:

$$E_{t-1} \ln p_{i,t} = \ln p_{i,t}, \tag{2.5}$$

where $E_{t-1} \ln p_{i,t}$ denotes the expectation in period $t-1$ regarding the price in the following period. That these expectations are rational is easy to see, since the deviations from the expected price (the forecasting error) has a zero expected value. This is indicative of weakly efficient markets since, if people could predict future price changes, they could make a profit at low risk. Still, it may be questioned whether, with such high number of missing observations, we still can trust the unit root test results. To decide this question, we carried out a Monte Carlo simulation (see Appendix 2.A). The results suggest that we can rely on the unit root tests, but we should rather prefer the KPSS. In addition, this suggests once more that no bias occurs in using these data and, hence, that they are MAR.

Table 2.2 Unit root tests on the level of the log of the Babylonian price series (*p*-values in parentheses)

	Barley	Cress	Dates	Cuscuta	Sesame	Wool
D-F	−2.931	−2.143	−1.817	−0.141	−2.758	−0.681
	(0.043)	(0.228)	(0.371)	(0.942)	(0.066)	(0.848)
KPSS	1.027	0.813	1.237	1.453	1.449	2.671
(<0.01)[a]	(<0.01)	(<0.01)	(<0.01)	(<0.01)	(<0.01)	

Note:
[a] <0.01 means that the null hypothesis can be rejected at 1% level of significance. Null hypotheses: D-F: non-stationarity, KPSS: stationarity.

Table 2.3 Unit root tests on the level of the first difference of the log of the price series (*p*-values in parentheses)

	Barley	Cress	Dates	Cuscuta	Sesame	Wool
D-F	−15.80	−8.483	−12.86	−7.413	−12.93	−9.222
	(0.000)	(0.000)	(0.000)	(0.000)	(0.000)	(0.000)
KPSS	0.057	0.047	0.052	0.402	0.104	0.163
	(>0.1)[a]	(>0.1)	(>0.1)	(>0.05)	(>0.1)	(>0.05)

Note:
[a] >0.1(> 0.05) means that the null hypothesis cannot be rejected at 10% (5%) level of significance. Null hypotheses: D-F: non-stationarity, KPSS: stationarity.

Market performance

The above analysis suggests that markets in Babylon can be seen as weakly efficient. However, as previously outlined, this does not say much about market performance because higher market efficiency as such is not necessarily correlated with institutional arrangements of markets other than the flows of information. Therefore, a concept of market performance has been developed that measures how well markets can adapt to unexpected (i.e. conditional) shocks.

That this is important can also be seen in Figure 2.1. Here we show polynomials of the price trends of several products in Babylon. Most notably, sesame has the lowest price movement over time. Hence, for example, the generic price fall in the second century BC affected sesame less than the other products. On the other hand, wool and cuscuta prices were affected much more strongly. This suggests that these last two products were inferior (less wanted) meaning that, in times of low prices, people bought other products so that the price fall in these two products was even bigger than in, for example, barley. Figure 2.1 also shows that with an increase in prices, the price of wool and cuscuta rose even more, as people moved away from the more preferred (and more expensive) barley to those two products. This example shows that simple economic mechanisms may also affect volatility without directly affecting market performance.

Other examples may also be found of economic, social and climatic factors influencing prices apparently without affecting the working of markets as such.

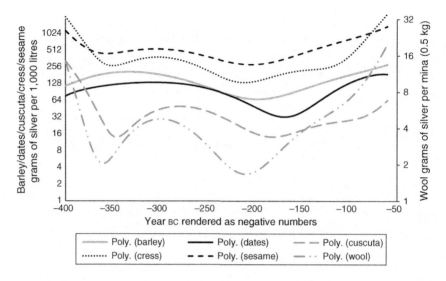

Figure 2.1 Long run movement of prices in Babylon.

Changes in climate may have affected barley differently from the way it affected dates (see Huijs *et al.*, Chapter 7, this volume). Beer was increasingly made of dates in the first millennium BC (cf. Stol 1994), but we cannot be sure if this changed in the later periods or if competition with wine was growing owing to the arrival of Greeks in Babylon under Antiochus IV. Beer may have been an export product (cf. Jursa 2010: 209; 221–4).

In the case of wool other factors may have played a role, something which we can hardly check. Babylonian textiles had been in demand for millennia. The products were marketed by Assyrian traders to Anatolia as early as the twentieth century BC (Veenhof 1972: 79–213) and Babylonian textiles must have been an export product in nearly all ancient times (cf. Jursa 2010: 220–1). In the biblical story of the exodus a certain Achan aroused God's wrath by stealing a golden garment from Shinear (Babylonia) worth 200 shekels of silver (Joshua 7: 21). The tomb of Cyrus was overlaid with Babylonian tapestry (Arrian, *Anabasis Alexandri*, 6. 29.5). We know that Babylonian textiles were much admired in the Mediterranean world, even as far away as Rome. The veil of the temple in Jerusalem was made of it (Josephus, *Jewish War*, 5. 215); the emperor Nero paid four million sesterces for one piece of Babylonian tapestry (Pliny, *Natural History*, 8. 196); Cato the Censor sold his Babylonian tapestry to finance the replastering of his farm; it was generally considered a sign of extreme luxury (Lucretius, *De rerum natura*, 4: 1029; Martialis, *Spectacula*, 8.28.17; Petronius, *Satyrica* 55.6); in the novel *Chaereas and Callirhoe* (8.8.14) by Charito a certain Demetrius possesses a ship with royal allure with a tent on it made of purple gold-stitched Babylonian cloth (cf. Morgan 2007: 29). So it may have been that the demand for textiles for some reason had increased. But something else may have happened. In the Neo-Babylonian period the Eanna temple owned large flocks of sheep, and it marketed wool to make money (cf. Kristin Kleber in Jursa 2010: 595–616). For some reason this activity may have stopped, as the city of Uruk and its temples began to decay after c. 100 BC, although of course this does not mean that the production of woollen textiles was not continued elsewhere in Babylonia. Without firm evidence it is difficult to pin-point the causes of increased prices.

These examples of changing production structures and changing geographical distribution of sheep rearing show that when one wants to calculate market performance, one should first deal with removing this expected price volatility. To measure the volatility caused by unexpected shocks, we first have to filter out the expected fluctuations. One example, as already mentioned, is agricultural structure, but one can think about other factors as well. An example is inflation. Inflation increases the price level and, as shown by Foldvari and Van Leeuwen (2011), when either an increasing or decreasing trend in prices exists, this will inflate volatility, causing an underestimation of market performance.

To remove this spurious component of volatility (i.e. country- and time-specific demand- and supply-related factors and the trend), Foldvari and Van Leeuwen use a conditional heteroscedasticity model, in which the variance of the residual term (the variance around the conditional expected value of the prices) is modelled, thereby filtering out the effect of the trend. The residual variance therefore captures, in a correctly specified model, only the effect of unexpected shocks. Hence, the lower the residual variance, the better markets can cope with shocks.

This exercise is reported in Table 2.4 for Babylon together with the corresponding CV values. Several things may be noticed. First, it is clear that the market performance measure is lower than the CV. This is caused by the removal of the expected volatility caused by agricultural structure, inflation etc. Second, we can see that difference is much smaller among the different products in the standard

Table 2.4 CV and market performance (standard error of the regression on first differences, log prices)

		CV	*Conditional volatility (i.e. inverse of market performance)*
Barley	Seleucid	0.74	0.50
	Parthian	0.73	0.85
Dates	Seleucid	0.85	0.51
	Parthian	0.62	0.48
Cuscuta	Seleucid	0.91	0.56
	Parthian	0.46	0.37
Cress	Seleucid	1.00	0.78
	Parthian	0.44	0.34
Sesame	Seleucid	0.79	0.50
	Parthian	0.42	0.28
Wool	Seleucid	0.42	0.18
	Parthian	0.54	0.35

error of the regression compared to the CV. This is logical since it is unlikely that major differences in market performance were in existence for the several products. Finally, we can test whether the mean of market performance in the Seleucid and Parthian periods was equal. We find that, with 95 per cent confidence, average market performance in both periods was equal.

For Babylon there are thus no major differences in market performance over time. This suggests that the factors affecting market performance, earlier in this text identified as trade, technology, storage, consumption, institutions and monetary shocks, remained about constant between c. 500 and 50 BC. However, even though these factors may have remained constant during Babylonian times, this was certainly not the case between 1 AD and the Industrial Revolution (as argued by Van Leeuwen *et al.*, Chapter 20, this volume).

Market efficiency versus market performance

Demand and supply

In the previous sections we showed that market performance and market efficiency are different concepts. However, whereas in Babylon markets were deemed weakly efficient, market performance was relatively low compared to later periods. At the same time, whereas Van Leeuwen *et al.* (Chapter 20, this volume) found that market performance did rise over time, the same was not necessarily true for market efficiency. This suggests that at best no relationship, and at worse an inverse relationship (see next section), exists between market performance and market efficiency.

Since any relationship between market efficiency and market performance takes place in a demand-and-supply situation, we have to start with defining a standard demand and supply model for the Babylonian market. Even though we lack data on output, fortunately, we are still able to create a simple demand and supply model for the Babylonian economy. Let us start by assuming that the supply and demand of agricultural goods in ancient Babylon can be described with two equations. Let us start with supply:

$$\ln Q_{i,t}^S = \alpha_0 + u_t \quad u_t \sim \text{iid}(0, \sigma_u^2). \tag{2.6}$$

The demand equation can be written as:

$$\ln Q_{i,t}^D = \beta_0 + \gamma \ln P_{i,t} + \sum_{k=1}^{n_p} \beta_k \ln P_{k,t} + \omega Y_t + v_{i,t} \quad v_t \sim \text{iid}(0, \sigma_v^2), \tag{2.7}$$

the condition of equilibrium in market i:

$$\ln Q_{i,t}^S = \ln Q_{i,t}^D, \tag{2.8}$$

where Q_i denotes the quantity of i supplied or demanded (superscripts S and D), $u_{i,t}$ denotes the supply shocks (locusts, natural disasters, destructions of war, weather conditions). In Equation (2.6) we assume that the supply is not affected by price, which is an obvious simplification but we will show that this version can be estimated with the available data. In the demand equation P_i denotes the price of product i, while P_j is the price of product j (there are n_p number of other goods) that is either a substitute or a complement of product i. Y denotes aggregate income, and $v_{i,t}$ is a random variable capturing the effect of demand shocks (e.g. king or satrap visiting Babylon, wars, plagues). The aggregate income is not observed, so we assume that most of its effects are captured by a time trend. The latter is included because it is believed that Babylon underwent a loss of its importance and some of its population left in this period. If we accept that the per capita income remained roughly the same in the period (as it can be derived from the basic Malthusian model), lower population means lower aggregate income. So the trend should generally yield a negative coefficient in the case of normal goods, and a positive coefficient in the case of inferior goods.

Since we have no data on quantities, it is not possible to identify both equations. What one can estimate, knowing prices only, is a reduced form equation for the price of product i:[5]

$$\ln P_{i,t} = \frac{\alpha_0 - \beta_0}{\gamma} - \sum_{k=1}^{n_p} \frac{\beta_k}{\gamma} \ln P_{k,t} - \frac{\omega}{\gamma} Y_t + \frac{u_t - v_t}{\gamma}, \tag{2.9}$$

where we can assume that $\gamma < 0$, i.e. the quantity of product i demanded is negatively related to the price of product i's price, so that the signs of the coefficients in the reduced equation will have the opposite sign than in the supply Equation (2.6). Since γ is unknown, however, we cannot determine the coefficients of the original demand and supply equations. The system of equations is unidentified.

However, we can estimate the reduced Equation (2.9) from the partial equilibrium model. We report the parsimonious specifications only (except for the multiple imputation), that is, after sequentially removing regressors whose coefficients are not significantly different from zero by at least 10 per cent. Also, we report all specifications with four missing data treatment methods: listwise deletion, pairwise deletion, mean imputation and multiple imputation.

Listwise deletion means that the regression is carried out on observations where all regressors were observed. This approach strongly reduces the size of our sample.

Pairwise deletion means that the main statistics of each variable are calculated using all available observations, and the parameters of the regression are estimated from those statistics. It has been found that if the correlation is high among the variables, listwise deletion has better properties (Allison 2001).

Mean imputation is the third method, where the missing observations in the regressors are replaced by their sample mean (unconditional mean imputation). The missing values of the dependent variable are not imputed in this case, since that would lead to serious bias. This method is usually not recommended (see Little and Rubin 2002: 62) since it results in a serious underestimation of the variances and co-variances. Nevertheless, as our Monte Carlo simulations (Appendix 2.B) show, this method leads to inefficient (high standard errors) but unbiased parameter estimates.

Multiple imputation is a method based on a fully conditional specification carried out five times.

Bearing in mind these definitions, calculations for the figures of Tables 2.5 to 2.10 are based on the following: listwise deletion: observations with any of the variables having a missing value are excluded (default treatment method in most software packages). Pairwise deletion: summary statistics are calculated for each variable using all available observations. The coefficients are calculated from these statistics. Mean imputation: the missing values are replaced by the sample mean of the series. Multiple imputation: the missing values are imputed with a fully conditional specification method five times, using all available variables. The regression is run on each set of imputations, pooled estimates are reported.

With our previous assumption that the series are missing at random, we can now assume that none of the methods we used result in biased estimates – but the first three methods result in an inefficient estimation, so one needs to be critical with the reported t-statistics and the standard hypothesis tests. Seemingly, even though there is a difference in magnitude and standard error, there is no difference in the sign of the coefficients. Hence, the sign of the coefficient (if significant) is generally the same in all models, but the significance may be biased in the first three methods. Therefore, we prefer the fourth method, the multiple imputation method.

The results of the demand and supply model are quite telling. As above regression results show, barley, dates and cuscuta have relatively strong seasonality, while sesame, cress and wool do not. Equally, the *na*-metres variable, giving the distance in metres from the maximum level of the Euphrates River,[6] is negative for dates and cuscuta and positive for wool. In other words, the lower the water level, the lower the price for dates and cuscuta, while the higher the water level, the lower the price for wool. For cress, sesame and barley the height of the river is not statistically significant.

More importantly, as argued above, we can interpret the price coefficients (elasticities) as having the same sign as the price elasticities in the demand equation provided that we assume the products own price elasticity to be negative. This assumption is common in the literature. Positive price elasticity means that when the price of one product (the regressor) rises, the demand for the other product (whose price is the dependent variable) increases as well. This behaviour is typical of substitutes. A negative coefficient, on the other hand, means that when a product gets more expensive, the demand for the product on the left-hand side of the equation reduces, indicating that the products are complements. We warn against the oversimplified interpretation of these relationships. Two products can be substitutes or complements even if they are seemingly not closely related, simply because of the existence of a budget constraint and because they have different

Table 2.5 The partial equilibrium model results for barley, using the four missing data treatment methods

	Listwise deletion			Pairwise deletion			Mean imputation			Multiple imputation		
	coeff	t-stat	p-value	coeff	t-stat	p-value	coeff	t-stat	p-value	coeff	t-stat	p-value
Constant	-1.052	-1.318	0.195	0.048	0.134	0.894	0.550	5.619	0.000	-0.949	-3.708	0.016
Indates[a]	0.181	1.243	0.221	0.185	3.278	0.001	0.320	21.794	0.000	0.232	6.325	0.002
Inpmus[a]	-0.162	-1.263	0.214	-0.260	-3.639	0.000	-0.105	-4.513	0.000	-0.216	-6.721	0.001
Inpcres[a]	0.477	4.273	0.000	0.519	8.747	0.000	0.226	12.130	0.000	0.504	11.986	0.000
Inpses[a]	0.629	3.335	0.002	0.362	4.902	0.000	0.235	11.141	0.000	0.413	5.892	0.003
Inpwool[a]	-0.009	-0.054	0.957	0.154	1.897	0.060	0.150	6.583	0.000	-0.005	-0.065	0.951
na-metres	-0.057	-0.444	0.659	-0.177	-3.607	0.000	-0.034	-2.622	0.009	0.062	1.235	0.280
t	-0.0001	-1.241	0.222	-0.00004	-1.256	0.211	0.000005	1.650	0.099	-0.00005	-1.335	0.247
February	-0.051	-0.231	0.819	-0.139	-0.969	0.334	-0.020	-1.194	0.232	0.015	0.113	0.915
March	-0.073	-0.311	0.758	-0.195	-1.340	0.183	-0.024	-1.426	0.154	0.011	0.098	0.926
April	0.085	0.259	0.797	-0.164	-1.089	0.278	-0.012	-0.690	0.490	0.082	0.884	0.419
May	-0.858	-2.495	0.017	-0.474	-3.234	0.002	-0.047	-2.788	0.005	-0.228	-1.681	0.162
June	-0.935	-2.748	0.009	-0.332	-2.302	0.023	-0.046	-2.721	0.007	-0.408	-2.178	0.092
July	-0.685	-2.350	0.024	-0.203	-1.404	0.163	-0.030	-1.773	0.076	-0.287	-1.984	0.114
August	-0.677	-2.546	0.015	-0.218	-1.486	0.140	-0.042	-2.495	0.013	-0.306	-1.737	0.154
September	-0.489	-1.894	0.066	-0.293	-1.999	0.048	-0.042	-2.458	0.014	-0.262	-1.990	0.112
October	-0.472	-1.902	0.065	-0.149	-1.014	0.312	-0.032	-1.904	0.057	-0.228	-4.014	0.006
November	-0.057	-0.211	0.834	-0.187	-1.296	0.197	-0.034	-1.990	0.047	-0.112	-1.619	0.161
December	-0.126	-0.510	0.613	0.087	0.606	0.546	-0.003	-0.169	0.866	0.068	0.712	0.511
N	57			145			4,091			4,091		
R^2	0.860			0.799			0.304			0.805[b]		
DW	1.414			0.949			1.047			1.917[b]		

Notes:

[a] Lnpdates = $\log_n$ (dates price); Lnp nus = $\log_n$ (cuscuta price); Lnpses = $\log_n$ (sesame price); Lnpwool = $\log_n$ (wool price); Lnpcres = $\log_n$ (cress price).

[b] Calculated as the mean of the respective statistics of the five sets of estimates.

Table 2.6 The partial equilibrium model results for cress, using the four missing data treatment methods

	Listwise deletion			Pairwise deletion			Mean imputation			Multiple imputation		
	coeff	t-stat	p-value	coeff	t-stat	p-value	coeff	t-stat	p-value	coeff	t-stat	p-value
Constant	0.572	0.595	0.556	0.916	2.180	0.031	1.508	19.381	0.000	1.524	3.753	0.017
Lnpbar[a]	0.669	4.273	0.000	0.724	8.747	0.000	0.154	12.130	0.000	0.791	9.247	0.001
Lnpdates[a]	0.322	1.909	0.064	0.023	0.331	0.741	0.061	4.798	0.000	0.007	0.084	0.937
Lnpmus[a]	0.335	2.312	0.026	0.136	1.554	0.123	0.175	9.180	0.000	0.227	4.276	0.008
Lnpses[a]	−0.234	−0.933	0.357	0.022	0.230	0.818	0.294	17.211	0.000	−0.130	−1.429	0.221
Lnpwool[a]	−0.067	−0.341	0.735	0.092	0.954	0.342	0.173	9.189	0.000	0.155	1.390	0.234
na-meters	0.064	0.424	0.674	0.153	2.572	0.011	0.036	3.313	0.001	0.005	0.090	0.933
t	0.0002	1.920	0.062	−0.00003	−0.627	0.532	−0.000003	−1.247	0.213	0.0001	1.265	0.272
February	0.130	0.497	0.622	0.105	0.622	0.535	0.006	0.415	0.678	−0.046	−0.282	0.791
March	0.188	0.683	0.499	0.064	0.373	0.710	−0.003	−0.244	0.807	−0.070	−0.795	0.460
April	−0.044	−0.114	0.910	0.049	0.275	0.784	−0.004	−0.317	0.751	−0.092	−0.946	0.386
May	1.261	3.238	0.002	0.365	2.063	0.041	0.010	0.726	0.468	0.187	0.906	0.413
June	1.067	2.627	0.012	0.221	1.278	0.203	0.004	0.264	0.792	0.248	1.200	0.293
July	0.610	1.715	0.094	0.111	0.644	0.521	0.003	0.186	0.853	0.149	0.594	0.583
August	0.374	1.116	0.271	0.025	0.144	0.886	−0.006	−0.456	0.648	0.048	0.172	0.872
September	0.275	0.869	0.390	0.129	0.736	0.463	0.004	0.274	0.784	0.079	0.324	0.762
October	0.344	1.139	0.262	0.112	0.642	0.522	0.007	0.498	0.618	0.146	1.078	0.335
November	0.145	0.457	0.650	0.077	0.451	0.652	−0.004	−0.316	0.752	0.040	0.333	0.754
December	0.055	0.188	0.852	−0.164	−0.968	0.335	−0.012	−0.819	0.413	−0.164	−1.064	0.342
N	57			145			4,091			4,091		
R²	0.832			0.725			0.302			0.722[b]		
DW	1.164			0.701			0.999			1.942[b]		

Notes:

[a] Lnpbar = $\log_n$ (barley price); Lnpdates = $\log_n$ (dates price); Lnp mus = $\log_n$ (cuscuta price); Lnpses = $\log_n$ (sesame price); Lnpwool = $\log_n$ (wool price).

[b] Calculated as the mean of the respective statistics of the five sets of estimates.

Table 2.7 The partial equilibrium model results for dates, using the four missing data treatment methods

	Listwise deletion			Pairwise deletion			Mean imputation			Multiple imputation		
	coeff	t-stat	p-value	coeff	t-stat	p-value	coeff	t-stat	p-value	coeff	t-stat	p-value
Constant	0.310	0.354	0.725	0.814	1.501	0.136	0.175	1.765	0.078	1.396	8.838	0.000
Inpbar[a]	0.210	1.243	0.221	0.422	3.278	0.001	0.326	21.794	0.000	0.518	5.485	0.004
Inpmus[a]	0.110	0.789	0.435	0.349	3.211	0.002	0.438	19.433	0.000	0.250	2.466	0.065
Inpcres[a]	0.265	1.909	0.064	0.038	0.331	0.741	0.091	4.798	0.000	0.0003	0.002	0.998
Inpses[a]	0.300	1.336	0.189	0.069	0.570	0.570	0.111	5.137	0.000	0.008	0.117	0.912
Inpwool[a]	0.254	1.468	0.150	0.238	1.947	0.054	0.076	3.289	0.001	0.281	4.063	0.010
na-meters	0.026	0.188	0.852	-0.092	-1.188	0.237	-0.016	-1.207	0.227	-0.148	-2.274	0.079
t	-0.0004	-4.425	0.000	-0.0001	-2.759	0.007	-0.00001	-3.617	0.000	-0.0002	-8.222	0.000
February	-0.092	-0.386	0.701	0.132	0.608	0.545	0.012	0.683	0.495	0.090	0.663	0.538
March	0.056	0.222	0.825	0.129	0.585	0.559	0.018	1.022	0.307	0.125	1.210	0.276
April	0.262	0.748	0.459	-0.007	-0.031	0.976	0.011	0.650	0.516	0.028	0.509	0.616
May	-0.088	-0.222	0.826	0.039	0.171	0.865	0.013	0.765	0.444	0.207	1.011	0.365
June	0.264	0.664	0.510	0.152	0.684	0.495	0.016	0.931	0.352	0.256	1.513	0.197
July	0.433	1.322	0.194	0.088	0.400	0.690	0.007	0.413	0.680	0.181	1.300	0.253
August	0.569	1.929	0.061	0.396	1.792	0.076	0.041	2.367	0.018	0.449	3.423	0.019
September	0.418	1.481	0.147	0.321	1.437	0.153	0.035	2.023	0.043	0.438	3.783	0.012
October	0.156	0.561	0.578	0.110	0.494	0.622	0.006	0.376	0.707	0.217	1.594	0.174
November	-0.023	-0.081	0.936	0.015	0.068	0.946	-0.007	-0.394	0.694	0.138	1.872	0.098
December	0.035	0.132	0.896	0.037	0.170	0.865	0.00003	0.002	0.999	0.057	0.425	0.689
N	57			145			4,091			4,091		
R²	0.550			0.592			0.308			0.597[b]		
DW	0.944			0.714			0.904			1.901[b]		

Notes:
[a] Lnpbar = $\log_n$ (barley price); Lnp mus = $\log_n$ (cuscuta price); Lnpses = $\log_n$ (sesame price); Lnpwool = $\log_n$ (wool price); Lnpcres = $\log_n$ (cress price).
[b] Calculated as the mean of the respective statistics of the five sets of estimates.

Table 2.8 The partial equilibrium model results for cuscuta, using the four missing data treatment methods

	Listwise deletion			Pairwise deletion			Mean imputation			Multiple imputation		
	coeff	t-stat	p-value	coeff	t-stat	p-value	coeff	t-stat	p-value	coeff	t-stat	p-value
Constant	−0.434	−0.435	0.666	0.995	2.369	0.019	0.296	4.497	0.000	0.540	0.798	0.468
Inpbar[a]	−0.243	−1.263	0.214	−0.364	−3.639	0.000	−0.047	−4.513	0.000	−0.297	−3.865	0.015
Inpdates[a]	0.143	0.789	0.435	0.215	3.211	0.002	0.194	19.433	0.000	0.155	2.273	0.081
Inpcres[a]	0.359	2.312	0.026	0.137	1.554	0.123	0.116	9.180	0.000	0.199	3.343	0.024
Inpses[a]	0.343	1.338	0.189	0.346	3.832	0.000	0.065	4.572	0.000	0.422	5.017	0.006
Inpwool[a]	−0.104	−0.517	0.608	0.330	3.557	0.001	0.031	2.035	0.042	0.137	0.804	0.466
na-meters	−0.183	−1.181	0.245	−0.276	−4.921	0.000	−0.047	−5.288	0.000	−0.284	−5.664	0.004
t	−0.0002	−1.476	0.148	−0.0002	−5.657	0.000	−0.00001	−3.730	0.000	−0.0003	−4.708	0.009
February	−0.069	−0.253	0.801	−0.089	−0.523	0.602	−0.010	−0.849	0.396	0.032	0.233	0.826
March	−0.183	−0.641	0.526	−0.244	−1.422	0.158	−0.014	−1.187	0.235	−0.214	−2.222	0.077
April	−0.155	−0.386	0.701	−0.240	−1.345	0.181	−0.005	−0.397	0.691	−0.227	−2.434	0.058
May	−0.527	−1.182	0.244	−0.131	−0.729	0.467	0.008	0.696	0.487	−0.117	−1.714	0.134
June	−0.095	−0.208	0.836	0.089	0.513	0.609	0.010	0.916	0.359	0.011	0.091	0.931
July	0.011	0.029	0.977	0.051	0.293	0.770	0.003	0.224	0.823	0.031	0.322	0.760
August	0.164	0.468	0.642	−0.026	−0.150	0.881	−0.008	−0.724	0.469	0.035	0.343	0.746
September	0.291	0.889	0.380	−0.098	−0.554	0.581	−0.011	−1.000	0.317	0.062	0.920	0.390
October	0.141	0.443	0.660	0.172	0.989	0.325	0.007	0.633	0.527	0.208	2.192	0.080
November	0.333	1.028	0.310	0.097	0.562	0.575	0.008	0.681	0.496	0.256	1.797	0.140
December	−0.136	−0.448	0.657	0.100	0.585	0.559	−0.00003	−0.002	0.998	0.115	0.981	0.375
N	57			145			4,091			4,091		
R^2	0.550			0.550			0.180			0.590[b]		
DW	0.944			0.673			0.986			1.954[b]		

Notes:

[a] Lnpbar = $\log_n$ (barley price); Lnpdates = $\log_n$ (dates price); Lnpses = $\log_n$ (sesame price); Lnpwool = $\log_n$ (wool price); Lnpcres = $\log_n$ (cress price).

[b] Calculated as the mean of the respective statistics of the five sets of estimates.

Table 2.9 The partial equilibrium model results for sesame, using the four missing data treatment methods

	Listwise deletion			Pairwise deletion			Mean imputation			Multiple imputation		
	coeff	t-stat	p-value	coeff	t-stat	p-value	coeff	t-stat	p-value	coeff	t-stat	p-value
Constant	2.736	6.428	0.000	1.838	5.042	0.000	2.887	51.517	0.000	2.524	15.931	0.000
Inpbar[a]	0.353	3.335	0.002	0.440	4.902	0.000	0.126	11.141	0.000	0.471	6.149	0.003
Inpdates[a]	0.146	1.336	0.189	0.037	0.570	0.570	0.058	5.137	0.000	0.002	0.055	0.958
Inpmus[a]	0.128	1.338	0.189	0.300	3.832	0.000	0.078	4.572	0.000	0.355	5.556	0.004
Inpcres[a]	−0.093	−0.933	0.357	0.019	0.230	0.818	0.231	17.211	0.000	−0.095	−1.416	0.224
Inpwool[a]	0.328	2.930	0.006	0.125	1.389	0.167	0.282	17.400	0.000	0.290	6.873	0.001
na-meters	−0.014	−0.148	0.883	0.178	3.256	0.001	0.033	3.443	0.001	0.026	0.378	0.724
t	0.0002	2.962	0.005	0.0001	3.501	0.001	0.00001	2.981	0.003	0.0002	11.595	0.000
February	0.050	0.303	0.764	0.025	0.159	0.874	−0.002	−0.147	0.883	−0.083	−0.618	0.567
March	0.033	0.189	0.851	0.120	0.748	0.456	0.002	0.129	0.897	−0.006	−0.138	0.892
April	−0.145	−0.593	0.556	0.062	0.374	0.709	−0.007	−0.571	0.568	−0.041	−0.427	0.688
May	0.242	0.883	0.383	0.239	1.436	0.153	0.008	0.666	0.505	0.094	1.421	0.204
June	−0.156	−0.561	0.578	0.153	0.943	0.347	0.011	0.884	0.377	0.270	1.392	0.233
July	−0.074	−0.320	0.751	0.113	0.703	0.483	0.011	0.884	0.377	0.192	1.984	0.106
August	0.132	0.619	0.540	0.111	0.682	0.497	0.011	0.921	0.357	0.186	1.440	0.216
September	−0.034	−0.167	0.868	0.152	0.929	0.354	0.013	1.020	0.308	0.094	0.595	0.582
October	0.145	0.753	0.456	−0.037	−0.225	0.822	−0.002	−0.136	0.892	0.070	0.734	0.497
November	−0.077	−0.384	0.703	0.137	0.859	0.392	0.013	1.041	0.298	0.026	0.326	0.757
December	0.081	0.436	0.665	−0.009	−0.059	0.953	0.004	0.291	0.771	−0.040	−0.600	0.571
N	57			145			4091			4091		
R^2	0.855			0.638			0.327			0.726[b]		
DW	1.636			1.019			1.030			1.918[b]		

Notes:

[a] Lnpbar = $\log_n$ (barley price); Lnpdates = $\log_n$ (dates price); Lnp mus = $\log_n$ (cuscuta price); Lnpcres = $\log_n$ (cress price); Lnpwool = $\log_n$ (wool price); Lnpcres = $\log_n$ (cress price).

[b] Calculated as the mean of the respective statistics of the five sets of estimates.

Table 2.10 The partial equilibrium model results for wool, using the four missing data treatment methods

	Listwise deletion			Pairwise deletion			Mean imputation			Multiple imputation		
	coeff	t-stat	p-value	coeff	t-stat	p-value	coeff	t-stat	p-value	coeff	t-stat	p-value
Constant	-4.016	-8.742	0.000	-3.497	-14.685	0.000	-2.625	-49.455	0.000	-3.876	-41.025	0.000
Lnpbar[a]	-0.008	-0.054	0.957	0.179	1.897	0.060	0.070	6.583	0.000	-0.007	-0.066	0.950
Lnpdates[a]	0.206	1.468	0.150	0.122	1.947	0.054	0.035	3.289	0.001	0.153	3.763	0.015
Lnpmus[a]	-0.065	-0.517	0.608	0.274	3.557	0.001	0.032	2.035	0.042	0.121	0.776	0.480
Lnpcres[a]	-0.045	-0.341	0.735	0.077	0.954	0.342	0.118	9.189	0.000	0.123	1.320	0.255
Lnpses[a]	0.550	2.930	0.006	0.120	1.389	0.167	0.245	17.400	0.000	0.305	6.822	0.001
na-meters	0.214	1.788	0.082	0.186	3.493	0.001	0.020	2.276	0.023	0.203	2.882	0.043
t	0.0002	2.079	0.044	0.0002	6.925	0.000	0.00001	5.237	0.000	0.0002	9.767	0.000
February	-0.085	-0.395	0.695	0.015	0.100	0.921	0.005	0.402	0.687	-0.029	-0.274	0.796
March	-0.223	-0.994	0.326	0.157	0.999	0.319	0.010	0.856	0.392	0.045	0.313	0.768
April	-0.047	-0.149	0.882	0.350	2.178	0.031	0.025	2.159	0.031	0.176	1.572	0.181
May	0.045	0.125	0.901	0.222	1.358	0.177	0.017	1.453	0.146	0.059	0.322	0.763
June	0.490	1.394	0.171	-0.017	-0.107	0.915	0.007	0.582	0.561	-0.103	-0.605	0.576
July	0.034	0.111	0.912	0.011	0.070	0.944	0.010	0.844	0.399	-0.070	-0.448	0.676
August	-0.394	-1.453	0.154	-0.055	-0.346	0.730	0.006	0.498	0.619	-0.186	-0.898	0.418
September	-0.249	-0.963	0.341	0.051	0.318	0.751	0.014	1.190	0.234	-0.150	-0.978	0.379
October	-0.454	-1.885	0.067	-0.042	-0.262	0.793	0.010	0.825	0.409	-0.209	-1.027	0.360
November	-0.398	-1.582	0.122	-0.058	-0.371	0.711	0.002	0.166	0.868	-0.234	-1.698	0.158
December	-0.297	-1.266	0.213	-0.072	-0.463	0.644	0.002	0.164	0.870	-0.035	-0.184	0.863
N	57			145			4091			4091		
R^2	0.793			0.654			0.239			0.661[b]		
DW	1.165			0.504			0.899			1.925[b]		

Notes:
[a] Lnpbar = $\log_n$ (barley price); Lnpdates = $\log_n$ (dates price); Lnp mus = $\log_n$ (cuscuta price); Lnpses = $\log_n$ (sesame price); Lnpcres = $\log_n$ (cress price).
[b] Calculated as the mean of the respective statistics of the five sets of estimates.

Table 2.11 Signs of the significant coefficients (from the multiple imputation method)

	Barley	Cress	Dates	Cuscuta	Sesame	Wool
Barley		+	+	−	+	0
Cress	+		0	+	0	0
Dates	+	0		+	0	+
Cuscuta	−	+	+		+	0
Sesame	+	0	0	+		+
Wool	0	0	+	0	+	

utilities for the consumer. For example, we find in Table 2.11 that wool was a substitute for dates.

Obviously, by this finding we do not mean that people used wool for the same purpose as dates. What we argue is that if the price of wool rose, people reduced their consumption of wool and increased that of dates. This is absolutely not illogical, since this is exactly what Engel's Law states: once real income drops (through price changes for example), the proportion of foodstuffs in the consumption basket should increase and vice versa. Another interesting finding is that cuscuta and barley are complements. This either speaks against the argument that what we call 'cuscuta' was used in the production of dates beer, or it suggests that the amount of cuscuta used in dates beer was so small that it did not affect its prices.

Market efficiency versus market performance

It is thus clear from the existence of substitute and complement relationships between the different products in Babylon that market relations exists. This allows us to directly compare market efficiency and market performance. Let us start with a supply equation:

$$q_t^s = \alpha_0 + \alpha_1 E_{t-1} p_t + \varepsilon_t \varepsilon_t \sim \text{iid}(0, \sigma_\varepsilon^2), \tag{2.10}$$

where $E_{t-1} p_t$ denotes the expectation in $t-1$ about the prices in period t. Now we create a similar demand equation:

$$q_t^d = \beta_0 + \beta_1 p_t + \eta_t \eta_t \sim \text{iid}(0, \sigma_\eta^2). \tag{2.11}$$

We assume that expectations regarding future prices can be modelled as an AR(1) process, which is essentially equal to our Equation (2.1):

$$E_{t-1} p_t = \gamma p_{t-1}. \tag{2.12}$$

The equilibrium price is therefore:

$$p_t = \frac{\alpha_0 - \beta_0}{\beta_1} + \frac{\alpha_1 \gamma}{\beta_1} p_{t-1} + \frac{\varepsilon_t - \eta_t}{\beta_1}, \tag{2.13}$$

or, in first differences,

$$\Delta p_t = \frac{\alpha_0 - \beta_0}{\beta_1} + \left[\frac{\alpha_1 \gamma}{\beta_1} - 1 \right] p_{t-1} + \frac{\varepsilon_t - \eta_t}{\beta_1}. \tag{2.14}$$

The market is weakly efficient if:

$$\gamma = \frac{\beta_1}{\alpha_1}, \tag{2.15}$$

that is, if present prices do not contain any information on price changes.

The variance of the price is:

$$Var(p_t) = \frac{\sigma_{\varepsilon_t}^2 + \sigma_{\eta_t}^2}{\beta_1 - \alpha_1 \gamma}. \tag{2.16}$$

Hence, the closer gamma gets to β_1/α_1 (the more efficient the market is) the higher the variance of prices gets. This is not surprising at all, since the price in year t has no information about changes of prices between t and $t+1$ if the process has a unit root. In this case the variance is expected to grow to infinity as the sample increases in length. In other words, in principle we find that the more efficient a market is, the higher unconditional volatility gets. This is, however, a spurious result that is based on the variance of the prices rather than of the standard deviation of residual as outlined earlier. Hence, it falls victim of neglecting the possible trend in prices and the inflation of variance due to non-stationarity. The approach suggested by Foldvari and Van Leeuwen (2011), directly estimating the residual variance from a specification like Equation (2.14), results in the two measures (market efficiency and market performance) being independent.

One has to be cautious in accepting the above apparent lack of statistical relationship between market efficiency and performance, as it was assumed that the size of the shocks was completely independent of the factors that would improve market efficiency. Of course we will find that market efficiency as well as market performance may increase over time if both the quality of institutions as well as the availability of price information has increased over the past centuries. So, while in the short run we can expect that the two measures will not be related, in the long run they might.

Conclusion

The discussion of the presence of markets in ancient societies has undoubtedly led to a victory of market-thinking. However, the exact definition of market development is less clear. In this chapter we put side by side the two main methodologies used to analyse markets in the long run: market efficiency and market performance. Even though other methods also exist, only these two methods have been used to quantify market behaviour in an economic manner over time.

There is, however, a big difference between market efficiency and market performance. The former relates to the predictability of prices (the less predictable, the more efficient the market), and thus focuses on the flows of information available to the agents in the market. However, there is no specific reason to assume that these flows of information became much better at any time up to the nineteenth century AD; in other words, it remains to be seen if market efficiency is better in the nineteenth century AD than it was in the third century BC. We do find that in Babylon in the third century BC efficient markets already existed. Market performance, however, looks at how markets deal with unpredictable shocks such as natural disasters. The stronger its underlying institutions are (often defined as storage, trade, technology, consumption and government intervention), the better markets can handle these shocks. These factors clearly improve over time. Whereas we found that in Babylon average market performance was 0.48, this declined to roughly 0.2 (i.e. market performance improved as argued earlier in the chapter) in the early modern period in some regions (cf. Van Leeuwen *et al.*, Chapter 20, this volume).

The increase in market performance over time combined with an uncertain development of market efficiency already suggests that the relation between the two measures is at best weak. We can formally describe this relationship starting from a demand and supply model. We found that in Babylon a demand and supply model existed. Although, because of lack of data on quantities, the model remains unidentified and we therefore cannot interpret the level of the coefficients, still we can establish the presence of a demand–supply relationship. We find that commodity prices were strongly interrelated (through substitution and complementarity), suggesting a working market mechanism.

Using this relationship, we find a positive relation between market efficiency and the CV – the higher the market efficiency, the higher the CV. However, this is a spurious result as it takes into account conditional variance and time trends. Using the proposed measure for market performance (standard error of the regression on first differences, log prices), there is no relation between market efficiency and market performance. However, this is all under the assumption that the underlying factors that drive market performance and market efficiency are unrelated: if factors increasing market performance also affect market efficiency, there may be a long run positive correlation between both measures.

Appendix 2.A: Monte Carlo simulation of unit root tests with data missing at random

We assume that series y is a random walk process with 3,500 observations:

$$x_t = x_{t-1} + \varepsilon_t, \text{ with } x_0 = 2.5, \text{ and } \varepsilon \sim N(0, 0.2). \tag{2.17}$$

The missingness is simulated based on the results from an LPM regression on the availability dummy of barley prices, which yields (t-statistics in parentheses):

$$D_t^{\text{missing}} = \underset{(12.3)}{0.0534} + \underset{(27.3)}{0.51} \cdot D_{t-1}^{\text{missing}} + u_t, \tag{2.18}$$

where we find that the standard error of the residual u is about 0.27. This formula simply reflects the autocorrelation in the probability of an observation surviving.

Table 2.12 Results from the Monte Carlo simulation for the D-F test with non-stationary data[a]

	Level of significance		
	1%	*5%*	*10%*
Dickey-Fuller (one-sided test)	−2.73	−2.02	−1.65

Note:
[a] Average number available of observations = 375.7.

Table 2.13 Results from the Monte Carlo simulation for the KPSS test with non-stationary data[a]

	Level of significance		
	1%	*5%*	*10%*
Asymptotic critical values (Kwiatkowski *et al.*, 1992)	0.739	0.463	0.347
% cases with smaller test statistics than the asymptotic critical value	2.14%	0.56%	0.26%

Note:
[a] Average number available of observations = 375.7.

Using this relationship we estimate the probability of an observation surviving. If this is less than 0.5, the observation is deleted, otherwise it is kept. This random simulation of the missingness means that the number of available observations changes by each iteration. Hence, we report the mean of the available observations in the summary table. Finally, we carry out D-F and KPSS unit root tests and observe the test statistics (*t*-statistics reported from the D-F auxiliary regression and the KPSS LM statistics). This procedure is repeated 10,000 times. The results for the D-F tests are reported in Table 2.12.

Kwiatkowski *et al.* (1992) report asymptotic critical values for the KPSS test. In Table 2.13 we report the share of those experiments, where the Lagrange Multiplier (LM) test statistics proved to be less than the asymptotic critical values (this is our estimate of the chance of Type-II error).

We find that if *x* is indeed a random walk process, we would erroneously reject the null hypothesis of stationarity in at most 2.14 per cent of the cases, which is acceptable.

Finally, we may experiment with a specification that differs from (2.17) only in so far that the autoregressive coefficient is now set to 0.99. These series are now stationary even though the effect of shocks will fade away very slowly. Now we can use the KPSS to test the null of stationarity (see Table 2.14).

The critical values are lower than the asymptotic critical values by Kwiatkowsky *et al.* (1992), so we can conclude that if we can reject the null hypothesis of

Table 2.14 Results from the Monte Carlo simulation for the KPSS and D-F tests with stationary data[a]

	Level of significance		
	1%	*5%*	*10%*
KPSS critical values with the autoregressive coefficient being 0.99	0.129	0.205	0.263
% cases when the D-F test would have led to false acceptance of the null hypothesis of non-stationarity	95.0%	82.6%	70.6%

Note:
[a] Average number available of observations = 376.3.

stationarity using their critical values we can safely argue that the series are non-stationary, even with a large number observations missing not at random. On the other hand, if we had used the critical values for the D-F test as in Table 2.12 (which are lower than suggested by MacKinnon (1996)), we would not have rejected the null hypothesis that *y* is a random walk process in 70.6–95 per cent of the cases. With the critical values suggested by MacKinnon this ratio would have been even higher. This is indicative that we should prefer the KPSS test.

Appendix 2.B: Monte Carlo simulation of static regression with data missing at random

The data generating process (DGP) is assumed to be very similar to that described in Appendix 2.A. We first create 3,500 observations with the same formula as in (2.17). Then we create variable *y* as follows:

$$y_t = 0.5 + 0.3x_t + e_t e \sim N(0, 0.3). \tag{2.19}$$

That is, we create two co-integrated series. This is what we expect in the case of related prices when they are determined by market mechanisms. Also, this is what our regression results suggest. That the two series are co-integrated means from an estimation perspective that the coefficients can be estimated with an ordinary least-squares (OLS) procedure as it is consistent.

The missingness of the two series is simulated independently. In the case of series *x* we used the same method as described in (2.18). For series *y* we used the same method, but with different coefficients (we used our dates price series to derive the coefficients):

$$D_t^{\text{missing}} = \underset{(13.1)}{0.0469} + \underset{(20.9)}{0.53} \cdot D_{t-1}^{\text{missing}} + v_t, \tag{2.20}$$

where we find the standard deviation of *v* to be 0.25.

Table 2.15 Results from the Monte Carlo simulation

Method	Statistics	Constant	Slope	Average number of observations
Whole sample	average	0.500	0.300	3,500
	std dev	0.009	0.001	
Listwise deletion	average	0.500	0.300	143.8
	std dev	0.049	0.007	
Mean imputation	average	0.500	0.300	342.9
	std dev	0.122	0.007	

This procedure led to a dataset very similar to the observed data, even though of the 3,500 theoretical observations, only 145 were on average available for regression analysis (where the two series overlapped). The estimation has been repeated 10,000 times. We report the results in Table 2.15.

The results in Table 2.15 suggest that although neither method should lead to biased parameter estimates, the efficiency of the estimation reduces.

Notes

1 The primitivism–modernism distinction (Finley vs Rostovtzeff) can also be viewed in terms of substantivism–formalism. More on this in Chapter 1, this volume.

2 They phrased it as 'market efficiency' but, as argued here, market performance captures the meaning better.

3 There is actually a discussion about what this product is. Most authors nowadays argue that it is cuscuta, but some others have argued for mustard. See Chapter 1, this volume.

4 One should bear in mind that the runs-test is by no means a test of any of the above mentioned hypotheses (MCAR, MAR, MNAR). The runs-test null hypothesis is simply that the data occur in a purely random manner. But even if that is the case, they could theoretically be correlated with any other variables we use in the further analysis, making them MAR or MNAR.

5 One may argue that the previous model is far too simple, and expectations regarding future prices should play a role in the market mechanisms. We can easily rewrite the model to include expectations:

(i)   supply: $\ln Q_{i,t}^S = \alpha_0 + \alpha_1 \ln(E_{t-1} P_{i,t}) + \sum_{k=1}^{np} \alpha_{k+1} \ln(E_{t-1} P_{k,t}) + u_t,$

(ii) demand: $\ln Q_{i,t}^D = \beta_0 + \gamma \ln P_{i,t} + \sum_{j=1}^{np} \beta_j \ln P_{j,t} + \omega Y_t + v_t,$

(iii) condition of equilibrium in market: $\ln Q_{i,t}^S = \ln Q_{i,t}^D.$

In equilibrium:

$$\ln P_{i,t} = \frac{\alpha_0 - \beta_0}{\gamma} - \sum_{j=1}^{np} \frac{\beta_j}{\gamma} \ln P_{j,t} - \frac{\omega}{\gamma} Y_t + \frac{\alpha_1}{\gamma} \ln(E_{t-1} P_{i,t})$$

$$+ \sum_{k=1}^{np} \frac{\alpha_{k+1}}{\gamma} \ln(E_{t-1} P_{k,t}) + \frac{u_t - v_t}{\gamma},$$

which we can rewrite under the assumption of rational expectations, i.e. prices are expected not to change from one period to the next, as follows:

$$\ln P_{i,t} = \frac{\alpha_0 - \beta_0}{\gamma} - \sum_{j=1}^{n_p} \frac{\beta_j}{\gamma} \ln P_{j,t} - \frac{\omega}{\gamma} Y_t + \frac{\alpha_1}{\gamma} \ln P_{i,t-1}$$

$$+ \sum_{k=1}^{n_p} \frac{\alpha_{k+1}}{\gamma} \ln P_{k,t-1} + \sum_{j=1}^{n_z} \frac{\alpha_{j+k+1}}{\gamma} Z_{jt} + \frac{u_t - v_t}{\gamma},$$

which is basically an ARDL(1,1) or ARX(1,1) model, where we explain the prices not only by contemporary prices of other products, but by lagged prices as well. Unfortunately this specification would leave us with too few observations and as such cannot be estimated with the current number of missing observations and the usual methods of data imputation result in bias in dynamic specifications.

6 The Babylonian astronomers measured the daily level of the river from the assumed peak flood downwards, measured in $na = 1/6$ of a cubit $= 8.33$ cm. See Huijs *et al.* (Chapter 7, this volume). We give the measurement here in metres.

Bibliography

Allison, P. D. 2001. *Missing Data*, Thousand Oaks CA: SAGE.

Andreau, J. 2002. 'Twenty Years after Moses I. Finley's *The Ancient Economy*', in *The Ancient Economy*, edited by W. Scheidel and S. von Reden, London: Routledge: 33–49.

Dilley, R. 1996. 'Market', in *Encyclopedia of Cultural Anthropology*, edited by D. Levinson and M. Ember, New York: Henry Holt: 728–32.

Fama, E. 1970. 'Efficient Capital Markets: A Review of Theory and Empirical Work', *Journal of Finance*, 25: 383–417.

Feinman, G. M. and Garraty, C. P. 2010. 'Preindustrial Markets and Marketing: Archaeological Perspectives', *Annual Review of Anthropology*, 39: 167–91.

Finley, M. I. 1973. *The Ancient Economy*, London: Chatto and Windus.

Foldvari, P. and Van Leeuwen, B. 2011. 'What Can Price Volatility Tell Us about Market Efficiency? Conditional Heteroscedasticity in Historical Commodity Price Series', *Cliometrica*, 5: 165–86.

Jursa, M. 2010. *Aspects of the Economic History of Babylonia in the First Millennium BC: Economic Geography, Economic Mentalities, Agriculture, the Use of Money and the Problem of Economic Growth* (with contributions by J. Hackl, B. Janković, K. Kleber, E. E. Payne, C. Waerzeggers and M. Weszeli), Münster: Ugarit Verlag.

Kwiatkowski, D., Phillips, P., Schmidt, P. and Shin, Y. 1992. 'Testing the Null Hypothesis of Stationarity against the Alternative of a Unit Root', *Journal of Econometrics*, 54: 159–78.

Lie, J. 1997. 'Sociology of Markets', *Annual Review of Sociology*, 23: 341–60.

Little, R. J. A. 1988. 'A Test of Missing Completely at Random for Multivariate Data with Missing Values', *Journal of the American Statistical Association*, 83 (404): 1198–202.

Little, R. J. A. and Rubin, D. B. 2002. *Statistical Analysis with Missing Data*, Oxford: John Wiley & Sons.

MacKinnon, J. G. 1996. 'Numerical Distribution Functions for Unit Root and Cointegration Tests', *Journal of Applied Econometrics*, 11 (6): 601–18.

McKnight, P. E., McKnight, K. M., Figueredo, A. J. and Sidani, S. 2007. *Missing Data: a Gentle Introduction*, New York: Guilford Press.

Morgan, J. R. 2007. 'The Representation of Philosophers in Greek Fiction', in *Philosophical Presences in the Ancient Novel*, edited by J. R. Morgan and M. Jones, Groningen: Barkhuis Publishing & Groningen University Library: 23–51.

Polanyi, K. 1968. *Primitive, Archaic, and Modern Economics: Essays of Karl Polanyi*, Garden City NY: Anchor Books/Doubleday.

Romero, N. E., Ma, Q. D.Y., Liebovitch, L. S., Brown, C. T. and Ivanov, P. Ch. 2010. 'Correlated Walks Down the Babylonian Markets', *Europhysics Letters*, 90 (1): 18004-p1–18004-p6.

Slotsky, A. L. 1997. *The Bourse of Babylon. Market Quotations in the Astronomical Diaries of Babylonia*, Bethesda MD: CDL Press.

Slotsky, A. L. and Wallenfels, R. 2009. *Tallies and Trends; the Late Babylonian Commodity Price Lists*, Bethesda MD: CDL Press.

Stol, M. 1994. 'Beer in Neo-Babylonian Times', in *Drinking in Ancient Societies. History and the culture of Drinks in the Ancient Near East*, edited by L. Milano, Padua: Sargon: 155–83.

Temin, P. 2002. 'Price Behavior in Ancient Babylon', *Explorations in Economic History*, 39: 46–60.

Van der Spek, R. J. 2005. *Commodity Prices from Babylon (385–61 BC)*, www.iisg.nl/hpw/data.php#babylon

—— Forthcoming. 'The Volatility of Prices of Barley and Dates in Babylon in the Third and Second Centuries BC', in *Documentary Sources in Ancient Near Eastern and Greco-Roman History: Methodology and Practice*, edited by H. D. Baker and M. Jursa, Oxford: Oxbow Books.

Van der Spek, R. J. and Mandemakers, C. A. 2003. 'Sense and Nonsense in the Statistical Approach of Babylonian Prices', *Bibliotheca Orientalis*, 60: 522–37.

Vargyas, P. 2001. *A History of Babylonian Prices in the First Millennium BC. 1. Prices of the Basic Commodities*, Heidelberg: Heidelberger Orientverlag.

Veenhof, K. R. 1972. *Aspects of Old Assyrian Trade and Its Terminology*, Leiden: E.J. Brill.

3 Analysis of historical time series with messy features

The case of commodity prices in Babylonia[1]

Siem Jan Koopman and
Lennart Hoogerheide

Introduction

In this chapter we discuss the multivariate analysis of historical time series that typically are subject to messy features such as missing observations and outlying observations. Our primary motivation is the multiple analysis of monthly commodity prices in Babylonia between 385–61 BC. We consider monthly price series for barley, dates, mustard, cress, sesame and wool. As can be expected, the data set is far from complete. The monthly time series spans over 300 years and hence we could have 3,888 observations for each price series. However for most series we only have around 530 monthly observations available. This means that the vast majority of data entries are missing, and we need to treat 3,358 missing observations in the analysis.

Further, data on the available prices stretch over a long period of more than three centuries. The treatment of commodities and market conditions changed greatly in Babylonia during this long and hectic period. The time series of prices is subject to outliers and structural breaks due to periods of war and other disasters. In times of turmoil, the supply of commodities typically reduces and their availability becomes scarce. As a result, prices typically rise and often to very high levels. Other contributions to this volume discuss further particularities of this data set and related sets. Our contribution concentrates on the statistical treatment of these historical data sets.

Different statistical methodologies for the analysis of time series analysis are available (see Ord 1990), but it is not our purpose to provide an overview of them here. In our contribution we discuss the class of unobserved components time series (UCTS) models for both univariate and multivariate analyses. A complete treatment is presented in Harvey (1989), who refers to such models as 'Structural Time Series Models'. An up-to-date discussion of univariate UCTS models is presented later in this chapter. Statistical analysis based on UCTS models relies mainly on the representation of the model in state space form. Once the model is framed in this way, the Kalman filter and related methods can be used to estimate

the dynamic features of the model, and also for the computation of the likelihood function. We will introduce the state space form and the related methods in
this chapter. We will argue that in particular the Kalman filter plays a central role
in time series analysis as it is general and can handle missing entries in a time
series routinely. We also demonstrate the generality of the UCTS model and the
Kalman filter by showing how the univariate UCTS model and its treatment can
be generalized towards a multivariate statistical analysis of a multiple time series.

The UCTS methodology is illustrated for our six monthly time series of commodity prices for barley, dates, mustard, cress, sesame and wool. We first analyse
each time series by an univariate UCTS model, and show that we can obtain accurate estimates of the evolution of the price levels over a time span of 600 years.
We discuss how outliers and structural breaks affect the analysis and how we can
allow for these irregularities in the time series. A complete multivariate analysis
is also considered: in particular we investigate how common the price evolutions
have been for the different commodities.

Subsequently we discuss in detail our time series methodology based on UCTS
models. We also discuss general state space methods. We introduce a number of
interesting multivariate extensions for the UCTS methodology and, finally, we
present the empirical study for the six monthly time series of commodity prices for
barley, dates, mustard, cress, sesame and wool in Babylonia between 385–61 BC.

Unobserved components time series models

The univariate UCTS model that is particularly suitable for many economic data
sets is given by:

$$y_t = \mu_t + \gamma_t + \psi_t + \varepsilon_t, \quad \varepsilon_t \sim \text{NID}(0, \sigma_\varepsilon^2), \quad t = 1, \ldots, n, \tag{3.1}$$

where μ_t, γ_t, ψ_t, and ε_t represent trend, seasonal, cycle, and irregular components,
respectively. The trend, seasonal, and cycle components are modelled by linear
dynamic stochastic processes that depend on disturbances. The components are
formulated in a flexible way and they are allowed to change over time, rather than
being deterministic. The disturbances driving the components are independent of
each other. The definitions of the components are given below, but a full explanation of the underlying rationale can be found in Harvey (1989, Chapter 2) where
model (3.1) is referred to as the 'Structural Time Series Model'. The effectiveness
of structural time series models compared to autoregressive integrated moving
average (ARIMA)-type models is discussed in Harvey et al. (1998). They stress
that time series models based on unobserved components are particularly effective when messy features are present in the time series – such as missing values,
mixed frequencies (monthly and quarterly seasons of time series), outliers, structural breaks and non-linear non-Gaussian aspects. An elementary introduction
and a practical guide to unobserved component time series modelling is provided
by Commandeur and Koopman (2007).

Trend component

The trend component can be specified in many different ways. Two examples are given below.

Local level

The trend component can simply be modelled as a random walk process and is then given by:

$$\mu_{t+1} = \mu_t + \eta_t, \quad \eta_t \sim \text{NID}(0, \sigma_\eta^2), \tag{3.2}$$

where $\text{NID}(0, \sigma^2)$ refers to a normally independently distributed series with mean zero and variance σ^2. The disturbance series η_t is therefore serially independent and mutually independent of all other disturbance series related to y_t in (3.1). The initial trend μ_1 is for simplicity treated as an unknown coefficient that needs to be estimated together with the unknown variance σ_η^2. The estimation of parameters is discussed later in this chapter. Harvey (1989: §2.3.6) defines the *local level model* as $y_t = \mu_t + \varepsilon_t$ with μ_t given by (3.2). In the case where $\sigma_\eta^2 = 0$, the observations from a local level model are generated by a NID process with a constant mean μ_1 and a constant variance σ^2.

Local linear trend

An extension of the random walk trend is obtained by including a stochastic drift component:

$$\mu_{t+1} = \mu_t + \beta_t + \eta_t, \quad \beta_{t+1} = \beta_t + \zeta_t, \quad \zeta_t \sim \text{NID}(0, \sigma_\zeta^2), \tag{3.3}$$

where the disturbance series η_t is as in (3.2). The initial values μ_1 and β_1 are treated as unknown coefficients. Harvey (1989: §2.3.6) defines the *local linear trend model* as $y_t = \mu_t + \varepsilon_t$ with μ_t given by (3.3).

In the case where $\sigma_\zeta^2 = 0$, the trend (3.3) reduces to $\mu_{t+1} = \mu_t + \beta_1 + \eta_t$ where the drift β_1 is fixed. This specification is referred to as a *random walk plus drift* process. If in addition $\sigma_\eta^2 = 0$, the trend reduces to the deterministic linear trend $\mu_{t+1} = \mu_1 + \beta_1 t$. When $\sigma_\eta^2 = 0$ and $\sigma_\zeta^2 > 0$, the trend μ_t in (3.3) is known as the integrated random walk process which can be visualized as a smooth trend function.

Seasonal component

To account for the seasonal variation in a time series, the component γ_t is included in model (3.1). More specifically, γ_t represents the seasonal effect at time t that is associated with season $s = s(t)$ for $s = 1, \ldots, S$ where S is the seasonal length ($S = 4$ for quarterly data and $S = 12$ for monthly data). The time-varying seasonal component can be established in different ways.

Fixed trigonometric seasonal

A deterministic seasonal pattern can be constructed from a set of sine and cosine functions. In this case the seasonal component γ_t is specified as a sum of trigonometric cycles with seasonal frequencies. Specifically, we have:

$$\gamma_t = \sum_{j=1}^{\lfloor S/2 \rfloor} \gamma_{j,t}, \quad \gamma_{j,t} = a_j \cos(\lambda_j t - b_j), \tag{3.4}$$

where $\lfloor \cdot \rfloor$ is the floor function, $\gamma_{j,t}$ is the cosine function with amplitude a_j, phase b_j, and seasonal frequency $\lambda_j = 2\pi j / S$ (measured in radians) for $j = 1, \ldots, \lfloor S/2 \rfloor$ and $t = 1, \ldots, n$. The seasonal effects are based on coefficients a_j and b_j. Given the trigonometric identities:

$$\cos(\lambda \pm \xi) = \cos\lambda \cos\xi \mp \sin\lambda \sin\xi, \quad \sin(\lambda \pm \xi) = \cos\lambda \sin\xi \pm \sin\lambda \cos\xi, \tag{3.5}$$

we can express $\gamma_{j,t}$ as the sine-cosine wave:

$$\gamma_{j,t} = \delta_{c,j} \cos(\lambda_j t) + \delta_{s,j} \sin(\lambda_j t), \tag{3.6}$$

where $\delta_{c,j} = a_j \cos b_j$ and $\delta_{s,j} = a_j \sin b_j$. The reverse transformation is $a_j = \delta_{c,j}^2 + \delta_{s,j}^2$ and $b_j = \tan^{-1}(\delta_{s,j} / \delta_{c,j})$. The seasonal effects are alternatively represented by coefficients $\delta_{c,j}$ and $\delta_{s,j}$. When S is odd, the number of seasonal coefficients is $S - 1$ by construction. When S is even, variable $\delta_{s,j}$, with $j = S/2$, drops out of (3.6) since frequency $\lambda_j = \pi$ and $\sin(\pi t) = 0$. Hence for any seasonal length $S > 1$ we have $S - 1$ seasonal coefficients, as in the fixed dummy seasonal case.

The evaluation of each $\gamma_{j,t}$ can be carried out recursively in t. By repeatedly applying the trigonometric identities (3.5), we can express $\gamma_{j,t}$ as the recursive expression:

$$\begin{pmatrix} \gamma_{j,t+1} \\ \gamma_{j,t+1}^+ \end{pmatrix} = \begin{bmatrix} \cos\lambda_j & \sin\lambda_j \\ -\sin\lambda_j & \cos\lambda_j \end{bmatrix} \begin{pmatrix} \gamma_{j,t} \\ \gamma_{j,t}^+ \end{pmatrix}, \tag{3.7}$$

with $\gamma_{j,0} = \delta_{c,j}$ and $\gamma_{j,0}^+ = \delta_{s,j}$ for $j = 1, \ldots, \lfloor S/2 \rfloor$. The variable $\gamma_{j,t}^+$ appears by construction as an auxiliary variable. It follows that the seasonal effect γ_t is a linear function of the variables $\gamma_{j,t}$ and $\gamma_{j,t}^+$ for $j = 1, \ldots, \lfloor S/2 \rfloor$ (in the case where S is even, $\gamma_{j,t}^+$, with $j = S/2$, drops out).

Time-varying trigonometric seasonal

The recursive evaluation of the seasonal variables in (3.7) allows the introduction of a time-varying trigonometric seasonal function. We obtain the stochastic trigonometric seasonal component γ_t by having:

$$\begin{pmatrix} \gamma_{j,t+1} \\ \gamma_{j,t+1}^+ \end{pmatrix} = \begin{bmatrix} \cos \lambda_j & \sin \lambda_j \\ -\sin \lambda_j & \cos \lambda_j \end{bmatrix} \begin{pmatrix} \gamma_{j,t} \\ \gamma_{j,t}^+ \end{pmatrix} + \begin{pmatrix} \omega_{j,t} \\ \omega_{j,t}^+ \end{pmatrix},$$

$$\begin{pmatrix} \omega_{j,t} \\ \omega_{j,t}^+ \end{pmatrix} \sim \text{NID}(0, \sigma_\omega^2 I_2), \tag{3.8}$$

with $\lambda_j = 2\pi j / S$ for $j = 1, \ldots, \lfloor S/2 \rfloor$ and $t = 1, \ldots, n$. The $S - 1$ initial variables $\gamma_{j,1}$ and $\gamma_{j,1}^+$ are treated as unknown coefficients. The seasonal disturbance series $\omega_{j,t}$ and $\omega_{j,t}^+$ are serially and mutually independent, and are also independent of all the other disturbance series. In the case where $\sigma_\omega^2 = 0$, equation (3.8) reduces to (3.7). The variance σ_ω^2 is common to all disturbances associated with different seasonal frequencies. These restrictions can be lifted and different seasonal variances for different frequencies λ_j can be considered for $j = 1, \ldots, \lfloor S/2 \rfloor$.

The random walk seasonal

The random walk specification for a seasonal component is proposed by Harrison and Stevens (1976) and is given by:

$$\gamma_t = e_j' \gamma_t^\dagger, \quad \gamma_{t+1}^\dagger = \gamma_t^\dagger + \omega_t^\dagger, \quad \omega_t^\dagger \sim \text{NID}(0, \sigma_\omega^2 \Omega), \tag{3.9}$$

where the $S \times 1$ vector $\gamma_t^\dagger$ contains the seasonal effects, e_j is the jth column of the $S \times S$ identity matrix I_S, $S \times 1$ disturbance vector $\omega_t^\dagger$ is normally and independently distributed with mean zero and $S \times S$ variance matrix $\sigma_\omega^2 \Omega$. The seasonal effects evolve over time as random walk processes. To ensure that the sum of seasonal effects is zero, the variance matrix Ω is subject to restriction $\Omega \iota = 0$ with ι as the $S \times 1$ vector of ones. The seasonal index j, with $j = 1, \ldots, S$, corresponds to time index t and represents a specific month or quarter. A particular specification of Ω that is subject to this restriction is given by $\Omega = I_S - S^{-1} \iota \iota'$. Due to the restriction of Ω, the S seasonal random walk processes in $\gamma_t^\dagger$ do not evolve independently of each other. Proietti (2000) has shown that the time-varying trigonometric seasonal model with specific variance restrictions is equivalent to the random walk seasonal model (3.9) with $\Omega = I_S - S^{-1} \iota \iota'$.

Harvey (1989: §2.3–2.5) studies the statistical properties of time-varying seasonal processes in more detail. He concludes that the time-varying trigonometric seasonal evolves more smoothly over time than time-varying dummy seasonals.

Cycle component

To capture business cycle features from economic time series, we can include a stationary cycle component in the UCTS model. For example, for a trend-plus-cycle model, we can consider $y_t = \mu_t + \psi_t + \varepsilon_t$. Next we discuss various stochastic specifications for the cycle component ψ_t.

Autoregressive moving average process

The cycle component ψ_t can be formulated as a stationary autoregressive moving average (ARMA) process and given by:

$$\varphi_\psi(L)\psi_{t+1} = \vartheta_\psi(L)\xi_t, \quad \xi_t \sim \text{NID}(0, \sigma_\xi^2), \tag{3.10}$$

where $\varphi_\psi(L)$ is the autoregressive polynomial in the lag operator L, of lag order p with coefficients $\varphi_{\psi,1}, \ldots, \varphi_{\psi,p}$ and $\vartheta_\psi(L)$ is the moving average polynomial of lag order q with coefficients $\vartheta_{\psi,1}, \ldots, \vartheta_{\psi,q}$. The requirement of stationarity applies to the autoregressive polynomial $\varphi_\psi(L)$ and states that the roots of $|\varphi_\psi(L)| = 0$ lie outside the unit circle. The theoretical autocorrelation function of an ARMA process has cyclical properties when the roots of $|\varphi_\psi(L)| = 0$ are within the complex range. It requires $p > 1$. In this instance the autocorrelations converge to zero when the corresponding lag is increasing, but the convergence pattern is cyclical. This implies that the component ψ_t has cyclical dynamic properties. Once the autoregressive coefficients are estimated, it can be established whether the empirical model with ψ_t as in (3.10) has detected cyclical dynamics in the time series. The economic cycle component in the model of Clark (1987) is specified as the stationary ARMA process (3.10) with lag orders $p = 2$ and $q = 0$.

Time-varying trigonometric cycle

An alternative stochastic formulation of the cycle component can be based on a time-varying trigonometric process such as (3.8) but with frequency λ_c associated with the typical length of an economic business cycle, say between 1.5 and 8 years, as suggested by Burns and Mitchell (1946). We obtain:

$$\begin{pmatrix} \psi_{t+1} \\ \psi_{t+1}^+ \end{pmatrix} = \varphi_\psi \begin{bmatrix} \cos\lambda_c & \sin\lambda_c \\ -\sin\lambda_c & \cos\lambda_c \end{bmatrix} \begin{pmatrix} \psi_t \\ \psi_t^+ \end{pmatrix} + \begin{pmatrix} \kappa_t \\ \kappa_t^+ \end{pmatrix}, \tag{3.11}$$

where the discount factor $0 < \varphi_\psi < 1$ is introduced to enforce a stationary process for the stochastic cycle component. The disturbances and the initial conditions for the cycle variables are given by:

$$\begin{pmatrix} \kappa_t \\ \kappa_t^+ \end{pmatrix} \sim \text{NID}(0, \sigma_\kappa^2 I_2), \quad \begin{pmatrix} \psi_1 \\ \psi_1^+ \end{pmatrix} \sim \text{NID}\left(0, \frac{\sigma_\kappa^2}{1 - \varphi_\psi^2} I_2\right),$$

where the disturbances κ_t and κ_t^+ are serially independent and mutually independent, also with respect to disturbances that are associated with other components. The coefficients φ_ψ, λ_c and σ_κ^2 are unknown and need to be estimated together with the other parameters.

This stochastic cycle specification is discussed by Harvey (1989: §2.3–2.5), where it is argued that the process (3.11) is the same as the ARMA process (3.10) with $p = 2$ and $q = 1$ and where the roots of $|\varphi_\psi(L)| = 0$ are enforced to be within the complex range.

Linear Gaussian state space models

The state space form provides a unified representation of a wide range of linear time series models; see Harvey (1989), Kitagawa and Gersch (1996) and Durbin and Koopman (2012). The linear Gaussian state space form consists of a transition equation and a measurement equation. We formulate the model as in (de Jong 1991), that is:

$$y_t = Z_t \alpha_t + G_t \varepsilon_t, \quad \alpha_{t+1} = T_t \alpha_t + H_t \varepsilon_t, \quad \varepsilon_t \sim \text{NID}(0, I), \tag{3.12}$$

for $t = 1, \ldots, n$, where ε_t is a vector of serially independent disturbance series. The $m \times 1$ state vector α_t contains the unobserved components and their associated variables. The measurement equation is the first equation in (3.12) and it relates the observation y_t to the state vector α_t through the signal $Z_t \alpha_t$. The transition equation is the second equation in (3.12) and it is used to formulate the dynamic processes of the unobserved components in a companion form. The deterministic matrices T_t, Z_t, H_t and G_t, possibly time-varying, are referred to as system matrices and they will often be sparse and known matrices. Specific elements of the system matrices may be specified as functions of an unknown parameter vector.

Unobserved component models in state space form

To illustrate how the unobserved components discussed in the previous section can be formulated in the state space form (3.12), we consider the basic structural model as given by:

$$y_t = \mu_t + \gamma_t + \varepsilon_t, \quad \varepsilon_t \sim \text{NID}(0, \sigma_\varepsilon^2), \tag{3.13}$$

with trend component μ_t as in (3.3), seasonal component γ_t as in (3.8) with seasonal length $S = 4$ (quarterly data) and irregular ε_t as in (3.1). We require a state vector of five elements and a disturbance vector of four elements; they are given by:

$$\alpha_t = (\mu_t, \beta_t, \gamma_t, \gamma_{t-1}, \gamma_{t-2})', \quad \varepsilon_t = (\varepsilon_t, \eta_t, \zeta_t, \omega_t)'.$$

The state space formulation of the basic decomposition model is given by (3.12) with the system matrices

$$T_t = \begin{bmatrix} 1 & 1 & 0 & 0 & 0 \\ 0 & 1 & 0 & 0 & 0 \\ 0 & 0 & -1 & -1 & -1 \\ 0 & 0 & 1 & 0 & 0 \\ 0 & 0 & 0 & 1 & 0 \end{bmatrix}, \quad H_t = \begin{bmatrix} 0 & \sigma_\eta & 0 & 0 \\ 0 & 0 & \sigma_\zeta & 0 \\ 0 & 0 & 0 & \sigma_\omega \\ 0 & 0 & 0 & 0 \\ 0 & 0 & 0 & 0 \end{bmatrix},$$

$$Z_t = \begin{pmatrix} 1 & 0 & 1 & 0 & 0 \end{pmatrix}, \quad G_t = \begin{pmatrix} \sigma_\varepsilon & 0 & 0 & 0 \end{pmatrix}.$$

Here the system matrices T_t, H_t, Z_t and G_t do not depend on t; the matrices are time-invariant. The standard deviations of the disturbances in H_t and G_t are fixed, unknown and need to be estimated. The corresponding variances are σ_η^2, σ_ζ^2, σ_ω^2 and σ_ε^2. It is common practice to transform the variances into logs for the purpose of estimation; the log-variances can be estimated without constraints. The unknown parameters are collected in the 4×1 parameter vector θ. Estimation of θ can be carried out by the method of maximum likelihood, as discussed later.

For the trend component μ_t in (3.3) the initial variables μ_1 and β_1 are treated as unknown coefficients. For the dummy seasonal component γ_t in (3.8) with $S = 4$, the initial variables γ_1, γ_0 and γ_{-1} are also treated as unknown coefficients. Given the composition of the state vector above, we can treat α_1 as a vector of unknown coeffients. We can estimate α_1 simultaneously with θ by the method of maximum likelihood or we can concentrate α_1 from the likelihood function. We also discuss the initialization issues later.

Kalman filter

Consider the linear Gaussian state space model (3.12). The predictive estimator of the state vector α_{t+1} is a linear function of the observations $y_1, \ldots, y_t$. The Kalman filter computes the minimum mean square linear estimator (MMSLE) of the state vector α_{t+1} conditional on the observations $y_1, \ldots, y_t$, denoted by $a_{t+1|t}$, together with its mean square error (MSE) matrix, denoted by $P_{t+1|t}$. We will also refer to $a_{t+1|t}$ as the state prediction estimate with $P_{t+1|t}$ as its state prediction error variance matrix. The Kalman filter is given by:

$$v_t = y_t - Z_t a_{t|t-1}, \qquad F_t = Z_t P_{t|t-1} Z_t' + G_t G_t',$$

$$M_t = T_t P_{t|t-1} Z_t' + H_t G_t', \qquad t = 1, \ldots, n,$$

$$a_{t+1|t} = T_t a_{t|t-1} + K_t v_t, \qquad P_{t+1|t} = T_t P_{t|t-1} T_t' + H_t H_t' - K_t M_t',$$

$$(3.14)$$

with Kalman gain matrix $K_t = M_t F_t^{-1}$, and for particular initial values $a_{1|0}$ and $P_{1|0}$. The one-step-ahead prediction error is $v_t = y_t - \mathrm{E}(y_t|y_1, \ldots, y_{t-1})$ with variance $\mathrm{Var}(v_t) = F_t$. The innovations have mean zero and are serially independent by construction so that $E(v_t v_s') = 0$ for $t \neq s$ and $t, s = 1, \ldots, n$.

Before the MMSLE $a_{t+1|t}$ and the MSE $P_{t+1|t}$ are computed in the Kalman filter, the MMSLE of the state vector α_t conditional on $y_1, \ldots, y_t$, denoted by $a_{t|t}$, and its corresponding MSE matrix, denoted by $P_{t|t}$, can be computed as:

$$a_{t|t} = a_{t|t-1} + P_{t|t-1} Z_t' F_t^{-1} v_t, \qquad P_{t|t} = P_{t|t-1} - P_{t|t-1} Z_t' F_t^{-1} Z_t P_{t|t-1}.$$

$$(3.15)$$

It then follows that:

$$a_{t+1|t} = T_t a_{t|t}, \qquad P_{t+1|t} = T_t P_{t|t} T_t' + H_t H_t'.$$

Formal proofs of the Kalman filter can be found in Anderson and Moore (1979), Harvey (1989) and Durbin and Koopman (2012).

Likelihood evaluation

The Kalman filter can be used to evaluate the Gaussian likelihood function via the prediction error decomposition, see Schweppe (1965), Jones (1980) and Harvey (1989: §3.4). Given a model as described previously for y_t, we denote the joint density of $y_1, \ldots, y_n$ by $p(y_1, \ldots, y_n)$ and the prediction error decomposition is then given by:

$$p(y_1, \ldots, y_n) = p(y_1) \prod_{t=2}^{n} p(y_t | y_1, \ldots, y_{t-1}).$$

The predictive density $p(y_t | y_1, \ldots, y_{t-1})$ is Gaussian and has mean

$$E(y_t | y_1, \ldots, y_{t-1}) = Z_t a_{t|t-1}$$

and variance

$$\text{Var}(y_t | y_1, \ldots, y_{t-1}) = Z_t P_{t|t-1} Z_t' + G_t G_t' = F_t.$$

For a realized time series $y_1, \ldots, y_n$, the log-likelihood function is given by:

$$\ell = \log p(y_1, \ldots, y_n) = \sum_{t=1}^{n} \log p(y_t | y_1, \ldots, y_{t-1})$$

$$= -\frac{n}{2} \log(2\pi) - \frac{1}{2} \sum_{t=1}^{n} \log|F_t| - \frac{1}{2} \sum_{t=1}^{n} v_t' F_t^{-1} v_t. \tag{3.16}$$

The one-step-ahead prediction errors v_t and their variances F_t are computed by the Kalman filter for a given value of the parameter vector θ. To make the dependence of the likelihood function on the parameter vector θ explicit, we can write $\ell = \ell(\theta)$.

Parameter estimation

In a state space analysis we are concerned with two groups of parameters that need to be estimated for a given model specification. The first group is contained in parameter vector θ; see previous section introducing unobserved component models in state space form for an illustration. The second group consists of initial variables for the unobserved (non-stationary) processes and the regression coefficients such as δ in (3.13). The initial conditions for unobserved stationary processes can be derived from the theoretical autocovariance function.

Maximum likelihood estimation of θ

The log-likelihood function (3.16) can be maximized with respect to θ numerically using a numerical quasi-Newton method. For example, the method of Broyden–Fletcher–Goldfarb–Shanno (BFGS) is generally regarded as computationally efficient in terms of convergence speed and numerical stability; see Nocedal and Wright (1999). The BFGS iterative optimization method is based on information from the gradient (or score). Analytical and computationally fast methods for computing the score for a current value of θ in a state space analysis have been developed by Koopman and Shephard (1992). The BFGS method is terminated when some pre-chosen convergence criterion is satisfied. The convergence criterion is usually based on the gradient evaluated at the current estimate, the parameter change compared to the previous estimate, or the likelihood value change compared to the previous estimate. The number of iterations required to satisfy these criteria depends on the choice of the initial parameter values, the tightness of the chosen criterion and the shape of the likelihood surface.

An alternative method for maximum likelihood estimation is the EM-algorithm; see Shumway and Stoffer (1982) and Watson and Engle (1983) in the context of a state space analysis. The basic EM procedure works roughly as follows. Consider the joint density $p(y_1, \ldots, y_n, \alpha_1, \ldots, \alpha_n)$. The Expectation (E) step takes the expectation of the state vectors conditional on $y_1, \ldots, y_n$ and the Maximization (M) step maximizes the resulting expression with respect to θ. The E step requires the evaluation of the estimated state vector using a smoothing algorithm related to the Kalman filter (de Jong 1989). The M step is usually carried out analytically and is simpler than maximizing the full likelihood function directly. Given the 'new' estimate of θ from the M step, we return to the E step and evaluate the smoothed estimates based on the new estimate. This iterative procedure converges to the maximum likelihood estimate of θ. Under fairly weak conditions it can be proved that each iteration of the EM-algorithm increases the value of the likelihood. As a result, the EM converges to a maximum of the likelihood. In practice it is often found that while the EM gets to a neighbourhood of the maximum quickly, it converges to the maximum slowly. Therefore a mix of EM and direct maximization is often advocated. When θ only contains parameters in G_t and H_t, Koopman (1993) shows that the EM can be modified toward a fast and simple procedure.

Estimation of initial states

The non-stationary trend and seasonal components, as discussed earlier in this chapter, rely on initial variables that are treated as fixed unknown coefficients. We have also shown that these initial states are collectively placed in α_1. We can therefore concentrate on the estimation of the initial state vector α_1.

Preferably we estimate α_1 jointly with θ by the method of maximum likelihood, as discussed above. However, numerical problems may arise when the likelihood function is maximized with respect to a high-dimensional parameter vector that joins θ and α_1. Fortunately, the direct maximization with respect to α_1 can be avoided since the one-step-ahead prediction error v_t is a linear function of the initial state α_1, that is, $v_t = v_t^o + v_t^\alpha \alpha_1$ where v_t^o is equal to v_t when the Kalman filter (3.14) is started with $a_{1|0} = 0$ and $P_{1|0} = 0$ and v_t^α is a function of the system matrices Z_t, T_t, G_t and H_t. Given this linear dependence, the initial state vector can be derived from from the log-likelihood function in the usual way. We then maximize the concentrated likelihood with respect to θ. The implementation of this approach was developed by Rosenberg (1973).

Tunnicliffe-Wilson (1989) and Harvey and Shephard (1990) argue convincingly that the maximum likelihood estimation of α_1 can lead to bias in the estimation of unknown variances in θ; for example, it can increase the probability that a variance is estimated as zero while the true variance is not zero. They advocate the estimation of θ via the maximization of a *marginal* or *diffuse* likelihood function with respect to initial state α_1. In a state space analysis, this approach can be embedded within a unified treatment for the initialization of the Kalman filter with respect to initial states; see Ansley and Kohn (1985), de Jong (1991) and Koopman (1997). Francke *et al.* (2010) subsequently argued that the strict implementation of the marginal likelihood function for models with initial states is preferred for parameter estimation.

Stationary conditions for the initial state

When the state vector only contains stationary variables, the initial conditions for α_1 can be obtained from the theoretical autocovariance function. In a time-invariant stationary state space model we have $\alpha_{t+1} = T\alpha_t + H\varepsilon_t$ with $E(\alpha_t) = 0$ and $P = \text{Var}(\alpha_t)$ for $t = 1, \ldots, n$. It follows that $P = TPT + HH'$ with solution:

$$\text{vec}(P^*) = (I - T \otimes T)^{-1}\text{vec}(HH').$$

Efficient algorithms for solving Riccati equations can be used to compute P^* when its dimension is large, as discussed in Anderson and Moore (1979) and Hindrayanto *et al.* (2010). Since this solution also applies to α_1, we can initialize the Kalman filter (3.14) with $a_{1|0} = 0$ and $P_{1|0} = P^*$.

In most models, the initial state vector α_1 contains initial stationary and non-stationary variables; see also the illustrations in the earlier section of this chapter introducing unobserved component models in state space form. The Kalman filter initialization methods of de Jong (1991) and Koopman (1997) account for such general model specifications.

Diagnostic checking

The assumptions underlying the models in the section initiating our discussions of unobserved component time series models are that all disturbances, such as ε_t, η_t and κ_t, are normally distributed, are serially and mutually independent and have constant variances. Under these assumptions the standardized one-step-ahead prediction errors (or *prediction residuals*) are given by:

$$e_t = \frac{v_t}{\sqrt{F_t}}, \quad t = 1, \ldots, n. \tag{3.17}$$

The prediction residuals are also normally distributed and serially independent with unit variance. We can investigate whether these properties hold by means of the following large-sample diagnostic tests:

Normality

The first four moments of the standardised forecast errors are given by:

$$m_1 = \frac{1}{n} \sum_{t=1}^{n} e_t, \quad m_q = \frac{1}{n} \sum_{t=1}^{n} (e_t - m_1)^q, \quad q = 2, 3, 4.$$

Skewness and kurtosis are denoted by M_3 and M_4, respectively, and when the model assumptions are valid they are asymptotically normally distributed as:

$$M_3 = \frac{m_3}{\sqrt{m_2^3}} \sim N\left(0, \frac{6}{n}\right), \quad M_4 = \frac{m_4}{m_2^2} \sim N\left(3, \frac{24}{n}\right),$$

(see Bowman and Shenton (1975)). Standard statistical tests can be used to check whether the observed values of M_3 and M_4 are consistent with their asymptotic densities. They can also be combined as:

$$M_N = n\left\{\frac{S^2}{6} + \frac{(K-3)^2}{24}\right\},$$

which asymptotically has a χ^2 distribution with two degrees of freedom under the null hypothesis that the normality assumption is valid. The *QQ plot* is a graphical display of ordered residuals against their theoretical quantiles. The 45 degree line is taken as a reference line (the closer the residual plot to this line, the better the match).

Heteroscedasticity

A simple test for heteroscedasticity is obtained by comparing the sum of squares of two exclusive subsets of the sample. For example, the statistic:

$$H(h) = \frac{\sum_{t=n-h+1}^{n} e_t^2}{\sum_{t=1}^{h} e_t^2},$$

is $F_{h,h}$-distributed for some preset positive integer h, under the null hypothesis of homoscedasticity.

Serial correlation

The correlogram of the prediction residuals should not reveal significant serial correlation. A standard portmanteau test statistic for serial correlation is based on the Box–Ljung statistic suggested by Ljung and Box (1978). This is given by:

$$Q(k) = n(n+2) \sum_{j=1}^{k} \frac{c_j^2}{n-j},$$

for some positive integer k, where c_j is the jth correlation:

$$c_j = \frac{1}{nm_2} \sum_{t=j+1}^{n} (e_t - m_1)(e_{t-j} - m_1).$$

Although these statistics can be used for formal hypothesis testing, in practice they are used as diagnostic tests. Diagnostic graphic tools can be even more informative and they include a time series plot, a histogram and a correlogram of the prediction residuals.

Missing values

A convenient property of the Kalman filter and related methods is their ability to account for missing observations in a data set. In a relatively straightforward manner, the filter can be amended when it is confronted with missing data. Some calculations are skipped while other calculations do not need to be changed. This feature is of high practical relevance as many data sets have at least some data points not available. In our context, it also offers a solution to the forecasting problem since we can regard the future observations as a set of missing observations.

The Kalman filter produces one-step-ahead predictions of the state vector as denoted by $a_{t+1|t}$ with its error variance matrices $P_{t+1|t}$ for $t = 1, \ldots, n$. In the Kalman filter, if y_τ is missing, we do not know its value or its one-step-ahead prediction error v_τ. The missing information on v_τ can be reflected by having $F_\tau \to \infty$ as this indicates that we have no information about v_τ. The consequences of having $F_\tau \to \infty$ in the Kalman filter is that $K_\tau \to 0$ while the remaining computations in the Kalman filter can still be carried out. The prediction step of the Kalman filter reduces to:

$$a_{t+1|t} = T_t a_{t|t-1}, \quad P_{t+1|t} = T_t P_{t|t-1} T_t' + H_t H_t', \tag{3.18}$$

for $t = \tau$ as $F_\tau \to \infty$. Note that $a_{t|t} = a_{t|t-1}$ and $P_{t|t} = P_{t|t-1}$ for $t = \tau$. The implementation of a Kalman filter with missing data entries is straightforward and relies simply on a conditional statement: if y_t is observed, carry out the Kalman filter as in (3.14); if y_t is missing, carry out the prediction step (3.18). Missing entries are allowed throughout the data sample $y_1, \ldots, y_n$, individually and in blocks.

This treatment of missing values can be adapted for the computation of forecasts and their forecast error variances. After the last observation, we add a series of missing values to the data set and carry on with the Kalman filter, which treats the future observations as missing values in the way described above. We then effectively obtain the state prediction estimates $a_{n+h|n}$ and its prediction error variance matrix $P_{n+h|n}$ for $h = 1, 2, \ldots$. The observation forecasts $\hat{y}_{n+h|n} = \mathrm{E}(y_{n+h}|y_1, \ldots, y_n)$ and its error variance matrix $V_{n+h|n} = \mathrm{Var}(y_{n+h} - \hat{y}_{n+h}|y_1, \ldots, y_n)$ are then computed by:

$$\hat{y}_{n+h|h} = Z_{n+h}a_{n+h|n}, \quad V_{n+h|n} = Z_{n+h}P_{n+h|n}Z'_{n+h} + H_{n+h}H'_{n+h},$$

for $h = 1, 2, \ldots$. This simple treatment of missing observations and forecasting is one of the attractions of state space analysis.

Multivariate extensions

At the start of this chapter we set out a comprehensive class of unobserved components time series models. In economic theory one focuses on the dynamic relationships between variables. Hence the need of econometricians to simultaneously analyse and model a multiple set of related time series. The multivariate analysis of time series is a challenging task because the dynamic interactions between time series can be intricate and the number of parameters in a model can increase rapidly. In this section we will highlight a number of multivariate extensions of decomposition models together with a number of applications.

Multivariate trend model

The decomposition models can easily be extended to the modelling of multivariate time series. For example, letting y_t denote a $p \times 1$ vector of observations, the multivariate local level model for y_t is given by:

$$y_t = \mu_t + \varepsilon_t, \quad \varepsilon_t \sim \mathrm{NID}(0, \Sigma_\varepsilon),$$

$$\mu_{t+1} = \mu_t + \xi_t, \quad \xi_t \sim \mathrm{NID}(0, \Sigma_\xi), \tag{3.19}$$

for $t = 1, \ldots, n$, where μ_t, ε_t, and ξ_t are $p \times 1$ vectors and Σ_ε and Σ_ξ are $p \times p$ variance matrices. In what is known as the *seemingly unrelated time series equations model* (3.19), the series are modelled as in the univariate situation, but the disturbances driving the level components are allowed to be instantaneously correlated across the p series. When slope, seasonal, or cycle components are involved, each of these three components also has an associated $p \times p$ variance matrix allowing for correlated disturbances across series.

The dynamic properties implied by the trend decomposition model (3.19) further depend on the specifications of the variance matrices Σ_ε and Σ_ξ. When both variance matrices are of full rank, the dynamic interactions between the time series can alternatively represented by:

$$y_t = \Lambda_\xi \mu_t^\dagger + \Lambda_\varepsilon \varepsilon_t^\dagger, \quad \mu_{t+1}^\dagger = \mu_t^\dagger + \xi_t^\dagger, \quad \varepsilon_t^\dagger \sim \text{NID}(0, \mathcal{D}_\varepsilon), \quad \xi_t^\dagger \sim \text{NID}(0, \mathcal{D}_\xi),$$

$$(3.20)$$

where the various terms are defined implicitly by relating the terms in (3.19) with those in (3.20) via:

$$\mu_t = \Lambda_\xi \mu_t^\dagger, \quad \varepsilon_t = \Lambda_\varepsilon \varepsilon_t^\dagger, \quad \Sigma_\varepsilon = \Lambda_\varepsilon \mathcal{D}_\varepsilon \Lambda_\varepsilon', \quad \Sigma_\xi = \Lambda_\xi \mathcal{D}_\xi \Lambda_\xi',$$

where $\mathcal{D}_\varepsilon$ and $\mathcal{D}_\xi$ are $p \times p$ variance matrices. Since we have assumed full rank variance matrices, it is also true that $\mu_t^\dagger = \Lambda_\xi^{-1} \mu_t$ and, similarly, $\varepsilon_t^\dagger = \Lambda_\varepsilon^{-1} \varepsilon_t$. The representation (3.20) shows in a more transparent, direct way of how the time series relate to each other. The loading matrix Λ_ξ typically determines the long-term movements or dynamics between the variables, whereas the loading matrix Λ_ε links the contemporaneous shocks in the time series.

The matrices Λ_x and $\mathcal{D}_x$ can be regarded as the result of the variance matrix decomposition of Σ_x, for $x = \varepsilon, \xi$. The variance decomposition $\Sigma_x = \Lambda_x \mathcal{D}_x \Lambda_x'$ is not unique, for $x = \varepsilon, \xi$. Since the number of coefficients in Σ_x is $\frac{1}{2} p(p+1)$, all elements in the $p \times p$ matrices Λ_x and $\mathcal{D}_x$ cannot be identified in the model. An appropriate set of identification restrictions is obtained by assuming that Λ_x is a lower (or upper) triangular matrix with unit values on the diagonal and that $\mathcal{D}_x$ is a diagonal matrix consisting of positive values. The restrictions imply the Cholesky decomposition of Σ_x. For given values of Λ_x and $\mathcal{D}_x$, the trend can still be transformed without affecting the model for y_t itself. For all orthonormal $p \times p$ matrices B and C, such that $B'B = I_p$ and $C'C = I_p$, we can reformulate the model as:

$$y_t = \Lambda_\xi^* \mu_t^* + \Lambda_\varepsilon^* \varepsilon_t^*, \quad \mu_{t+1}^* = \mu_t^* + \xi_t^*, \quad \varepsilon_t^* \sim \text{NID}(0, C\mathcal{D}_\varepsilon C'),$$
$$\xi_t^* \sim \text{NID}(0, B\mathcal{D}_\xi B'),$$

$$(3.21)$$

where:

$$\Lambda_\xi^* = \Lambda_\xi B', \quad \mu_t^* = B\mu_t^\dagger, \quad \Lambda_\varepsilon^* = \Lambda_\varepsilon C', \quad \varepsilon_t^* = C\varepsilon_t^\dagger,$$

for $t = 1, \ldots, n$. The transformations based on B and C can be exploited to obtain a loading structure that suits an economic interpretation. We emphasize that the statistical dynamic properties of y_t are the same for all model specifications (3.19), (3.20) and (3.21).

Common trends and cycles

When the variance matrix of the trend disturbance Σ_ξ has not full rank, the multivariate local level model (3.19) implies a common trend component for y_t. In other words, when rank$(\Sigma_\xi) = r < p$, the underlying trends of the p time series in y_t depend on a smaller set of r common trends. In terms of the model representation (3.20), the dimensions of the matrices Λ_ξ and $\mathcal{D}_\xi$ are $p \times r$ and $r \times r$, respectively. Hence, the trend vector $\mu_t^\dagger$ represents the common trends and has dimension $r \times 1$, since the time series in y_t can all have different locations. The locations of r time series can be determined by the r trends in $\mu_t^\dagger$. The locations of the remaining $p - r$ time series in y_t are then adjusted by the constant vector $\bar{\mu}$ in:

$$y_t = \bar{\mu} + \Lambda_\xi \mu_t^\dagger + \varepsilon_t, \quad \mu_{t+1}^\dagger = \mu_t^\dagger + \xi_t^\dagger, \tag{3.22}$$

where $\bar{\mu}$ consists of r zero and $p - r$ non-zero values. Common trends in a model allow interesting economic relations and are related to the concept of cointegration, see Stock and Watson (1988) and Anderson and Vahid (2011) where common cycles and trends are studied using vector autoregressive models.

Common dynamics can also be introduced for other unobserved components in the model. In particular, common drifts and common cycles are of interest in economic time series. The basic formulation of a model with common trends and cycles is given by:

$$y_t = \bar{\mu} + \Lambda_\xi \mu_t^\dagger + \Lambda_\kappa \psi_t^\dagger + \varepsilon_t, \tag{3.23}$$

where $\mu_t^\dagger$ is the $r_\mu \times 1$ vector of common trends and vector $\psi_t^\dagger$ contains the r_ψ common cycles. The loading matrices Λ_ξ and Λ_κ have dimensions $p \times r_\mu$ and $p \times r_\psi$, respectively. We can adopt one of the cycle specifications discussed in the earlier section on cycle components and generalize these to multivariate processes. For example, a multivariate version of the ARMA process (3.10) can be considered, see Shumway and Stoffer (2006, Chapter 5.7). The multivariate version of the cycle process (3.11) is known as the similar cycle since the discount factor φ_ψ and the cycle frequency λ_c are common to all individual cycles: see the discussion in Harvey and Koopman (1997). We define the similar cycle process for $\psi_t^\dagger$ in (3.23) by:

$$\begin{pmatrix} \psi_{t+1}^\dagger \\ \psi_{t+1}^+ \end{pmatrix} = \varphi_\psi \left\{ \begin{bmatrix} \cos \lambda_c & \sin \lambda_c \\ -\sin \lambda_c & \cos \lambda_c \end{bmatrix} \otimes I_{r_\psi} \right\} \begin{pmatrix} \psi_t^\dagger \\ \psi_t^+ \end{pmatrix} + \begin{pmatrix} \kappa_t^\dagger \\ \kappa_t^+ \end{pmatrix}, \tag{3.24}$$

where the auxiliary cycle vector ψ_t^+ has dimension $r_\psi \times 1$, the discount factor φ_ψ and cycle frequency λ_c remain scalars and $\otimes$ is the Kronecker matrix product operator. The $r_\psi \times 1$ disturbance vectors $\kappa_t^\dagger$ and κ_t^+ together with the initial conditions for the cycle vectors are given by:

$$\begin{pmatrix} \kappa_t^\dagger \\ \kappa_t^+ \end{pmatrix} \sim \text{NID}(0, I_2 \otimes \mathcal{D}_\kappa), \quad \begin{pmatrix} \psi_1^\dagger \\ \psi_1^+ \end{pmatrix} \sim \text{NID}\left(0, \frac{1}{1 - \varphi_\psi^2} I_2 \otimes \mathcal{D}_\kappa\right),$$

and the cyclical disturbance series $\kappa_t^\dagger$ and κ_t^+ are serially independent and mutually independent. It follows for the cycle component $\psi_t = \Lambda_\kappa \psi_t^\dagger$ in (3.23) that:

$$\mathrm{E}(\psi_t) = 0, \quad \mathrm{Var}(\psi_t) = \Lambda_\kappa \mathcal{D}_\kappa \Lambda_\kappa',$$

for $t = 1, \ldots, n$. The individual cycle processes in $\psi_t^\dagger$ are mutually independent of each other while those in ψ_t are correlated with each other.

In the decomposition model (3.23) for y_t with trend and cycle components, only time series with coincident cycles are viable candidates for inclusion in the model for y_t. It can be of economic interest to investigate whether leads or lags of economic variables are appropriate for its inclusion in y_t. For this purpose, the model can be modified to allow the base cycle ψ_t to be shifted for each time series. The phase shift mechanism proposed by Rünstler (2004) allows the cycle process ψ_t to be shifted ν time periods to the right (when scalar $\nu > 0$) or to the left (when $\nu < 0$) by considering:

$$\cos(\nu \lambda_c) \psi_t + \sin(\nu \lambda_c) \psi_t^+, \quad t = 1, \ldots, n.$$

The shift ν is measured in real-time so that $\nu \lambda_c$ is measured in radians and due to the periodicity of trigonometric functions the parameter space of ν is restricted within the range $-\frac{1}{2}\pi < \nu \lambda_c < \frac{1}{2}\pi$. Individual cycles in ψ_t can be shifted differently by having different ν values. For the ith equation of (3.23), we may have:

$$y_{it} = \bar{\mu}_i + \Lambda_{\xi,i} \mu_t^\dagger + \cos(\nu_i \lambda_c) \Lambda_{\kappa,i} \psi_t^\dagger + \sin(\nu_i \lambda_c) \Lambda_{\kappa,i} \psi_t^+ + \varepsilon_{it},$$

where z_{it} is the ith element of z_t for $z = y, \varepsilon$, $\bar{\mu}_i$ is the ith element of $\bar{\mu}$ and $\Lambda_{x,i}$ is the ith row of Λ_x for $x = \xi, \kappa$ with $i = 1, \ldots, p$. For identification purposes, we assume that a specific equation j contains the contemporaneous base cycle with $\nu_j = 0$. The remaining $p - 1$ ν_i's can be determined uniquely and their corresponding cycles then shift with respect to the base cycle $\Lambda_{\kappa,j} \psi_t^\dagger$. More discussions on shifted cycles together with an empirical illustration for constructing a business cycle from a panel of macroeconomic time series are provided in Azevedo *et al.* (2006).

State space representation and parameter estimation

The UCTS models discussed here can be represented in state space form including their multivariate versions. The multivariate trend and cycle decomposition model with common components and possibly with shifted cycles remains linear with respect to the time-varying unobserved components and can therefore be represented in state space form. Kalman filter and related methods discussed in the previous section are applicable to multivariate time series models. The methodology of estimation and forecasting remains as for the univariate model. However, the dimensions for both the state vector α_t and the parameter vector θ are typically larger and computations are more time-consuming. It is therefore important that all necessary computations are implemented in a numerically stable and efficient manner; see the discussions in Koopman *et al.* (1999, 2008).

A time series analysis of commodity prices in Babylonia

Figure 3.1 shows six monthly time series of commodity prices for barley, dates, mustard, cress, sesame and wool in Babylonia between 385 and 61 BC. The series length is for 3,888 observations but we only have 530 prices available. The vast majority of the data are therefore missing. The data are transformed into logarithms in the graphs and for all analyses. In the earlier years of our sample, less data are available while in the later years more prices are observed. Some common features in the evolution of the log-prices emerge. For all commodities, the prices are increasing in the years towards 300 BC while in the following years up to 150 BC the prices are slowly falling. In the last century of our sample, say from 150 BC, the prices are increasing for most commodities. All time series are subject to outliers; some of them can be identified with specific historical events.

Univariate decompositions

In our first set of analyses, we aim to decompose the dynamic features of the time series in level, cycle, seasonal and irregular processes. This provides an insight

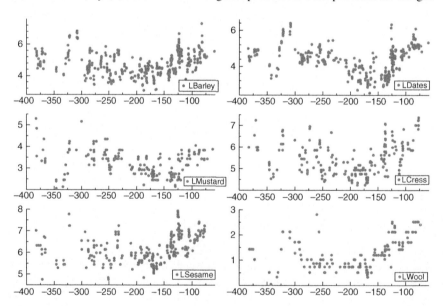

Figure 3.1 Monthly commodity prices in Babylonia.

Note:
Monthly time series of commodity prices (in logs) in grams of silver per hectolitre for barley, dates, mustard, cress and sesame, and per pound (*mina*, c. 500 g) for wool (*y*-axis) in Babylonia between 385 and 61 BC. The *x*-axis displays BC years as negative numbers.

into the major properties of the monthly time series. The UCTS model that we consider is given by:

$$y_t = \mu_t + \psi_t + \gamma_t + \varepsilon_t,$$

where y_t is an univariate time series of monthly commodity prices and where we treat the level component μ_t as the random walk process (3.2), the cycle ψ_t as the trigonometric cycle process (3.11), the seasonal γ_t as the sum of time-varying seasonal trigonometric terms (3.8) and the irregular ε_t as Gaussian white noise. The model is framed in state space and the Kalman filter plays a central role in the analysis. Hence the treatment of missing values is straightforward and we can carry out the analysis in a standard fashion.

The resulting decomposition for all six time series are displayed in Figure 3.2. We present only the estimated level (or trend) and the cycle components for each monthly price series. The seasonal component has to be estimated significantly only for the barley prices but it is found that these seasonal effects are not varying over time. We have kept the seasonal component inside the model for barley but for

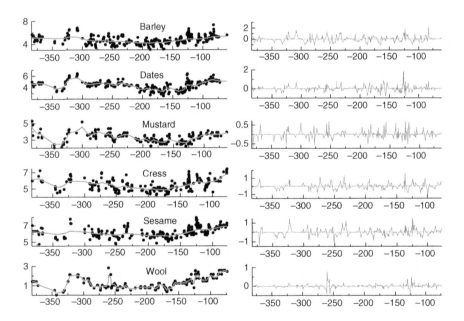

Figure 3.2 Univariate decompositions of commodity prices in Babylonia.

Note:
The graphs on the left present the estimated level (or trend) components for the monthly time series of commodity prices (in logs) in grams of silver per hectolitre for barley, dates, mustard, cress and sesame, and per pound (*mina*, c. 500 g) for wool (*y*-axis) in Babylonia between 385 and 61 BC. The graphs on the right present the estimated cycle components. The *x*-axis displays BC years as negative numbers.

all other series we have removed the seasonal component γ_t from the model specification. The estimated irregular components are not displayed. In some series the irregular component is estimated to have a very small variance and in other series the model has captured only some of the outliers in the series. The estimated cycle component is of key interest and we find that this effect clearly takes out movements in the time series that last for a small number of years. We may want to interpret these dynamic features as economic cyclical effects in commodity prices.

When we take a closer look at the estimated levels and cycles, we can identify some common movements. In particular the evolution of the level effect in the series appear to be common across the data for dates, mustard, cress and sesame while barley and wool appear to be subject to somewhat different dynamics. The estimated cycle components also present some common features among the different commodities but they are less strong and not so convincing. The cycle for wool is certainly somewhat different. To investigate the commonalities in the price series more accurately, we next consider a multivariate analysis for barley, dates, mustard, cress and sesame. We exclude wool from this analysis.

Multivariate decomposition

In the multivariate analysis, we simultaneously decompose the dynamic features in the time series of barley, dates, mustard, cress and sesame. We include the components for level, cycle and irregular. In the case of barley we include fixed seasonal dummies to capture the significant seasonal effects. This joint analysis of the series may provide an insight into common properties of the monthly time series. The multivariate UCTS model that we consider is then given by:

$$y_t = \mu_t + \psi_t + \varepsilon_t,$$

where y_t is the 5×1 vector of monthly commodity prices for barley, dates, mustard, cress and sesame, while we treat the level component μ_t as the multivariate random walk process in (3.19), the cycle vector ψ_t as the similar cycle process (3.24) and the irregular ε_t as the vector of Gaussian white noise processes. The model is framed in state space and the Kalman filter is adapted to this multivariate setting as previously discussed. The treatment of missing values remains straightforward and our analysis remains to rely on standard state space methods.

After a first analysis based on our multivariate decomposition, it becomes very clear that the estimated variance matrix of the level component μ_t (e.e. Σ_η), has a rank close to one. The four smallest eigenvalues of this variance matrix are very close to zero in comparison to the largest eigenvalue. Hence we have changed the decomposition model towards a model with only a single common level in its specification; see the discussion in the earlier section on common trends and cycles. The results of the analysis based on this model are discussed below.

The common features in the level component appear most strongly for barley, dates and cress, although the common level captures the main movement in all

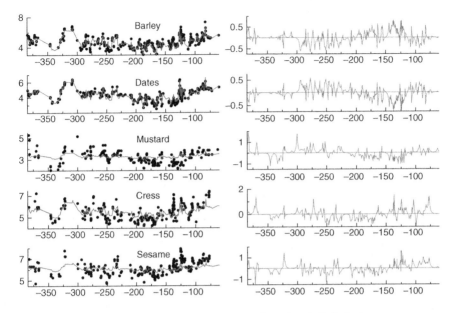

Figure 3.3 Multivariate decompositions of commodity prices in Babylonia.

Note:
The graphs on the left present the estimated elements of the vector level component for the monthly time series of commodity prices (in logs) in grams of silver per hectolitre for barley, dates, mustard, cress and sesame (*y*-axis) in Babylonia between 385 and 61 BC. The graphs on the right present the estimated elements of the vector cycle component. The *x*-axis displays BC years as negative numbers.

commodity prices. The cycle components do not appear to share many commonalities. In other words, the deviations from the time-varying level component are mostly adjusting differently in the shorter term (see Figure 3.3). However, a strong and persistent negative correlation appears in the estimated cycle components for the price series of barley and dates. This is an interesting finding as it suggests that in Babylonia, barley and dates were stronger substitutes for each other than mustard, cress and sesame were for each other.

Conclusion

In this chapter we have reviewed time series analyses based on unobserved components time series (UCTS) models, both in univariate and multivariate versions. The methodology is general and enables the handling of messy features in time series. An empirical analysis is presented for a set of historical time series from Babylonia. The six time series consist of monthly commodity prices, in logs, but in the vast majority of months, the prices have not been available. We have shown that the Kalman filter can handle such missing observations as part of the analysis when it needs to treat both univariate and multivariate models. Consequently, we may conclude that a time series analysis based on unobserved components is effective in identifying the main dynamic features in the commodity prices for barley, dates, mustard, cress and sesame in Babylonia between 385 and 61 BC.

Note

1 We thank the participants of the KNAW Colloquium 'The efficiency of Markets in Pre-industrial societies: the case of Babylonia (c. 400–60 BC) in comparative perspective', 19–21 May 2011 in Amsterdam. The discussions have been very insightful.

Bibliography

Anderson, B. D. O. and J. B. Moore. 1979. *Optimal Filtering*, Englewood Cliffs: Prentice-Hall.

Anderson, O. D. and F. Vahid. 2011. 'VARs, Cointegration and Common Cycle Restrictions', in *Oxford Handbook on Economic Forecasting*, edited by M. P. Clements and D. F. Hendry, Oxford: Oxford University Press, pp. 9–34.

Ansley, C. F. and R. Kohn. 1985. 'Estimation, Filtering and Smoothing in State Space Models with Incompletely Specified Initial Conditions', *Annals of Statistics 13*, 1286–1316.

Azevedo, J. V., S. J. Koopman, and A. Rua. 2006. 'Tracking the Business Cycle of the Euro area: a Multivariate Model-based Band-pass Filter', *J. Business and Economic Statist. 24*, 278–290.

Bowman, K. O. and L. R. Shenton. 1975. 'Omnibus Test Contours for Departures from Normality based on $\sqrt{b_1}$ and b_2', *Biometrika 62*, 243–50.

Burns, A. and W. Mitchell. 1946. 'Measuring Business Cycles', Working paper, NBER, New York.

Clark, P. K. 1987. 'The Cyclical Component of U.S. Economic Activity', *The Quarterly Journal of Economics 102*, 797–814.

Commandeur, J. J. F. and S. J. Koopman. 2007. *An Introduction to State Space Time Series Analysis*, Oxford: Oxford University Press.

de Jong, P. 1989. 'Smoothing and Interpolation with the State Space Model', *J. American Statistical Association 84*, 1085–8.

——— 1991. 'The Diffuse Kalman Filter', *Annals of Statistics 19*, 1073–83.

Durbin, J. and S. J. Koopman. 2012. *Time Series Analysis by State Space Methods*, 2nd edition, Oxford: Oxford University Press.

Francke, M., S. J. Koopman, and A. de Vos. 2010. 'Likelihood Functions for State Space Models with Diffuse Initial Conditions', *Journal of Time Series Analysis 31*, forthcoming.

Harrison, J. and C. F. Stevens. 1976. 'Bayesian Forecasting (with discussion)', *J. Royal Statistical Society B 38*, 205–47.

Harvey, A. C. 1989. *Forecasting, Structural Time Series Models and the Kalman Filter*, Cambridge, UK: Cambridge University Press.

Harvey, A. C. and S. J. Koopman. 1997. 'Multivariate Structural Time Series Models', in *Systematic Dynamics in Economic and Financial Models*, edited by C. Heij, H. Schumacher, B. Hanzon, and C. Praagman, Chichester: John Wiley and Sons, pp. 269–98.

Harvey, A. C. and N. Shephard. 1990. 'On the Probability of Estimating a Deterministic Component in the Local Level Model', *J. Time Series Analysis 11*, 339–47.

Harvey, A. C., S. J. Koopman, and J. Penzer. 1998. 'Messy Time Series: A Unified Approach', in *Advances in Econometrics, Volume 13*, edited by T. B. Fomby and R. Carter Hill , New York, NY, USA: JAI Press, pp. 103–143.

Hindrayanto, I., S. J. Koopman, and M. Ooms (2010). 'Exact Maximum Likelihood Estimation for Non-stationary Periodic Time Series Models', *Computational Statistics & Data Analysis 55*, 2641–54.

Jones, R. H. 1980. 'Maximum Likelihood Fitting of ARIMA Models to Time Series with Missing Observations', *Technometrics 22*, 389–95.

Kitagawa, G. and W. Gersch. 1996. *Smoothness Priors Analysis of Time Series*, New York: Springer Verlag.

Koopman, S. J. 1993. 'Disturbance Smoother for State Space Models', *Biometrika 80*, 117–26.

—— 1997. 'Exact Initial Kalman Filtering and Smoothing for Non-stationary Time Series Models', *J. American Statistical Association 92*, 1630–8.

Koopman, S. J. and N. Shephard. 1992. 'Exact Score for Time Series Models in State Space Form', *Biometrika 79*, 823–6.

Koopman, S. J., N. Shephard, and J. A. Doornik. 1999. 'Statistical Algorithms for Models in State Space Form using SsfPack 2.2.', *Econometrics Journal 2*, 113–66. www.ssfpack.com/.

—— 2008. *Statistical Algorithms for Models in State Space Form: SsfPack 3.0*, London: Timberlake Consultants.

Ljung, G. M. and G. E. P. Box. 1978. 'On a Measure of Lack of Fit in Time Series Models', *Biometrika 66*, 67–72.

Nocedal, J. and S. J. Wright. 1999. *Numerical Optimization*, New York: Springer Verlag.

Ord, J. K. 1990. *Time Series*, Sevenoaks: Edward Arnold.

Proietti, T. 2000. 'Comparing Seasonal Components for Structural Time Series Models', *International Journal of Forecasting 16*, 247–260.

Rosenberg, B. 1973. 'Random Coefficients Models: the Analysis of a Cross-section of Time Series by Stochastically Convergent Parameter Regression', *Annals of Economic and Social Measurement 2*, 399–428.

Rünstler, G. 2004. 'Modelling Phase Shifts among Stochastic Cycles', *Econometrics Journal 7*, 232–248.

Schweppe, F. 1965. 'Evaluation of Likelihood Functions for Gaussian Signals', *IEEE Transactions on Information Theory 11*, 61–70.

Shumway, R. H. and D. S. Stoffer. 1982. 'An Approach to Time Series Smoothing and Forecasting using the EM Algorithm', *J. Time Series Analysis 3*, 253–64.

—— 2006. *Time Series Analysis and Its Applications: With R Examples*, 2nd edition, New York: Springer-Verlag.

Stock, J. H. and M. Watson. 1988. 'Testing for Common Trends', *J. American Statistical Association 83*, 1097–107.

Tunnicliffe-Wilson, G. 1989. 'On the use of Marginal Likelihood in Time Series Model Estimation', *J. Royal Statistical Society B 51*, 15–27.

Watson, M. W. and R. F. Engle. 1983. 'Alternative Algorithms for the Estimation of Dynamic Factor, MIMIC and Varying Coefficient Regression', *J. Econometrics 23*, 385–400.

4 Market performance and welfare

Why price instability hurts

Karl Gunnar Persson

Introduction

Throughout history price instability of necessities (basic food such as grain) has concerned rulers and their subjects. Rulers feared the political consequences of price volatility, while the common people were hurt by it. Grain supply policies have therefore been practiced, not always with much success, from antiquity to the present. Food markets have also been studied by economists from the formative years of classical economics to modern development economics. We will explore the insights from centuries of economic thought in this chapter.

What makes grain so special? There are at least five exceptional characteristics which made grain markets more volatile than most other product markets.

1 For poor people, grain, and products made of grain, which include bread, porridge, meat and beer, was the major source of calories and nutrients and it had few close substitutes.
2 Unlike other markets grain is produced once a year but consumed throughout the year. This implies that an economy must store (maintain substantial inventories of) grain until the next harvest. Since grain storage is costly, the price usually increased in the period from one harvest until the next harvest.
3 Compared to most other goods (for example, cloth), grain production is less controllable by human intervention and more subject to natural calamities. Serious production shortfalls, harvest failures, were therefore quite frequent in pre-industrial times.
4 Grain price volatility was mainly driven by supply changes because demand was not very sensitive to income shocks (but this changed with the introduction of new crops such as potatoes and the rise in per capita income in the Industrial Revolution).
5 Grain is perishable and carry-over stocks (grain stored from one harvest year to the next) were usually a small fraction of yearly consumption for reasons we will discuss below. The implication is that the current harvest determines supply and prices, cf. point 4 above.

Although the correlation between harvest outcomes of different types of grain is positive, it is low enough to reduce risk if farmers diversify into winter and spring crops and into different grains.

These peculiarities make the demand for grain *price inelastic*, which means that the volume demanded is relatively insensitive to levels and changes of price. As a consequence a small shock to the yearly output, the harvest, will have large effects on the price of grain. For example, an elasticity of −0.1 implies that a negative output shock of just 1 per cent will increase prices by 10 per cent while an elasticity of −0.5 means that the harvest shortfall had to be 5 per cent to generate a price increase of 10 per cent. The extent of price inelasticity of demand is in itself a matter of controversy.[1] Nobel laureate Fogel (1992) represents what increasingly is considered an outlier position, arguing that price elasticity for grain was down to around or even below −0.2 for pre-industrial Europe. However, these suggestions are implausible. We know that harvest shortfalls of 20 per cent were quite common and they would, following Fogel, cause spikes in prices of more than 100 per cent, which are extremely rare. The Fogel position is linked to a particular view of the predicament of the pre-industrial economy, which suggests that harvest shortfalls were *not* the major problem. Instead focus is directed on failures in the institutional setting in the provision and distribution of available food. A similar proposition has been applied to twentieth-century famines in developing nations by Sen (1981). The argument is that the shortfall has been exaggerated. Had the entitlements – the purchasing power – of the poor been maintained, famines could in many instances have been evaded, it has been suggested. Institutional and political failures rather than food availability were the primary problem.

Fogel's position was challenged by Persson (1999) and later Barquin (2005) was unable to replicate Fogel's results despite using Fogel's data. Persson argued that harvest shortfalls were substantial and, using early nineteenth-century data, estimated pre-industrial elasticities to lie between −0.6 and −0.7. Campbell and Ó Gráda (2011) have corroborated these results for medieval England using newly collected yield and price data.

If Fogel had been right, the problem was not primarily large shocks to supply, but here Campbell and Ó Gráda (2011) refuted Fogel by detailing estimates of the magnitude and frequency of medieval shortfalls. More controversially they claim that variance in yields fell and demand is reported to become more inelastic before the Industrial Revolution in England.

A common modern yardstick for a *growth disaster* is a decline of 10 percent of output, gross domestic product (GDP) or industrial output, from year to year. For the Industrial era this has occurred about once in a lifetime (or less), but in pre-nineteenth-century agriculture it happened very often.[2] If we look at a single crop such as wheat, the most sensitive of grains, the probability of a 10 per cent shortfall was very high, say, one in every third or fourth year. It is more useful to look at the probability of a joint shortfall of all three major grains, wheat, barley, and oats or rye when cultivated. The probability of a joint harvest shock in the three major crops was about 0.2 for a 10 per cent shortfall and 0.1 for a 20 per cent shortfall. That represents an event occurring every ten years. So farmers would be right to diversify into several crops – as well as winter and spring crops – to reduce risks, and this is what they did. The worst consequences were linked to consecutive so-called back-to-back shortfalls which were, however, less frequent. The probability of two consecutive joint shortfalls of 10 per cent was 0.07, which represents an event happening every 15 years.

There are both short-term and long-term consequences of frequent growth disasters. The short-term impact relates to the disruption of consumption and the long-term effects are more ambiguous as they relate to investment and growth of output. We will discuss both types of consequences.

Market performance by means of market integration

How can economies handle large shocks to minimize negative consequences (i.e. how can an economy increase market performance)? We have mentioned crop diversification (or consumption diversification: see Foldvari and Van Leeuwen, Chapter 2, this volume) as one possibility. There are several other possibilities. The first one is an increase in output per hectare as a result of technical progress or commercialization and specialization. However, this was limited before the nineteenth century. Two other possibilities to smooth erratic production outcomes are geographical integration of markets (i.e. trade) and intertemporal integration (i.e. storage from one harvest year to the next).

Since storage is often seen as being too small to have been of much influence (e.g. McCloskey and Nash 1984), this suggests that it is largely the geographical integration of markets (i.e. trade) that is able to reduce price volatility and increase market performance. Indeed, local output shocks in an isolated, non-trading, economy (where markets are poorly integrated and nominal wages are fairly rigid in the short and medium run) create large price effects given the low price elasticity and hence volatility in real income and consumption. That means that the region or nation had to rely on its own output, the yearly harvest. The Greek philosopher Aristotle famously suggested that local output shocks were not correlated.[3] As a consequence harvest outcomes would cancel out in a wider geographical area. In a more technical language, the insight supposes that local deviations from normal or average harvest were stochastic with a zero mean, implying a constant global output. In a given year some regions had a bumper harvest, some had a normal harvest while others had a poor harvest due to impact of natural events. This implies that trade between regions could dampen supply shocks and hence price and consumption volatility. Aristotle naturally situated his argument in the Mediterranean where access to comparatively cheap maritime transport made interregional trade possible. If, say, Sicily, had a poor harvest Tuscany might have a good one and trade would ease the shortage in one region and dampen price increases in Sicily, while exports from Tuscany softened the price fall there.

Aristotle's argument is important because it implicitly relied on the insight that local harvest outcomes within a wider geographical area are independent or uncorrelated, and the implication is that trade and market integration can be expected to dampen local price volatility because it dampens local supply volatility. Market integration means that local producers lose market power and become price-takers rather than price-makers. Aristotle's argument was refined and developed by the French Enlightenment thinkers (scornfully nicknamed *les économistes* by contemporaries) into a forceful argument for free internal as well as external trade in grain (Persson 1999, Chapter 1). That argument preceded the comparative advantage argument for free trade, but it was of course less general, mostly applicable to products where the local harvest varied a lot while global output was roughly constant. It also had an impact on late eighteenth- and early nineteenth-century grain trade policies.

The second possibility is storage. In a given locality the intertemporal correlation of harvest outcomes is positive but not large, making intertemporal 'integration' an alternative or supplement to geographical trade. However, the little evidence we have suggests that carry-over stocks were quite small. There are several reasons for this. Grain is perishable, which means that a substantial proportion of stocks were wasted. The number of years you could carry over grain was limited to two or three years, depending on climate and the sophistication of granary-technology, which improved over time. Profitable storage is based on the expectation of increasing prices from one harvest to the next or over a longer period to cover the costs for carry-over storage. There are, however, large risks involved in carry-over storage speculation. There is strong evidence that the seasonal pattern of grain prices generally displays a strong fall in prices around the harvest, which means that carry over from before to after the harvest is, as a rule, unprofitable. The reason for a regular all-year low around the harvest is something of a puzzle. You would expect producers to hold on to their harvest and wait until prices recover. However, that would require fairly well-functioning capital markets, but capital markets were far from perfect. In their absence, cash-constrained producers were forced to sell prematurely to meet lenders' demands of repayment of loans made during the growing season. In many instances the moneylenders were also grain merchants and could orchestrate the massive sell-off just after the harvest, by having loans mature close to the harvest. We need more detailed micro studies of producers and merchant-lender relationships to clarify these issues. The repeated pattern of all-time low at harvest time is consistent with the proposition that the carry-over storage was not substantial. As noted above, this is largely based on profit motives. However, storage might also take place for non-profit motives. For example, public granaries were, in some locations, an alternative (see for example in China: Liu, Chapter 12, this volume), but these institutions were often unstable and occasionally starved by lack of continuous funding from local or central governments. Yet another possibility is what is called the 'convenience yield', i.e. storage by individuals used to fence off starvation rather than to make a monetary profit. Alhough Foldvari and Van Leeuwen (Chapter 18, this volume) find some evidence for the existence of non-profit storage, in this chapter we are only concerned with the market effects and will from here on focus only on market integration as an effect reducing price volatility.

Welfare consequences of market performance: survival probabilities[4]

Excluding intertemporal redistribution as a major supply and price stabilizing force, the viable alternative to smoothen supply when local harvests varied was geographical market integration. This was inhibited by transport costs over long distances and as a consequence price volatility was high. Regional price differences must be fairly high to trigger off arbitrage and trade. But the consequences of price volatility of grain are not the same for producers of grain as they are for consumers of grain.

In a poorly integrated market local prices of grain move *inversely* with local harvest changes. Furthermore, with a price elasticity smaller than -1 the income would actually fall for a farmer when output was above normal, and increase when it was below. For net consumers of grain (and this included the non-agrarian labour force and rural workers and small farmers), this inverse relationship meant that their consumption fell in years of bad harvests as a consequence of falling availability of food and the limited purchasing power of the poor. Under fairly general conditions, when living standards for part of the population are close to subsistence minimum, such a situation decreases the average survival probabilities of the population.

It is worthwhile spelling out these conditions in some detail: the following simplified exposition is inspired by Martin Ravallion's (1988) argument as originally applied to famines in contemporary developing nations.

We take the survival probability function to increase in consumption but at a decreasing rate, except for extremely low levels of consumption, as depicted in Figure 4.1. The survival probability schedule is derived from a health production function, not spelled out here, where survival depends on consumption and the personal constitution of individuals (i.e. of how fit, strong, disease-resistant a person is). The characteristic of that function is that there is a trade-off between consumption and personal constitution. At very high levels of consumption a unit decrease in consumption will increase claims on personal constitution much less than a unit decrease in consumption at low levels of consumption. The shape of the survival probability schedule depends on how personal constitution is distributed in the population. A single peaked normal density distribution with a long right hand tail will generate the shape as in Figure 4.1. We define real consumption, c, as the nominal wage (assumed constant in the short run) divided by the price of grain, which means that real consumption varies inversely with the price of grain. The survival probability s takes values between 0 and 1, where 1 implies that survival from one period to next is assured by a probability of 100 per cent.

The disadvantages of price and hence consumption volatility are clearly seen in Figure 4.1. Recall that c is defined as the constant nominal wage deflated by the price of grain. Then at a constant price, real consumption will remain stable at $c\#$ and the survival probability constant at $s\#$. If prices, and hence real consumption, vary and successively take values c^* and c' respectively, the survival probability will oscillate between a low s^* and a high s'. Given the shape of the survival probability function, the impact of a unit fall in real consumption, from $c\#$ to c^*, will have a larger negative effect on survival probability than the positive effect of a unit increase in consumption from $c\#$ to c'. In other words the absolute value of the decline from $s\#$ to s^* is larger than that of $s\#$ to s' (i.e. a harvest failure will increase the price and, hence, lower the consumption. This leads to a strong

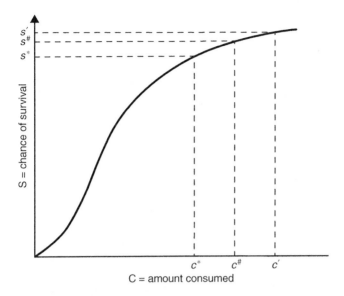

Figure 4.1 The survival probability function.

reduction in *s*. If there is an abundant harvest, prices will drop, consumption will increase and *s* will rise, but by less than the amount of the drop which occurred during a similar drop in the harvest). As a consequence long-term survival probabilities of a population will be lower in a non-integrated economy. Mortality risks would be higher. The intuition is straightforward: consumption has diminishing returns in terms of survival probability.[5]

The argument can be generalized if we re-interpret *s* to be the transition probability to a well-defined state of human well-being. You can, for example, define a state of health that permits growth of physical and mental attributes necessary to sustain normal work effort and participation in social life. For the same reason as spelled out above, price and consumption stability is preferable to volatility because over a longer period the long-term share of the population enjoying that particular state of human well-being will be larger. It is also possible that deprivation of the desired state of human well-being can cause 'hysteresis' effects – that is, making it difficult to regain the original state. A related argument is that the transitory decrease in the transition probability to the defined state of health can provoke irreversible effects, for example physical stunting and future increased incidence of diseases.

The effect of market performance on the incentives of the producers of food

We outlined earlier that price volatility and, consequently, market performance, were mainly driven by supply side factors, most notably by trade. We turn now to the impact of price volatility on producers of food. Producers are, however, not a homogenous group. As the subsequent exposition makes clear, it matters a lot whether producers are permanently producing a surplus for the market or, typical for small-scale farmers, a surplus only in periods of good harvest conditions. The Enlightenment economists in late eighteenth-century France and their disciples in the rest of Europe argued that price volatility had disincentive effects on investments because of the inverse relationship between output and price for producers in a non-integrated market. Because local harvest outcomes affected local prices, and with elasticities lower than -1, revenue would actually fall when output increased. Part of this argument suffers from a fallacy of composition. It was, of course, frustrating for a farmer to see the prices and revenue fall when the harvest was plentiful. However, individual effort had little impact on aggregate harvest outcomes, and hence little effect on local prices even in a segmented market. It is therefore not obvious that this particular disincentive effect was predominant.

There is, however, a more rewarding argument in the Enlightenment literature. Large landowners might have a marketable surplus of grain to sell in bad as well as good harvest years. But for ordinary leaseholders and small to medium landholders (most of) the marketable grain was swept away when the grain harvest fell much below the average. Therefore large segments of the farming population derived little comfort in the high prices following a harvest failure. Besides, it was argued that the total revenue (price per unit of grain times output) curve was actually shaped as an inverted U, implying that revenue was at its lowest when the harvest failed and also when the harvest was plentiful. Now, this is not very likely, but the Enlightenment thinkers implicitly assumed that point-elasticities changed as output changed, which is plausible. The question is by how much. Demand is likely to become more price-elastic when prices soar, and the other way round. Given the fact that the real purchasing power of consumers falls when prices soar, the public will be increasingly sensitive to further price increases. This observation lies behind Figure 4.2, which meets the Enlightenment economists halfway.

Assume a unit price of grain to be 1; then the straight 45 degree line is the total revenue for a farmer in a perfectly integrated market. Price, by definition, is not affected by individual or local output in a perfectly integrated market, but remains constant since global output is constant and trade smoothens local supply deviations (in other words, since local output shocks are assumed to be uncorrelated and if there is trade, prices will always have their average value, which is here assumed to be 1; this means that having twice the output results in twice the income, i.e. a 45 degree line).

This changes when a market is not integrated, the *TRni* curve is the total revenue curve for a farmer in a non-integrated market. Had point-elasticities been constant across harvest outcomes, this schedule would have been a straight line with a negative slope. But if point-elasticities converge to -1 as output falls, it will have a shape as in Figure 4.2. Total revenue increases but at a decreasing rate as output falls.[6]

The distance c in Figure 4.2 is the loss in revenue that a farmer in a perfectly integrated market suffers when the harvest outcome is down at b, relative to the

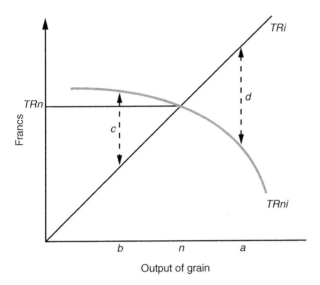

Figure 4.2 Total revenue of a representative farmer in an integrated and in a non-integrated market.

corresponding case of a farmer in a non-integrated market. However, the gain *d* in a good harvest *a* is actually larger than the loss. Of course, the argument depends crucially on the idea that as grain becomes ever more scarce, demand will be increasingly sensitive to further price increases. It is also easy to see that the inverse price reactions have asymmetric revenue effects compared to a case of stable output in a non-integrated market. At a normal harvest, *n*, the total revenue is *TRn*. A decline in output to *b* increases total revenue a little, while the decline in revenue from *TRn* is large when output increases to *a*. The obvious implication is therefore that total revenue over an extended period of price volatility is *lower* than in the case of stable prices in a non-integrated market.

Is there some way we can find firmer ground for the belief shared by the insights of the contemporaries in pre-industrial economies, that bad harvests were as bad for investments as good harvests as long as local markets were not integrated? Yes, there is! A bad harvest increases total revenue, but not enough to compensate for the loss of revenue in a good harvest. If investments are linked to long-run average revenue, investment will be hurt in the case of price volatility (which lowers long-run revenue as we just showed) relative to the case of stable prices.

Consider next the case of a bumper harvest. The effect on total revenue of a representative farmer will be negative and the income effect on demand for investments will therefore be negative. However, the relative price of food falls, assuming that prices for other goods are unaffected by the fall in grain prices. Consequently, there will be a positive substitution effect away from investment goods, the relative price having increased, to consumption of grain. So in this light bumper harvests are not good for investments. Investments are harmed by the joint negative sign of the income and substitution effect. If we look at the perfectly integrated market, there are no changes in relative prices, so we can discard substitution effects entirely. And when it comes to the income effect, it is positive since a bumper harvest increases total revenue of a representative farmer.

Summing up in a few words: segmented markets are bad for consumers because of the price volatility effects discussed in the previous section. Furthermore, price volatility is bad for producers because when prices are high, they have little to market and when they have much to bring to the market, prices are generally low.

We know that negative shocks in the modern economy often have long-run effects. There is little understanding on how the frequent harvest shortfalls in pre-industrial economies influenced human mentalities and behaviour. Did they foster a fatalistic mentality? If so, human effort was constrained. Conversely one could argue that being at the mercy of the elements stimulated human ingenuity to control nature. Price volatility probably also favoured a type of contract, the share-cropping system, which constrained production. In share-cropping the farmer parts with a given proportion, often 50 per cent of the harvest, paid as rent to the landlord. This constrains production because the farmer will keep only half of the marginal product (as opposed to a fixed rent contract where the farmer keeps the entire marginal product). So if the farmer is willing to work until the marginal product is 10 units, the share-cropper will stop working when the marginal output is 20 units. However, in a world in which prices varied inversely with harvest volumes, the share-crop contract was easier to honour for a farmer. Payment was made in kind rather than in money and share-crop farmers did not accumulate burdensome and often insurmountable arrears of rents, which fixed rent farmers usually did. This was in fact the process which led to many leaseholders losing their lease and becoming proletarianized.

Deadweight loss and failed trade in imperfect markets[7]

As we have seen, imperfectly integrated markets not only exhibit price volatility, but this price volatility is also the cause of sub-optimal investment behaviour and income for producers. However, in practice markets were not integrated or autarkic but rather an intermittent form. Indeed, one important characteristic of pre-modern grain markets was the slow adjustment after violations of (departures from) the law of one price. For a bilateral market situation where markets *actually trade* we can define the law of one price equilibrium as the condition:

$$|Price\ in\ Amsterdam - Price\ in\ Danzig| = Transport\ and\ transaction\ cost$$
$$between\ the\ markets.$$

This condition can be read as meaning that the absolute difference in the price of a strictly identical good in two markets should be equal to the transport and transaction costs between the two markets.

That condition was generally violated in pre-industrial markets. The law of one price is in modern parlance not a state in which economies rest but an 'attractor' or 'error correction mechanism' that ensures that violations are transitory. Violations of the law of one price signal arbitrage opportunities not yet exploited, but which ensure that violations cannot depart permanently from the equilibrium.

The important question is whether trade in imperfect real markets differs from trade in perfect equilibrium markets. Theoretical economists tend to discard the argument entirely by assuming that trade only takes place at market clearing prices (the price when supply and demand match perfectly). But economics is still in need of a good story to explain *how* market clearing prices come about. Very few markets are like auctions, for example. Studies of actual markets tend to suggest that trade takes place at prices which are not market clearing. There are situations of excess supply when sellers cannot sell even fractions of their commodities at the prevailing price, and situations of excess demand when buyers are willing to buy more at the prevailing price but find no suppliers coming forward with their produce. The nineteenth-century commercial press talked about 'dull' markets to describe these situations, and were explicit about whether buyers or sellers were hesitant. In real economies there are frictions caused by uncertainty, menu costs and inertia, making price adjustments slow. Adjustment speed is linked to a number of conditions which were endemic in pre-industrial markets. First, markets were often thin, i.e. few participants were active. Second, information was unreliable and travelled slowly. That did not mean that trade was absent, but it was frequently constrained below equilibrium levels.

One way to consider these frictions is as a sort of tax equivalent in the measurement of dead weight loss. The argument is illustrated in Figure 4.3. We consider exchange between two markets separated by distance: hence transport and transaction costs will be incurred. The supply schedule for the exporting market is depicted by S. The price on the vertical axis is the price in the importing market, which implies that S is defined as the price per unit at the point of origin plus the transport and transactions costs to the destination market. The downward sloping demand curve D is the demand schedule for the importing market. The law of one price equilibrium would set the price at P^{eq} and the quantity traded at Q^{eq}. Now consider the possibility that actual price is above that equilibrium, say, at P^*. At that price the suppliers are willing to supply a lot more (Q^*) than the buyers are willing to take: a situation of excess supply, or constrained demand. Sellers will chase buyers and offer lower prices, and this is probably the process by which price eventually adjusts to the equilibrium.

The area below the demand curve and the straight line between P^{eq} and the intersection of the demand and supply schedules in equilibrium represents the consumer surplus and the area between that straight line and the supply schedule represents the producer surplus. The sum of the producer and consumer surpluses is A + B + C + D. But at the price P^* the consumer surplus A is transferred to the seller and is therefore not a loss to the society, although it changes the distribution of consumption possibilities. You can interpret it as a tax benefitting the producers

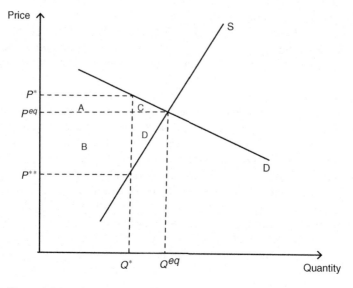

Figure 4.3 Deadweight loss and missing trade.

and harming the consumers. But there *is* a loss for all, for society: the deadweight loss, represented by the triangle $C + D$.

We can also describe a case of excess demand or constrained supply using Figure 4.3. Imagine that price is P^{**}. At that price suppliers are willing to supply Q^* but buyers are willing to purchase more than that and can be expected to bid up prices. In this situation the producer surplus B is transferred to consumers in the form of below equilibrium prices, but there remains again the deadweight loss of $C + D$.

What determines the magnitude of the deadweight loss? First the demand and supply elasticities (the slopes of the demand and supply schedules), and second the extent and persistence of deviations from equilibrium price. Over time, as information technology advances, the extent and persistence of these deviations decline.

Ejrnæs and Persson (2010) made estimates of the magnitude of deadweight loss in transatlantic grain trade and found that it fell considerably as information technology improved in the second half of the nineteenth century. With the telegraph and the commercial press reporting prices with just one day's delay, deviations from equilibrium price declined considerably. The magnitude of the deadweight loss as a tax is usually measured as a fraction of GDP, but Ejrnæs and Persson estimated it as a fraction of the total value of equilibrium trade. In an upper-bound estimate the deadweight loss fell from about 3.5 per cent in the pre-telegraph era (that is, the actual trade was 3.5 per cent smaller than the hypothetical case of market clearing prices) to a mere 0.5 per cent after the transatlantic cable had come into operation.

The fall in transatlantic transport costs has traditionally been advanced as a major factor in improving market integration and market efficiency.[8] It turns out, however, that if freight costs are also interpreted as a tax, the fall in the number of deviations from equilibrium price in the second half of the nineteenth century was more important in reducing deadweight loss than the decline in transatlantic transport costs.

For readers not comfortable or familiar with the concept of deadweight loss an alternative, intuitively more appealing, approach can be derived simply by concentrating on the (relative) volume of missing trade. Again look at Figure 4.3. In equilibrium, traded quantities are Q^{eq} and any other price would actually constrain trade. If price is above P^{eq} it is a case of demand constraint and if price is below P^{eq} it is a matter of supply constraint. One measure of missing trades would simply be to estimate the deviations from equilibrium trade. Again, these losses can be substantial but are sensitive to the elasticity of supply and demand. In the pre-telegraph era, missing trade in transatlantic trade was almost 14 per cent of equilibrium trade in an upper-bound estimate, but down to 5 per cent in a lower-bound estimate. As in the case of deadweight loss, these figures fell considerably after the introduction of telegraph. But the pre-telegraph estimates might be plausible estimates in intra-European long distance trade in the pre-modern era.

Conclusion

We have identified a series of welfare losses in pre-modern grain markets that were due to lesser market performance. The poor market performance is largely as a result of less efficient trade.

The welfare effects impact suppliers as well as society as a whole. The first set of problems applies to necessities with inelastic demand. Large price swings are generated by harvest shortfalls, which cause disruptions in real income and consumption. The effects of a fall in consumption cannot be compensated by ensuing above average consumption. It is partly a problem of irreversible effects of extreme poverty, the most serious of course being premature death. However, there are other irreversible effects such as permanent stunting, disruptions of mental development and health-induced abortions. We also argued that net producers of grain suffered from the inverse relationship of changes in output and price, which reduced long-run total revenue for the representative farmer compared to the long-run total revenue of the same farmer in a situation of price stability. We also noted that in a segmented market the relative price of investment goods increased in a good harvest.

For society as a whole, imperfect trade (and hence, lower market performance) refers to a wider set of pre-modern commodity markets and relates to imperfections and frictions in markets which are thin and plagued by inadequately informed traders. In such markets potential trade is 'lost', i.e. not realized, because price can remain above or below the market clearing price. As a consequence, the value of actual trades is lower, demand constrained and supply constrained, relative to the potential or market clearing level, respectively. What matters here is the speed and accuracy of information flows, a problem that was not adequately solved until the introduction of the telegraph and the specialized commercial press.

Notes

1 Elasticity can be estimated by the function $e = -$(standard deviation of output/standard deviation of price) or alternatively as $\ln(q_t) = a + b\ln(p_t)$ where q is output, p is price, a is a constant and b the estimated elasticity. These two methods generate approximately the same results.
2 As a comparison, the 2008 recession was associated with a fall in GDP of about 5 per cent, although industrial production fell by more than 10 per cent in a number of trade-intensive nations, and world trade by as much as 30 per cent.
3 Aristotle, *Politica* I 1259a on opportunities to make profit from insider knowledge concerning coming harvests. Cf Aristotle, *Meteorologica* 2.4. for the diversity of the Mediterranean climate; Garnsey 1988: 9.
4 This and the following section are based on Persson (1999).
5 In Figure 4.1 there is a section at very low consumption and survival probability where there are increasing returns in terms of survival probability. The particular shape of the survival probability curve depends on the distribution of personal characteristics, as described in the text. It is unlikely that actual economies, present or historical, can be found with survival probabilities and consumption levels as low as those shown.
6 Enlightenment thinkers believed (implicitly) that elasticities became larger than -1 at low output, thereby generating the inverted U-shape of the total revenue curve.
7 This section is based on Ejrnæs and Persson (2010).
8 For a critical examination of this argument see Persson (2004).

Bibliography

Barquin, Gil, R. 2005. 'The Elasticity of Demand for Wheat in the 14th to 18th Centuries', *Revista de Historia Económica – Journal of Iberian and Latin American Economic History*, 23: 241–68.

Campbell, B. M. S. and Ó Gráda, C. 2011. 'Harvest Shortfalls, Grain Prices and Famines in Pre-Industrial England', *Journal of Economic History*, 71: 859–86.

Ejrnæs, M. and Persson, K. G. 2010. 'The Gains from Improved Market Efficiency: Trade Before and After the Transatlantic Telegraph', *European Review of Economic History*, 14: 361–81.

Fogel, R. W. 1992. 'Second Thoughts on the European Escape from Hunger: Famines, Chronic Malnutrition and Mortality rates', in *Nutrition and Poverty*, edited by S. R. Osmani, Oxford: Clarendon Press: 243–86.

Garnsey, P. D. A. 1988. *Famine and Food Supply in the Graeco-Roman World. Responses to Risk and Crisis*, Cambridge: Cambridge University Press.

McCloskey, D. N. and Nash, J. 1984. 'Corn at Interest: the Extent and Cost of Grain Storage in Medieval England', *American Economic Review*, 74(1), 174–87.

Persson, K. G. 1999. *Grain Markets in Europe, 1500–1900: Integration and Deregulation*, Cambridge: Cambridge University Press.

—— 2004. 'Mind the Gap! Transport Costs and Price Convergence in the 19th Century Atlantic Economy', *European Review of Economic History*, 8: 125–47.

Ravallion, M. 1988. *Markets and Famines*, Oxford: Clarendon Press.

Sen, A. K. 1981. *Poverty and Famines: an Essay on Entitlement and Deprivation*, Oxford: Clarendon Press.

Part II

Market performance in Babylonia and the Mediterranean in antiquity

5 Market performance and market integration in Babylonia in the 'long sixth century' BC

Michael Jursa

Introduction

This chapter, drawing mostly on Jursa 2010, begins by surveying the principal characteristics of the Neo-Babylonian economy in the period between the fall of the Assyrian Empire (612 BC) and the Babylonian revolts against Xerxes in 484 BC. It then goes on to address the implications of the proposed model for the issue of market performance (and, more specifically, market integration in sixth-century BC Babylonia), and for an understanding of the Babylonian economy in later centuries in general.

The economy of Babylonia in the first millennium BC does not differ from that of earlier periods of Mesopotamian history with regard to the fundamental features of economic life. Economic activities were determined to a large extent by environmental conditions (Potts 1997; Liverani 1998). Four principal ecological zones can be distinguished: the central alluvial plain, criss-crossed by rivers and irrigation canals, swampy river deltas and generally deeper lying areas with little or no drainage; the reed forests in which hunters, fishers and bird catchers operated; the steppe bordering on the alluvium – the realm of the shepherds; and the cities. These zones were exploited in distinctive ways: irrigation agriculture had its place in the plain; hunting and fishing in the marshes; sheep breeding on the plains and the steppe, according to a seasonal rhythm; and artisanal production and administration in the city.

Irrigation agriculture was the mainstay of the economy. Importantly, the Babylonian agrarian system had two leading crops, barley and dates, whose potential for nutrition was roughly equal, but it depended on specific circumstances whether this potential was realized. The most distinctive trait of arable farming consisted of the use of the seeder plough, an ingenious implement allowing high returns on seed. Cereal farming (producing mostly barley) was therefore an extensive form of cultivation, economizing on scarce resources – water, seed and labour – while making comparatively lavish use of land. On the other hand, date gardening, the second distinctive agrarian regime abundantly attested in this period, implied a far more intensive use of land (and water). Typically, date groves were also used for vegetable gardening, fruit trees and even grain farming. Returns were higher than for simple arable farming, as were labour requirements.

Within this basic matrix, the period under discussion exhibits a set of interdependent characteristics that cumulatively transformed the nature of the economy in important ways (Jursa 2010). By the eighth century BC, the climatic anomaly that had contributed substantially to the crisis of the Near Eastern world around the turn of the millennium had passed The climate grew wetter, the conditions for arable agriculture in the alluvial floodplain of southern Mesopotamia improved markedly, and the population increased (for a similar line of reasoning for the second century BC see Huijs *et al.*, Chapter 7, this volume). The rate of urbanization increased as well; larger cities grew at a faster rate than smaller settlements (Adams 1981). Economic development was impeded during much of the seventh century by political unrest and war, but after the rise of the Neo-Babylonian Empire at the end of the seventh century, Babylonia could reap the benefits of peace, and, importantly, of empire, as it had become the centre of a state spanning from the Levant in the west to the foothills of the Iranian plateau in the east. The economy gained considerable impetus from this felicitous combination of ecological, demographic, socio-economic and political factors. During the roughly 140 years following the fall of Assyria, agrarian production in Babylonia increased considerably; also, it was frequently not aimed at subsistence production but at the market. A substantial (but unquantifiable) part of the urban population worked in non-agrarian occupations, and there was a high degree of labour specialization. For the first time in Mesopotamian history, one can make the case for a substantial part of the urban and rural workforce consisting, not of compelled labourers, but of free hirelings who received paid money wages. Economic exchange was monetized to a greater degree than ever before in Mesopotamian history. Among the urban population, few can have remained entirely untouched by the monetary economy. Finally, the available indications for consumption patterns point to a higher level of prosperity in comparison to earlier periods of Babylonian history.

The overall development of the Babylonian economy in the 'long sixth century' is best described, and explained, by reference to what might be called a 'commercialization model.'[1] As is also frequently suggested for other periods (e.g. Dyer 2005), population growth can be seen as a stimulus for commercial development and technological progress; rising demand generates positive feedback in the economy which offsets (for a while) the Malthusian threat accompanying demographic growth. Urbanization allows an increasing division of labour and economic specialization, and thus contributes to an increase in labour productivity. As administrative, religious and economic centres, cities are foci of high consumption and depend on an increasing pool of non-agricultural labour. They stimulate the production of a growing agricultural surplus by offering market opportunities, and, importantly in the case of Mesopotamia, they can also furnish manpower that allows an intensification of agricultural production. Patterns of agrarian development can thus be explained: following J.H. von Thünen and his classic *Agrarkreise* model (Roncaglia 2003: 303; Hatcher and Bailey 2001: 131ff.), proximity to a city and its consumers should increase a process of commercialization of exchange and lead to an intensification of agricultural production, whereas further away from the urban centre, agrarian regimes aiming at self-sufficiency of producers and characterized by extensive production are more common. Urbanization and the commercialization of agrarian production are thus mutually reinforcing processes.

According to the model, the interplay of intensification and market-orientation of agricultural production, urbanization, increasing division of labour and technological improvements should lead to an increased productivity per capita and thus to intensive economic growth. This implies in theory an increase in real incomes and hence in economic 'well-being' throughout society. It also implies that of the three principal modes of economic exchange, the commercial mode of exchange should play an (increasingly) important role in comparison to the redistributive mode and perhaps also of the reciprocal mode of exchange.

The commercialization model can be tested against the available documentation dating to the period (Jursa 2010: 785ff.): as postulated by the model in its traditional form, there is evidence for demographic growth and increasing urbanization; for agrarian expansion; for increasing monetization of exchange; for the presence of markets and market-supporting institutions; for subsistence strategies of private and institutional households that do not aim at self-sufficiency, but rely to a large degree on the market; there is a marked division of labour and labour specialization, labour is frequently hired, rather than constrained; and, crucially, the state functions as a catalyst sustaining the process of agrarian change, monetization and commercialization of economic life by channelling tribute and booty from the imperial periphery into the economy of the imperial centre.

In the present chapter we focus on monetization as one factor conducive to advance the creation of a working market and, on the other hand, on price development as a measure of the performance of these markets. Both factors are an extension of the points made in Jursa (2010).

The use of silver and the increasing monetization of economic exchange

Exchange in sixth-century Babylonia was monetized to a significant degree (Jursa 2010: 469ff.; Graslin-Thomé 2009: 238ff.).[2] The most common money medium was silver, which was weighed and came in certain forms and in specified degrees of purity. Other metals were used to a much lesser degree in this period.[3] For an analysis of silver usage, it is necessary, because of the structurally different form of the data, to distinguish between the institutional sector of the economy, the 'world' of the large temple households, and the private sector of the economy.

In comparison with eighth-century data, the sixth-century temple archives (of the Ebabbar and the Eanna temples) show that the range of economic situations in which silver money was used had expanded substantially. Silver was the near-exclusive means of payment for all transactions reaching beyond the confines of the temple households. Owing primarily to the importance of cash-crop agriculture (the principal source of the temple's money income) and of hired labour which was paid for in silver, the temples could not have functioned without monetized exchange with the outside economy. The fact that the temples' exchange with the external economy was largely monetized implies that the role of silver money in this external economy, which is documented more sketchily in the private archives, was equally important.

The redistributive household model postulates that temple-internal transactions were generally conducted in kind (see for example Renger 2007). However, up to a fifth of the internal payments attested in the archives were in fact made in cash. Monthly salaries (or 'rations') that were normally paid in kind to temple dependents were frequently substituted by silver payments, and we find also frequent instances of money use in the prebendary economy, where the incomes of priests could be paid in silver rather than in kind, as was traditional. Also 'travel rations' – distributions intended for provisioning temple dependents while away from home – routinely contained a silver component (Janković 2008). All this points in the same direction: clearly, it was common to conduct low-value transactions with silver.

The importance of silver-based transactions for the non-institutional sector of the economy emerges also from the private archives of city dwellers (Jursa 2010: 624ff.). Silver was a common means of hoarding wealth (for those who had any wealth to hoard). It appears frequently in dowry lists and estate divisions, while staples do not. This is exactly the opposite of the situation in the Old Babylonian period, around 1650 BC: a good example for the inadvisability of focusing too strongly on the 'longue durée' of the Mesopotamian economy (Jursa 2010: 806ff.). Valuable items – land as well as movable goods such as animals or slaves – were as a rule bought and sold for silver only. As an illustration of the change, we quote a sale document dating to the mid-tenth century BC, i.e. from before the economic transformations of the long sixth century. In this text, a plot is sold for:

> 1,000 shekels of silver, viz. 4 slaves for 240 (shekels) of silver, 4 leading oxen for 120 (shekels) of silver, 6 Amorite donkeys for 180 (shekels) of silver, 10 shekels of red gold for 120 (shekels) of silver, 44 (*kurru*) of barley, per *sūtu* 6 *qa*, for 98 (shekels) of silver, 5 *kurru* of wheat for 20 (shekels) of silver, 12 *kurru* emmer wheat for 24 (shekels) of silver, 1 (*kurru*) of cress for 6 (shekels) of silver, 3 *kurru* 1 *sūtu* oil, per *sūtu* 3 *qa*, for 91 (shekels) of silver, 3 *ṣibtu*-garments (made) of *naḫlaptu*-cloths, in addition to *loincloths* and blankets? for 28 (shekels) of silver, . . ., 2 *reins* (made of cloth) for 7 <(shekels) of silver>, 1[black?] *naḫlaptu*-garment for 7 <(shekels) of silver>, 6 iron [.].. -knives ≪for 10≫ [(rev.)] for 12 (shekels) of silver, 21 sheep for 21 (shekels) of silver, 2 bows *ditto* 8 (shekels) of silver, 1 copper spade for 1 (shekel) of silver, 2 old sacks for 2 (shekels) of silver . . . all in all 1,000 (shekels) of silver.
>
> (Weszeli 2010)

In this text, a large variety of goods, from slaves to sacks, is exchanged against real estate. Silver is used simply as a standard of value, to achieve the necessary conversions. Large-value transactions that were reckoned in silver but were conducted in kind in this way never occur in our period; simple silver payments – payments involving the transfer of physical silver, that is – are the rule.

But also (comparatively) low-value commodities changed hands for silver; 'cheap' monies (barley, wool, base metals) and barter were not the only means of acquiring items of everyday consumption. For goods whose money values ranged between 1 and 4 shekels of silver (which is 40 to 160 per cent of the median monthly wage, 2.5 shekels, around 550 BC), silver was demonstrably the predominant means of payment. For goods costing less than a shekel, there is documentation that silver amounts as small as 1/40 of a shekel, 0.208 g (the equivalent of 3 litres of barley) actually changed hands. But as low-value transactions were normally not recorded in writing it is impossible to establish the proportion of silver transactions in the total of transactions involving everyday goods. Even a superficial comparison of prices (or equivalents) of dates and barley attested in earlier Mesopotamian sources with Neo-Babylonian prices (see below) shows that the purchasing power of silver in our period of the long sixth century had diminished to between half and a third of what it had been in these earlier periods.[4]

Silver was the usual means of paying house rents; agricultural rents on the other hand were normally paid in kind in the sixth century. Only in the fifth century do field rents reckoned in silver money appear more frequently.[5] Lending and borrowing at interest as a genuine independent business activity usually involved money loans, not loans of staples. Only few debts in kind bore interest. Silver was also the normal form in which wealth was invested in business partnerships; staples (dates or barley) occur only infrequently in this context.

The extent to which silver money was used for hiring labour and in the context of taxation is an important indication of the degree to which the economy as a whole was monetized. There was a close link between taxation in a wider sense and the hiring of labour because of the ubiquitous practice of hiring substitutes for state-imposed labour obligations. Wages in kind were frequently paid to slaves and for part-time employment or to those on very low wages, but even in these cases silver wages were not unusual. Free hirelings who were demonstrably employed full-time, e.g. as harvesters or builders or for other strenuous duties, nearly always received silver wages. Hired labour was an ubiquitous phenomenon, as is beautifully illustrated by a letter written around 550 BC (CT 22, 133). A temple weaver is quoted as saying to his superior: 'Let [my lord] give (me) money (*kaspu*) to hire labourers. I am beleaguered (*lamû'inni*) by men who are for hire, and my work cannot be done without the(se) hirelings.'

Importantly, hired mass labour, rather than compelled labour, was the backbone of the labour force temples provided for the royal building projects to which they were required to contribute. These undertakings brought large amounts of money into circulation among the less affluent strata of the free population, both urban and rural. The agency of the crown played a major role in this respect: in the final count it provided a large part of the funds that enabled the ambitious building projects of the period. The vast amounts of surplus silver that the Neo-Babylonian monarchy could spend in this way originated in the benefits of empire: the spoils taken in Assyria, the tribute received from subjected provinces and vassal states in Syria. The process of monetization of economic exchange in the sixth century would not have been as far-reaching as it was, had it not been for these political background conditions.

In the realm of taxation and payments for substitute labour service, silver money predominated (Jursa 2010: 645ff.). A few types of taxes called for payment in kind, but silver was used for the large majority of payments made in connection with state-imposed obligations, even before the 'tax reforms' of Darius. However, the link between these obligations and the attested payments was not straightforward. Both under the Neo-Babylonian monarchy and under Persian rule, the state was not so much interested in taxes paid by individual Babylonian households as in forced labour and military service – the 'tax system' was geared towards the mobilization of manpower for the crown rather than towards the acquisition of funds. Nevertheless this system had an effect on the use of money and on the monetization of the economy. To discharge their obligations, heads of households that were subject to royal demands for labour service hired substitute labourers or soldiers (who had to be paid in cash) if they could afford to do so. Private taxpayers therefore had to have access to silver: landowners at least were to some extent forced into the market for staples. Agricultural producers without additional sources of income had to sell some of their crops for cash, otherwise they would have lacked the means required for dealing with the demands made by the state. In addition, indirect taxes (harbour taxes etc.), and occasionally genuine direct taxes extracted on the basis of land-for-service schemes, were payable in silver.

Before the fall of Babylonia to the Persians, money spent on corvée labour was used locally. The principal recipients were large numbers of hirelings of urban and rural origin; this assured a wide circulation of this silver also among the poorer strata of society. The Achaemenid period brought little change in the system before the final decades of the reign of Darius at the earliest (there was no widespread shift from taxation in kind to money taxes under Darius: in Babylonia, money had been the preferred means of taxation-related payments already under the Neo-Babylonian kings). However, the cumulative load of labour and service obligations increased and probably peaked under Darius. The most important novelty of the period was the forced service of Babylonian corvée workers and soldiers outside the country, particularly in Elam. This caused a flow of cash out of Babylonia, even though the system was set up in such a way that a substantial part of the silver that was spent for this endeavour eventually ended up in local circulation again (because it was paid to substitute workers and soldiers of local, i.e. Babylonian, origin; Jursa and Waerzeggers 2009). In the private sector of the economy at least, the financing of the different royal levies was organized in a decentralized, sometimes obviously improvised, *ad hoc* manner, but generally Babylonians ended up paying other Babylonians to do the necessary work. The members of Babylonian labour gangs that were sent to do service abroad were hired locally, i.e. in the taxpayers' cities of origin, and kept their local ties intact.

Overall the Babylonian sources contradict the assumption that increasing tax demands under Darius might have dramatically drained the cash resources of the country (Jursa 2011). The bulk of 'tax money' was not hoarded, but spent for labour in one way or another. There was also no shortage of silver during any part of this king's reign. On the contrary, it is reasonable to assume that the system of taxation and labour mobilization continued to contribute to the increased circulation of money among the less affluent parts of the population under Darius, at the end of the sixth century.

In sum, it is clear that the role of silver in the economy expanded in the late seventh and the sixth century. This development can be placed into historical context: it must be connected with the political circumstances of the late seventh and the sixth century when Babylonia was at the centre of an empire which drew, by compulsion or through trade, large amounts of wealth from the entire Near East. This allowed the purchasing power of silver to fall far enough (in comparison with earlier periods of Babylonian history) to allow also low-value silver transactions (for an analysis of the purchasing power of the fourth to first centuries BC, see Van der Spek *et al.*, Chapter 19, this volume). The spending policy of the Neo-Babylonian kings contributed substantially to this development by bringing large amounts of money into circulation. Few residents of Babylonian cities can have remained entirely untouched by the money economy. For the rural population, the monetization of economic exchange will have been less far-reaching than for city dwellers. Nevertheless, much money flowed into the countryside from the city as payment for crops and for the labour of rural hirelings working in the city or on the large-scale public building projects in the countryside. The rural population, even subsistence farmers living in villages, certainly had many uses for money. There was a need to pay direct taxes and various indirect taxes and fees, such as harbour dues, gate taxes and the like. Substitutes fulfilling corvée duties or military service obligations incumbent on rural landowners received money wages, and the products of city-based craftsmanship also had to be paid with money. As stated above, however, agricultural rents were not normally paid in cash in the sixth century, and field rents payable in money became common only in the fifth century. For these reasons, it is prudent to assume that while money had percolated into the countryside, its overall impact on the rural economic environment was (still) less profound than in the case of the urban economy.

Price development and the working of the market

Having established the existence of commodity markets and their overall economic importance, the next question to answer is how well these markets performed. This can be done by an analysis of the extant price data (see the introduction to this volume and Chapter 2 by Foldvari and Van Leeuwen). We begin by presenting some of the available data. All prices are in silver.

Between 590 BC and the end of the sixth century, the data are sufficient for establishing the general trend of price developments. As shown in Figure 5.1, prices decrease until after –560, when they fall below the iconic 1 shekel per *kurru* level. After –550 they increase dramatically and peak towards the end of the century. The price level attained during these years is extraordinary: according to the astronomical diaries, prices of over 500 grams per tonne appear only rarely: in the late fifth century, in the late fourth century (in particular during the period of crisis

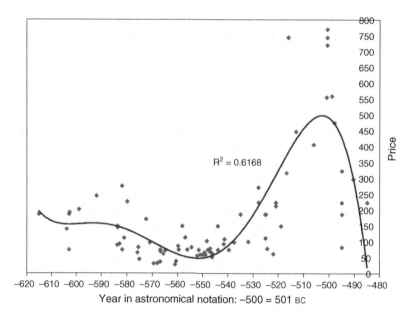

Figure 5.1 Barley prices in Babylonia in the sixth century BC.

Source: Jursa (2010: 443ff).

Note:
Barley prices (grams of silver per tonne): 85 price observations.

after the death of Alexander) and occasionally in the first century (Vargyas 2001: 64ff.; Pirngruber 2012; Van der Spek 2005). At the beginning of the fifth century, prices decreased to some degree: this section of the trend line is based on eight price observations from 501 to 487 BC. These are more data than have been available in the past, but the end of the period is still poorly documented. The median price is 111.6 grams per tonne, the mean price 190.5 grams per tonne.

The general development of sesame prices, as shown in Figure 5.2, resembles that of barley: prices decrease until −550. From about −540 onwards, somewhat later than barley prices, they increase sharply and peak towards the end of the century. As in the case of barley, the price level attained in these years is quite high: such prices recur rarely in the price data of the astronomical diaries, examples being during the late fifth century and in the late fourth century during the period of crisis after the death of Alexander (see Appendix, this volume). The subsequent decrease suggested by the trend line is based on evidence roughly as trustworthy as the identical development observed for barley: we have seven price observations from after the turn of the century. The median price is 844.3 grams per tonne, the mean price 1120.6 grams per tonne.

The by now expected sharp increase in prices at the end of the century is also present for dates, as shown in Figure 5.3. However, it starts much later than was

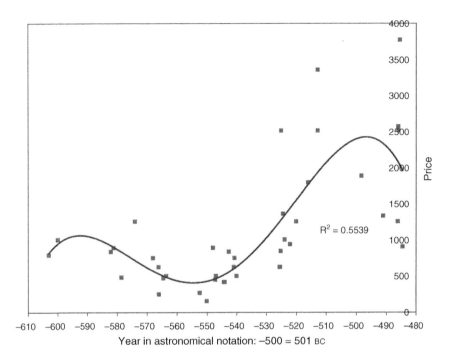

Figure 5.2 Sesame prices in Babylonia in the sixth century BC.

Source: Jursa (2010: 452ff).

Note:
Sesame prices (grams of silver per tonne): 40 price observations.

the case for barley and sesame, at around 520 BC. It is preceded by several decades of essentially stable prices; at best there is a moderate rise around the middle of the century, followed by an even more moderate decline during the early Persian period. The price level attained at the end of the century is high, but not quite as high as the prices cited by the astronomical diaries for the difficult post-Alexander years and other periods of crisis. The mean price is 77.3 grams per tonne and the median is 62 grams per tonne. It should be noted that the data prices exhibit evidence for price discrimination: larger consignments of dates tended to change hands at cheaper prices than smaller ones (Jursa 2010: 589f.).

As shown by Figure 5.4, the general trend for wool prices would seem to be more or less identical to that observed for barley. However, there are very few price observations for the Achaemenid period (post 539 BC).[6] The mean price is 4.7 grams of silver per kg, the median 4.2 grams of silver per kg.

For sheep prices, only from about −570 onwards is the information sufficiently dense to warrant an interpretation of the trend line (see Figure 5.5). Prices first remain stable (at less than 2 shekels per sheep). They start to increase in the early −540s, i.e. during the reign of Nabonidus, and peak around −505, i.e. in the

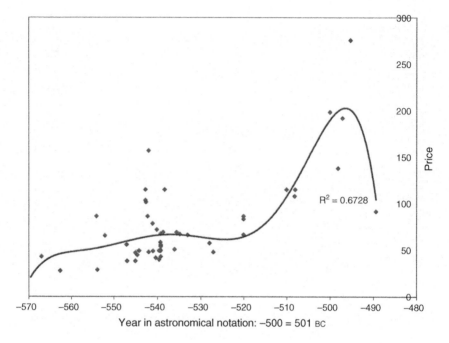

Figure 5.3 Date prices in Babylonia (sales only) in the sixth century BC.

Source: Jursa (2010: 592ff).

Note:
Date prices (grams of silver per tonne): of the available price data, we use 53 quotations, all referring to the sale of dates, most of them coming from Sippar. This means that the economic setting is demonstrably the same for all prices. This increases the value of the data.

middle of Darius' second decade. Afterwards they fall again to the level of −530. The mean price is 3.47 shekels, and the median 3 shekels exactly.

The distribution of slave price attestations throughout the century is sufficiently even (see Figure 5.6) to allow a reconstruction of price behaviour from the beginning of the sixth century until its end. Prices fall at the beginning of the century and then remain fairly stable until close to −550. Then they rise and peak around the year −510. This is followed by a decrease to the level attained at −535. In other words, the price trend is very similar to that of sheep. The mean price is 64.65 shekels, and the median is 58 shekels.

Prices of agricultural land are well documented, but hard to use for statistical purposes: land is a commodity of very variable quality, but these differences in quality are always reflected in detail in the sources. The following scatter graph (Figure 5.7) presents the most homogenous subsection of data available, the prices of date gardens in the central Babylonian region of Borsippa and Babylon.

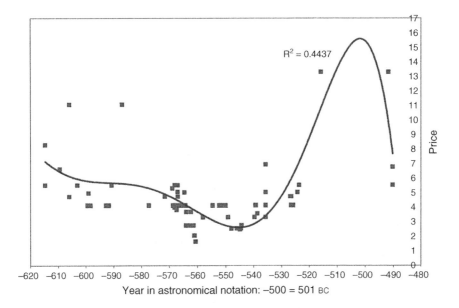

Figure 5.4 Wool prices in Babylonia in the sixth century BC.

Source: Kleber in Jursa (2010: 603ff.) and Jursa (2010: 616f).

Note:
Wool prices (grams of silver per kilogram): the scatter graph is based on 85 price observations. Most of them come from wool sales. Until the middle of the century, most of the data are from Uruk in southern Babylonia, later data come predominantly from Sippar in the north of the country.

As expected, the data shown in Figure 5.7 for real estate prices scatter widely ($R^2 = 0.21$): numerous factors could come into play and cause a wide range of price differences even within the same general category of land, as is the case here for productive date gardens. Still, the trend line can be given some weight for the period after -550: for this period it is based on adequate data. At first there is very little discernable movement, but in the mid -520s prices begin to rise. However, the increase is modest in comparison to the soaring commodity prices of this part of the sixth century. At the most it will have led to an increase of ('only') about 60 to 80 per cent over the level prevalent during the reign of Nabonidus. Other data series exhibit at least a tripling of price levels by -510: garden prices were undoubtedly affected by the general price trend of the century's final decades, but to a significantly lesser extent. The mean of the prices included in this graph is 384 shekels per *kurru*, and the median 371 shekels per *kurru*. The coefficient of variation is 0.42.

The following graph (Figure 5.8) compares the development of these price series.[7]

Figure 5.8 shows that those data sets that contain sufficient information (slaves and barley) suggest falling prices at the beginning of the century. This trend was

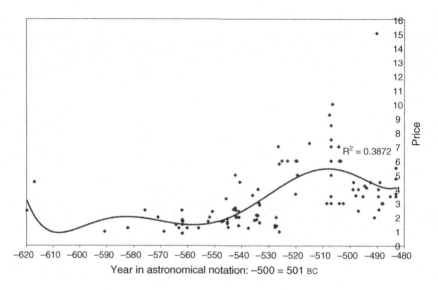

Figure 5.5 Sheep prices in Babylonia in the sixth century BC.

Source: Jursa (2010: 735ff).

Note:
Sheep prices: 103 price quotations, mostly from Sippar, mostly reflecting the same economic situation: a temple purchasing sheep from private sellers. Prices are in Babylonian silver shekels (8.3 g).

reversed around the middle of the century, when barley, sheep, date and slave prices all started to increase: the general increase in prices began before the fall of the Babylonian Empire to the Persians in 539 BC. Only in the case of dates there was a slight interim reprieve from roughly −540 to −520, i.e. until the beginning of the reign of Darius. The increase was dramatic in case of barley and less pronounced, but still quite strong, for the other commodities. Even the otherwise very stable garden prices exhibit a moderate increase in step with this general trend. The increase culminated around −510 or slightly later; the very end of the sixth century and the beginning of the fifth experienced falling prices again.

The data concern diverse commodities that depend on different supply and demand structures and come from sources of different geographical and socio-economic origin. Seasonal variations,[8] short-term price crises for individual goods and generally the high volatility of prices mean that we can exclude the possibility that we are dealing with administered prices (as has been suggested by some scholars in the past). Nevertheless the prices, with exception of the land prices, follow roughly the same long-term trend. This means that they reflect a single economic system, the monetized sector of the Babylonian economy, and that in this sector of the economy prices were determined primarily by the interplay of supply and demand (of goods and money) – no other mechanism could have yielded a similar

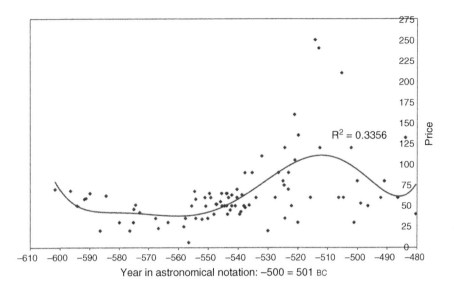

Figure 5.6 Slave prices in Babylonia in the sixth century BC.

Source: Jursa (2010: 741ff).

Note:
Slave prices. The scatter graph contains 90 price observations. To achieve maximum coherence of the data, only adult male slaves have been taken into account. Since most prices were gleaned from slave sale contracts from private archives, the economic setting is the same for nearly all the texts. Prices are in shekels.

consistent result (see also Foldvari and Van Leeuwen, Chapter 2, this volume, on the supply-demand model in Babylon).

The land prices follow the general trend only in a very mitigated fashion. From a legal viewpoint, land could be sold freely, but it is possible, especially in the realm of the Borsippean priesthood (a social group that insisted very strongly on its exclusive nature and was not at all open to outsiders), that land transactions were subject to social constraints that influenced price development. Other factors, such as the increase of the tax load attached to landownership, may have rendered land less attractive, relatively speaking. They thereby counteract the general trend towards a steep price increase in the second half of the reign of Darius.

The reasons for the price development in the sixth century cannot be discussed here in detail. Suffice it to say that the decreasing prices in the first half of the sixth century are easily explained in view of the general economic recovery and expansion of the time, while the rising prices thereafter, especially the steep increase of prices after −520 and the subsequent decrease around the turn of the century are more difficult to understand. Monetary factors are most likely decisive for the general increase visible in practically all commodities, which can be seen as the result of 'inflation', i.e. the devaluation of ever more ubiquitous silver that was imported

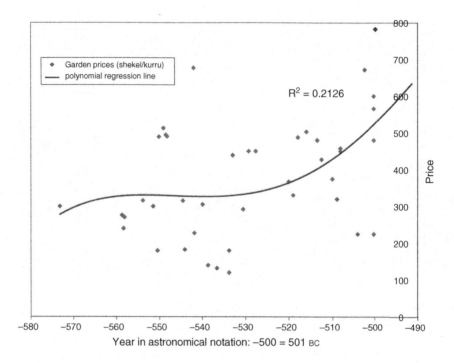

Figure 5.7 Garden prices in Babylon and Borsippa in the sixth century BC.

Source: Jursa (2010: 457ff).

Note:
Prices are in shekels per *kurru* of land (1 *kurru* = 1.35 ha in this case); there are 41 price observations.

into Babylonia by the state as spoils from the imperial periphery and was subsequently brought into circulation through state spending (see Jursa 2010: 745ff.). The peak in commodity prices, especially the soaring prices of barley, are likely to be the result of a series of supply shocks – there is evidence for failed barley harvests, for instance in the reign of Cambyses (Kleber 2012). During the later reign of Darius, we see also the effects of the demands made on Babylonian resources by Babylonia's Persian overlords: goods and labour, much more than cash resources, were requisitioned in various ways and employed in western Iran, especially in and around Susa (Jursa and Waerzeggers 2009; Tolini 2011: 241ff.) – heavy demands that certainly contributed to the developing crisis which culminated in the Babylonian uprising against Xerxes in 404 BC (Waerzeggers 2003/2004).[9]

Market integration and market performance

What do these prices and the background material we have tell us about market performance and, more specifically, market integration (i.e. trade)? The institutional infrastructure on which commercial exchange depended – the market

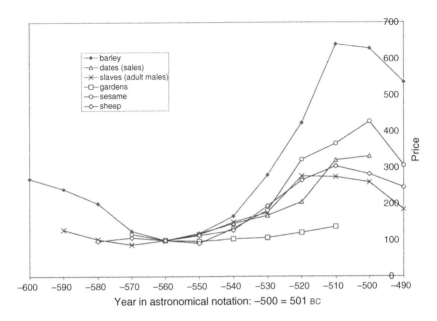

Figure 5.8 Comparison of the price development of commodities, slaves and land in Babylonia in the sixth century BC.

Source: Jursa (2010: 746).

Note:
We use moving ten-year averages, whose values for −560 have been set at index = 100.

places – are only occasionally mentioned in the sources: we hear about *sūqu* 'street market', *kāru* 'harbour district, commercial quarter', and about buying and selling at city gates (Graslin-Thomé 2009: 158ff., Jursa 2010: 641ff.). The commodity prices demonstrably reflect a single economic system, the monetized sector of the Babylonian economy. In this sector of the economy prices were determined primarily by the interplay of supply and demand. The evidence for factor markets is more ambiguous (this is discussed in detail in Jursa 2014). A labour market of sorts existed; the available wage data appear to be congruent with the assumption that wages followed the general price trend, especially in the second half of the sixth century, but real statistical proof cannot be given. We have already pointed out that the land market was not fully synchronized with the commodity markets. Finally, one should probably not speak of a 'capital market.' Credit for productive purposes was available, but the mechanisms which brought investors and businessmen together, while poorly understood, are as likely to have been social as strictly economic. Interest rates were potentially subject to negotiation between the parties concerned, but custom (and in part also interference by cities and later the crown) strongly promoted a standard rate of 20 per cent p.a.

Babylonia was embedded in a network of long-distance trade routes that brought into the country precious metals and other materials that were not available locally. This commerce was at least in part in the hand of state merchants, but private traders are also attested. The volume of this trade (to which one has to add the important contribution of tribute and booty) was considerable, notwithstanding the comparative dearth of textual information (Graslin-Thomé 2009). As for economic interaction within Babylonia, a survey of Babylonian economic geography shows that it is justified to consider the country in the long sixth century a single integrated economic space (Jursa 2010: 62ff.). All its regions were interacting with the centre, Babylon, and to a lesser degree with each other, especially along the (western) Euphrates route. Of the well-documented cities, only Nippur was anomalous; its region was comparatively isolated. Goods and people could, and did, travel freely. Bulk transport of staples across the entire country was feasible at moderate cost because of the ubiquitous availability of water transport. This is well illustrated by a letter fragment from southern Uruk in which temple officials are informed by their agents about grain prices in the centre and the north of the country: '(beginning lost) ... the prices which the servant has written us about, viz. 48 litres of barley in Babylon and Borsippa for 1 shekel (of silver), and 60 litres of barley in Sippar and Opis ...' (W 3381 z). Shipping grain from Uruk in the south upstream to Sippar in the north of the country, over a distance of somewhat less than 300 km, cost about 10 per cent of the value of grain shipped, excluding tax; with tax, the total cost amounted to close to 20 per cent (Weszeli in Jursa 2010: 144f.). In comparison to the prohibitively high costs of land transport, these relatively low transaction costs can be considered one of the main advantages of Babylonia over many other pre-modern economies. On the other hand we can exclude on this basis the idea that even water transport of bulk goods was feasible for much longer distances: getting a cargo of barley from Uruk to central Syria along the Euphrates would have been prohibitively expensive. Babylonia was an integrated economic space, but for agricultural products it was basically also a closed space.

Efficient transport and the resulting low transaction costs have a direct bearing on market performance. Nevertheless, the case for market performance in Babylonia should probably not be overstated. Just as in the case of Egypt in late antiquity, for which a similar argument has been made (Rathbone 1997), we are dealing with 'comparatively' integrated markets that were performing 'comparatively' well: market failures were a common occurrence. Several of the most explicit references to (physical) markets as places of buying and selling in fact refer to market failures – they point out that there was nothing to buy or sell.[10] As discussed by Bert van der Spek et al., Chapter 1 and Van Leeuwen et al., Chapter 20, this volume, the volatility of commodity prices in Babylonia points to a relatively low degree of market integration (although not worse than in the medieval Middle East) – much of the short-term variation in prices may well have resulted from problems of distribution rather than from actual scarcity or oversupply throughout the country.[11] 'Supply and demand were not easily paired. Commerce could only react slowly to sudden market developments.'[12]

Dismissing, *inter alia* Rathbone's claim for Egypt having an integrated market for wheat and wine, Bang has suggested a 'new' concept to describe the nature of markets of complex agrarian societies, the *bazaar* (Bang 2006: 77ff.). Basing his ideas on data from the pre-industrial Middle East and North India, he sees the *bazaar* as a 'particular socio-economic system', 'a place of high risk and uncertainty where bottlenecks, asymmetries and imbalances were endemic'. Bang (2006: 79) goes on to say:

> It combines the presence of peddlers and small retailers with large whole-sale merchants and long-distance trade while at the same time recognising that these categories were ... fluent and ... not ... clearly distinct... [The term]... can be used to denote a stable and complex business environment characterized by uncertainty, unpredictability and local segmentation of markets.

In other words, a plethora of external factors (institutional and otherwise) might limit the performance of the market – especially the last point, the juxtaposition of a stable institutional background for commerce with instability resulting from contingent external factors. This factor is useful and particularly applicable to the Babylonian evidence.

For Bang, economic agents in the *bazaar* developed typical sets of behaviour which minimized commercial risk in this environment, but at the same time perpetuated the general condition of unpredictability and volatility (Bang 2006: 80ff.). These strategies include parcelling of capital, low standardization of products, opportunistic speculation (to allow profiting from irregular and excessively high local prices) and the formation of segmented social networks.

The strategy of *parcelling of capital* could also be made for Babylonia: we have pointed out above that trading companies tended to operate with only modest amounts of money, even though the available legal instruments would have allowed a greater accumulation of capital with multiple investors.

Low standardization of products applies especially to prestige goods and items procured through long-distance trade; we can assume that also in Babylonia 'merchants ... attempted to profit on variability' (Bang 2006: 82), but it cannot be proved.[13]

Opportunistic speculation, on the other hand, was certainly part of the world of Babylonian trade: there was an awareness of seasonal as well as regional price differences which were exploited by 'harvest loans' and similar transaction types.

Finally, the assumption that the archetypical *bazaar* trader operated in *segmented social networks* fits the prosopographical data of some of the larger entrepreneurial archives of our period very well (Waerzeggers: Forthcoming).

Bang's *bazaar* economy is clearly a useful heuristic concept that helps further the understanding of Babylonia in the first millennium BC, but it should be developed further, taking into account the particular ecological and economic background conditions of the time. We would follow Rathbone (1997) rather than Bang (2006: 64ff.) and assume that ubiquitous cheap river transport must have allowed Egypt of late antiquity, or Babylonia, for that matter, to achieve a higher degree of market integration than found in other pre-modern economies lacking this eco-logical advantage – even if market integration and market performance may still have been 'low' by contemporary (or, which is more relevant, by early modern) standards.

Market performance, or market stability, expressed in terms of price volatility, can be quantified. We use here the standard method of measuring volatility by means of the 'coefficient of variation' (CV), i.e. the standard deviation of a price series divided by its mean. The data are summarized in Table 5.1. Prices are in shekels of silver per item (sheep, slaves), 1 *kurru* of staples (barley, dates, sesame), 5 minas (wool), or 1 *kurru* of surface area (date gardens).

Table 5.1 presents the median and mean prices for the entire data series and for the final three decades of the Neo-Babylonian period, a phase of generally low and relatively stable prices. The CVs for the latter period are significantly lower than for the former period, and they are also quite similar to each other: those for barley, dates and sesame range from 0.42 to 0.47; only that of wool is considerably lower (0.22). This reflects the comparatively stable economic conditions prevail-ing during the middle of the sixth century. In contrast, the CVs of barley, sesame and dates for the whole data series range from 0.6 to 0.99 – the difference is the result of inflation and the supply crisis for barley of the final decades of the sixth century. The CVs for the prices attested in the Babylonian astronomical diaries fall into the same order of magnitude as our results, especially when compared to the results for the sixth century as a whole (see Table 5.1 and Van Leeuwen *et al.*, Table 20.1, Chapter 20, this volume). For dates, Van Leeuwen *et al.* have calcu-lated a CV of 0.93 for the period of 500 to 220 BC, of 0.71 for the period of 220 to 120 BC and of 0.68 for both periods. This can be compared, for example, with the data compiled in Söderberg (2004/5, Table 2). Grain prices in Mamluk Egypt

Table 5.1 Median and mean prices and coefficients of variation (Babylonia, sixth century BC)

	All data (sixth century)			c. 570–539 BC		
	mean	median	CV	mean	median	CV
Barley	2.56	1.5	0.99	1.04	1	0.42
Dates (sales)	1.32	1.01	0.6	1.07	0.91	0.43
Sesame	13.37	10.07	0.77	6.81	6	0.47
Sheep	3.36	3	0.58	2.05	1.81	0.43
Slaves	64.65	58	0.64	49.62	50	0.31
Wool	1.4	1.25	0.49	1.28	1.25	0.22
Date gardens	384	371	0.42	336	300	0.43

(AD 1250–1517) have CVs of around 0.79–0.85; in medieval Europe (AD 1260–1512), variation was lower: e.g. London 0.412, Tuscany 0.414, Leiden 0.39; and there were exceptional values in Valencia 0.161 and Stift Klosterneuburg 0.726. Early modern data tend to have lower CVs, but are not hugely different.

Such figures lend plausibility to our Babylonian data. A comparison of these findings with the data culled from the Babylonian astronomical diaries shows little evidence of significantly changing market performance between the sixth century and the first century BC, while market performance was higher (and price volatility lower) in medieval and early modern Europe (Van Leeuwen *et al.*, Chapter 20, this volume). Hence, in Babylon we are certainly dealing with an often unstable market and a high volatility of prices, and there was always the possibility of supply crises. Nevertheless, it is an indication of the relatively good *performance* of the Babylonian market that the volatility of commodity prices in sixth-century Babylonia, as measured by the CV, comes so close to that encountered in these much later economies.

Market integration and performance: regional diversity and further questions

The foregoing conclusions are based on a comparatively crude statistical analysis of the data. One way to consolidate our understanding might be to carry out a quantitative analysis of the interrelation between different commodity prices, in particular between barley and dates, to explore further the effects of the Babylonian dual-crop regime on prices. This issue remains to be investigated; here, a different approach will be taken.

The available price data come mostly from two sites, Sippar in the north of Babylonia and Uruk in the south. On the basis of qualitative information, the basic integration of all of Babylonia into one economic space has been established, as we have already discussed. Nevertheless it would be desirable to provide also a quantitative argument, on the basis of a comparison, rather than a conflation, as above, of the Sipparean and Urukean data sets: price levels might be marginally, or even more than marginally different. Unfortunately, apart from the anomalous case of wool, only the data set for barley exhibits a sufficient degree of temporal overlap of the data from Sippar (and generally from northern Babylonia) with the data from Uruk (Figure 5.9).

Between −580 and −530 the data series overlap and are sufficiently dense to warrant an analysis of the price trends. For much of this period, Urukean barley is cheaper than barley in northern Babylonia. Uruk prices catch up with Sippar prices around the time of the conquest of Babylonia by Cyrus (539 BC). In fact, the price increase that begins in the second decade of Nabonidus' reign is noticeable in both cities/regions, even though for Uruk we do not have data for the reign of Darius (post −522), when barley prices in Sippar reached unprecedented heights. The difference in price levels that we see between c. 580 and 550 BC is pleasing, as it conforms to expectations. The south of Babylonia, especially the Sealand around and south of Uruk, was much more a grain-producing region than

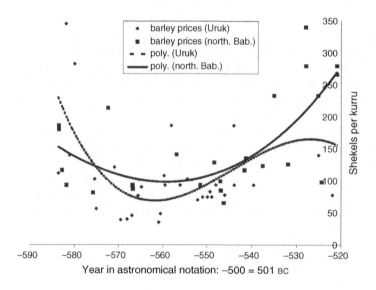

Figure 5.9 Comparison between barley prices in Uruk and northern Babylonia in the sixth century BC.

Source: Jursa (2010: 443ff. and 592ff.).

the north, where there was a strong tendency to favour horticulture over arable farming. This agrarian imbalance is reflected in our prices. The market did not level out these fundamental differences (nor was it likely to have done so: after all, the distance between the two regions is substantial). It is perhaps more remarkable that the difference was not more noticeable – another indication of the relative performance of the Babylonian market. The north-south divide in the price level of barley is also reflected in wage levels. During the reign of Nebuchadnezzar, the Eanna temple of Uruk generally paid its dependents lower wages in kind than the Ebabbar temple of Sippar in the north (Jursa 2010: 296ff.). A Urukean temple serf normally received 90 litres of barley or dates (or the equivalent in silver money), sometimes even less. The Sipparean norm, however, was 180 litres, a wage level that Eanna reached in a consistent way only late during the reign of Nabonidus, in the –540s, when according to our price data barley prices in the south had caught up with barley prices in the north. This observation has two methodological consequences. First, it proves the existence of a connection between the institutional wage standard (and by extension also the wage standard for free hired labour) and the general price level, which thereby illustrates (again) how the market had formed (transformed) even the core areas of the institutional economy. Second, institutional wage levels, even regarding wages in kind, can be used as proxy data for prices and indirectly also for money wages paid to institutionally unattached, free labourers.

Conclusion

The quantitative data culled from Babylonian sources of the sixth century BC, and (summarily) presented here, reflect an economic system that had a complex agrarian base and relied strongly on monetary exchange and on market mechanisms that were performing relatively well. Nevertheless, markets remained sensitive to outside shocks and mismatches in supply and demand.

The various phenomena characteristic of the 'commercialization model' that was described in the introduction are traceable in the source data and can be integrated into a coherent whole. A comparatively far-reaching monetization of economic exchange went hand in hand with demographic expansion, increasing urbanization and agrarian change. This in turn led to a dynamic economic system that was strongly market-oriented (although household-internal subsistence production continued to be important) and produced a modicum of economic growth (also in terms of productivity per capita), mostly by exploiting the potential of the Babylonian dual-crop agriculture and the presence of fairly efficient commodity (and in part factor) markets, and by benefitting from the massive royal investment of the 'spoils of empire' in the agrarian and urban infrastructure.

The interplay of long-term demographic and agrarian change with more contingent factors, including political history, turned the sixth century into an unusually prosperous phase of Babylonian history. Towards the end of this phase, however, the new Persian overlords of Babylonia started to over-exploit the rich province. They thereby contributed to – if not actually triggered – the development of a sequence of economic and political crises. At the end of these came the Babylonian rebellions against Xerxes and the far-reaching socio-economic change in their aftermath.

Notes

1 For variants of this basic model that have been applied to ancient and medieval economies see, for example, Hatcher and Bailey (2001: 121ff.), Hopkins (1978) and Millett (2001). For its application to the present period, see Jursa (2010: 783ff.).

2 Note: 1 Babylonian shekel = 8.3 g; 1 *kurru* = 180 l = 144 kg (dates), 111.6 kg (barley), 99 kg (sesame).

3 Cf. also Graslin-Thomé (2009: 357). Copper and tin were used very rarely indeed according to the extant sources (Jursa 2010: 474), but there is some evidence that at least the Eanna temple occasionally used gold as a means of purchase (PTS 2267, YOS 17, 360, etc.: the dossier remains to be studied in detail).

4 See Jursa (2010: 630 note 3337): Old Babylonian (1800–1600 BC) barley prices are generally below 0.75 shekel per *kurru* (0.021 g per litre) during the reign of Samsuiluna; they increase to around 1.5 or more (>0.042 g per litre) during the reign of Ammiṣaduqa. Ur III merchant accounts (around 2020 BC) state that 1 litre of barley equals roughly 0.028 g of silver and 1 litre of dates 0.019 g. The median price for barley in the sixth century is 0.069 g, the mean, 0.118 g; the median price for dates is 0.047 g per litre, the mean, 0.061 g.

5 Numerous references to field rents that were payable in silver can be found, for instance in the Murašû archive (BE 10, 100, 103, 111, 112, etc.).

6 Proxy data (prices of woollen garments, sheep prices) suggest that wool prices did indeed follow the general trend in this period.

7 The wool prices have been excluded from this comparison, because their moving ten-year averages cannot be plotted after −530.

8 Seasonal variations can be shown to have existed by statistical means in the case of barley (Jursa 2010: 449f.); for dates, this is more difficult as the large majority of prices are post-harvest prices. However, the texts show that Babylonians were aware of the seasonality of agrarian prices and exploited this phenomenon.

9 The socio-economic changes after this violent episode of Babylonian history were far-reaching, and affected many of the phenomena which we have drawn on for the development of the model for the sixth-century economy presented here. They led to fundamental changes in the overall makeup of the economy that are not discussed here (see, preliminarily, Jursa 2014).

10 Jursa (2010: 642). But it should be taken into account that these statements come from letters which report the exceptional, not the ordinary.

11 See also, e.g. Van der Spek and Mandemakers (2003: 532). But the point concerns not so much integration in the 'world market' – this is excluded for staples at least – but market integration from a purely Babylonian perspective.

12 Bang (2006: 61), on the economy of late antiquity. See also his book-length study (Bang 2008), on which see Von Reden (2010).

13 The most recent study of Mesopotamian merchants of the first millennium can be found in Graslin-Thomé (2009: 383ff.).

Abbreviations

For the abbreviations used in this article see:

M. Roth *et al.* (eds.) *The Assyrian Dictionary of the Oriental Institute of the University of Chicago.* Volume 20. Chicago: Oriental Institute: vii-xxix, online: http://oi.uchicago.edu/research/pubs/catalog/cad/.

Archiv für Orientforschung 48/49 (2007/8) 311 ff., online: http://orientalistik. univie.ac.at/fileadmin/documents/Abkürzungen_gesamt_ONLINE_Liste_1x.pdf.

Bibliography

Adams, R. McC. 1981. *Heartland of Cities, Surveys of Ancient Settlement and Land Use on the Central Floodplain on the Euphrates*, Chicago: University of Chicago Press.

Andreau, J., Briant, P. and Descat R., eds. 1997. *Economie Antique. Prix et Formation des Prix dans les Economies Antiques*, Saint-Bertrand-de-Comminges: Musée archéologique départemental.

Baker, H. D. and Jursa, M., eds. Forthcoming. *Documentary Sources in Ancient Near Eastern and Greco-Roman History: Methodology and Practice*, Oxford: Oxbow Books.

Bang, P. F. 2006. 'Imperial Bazaar: Towards a Comparative Understanding of Markets in the Roman Empire', in *Ancient Economies, Modern Methodologies. Archaeology, Comparative History, Models and Institutions*, edited by P. F. Bang, M. Ikeguchi and H. G. Ziche, Bari: Edipuglia: 51–88.

—— 2008. *The Roman Bazaar. A Comparative Study of Trade and Markets in a Tributary Empire*, Cambridge: Cambridge University Press.

Dercksen, J.-G. 1999. *Trade and Finance in Ancient Mesopotamia*, Istanbul: Nederlands Historisch-Archaeologisch Instituut.

Dyer, Christopher. 2005. *An Age of Transition? Economy and Society in the Later Middle Ages*, Oxford: Oxford University Press.

Fernea, R. A. 1970. *Shaykh and Effendi. Changing Patterns of Authority among the El Shabana of Southern Iraq*, Cambridge (MA): Harvard University Press.

Graslin-Thomé, L. 2009. *Les Echanges à Longue Distance en Mésopotamie au Ier Millénaire. Une Approche Economique*, Paris: De Boccard.

Hatcher, J. and Bailey, M. 2001. *Modelling the Middle Ages. The History & Theory of England's Economic Development*, Oxford: Oxford University Press.

Hopkins, K. 1978. 'Economic Growth and Towns in Classical Antiquity', in *Towns in Societies. Essays in Economic History and Historical Sociology*, edited by P. Abrams and E. A. Wrigley, Cambridge: Cambridge University Press: 35–77.

Janković, B. 2008. 'Travel Provisions in Babylonia in the First Millennium BC,' in *L'archive des Fortifications de Persépolis. État des questions et perspectives de recherches*, edited by P. Briant, Wouter F. M. Henkelman and Matthew W. Stolper, Paris: De Boccard: 429–64.

Jursa, M. 2008. 'The Remuneration of Institutional Labourers in an Urban Context in Babylonia in the First Millennium BC', in *L'archive des Fortifications de Persépolis. État des questions et perspectives de recherches*, edited by P. Briant, Wouter F. M. Henkelman and Matthew W. Stolper, Paris: De Boccard: 387–427.

—— 2010. *Aspects of the Economic History of Babylonia in the First Millennium BC: Economic Geography, Economic Mentalities, Agriculture, the Use of Money and the Problem of Economic Growth*. With contributions by J. Hackl, B. Jankovic, K. Kleber, E. E. Payne, C. Waerzeggers and M. Weszeli, Münster: Ugarit-Verlag.

—— 2011. 'Taxation and Service Obligations in Babylonia from Nebuchadnezzar to Darius and the Evidence for Darius' Tax Reform', in *Herodot und das Persische Weltreich – Herodotus and the Persian Empire*, edited by R. Rollinger, B. Truschnegg and R. Bichler, Wiesbaden: Harrassowitz-Verlag: 431–48.

—— 2014. 'Factor Markets in Babylonia from the Late Seventh to the Third Century BCE', *Journal of the Economic and Social History of the Orient*, 57(2): 173–202.

Jursa, M., with contributions by Waerzeggers, C. 2009. 'On Aspects of Taxation in Achaemenid Babylonia: New Evidence from Borsippa', in *Organisation des Pouvoirs et Contacts Culturels dans les Pays de L'empire Achéménide*, edited by P. Briant and Michel Chauveu, Paris: De Boccard: 237–69.

Kleber, K. 2012. 'Famine in Babylonia. a Microhistorical Approach to an Agricultural Crisis in 528–526 BC', *Zeitschrift für Assyriologie*, 102: 219–44.

Liverani, M. 1998. *Uruk La Prima Città*, Rome: Editori Laterza.

Millett, P. 2001. 'Productive to Some Purpose? The Problem of Ancient Economic Growth', in *Economies beyond agriculture in the classical world*, edited by D. J. Mattingly and J. Salmon, London: Routledge: 17–48.

Pirngruber, R. 2012. *The Impact of Empire on Market Prices in Babylon in the Late Achaemenid and Seleucid periods, ca. 400–140 B.C.* Unpublished Thesis, VU University Amsterdam.

Potts, D. T. 1997. *Mesopotamian Civilization. The Material Foundations*, London: Cornell University Press.

Rathbone, D. W. 1997. 'Prices and Price-formation in Roman Egypt', in Andreau, Briant and Descat 1997: 183–244.

Renger, J. 2007. 'Economy of Ancient Mesopotamia: a General Outline', in *The Babylonian World*, edited by G. Leick, London: Routledge: 187–97.

Richardson, S. 2002. *The Collapse of a Complex State: A Reappraisal of the End of the First Dynasty of Babylon, 1683–1597 B. C.*, Unpublished thesis, Columbia University, New York.

Roncaglia, A. 2003. *La Richezza Delle Idee. Storia del Pensiero Economico*, Bari: Editori Laterza.

Söderberg, J. 2004. 'Prices in the Medieval Near East and Europe', www.iisg.nl/hpw/papers/soderberg.pdf (accessed 31 July 2009).

Tolini, G. 2011. *La Babylonie et l'Iran. Les Relations d'une Province avec le Coeur de L'empire Achéménide* (539–331 *avant notre Ere*). Unpublished thesis, Université de Paris I, Paris.

Van der Spek, R. J. 2005. *Commodity Prices from Babylon (385–61 BC)*, www.iisg.nl/hpw/data.php#babylon.

Van der Spek, R. J. and Mandemakers, C. A. 2003. 'Sense and Nonsense in the Statistical Approach of Babylonian Prices', *Bibliotheca Orientalis*, 60: 522–37.

Vargyas, P. 2001. *A History of Babylonian Prices in the First Millennium BC. 1. Prices of the Basic Commodities*. Heidelberg: Heidelberger Orientverlag.

Von Reden, S. 2010. 'Review of Bang 2008', *Gnomon*, 82(8): 720–4.

Waerzeggers, C. 2003/2004. 'The Babylonian Revolts Against Xerxes and the "End of Archives" ', *Archiv für Orientforschung*, 50: 150–73.

—— 2010. *The Ezida Temple of Borsippa. Priesthood, Cult, Archives*, Leiden: Nederlands Instituut voor het Nabije Oosten.

—— Forthcoming. *Return to Babylon. Migration and Social Mobility in Babylonia from Nebuchadnezzar II to Xerxes. A Case Study*, Leuven: Peeters.

Weszeli, M. 2010. 'A New Boundary Stone of the Reign of Nabû-mukin-apli (978–943 BC)', *Revue d'Assyriologie*, 104: 99–130.

6 Prices and related data from northern Babylonia in the Late Achaemenid and Early Hellenistic periods, c. 480–300 BC[1]

Johannes Hackl and Reinhard Pirngruber

Introduction

This chapter presents a preliminary survey of price data and rations culled from legal and administrative documents[2] as well as so-called astronomical diaries (ADs) from Late Achaemenid and Early Hellenistic northern Babylonia. The textual material under consideration offers datasets for a whole range of commodities to be used in the analysis of price behaviour in the period following the 'long sixth century'.[3] However, the investigation of price developments is fraught with problems during the period under consideration, mainly owing to the incompleteness of the data. The near-absence of usable data from especially the fifth century BC, rendering exact reconstructions of price behaviour impossible, can be correlated to a general scarcity of archival texts post-dating the second year of Xerxes (484 BC). Likewise, the ADs,[4] the richest source of commodity prices from the Late Achaemenid, Seleucid and Parthian periods, offer little information on the fifth and early fourth centuries BC. However, the small number of attestations notwithstanding, some general trends can be described anyway.

Since a substantial part of the archival texts from northern Babylonia still remains unpublished, some introductory remarks are in order. The following section is intended to give a concise survey of the time span und text corpus under consideration. In the next section, some selected datasets are presented under due consideration of material from the 'long sixth century' and smaller contemporary files from non-cuneiform sources. The chapter goes on to provide an overview of the price quotations for the ADs for the period in question, and the final section summarizes the results obtained.

Late Achaemenid and Hellenistic archival texts from northern Babylonia: time span and text corpus

The beginning of the period under consideration is marked by the suppression of the Babylonian revolts against Xerxes (484 BC). The remainder of the fifth century and the larger part of the fourth century BC Babylonia remained largely unaffected by major political events of greater impact. Only the events following the advent of the Macedonian king Alexander the Great in Babylon in 331 BC would change the political landscape of the ancient Near East substantially. The last three decades of the fourth century BC saw Babylonia pass from Achaemenid to Macedonian rule, culminating in the establishment of the Seleucid dynasty in 305 BC.[5] The extensive armed conflicts that took place between several leading generals of the Macedonian army after Alexander's early death in 323 BC entailed an extended period of continuous fighting in and around Babylon, which peaked in 310/09 BC with a final abortive attempt of Antigonus Monophthalmus (the 'One-Eyed') and his troops led by his son Demetrius to wrest Babylonia from Seleucus.[6]

It is the textual material drafted in this period (early fifth to early third century BC) on which the discussion in this chapter draws. In the period spanning the later portion of the reign of Seleucus I and the reigns of the following Seleucid (and Parthian) rulers, documentation becomes less dense. Apart from a few dozen contextually isolated legal records, the later Seleucid textual material is made up by only two archives: the Abu-ul-īde[7] and Rahim-Esu archives.[8] The latter also stands at the end of cuneiform writing tradition in the context of economic record keeping (94/3 BC).

Studies carried out on the basis of the extant Babylonian textual record from the later period are hampered by several factors. As mentioned above, the documentation from the later fifth century (BC) onwards (henceforth post-484 BC period) is far less abundant than that of the 'long sixth century'. Also, the chronological and geographical distribution of the material is skewed: only some 2,000 tablets are available in publication, less than 700[9] of which were drawn up in northern Babylonia.[10] The larger part of the material stems from central and southern Babylonia, particularly from Nippur and Uruk respectively, and with the exception of the extensive but atypical Muraŝû archive from Late Achaemenid Nippur (more than 800 tablets),[11] the bulk of the available cuneiform documentation dates from the Hellenistic period (Uruk).[12] What is more, the post-484 BC material cannot compete with the sixth-century BC corpus in terms of the wide variety of subjects treated. Amongst other reasons, this is because some text types are obviously no longer committed to cuneiform writing. The fact that so few tablets have come down to us makes it impossible to present a picture as coherent and accurate as the one that can be drawn for the 'long sixth century'.

The reasons for the scant cuneiform documentation (in the context of record keeping) in particular in northern Babylonia after the suppression of the revolts against Xerxes, have been debated extensively. Probably the main reason is what is now commonly referred to as 'the end of archives'[13] in the second year of Xerxes (484 BC), the result of the reprisals taken against the major temples and urban elites of those northern Babylonian cities such as Babylon and Borsippa who had instigated, or at least supported, the revolts against Xerxes. Furthermore, the supposedly diminishing importance of the Akkadian language (especially during the second half of the first millennium BC) and the decreasing use of clay tablets in favour of perishable writing materials like papyrus and leather are also often cited in this context.[14] Finally, straightforward reasons include accidents of recovery and the overall poor state of preservation of the textual material. The latter also seems to be the reason why the post-484 BC material from northern Babylonia has only received limited scholarly attention, as reflected in the number of published texts.

Price data and rations from the post-484 BC period

The brief sketch of the political developments during the Late Achaemenid and Early Hellenistic period outlined above gives rise to the question of whether these events are reflected in the legal and administrative textual record from Babylonia. Despite a general continuity in these texts, significant differences are indeed to be noted between Achaemenid and Seleucid legal texts, in both form and content.[15] It is reasonable to assume that some of these formal changes were responses to changing conditions of the juridical or commercial environment in which texts were written, and that some of the changes in the environment were themselves results of the above-mentioned political developments.[16] In the present context, however, we are less interested in formal changes than in economic changes that can be inferred from the data preserved in the archival texts from northern Babylonia: prices (slaves, livestock, houses and arable land), rents and wages (house letting and boat rentals; hirelings and slaves), interest rates (silver and staple goods) and rations for temple personnel. The paucity of the data that are to be found in our material notwithstanding, at least some datasets lend themselves to comparison with the well-documented 'long sixth century' so that a few (diachronic) trends or some (synchronic and diachronic) patterns can be discerned. In this section, (a) slave prices, (b) house rents, (c) interest rates (silver) and (d) rations are investigated. The selection of these particular datasets is based on the following considerations: each dataset has sufficient attestations to cover a large part of the period under consideration (this does not apply to slave prices; however, slave prices are to be considered anyway, as they are an important source of information for the development of prices in general in the 'long sixth century');[17] surveys of attestations from the sixth-century BC corpus have been compiled by earlier studies (this does not hold true for the house rents, for which a corresponding survey is given below); and the categories treated here are not included in the ADs and hence offer complementary data. Note that there are too few attestations to allow for a statistical treatment of the material presented here. On the basis of new data, the present study rather aims to re-examine price trends and so forth that have been described by previous studies.

Slave prices

The table and scatter graph in Jursa (2010: 741–44) and Jursa, this volume, Figure 5.6, containing ninety slave price observations (adult male slaves) from the 'long sixth century' that were mostly gleaned from slave sale contracts from private archives is followed by a detailed discussion of the distribution of price attestations throughout the 'long sixth century'. The mean price is 64.65 shekels, the median price 58 shekels (c. 600–480 BC). Figure 6.1 (the same as Figure 5.6,

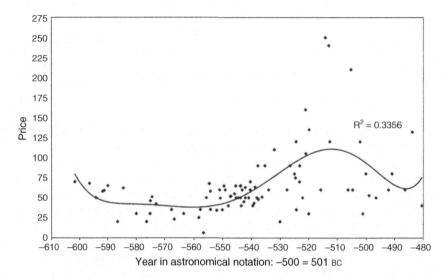

Figure 6.1 Slave prices (in shekels) in Babylonia in the sixth century BC.

Source: Jursa (2010: 744, Figure 27).

reproduced here for convenience) shows the distribution of slave prices in the 'long sixth century'.

The distribution of price attestations drawn from the late material does not allow for a reconstruction of the price behaviour of the entire period. Slave price observations are only available for the fifth century BC (roughly until the end of the reign of Artaxerxes I (465–424 BC)). What is more, in several instances regnal years in the date formula and/or operative section of the text are lost, rendering an exact dating impossible. The mean price for adult male slaves (Table 6.1) in this period is 97.57 shekels, and 69.5 shekels for adult female slaves (Table 6.2). Also note the unusually high price of the two male and female slaves sold together (Table 6.3) in YBC11572 (7 Art I = 458/7 BC).

As has been stated above, the mean price of adult slaves for the 'long sixth century' is 64.65 shekels. For the Early Achaemenid period (1 Cyr = 538 BC to 2 Xer = 484 BC), however, the mean price is considerably higher (89.6 shekels) with price peaks during the first two decades of Darius I (522–486 BC). It can be stated that the price observations culled from the fifth century BC material roughly correspond to the price level attested between 520 and 500 BC.

House rents

There are no comprehensive surveys of house rents attested in the 'long sixth century' and later centuries.[18] Oppenheim (1936), a detailed but to some extent outdated study on house letting in Babylonia and other aspects of rent law, only comments on the range of annual house rents, but refrains from presenting a list of

Table 6.1 Slave prices, late Achaemenid Babylonia (adult males)

Reference	Date	Origin	Price (shekels)
BM 40543	[...] Xer (486–465 BC)	Babylon	83
YBC 11614	[Xer/Art I]	Borsippa	80
RA 97: 127 (BM 54143)	8 Art I (457/6)	Kutha	90
Iraq 54 135 no. 6	28 Art I (437/6)	[Dilbat?]	90
VS 5, 141	[39+ Art I] (426–424)	Borsippa	120[a]
VS 5, 142	[... Art I] (465–424)	Borsippa	120
RA 97: 119 (BM 54073+)	[... Art I]	Cutha	100
BM 78977	[... Art]	[Babylon?]	20[b]

Notes:
[a] Two male slaves are sold for 240 shekels.
[b] The price might suggest that a child or an adolescent male is sold here, but the text does not give pertinent information.

Table 6.2 Slave prices, late Achaemenid Babylonia (adult females)

Reference	Date	Origin	Price (shekels)
VS 5, 118	8 Xer (478/7)	Borsippa	120
VS 5, 128	[...] Art I	[Babylon/Borsippa?]	30
BM 35393	9 Art	[Babylon]	40
PSBA 5, 103ff. (BM 47361)	23 Art	Babylon	68
ZA 79: 95f. (BM 62588)	35 Art	Borsippa region	60[a]
BM 79026	[... Art]	[Babylon?]	65

Note:
[a] Three female slaves are sold for 180 shekels.

Table 6.3 Slave prices, late Achaemenid Babylonia (adult male and female sold together)

Reference	Date	Origin	Price (shekels)
YBC 11568	20 Xer (466/5)	Borsippa	180
YBC 11572	7 Art I (458/7)	Borsippa	300

the attestations.[19] This is probably because, as a rule, house rental contracts do not stipulate the size of the house or plot that is to be rented out. Hence, an assessment of the average ratio of house size to rent, that is price per reed (12.25 m²), is impossible. What is more, houses are a commodity of very variable quality, an attribute which is rarely specified in the rental contracts at our disposal. For the present study, however, it can be argued that the range of house plot sizes (and also the quality of the houses rented out) was more or less the same during the period under discussion and in the sixth century BC.[20] A comparison of the annual house rents between these two periods thus seems warranted.

For the purpose of comparing house rents throughout the 'long sixth century' and later centuries, attestations from the sixth-century BC corpus have

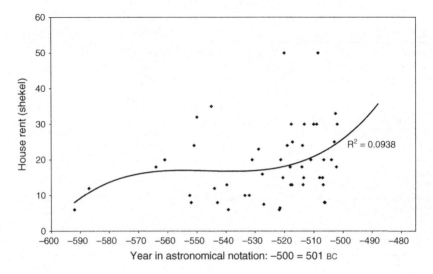

Figure 6.2 House rents in Babylonia in the sixth century BC.

Note:
The graph is on a three degree polynomial scale in order to facilitate comparison with the graph on date garden prices in Jursa (2010: 460, Figure 12).

been collected as well. Table 6.4 and the scatter graph in Figure 6.2 contain data on 51 house rents. Only complete houses have been taken into account (rental contracts concerning the letting of side wings[21] and other parts of the building were not included). Most house rents were gleaned from house rental contracts from private archives (Egibi, Nappāhu, etc.).[22] House rents paid in kind (*Alimentations-Mietverträge*)[23] have not been taken into account.

The distribution of house rent attestations throughout the century is sufficiently even to allow a reconstruction of the development of house rents from the latter half of the reign of Nabonidus (Nbn) until the end of the sixth century BC. Rents remain fairly stable until close to 520 BC, and then they rise and peak towards the end of the century. This trend is quite similar to that of land prices at that time, as evidenced by date garden prices in the vicinity of the cities of Babylon and Borsippa (see Jursa 2010: 460, Figure 12). The mean price of house rents is 18.69 shekels, the median price 18 shekels. Despite the fact that the r^2 (coefficient of determination) is unsatisfactorily low – mainly due to wide range of the price attestations, which are usually scattered between 10 and 30 shekels in the period 520–500 BC – the price behaviour shown in the graph fits the general trend as suggested by land prices and the prices of other commodities.[24] This also becomes evident if an examination of the data are limited to rents prior to the reign of Darius I (roughly before 520 BC) on the one hand, and to rents post-dating that date on the other hand. The results are then as follows: the mean price until 520 BC is 14.83 shekels and afterwards is 21.65 shekels.

Table 6.4 House rents in Babylonia in the sixth century BC and later

Reference	Date	Origin	House rent p.a. (shekels)
YOS 17, 5	13 Nbk II (592 BC)	Babylon	6
NCBT 899	18 Nbk II (587)	Babylon	12
BM 29748	41 Nbk II (564)	Borsippa	18
NBC 4513	1 AM (561)	Uruk	20
VS 5, 23	4 Nbn (552)	Babylon	10
YOS 6, 85	4 Nbn (552)	Uruk	8
Nbn. 224	5 Nbn (551)	Babylon	24
Nbn. 238	6 Nbn (550)	Babylon	32
Nbn. 500	11 Nbn (545)	Babylon	35
Nbn. 597	12 Nbn (544)	Babylon	12
VS 5, 32	13 Nbn (543)	Babylon	8
Nbn. 1030	17 Nbn (539)	Babylon	13
BM 114446	acc Cyr (539)	Uruk	6
Cyr. 228	6 Cyr (533)	Babylon	10
AnOr 8: 58	7 Cyr (532)	Uruk	10
BIN 1, 118	8 Cyr (531)	Uruk	20
Camb. 117	2 Cam (528)	Babylon	23
Camb. 182	3 Cam (527)	Babylon	16
Camb. 184	3 Cam (527)	Babylon	7.5
BM 26689	1 Nbk IV (521)	Borsippa	6
VS 5, 59	1 Dar I (521)	Babylon	6.5[a]
Dar. 25	1 Dar I (521)	[...]	20
VS 5, 61	2 Dar I (520)	Babylon	15
Dar. 64	3 Dar I (520)	Babylon	50
BM 26566	3+ Dar I (520?)	Borsippa	24
VS 5, 64	4 Dar I (519)	Babylon	18
VS 5, 67	5 Dar I (518)	Babylon	13
Dar. 191	5 Dar I (518)	Babylon	30
VS 5, 67	5 Dar I (518)	Babylon	13
VS 5, 68	5 Dar I (518)	Babylon	25
CTMMA 3, 97	8 Dar I (514)	Babylon	18
JCS 28 no. 46	9 Dar I (513)	Babylon	24
BRM 1, 74	9 Dar I (513)	Babylon	13
Dar. 256	9 Dar I (513)	Babylon	15
BM 96160	9 Dar I (513)	Borsippa	30
VS 6, 201	11 [Dar I] (511)	Babylon	20
Dar. 330	12 Dar I (510)	Babylon	30
NBC 6208	13 Dar I (509)	Sippar	30
Dar. 378	14 Dar I (508)	Babylon	50
Dar. 424	14 Dar I (508)	Babylon	15[a]
VS 5, 78	15 Dar I (507)	Babylon	15
VS 5, 81	16 Dar I (506)	Babylon	13
VS 5, 82	16 Dar I (506)	Babylon	20
Dar. 428	16 Dar I (506)	Babylon	8
NBC 8406	16 Dar I (506)	Borsippa	8
VS 5, 84+	18 Dar I (504)	Babylon	20
Dar. 485	19 Dar I (503)	Babylon	25
Dar. 499	20 Dar I (502)	Babylon	33
VS 4, 154	20 Dar I (502)	Babylon	18[a]
BM 96183	20 Dar I (502)	Borsippa	30+
BM 25628	34 Dar I (488)	Borsippa	7

Note:
[a] The rent actually specified is a monthly one or given for several months.

Table 6.5 House rents in Babylonia in the post-484 BC period

Reference	Date	Origin	House rent p.a. (shekels)
BM 79000	1 Art I (464)	[Babylon]	20
RA 97: 74 (BM 54078)	7 Art I (458)	Kutha	20
NBDMich. 2	9 Art I (456)	Babylon	6
NBDMich. 13	9 Art I (456)	Babylon	12
NBDMich. 14	9 Art I (456)	Babylon	16
VS 5, 119	8 Art II (397)	[Babylon]	20
TEBR 72	35 Art II (370)	[Babylon]	48
OECT 12, A 79	43 Art II (362)	[...]	30
BM 95518	[28] Art I/II (437/377)	[Babylon]	14
BM 36322	1 Art (464)	[Babylon]	20
BM 40786	[...] Art	[Babylon]	20
ZA 3: 152f.	[... Art]	[Babylon]	6
BM 47469	8 Phi (316)	Babylon	6
CT 49, 107+	37 SE (275)	Babylon	6

House rents in the post-484 BC period (see Table 6.5) are very similar to those of the sixth century BC (the arithmetic mean of the house rents given in Table 6.6 is 17.43 shekels). More precisely, they are more expensive than house rents before −520, but not quite as high as those attested in the first two decades of the reign of Darius I (roughly 520–500 BC). Unfortunately, it is not possible to illustrate the data from the post-484 BC period in a scatter graph, as for some of the attestations dating from the reign of an Artaxerxes it is not clear which of the three kings bearing that name (Artaxerxes I: 465–424 BC; II: 405–359; III 359–338) they should be attributed to. What is more, there are not enough data to investigate the subsequent development during the transition from Achaemenid to Macedonian rule and the following Seleucid period.

Interest rates for silver

A comprehensive study on interest rates in the 'long sixth century' and later centuries can be found in Jursa (2010: 490–99) (see Table 6.6 and also Van Leeuwen *et al.*, 2011, 184ff). The following is a brief summary of the principal findings presented there. In the sixth century BC, rates below 20 per cent p.a. must be considered exceptional. Occasional deviations from the 20 per cent rate are most likely to be the result of negotiations between the parties. From the reign of Artaxerxes I interest rates tend to exceed 20 per cent more often – based on the data gleaned from Late Achaemenid texts, it seems that interest rates of 20 to 40 per cent p.a. were the norm in this period.[25]

Little can be added on the basis of the new textual material from northern Babylonia. Only some additional attestations of the 20 per cent rate show that the standard rate of the 'long sixth century' was more frequently used in the fifth century BC than is suggested by Table 57 in Jursa (2010: 497ff). However, this has no bearing on the general trend of the development of interest rates. Interest

Table 6.6 Interest rates in Babylonia, 471–177 BC, paid in silver

Reference	Date	Origin	Rate (per cent, p.a.)
BM 54670	15 Xer (471)	[Babylon]	20
BM 54671	11 Art I (454)	Kutha	20
BM 54066	20 Art I (445)	[Babylon]	40
AMI 23: 175f.	28 Art I (437)	Borsippa region	20
OECT 10, 205	30 Art I (435)	Kiš	24[a]
BM 46716	31+ Art I (434?)	Babylon	20
BM 54674	32 Art I (433)	Babylon	20
BM 40550	2 Dar II (422)	Babylon	40
VAT 15755 = *FuB* 14, 23 n.13	6 Dar II (418)	[Babylon]	60
VAT 13393 = *FuB* 14, 28f. n. 2	7 Dar II (417)	[Babylon]	30
BM 62456	[...] Dar II	[...]	40
AuOr 15, 186, Nr. 37	[Art I/Dar II]	[Babylon]	20
BE 8/1, 121	1 Art	Borsippa	20
BM 47643	3 Art	[Babylon?]	20
BM 36359	15 Art	Babylon	40
BM 61513	18 Art	[Babylon]	20
BM 65397	25 Art	[Borsippa?]	20
EPHE 426	28 Art	[Babylon?]	40
CT 49, 34	3 Ant (315)	Babylon	40
AION *Suppl.* 77, A2–6	4 Ant (314)	Babylon	40
AION *Suppl.* 77, A2–10	6 Alx IV (311)	Babylon	40
BM 46856	35 SE (277)	[Babylon?]	20
CT 49 106	35 SE (277)	Babylon	40
CT 49 111	42 SE (270)	Babylon	40
BM 31454	44 SE (268)	Babylon	80
AION *Suppl.* 77, 15	[35–46] SE (277–66)	[Babylon]	40
BM 31728+	51 SE (261)	Babylon	40
CT 49 116	[35–49] SE (277–63)	[Babylon]	40
CT 49 112	[35–55] SE (277–27)	[Babylon]	40
CT 49 121	54 SE (268)	[Babylon]	40
BM 41582	116 SE (196)	Babylon	23.75
Persika 9: 214, 6	135 SE (177)	Kutha	30[a]

Note:

[a] The monthly interest rate is not calculated per mina, but on the basis of the actual debt.

rates of less than 20 per cent appear frequently only in the seventh and early sixth centuries BC, interest rates above 20 per cent are common in the fifth century BC and later. The trend towards rising interest rates continues into the early Seleucid period during which rates of 40 per cent p.a. are attested quite frequently.[26]

Tendentiously, even higher interest rates (5 per cent per month, hence 60 per cent per year, plus compound interest) are attested in roughly contemporary

Aramaic papyri from another part of the Achaemenid Empire, Elephantine in Egypt.[27] The fact that both attestations are at the high end of the interest rates spectrum found in Babylonia in the same period may reflect the less urbanized, and also less monetized environment of the Jewish military colony on an island in the Nile River, especially when considering the rather low principals loaned (3.5 and 4 shekels of silver, respectively).

Rations as salaries paid in kind

A detailed study of the diachronic development of the Babylonian institutional ration system can be found in Jursa (2008). The paper not only demonstrates that the ration system in Babylonia underwent several fundamental changes during the first millennium BC, but also identifies the standard rations for different periods and institutional environments. The best documented cases are the ration systems of the Eanna (Uruk) and Ebabbar temples (Sippar) (both archives date from the 'long sixth century'). On the basis of the available material, Jursa concludes that the common standards for rations paid in kind were (nearly) the same in both temples. The monthly cost of maintaining an adult or trained worker ranged between 90 and 180 litres of dates or barley.[28] In view of daily energy requirements, it is assumed that a significant part was meant for exchange (supplementary foodstuff) or used to feed wives and children. The latter supposition is also supported by the fact that women and children were normally not included in the redistributive system. The fact that the size of the rations is quite substantial is indicative of them being also used as a means of exchange. In addition, Jursa suggests abolishing the common term 'ration' in favour of 'salary (paid in kind)', since these payments do not seem to have been calculated on the basis of the nutritional requirements of the recipients, but more generally, on the cost of living.[29]

The ration lists of the Late Achaemenid and Early Hellenistic Esangila archive (comprising more than 140 of such lists, of which around fifty are preserved well enough to yield usable data) suggest a different system of remuneration, apparently closely tied to the prebendary system.[30] In contrast to Sippar and Uruk during the 'long sixth century', separate ration lists are drawn up for women, and sons are mentioned together with their fathers, receiving the same rations. Since rations issued to a group (recipient + brother(s) and/or son(s)) are as a rule a multiple of what would have been given out to a single recipient, it is assumed that only working persons are mentioned.

Table 6.7 Rations in late Achaemenid Babylonia paid to *širkus*

Text	Date	Recipient(s)	Ration	Monthly ration p.p.	Period
BM 78964 (barley)	8 Art II/III (397/51)	1(×1+)	0;1.4	60 l	[...]
BM 78976 (barley/dates)	8 Art II/III (397/51)	1(×5)	0;1.4	60 l	MN 4–6
		1 + 1 son	0;2.5.3?	52,5 l	

Table 6.8 Rations in late Achaemenid Babylonia paid to reed workers

Text	Date	Recipient(s)	Ration	Monthly ration p.p.	Period
BM 87230 (barley)	8 Art (457/ 397/ 351)	1 + 1 brother (×2)	0;3.2	60 l	MN [3]–4
		1	0;1.4	60 l	
EAH 241 (barley)	12 Art (453/ 393/ 347)	1 + 2 sons	1;2.3	85 l	MN 10
		1	1;0	180 l	
		1 + 1 brother	0;3.2	60 l	
		1 (×2)	0;1.4	60 l	
		1 + 4 sons	1;1.4	48 l	
BM 78998 (barley)	16 Art (449/ 389/ 343)	1 + 3 sons	1;3.4.3	78,75 l	MN 6
		1 + 2 sons	1;2.3	85 l	
		1 + 1 brother	0;3.2	60 l	
		1 + 4 sons	1;2.0.3	51 l	
		1 (×2)	0;1.4	60 l	
		1 + 1 son (×2)	0;2.5.3	52,5 l	
		1	0;1.1.3	45 l	
		1 + 2 brothers	1;0	60 l	
CT 44, 80 (barley)	17 Art (448/ 388/ 342)	1 + 3 sons (×2)	1;3.4.3	78,75 l	MN [2]–8
		1 + 1 brother	0;3.2	60 l	MN 2–[8]
		1 + 4 sons	1;2.0.3	51 l	
		1 (×2)	0;1.4	60 l	
		1 + 1 son (×2)	0;2.5.3	52,5 l	
		1	0;1.1.3	45 l	
		1 + 2 brothers	1;0	60 l	

According to Table 7 given in Jursa (2008), 90 litres seem to have been the standard ration for men, and 45 litres for women. This is corroborated by some thirty additional published and unpublished ration lists that are not included in Jursa (2008, Table 7). Despite the recognized standard, these lists display a great variety of rations. Jursa argues that this variety can be accounted for by a different system of remuneration which was in use in Babylon at that time.[31] According to Jursa it seems highly unlikely that the complete absence of references to prebends in the Esangila material – e.g. the term *pappasu* being the *terminus technicus* for 'prebendary income' both in Sippar and Uruk during the 'long sixth century', is never used in these texts – is indicative of the abolishment of the prebendary system. Rather, one might suggest that the disbursement of prebendary income is 'concealed' by the fact that the prebend owners received *kurummatu* rations instead of *pappasu*.[32] The fact that the majority of the groups of recipients is made up by the typical professions involved in the organization and operation of the prebendary system of Esangila (groups (2) and (3) in Jursa (2008: 417)), lends additional support to this assumption. Hence, the comparatively broad variety in rations can be explained with the basic organization of the prebendary system.

Because the number of days per month for which the owners of the prebends received prebendary income is likely to vary with each recipient (or group of recipients), the rations given out are calculated on the basis of the actual service period. Also, the type of prebend is likely to have a bearing on how the prebend owners were remunerated for their services.[33]

As touched upon above, both group (2) and group (3) of the professions receiving rations are well-attested in the Esangila archive. Recipients of group (1), the non-prebendary professions, however, are rare (note that they are not represented in Table 7 given in Jursa (2008) on the basis of which the 90 litres standard has been calculated). Yet there are five ration lists among the unpublished Esangila texts recording the disbursement of barley (or dates?) to professions of group (1): temple oblates (*širkus*) and reed workers (see Table 6.7 and Table 6.8).[34] It is noteworthy that the average ration paid to men of these two groups, 65 litres, is well below the standard of 90 litres per month attested for groups (2) and (3).

Price data from the astronomical diaries[35]

The ADs are a set of cuneiform tablets recording a variety of observed celestial, climatic, ecological and economic phenomena, as well as giving accounts of historical events. They comprise the largest collections of observational data available from the Ancient World, consisting of hundreds of tablets dating from the period c. 650–60 BC. The better part of the preserved information usually relates to astronomical observations, yet the ADs are at the same time the single most important source for the history of Late Achaemenid and Seleucid Babylonia. Additionally, they contain unique economic data consisting of several hundred quotations of the silver equivalents of six different commodities, including the staple foods barley and dates (cf. Van der Spek *et al.*, Chapter 1, this volume).

Unfortunately for the purposes of this chapter, the earliest period for which ADs are attested, the sixth and fifth centuries BC, are very scarcely documented. Nevertheless an attempt can be made to analyse the few scattered price quotations from the ADs from the fifth century BC (collected below in Table 6.9) as well as the somewhat less slender number of observations from the fourth century BC material, along with the much denser information of the 'long sixth century'. The best-documented period of 575–535 BC was also characterized by very low barley prices, ranging mostly below 1 shekel per *kurru* (4.64 g. per hl), before a dramatic increase in prices set in around 540 BC, peaking around the year 500 BC, when prices arrived at a level of 10 shekels per *kurru*. Afterwards, prices fell again to a level between 3 and 4 shekels per *kurru*.[36]

As far as the scanty evidence at our disposal allows us to see, the ensuing decades of the fifth century were characterized by a very high price level. According to Astronomical Diary of year 419–8 (ADART no. −418), the most informative source on prices for that period, prices of barley, the most frequently attested commodity, fluctuated in 419/8 BC very much in line with the usual seasonal pattern of decreasing prices in the period immediately following the harvest in the month of *ayaru* (II)[37] between 5 and 10 shekels per *kurru*; the mode and

Table 6.9 Commodity prices from the Babylonian astronomical diaries from the fifth century BC

Diary (and Babylonian month)	Date BC	Commodity	Equivalent (litres/shekel)[a]	Price (shekels/kurru)
ADART no. −461 (VI)	08/07–06/08 462	Sesame	6	30
ADART no. −453 (X)	03/01–31/01 452	Barley	18-15-18	10-12-10
		Dates	48	3.75
		Cuscuta	144	1.25
		Sesame	8	22.5
ADART no. −418 (I)	27/03–25/04 419	Barley	24–23	7.5–7.83
		Dates	16.5	7–8
		Cuscuta	144	1.25
		Cress	18	10
		Sesame	6	30
		Wool	1	180
ADART no. −418 (II)	26/04–24/05 419	Barley	24-18-24[b]	7.5-10-7.5
		Dates	17?	10.6
		Cuscuta	120	1.5
		Cress	13	13.85
		Sesame	5?	36
		Wool	1	180
ADART no. −418 (III)	25/05–23/06 419	Barley	30–36	6–5
		Cress	16?	11.25
		Sesame	5	36
		Wool	1	180
ADART no. −418 (IV)	24/06–22/07 419	Barley	34?–31	5.29–5.80
		Wool	1	180
ADART no. −418 (XII)	15/02–15/03 418	Barley	21–24	8.57–7.5
		Dates	52.5	3.43
		Cuscuta	90	2
		Cress	18	10
		Sesame	6	30
		Wool	5/6	216
ADART no. −418 (XII$_2$)	16/03–14/04 418	Barley	25	7.2
		Dates	48–49.5	3.75–3.63
		Cuscuta	120	1.5
		Cress	18	10
		Sesame	6	30
		Wool	1	150

Notes:

[a] Minas (0.5 kg) in the case of wool. In several cases, separate prices are given for barley for the beginning, the middle, and the end of the month, also, for barley and dates a second price is given occasionally for the end of the month.

[b] The equivalent for this particular price quotation is 1 shekel and one-eighth rather than the usual 1 shekel.

mean were 7.5 shekels/kurru and 7.85 shekels/kurru respectively. A look at the only other diary from this century confirms this impression: in the pre-harvest season of 452 BC, the barley price oscillated between 10 and 12 shekels for a *kurru*. The general impression is thus one of high prices prevailing throughout the fifth century BC, comparable to those of the last decades of the sixth century BC. The price decrease of the first decade of the fifth century BC seems to have been a temporary one only. However, we cannot exclude the possibility that our extant prices are among the highest of the fifth century BC. The evidence at our disposal is simply not adequate to sustain any certain conclusions.

The few pertinent price data from private archives published thus far cannot help us any further here. Two higher (i.e. more favourable) barley equivalents of 100 and 90 litres per shekel are attested in the fifth century BC. However, the latter (BE 8, 158) from Nippur stems from an internal transaction of a temple and thus likely represents a fixed rate rather than a genuine price shaped by the interplay of supply and demand.[38] The former dates to September 429 BC, and in this text (ROMCT 2, 49), 6,000 litres of barley (33 *kurru*, 1 *pānu*, and 4 *sūtu*) are specified as the equivalent of 1 mina (= 60 shekels) of silver. The transaction in question, however, was a sale of wool by a temple, and again the equivalent given is thus not a genuine price. In addition, the text stems from the rural region of Nippur and is thus not necessarily indicative of conditions in or around the city of Babylon. The moderate equivalent of 60 litres per shekel (3 shekels per *kurru*) given by Vargyas (2001, 64) for August 485 BC is misplaced, as the text (CT 49, 150) actually dates to the Parthian period.[39] Summing up, the impression is one of rather high prices throughout the fifth century BC – the prices of 3 to 4 shekels per *kurru* of the first decades seem to be on the lower side when compared to the prices prevailing in the second half. The scarcity of data, again, renders every conclusion uncertain.

During the fourth century BC, the barley price data align better with the mean price ranging between 3 and 4 shekels per *kurru* found in the 490s BC.[40] The mean of the fourth century BC sample is 3.37 shekels per *kurru* (corresponding to an equivalent of 70 litres per shekel). As is the general rule with foodstuffs, the value of the median (2.79) is lower than the mean of the sample due to demand inelasticity.[41] These values are much lower than the high prices seemingly prevailing during the fifth century BC, our reckoning of which, it must be kept in mind, relies on few data only. Overall, the sample is characterized by a rather high price volatility compared to the ensuing Seleucid period, c. 300–140 BC, as indicated by the standard deviation of 1.79. Price volatility is especially high in the period between 385 and 366 BC, when the barley price oscillated between 1.82 shekels/*kurru* in March/April 370 BC and 7.5 shekels/*kurru* in January 372 BC.

All the other commodities of the ADs exhibit a substantially lower mean during the fourth century BC than in the fifth century BC. For dates, the mean diminishes from 4.42 to 2.02 shekels per *kurru*,[42] for sesame from 30.64 to 9.27 shekels per *kurru*. Also the overall pattern of the comparison of the prices of both commodities with their respective sixth century BC values is similar to that of barley: the fifth century BC values align best with the price peak prevailing in the last decades or so of the sixth century BC, whereas the fourth century BC prices are comparable to

Table 6.10 Price volatility of barley, dates and sesame in Babylonia, 400–330 BC

Commodity	Mean price (shekels per kurru)	Standard deviation (400–330 BC)
Barley	3.37	1.79
Dates	2.02	0.82
Sesame	9.67	5.56

the prices of the first decade of the fifth century BC, but are higher than the overall sixth century BC level. For example, for dates, the mean of the fourth century BC (2.02) lies quite clearly above the mean of the 'long sixth century' mean of 1.24 shekels per *kurru*, but slightly below the values for early fifth century BC.[43] As can be seen in Table 6.10 above, the level of price volatility is elevated for all of the commodities attested in the ADs during the period between c. 400 and 330 BC.

Summing up our findings for the Late Achaemenid data, we firstly note that the mean prices are in general higher than the low mid-sixth-century BC prices, but substantially lower than the high prices caused by the monetization shock in the last quarter of the sixth century BC. Any direct comparison between the two datasets is, however, rendered problematic by the scarcity of price data throughout the fifth century BC, leaving all attempts at such a comparison on a shaky ground. The general impression is one of a fairly high price level in this period.

Conclusion

The (very) limited amount of usable price data (especially that of agrarian goods) combined with the fluctuation of the commodity prices culled from the ADs, as well as the (near)-absence of wage data from the post-484 BC period make studying price behaviour and so forth in this period difficult. Nevertheless, some general remarks based on the datasets presented above can be given anyway.

The most interesting information available concerns house rents. The scatter graph of house rents from the 'long sixth century' is based on somewhat fewer attestations than would be desirable (i.e. eighty to over one hundred), but when compared with other price series, it is obvious that the data are very homogenous in their economic background. During the period from the later years of Nabonidus to the reign of Darius I it can be demonstrated that the development of house rents followed the prices of land (and also that of non-agrarian goods).[44] Hence, it is reasonable to assume that house rents from the post-484 BC period are also indicative of price developments during that time. Note that the price level of the house rents collected here is very similar to that attained in the second half of the sixth century BC, but well below the price level during the reign of Darius I.

The rations paid to male temple dependants as salaries in kind that are recorded in the ration lists from the Late Achaemenid and Early Hellenistic period, 90 litres per month, roughly correspond to those attested for the Eanna temple in Uruk during the period of the Neo-Babylonian Empire (Nebuchadnezzar to early

Nabonidus).[45] Rations paid to adult males performing non-prebendary professions, however, are considerably lower. They only received an average of 65 litres per month. Since it has been shown that there is a connection between the institutional wage standard and the general price level in the 'long sixth century', data on the latter are especially important, as they may serve as proxy data for the scarce direct information on wage levels and even money wages paid to non-institutional labourers in this period. Moreover, the striking difference between the 'prebendary' and 'non-prebendary' rations can be marshalled in favour of interpreting the 90 litres payments as being a combination of prebendary income and 'rations' proper. Of course, it has to be borne in mind that the number of attested entries is very limited. Even small amounts of additional information might affect the calculated mean considerably. However, an income of 65 litres of barley per month for an unskilled labourer is a priori not unlikely in this period, as this amount would correspond to a hypothetical silver wage of circa 1 shekel per month (according to the evidence from the ADs): as noted previously, the average price of the years 400–330 BC of 3.37 shekels per *kurru* corresponds to a barley equivalent of 70 litres for 1 shekel.

The high prices for adult slaves attested for the post-484 BC period are unexpected, as they do not fit the rather low price level suggested by house rents and rations. Given the scarcity of the attestations (seven), however, one should be wary of over-interpretation.

The additional attestations for interest rates paid in silver follow the general trend described in Jursa (2010: 497). The issue of the clearly increasing interest rates during the later period, also attested in the Aramaic documentation from Egypt, is in need of a more detailed treatment that draws on a wider range of sources.

As regards prices of agrarian goods, the most striking phenomenon of the fourth century BC is the rather high level of price volatility manifest in the large range of prices in the period between c. 385 and 369 BC. In the absence of a convincing mono-causal explanation of these phenomena, the most satisfactory and probable interpretation of the pattern of the fourth century BC is an interplay of several smaller factors detrimental to market performance. As regards political history, the particularly volatile prices of the years 385–369 BC saw much bellicose imperial activity in various parts of the Achaemenid Empire, most prominently several abortive attempts at the re-conquest of Egypt during the 370s BC involving the Great King himself. A number of ominous references repeatedly point to various difficulties in Babylonia in this period, including disease (ADART no. −382) and famine (ADART no. −373A). These troubling situations may have been caused by these unsuccessful military enterprises, as warfare in other provinces could equally affect Babylonia in various ways (drain of monetary resources and manpower, to state the most obvious).[46] Possibly the more influential factor hampering a smooth working of the market for agricultural produce in the Late Achaemenid period lies in the changed institutional framework of the country in the period after the revolts against Xerxes in 484 BC. The clearest symptom of this new regime was a much tighter and more direct grip on part of the crown on essential resources and mainly agricultural land[47] – a good example is the management of temple-land directly by crown agents as evidenced by several texts (cf. Stolper 1985: 42) – as well as an unprecedented reliance on agricultural entrepreneurs for the exploitation of the land, who further destabilized market performance by pooling the relevant means of production in their own hands.

Finally, it should again be emphasized that the scarcity of usable data are a real impediment for the study of price behaviour during the post-484 BC period. Because of that, the aim of this chapter was, above all, the presentation of new data that can be used by future studies, especially those focusing on the development of price behaviour and economic changes in Late Achaemenid and Hellenistic Babylonia in general.

Notes

1 Abbreviations are those of the *Archiv für Orientforschung* 48/49 (2001/02): 311ff. and Jursa (2005: 153ff.). J. Hackl's research on the present subject is based on the work conducted under the auspices of the START Project 'The Economic History of Babylonia in the First Millennium BC' Y 180, led by Michael Jursa at the University of Vienna and funded by the Austrian Science Fund (FWF). The broader-based investigation leading to the preparation of the article that underpins this chapter was carried out in the context of an ongoing project entitled 'Official Epistolography in Babylonia in the First Millennium BC' as part of a National Research Network ' "Imperium" and "Officium" – Comparative Studies in Ancient Bureaucracy and Officialdom' S 10803-G18, also funded by the Austrian Science Fund. R. Pirngruber's research took place within the framework of the project 'On the Efficiency of Markets for Agricultural Produce in Pre-industrial Societies: the Case of Babylonia, c. 400–c. 60 BC' led by R. J. van der Spek and funded by The Netherlands' Organization for Scientific Research (NWO), and was carried out at the VU University Amsterdam. J. Hackl provided the sections on the data from the archival texts, R. Pirngruber the section on the data from the ADs; the drafting of the final manuscript and remaining two sections are the joint work of the two authors. We owe particular thanks to M. Jursa and R. J. van der Spek for offering aid, criticism and advice.
2 This material is the subject of J. Hackl's forthcoming dissertation on Late Achaemenid and Hellenistic archival texts from northern Babylonia.
3 On this term see Jursa (2010: 4ff.). It refers to a time span of some 150 years beginning with the ascent of the Neo-Babylonian Empire in 626 BC and ending in the second year of Xerxes (484 BC). See also Jursa, Chapter 5, this volume.
4 The editio princeps of the ADs is Sachs and Hunger (1988, 1989 and 1996). For more information see Van der Spek *et al.*, Chapter 1.
5 See the convenient historical summary in Boiy (2004: 99ff.).
6 See most recently Boiy (2007: 40ff. and 111ff.) on the political events during the Wars of the Diadochi. See Van der Spek (2000: 299ff.) and Pirngruber (2012: 38ff., 90ff. and 104ff.) for the economic repercussions of this conflict.
7 On this archive see most recently Jursa (2006). Also called the Mūrānu archive after the principal descendant of Abu-ul-īde.
8 On this archive see Van der Spek (1998). In general, also Jursa (2005: 75f).
9 Major publications of Late Achaemenid and Hellenistic textual material from northern Babylonia (in selection) are San Nicolò and Ungnad (1935), Kennedy (1968), Jakob-Rost and Freydank (1972), Joannès (1982), McEwan (1984), Stolper (1992, 1993, 2004, 2007), Van der Spek (1998), Jursa (2003, 2006). Around 600 texts, mainly in the

collections of the British Museum, can now be added of which copies or transliterations are available to the present author.

10 In comparison, from the 'long sixth century' about 16,000 tablets are available in publication and many more remain unpublished or unread. See Jursa (2010: 6).

11 The pertinent literature on this archive is conveniently summed up in Jursa (2005: 113f).

12 Oelsner (1975/1976: 312ff.10) gives a list of the Late Achaemenid sources then available; for material published since then see the pertinent sections in Jursa (2005) and note 9. Basic bibliographical information on the texts dated to the Hellenistic period can be found in Oelsner (1986) with additions in Stolper (1994), Boiy (2004) and Corò (2005).

13 It has recently been shown that the uprisings at the beginning of the reign of Xerxes led to reprisals against the northern Babylonian elites which resulted in a break in the documentation. See Waerzeggers (2003/2004), Kessler (2004), Oelsner (2007) and Baker (2008a).

14 See e.g. Invernizzi (2003: 309ff.).

15 Important studies are: Krückmann (1931), Lewenton (1970) and Doty (1977), all of which are based on textual material from Hellenistic Uruk. See also Oelsner (1978 and 1981).

16 See the discussion in Stolper (1994).

17 See Jursa (2010: 233f. and 741ff.).

18 Note that the Babylonian private house of the first millennium BC will be treated in Baker (forthcoming).

19 Oppenheim (1936: 64).

20 The majority of the textually 'attested' houses measure well below 200 m^2. See Baker (2004: 56–62).

21 On side wings see most recently (Baker 2008b).

22 On these two major archives see Jursa (2005: 65f. and 68f.) with basic bibliographical information.

23 See Ries (1993–7: 176).

24 See the graph in Jursa (2010: 746, Figure 28).

25 A detailed discussion of recognized standard interest rates regulated by the nishu ('tariff') clause can be found in Jursa (2010: 494ff.).

26 On penalty clauses in the context of interest rates see Jursa (2006: 161ff.).

27 Porten and Yardeni (1989), texts B 3.1 (9 Art.) and B 4.2 (before 36 Art.).

28 On rations paid in silver see Jursa (2008: 404ff.).

29 Jursa (2008: 411f.).

30 See the discussion in Jursa (2008: 417).

31 Jursa (2008: 417).

32 For a detailed study of the remuneration system of the Esangila temple during the Late Achaemenid and Early Hellenstic periods see now Hackl (2013: 380–93).

33 See most recently Corò (2005) and Waerzeggers (2010).

34 CT 44, 80 (caption broken) also belongs to this group of ration lists, as is suggested by prosopographical evidence.

35 The following remarks condense Pirngruber (2012: 27–37), which provides a fuller account especially the period 400–330 BC and which also includes Table 6.9.

36 Jursa (2010: 447–448). We chose shekels (8.33 grams) of silver per kurru (180 litres) as unit of measurement to provide easy comparison with M. Jursa's data. For the utility of converting equivalents into genuine prices see the arguments in Van der Spek and Mandemakers (2003).

37 This year can thus be added to the list in Van der Spek and Mandemakers (2003: 526–8).

38 The text dates to 423/2 BC (year 2 of Darius II), see also comment 44 in Vargyas (2001: 80). That the context of price data are indeed relevant has been demonstrated by Jursa

(2010: 587), according to which internal transactions within the temple household tend to stick to an ideal price (180 litres per shekel of silver in the sixth century BC).

39 Additionally, the equivalent stated in line 8 amounts to 90 rather than 60 litres per shekel (6 shekels for 3 kurru of barley). See also Van der Spek (1998: 223–6) for this text.

40 See the last entries in Table 49 in Jursa (2010: 443–7). For the whole sixth century BC, the mean was lower at 2.56 shekels per kurru (Jursa 2010: 448).

41 On that point see also Van der Spek and Mandemakers (2003: 523–4).

42 Not counting the dubious reading of 17 litres per shekel of ADART no. −418, month II, which would raise the mean of the earlier cluster to 5.45.

43 Jursa (2010: 586, and 592–4). See in particular the latest values from Darius I, year 17 (505/4 BC) onwards.

44 See the graph in Jursa (2010: 746, Figure 28), and Jursa, this volume, Figure 5.8, illustrating the development of the prices of agrarian and non-agrarian goods.

45 The situation in northern Babylonia (Sippar) is different. See the discussion in Jursa (2010: 296ff.).

46 See Van der Spek (2000) and Pirngruber (2012, 94ff. *passim*). The best documented example in the corpus of the ADs is the outbreak of the First Syrian War in 274/3 BC, leading to a significant increase of the barley price, probably due to a demand shock caused by military convocation.

47 For this interpretation (adding an economic perspective to the insights of Waerzeggers (2003/2004) and Kessler (2004) see now Jursa (2014).

Abbreviation

ADART = Sachs, A.J. and Hunger, H. 1988. *Astronomical Diaries and Related Texts from Babylonia*. Vol. I. *Diaries from 652 B.C. to 262 B.C.* Vienna: Verlag der Österreichischen Akademie der Wissenschaften.

Bibliography

Baker, H. D. 2004. *The Archive of the Nappāhu Family*, Vienna: Institut für Orientalistik der Universität Wien.

—— 2008a. 'Babylon in 484 BC: the Excavated Archival Tablets as a Source for Urban History', *Zeitschrift für Assyriologie*, 98: 100–16.

—— 2008b. 'The Layout of the Ziggurat Temple at Babylon, *NABU*, 2008 no. 27.

—— Forthcoming. *The Urban Landscape in First Millennium B.C. Babylonia*.

Boiy, T. 2004. *Late Achaemenid and Hellenistic Babylon*, Leuven: Peeters.

—— 2006. 'Aspects chronologiques de la période de transition (350–300)', in *La transition entre l'Empire achémenide et les royaumes hellénistiques*, edited by P. Briant and F. Joannès, Paris: De Boccard: 37–100.

—— 2007. *Between High and Low. A Chronology of the Early Hellenistic Period*, Frankfurt am Main: Verlag Antike.

Corò, P. 2005. *Prebende templari in età seleucide*, Padua: S.A.R.G.O.N. Editrice e Libreria.

Doty, L. T. 1977. *Cuneiform Archives from Hellenistic Uruk*, Ann Arbor, MI: University Microfilms International.

Hackl, J. 2013. *Materialien zur Urkundenlehre und Archivkunde der spätzeitlichen Texte aus Nordbabylonien*, unpublished PhD thesis, University of Vienna.

Invernizzi, A. 2003. 'They Did Not Write on Clay: Non-cuneiform Documents and Archives in Seleucid Mesopotamia', in *Ancient Archives and Archival Traditions. Concepts of Record-Keeping in the Ancient World*, edited by M. Brosius, Oxford: Oxford University Press: 302–22.

Jakob-Rost, L. and Freydank, H. 1972. 'Spätbabylonische Rechtsurkunden aus Babylon mit aramäischen Beischriften', *Forschungen und Berichte*, 14: 7–35.

Joannès, F. 1982. *Textes économiques de la Babylonie récente*, Paris: Éditions Recherche sur les Civilisations.

Jursa, M. 2003. 'Spätachämenidische Texte aus Kutha', *Revue d'Assyriologie*, 97: 43–140.

—— 2005. *Neo-Babylonian Legal and Administrative Documents: Typology, Contents and Archives*, Münster: Ugarit Verlag.

—— 2006. 'Agricultural Management, Tax Farming and Banking: Aspects of Entrepreneurial Activity in Babylonia in the Late Achaemenid and Hellenistic Periods', in *La transition entre l'Empire achémenide et les royaumes hellénistiques*, edited by P. Briant and F. Joannès, Paris: De Boccard: 137–222.

—— 2008. 'The Remuneration of Institutional Labourers in an Urban Context in Babylonia in the First Millennium BC', in *L'archive des Fortifications de Persépolis. État des questions et perspectives de recherches*, edited by P. Briant W. F. M. Henkelman and M.W. Stolper, Paris: De Boccard: 387–427.

—— 2010. *Aspects of the Economic History of Babylonia in the First Millennium BC. Economic Geography, Economic Mentalities, Agriculture, the use of Money and the Problem of Economic Growth*, with contributions by J. Hackl, B. Janković, K. Kleber, E. E. Payne, C. Waerzeggers and M. Weszeli, Münster: Ugarit Verlag.

—— 2014. 'Factor Markets in Babylonia from the Late Seventh to the Third Century BCE', *Journal of the Economic and Social History of the Orient*, 57(2): 173–202.

Kennedy, D.A. 1968. *Babylonian Tablets in the British Museum*. Part XLIX. *Late-Babylonian Economic Texts* (= CT 49), London: The Trustees of the British Museum.

Kessler, K. 2004. 'Urukäische Familien versus babylonische Familien: Die Namengebung in Uruk, die Degradierung der Kulte von Eanna und der Aufstieg des Gottes Anu', *Altorientalische Forschungen*, 31: 237–62.

Krückmann, O. 1931. *Babylonische Rechts – und Verwaltungsurkunden aus der Zeit Alexanders und der Diadochen*. PhD thesis. Berlin.

Lewenton, U. 1970. *Studien zur keilschriftlichen Rechtspraxis Babyloniens in hellenistischer Zeit*. PhD thesis. Münster.

McEwan, G.J.P. 1984. *Late Babylonian Texts in the Ashmolean Museum*, Oxford: Clarendon Press.

Oelsner, J. 1975/6. 'Zwischen Xerxes und Alexander: babylonische Rechtsurkunden und Wirtschaftstexte aus der späten Achämenidenzeit', *Welt des Orients*, 8: 310–18.

—— 1978. 'Kontinuität und Wandel in Gesellschaft und Kultur Babyloniens in hellenistischer Zeit', *Klio*, 60: 101–16.

—— 1981. 'Gesellschaft und Wirtschaft des seleukidischen Babylonien: einige Beobachtungen in den Keilschrifttexten aus Uruk', *Klio*, 63: 39–44.

—— 1986. *Materialien zur babylonischen Gesellschaft und Kultur in hellenistischer Zeit*, Budapest: Eötvös University: Assyriology.

—— 2007. 'Das zweite Regierungsjahr des Xerxes (484/3 v. Chr.) in Babylonien', *Wiener Zeitschrift für die Kunde des Morgenlandes*, 97: 289–303.

Oppenheim, A.L. 1936. *Untersuchungen zum babylonischen Mietrecht*, Vienna: Selbstverlag des Orientalischen Institutes der Universitäat.

Pirngruber, R. 2012. *The Impact of Empire on Market Prices in Babylonia in the Late Achaemenid and Seleucid periods, ca. 400–140 B.C.*, unpublished thesis, VU University Amsterdam.

Porten, B. and Yardeni, A.1989. *Textbook of Aramaic Documents from Ancient Egypt*. Volume 2: *Contracts*, Winona Lake, IN: Eisenbrauns.

Ries, G. (1993–7) 'Miete. B. II. Neubabylonisch', *Reallexikon der Assyriologie*, 8: 174–81.

Sachs, A. and Hunger, H. 1988. *Astronomical Diaries and Related Texts from Babylonia*. Volume 1: *Diaries from 652–262 B.C.*, Vienna: Verlag der Österreichischen Akademie der Wissenschaften.

—— 1989. *Astronomical Diaries and Related Texts from Babylonia*. Volume 2: *Diaries from 261–165 B.C.*, Vienna: Verlag der Österreichischen Akademie der Wissenschaften.

—— 1996. *Astronomical Diaries and Related Texts from Babylonia*. Volume 3: *Diaries from 164–61 B.C.*, Vienna: Verlag der Österreichischen Akademie der Wissenschaften.

San Nicolò, M. and Ungnad, A. 1935. *Neubabylonische Rechts – und Verwaltungsurkunden*. *Band I: Rechts – und Wirtschaftsurkunden der Berliner Museen aus vorhellenistischer Zeit*, Leipzig: Hinrichs.

Slotsky, A.L. 1997. *The Bourse of Babylon. Market quotations in the Astronomical Diaries of Babylonia*, Bethesda MD: CDL Press.

Stolper, M.W. 1985. *Entrepreneurs and Empire. The Murašû Archive, the Murašû Firm, and Persian rule in Babylonia*, Istanbul/Leiden: Nederlands Archaeologisch-Historisch Instituut te Istanbul.

—— 1992. 'Late Achaemenid Texts from Dilbat', *Iraq*, 54: 119–39.

—— 1993. *Late Achaemenid, Early Macedonian, and Early Seleucid Records of Deposit and Related Texts*, Napoli: Istituto Universitario Orientale.

—— 1994. 'On Some Aspects of Continuity between Achaemenid and Hellenistic Babylonian Legal Texts', in *Achaemenid History VIII. Continuity and Change*, edited by H. Sancisi-Weerdenburg, A. Kuhrt, and M.C. Root, Leiden: Nederlands Instituut voor het Nabije Oosten: 329–51.

—— 2004. 'The Kasr Texts, the Rich Collection, the Bellino Copies, and the Grotefend Nachlass', in *Assyria and Beyond: Studies presented to Mogens Trolle Larsen*, edited by J.G. Dercksen, Leiden: Nederlands Instituut voor het Nabije Oosten: 511–50.

—— 2007. 'Kasr Texts: Excavated but not in Berlin', in *Studies Presented to Robert D. Biggs, June 4, 2004. From the Workshop of the Chicago Assyrian Dictionary*, edited by M. T. Roth, W. Farber, M. W. Stolper and P. von Bechtolsheim, Volume 2, Chicago: University of Chicago Press: 243–83.

Van der Spek, R.J. 1993. 'The Astronomical Diaries As Source for Achaemenid and Seleucid History', *Bibliotheca Orientalis*, 50: 91–101.

—— 1998. 'Cuneiform Documents on Parthian History: the Rahimesu Archive. Materials for the Study of the Standard of Living', in *Das Partherreich und seine Zeugnisse*, edited by J. Wiesehöfer, Stuttgart: Steiner Verlag: 205–58.

—— 2000. 'The Effect of War on the Prices of Barley and Agricultural Land in Hellenistic Babylonia', in *Économie antique. La guerre dans les economies antiques*, edited by J. Andreau, P. Briant and R. Descat, St.-Bertrand-des-Comminges: Musée Archéologique Départemental: 293–313.

Van der Spek, R. J. and Mandemakers, C. 2003. 'Sense and Nonsense in the Statistical Approach of Babylonian Prices', *Bibliotheca Orientalis*, 60: 521–37.

Van Leeuwen, B., Foldvari, P. and Pirngruber, R. 2011. 'Markets in Pre-industrial Societies: Storage in Hellenistic Babylonia in the Medieval English Mirror', *Journal of Global History*, 6: 169–93.

Vargyas, P. 2001. *A History of Babylonian Prices in the First Millennium BC*, Volume 1: *Prices of Basic Commodities*, Heidelberg: Heidelberger Orientverlag.

Waerzeggers, C. (2003/2004) 'The Babylonian Revolts against Xerxes and the "End of Archives"', *Archiv für Orientforschung*, 50: 150–73.

—— 2010. *The Ezida Temple of Borsippa. Priesthood, Cult, Archives*, Leiden: Nederlands Instituut voor het Nabije Oosten.

7 Climate, war and economic development

The case of second-century BC Babylon[1]

Joost Huijs, Reinhard Pirngruber and Bas van Leeuwen

Introduction

Economic development in Babylon during the Seleucid (305–141 BC) and Parthian (141 BC–AD 226)[2] periods has been a topic of research for quite some time. Studies so far have focused on salinization, monetary shocks, wars and other factors,[3] but few have looked at a factor that has recently emerged in the literature as an important factor in the development of early economies: climate.

In this chapter we therefore investigate climate as an explanatory factor in economic development in Babylon. We focus especially on the period of remarkably low prices of barley and dates, the two basic staples, between c. 220 and 150 BC. Whereas several hypotheses have been brought forward regarding the decline in the date prices from c. 200 BC onwards (Aperghis 2004; Van der Spek 2004),[4] there is much less controversy as to why prices increased again during the early Parthian period. Generally, this price increase is attributed to the unrest and wars of that period which, according to this line of argument, caused the Babylonian economy to stagnate.[5] Yet Foldvari and Van Leeuwen (2012) find no evidence for decreasing per capita incomes, and likewise, neither trade, nor technological development, nor consumption levels seem to have declined. For example, in the Sassanid period complex irrigation systems were in use which partially originated from Parthian times (Adams and Nissen 1972; Adams 1981). This may suggest that the economy, and more specifically markets, were as efficient during the Parthian period as before. Indeed, Van Leeuwen *et al.* (Chapter 20, this volume), who define market performance as the ability of the market to adapt to unexpected (that is, exogenous) shocks, show that performance in the Parthian period is not significantly different from that in the Seleucid period.[6]

Thus, even though the attestations of armed conflict increased in Babylon during the early Parthian period, their connection with a stagnating or regressing economic development is questionable. Conversely, it is doubtful whether the price rise during the early Parthian period can be contributed solely to warfare. Also, prices had already started to rise during the 150s BC, and thus still during the late Seleucid period (see Figure 7.1), about 15 years before the Parthian takeover in 141 BC.

The possibility that the decline and following upswing (which are of about the same magnitude) are related has hitherto not been considered in the scholarly

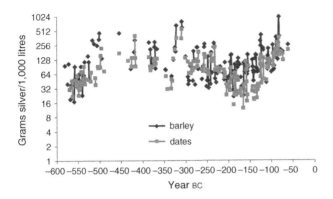

Figure 7.1 Annual barley and dates prices in Babylon (grams of silver per 1,000 litres).

Sources: Slotsky (1997); Vargyas (2001); Slotsky and Wallenfels (2009); Jursa (2010); Van der Spek (2005; forthcoming); Appendix, this volume.

discourse. Prices started to decline around 220 BC, the first signs of reversal became visible around 160 BC (see Figure 7.1). In the next section we study the price decline in the period c. 220–160 BC combined with the following price rise. We find that this pattern is best explained by a supply-centred approach. The available evidence suggests that part of the explanation may lie in improved climatic circumstances for the growth of the main staples. If this is true, it means that deteriorating climatic circumstances may also be at the root of the price increase in the Parthian period.

This hypothesis of the impact of changing climate on the price development in the second century BC can be tested further, since the literature on the effects of climate on the economy suggests a negative correlation between climate and social unrest: the better the climate, the smaller should be the number of instances of armed conflict (Zhang *et al.*, 2007). If this is true, we expect a relatively low level of conflict until about the 150s BC, when the climate was relatively beneficial, and a rise thereafter in the Parthian period. Therefore, in subsequent sections we look at the attestations of wars and unrest in the Seleucid and Parthian periods. We do indeed find that incidences of warfare decreased until the middle of the second century BC, as did their effect on prices. Both in the early Seleucid and the Parthian periods, the occurrences of war were more numerous, and had a stronger impact.

Price development during the second century BC: the price decline c. 220–160 BC and the subsequent increase c. 160–100 BC

To analyse why the level of prices was comparatively low during the second century BC, we start by placing the several competing theories in a demand-supply framework.

Demand-supply model: evaluation of earlier hypotheses

For the price decline in second-century BC Babylon several hypotheses have been formulated.

Aperghis (2004: 84, 146) argued that a tax reduction by Antiochus III in Babylon in 208 BC caused the prices of dates and, correspondingly, of cuscuta, to go down.[7]

A second hypothesis was put forward by Van der Spek (2004: 322), who postulated that the promulgation of a royal decree during the reign of Antiochus III (222–187 BC), encouraging the expansion of date gardens, would have increased the relative supply of dates and, hence, reduced the price of dates relative to barley.

A third theory is that the supply situation of barley in particular worsened because of increased salinization (Jacobsen and Adams 1958).

A fourth theory is that a reduction of the amount of silver in the economy increased purchasing power (Van der Spek *et al.*, Chapter 19, this volume).

A final possibility, which has so far not been considered for Hellenistic Babylonia, is that climatic change affected the supply of both barley and dates. Such an argument has, for example, been applied to the fifteenth century AD, where Zhang *et al.*, (2007: 19216) argued that a strong change in average temperature in Europe affected agricultural output.

We can make these five hypotheses slightly more formal by placing them in a simple demand-supply framework (see Figure 7.2). The curves *S* give the supply for barley and dates respectively, and the lines denoted by *D* indicate the demand of both crops. *Q* denotes the quantity of the commodity, and *P* its price. As Figure 7.2 shows, the *demand curve* for dates is much steeper than that of barley (the quantity of the demand for dates thus extends over a smaller range than that of barley); *dates* are thus the *less elastic commodity*. We can phrase this differently: if the price of dates goes down from *Pdat* to *Pdat1*, people will not consume notably more dates. However, if the price of barley goes down from *Pbar* to *Pbar1*, people will switch from dates and start consuming more barley. The reason for this is that dates are the inferior (i.e. less demanded) product: people will prefer barley over dates in the event of a general price decrease.

The price elasticity of a good in antiquity is difficult to establish. However, a well-established fact is that the price elasticity of inferior (less demanded) products is lower. This implies that people will only buy it while at subsistence level, because that good is cheaper and because it generates more kcalories. In both cases, this is dates. However, we can test elasticities using data on prices and quantities of barley and dates from present-day societies in which these staples play an important role. The *price* elasticity of demand can be written as:

$$E_d = \frac{\Delta Q_d / Q_d}{\Delta P / P},$$
(7.1)

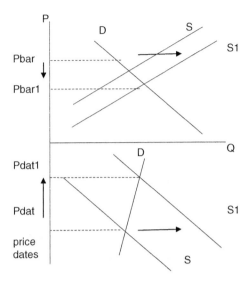

Figure 7.2 Supply and demand model for barley and dates.

which says that the *price* elasticity of demand is equal to the percentage change in the quantity demanded divided by the percentage change in the price. Using the quantity and price data from the Food and Agriculture Organization of the United Nations (FAO) for the period 1960–90, we can calculate the average *price* elasticity for dates for Saudi Arabia, Qatar and Yemen, all countries with dates and barley as basic commodities, as −0.6 for barley and −0.3 for dates.[8] Hence, (the absolute value of) the elasticity is higher for barley than for dates.

With this simple demand and supply model from Figure 7.2, we can look at the effects that an increasing or decreasing supply of dates and barley would have on prices. The above five hypotheses on the price decline can be classified as a negative supply shock (salinization), a positive supply shock for dates only (lower taxes; increasing number of date orchards), a positive supply shock for both barley and dates (climate), and a positive demand shock for both commodities (silver increases in value).

If there is a negative supply shock (salinization), the supply curves (*S*) will move to the left, which increases prices of both barley and dates. Since we can clearly see from Figure 7.1 that the prices in reality went down, we can readily dismiss this hypothesis. Lowering of taxes for dates, and also increasing the number of date gardens, may create a positive supply shock for dates, which can be viewed as a shift in the supply curve of dates (*S*) to the right. When the supply of dates increases, prices will fall. However, since the demand for dates is less elastic, people will not buy significantly more dates. Consequently, a positive supply shock will lead to a very fast decline of date prices. However, it may be argued that as the budget of each individual becomes higher, people will start demanding more barley. Hence, the barley demand curve will shift to the right. This means that more barley is demanded for higher prices. This scenario is unlikely since not only does Figure 7.1 show that both barley and date prices went down, although prices fell less for barley than for dates, but also in this scenario date prices would have fallen first, while in reality we see that barley prices decreased first. Moreover, these scenarios cannot account for the price decline discernible in other commodities such as sesame and cress.

The fourth hypothesis (climate) is that there may be a positive supply shock for both barley and dates. In this case, the supply curves of both barley and dates shift to the right (for the same price, more is supplied). This implies that the prices of both barley and dates will go down, but the prices of dates go down further than those of barley (since dates are the less elastic commodity), which is exactly what we find in Figure 7.1. The final hypothesis is that a decrease in silver in circulation in Babylon took place and, hence, an increase in purchasing power. Van der Spek *et al.* (Chapter 19, this volume) found that a decrease in silver in circulation will decrease the prices of dates more than that of barley. These last two hypotheses are thus credible. In the light of a similar decline in prices in other regions during the second century BC (Van Leeuwen *et al.*, Chapter 20, this volume), we present in the following section some evidence to corroborate the notion that climatic development had at least some impact on prices in second-century BC Babylonia.

Temperature: ice core data

Except for indirect evidence via a demand-supply model, the thesis of climate change is difficult to substantiate for ancient economies in general (but see Johnson and Gould 1984). Fortunately, we do have some data to help us go deeper into this question. These data can be split up into more general data with a higher frequency (such as Greenland ice core data), and more local data, which unfortunately often have a much lower time frequency.

The data with the highest frequency (i.e. annual) is the ice core data from Greenland. Although usually considered to be representative of the climatic development of the northern hemisphere (cf. Wick *et al.*, 2003: 672: the Younger Dryas, 12,800–11,500 BP), some scholars have argued for caution in the light of the fact that these data are often in antiphase with the climate in northern Europe, as a result of the North Atlantic oscillation. Likewise there is the danger, because of the method by which these data are measured, that they are indicative of rather localized weather changes only. Nevertheless, extrapolation of the long-run trend in climate seems possible, but preferably in connection with other evidence.

The main idea is that temperature is affected by the oceans, where over time moisture evaporates and turns into snowfall on Greenland. Since fresh water contains lighter isotopes (^{16}O) than ocean water (^{18}O), an increasing proportion of ^{18}O isotopes indicates less fresh water (rain and moisture) and thus colder weather.[9] This means that the lower the value in Figure 7.3, the colder the temperature was.[10] In general, a decline of the ^{18}O by 2.2 per mille indicates a decline in temperature of roughly 1 degree Celsius. Since temperature is strongly related

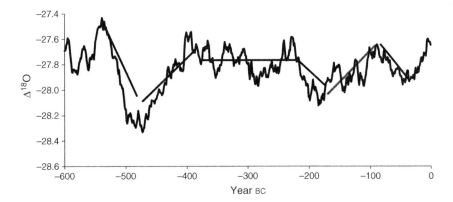

Figure 7.3 Graph showing 41-year moving average of $\Delta^{18}O$ (%, parts per thousand) annual averages, 600 BC–AD 1.

Source: Langway *et al.* (1985).

to agriculture, and especially so in pre-industrial societies (Zhang *et al.*, 2007; Campbell *et al.*, 2007), this has a direct bearing on agricultural output and, hence, prices.[11]

As shown in Figure 7.3, remarkable troughs can be found in the ice core data, most notably between c. 520 and c. 460 BC when a decline of up to two degrees took place. A similar scenario of decreasing temperature took place between c. 230 and 180 BC (roughly 1 degree), followed by a gradual rise until c. 80 BC. However, whereas the first distinct drop in temperature cannot be associated with lower prices in Babylonia, for the second (and later) drops such a correlation can be made plausible (see Figure 7.4).

The question is therefore why the drop in temperature as evidenced by the ice core data between c. 520 and 460 BC did not result in lower prices. There are two possible explanations. First, current theories suggest that the effects of climatic circumstances during this period were outweighed by those of structural growth during the sixth century BC and the following decline, especially after 484 BC.[12] Basically, these theories suggest that increasing monetization entailed inflation-like symptoms in the second half of the sixth century BC, constituting a counterweight to a potential drop in prices due to climatic change in the last quarter of the sixth century BC. A second explanation, as outlined earlier, is that the Greenland ice core data around this time show a *local* temperature fluctuation that is not representative of the remainder of the northern hemisphere. Indeed, there is some evidence that this might be the case. For example, the dendrochronological data outlined below and in Figure 7.5, as well as the Dead Sea and Lake Van data discussed in the next section, do not show a significant variation in temperature. Rather the opposite occurred at Lake Van, where an increase of moisture is shown by the oxygen isotopes and the Mg/Ca values. These apparently favoured the growth of Pastacia shrubs that demand mild winters (Rossignol-Strick 1999).

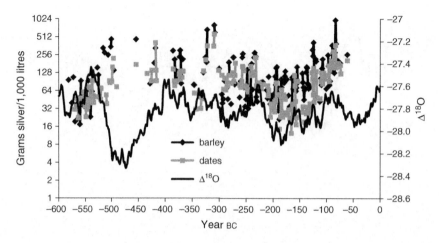

Figure 7.4 Graph showing 41-year moving average of Δ^{18}O annual averages (i.e. indicative of temperature) versus barley and date prices (grams of silver per 1,000 litres), 600 BC–AD 1.

Sources: Slotsky (1997); Vargyas (2001); Slotsky and Wallenfels (2009); Jursa (2010); Van der Spek (2005; forthcoming); Appendix, this volume; Langway *et al.* (1985).

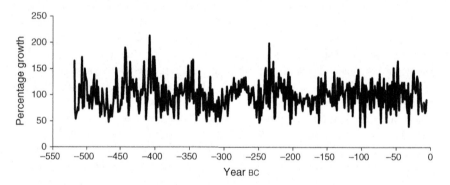

Figure 7.5 Buxus chronology from Ferra (Italy) for the period 518 to 5 BC.

Source: Kuniholm *et al.* (1992).

All available evidence seems to show that between c. 230 and 180 BC, there did indeed occur a strong decrease in both prices and temperature, which then increased in tandem again after 160 BC until c. 80 BC. Unfortunately, we have very little data beyond that point.

Corroborative evidence can also be found by using a series of dendrochronology (i.e. growth of tree rings) from Ferrara (Italy).

We do indeed find a period of decline of the buxus growth indicative of cold and wet weather between c. 220 and 160 BC which nicely matches the ice core data showing a decline in average temperatures in the same period.

Humidity: regional lake data

It thus appears that there is a positive correlation between the ice core temperatures in Greenland and the average price level in Babylon around the turn of the third century to the second century BC. This correlation is around 15 per cent. This may sound counter-intuitive, but lower temperatures may actually induce more rain, benefiting the growth of staple crops in warmer regions such as Babylonia. These lower temperatures may also have as side effect not only that it rains more heavily, but also that it rains more often, thus further stimulating barley growth.

There is a way to cross-check the climatic evidence, and especially the moisture data, by using sediments from lakes located in the Middle East. We use data from two different lakes.

Lake Van is located in south-east Turkey, and is considered representative of the vegetation responding to the climate in the Near East in general under the condition that species-related threshold levels are crossed (Wick *et al.*, 2003: 673). The lake contains many types of sediment including Δ^{18}O-levels which we described earlier when discussing the Greenland ice core. However, as indicated by Wick *et al.* (2003: 667),

> the high Δ^{18}O concentrations recorded at Lake Van are characteristic of terminal lakes and comparable to those measured in African lakes. Oxygen-isotope enrichment in closed systems is primarily controlled by fractionation processes connected to evaporation. The latter strongly depends on relative humidity and, to a lesser degree, on temperature.

See also Casanova and Hillaire-Marcel (1993), and Gat and Bowser (1991). According to Figure 4 in Wick *et al.*, (2003), the Δ^{18}O concentrations drop during the sixth and the second centuries BC, suggesting that in the period of cooling down, we are also confronted with a wetter climate.

These results receive corroboration by the second suitable testing case for moisture, namely the Dead Sea data. Bookman *et al.* (2004, Figure 7) show that around 250 BC the climate in the Middle East became significantly wetter. Interestingly, no such wet climate is found in the sixth century BC. Hence, it is possible that the wetter climate in the sixth century BC was mainly due to local circumstances in Lake Van while there is evidence that the wetter (and colder) climate of the second century BC took place throughout the entire Middle East.[13]

Irrigation: river level data

The preceding evidence of increases in moisture in the sixth and fourth centuries BC only form a partial explanation for the increased agricultural output, since Iraq was largely dependent on irrigation fed from the Euphrates and Tigris Rivers. Yet, here also climate may play a role. Fortunately, we do have some information on the level of the Euphrates River in Babylon between c. 400 and 60 BC. These data are taken from the astronomical diaries (ADs),[14] which contain monthly notations of the river level of the Euphrates, mostly given in *na* (the distance from the peak

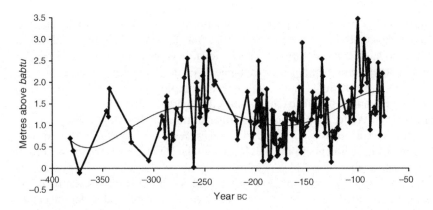

Figure 7.6 Annualized[a] river level of the Euphrates, *babtu* expressed in metres (with 5th
       degree polynomial).

Note:
[a] We converted monthly data in annual data. Since some years do not have data for all months, we
corrected for seasonal effects.

flood level downwards), and sometimes in *babtu* (the distance from the lowest
level upwards). Fortunately, we are able to convert *na*-levels into *babtu*-levels,
and the latter into metres (Figure 7.6).

A comparison of the ice core data (Figure 7.3) and the river level data
(Figure 7.6) demonstrates a remarkable parallelism. The period of c. 290 to 230 BC
is characterized by a rise in both temperature and river level. A fall in both
can be observed in 230–180 BC, and a rise again in 180–80 BC. This suggests
that during periods of cooling down, the water level of the Euphrates decreased.
Although counter-intuitive at first glance, this is not really surprising given that
the Euphrates draws much of its water from the snow in the mountains of Turkey
around Lake Van: with falling temperatures less melting water will find its way into
the river in winter, but an increased amount during spring. In addition, as we have
already observed, humidity also increased, causing river levels on average to rise.

This is of course only part of the story, since water has to be available in the right
amount and at the right time of the year. For example, the date harvest usually took
place in the seventh month of the Babylonian calendar (roughly October), whereas
the barley harvest took place in early spring. Figure 7.7 shows the water level in
babtu (expressed in metres) per month during the third and second centuries BC.
The main finding is that the water level of the Euphrates was higher in 220–140 BC
during the first half of the year when barley was ripening on the fields (for a similar
result see Hecker and Kamminga 1989), and especially during the spring flood
(see the values for April and May), caused by a wetter climate in the mountains
of Lake Van (more snowfalls, more melting water). The net effect was a higher
output of barley, as more water was available for irrigation purposes (e.g. Yau
et al., 2011). What remains to be explained is the enormous drop in the river level

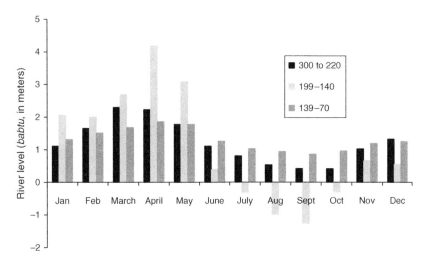

Figure 7.7 Monthly river level of the Euphrates between 300–220, 220–140, and 140–70 BC in *babtu* (metres).

Note:
ᵃ This is calculated from *babtu* meaning a notional (and so far unknown) low water level. A negative *babtu* therefore does not mean there is no water in the Euphrates.

that took place after the spring flood in April and May and is best visible in the months from June to September in the period 220–140 BC in the light of lower temperatures.

All in all it seems that there is plenty of evidence that climatic changes had quite some impact on prices in second-century BC Babylon. Climate was characterized by lower temperatures and increased average moisture (but lower moisture during the ripening of barley) as appears both from our gramineae/NAP index, the Δ^{18}O-levels in Lake Van, and from the evidence of increased levels of the Euphrates River during the growing seasons of barley. The result of all these climatic developments seems to have been a decidedly positive impact on agricultural output and in particular the barley supply, whereas the evidence of positive influence on dates is more tenuous (see Foldvari and Van Leeuwen, Chapter 2, this volume). This is also what emerges from Figure 7.1 where we observe that barley prices go down first, suggesting that the change in climate has primarily a positive effect on barley and, via the price elasticities, on dates. Yet according to the law of supply and demand, a rise in barley output will lower the price of barley, which means that more people were able to switch from dates to barley – which in turn, since dates is the less elastic product, means a faster decrease in the date price compared to barley. Likewise, in the early Parthian period when climate deteriorated again, this same phenomenon caused the prices of barley to start rising before those of dates. Due to the increase in barley prices, more people switched to dates and,

Table 7.1 Domestic warfare and warfare abroad as a percentage of the historical sections in the Babylonian astronomical diaries, 299–50 BC

	Domestic warfare/ historical sections	Warfare outside city/ historical sections	Total warfare/ historical sections
299–221 BC	20.0%	4.4%	24.4%
220–142 BC	8.3%	13.9%	22.2%
141–101 BC	32.7%	13.5%	46.2%
100–50 BC	34.0%	6.0%	40.0%

because of lower price elasticity of the latter, prices of dates accordingly went up faster than those of barley.

Climate, warfare and prices

In the previous sections we stressed that the decline in prices between c. 220 and 160 BC was at least partially caused by climatic changes. According to standard climate theory, a higher agricultural output due to better climatic circumstances often leads to a reduction in the instances of armed conflict (Zhang *et al.*, 2007). Therefore if we find a decline in the number of instances of warfare – here defined as armed conflicts both on an imperial (warfare against other kingdoms or external invaders) and local (local revolts, raids of nomadic tribes, etc.) scale – as well as of its impact on prices, we have an additional argument for the importance of climate in explaining the price decline in the second century BC. The decline of warfare in the second century BC is not easy to ascertain though. One possible way to test both hypotheses is to look at warfare in Babylon and warfare outside Babylon. Table 7.1 clearly shows that although the number of wars and revolts outside Babylon increased in the late Seleucid period (accompanying the gradual weakening and dissolution of the empire), this was not the case for armed conflicts within Babylon.[15] On the contrary, we find that armed conflicts within Babylon declined in the late Seleucid period, in parallel with the improvement in climate. In the early Parthian, and even more so during the later Parthian period, we find that the amount of wars and rebellions inside Babylonia increased again,[16] together with a deterioration in climate.

To test our assumptions on warfare more formally, we regress the growth of prices on a month dummy and a dummy indicating war inside Babylon and a dummy indicating warfare outside Babylon. Table 7.2 reports the results for the periods c. 300–200 BC and 220–130 BC,[17] hence covering the period with relatively unfavourable climatic circumstances as well as the period with more favourable circumstances. From the regressions it is clear that for both periods the role of seasonality was limited. This may be caused by the fact that we used price changes rather than levels.

The only period for which we find some effect is at the end of the year in the months preceding the new barley harvest, when there is a price rise. There are some differences, however, when we look at wars inside and outside Babylon. For

Table 7.2 Regression of the price changes of barley, 300–130 BC

Dependent variable: Dlnbarey

	300–200 BC		220–130 BC	
	Coefficient of regression	t-value	Coefficient of regression	t-value
February[a]	−0.009	−0.14	0.022	0.34
March	−0.029	−0.43	0.023	0.38
April	0.007	0.11	0.039	0.53
May	−0.074	−1.13	−0.132	−1.99
June	−0.081	−1.21	−0.024	−0.36
July	0.019	0.28	0.054	0.75
August	0.021	0.26	0.023	0.33
September	0.012	0.18	0.032	0.50
October	0.000	0.00	0.061	1.01
November	0.078	1.18	0.089	1.46
December	0.176	2.40	0.036	0.57
War inside Babylon	0.603	3.54	0.019	0.31
War outside Babylon	−0.051	−0.43	0.017	0.27
Constant	−0.021	−0.47	−0.029	−0.57
Obs.	136		114	
R^2	0.207		0.175	

Note:
[a] January is the omitted variable.

the period 300–200 BC we find that the effect of a domestic war on a price increase is clearly positive and significant with a regression coefficient of 0.6. A war outside Babylon, however, does not have an appreciable effect on prices changes, suggesting that on average wars outside Babylon had little effect on the prices in the city, even in a period with unfavourable climatic conditions. The same regression, now for the period 220–130 BC, shows insignificant coefficients for the effects of wars both inside and outside Babylon. No doubt some wars will have had an effect but it does seem that the effect of wars on price levels is smaller in the second century BC, which was dominated by more favourable climatic circumstances, compared to the third century BC.

The preliminary conclusion therefore seems to be that especially during the early Seleucid period we find a strong effect of domestic armed conflict on prices. This was also the period with less moisture and higher temperatures, resulting in less agricultural output. For the late Seleucid period, we find that climate has a strong effect on prices: the lower the river level (and higher moisture), the higher the agricultural output for barley (and possibly dates). This matches well with the climate theories that suggest that the more favourable agricultural climate in the second century BC led to less warfare. Hence, the reduction in local warfare in the period 220–160 BC also conforms to the expectations of climate theory.

A historical analysis of the relation between warfare and prices

It is clear from the discussion above that there exists a high level of correlation between climate and price levels in Babylon. This became especially manifest in the second century BC, when favourable climatic circumstances were one of the factors driving down prices, date prices more than barley prices. In the previous section we argued, following climate theory, that there was an alternative way to look at this phenomenon: if climate improved and, hence, agricultural output increased, we often expect a lower incidence of warfare (or a lower effect of warfare on prices). Indeed, expressed as a percentage of the historical sections in the ADs, it looks as if the number of disturbances inside Babylon went down in the second century BC, even though the number of foreign wars increased (see Table 7.1). However, foreign wars had only a limited effect on the price level in general, while the effect of domestic wars on prices decreased markedly in the second century BC (see Table 7.2). Clearly, this analysis is on a macro level, but wars can have very different effects depending on where they are fought, who is fighting them and, even more importantly, who lost. Therefore, we try to go into more detail on warfare in the Seleucid and Parthian periods, to see if our assertions on the weaker role between price rises and domestic warfare in the second century BC also hold at a micro level.

Seleucid period

We find for the Seleucid period that there is indeed good evidence that warfare not only occurred more frequently during the third century BC as compared to the second, but equally that warfare had a much stronger impact on the commodity

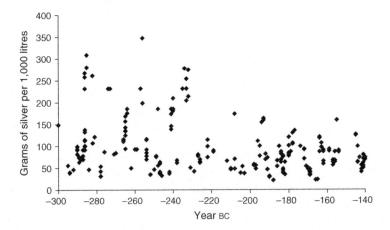

Figure 7.8 Monthly barley prices during the Seleucid period, c. 300 BC–c. 140 BC (grams of silver per 1,000 litres).

Sources: Slotsky (1997); Vargyas (2001); Slotsky and Wallenfels (2009); Van der Spek (2005; forthcoming); Appendix, this volume.

Table 7.3 Commodity prices in Babylonia in grams of silver per 1,000 litres

Commodity	Seleucid mean price (300–141 BC)	Seleucid peak price (230s BC)	Parthian mean price (141–60 BC)	Parthian peak price (83, 126, 77, 126[a] BC)
Barley	96.85	308.52	218.58	2,380.00
Dates	65.46	231.39	101.08	555.33
Cress	219.58	793.33	484.93	1,586.67
Sesame	382.34	1,388.33	910.67	2,776.67

Note:
[a] There were two peaks in 126 BC.

prices during the earlier period. Even a quick glance at the graph of monthly barley prices of the Seleucid period (Figure 7.8) shows that in the years up to the beginning of the reign of Antiochus III (222–187 BC), outliers were in general of a much larger magnitude than afterwards.[18]

Some of these outlying data can be shown to correlate to periods of warfare in or even outside of Babylonia. A good case in point is the cluster of high barley prices prevailing in the 230s BC, with the maximum price amounting to 308.52 grams of silver per 1,000 litres in January 232 BC, compared to a mean value of this commodity in the Seleucid period of 96.85 grams of silver. The historical sections of the ADs provide us with several glimpses into the events in Babylon during these years. The impression conveyed by these, unfortunately often fragmentary, reports is one of a country in troubled times, afflicted by various difficulties and especially internal strife. Repeatedly, fighting between different factions in the city is mentioned. In summer 238 BC, a skirmish is reported between loyalist royal troops from the citadel and a group of unidentified rebels, who earlier had succeeded in capturing the royal palace in the city. In September/October 235 BC, it seems that again a General revolted from the central authority; a connection to the events of three years earlier cannot be excluded. In winter 230/229 BC, fighting in the city is recorded again.[19] Additionally, natural disasters seem to have aggravated this already precarious situation, a locust invasion in 238 BC is mentioned (but cannot be correlated directly to a price increase). The events of these years were obviously accompanied by an elevated mortality rate, as is reported in the same sources (ADART III no. −237).

It is noteworthy that not only was the barley price clearly above average in this period, but also prices for dates, cress and sesame show clear peaks in the 230s BC (see Table 7.3).

It is also noticeable that conflicts fought in other parts of the empire occasionally left their mark in the price data of the ADs. The very high barley prices prevailing between autumn 274 BC and spring 273 BC are best interpreted as caused by a demand shock resulting from an army conscription in Babylon in connection with preparations for the First Syrian War.[20] Cress prices were also well above average in the same period, arriving at a maximum price of 1041.25 grams of silver per 1,000 litres.

This impression of exogenous shocks causing wide oscillations in the Babylonian commodity prices, with episodes of warfare taking pride of place, changes dramatically in the last quarter of the third century BC. Very tellingly, the largest outlier of the period between c. 220 and 156 BC was caused not by an armed conflict but simply by the phenomenon of seasonal fluctuation. In April 208 BC, barley stood at 173.54 grams of silver per 1,000 litres – which is a small number for an outlier considering the evidence from the earlier Seleucid period – but already the following month, with the arrival of the new barley harvest, prices recovered to a level at and even below average.[21] Price fluctuations that can be securely correlated to instances of warfare are even sparser and of less magnitude than before. The AD for the year 145/4 BC, for example, attests to the bellicose (?) activities of a certain Aria'bu,[22] the presence of various diseases in the country, as well as to preparations made to ward off the impending invasion by the Elamite king Kamnaskires, which finally did happen later the same year. Unfortunately no prices are extant from this later episode, but during Aria'bu's operations in autumn 145 BC, the barley price stood at 126.21 grams of silver per 1,000 litres. This is indeed (about 30 grams) above the mean value for the whole Seleucid period, and even more (about 50 grams) if one was to consider only the prices of the latter half of that period to the end of which this incident dates.[23] However, not even one year later, in the summer and autumn of 144 BC, the price level of barley was back to a level at about average. The defeat of the Babylonian troops against the Elamite kings and the latter's plundering of the countryside is graphically described in the diary (ADART III no. −144, r20–r22):

> Kamnaskires, the king of Elam, marched around victoriously in the towns and canals of Babylonia and this [.. .. ..] they plundered, their spoil they carried off. The people, their [.. .. ..] and their animals in fear of this Elamite to [.. .. ..] Fear and panic was in the land.

But these events have left virtually no traces in the price data at a few months distance from the moment when they occurred. And even at the time of their actual occurrence, the effects were meagre compared to the effects of warfare in the third century BC.

Parthian period

Several instances of armed conflict follow the Parthian takeover of Babylon in 141 BC. A clear example is the first Seleucid campaign to try to re-conquer their lost territory in Mesopotamia, starting in 139/8 BC.[24] For two years Babylonia was the stage of military operations of royal Seleucid and Parthian armies. The regions of Elam and Mesene also got involved. Numerous troops will have taken part in these manoeuvres and fights. With exception of *kasû*, all foodstuffs exhibited a strong rise in prices and peaked at between two and five times their starting level. Nevertheless, since the price rises in question often did not reach the long-term Parthian averages, the population may have coped fairly well with these.

An example is provided by the barley price: its average level during the Seleucid campaign was 144 grams of silver per 1,000 litres, while in the whole Parthian period it was 219 grams (see Table 7.3). Thus the barley price average during this Seleucid campaign and its aftermath was more than 30 per cent lower than this product's long-term average. We did not include a correction for inflation though and, hence, the effect on the population might have been larger than may appear at first sight. In addition, we see that the cushioning effect on high prices of barley and dates which both harvests normally exert (see Table 7.2 and the events of year 208 BC noted above), stops occurring in spring 138 BC. This suggests that only after two years of warfare, the fighting started to eclipse the regular, yearly pattern of price developments, basically determined by seasonality. The prevailing low prices thus strongly counteracted price increases during the period of war.

Whereas the wars of the 130s BC constituted a reaction to the Parthian conquest of Mesopotamia in 141 BC from the Seleucid side, this picture changes during the 120s BC into one of predominance of domestic conflict (see Table 7.1), which is manifest in the numerous recordings of small-scale local warfare, rebellion, and incursions of Arab tribes. These Arab raids could well be seen as a symptom of unfavourable climatic change that took place in that period, as the desert nomads are likely to suffer in a very direct manner from increased temperature and drought. In particular, the sharp rise in temperature is clearly visible for the decades between 160 and 120 BC (see Figures 7.3 and 7.4), and the starting point of the frequently recurring raids in 130 BC may therefore not be coincidental. These crisis years culminated in 126–124 BC with extreme prices, after which foodstuff prices stabilized around their long-term Parthian averages until c. 80 BC.

In short, alongside the increasingly unfavourable climate, we witness the steady rise in prices back to and even beyond the pre–220s BC levels, to a certain extent amplified by warfare circumstances. This development mirrors the events that we have seen occurring in the 220s BC, in which a decline in prices appears to have been rooted in favourable climatic changes. The main difference is that the increase in date prices was faster than that for barley, suggesting a relative shift in favour of dates, which points all the more – via the inverse of the mechanism that occurred at the end of the third and start of the second century BC – at a reduction in supply that, due to differences in elasticities of the different products, affected dates more strongly.

Conclusion

In this chapter we have discussed the price decline in the later Seleucid and the following price increase in the early Parthian periods by looking at the two phenomena in tandem. A simple demand and supply model suggests that the decline in prices during the late Seleucid period may have been caused by an increase in the supply of the main staple crops. This also explains why date prices in Babylon declined more than barley prices: given the inelastic nature of the demand for dates, an increase in the supply of barley (and/or dates) results in a faster decrease of date prices, compared to barley prices. We see the same process at work in the sixth century BC (cf. Jursa, Chapter 5, this volume).

Using all kinds of climatic evidence, we find that postulated the supply increase of barley is at least partly caused by climatic factors. Using Greenland ice core data, we found that from c. 400 BC onwards there was a strong correlation between temperature and prices: the cooler the climate, the better the growth of barley. Lake sediment data from Lake Van and the Dead Sea, as well as dendrochronological data, showed that this period also experienced increased moisture and a higher level of the Euphrates River. Yet whereas the average river level increased from around the middle of the second century BC, this was unevenly distributed over the year, with most water being available during the spring (which is the growing season for barley).

Our findings thus suggest that climate especially favoured the agricultural output of barley and, mainly via elasticity, affected also the production of dates (because nutritional patterns tended towards an increased consumption of barley at the expense of dates in the late Seleucid period). For the price rise in the early Parthian period, this mechanism worked exactly the other way around. So far, however, it is based on indirect evidence of a supply and demand model combined with some direct climatic evidence from the ice core data, a regional moisture index and the level of the Euphrates River. But there is an alternative way to review its plausibility. According to climate theory, a better climate would result in more abundant harvests and a lower number of armed conflicts. Therefore, our finding that the effect of warfare on price level declined in the second century BC strengthens the point that climatic factors played a role in the price decline in that period. Conversely, during the early Seleucid period, with less favourable climatic circumstances, regression analysis shows that armed conflicts had a stronger effect on the price level. These findings are also confirmed when we examine at a micro level wars fought during the third and first centuries BC.

Notes

1 We thank Hans Renssen, VU University, Amsterdam, for his comments on climatic issues in an earlier draft. He is, of course, not responsible for opinions expressed here.
2 Unfortunately, the abundant price documentation of the ADs stops in the 60s BC.
3 For example, Adams and Nissen (1972), Van der Spek (2000) and Aperghis (2004).
4 Commodities other than dates received much less attention, partly due to the fact that the price decline in the first half of the second century BC was less pronounced; see Pirngruber (2012: 59ff.).
5 Grainger (1999: 315, 319), for example, speaks of declining living standards in the Parthian period, which he partly attributes to political vicissitudes.
6 Their explanation is that the level of urbanization, as well as the costs of production and transaction costs, do not significantly change between the Seleucid and Parthian periods, and therefore that the ability of markets to respond to exogenous shocks does not change.
7 These first two hypotheses were discussed in greater detail by Pirngruber (2012, 59ff.). Cuscuta is used as a condiment in the production of date beer and its price is therefore likely to be correlated with the price of dates. However, for a different view see Foldvari and Van Leeuwen, Chapter 2, this volume.

8 FAO (2011a) and FAO (2011b). Of course these values have to be negative in order to get a demand equation. Furthermore, we do not distinguish between a demand and supply elasticity.

9 These data are represented as $\Delta^{18}O$, which is the ratio of the oxygen isotopes ^{18}O and ^{16}O in water. These ratios, taken from melting water of the ice core, tell us something about the temperature of the surroundings when the water froze. The reasoning behind this is that in a colder climate more water has been stored in the form of ice and snow on the continents, containing relatively few ^{18}O (and much ^{16}O), compared to the oceans containing relatively more ^{18}O (and less ^{16}O). Liquid water that contains the heavier ^{18}O molecules condenses first and falls like rain. Hence, if water travels from warm to cold, the more north (i.e. to colder areas) you go, the more ^{16}O molecules liquid water will contain. This means that if the global temperature increases, more ^{18}O molecules will end up in the Greenland ice core. On average an increase of 0.22 per cent $\Delta^{18}O$ is about equal to an increase in temperature of 1 degree Celsius (Wick *et al.*, (2003: 667): 0.35 per cent, with parallel increase of relative humidity of 0.02 per 1 degree Celsius).

10 One caveat with these data are that before AD 700 they may be off the mark by 7 years. However, our analysis of price drops during two centuries will not be affected.

11 Campbell *et al.*, (2007) estimate for England that a 1 degree rise in summer temperature leads to a 5 per cent increase in grain harvest. However, the reverse is true for regions in the Middle East where a cooling down may lead to higher agricultural output.

12 See Jursa (2010: 462–8, 783–800) for the process of increasing commercialization and monetization during the sixth century BC, and Jursa (forthcoming) for the decline in the fifth century BC. For the higher prices in the late Achaemenid period see also Hackl and Pirngruber, Chapter 6, this volume, and Van der Spek (2011).

13 There is still another way to test for moisture. Dividing the arboreal pollen (which thrive in wet weather) by the non-arboreal pollen (which thrive in dry weather), we obtain an index of moisture (el-Moslimany 1990: 347–8). A calculation of this index (the gramineae/Nap index) also indicates that an increase in humidity seems to have occurred in the second century BC.

14 Daily observations of the celestial sky and events of earth written down in cuneiform script by Babylonian scholars. Cf. Van der Spek *et al.*, Chapter 1, this volume.

15 Warfare in other provinces or even outside the Seleucid Empire (e.g. in Egypt) usually left no traces in the Babylonian price data, cf. Pirngruber (2012, 90ff.). For a history of the later Seleucid Empire see Ehling (2008).

16 The increase in incidences of warfare during the Parthian period, even though strengthening our argumentation, may have been not as strong as this table suggests. This impression is mainly caused by a formal development in the ADs: in the Parthian period we do not only have more, but also more exhaustive historical sections (Pirngruber 2012).

17 We chose 130 BC as end point in order to have a sufficient amount of observations. This is justifiable insofar as date prices started to rise only after quite a time lag compared to barley.

18 Not considered in this discussion are the enormously high prices of the last quarter of the fourth century BC, during which the continuous warfare between the generals of Alexander the Great for the division of his empire wreaked great havoc upon Babylonia. In spring 309 BC, the price for barley was 1110.67 grams of silver per 1,000 litres. For a political history of Babylonia during these years see Boiy (2004: 117–37), see also Van der Spek (2000: 299–305) on the price data of that period.

19 The diaries testifying to the instable political situation are ADART II, −237, −234A, −230A + B and −229A. A very brief commentary to these passages is provided by Del Monte (1997: 49–52) and Van der Spek (2006: 297–301). The evidence is also discussed in Pirngruber (2012, 77f.).

20 On the price data of these years see Van der Spek (2000: 305–7), discussing also other measures possibly imposed on the population of Babylonia in context with the war preparations. See also Boiy (2004: 141–3).

21 Barley arrived a second time at 173.54 grams of silver per 1,000 litres during the later Seleucid period, in October 194 BC. Unfortunately, there are no sources extant on the political situation in Babylonia in that period. A connection to the western campaigns of Antiochus III – in the form of an army conscription similar to the pattern provided by the data of 274/3 BC pertaining to the First Syrian War – cannot be excluded but has to remain speculative. Another supply shortfall, however, can be excluded because in this second instance the rise in the barley price was accompanied by a price rise in the other commodities as well.

22 The passage in question is broken. However, the remaining words (e.g. *illatu*, hostile troops) point to a bellicose context. See Del Monte (1997: 95–100) for a discussion of this diary.

23 The mean value (in grams of silver per 1,000 litres) for the later Seleucid period, i.e. the years between c. 230 and 140 BC, amounts to 73.39 (as compared to 96.85 for the whole period).

24 See Del Monte (1997: 105ff.) but cf. Van der Spek (1997/1998: 172–3) for the decisive battle and its exact date. A second attempt at re-conquest took place in 130/29 BC; see Del Monte (1997: 130ff.); Josephus, *AJ* XIII 236–44; Justinus, *Epit.* XXXVIII 10.8–10, 42.14; Le Rider (1965: 155–6, 337–8 with pl. 31.321 and pl. 13.D-L, types LR 109–10).The price developments are not that well preserved, but seem to be rather comparable to the developments of 139–137 BC.

Abbreviation

ADART III = Sachs, A. J. and Hunger, H. 1996. *Astronomical Diaries and Related Texts from Babylonia*. Vol. III. *Diaries from 164 to 61 B.C.* Vienna: Verlag der Österreichischen Akademie der Wissenschaften.

Bibliography

Adams, R. McC. 1965. *Land behind Baghdad; a History of Settlement in the Diyala Plains*, Chicago: Chicago University Press.
—— 1981. *Heartland of Cities*, Chicago: Chicago University Press.
Adams, R. McC. and Nissen, H. J. 1972. *The Uruk Countryside; the Natural Setting of Urban Societies*, Chicago: Chicago University Press.
Aperghis, G. G. 2004. *The Seleukid Royal Economy; the Finances and Financial Administration of the Seleukid Economy*, Cambridge: Cambridge University Press.
Boiy, T. 2004. *Late Achaemenid and Hellenistic Babylon*, Leuven: Uitgeverij Peeters.
Bookman, R., Enzel, Y., Agnon, A. and Stein, M. 2004. 'Late Holocene Lake Levels of the Death Sea', *Geological Society of America Bulletin*, 116: 555–71.
Campbell, B., Kelly, M. and Ó Gráda, C. 2007. 'Weather, Living Standards and Population Growth before the Industrial Revolution', Unpublished paper: Belfast University.
Casanova, J. and Hillaire-Marcel, C. 1993. 'Carbon and Oxygen Isotopes in African Lacustrine Stromatolites: Palaeohydrological Interpretation', in *Climate Change in Continental Isotopic Records*, edited by P. K. Swart, K. C. Lohmann, J. McKenzie and S. Savin, Geophysical Monograph Series 78, Washington DC: Wiley-AGU: 123–33.
Del Monte, G. F. 1997. *Testi dalla Babilonia Ellenistica*; volume I: *Testi Cronografici*, Pisa: Istituti Editoriali e Poligrafici Internazionali.

Ehling, Kay 2008. *Untersuchungen zur Geschichte der späten Seleukiden (164–63 v.Chr.). Vom Tode des Antiochos IV. bis zur Einrichtung der Provinz Syria unter Pompeius*, Stuttgart: Franz Steiner Verlag.

Emeis, K-C., Struck, U., Schulz, H. M., Rosenberg, R., Bernasconi, S., Erlenkeuser, H., Sakamoto, T. and Martinez-Ruiz, F. 2000. 'Temperature and Salinity Variations of the Mediterranean Sea Surface Waters Over the Last 16,000 Years from Records of Planctonic Stable Oxygen Isotopes and Alkenone Unsaturation Ratios', *Palaeogeography, Palaeoclimatology, Palaeoecology*, 158: 259–80.

FAO = Food and Agriculture Organization of the United Nations 2011a. 'Price Archive', http://faostat.fao.org/site/570/default.aspx#ancor (accessed 13 April 2011).

—— (2011b). 'Production: Crops', http://faostat.fao.org/site/567/default.aspx#ancor (accessed 13 April 2011).

Foldvari, P. and Van Leeuwen, B. 2012. 'Comparing Per Capita Income in the Hellenistic World: the Case of Mesopotamia', *Review of Income and Wealth*, 58: 550–68.

Gat, J. R. and Bowser, C. 1991. 'The Heavy Isotope Enrichment of Water in Coupled Evaporative Systems', *Stable Isotope Geochemistry*, 3: 159–68.

Grainger, J. D. 1999. 'Prices in Hellenistic Babylonia', *Journal of the Economic and Social History of the Orient*, 42: 303–50.

Hecker, K. and Kamminga, J. 1989. 'Untersuchungen zur Klimageschichte Mesopotamiens zwischen 4500 und 2000 v.h. anhand keilschriftlicher Quellen', in Bundesministerium für Forschung und Technologie, Projektträger Gesellschaft für Strahlen – und Umweltforschung (ed.) *Klimaforschungsprogramm, Statusseminar, 10.01–12.01 1989, Konferenzbericht*, München: Gesellschaft für Strahlen – und Umweltforschung mbH München (GSF): 473–6.

Jacobsen, T. and Adams, R. McC. 1958. 'Salt and Silt in Ancient Mesopotamian Agriculture', *Science*, 128: 1251–8.

Johnson D. L. and Gould, L. 1984. 'The Effect of Climate Fluctuations on Human Populations: a Case Study of Mesopotamian Society', in *Climate and Development*, edited by A. K. Biswas, Dublin: Tycooly/UNEP: 117–38.

Jursa, M. (with contributions by J. Hackl, B. Jankovic, K. Kleber, E.E. Payne, C. Waerzeggers and M. Weszeli). 2010. *Aspects of the Economic History of Babylonia in the First Millennium* BC: *Economic Geography, Economic Mentalities, Agriculture, the Use of Money and the Problem of Economic Growth*, Münster: Ugarit Forschungen.

Jursa, M. Forthcoming. 'On the Problem of the Existence of Factor Markets in Babylonia from the Long Sixth Century to the End of Achaemenid Rule', *Journal of the Economic and Social History of the Orient*, forthcoming.

Kuniholm, P. I., Griggs, C. B., Tarter, S. L. and Kuniholm, H. E. (1992 [1995]) 'A 513-Year Buxus Chronology for the Roman Ship at Comacchio (Ferrara)', *Bollettino di Archeologia*, 16–18: 291–9.

Langway, Jr., C. C., Oeschger, H. and Dansgaard, W., eds. 1985. *Greenland Ice Core: Geophysics, Geochemistry and Environment*, Washington DC: American Geophysical Union.

Le Rider, G. 1965. *Suse sous le Séleucides et les Parthes; les Trouvailles Monetaires et l'Histoire de La Ville*, Paris: Librairie Orientaliste Paul Geuthner.

el-Moslimany, A. P. 1990. 'Ecological Significance of Common Nonarboreal Pollen: Examples from Drylands of the Middle East', *Review of Palaeobotany and Palynology*, 64: 343–50.

Pirngruber, R. 2012. *The Impact of Empire on Market Prices in Babylon in the Late Achaemenid and Seleucid periods, ca. 400–140* BC, unpublished thesis, VU University, Amsterdam.

Rossignol-Strick, M. 1999. 'The Holocene Climatic Optimum and Pollen Records of Sapropel 1 in the Eastern Mediterranean, 9000–6000 BP', *Quaternary Science Reviews*, 18: 515–30.

Slotsky, A. L. 1997. *The Bourse of Babylon; Market Quotations in the Astronomical Diaries of Babylonia*, Bethesda MD: CDL Press.

Slotsky, A. L. and Wallenfels, R. 2009. *Tallies and Trends; the Late Babylonian Commodity Price Lists*, Bethesda MD: CDL Press.

Van der Spek, R. J. 1997/1998. 'New Evidence from the Babylonian Astronomical Diaries Concerning Seleucid and Arsacid History', *Archiv für Orientforschung*, 44/45: 167–75.

—— 2000. 'The Effect of War on the Prices of Barley and Agricultural Land in Hellenistic Babylonia', in *économie Antique; La Guerre dans les économies Antiques*, edited by J. Andreau, P. Briant and R. Descat, Saint-Bertrand-de-Comminges: Musée archéologique départemental de Saint-Bertrand-de-Comminges: 293–313.

—— 2004. 'Palace, Temple and Market in Seleucid Babylonia', in *Le Roi et l'Économie. Autonomies Locales et Structures Royales dans l'économie de l'Empire Séleucide. Actes des Rencontres de Lille (23 juin 2003) et d'Orléans (29–30 janvier 2004*, edited by V. Chankowski and F. Duyrat, Paris: De Boccard: 303–32.

—— 2005. *Commodity Prices from Babylon (385–61 BC)*, http://www.iisg.nl/hpw/data. php#babylon (last accessed April 2013).

—— 2006. 'How to Measure Prosperity? the Case of Hellenistic Babylonia', in *Approches de l'économie hellénistique*, edited by R. Descat. Paris: De Boccard: 287–310.

— 2011. 'The "Silverization" of the Economy of the Achaemenid and Seleukid Empires and Early Modern China', in *The Economies of Hellenistic Societies, Third to First Centuries*, edited by Z. H. Archibald, J. K. Davies and V. Gabrielsen, Oxford: Oxford University Press: 402–20.

—— Forthcoming. 'The Volatility of Prices of Barley and Dates in Babylon in the Third and Second Centuries BC', in *Documentary Sources in Ancient Near Eastern and Greco-Roman History: Methodology and Practice*, edited by H. D. Baker and M. Jursa, Oxford: Oxbow Books.

Vargyas P. 2001. *A History of Babylonian Prices in the First Millennium BC. 1. Prices of the Basic Commodities*, Heidelberg: Heidelberger Orientverlag.

Wick, L., Lemcke, G. and Sturm, M. 2003. 'Evidence of Lateglacial and Holocene Climatic Change and Human Impact in Eastern Anatolia: High-resolution Pollen, Charcoal, Isotopic and Geochemical Records from the Laminated Sediments of Lake Van, Turkey', *The Holocene*, 13: 665–75.

Yau Sui-Kwong, Nimah, M., and Farran, M. 2011. 'Early Sowing and Irrigation to Increase Barley Yields and Water Use Efficiency in Mediterranean Conditions', *Agricultural Water Management*, 98: 1776–81.

Zhang, D. D., Brecke, P., Lee, H. F., He, Y.-Q. and Zhang, J. 2007. 'Global Climate Change, War, and Population Decline in Recent Human History', *Proceedings of the National Academy of Sciences of the United States of America*, 104: 19214–19.

8 Mediterranean grain prices in classical antiquity

Dominic Rathbone and Sitta von Reden

Introduction

As a contribution to the overall objective of this volume to collate grain prices in the Mediterranean and surrounding regions from ancient Babylonia to modern Europe in order to analyse and compare their variability as an indicator of market performance, our chapter has two primary aims. First, to construct and present the first ever comprehensive list of attested prices of wheat and barley from the Greek, Hellenistic, Roman and early Byzantine worlds over the long millennium from the late fifth century BC to the early eighth century AD – with the exception of the great series of barley prices from ancient Babylonia, which is dealt with separately in this volume by Van der Spek and his team in Chapters 2, 3, 6, 7, 18 and 19. In our list we have tried to combine the traditional pedantic accuracy of ancient historians in reporting and interpreting the ancient prices with the more user-friendly approach of converting all prices into their equivalent in grams of silver per hectolitre of grain so they can be used for direct comparisons within antiquity and with later periods. Second, to investigate what our price data – sometimes rich, most often sparse – can or cannot tell us about market performance across the areas and ages we cover. We assess and comment on the frequent long-term stability of ancient prices, the extent and probable causes of volatility, and the apparent differences between regions and eras, some of which seem to represent significant changes in the nature of the market. In this chapter we locate our analysis of prices in broader considerations of institutions and mentality which we believe shaped or at least strongly influenced the nature of markets in our worlds and hence the grade of market performance.

A brief glance at our tables of attested prices (see Tables 8.1 and 8.2 later, and the Appendix) will reveal to historians of later periods, and of ancient Babylonia, the overall paucity of our data and their heterogeneity. Only from Egypt under Ptolemaic, Roman and Byzantine rule do we have a long-term series, albeit skeletal, of prices from private transactions attested in documents. Athens of the fifth to fourth centuries BC and Delos in its phase of independence from 314 to 167 BC provide limited series of data recorded in public inscriptions. Most of our other prices are very scattered in time and place, and are cited in literary or epigraphic texts with a rhetorical purpose to emphasize broader points such as the intensity of a siege, fertility of an area or generosity of a benefactor, or are government attempts to set prices in a particular political context. Because of the distribution and nature of the evidence, and also for metrological reasons, we present our data in a number of tables, as listed here, and structure our discussion by these tables, which can be found in the Appendix to this chapter.

A8.1   Multipliers for converting ancient grain prices into grams of silver per hectolitre

A8.2   Wheat prices at Athens, fifth to fourth centuries BC

A8.3   Barley prices at Athens (and elsewhere), fifth to fourth centuries BC

A8.4   Wheat prices at Delos, third to second centuries BC

A8.5   Barley prices (*krithē* and *alphita*) at Delos, third to second centuries BC

A8.6   'Market' prices of wheat in Egypt, 330–30 BC

A8.7   Variation of *olyra* prices in Egypt in 159/8 BC

A8.8   Conversion rates of wheat into cash and *vice versa* in Egypt, 330–30 BC

A8.9   Penalty prices in Egypt, 330–30 BC

A8.10 Grain prices in Rome, Italy and the west, third century BC to fifth century AD

A8.11 Grain prices in the Greek east (excluding Delos and Egypt), third century BC to sixth century AD

A8.12 Private wheat prices in Egypt, 30 BC to third century AD

A8.13 Private penalty prices for wheat in Egypt, 30 BC to second century AD

A8.14 Wheat prices set by the state in Egypt, first to third centuries AD

A8.15 Wheat prices in Egypt, fourth century AD

A8.16 Barley prices in Egypt, first to fourth centuries AD

A8.17 Grain prices in Egypt, fifth to early eighth centuries AD

No scholar since Heichelheim (1930, cf. 1954/5) has been brave or foolish enough to try to collect the price data for grain (let alone other goods and wages) for classical antiquity as a whole, and Heichelheim never published his Roman and Byzantine data. In more recent times there have been collections of data for particular areas and periods which we have gratefully used as bases for our tables, although we have checked the references and made various amendments and have devised our own system of comparing prices.[1] Our aim to cover the whole of classical antiquity (except Babylonia) has, frankly, proved too ambitious. We trust that most of our tables are pretty complete and accurate, but suspect we may have missed some prices in classical Greece outside Athens and in the cities of the Hellenistic and Roman worlds. Even with modern technology, there is no easy and reliable way to search the ever-expanding corpora of inscriptions, papyri and other texts for prices of grain. Because of our own lack of expertise, we do not list all the grain prices for Judaea attested in rabbinic sources or those from Byzantine Egypt, but summarize the work of others.[2] This is not a great problem because even for areas we have examined ourselves, the best that we can normally manage is to establish the parameters of 'normal' prices, and the rabbinic prices are in any case generalizing statements, not from actual sales.

There are advantages in comparing prices of grain, rather than of a commodity such as wine. Although for Roman Egypt we have many more wine prices than grain prices (but probably fewer elsewhere in the ancient world), the range of quality of a grain like wheat was far more restricted, so price did not vary much for quality. Grain, furthermore, was the most important component of most ancient diets, making its price a privileged indicator of living standards. However, consumption of grains was variable by region and perhaps by status. Wheat was the preferred grain of the Graeco-Roman world, even if barley was still often consumed (and fed to animals doing heavy work); hence most of our attested grain prices are for wheat, the socially favoured and most traded grain. Egyptian *olyra* and Roman *far*, both forms of emmer wheat, seem to have been rural subsistence staples, little traded. We have included prices of barley, when we have them, in our tables, but only have enough for Ptolemaic and Roman Egypt to justify separate tables. Barley prices can occasionally be used to supplement gaps in the evidence for wheat prices, but our main interest is to look for variation in the price ratio between wheat and barley as a possible indicator of structural changes in the production and distribution of grains in classical antiquity.

Our sparse and disparate data raise various problems of methodology. Metrological issues are discussed in the next section. One methodological qualification has to be made at the outset. The number of extant prices, even in the case of grain, is far from sufficient to substantiate arguments in purely quantitative terms. The raw data can be, and have been, used in arguments for widely different pictures of price formation, both for Mediterranean-wide market integration and also for local and regional price formation.[3] Prices themselves can be regarded as typical, normal or abnormal, and as influenced by administrative pressure, market forces or popular sentiment. It is therefore the social and economic structures, institutions and politics, including the nature and level of monetization, which we bring to bear on the interpretation of the data, the incentive systems and normative influences that shaped economic behaviour as well as the social, technological and environmental conditions which are generally thought to have impacted on communication and price formation. Any quantitative analysis of ancient price data are dependent on some prior assumptions about the economies of which they were part. As will be argued in the course of this chapter, while none of these were insulated economies with totally independent dynamics of price formation, they were not, in the classical Greek and Hellenistic world, part of a fully integrated monetary economy in which interregional market forces set the levels of prices across local markets; the Roman world, however, did bring considerably greater integration.

Metrology and method

The basic problem of comparing prices and earnings over large areas and long periods lies in the regional and chronological variation in the measures and units of value (coinages) used, and our imperfect knowledge of those values. Here, following the general practice of this volume, we convert ancient grain prices into their equivalent in grams of silver per hectolitre of grain. This has advantages and disadvantages. The principal advantage is that most states in classical antiquity used silver coinages of an extremely high purity, and our knowledge, from numismatic studies, of the target weight to which coins were minted is fairly good. One problem is that in the later third to mid-fourth century AD the Roman government debased and reformed its silver coinage out of existence, and the new long-lasting monetary system which replaced it was based on a gold coin, the *solidus*; fortunately we have a fixed official valuation of silver bullion in terms of *solidi* which we can use for conversion. In fact gold coins had also been used in the Principate alongside silver, so we can compare earlier values in gold. There is an advantage too in calculating our equivalents in terms of volume (hectolitres) of grain rather than weight (tonnes) because the evidence for the densities of ancient grains is not straightforward (see below).

The main disadvantage of using silver as our standard of value is that it was itself a commodity, subject to fluctuations in value. This disadvantage applies to all the other chapters in this volume, but is particularly evident here because of our geographical and chronological range. A related issue is how to deal with debasement, when a government reduced the silver content (or gross weight) of a coin without reducing its face value. Heichelheim's solution to these problems, which was to index prices from different monetary systems by selecting pairs of more or less contemporary prices as baseline equivalents, was arbitrary and produced a complicated graph comparing levels of change rather than levels of prices which is extremely difficult to read and comprehend.[4] Ideally, in a fuller study, we would check variances over time between coin values and a basket of other goods and earnings to look for changes in the purchasing power of our coinages. Here, however, where the focus is on the variability of prices, what matters first is to identify the discrete periods of different price levels within which to analyse variability. Even to compare and explain price levels across these periods, we think it more transparent to use the silver equivalent of the face values of our coin-units – and we also give the ancient prices so that readers can see the patterns in the original pricing – and then to discuss in our analyses the evident or possible effects of changing bullion values and debasements. We have a fair idea of what to expect. Bullion values plummeted, for example, following Alexander the Great's distribution of the Persian royal treasures and Augustus' spending of the accumulated wealth of Cleopatra VII. We have good numismatic evidence for the weight reduction of the Attic drachma, and other Greek coinages in the early second century BC, and the slow but eventually total debasement of the Roman *denarius* and Alexandrian tetradrachm in the later second and third centuries AD. We note, incidentally, that ancient coinages had a high ability to maintain a token value because states normally dominated the bullion supply (by owning mines and holding huge reserves, e.g. as temple offerings) and because there were no foreign competitor coinages to cause exchange problems. We therefore are happy here to use the silver bullion equivalent to the face values of our coinages as the best, or least bad, working common measure of value.

Most grain prices from classical antiquity can be converted with reasonable certainty into modern equivalents because of the dominance of the well-known Attic (Athenian) and then Roman standards of coinage and measurements. However, since there has been no general study of ancient metrology since Hultsch (1882), and because old erroneous values go on being used in modern studies, we explain briefly below which values we use and why.[5] We summarize our assumptions in Table A8.1, where we list the multipliers for converting the principal ancient prices in equivalent in grams of silver per hectolitre. Variant coins (e.g. the *chrysous*) and measures (e.g. the *kophinos*), which occur only once or twice, are discussed in the relevant table of prices. In the tables and our discussions we use the following abbreviations for the main coins and dry measures: dr. = drachma; ob. = obol; tal. = talent; *den.* = *denarius*; HS = sesterce; *sol.* = *solidus*; and *med.* = *medimnos*; *mod.* = *modius Italicus*; *mod. castr.* = *modius castrensis*; *art.* = *artaba*. We round up equivalents in grams of silver per hectolitre to one decimal place if they are less than 100; for values of 100 and over we calculate to the nearest round number. Most of the documented private sales were for a few measures of grain, so we only specify the quantity if it was exceptionally large.

In classical Athens the principal coin was the silver *drachma* which numismatic studies have shown was minted at a target weight of 4.32 g.[6] The normal measure of capacity used for grains was the *medimnos*, which official measures found in the Athenian agora indicate was equivalent to around 53.0 l.[7] Already in the fifth and fourth centuries BC Attic standards of coins and measures had been adopted by most Greek states in the Aegean and Sicily, and they were then spread through much of the Hellenistic world by Alexander the Great and his successors, although some states, notably Ptolemaic Egypt, used other standards. Delos used the Rhodian standard for their coinage, but converted prices into the more common Athenian one for public accounting purposes.[8] In the 170s BC the Attic drachma was apparently reduced in weight to around 4.20 g, and similar weight reductions happened to some other Greek coinages. But the theoretical target weight of the Athenian drachma remained the same, and so we ignore this for calculating the silver bullion equivalents of prices in our tables.[9]

The silver coinage of Hellenistic Egypt was lighter than the Athenian standard. In 310 BC the Ptolemaic silver drachma was reduced from its former Attic weight of 4.32 g to 3.9 g, and then to 3.56 g in 306/5 BC. Within Egypt Ptolemaic silver coins were exchanged for Attic-standard coins at the value of 1:1, but elsewhere 1 Attic drachma was equivalent to 1 drachma and 1 obol of Ptolemaic coinage.[10] The silver drachma was part of a tri-metallic currency system in which drachmas and tetradrachms were minted in silver, obols, half-obols and smaller fractions in bronze, and large pieces equivalent to 20 and 60 silver drachmas in gold. Ptolemy II changed the gold denominations, which does not concern us here, but also increased the importance of bronze in the tri-metallic system by minting values up to 1 drachma in that metal. This proved fatal in the long-term, but during most of the third century BC 1 bronze drachma was equivalent to 1 drachma in silver. In payments to the state, an agio of 10 per cent was added if obligations expressed in silver were paid in bronze coinage.[11]

By the reign of Ptolemy IV (220–205/4 BC) the equivalence between the silver and bronze drachma could no longer be maintained. It seems that at first the bronze drachma was merely re-tariffed at half the value of the silver drachma. This led to a nominal increase of prices by 100 per cent within Egypt, as now twice the

Table 8.1 The changing tariff of the Ptolemaic bronze currency

Period	Date	Tariff
1	c. 265–220 BC	1 silver drachma = 1 dr. bronze
2	c. 220–200 BC	1 silver drachma = 2 dr. bronze
3	c. 200–183 BC	1 silver drachma = 60 dr. bronze
4	183–176/168 BC	1 silver drachma = 120 dr. bronze
5	176/68–130 BC	1 silver drachma = 240 dr. bronze
6	c. 130–30 BC	1 silver drachma = 300, 400 or 600 dr. bronze

amount of bronze coinage (the common currency) had to be given in exchange for obligations formerly expressed in terms of the equivalence between silver and bronze. But this did not stabilize the currency system.[12] It seems that subsequently bronze coins, and prices expressed in that standard, were valued against silver at their real metallic relationship of value, which was conventionally set at 1:60. Thus 1 silver drachma was now worth 60 drachmas in the bronze standard, leading to a nominal increase of prices by a factor of 60. During the second century BC there were further monetary changes of that kind, leading to a (nominal) price increase of a further 100 per cent from 183 BC onwards (silver:bronze 1:120), and of another 100 per cent (1:240) around 176 BC or later, possibly because the weight of the bronze drachma was then halved. From 168 BC, however, pre-183 BC price levels are also found.[13]

After 130 BC further monetary manipulation affected price levels. From demotic documents we can see that 4 drachmas were no longer reckoned to the *statēr* (the 'tetradrachm') but 20 drachmas.[14] At the same time, the value relationship between bronze and silver became flexible according to a variable price of the silver *statēr*. Thus we have evidence for silver drachmas being reckoned at 300, 400 and 600 dr. bronze.[15] Extant prices in the papyri thus can reflect different relationships of value between silver and bronze at the rate of 1:300, 1:400 and 1:600. To translate the Egyptian price levels from different periods into grams of silver, we have used the model set out in Table 8.1.[16]

The normal measure of capacity for grains in Egypt was the *artaba*, a name of Persian origin. It seems, despite local variants, that a standard official size was dominant for measuring grain in the evidence we are presenting here.[17] The official Ptolemaic *artaba* was probably slightly different to that of the Roman period, but because firm evidence is lacking, we round up the Roman-period value to an approximate 40 l.[18]

The basic Roman weights and measures, which helpfully remained standard from the early Republic into Byzantine times, are known exactly because the units of weight, length and capacity were linked by round-number definitions which provide a check on empirical evidence.[19] The standard measure of capacity of grain was the *modius* (*Italicus*) equivalent to 8.62 l, although by the fourth century AD the state sometimes used the *modius castrensis* ('of the camp') equal to 1.5 *modii Italici*, that is 12.93 l. Much of our evidence for the Roman world comes from Greek writers who used the roughly correct ratio of 6:1 in converting *modii* into *medimnoi*, and the implied 51.72 l seems to have become the official value of the *medimnos* in Greek states as they came under direct Roman rule. So too the standard *artaba* in Egypt was made equal to 4.5 *modii Italici*, that is 38.78 l, and the Judaean *se'ah* seems to have been adjusted to equal the *modius*.[20] Throughout our period the basic Roman (and Byzantine) unit of weight, by which coins were minted, was the pound (*libra*) equivalent to 323 g. In 212/1 BC the Romans introduced the silver *denarius*, which by the mid-second century BC had become the most important Roman coin in circulation. From 212/1 to 157 BC the *denarius* was minted at an official target weight of 72 to the Roman pound of silver (4.49 g), from 156 BC to AD 64 at 84 to the pound (3.85 g), and from AD 64 (Nero's reform) to the later third century AD at 96 to the pound (3.36 g). The principal unit of account, used by the Romans for prices and so on, down to 141 BC was the *as*, of which there were 10 to the *denarius*; from 140 BC on it was the *sestertius* (abbreviated HS), with 4 sesterces, each of 4 *asses*, to the *denarius*. To express Roman prices on the *denarius* system, Greek writers simply used the drachma to stand for the *denarius*, and rounded asses and sesterces to the nearest obol. Some communities in the eastern provinces were allowed to continue minting Greek-style coinages, but tied to the Roman standard even if the silver content was less, so that the drachma and *denarius* were, in face value, equivalent. In Egypt the main circulating coin remained the Alexandrian tetradrachm (4 dr.) which, although it was a billon coin with little silver content, was deemed equivalent to a *denarius*. From AD 238 onwards the *denarius* was progressively replaced by the so-called *antoninianus*, a coin with notionally 150 per cent of the silver content of the *denarius* but tariffed at 2 *denarii*, which had briefly been minted in AD 215–219; we do not alter our multiplier for converting the wheat prices of AD 238 to 274, which all come from Egypt, but discuss this later in the chapter.

The details and effects of the reforms of Roman coinage in AD 274 by Aurelian and in AD 294–6 and 301 by Diocletian are still unclear and disputed.[21] The only wheat prices we have for AD 275 to 300 come from Egypt, where the Alexandrian tetradrachm remained in production and use into AD 295/6. However, we believe that the tetradrachm was pegged to Aurelian's new billon coin, which replaced the *antoninianus*, and that its mark of 20:1 denoted that this new coin was notionally on the old *denarius* standard (96 per lb) but tariffed at 20 *denarii*, because this provides a plausible multiplier for converting the now higher Egyptian wheat prices into a silver equivalent.[22] In AD 296/7 Diocletian replaced the tetradrachm in Egypt with elements of his new mainstream coinage, although local practice long remained to reckon in tetradrachms equivalent to the new *denarius*, but we have no wheat prices until after his second coinage reform and Edict on Maximum Prices, both of AD 301. We can calculate the silver equivalent of prices in his Edict because we know the target weight of his new *denarius*.[23] For most of the rest of the fourth century AD, however, prices of all goods, including gold and silver, expressed in drachmas (and talents), show continuing and dramatic inflation. That means that we can only calculate silver equivalents of wheat prices, which all but one come from Egypt, for which we have contemporary silver bullion prices.

Meanwhile, in AD 312 Constantine had started minting the *solidus*, the standard gold coin, at 72 to the pound (4.49 g), which in the last decades of the fourth century AD became the universal standard of the monetary systems of the late Roman, Byzantine and Arab worlds. Although, as we will see, the purchasing power of gold seems to have rocketed in late antiquity, the relative value of silver seems to have fallen slightly but then stayed stable. The traditional gold:silver ratio of 1:12, used by Augustus, Nero and Diocletian for their coinage reforms, which must, despite market fluctuations, have been the generally accepted norm, is last attested around AD 307/8.[24] By AD 397 a new ratio of 1:14.4 appears as the official norm, which is also attested in fiscal documents from Egypt dateable by their script to the fifth century AD, and the AD 397 ruling was incorporated in Justinian's law code of the mid-sixth century AD, which implies its continuing validity.[25] We suspect that the setting of this new ratio was part of the establishment of the dominance of the new *solidus*, and so use it for converting wheat prices in *solidi* from the mid-fourth century AD onwards into a silver equivalent.

As a coda, we explain how users of our data can, if they wish, convert our equivalent values in grams of silver per hectolitre of wheat into grams of silver per tonne.[26] The density of grains varies by type and region of production, and barley may be more or less processed before sale. Most densities given in ancient sources lie within the modern ranges, but because there clearly was variation, and precision is unattainable, we suggest using approximate generalized densities of 78 kg/hl for wheat and 60 kg/hl for barley. To convert silver values in g/hl for wheat into g/tonne, multiply by 12.82, and for barley, by 16.67.

Grain prices in the eastern Mediterranean (c. 420–30 BC)

Sitta von Reden

Grain markets and the grain trade

During the period under consideration the commercial distribution of grain in the Greek world was a free enterprise. It took place in local markets (*agorai*) on the one hand and foreign markets (*emporia*) on the other, the latter being situated typically in harbours at some distance from the major town centre. The physical distinction between *emporia* and *agorai* is a direct manifestation of commercial exchange taking place at two levels in Greek cities: firstly at the local level, largely regulated by free supply-and-demand mechanisms, and secondly in connection with the external world, which was far more controlled by political interference, incentive structures created by public institutions, and direct legislation. These two markets, it can be argued, were not fully related to each other, and their interdependent price formation was frequently controlled by administrative regulation.[27]

At the local level, primary producers either themselves or through agents sold their surplus at the farm gate and in local markets to either consumers or middlemen who sold it on in other local markets or the harbour.[28] From such second-level markets connected to places beyond the borders of a town or *polis*, the grain was transported by merchants (*emporoi*) along roads, by river or across the sea to places at closer or further distance. Long-distance trade of grain via the sea became frequent during the archaic period, as Greeks migrated and settled along the coasts of the western Mediterranean, Africa, the Levant and the Black Sea. Trade vessels carried mixed loads of various commodities and varied considerably in size. The smallest ships attested archaeologically were less than 14 m long with a carrying capacity of 20 tonnes or less. By the Hellenistic period, however, ships of a capacity nearing 150 tonnes seem to have been quite normal, and ships of 350–500 tonnes not rare.[29] Transport by land was expensive in comparison to sea-borne trade. For a bulky commodity like grain, a sea voyage is thought to have added c. 2 per cent per 100 miles to the costs, whereas freight charges for overland transport by mule or cart could make goods up to 50 per cent more expensive.[30] But such costs varied according to place and season, and probably decreased as road systems improved.

The Greek grain trade was stimulated by a high variability of local climates in the Mediterranean, the frequency of (often local) grain shortages and the high mobility of Greek populations and individuals.[31] At the household level temporary shortages were buffered by storage which is estimated to have made some peasant families independent of external supplies for more than twelve months.[32] But unequal storage facilities and the control over surplus put poorer families at the whim of large proprietors who are known to have speculated with the seasonal variation of supply and demand, as well as with impending scarcity.[33] Such speculators could drive up prices in the local market, or alternatively, demonstrate public spirit by deliberately refraining from withholding stores. Conversely, governments could prohibit export of staple foods in order to protect local exchange, which had effects on the supply of the *emporion* as well as other markets in the region. The supply of places with low productivity relative to the size of the population, such as Attica, entailed increasing pressure to secure grain from grain-rich places such as Sicily, Egypt, some Cycladic islands and areas around the Black Sea.[34] But even in places of high productivity, shortages and food crises are attested, and the food supply of Greek cities became a structural problem as larger parts of the population lived in cities and cities grew in size.[35]

Long-distance enterprise was from the late fifth century BC onwards usually, though not always, financed by maritime loans.[36] These loans were used to finance or part-finance the acquisition of the cargo as well as any further costs for the boat and crew, and were repayable on the safe return of the boat at the home port. Boats and cargo served as security for the loans, and if they were lost, neither the debtor nor a third party had to pay up for the forfeited loan. It was a flexible system of credit suited to the social position of traders who neither had landed property themselves nor could provide civic surety for them. They carried high interest rates and occasionally led to legal trouble. But they were a financial institution crucial for the development of large-scale and long-distance trade, and provided an instrument with which individuals and governments could influence effectively directions and intensity of the grain trade.[37]

Throughout the Greek world we find other institutions beyond the market that influenced the supply, demand and price setting of grain.[38] The oldest institution was benefaction (*euergesia*), which meant that a benefactor from his own resources made available cheaper grain by making donations of grain or money, or by reducing harbour taxes and interest rates connected with the grain trade, thus encouraging traders to direct their supplies to the city in need. In turn, the population thanked him with public honours, inscriptions and privileges, which created a viable incentive structure. There is some evidence, however, that benefactors did not always set favourable prices on their own accord, but were strongly encouraged to do so by the pressure of civic institutions. To extend this system of more or less voluntary benefaction, special grain commissioners – called *sitōnai* – who were appointed to be responsible for the grain supply in times of need are attested in Athens from the second half of the fourth century BC.[39] These were also of the class of benefactors and at times made gifts from their own resources, but also identified other benefactors, contracted with traders, and made available grain at lower prices by whatever means they could think of. Some are known to have established grain funds (*sitōnika*) in their cities supplied by special taxes or collective donations which served to reduce grain price in times of emergency.[40] Both the need for euergetism and grain commissioners show that, while in principle the grain trade was free, the market alone did not function adequately for all parts of the population.

The third strategy to support the supply of grain and stabilize market prices was regulation. Greek *poleis* hardly ever provided free grain to their citizens before the second century BC, but they designed laws and special taxes to control grain prices, the relationship between prices in *emporia* and *agorai*, as well as the size of imports to and exports from their markets. These were frequently one-off measures to deal with particular crises, but in Athens where the food supply became a notorious issue in the later fourth century BC, special regulations for grain imports and the local grain sale became permanent.[41] One such law provided that any trader who lived on Athenian territory was to transport grain to no other place than Athens. This law was also extended to those who, though not resident Athenians, had contracted maritime loans there. Offenders of both types were punished by death. In addition, prices were controlled during times of emergency by fixing the margin allowed to be added to the wholesale price on retail. Special grain wardens (*sitophylakes*), in addition to regular market officials (*agoranomoi, mētronomoi*), watched over the grain market both in the harbour and the city. Both official regulation and the institutions of benefaction increased the supply of city markets and influenced price formation. They cut prices in times of scarcity, and in the long term strengthened normative ideas about normal or acceptable prices.

Monetization

By the time of the late fifth century BC, the economy visible in our sources was fully monetized. This 'visible' economy is presented in literary texts, contracts, accounts, mint activity, coin circulation and so on, but cannot, of course, be taken as the economy in its entire social and geographical extension. In Athens, all wages, taxes, tributes and rents that we know of were paid in cash.[42] This does not mean that in any transaction that was settled in monetary terms, cash changed hands, but the monetary system of coinage served as the means of account. In Athens, where the coin supply was abundant, we can expect that most exchange was indeed cash exchange, and there is explicit evidence that in Athens loans were regarded as cheap and readily available (e.g. Xenophon *Poroi* 3.2; [Aristoteles] *Oikonomika* 1344 b 30 ff).[43] What happened beyond that 'visible' economy is difficult to tell. A unified coinage was a phenomenon of the *polis*, whereas regions with other political systems had either a variety of coinages, used foreign coins for limited purposes, or had no coined money at all. It is also believed that in rural areas exchange was less dependent on coinage than in cities, but these are arguments from silence and can hardly be proved. Greek mints coined money down to very small fractions (1 *chalkous* or 1/48 of a drachma), while in the course of the fourth century BC base metal coins (usually bronze) became increasingly popular for fractional denominations, suggesting increasing monetization and the need for small change in petty transactions.[44]

Greeks minted their precious metal coins on a variety of weight standards. This means that the weight of the standard coin (the so-called *statēr*) varied according to the local weight system adopted for the weighing of bullion. This poses greater problems for modern historians than it did for the users themselves. For, although the different value of coins of different coin system had to be kept in mind, they were easily interchanged on the basis of exchange rates which were common knowledge. Many *poleis* also adapted their weight systems to that of a dominant standard, such as that of Athens, Aigina or Miletos, depending on which exchange network they wished to integrate with.[45] Reasons for such currency alliances were as much political as they were economic and symbolical. Many extant confederacy contracts include clauses about common coinages, weights and measures (see below). Some problem for the acceptability of foreign coins was created by the nature of ancient coin design in that it reflected the political authority which guaranteed weight, purity and value of issues. Such problems of acceptability were often dealt with pragmatically. Thus some states outside Greece (e.g. Arabia, Egypt in the fifth century BC) minted coins not only to the most acceptable weight standard (such as the Athenian), but also with the design of the dominant coinage to make them most acceptable to users.

During the time of the Athenian League (479–403 BC), Athenian coinage became the dominant currency in the Aegean world. Athens as an economic centre and minter of a massive coinage, together with the monetary tribute it required from the league, made Athenian coinage not only the most desirable medium of exchange but also spread monetization throughout Greece. It is not mere coincidence that banks, maritime loans and a sophisticated law of contract appear in Athens during the second half of the fifth century BC. Within the Athenian sphere of influence we can speak of an almost unified coin system from the mid-fifth century BC onwards. The importance of Athenian coinage lasted beyond the decline of Athenian power. Philip and Alexander of Macedonia adopted the Athenian weight standard for their coinages in the fourth century BC, and this standard was also adopted for all imperial coinages after Alexander's death, except that of Egypt. Despite the perseverance of some other standards and local economies (most notably the Rhodian, Chian and Aiginetan standards as well as some new standards such as that of the Roman *denarius*), the co-existence of different coin systems cannot be regarded as a severe impediment to interregional market exchange based on coinage.

More important for our considerations are the different monetary habits with which the Greeks were confronted after the conquest of the Persian Empire in the Hellenistic period. Coinage was a Greek phenomenon, while the rest of the world had used and minted coins only for interacting with Greeks.[46] Thus the *shekel* introduced in most Persian territories as a unit of bullion continued to be so used under Hellenistic rule alongside coinage. In Asia and in Egypt, moreover, grain was current as a medium of payment in a large number of transactions, such as tax, wage and rental payments. Particularly in Egypt we have much evidence that wheat was used as a currency to pay rents and taxes, and to buy labour and commodities in the market.[47] Ptolemaic coinage, when introduced during the last quarter of the fourth century BC, was inserted into this monetary economy in grain which must not be confused with a barter economy. For grain was not just a medium of exchange, but the *artaba* of wheat functioned also as a standard of value and an accounting unit with a stable relationship of value to other grains and metal. Under the Ptolemies it was tariffed at an official relationship to the value of Ptolemaic coin units. The metrological relationship of value between wheat and coin was different from the market value of grain und seems to have been pegged to some customary relationship of value between different cereals and metals.[48] It does not seem, however, that this value was entirely artificial. As we shall see further below, the exchange rate between wheat and coin seems to have been re-tariffed at the end of the third century BC, either in the light of changes in the monetary economy, changing levels of market prices, or both.

The evidence

Three sets of evidence can be used for a quantitative analysis of grain prices in the eastern Mediterranean during the Classical and Hellenistic periods: public inscriptions and forensic oratory from Classical Athens (late fifth to late fourth centuries BC); accounts published on stone by the priests of the temple of Apollo on Delos from the late fourth to early second century BC; and the papyrological documentation of prices from Ptolemaic Egypt, most of which relates to the *chōra*, and consists of accounts and loan and tenancy contracts as well as some correspondence.

Athens

Table A8.2 suggests a normal price range of wheat price between 5 and 6 dr./*med.* in Athens between the end of the fifth and the fourth century BC. But what does 'normal price' mean and how was it established? The first three examples come from the accounts of the sale of confiscated property shortly before the Sicilian expedition in 415 BC (the so-called *Attic Stelai*). The sale is usually regarded to have been executed by the *polētai* (officials responsible for the sale of public property) in the form of an auction.[49] In this case, the entries of 6 dr. to 6 dr. 3 ob. would reflect prices derived in a situation of free competitive bidding. It has also been argued, however, that among the property sold according to the *stēlai* there were items (like outstanding rents) that are unlikely to have been sold by auction, and that the buyers of pieces of land or houses, by far the most important items of the confiscated property, were registered in the deme (district) in which the confiscated land was situated. The sale in front of the *polētai* was not an open auction but one that was controlled by the *boulē* (council) and the *archontai* (chief magistrates) who also had to confirm the sale of each item sold.[50] If this interpretation is adopted, the three first prices represent not so much competitive market prices, but prices which the *polis* regarded as 'right' in the interest of both the treasury and the citizen buyers. A similarly normative price is represented by the law concerning the sale of wheat offerings, as well as the prices at which the sales of wheat offerings of the Eleusinian temple were actually sold and recorded (nos. 10 and 11). Also a price recorded in an honorific decree to Herakleides (no. 12) can be regarded as a reflection of such normative price setting, if we consider that benefactors' prices were set by suggestions of the *polis*.[51] In this case, figures of 5 to 6 dr. do not represent market prices in the first instance, but prices that were regarded as normal or established by the citizens of Athens. This, then, is also the meaning of the term *kathestēkuia timē* occurring in Dem. 34.39 (no. 7) and Dem. 56.8 and 10 (without giving the level of that price).[52] While there will have been some real observations behind the perception of normal or established prices, the difference of perspective is important: it puts emphasis on civic power as a regulating mechanism for ancient grain markets even outside times of emergency. Civic control became stronger at times of severe emergency, and created then various forms of public rhetoric against mischievous dealers, pressure on benefactors and direct regulation (see above, and the much-discussed affair of Lysias 22). But it is important to realize that the evidence for long-term stability of prices is not the result of a perfect market across the Aegean.[53] Prices of 9 dr. per *medimnos* (no. 8), may, then, have been just as much in the normal range of market prices as 10 dr. per *artaba* in the *chōra* of Alexandria in the 320s BC (Table A8.6 no. 1).

Delos

On Delos during the time of its independence (314–167 BC), a board of commissioners (*hieropoioi*) responsible for the financial management of the temple of Apollo recorded on marble the annual income and expenditure of the temple for about 145 years.[54] They gave the income from rents of houses and estates under the control of the temple, the interest the god had earned on loans, income from concessions sold to farmers, payments to contractors, payment of wages to hired labourers and purchases of goods. This last payment was not for daily necessities, but for the supplies for ritual or food for labourers, or materials needed for the maintenance of the temple. The evidence in many cases provides minute detail about the development of prices over one year, or over a longer period, but it also raises a number of problems. In most cases, the *hieropoioi* published total sums expended rather than prices per unit or wages per day. They also tended to omit specifications of quality, volume, size or weight per unit. Any such information is lost for economic analysis. Also, because of the chance survival of the *stēlai*, data on prices do not spread evenly across the period. Often we cannot know whether a commodity was not needed, or not recorded, or the record not preserved. In the case of grain, it usually seems to have been supplied by the property of the temple, and only in exceptional circumstances was purchased by the *hieropoioi*. Thus our material is more meagre than we would wish, and might reflect periods of some economic pressure, rather than normal years. The purchase of wheat, it should be noted, was recorded only rarely, and then exclusively in relation to one particular purpose. It does not reflect the regular provision of the temple with wheat bought in the market.

On the positive side, there is no reason to doubt that the prices recorded were market prices.[55] There is also no indication that they were the result of any special negotiation with traders or local grain dealers. We are also in the happy position of having evidence for seasonal variation of grain prices (Table A8.4 nos. 1–8, 11–13): the high prices recorded in Delos for the months from September to December fall into the season when market prices ought to have risen for reasons of declining stores and the winter interruption of sea-trade. The fact that higher prices for the winter months recur in different years may confirm that we are witnessing a seasonal pattern rather than exceptional circumstances.[56] Comparison of these prices with the benefactor's price of the year 180 BC (nos. 9 and 10) may suggest, moreover, that price concessions were expected to be oriented towards low summer prices rather than annual averages. This might confirm, though it does not prove, our suggestion that normative or iconic prices were only marginally in line with economic reality.

Delian barley prices (Table A8.5), however, confuse any neat picture that has emerged so far. First of all, we see that consideration must be given to the form in which cereals were sold. Barley in particular could be sold in unprocessed or semi-processed form as grain or flour (*krithē* or *alphita*). The difference in price between unprocessed and semi-processed barley could, according to these data, be considerable and must make us wonder whether variation of cereal prices in other records, especially when used for rhetorical purposes, hide variations of quality and mode of sale which are important for understanding price levels. *Krithai* prices also show no sensitivity to seasonal availability: the highest price recorded comes from the month of July (just after the harvest), while the lowest was paid in November, when prices of wheat were recorded as being particularly high. There is also no obvious explanation for why the *hieropoioi* bought both wheat and *alphita* for feeding the *technitai* during the winter of 282 BC. Did they do so because wheat prices were exceptionally high during that winter? And did people normally supplement wheat with barley, if prices were high?

Egypt

The corpus of wheat prices from Ptolemaic Egypt is the largest of the three sets, comprising over 100 figures. Most belong to the period from c. 275 to c. 80 BC, that is, from the reign of Ptolemy II Philadelphos to the death of Ptolemy IX Soter II. Important periods of economic change in the first years of Ptolemaic rule on the one hand and the reign of Cleopatra VII on the other are not represented by these data. Also, our evidence concentrates in some areas of intensive Greek settlement in the Fayyum and the adjacent areas of the Oxyrhynchite and Heracleopolite nomes in Middle Egypt. Although there are reasons to believe that there were markets in the less Hellenized area of Upper Egypt, too, economic organization, Ptolemaic influence and the use of coined money varied considerably between Upper and Lower-Middle Egypt.[57] The southern regions of the Nile Valley in particular continued to be dominated by an old land tenure regime where the distribution mechanisms of surplus grain are likely to have been different from the practices represented by Greek papyri. Even within the areas of Greek occupation, our evidence tends to concentrate on the activities of a few groups of people: Greek cleruchs (*klērouchoi*, military settlers) and their agents, local administrative offices and the military. Most damaging to our picture of Egyptian price formation is the fact that the city of Alexandria is almost entirely excluded from the papyrological evidence.

The data can be divided into three categories: first, prices that are references to market prices, or have been accounted for as payments for grain purchased or sold (Table A8.6); second, conversion rates of cash into wheat or wheat into cash, recorded in contracts and accounts (Table A8.8) and, third, penalty prices payable in lieu of grain for unfulfilled rental obligations in kind (Table A8.9).

The entries of Table A8.6 come closest to market prices, but not all figures represent prices paid for grain in a market. Nos. 2–3, 8–10 and 19–20 might be regarded as direct references to prices prevalent in a market, but all others render account for payments of, and receipts for, grain sold under variable conditions. Some of these cereals were transacted internally on the estate from which most of the records come; others may have been sold from the threshing floor of the estate, which excluded any costs of transport. There were also various conditions in which grain could be sold: cleaned or uncleaned; sifted or unsifted; bleached or unbleached; there were also different measures used in different transactions and different districts of Egypt.[58] From the qualifications of rental payments stipulated in interpersonal contracts we know that these differences mattered.[59] In some cases, a monetary payment for grain accounted for may hide a conversion of cash and wheat, thus belong to the list of Table A8.8. In most cases we also do not know at what time of the year the grain was purchased or delivered, and whether the payment was part of a more complex set of negotiations which the transacting partners had agreed upon.[60]

All the prices of Table A8.8, furthermore, represent notional grain prices serving as conversion rates of kind into cash or *vice versa*. There was an official conversion rate of 2 dr. per *artaba* of wheat, which the government introduced for the conversion of payments made to the state (taxes, rents, wages, etc.). Individuals in private transactions could adopt this rate or negotiate their own rates of exchange and not adhere to the official one. Conversion rates were used in a great variety of circumstances. For example, employees on large agrarian estates or in local tax offices could commute their cash wages into wheat, or vice versa, either for consumption or for making further payments in kind. Landlords who according to some contracts provided monetary loans (so-called *katerga*) to their tenants for financing additional agrarian labour also commuted them into kind when adding them to the rent due at the end of the agrarian year. Moreover, certain tenancy contracts foresaw a full or part pre-payment (*prodoma*) of the rent as a loan in cash which was offset against the rent in kind at the end of the contractual period (e.g. no. 15). A similar construction was a sale with deferred delivery. In such cases a commodity (such as grain) was paid for in advance while the delivery of the good followed later. Often this was used as a substitute for a monetary loan which was repaid with interest in kind. The rate of exchange between cash and commodity was once again set in the contract.[61]

The penalty prices of Table A8.9 represent prices of a particular kind as well. Penalty prices (*epitima*) were agreed in private and royal contracts in the case that rental obligations were not fulfilled as stipulated.[62] Traditionally an unfulfilled rental obligation in grain was punished with a surcharge of 50 per cent on the original rent (*hēmiolion*). In pre-Ptolemaic Egypt it was paid in kind or wheat equivalent. Under the Ptolemies, contractual penalties came to be expressed in cash terms, converting the obligation in kind into cash at an official rate of exchange. It appears that the official conversion rate of 2 drachmas per *artaba* of wheat was applied here too, and that the penalty price was assessed therefore as twice the value of the original obligation in kind. Such penalty regulation seems to have been applied both in royal and interpersonal contracts which occasionally added explicitly that a contract was to be executed 'according to the rules of the king' (*kata to diagramma*, or *hōs pros basilika*).[63] From the end of the third century BC onwards the level of *epitima* change and they become more variable from contract to contract. Many of the changes in the level of the *epitima* can be explained by changes to the monetary system, but some problems remain (see column 4 of Table A8.8). Changes in the level of penalty prices, and a greater volatility of them, may be due to real price increases, to which the official rate responded, but they may also reflect errors in our understanding of monetary changes, or indeed a more flexible use of official conversion rates in interpersonal contracts (see the Introduction to this chapter). In principle, however, penalty prices represent a very static use of official rates of exchange, and responded little to short-term variation of purchase prices.

Our three sets of price information reflect prices in the Egyptian grain markets, but they do so in different ways. The first table gives market prices, but also prices negotiated under other circumstances; the second represents conversion rates that were pegged to an official conversion rate, but these were adopted flexibly in any individual transaction. Penalty prices, finally, reflect a notional relationship between wheat and cash and responded, if at all, slowly to changing market conditions. The degree to which they were negotiable seems to have been limited.

Market prices

We have three documents indicating the time of the sale (Table A8.6 nos. 4, 20 and 21, all dating to March). The harvest in Egypt started in late March/early April; thus these purchases took place shortly before the new harvest and prices might have been high. However, the document from which no. 21 is taken makes explicit reference to 'this year's grain' (*pyros eniausios*, P. Tebt. I 112, ll. 57 and 118), suggesting that the new harvest did not affect prices in any notable way. The few data which we have for seasonal variation of cereal prices in Egypt relate to *olyra* (Table A8.7) and, compared to the variation of wheat prices on Delos in 282 BC, it is negligible.

We have two documents relating to the city of Alexandria (Table A8.6 nos. 2 and 8). Unsurprisingly, they indicate significantly higher wheat prices in the capital than in the *chōra*. We have also one price from Thebes in Upper Egypt (no. 29), showing no particular difference from price levels in the Fayyum and adjacent areas. This accords with the findings in the next section for the Roman period, which do not support previous views that prices in Upper Egypt were lower than in Middle Egypt.[64] So too, although low penalty prices are attested in Thebes for the years 109 and 108 BC, even lower penalty prices are attested for the Arsinoite, Heracleopolite and Hermopolite nomes. There is no conclusive evidence for regional price variation between Upper and Lower Egypt during the Hellenistic period.

There is not much evidence for price controls in Egypt, nor for officials buying grain at special rates. We have two documents representing grain purchases by a tax office (nos. 20 and 21). But both documents belong to the same dossier representing the activities of one village clerk in Kerkeosiris during the late second century BC and cannot be regarded as significant. It may be noteworthy, however, that the price of 2 dr./*artaba* comes from a time when our calculation of penalty prices oscillated around 3 to 5 dr. (Table A8.9). Possibly the price of 2 dr./*art.* still reflects the official price set by the government as conversion rate in the third century BC.

Conversion rates

The items nos. 1, 3 and 4 in Table A8.8 represent the practice of private employees converting their monetary salary into payments in kind at an 'internal' rate. All three belong to the archive of Zenon, the manager of a large royal domain in the Fayyum. Nos. 2 and 6, belonging to the same archive, represent the rate at which Zenon converted *katerga* loans into grain to be added to the rent at the end of the agrarian year.[65] Nos. 8 and 9 represent cash salaries converted into wheat in a local tax office. It is notable that the conversion rates of the tax office are very close to those adopted by Zenon for converting salaries and cash loans of his employees and tenants into kind. Moreover, if our model of monetary changes is correct, such rates remained fairly similar over a period of 150 years. No distinction, furthermore, seems to have been made whether a landlord commuted cash loans back into kind, or an employee his wage into grain. It may also be noted that interpersonal conversion rates in this fragmentary sample are usually slightly lower than the official rate applied to unfulfilled contracts. They are also lower than market prices of that period.

Penalty prices

Table A8.9 shows that during the reigns of Ptolemy II and III *epitima* were set at 4 dr./*art.*, representing most likely twice the official conversion rate of 2 dr. attested in P. Col. I 54 (Table A8.8 no. 5). In about 220 BC, however, the official penalty price increased to 5 dr., representing a conversion rate of grain into cash of 2 1/2 dr. Soon afterwards penalty prices doubled to 10 dr. However, as we suggested in the Introduction, this increase reflects only a nominal increase of price levels due to monetary changes. Assuming that the model of monetary changes in the subsequent periods is also correct, *epitima* remained fairly stable for the next one and a half centuries, although oscillating around that level for reasons that might be monetary, or due to other reasons we do not know.

The level of official penalty prices suggests several things in relation to market prices. First, penalty prices may have been set in view of current or 'normal' market prices and responded, if slowly, to changes of such prices (e.g. Table A8.9 no. 10 of the year 222 BC, and several odd figures attested for the second century BC). An alternative, and in my view more likely, explanation of this link may be that notions of normal price in the market were derived from the level of official conversion rates and penalty prices. Such standardized prices stabilized market prices and created a limit to arbitrary fluctuations of price according to supply and demand. Secondly, it seems that the variation of prices was greater in the later Ptolemaic period than in the period of the first three Ptolemies which seems to have been more stable in terms of political power and monetary policy. But the variation of the prices set out in the table might also be due to insufficient knowledge of the monetary policy of the Ptolemies during the last two centuries BC. Alternatively, they may reflect a policy impossible to implement in practice, or a liberal handling of official exchange rates in private contracts.

Price formation in classical and Hellenistic Greece as evidence for market behaviour

In contrast to arguments about the Roman world, the economies of Greek cities, monarchies, leagues and empires throughout the Classical and Hellenistic periods are not assumed to have been connected by a network of interdependent price-setting markets. Starting with Moses Finley, who never addressed trade and exchange explicitly, the model of fragmented economies dominates modern interpretations of the economy in the eastern Mediterranean from the Archaic to the Hellenistic period. Since the work of Finley, models of trade and marketing have become more refined, paying attention to circulation patterns of coinages and goods, as well as to the political conditions under which regional and interregional exchange networks could emerge.[66] Thus in his influential analysis of the economy of Hellenistic Delos, Gary Reger argued, contrary to Rostovtzeff and Heichelheim, that local and regional supply rather than Mediterranean-wide market integration accounted for price movement in Delian prices.[67] The island of Delos was not a large-scale importer of grain from distant locations, but drew most of its imported grain from the immediate neighbourhood in the Cyclades. Only in exceptional circumstances was grain imported from greater distances. Changes of levels in price, moreover, could be explained by the changing political alliances of the island with nearby Athens and Rhodes. Prices of different goods in Delos did not rise and fall at the same time and do not suggest any form of economic cycles affecting the Hellenistic economy as a whole. In the wake of Reger's work, Greek economic historians have looked more intensely for regional economies which were partially and temporarily interconnected. The plural of the term refers both to different levels of the economy (according to commodities, social groups, consumption habits, transport patterns and modes of transaction) and to different economic zones created mostly, though not exclusively, by political, economic and monetary exchange.

One such economic zone was the Delian League, more aptly called the Athenian Empire here. The League not only was a tributary system that mobilized goods and money, but it also created a dominant political and economic centre of consumption, a dominant coinage, and a legal infrastructure that facilitated trade and exchange within and beyond the Empire.[68] The spread of Athenian coinage and its imitations as far away as Arabia and Egypt demonstrates the geographical dynamic of the economy of Athens.[69] Unfortunately, we lack the data to analyse the effects this dynamic had on the formation of prices in the Aegean. It has been argued, however, that the Athenian Empire was only one of many larger and smaller political alliances that created favourable conditions for cohesive regional economies. Armin Eich, for example, has collected a number of cases for what he calls 'small empires'. Small empires were characterized by economic integration created and maintained by the dominance of one political centre.[70] One such centre was fifth-century BC Thasos which dominated the region of its own hinterland and that of the Thracian mainland. Olynthus on the Chalcidice was another centre controlling a larger region in its neighbourhood. Corinth in the late fifth century BC was an example of a mother town exerting economic control over a number cities along the south coast of Aetolia up to Corcyra. In all these instances, the formation of a regional economic zone was a side effect of political alliance or dependence.

Other regional economic zones have been identified by their use of a common coinage or coin standard. Once again, the case of Athens during the time of the Athenian domination in the fifth century BC is the most prominent case. Arguably, the dominance of Athenian coinage during the time of the Athenian League developed for both political and economic reasons.[71] Andrew Meadows, moreover, has noted the spread of the Chian coin standard in the first half of the fourth century BC. This seems to have been initiated in the first instance by a political alliance which the Chians had formed with some towns on mainland Asia Minor.[72] Several towns, including the cities of Chios, had minted shortly after the end of the Peloponnesian War a common coinage minted with the letters ΣΥΝ (['coin'] of the *syn*[*machoi*]'). One side of the coin had a common design, the type of the other was chosen by each member town individually. The weight of the standard coinage was carefully chosen, for it was equal to 3 Chian drachmas and 2 Persian *sigloi*. The linkage of a region by a unified coinage seems to have been hugely successful, for soon after the issue of the alliance coinage a large number of surrounding cities adopted the Chian standard. Before the alliance coinage, the Chian standard had been used just locally by Chian cities; after the alliance coinage it is attested by coinages of fourteen towns in an extensive region along the coast of Asia Minor. By 375 BC the royal mints of the western Persian satrapies joined in. Some 1,000 coins deposited in a hoard at Halikarnassos in 341 BC were all coined on the Chian standard. Similar economic dynamics behind the use and circulation of coinage have been observed by Meadows in places under changing political domination. The city of Arados in Phoenicia interspersed its own coinage (posthumous Alexander coins) with imitations of Ptolemaic tetradrachms minted on the Ptolemaic standard. There was no political reason to do so. The imitations seem to have circulated in the second century BC in Phoenicia and Palestine, although the regions were then under Seleucid control. As Meadows suggests, the Seleucid kings from Antiochus V onwards were complicit in the maintenance not just of the Ptolemaic weight standard in this part of their realm, but also of recognizably Ptolemaic coin design.[73] There is little reason to doubt that they did so because the Ptolemaic coinage was the most acceptable in this economic zone. Yet once again, the effects of such coin networks, and the economic zones they reflect, cannot be related to extant price developments. So, while we have persuasive evidence against the notion of fragmented coinages prohibiting the formation of larger economic regions, we cannot demonstrate how the formation of such regions influenced price formation in the Greek world.

Another way of explaining price formation has been suggested by the quantity theory of money. Alain Bresson argued that the volume of money in circulation was an important influence on price levels, explaining variation both in the long term and in particular instances. The impact of the quantity of money could, first, be observed by the general rise in prices across commodities and wages towards the middle of the fifth century BC in Athens. It was caused by a demonstrably greater degree of mint output in Athens after 479 BC. There was, second, a decline in prices during the last quarter of the fifth century BC when coinage literally ran out at the end of the Peloponnesian War. The price cycles correlate clearly with the rise and decline of mining activities at Laurion in the course of the fifth century BC.[74] More dramatic were the effects of coin input on prices when the Achaemenid royal treasury was seized by Alexander the Great and minted into coins. It has been calculated that between the 320s and 294 BC 180,000 talents of silver equivalent rapidly bought into circulation some 200,000 talents of new silver coinage.[75] Bresson suggests that the drop of prices on Delos in the post 290s BC were the visible signs of the effects of the change in monetary quantity during the previous years. At that time, Bresson suggests, price levels went back to normal as the new level of coin input had gradually been absorbed by the costs of warfare. Prices on Delos climbed again at the beginning of the second century BC, which Bresson explains by Roman coinage arriving in the eastern economy.[76]

Bresson's argument shifts the question of price formation from the growth of markets to the question of the purchasing power of the people participating in markets. It rightly draws attention to the effects of increasing coin input in economies with a limited level of monetization (a question also addressed by Keith Hopkins in relation to the Roman world).[77] Problems arise when we attempt to link evidence for increasing mint output (or mining) with extant price data. As we saw above, even our best series of price data are circumstantial, isolated, or rhetorical. Volumes of money might reasonably be linked to evidence for changing levels of standardized or fixed payments (such as public wages, taxes, penalties, or army pay). The procedure becomes problematic if we try to correlate them with price variation which can be explained by many other possible causes.[78]

Most likely to be flawed is the argument by Hélène Cadell and George LeRider who explained the price increase in Egypt at the end of the third century BC by applying the quantity theory of money. Cadell and LeRider suggest that the amount of royal donations to soldiers after the battle of Raphia (attested by Polybius and the so-called Raphia decree), combined with (assumed) grain shortage due to the demands by the Ptolemaic army during the fourth Syrian War, created an oversupply of coinage which the economy could not absorb.[79] This caused inflation and subsequently the monetary changes in Egypt described above. However, real inflation cannot explain why, as noted previously, prices increased rhythmically and in recognizable steps over a period of 100 years. Moreover, it is now certain that only prices reckoned in bronze coinage were affected by the increase, while the value of silver coinage remained fairly unaffected.[80] It can also be asked whether coined money had the same effects on prices as in fully monetized economies, given that grain remained an important means of payment long after coinage was introduced for use in (some parts of) the economy of Egypt.[81] Thus, while we cannot exclude the possibility that changes of volumes of money in circulation were major factors for changes in price levels, both temporarily and in the long term, we are lacking the data to prove that link empirically.

My conclusions, therefore, are quite pessimistic. Extant prices cannot tell us much about the nature of markets and price formation in the Classical or Hellenistic world, despite the fact that they may well have been influenced by changing intensities of trade, greater interdependence of (some) markets, variable consumption patterns, volumes of money in circulation and so on. Some general observations can still be made. Firstly, there were strong notions of 'normal price' for grain which were different in different economic zones and under different economic circumstances. In the city of Athens, the idea of normal price in local markets and places of exchange ranged between 5 and 6 dr./*med.*; on Delos, normal prices seem to have been in the range of 6–10 dr./*med.* according to season. In the *chōra* of Ptolemaic Egypt wheat prices of 2 to 2.5 dr./*art.* seem to have enjoyed some official backing, and are likely to have affected prices in interpersonal exchange. In first-century BC Sicily, the equivalent of 2.5 to 3 dr./*art.*, too, seems to have been regarded as normal (Table A8.10 no. 15b). Such regional stability of price expectation over several generations, and even centuries, suggests a large degree of institutional pressure and little impact of changing economic trends and market forces.

We can observe, secondly, that massive deviations from normal price levels were frequent, both within and between regional economies (as can be seen especially from Table A8.10 and Table A8.11). If we can assume that multiples of normal grain prices were, and could be, paid by some people, we can assume that the distribution of grain during periods of shortage was a social rather than an economic problem.[82]

Monetization and coin circulation, thirdly, played a major role both for the formation of regional notions of 'normal price' and the formation of interdependent economic regions. It is likely, although it cannot be proved, that grain prices consolidated across the territory of Egypt as coined money became the main unit of account and means of payment in public and private transactions. Equally, the Athenian currency standard, represented by Athenian and posthumous Alexander coinages, created larger monetary networks and thus a greater degree of comparability of prices across regions. This may have affected, in particular circumstances, price formation according to accepted norms. We might speculate, for example, that the similarity of 'normal price' in rural Egypt and Sicily during the Hellenistic period was the result of close political and economic connections between Sicily and the Ptolemaic Empire, which is also reflected by imitations of Egyptian coin designs on Sicilian coinage during the third century BC.[83] I would suggest, however, that market development in the Classical and Hellenistic world should continue to be studied in relation to the formation of economic zones resulting from political alliances, leagues and empires, and the development of monetary networks that both went alongside political connections and outlived them in the long term. Within the economic zones thus identified, we need to address the question of the social composition of markets: which social groups participated in the monetized exchange of grain, and what people influenced the demand for grain in local market places? Who benefitted from official price regulation, grain donations and grain funds, and for whom were these measures designed? Did the range of people benefitting from grain at reduced price increase during the Hellenistic period, as a greater social range of people entered the market as a result of increasing monetization? And how much did changes in numbers and social composition of participants in monetized market exchange affect the economy of food distribution as a whole? These questions, though crucial for understanding of the role of markets in the ancient economy, cannot be analysed on the basis of price data.

Grain prices and their variability in the Roman world, 250 BC to AD 750

Dominic Rathbone

Grain prices in the Roman world: the data

In contrast to ancient Babylonia, we have remarkably few grain prices from the Roman world. That has not deterred scholarly interest, and it is reasonable to wonder whether anything new and sensible is left to be said. In this part of our chapter I outline what price data we do have and review the main recent discussions of the nature of the grain market or markets in the Roman world. I then re-assess the data newly collated in our tables, first by drawing out the main patterns and trends in the data, then by examining local price variability in more detail. Lastly I sum up what this new collation and assessment of the price data and their variability can tell us about how free and how integrated the grain markets of the Roman world were, and whether this enables us to assess Roman market performance.

My Roman world ranges across the millennium from roughly 250 BC to AD 750. It comprises two main chronological and geographical components: the last two centuries BC in which Rome gradually conquered the Mediterranean area and, continuing into the first century AD, much of central Europe, and the first to fourth centuries AD through which, despite crises, the Roman Empire flourished. With the aim of providing some link through to the mediaeval data presented in other studies in this volume, it also includes the fifth-century AD transition in the west, and Egypt under Byzantine into Arab rule. Politically in the two main periods Rome had an oligarchic government, dominated by the senate in the Republic and an emperor in the Principate (first to third centuries AD), with administration mostly devolved to the governors of provinces and the local councils of landowners which ran the cities-cum-territories, the basic social and administrative blocks of most of the Empire, although the fourth-century AD government was arguably more centralized and bureaucratic. Militarily Rome was the dominant power throughout; only on her eastern frontier did she face another complex imperial state, the Parthians and then Sassanians, in a stand-off punctuated by futile wars.

However, within these broad chronological and geographical parameters there are enormous variations in the survival of price data for grain. I begin with 250 BC because there is no earlier reliable grain price of any sort for Rome and Italy, and from then to around AD 500 we have just over thirty prices for the whole western empire (Table A8.10).

For Rome itself we have only two or three market prices of wheat (nos. 4, 13, 17), all from episodes of acute shortage – in 211/0 BC, around 100 BC (if I am right that this reflects the contemporary experience of the writer of the annalistic account followed by Dionysius, rather than being pure invention), and AD 6. From Pompeii, which has proved a big disappointment as a potential source of price data, we have just a couple of graffiti of uncertain interpretation (no. 21). Otherwise for Rome and the west we have nine cases of state-subsidized prices, including four sales of surplus state stock in the period 203 to 196 BC and the token price set for the monthly grain ration (*frumentatio*) to resident adult male citizens instituted in 123 BC, which lasted, with a gap, until the ration was made free in 59 BC (nos. 5–8, 11, 14, 20; cf. 1, 18). Other prices for Italy and the west are a mixed bag: three probably rhetorical prices to illustrate the fertility of the past or particular regions (nos. 2, 9–10), a handful of prices relating to shortages (nos. 3?, 19, 22, 25–26), and two moralizing literary passages (nos. 12, 24). More useful is the group of market and state purchase prices given by Cicero for Sicily in the 70s BC (nos. 15a–c), although we have to beware of some misrepresentation to strengthen his prosecution of the governor Verres for extortion. Our single documentary price comes from the northern frontier of Britain around AD 100 (no. 23), the north-west limit of the Roman world. For late antiquity we have four prices of disparate type and reliability (nos. 27–30).

The eastern Greek-speaking half of the Empire, leaving aside Egypt, is no better. From the period of conquest we have six documentary prices from Delos (Table A8.4 nos. 8–13; Table A8.5 nos. 16–19), and nine to twelve from elsewhere, of which ten relate to local shortages (Table A8.11 nos. 9–17, perhaps also 6–8). For the first three centuries AD we have another eleven prices (nos. 18–28), of which seven are shortage prices, and then one set of shortage prices each of the mid-fourth and late sixth century AD (nos. 29–30). The only province of the Roman Empire from which we have a significant, if limited, corpus of grain prices attested in documents is Egypt. From the first three centuries of Roman rule we have over forty wheat prices or sets of prices from private sales, most of the second to third centuries AD, say one for every six years (Table A8.12). For the earlier part of this period we have seven penalty prices from contracts (Table A8.13), which I list for completeness since they are notional, not actual prices, and also, for the whole period over thirty prices charged by the state for converting wheat dues into cash (*adaeratio*) or paid as compensation for requisitions (Table A8.14), which give an indication of what the state deemed to be a fair average price. For the fourth century AD we have another 26 wheat prices, private and public, which I list separately in Table A8.15 because the new monetary system of that time experienced constant inflation. For the first to fourth centuries we also have around fifty barley prices from both private and state transactions (Table A8.16), which I list for completeness and also for use of the cases with contemporary wheat prices where the price ratio between the two grains can be established. Lastly, I give a summary of an ongoing study of the grain price data from Byzantine and early Arab Egypt, that is from the fifth to early eighth centuries AD (Table A8.17), which, along with the private prices from Ptolemaic Egypt (Table A8.6), enables us to set the Roman-period grain prices from Egypt in a long-term context. It must be noted, however, that even the Egyptian data are not abundant in comparison with later datasets, and are limited by region mainly to Middle Egypt. We have no grain prices from Alexandria, the second city of the Roman Empire, or the Delta, and only a few from Upper Egypt.

These, in sum, are the data on which the modern views, summarized in the next section, are or claim to be based; whether they are in fact sufficient to form a basis for empirical conclusions may be doubted, but any hypothesis about grain prices in the Roman world must at least be able to accommodate them.

Grain markets in the Roman world: previous views

Some interpretations of the grain market in the Roman world argue for a single unified market centred on Rome, some instead argue for unintegrated regional, or even local, markets, and some try to follow a middle way. The disagreement is symptomatic of, and often explicitly located in, a broader debate about the extent to which the Roman economy in general was unified, monetized, sophisticated, prosperous, productive and capable of growth. It may be noted that most ancient historians nowadays tend to favour the view that the Roman economy was relatively simple and undeveloped.

The most straightforward argument for a unitary market centred on Rome is that advanced by Kessler and Temin (2008), adapted for its place of publication to foreground the monetary unity of the Empire which is implicit in the market argument.[84] Their regression analysis of six pairs of contemporaneous wheat prices from Rome (in fact Rickman's estimates) and an overseas location purports to find a direct, statistically robust, correlation between provincial wheat prices and distance (as the crow flies) from Rome. Their explanation is that Rome's political and monetary unification of the Mediterranean created a scale and ease of trade sufficient to unify prices which were set by the city of Rome as the massive centre of consumption of the surplus wheat produced in the provinces. This explanation has been advanced before in more general terms, but also with more coherent historical and economic background, by Hopkins (1980; 1995/6) and Von Freyberg (1998). In his 1980 chapter, rewritten and nuanced in the 1995/6 version, Hopkins argued that in order to meet Rome's monetized fiscal demands, which were mostly disbursed on military expenditure in the frontier provinces, the inner ring of civilian provinces had to increase production to sell goods to Rome and its army and hence gain the money to pay their taxes. This created a single unified monetary zone and market in which 'Rome was at the peak of a pyramid of rising prices'.[85] Von Freyberg, like Temin an economist, has applied 'terms of trade', or 'comparative cost', analysis to the Roman economy. He argues that throughout the Principate capital was transferred to Rome and Italy, mainly by ever-increasing taxation and the central issue ('sale') of imperial coinage, also through private Italian acquisition of estates in the provinces, and because of the central location of most imperial demand. The net result was to depress provincial prices and raise those in Rome and Italy, giving provincial production a significant comparative cost advantage and causing Italian production to stagnate. The main earlier study of ancient Mediterranean grain prices (and other data), had reached the opposite conclusion: Heichelheim, like his contemporary Rostovtzeff, believed that the Hellenistic monarchies had created a world economy in and around the eastern Mediterranean before their conquest by Rome, but that a crisis in the late second century BC, followed by unrelenting Roman imperial exploitation, caused a long-term rise in prices, but not wages, and thus economic depression in the eastern provinces.[86]

The main counterblast to this view is Erdkamp (2005), a wide-ranging study of the production and distribution of grain in the Roman Empire, indeed the only monograph to date on the topic. Erdkamp's principal argument is that the grain market of the Roman Empire resembled that of pre-industrial Europe as interpreted by Persson (1999). A combination of heavy taxation, small and autarkic production units and limitations of information and transport meant that there was too little tradeable surplus for specialist merchants or an integrated market to emerge. Hence there was huge price variation caused by local shortages, which could only be palliated by intervention by the local, or sometimes the imperial, authorities. Overall Erdkamp concludes that lack of confidence in the food supply deterred investment of capital away from agriculture into industrial production, and thus inhibited economic growth. Silver (2007) accepts the general picture but disagrees on one important point: in his view it was the political readiness of the authorities to intervene, and to cut the profits of producers and merchants to the benefit of consumers, which had caused the problem by encouraging improvident consumption and discouraging speculative storage. In general terms Erdkamp's thesis is in the Finleyan tradition of an undifferentiated Graeco-Roman economy in which, despite urbanization, trade was marginal. An alternative tweaking of the Finleyan picture is Bang (2008), which imagines the Roman economy, vaguely on a model of Mughal India, as a patchwork of 'bazaars', by which he seems to mean unintegrated local markets dominated by small-scale exchanges often influenced by clientelism, with high price variability, because various material and institutional factors made interregional trade difficult.[87]

A sort of middle way is advanced, at least implicitly, by Garnsey (1988). The crucial points that he makes are that in peacetime there are few known cases of people suffering prolonged food shortages, let alone famine, and that, with the partial exception of the *annona* of Rome, the direct acquisition, shipping and distribution of grain by civic and imperial authorities was rare, and their interventions were typically limited to encouraging shippers or discouraging profiteering. It follows that the absence of serious crises implies a reasonably efficient market in grain, supported by official intervention on occasion. Lastly, returning to the price data, Bransbourg (2012) demonstrates that the price analysis of Kessler and Temin (2008) is statistically flawed because of weaknesses in the evidence and its interpretation.[88] He uses the model of eighteenth-century French grain prices to argue that price relativities in the Roman Empire too will have been determined primarily by the ease or difficulty of transport to and from any local area. Indeed he claims that if the reliable Roman prices are reworked to allow for real transport distances they imply that, while inland areas were essentially on their own, coastal areas near ports did to some extent belong to a unified grain market centred on Rome, although he also suggests that prices in the eastern Mediterranean were generally higher than in the west.

Such is the range of views on the grain market in the Roman world. It may be noted that of the studies cited above, only two (Kessler and Temin (2008), Bransbourg

(2012)) actually present and discuss some price data, and only Heichelheim had actually made a systematic collection of the data. The following section therefore starts with prices before looking at the wider background.

Towards a re-assessment I: main patterns and trends

With the exception of the Egyptian data, the grain prices we have from the Roman world are too few and mostly too rhetorical to be suitable for a straight statistical analysis. The extraordinary prices claimed for sales in cities under siege (Table A8.10 nos. 3, perhaps 4, 29; Table A8.11 nos. 1, 13) or armies in desperate situations (Table A8.10 nos. 16, 19; Table A8.4 nos. 16, 17) are probably mostly fiction – note the sale which is variously reported as of wheat or a rat (Table A8.10 no. 3) – but in any case these prices are of no significance for normal variability and are not discussed further here. Crisis prices in peacetime cited as justification for state intervention or private benefactions are also inherently suspect, but may give some indication of the upper parameters, whether real or imagined, of variability, so are discussed, mostly in the next section. In the search for chronological and regional patterns, it is safest to start with the better data, and then to see how far the rest can be sensibly related to them.

For the Republican period, that is the third to first centuries BC (before the annexation of Egypt), I start with the Greek cities of the eastern Mediterranean where the indications, though few, are consistent that 5 to 6 dr. per *medimnos* of wheat (40.8–48.9 g/hl) were seen as the usual market range (with a variation of plus/minus 9 per cent around the median price), and 4 dr. (32.6 g/hl) as cheap (Table A8.11 nos. 2, 3, 5, 6b, 8, 9, 10, 11, 14). This range of variation is implausibly low, and suggests that our evidence privileges normative prices.[89] The two recorded prices lower than 4 dr. are both benefactions in northern Greece, where we may suspect that the honorand was in fact trying to make a virtue out of having to dump surplus stock imported from the Crimea (Table A8.11 nos. 6a, 7). This normal price level of 5 to 6 dr. goes back to Athens in the later fifth to fourth centuries BC (Table A8.2). While in the Nile Valley of Ptolemaic Egypt (third to first centuries BC) the normal range of wheat prices was 1.5 to 3 dr. per *artaba* on the silver standard (13–27 g/hl), that is less than half the Greek level; but with a higher range of variation of 33 per cent around the median, the two prices we have from Alexandria (Table A8.6 nos. 2, 8), of 270 and 249 BC, equivalent to 43.5 and 48.0 g/hl, are both within the normal Greek range.

In Sicily, which bridged the Greek east and Roman west and was renowned for its grain production, the normal price range of wheat in the 70s BC according to Cicero (Table A8.10 nos. 15a–c) was between HS 2 and 3 per *modius*; allowing for Cicero's forensic exaggeration of Verres' extortion, and comparing the prices of HS 3, 3.5 and 4 set by the senate for as compensation for extra levies, I reckon the normal range was more like HS 2 to 4 (22.3–44.7 g/hl), with 33 per cent variation around the median price, in effect a range which straddled those of the Greek cities and lower prices probably found in the Po Valley and Spain (see below).

For Rome and the west in this period we have no straightforward market prices. As the second war against Carthage (the Hannibalic war) turned in Rome's favour at the end of the third century BC, the Roman state was able to draw grain from Italy, Sicily, Sardinia and Spain. In 203, 201, 200 and 196 BC the aediles (junior magistrates) at Rome sold off surplus tax wheat for 4 and even 2 *asses* per *modius*, that is 20.9 and 10.4 g/hl (Table A8.10 nos. 5–8). In 202 BC merchants importing wheat from Sicily and Sardinia, probably for the state, had to give it to the shippers to cover the transport costs (Livy *Ad Urbe Condita* 30.38.5). Since these aediles are not presented as populists, 4 *asses* must represent the low end of the normal market range, and I guess that the average market price at Rome in the earlier second century BC was around 6 to 8 asses per *modius*, that is 31.3–41.8 g/hl, a level just below the normal Greek range and equivalent to cheap prices there. In 122 BC Gaius Gracchus instituted a monthly wheat distribution (*frumentatio*) to citizens at Rome which lasted into the Principate. For the monthly ration of 5 *modii* he set a subsidized price apparently of 2 *den.*, that is 17.9 g/hl, which lasted, with some brief interruptions, until 59 BC when the distribution was made free (Table A8.10 no. 11). In relation to the *denarius* Gaius' rather curious price per *modius* of 6 1/3 *asses* (which is how the price was officially cited) was the same as the price of 4 (old-style) *asses* charged by aediles in 203 and 201 BC, and maybe also in some years after 196 BC; given Roman traditionalism, Gaius may well have deliberately adopted their price.[90]

Guesstimates of the market price of wheat at Rome in the late Republic usually suppose that it was about twice the Gracchan price, say around HS 3 per *modius*, that is 33.5 g/hl.[91] However it is hardly plausible that wheat cost the same at Rome as in Sicily of the 70s BC, and a substantial state subsidy is implied by political opposition to the *frumentatio* because of its high cost.[92] I suspect that the prices in the annalistic account of the supposed grain shortage in Rome in 439 BC (Table A8.10 no. 13) reflect late Republican realities, and that HS 8 per *modius* probably represents the higher end of the normal market range in Rome of around 100 BC.[93] If the normal market range at Rome was say HS 6 to 8 per *modius* of wheat, that is 67.0–89.3 g/hl – a guess which I feel more likely to be low than high – the Gracchan price was around a quarter to a fifth of the norm. Putting the above guesstimates together, wheat at Rome in the late Republic cost between 50 per cent and 100 per cent more than in the Greek cities of the time, and twice as much as it probably had at Rome in the early second century BC. This is not surprising given Rome's continuing overseas conquests and development into an imperial metropolis, and may well have been part of a general rise in costs at Rome over the second century BC, and increasing economic differentiation of rich and poor.[94]

The other prices we have for Rome and the west in this period are of little use. The price for 250 BC of 1 *as* per *modius* is an iconic one-for-one price to denote the mythical happiness of the good old days, as emphasized by Pliny's specification of *far* (emmer wheat), the traditional grain of antique Rome (Table A8.10 no. 2, cf. no. 1); this was again the message in 74 BC when the aedile Seius distributed wheat at 1 *as* per *modius*, which he might more simply have given out gratis (no. 14). Polybius' prices for wheat in the Po Valley and in western Spain around 150 BC (nos. 9, 10) are probably exaggerations to underline the fertility he is claiming for those areas; the first is the iconic 1 *as* per *modius* again, but the 2.5 *asses* per *modius* in Spain possibly represents the bottom end of the price scale in the western provinces (including northern Italy) before the second-century BC rise. The contextless citation of Lucilius (no. 12), lastly, is opaque; at a guess it might be a jibe about some magistrate's profiteering from the requisition or sale of Sicilian wheat (measured by the *medimnos*).

The few market prices we have for Rome and Italy in the first and second centuries AD point to a continuation of the late Republican price range, equivalent after AD 64 to 58.5–78.0 g/hl, although two Italian benefactions which use a new iconic one-for-one price of 1 *den.* per *modius*, that is 39.0 g/hl, suggest that prices in most of Italy were somewhat lower than at Rome (Table A8.10 nos. 20–2, 25). Two isolated texts give prices in Africa and Britain more or less comparable to those in Italy (nos. 23, 26). The data for the Greek east (excluding Egypt) in this period are thin and equivocal. The normal price at Pisidian Antioch is said to have been a very low 3 to 3.33 dr. per *medimnos*, that is 19.5–21.9 g/hl; in a shortage the Roman governor of the province ordered sales at 1 *denarius* per *modius* (i.e. 6 dr./*med.*), the new iconic 'good times' price (no. 20). Two other cases imply that 4 dr. per *medimnos* was, as in previous centuries, a low price (Table A8.11 nos. 18, 25), so the norm in the Greek cities may still have been 5 to 6 dr., now 32.5–39.0 g/hl. However, the wheat prices in Judaea and beyond of 1 to 4 *den.* per *se'ah* given by the rabbinic tradition (no. 24) look very high, even if we suppose the normal range was 1 to 2 *den.*, that is 39.0–78.0 g/hl, with 33 per cent variation around the median price.[95]

Middle Egypt under Roman rule provides us with just enough documented private and state prices to be reasonably confident about the normal parameters of wheat prices, although they are far too few to generate a graph of year-on-year variation. The private price data show two long central periods of stable prices of wheat. First, from the AD 70s to 160s the normal price fluctuated between 6 and 12 Alexandrian dr. per *artaba*, that is 13.0 to 26.0 g/hl, with a variation of plus/minus 33 per cent around the median price (Table A8.12 nos. 6–17). This is remarkably similar to the 'normal' private prices of the Ptolemaic period which fluctuated between 13.4 and 26.7 g/hl, with a variation of plus/minus 33 per cent around the median (Table A8.6, excluding nos. 1, 2 and 8 from Alexandria). The Arsinoite prices of AD 45–7 (nos. 4–5, cf. 1–3) are within this range, but followed a particularly poor inundation, which may suggest that wheat prices in the earlier first century AD were somewhat lower, as might also the handful of penalty prices in contracts (Table A8.13). The prices set by the state are also lower in the earlier period (Table A8.14 nos. 1–8), but for Middle Egypt, and indeed Upper Egypt too, from the AD 70s into the third century AD were mostly a standard 8 dr. per *artaba*, which was presumably reckoned to be a fair if lowish price since the state both 'bought' and 'sold' wheat at this price (nos. 9–28).

Second, from the AD 190s to around 270 private prices of wheat normally fluctuated between 12 and 20 dr. per *artaba*, that is 26.0–43.3 g/hl, roughly double the previous range, with a variation around the mean of 25 per cent (Table A8.12 nos.

18–43). Curiously, the price set by the state seems to have remained at 8 dr. until at least AD 216, after which we have no attested cases until the time of the next price rise. In the AD 270s the prices of wheat, both private and public, rose slightly then jumped to a new level some ten times higher at over 200 dr. per *artaba*, say around 27 g/hl, which probably lasted until Diocletian's replacement of the Alexandrian tetradrachm with his new imperial coinage in AD 296 (Table A8.12 nos. 43–4; 7.3 nos. 30–3). Private and state prices for barley in Egypt show a similar pattern: a stable normal range from the AD 40s to 160s, which doubled to another stable range from the AD 160s to around 270, followed by a leap to a new level in the AD 270s to 290s (Table A8.16 nos. 3–16, 17–25, 26–7). Indeed the same pattern is visible in prices of other goods in Egypt from horses to houses, and also in wages.[96]

Scholars are in general agreement that the doubling of prices in Egypt between the AD 160s and the 190s must be a result of the Antonine plague, although we lack evidence to explain quite how it happened and it is not yet certain whether, as one might expect from comparison with the Black Death, the real value of wages rose relative to prices. The more dramatic rise in the AD 270s looks to have been the result of Aurelian's coinage reform of AD 274/5 which re-tariffed the silver coinage. If the explanations for these two rises are correct, similar price rises should have occurred throughout the Roman Empire. The dire lack of price data elsewhere makes this impossible to prove, but there are two supporting indications. One is that military pay was probably doubled by Septimius Severus in AD 197, and then increased again by his successor Caracalla.[97] The other is the increases in the fee (*entagion*) paid by athletes and Dionysiac artistes for entry into their universal professional associations, which was set by imperial regulation and presumably was the same throughout the Empire: in AD 194 one athlete paid 100 *denarii* at Naples, and later another 50 *denarii* at Sardis (for a separate reason?); in Egyptian cities in AD 264, 266 and 274 three artistes each paid 250 Attic drachmas or *denarii*, while in 288 another paid 850 *denarii*.[98] One last observation, to be discussed further below, is that the much higher notional silver equivalent of prices in the AD 190s to 270s was in effect compensated for by the Roman state through debasement of the *denarius* (and Alexandrian tetradrachm) and then its replacement with the relatively lighter *antoninianus* (as discussed previously), while Aurelian's coinage reform possibly brought the notional silver equivalence of wheat prices back nearer to pre-AD 190 levels.

The fourth century AD in Egypt saw constant and steep monetary inflation evident in the prices of a wide range of goods including gold and silver bullion. There is no scholarly agreement on the causes of this unique phenomenon in Graeco-Roman history, although in my view the root of the problem was that the state started levying taxes in bullion, in effect refusing to take back its own coinage at face value.[99] In his Edict on Maximum Prices of AD 301 Diocletian had set a ceiling for wheat of 100 *den.* per *modius castrensis*, equivalent to 26.0 g/hl, and for barley of 60 *den.* (Table A8.11 no. 27), which appears to have been deliberately lower than the price then current in the Greek cities.[100] In Egypt one wheat price just before, and another probably soon after the Edict were lower (Table A8.15

nos. 1–2), three prices, one official, of AD 304 to 311 were exactly the prescribed maximum (nos. 3–5), and then inflation struck and continued through to the AD 360s or 370s when the gold *solidus* finally established itself as a fixed monetary standard and prices consequently stabilized (nos. 6–26). A similar pattern is evident for barley, with one lower pre-Edict price and inflation from AD 315/6 to the 380s (Table A8.16 nos. 28–46). Because the price of silver also changed, we can only calculate silver equivalents of wheat prices for which we have near contemporaneous silver prices (Table A8.15 nos. 3, 16, 20, 24): the overall range is roughly 20–40 g/hl, slightly under the normal range for the AD 190s to 270, but the high prices all come from one compilation, so perhaps the normal upper parameter was rather lower. The two prices in gold from the fourth century AD (nos. 15, 26) both imply much lower silver equivalents of 12–20 g/hl, much the same as the normal range in the AD 40s/70s to 160s. For what it is worth, the two fourth-century AD wheat prices we have outside Egypt, both in gold, suggest lower prices than previously in Africa and fairly standard prices in Syrian Antioch (Table A8.10 no. 27; Table A8.11 no. 29).

Finally, the preliminary data from Byzantine into early Arab Egypt, all now on the gold standard of the *solidus*, show that wheat was normally sold at 12 to 8 *artaba* per *solidus* in the fifth and sixth centuries AD, equivalent in silver to 13.9–20.8 g/hl, and in the seventh into eighth centuries AD was somewhat lower at 13 to 9 *artaba* per *solidus*, that is 12.8–18.5 g/hl (Table A8.17 nos. 1, 2). The two isolated indications we have of prices in Africa and Italy are comparable (Table A8.10 nos. 28, 30); the only other eastern data, which are from Edessa (Mesopotamia) give a higher than normal price equivalent to 25 g/hl (Table A8.11 no. 30).

The overall patterns of price ranges in the Roman world, expressed as grams of silver per hectolitre, are summarized in Table 8.2. A fundamental issue is the helpfulness or not of using this standardized equivalent calculated from the face value of the various types of ancient coins. The general picture from the Greek and Roman worlds is that the private use of coins at their face value, even in the context of noticeable state reductions of weight or fineness, was remarkably tolerant and persistent – as long as tax rates were not raised. Thus the weight reductions of the Attic-standard drachma in the early second century BC and again under Nero did not affect the normal price of wheat in the Greek cities. Continuing debasement of the Alexandrian tetradrachm from the AD 210s to 270s, eventually to a mere silver wash, which went far beyond compensating for the doubling of prices in the AD 160s to 190s, had no effect on the normal range of wheat prices in Egypt. On the other hand, there can be problems. The doubling of wheat prices in late Republican Rome and the doubling in Egypt in the AD 160s to 190s do not indicate real increases in the price of wheat within those contexts insofar as other prices and wages rose too. These changes in the level of equivalence have to be interpreted in their broader economic context. The rise in Egypt was probably part of an empire-wide phenomenon caused by the demographic shock of the Antonine plague, which was in effect compensated for by monetary debasement under Marcus Aurelius. However the rise in late Republican Rome really did mean, in my view, that wheat and other prices there rose in real terms relative to those in the Greek world because

Table 8.2 Normal ranges of wheat prices in grams of silver per hectolitre

Period	Rome and west	Greek cities	Middle Egypt
500–301 BC		41–49 (Athens)	
300–1 BC	*31–42*[a] (Rome 250–150)	41–49	13–27
	67–89 (Rome 100–1)		
	22–45 (Sicily 70s)		
AD 1–200	*58–78* (Rome)	*33–39*	
	40–50 (Italy, provinces)	39–78 (Judaea)	13–26 (from 40s)
190s to 274			26–43
270s to 290s			c. 27
301		26 (Price Edict)	
c. 310–380			20–<40
	25– ?[b] (Africa)	33–50[b] (Syria)	12–20[b]
401–600			14–21[b]
601–750			13–19[b]

Notes:
[a] Guesstimates in italics.
[b] Prices set in *solidi*.

of its development as an imperial metropolis. So too in late antiquity there was a real leap in the purchasing power of gold – compare, for instance, the iconic Principate price of 1 *den.* per *modius* (Table A8.10 nos. 22, 25; Table A8.11 no. 20), equivalent to 3.33 g gold per hl, with the comparably low late antique commutation price of 40 *modii* per *solidus* (Table A8.10 no. 28; Table A8.17 no. 1n), equivalent to 1.30 g gold per hl – which accompanied the emergence of a new socio-economic order.[101] The conversion procedure is generally useful if used with care; the fundamental problem in reconstructing the history of wheat prices in the Roman world remains the lack of basic data.

Admittedly it requires the eye of faith to discern patterns in the data in Table 8.2. The main developments I see are as follows. There was a relatively integrated and stable market in wheat in the Greek cities from the fifth to fourth centuries BC. In the third to first centuries BC Ptolemaic Alexandria became part of this market, although prices remained much lower in the Nile Valley; prices in the western Mediterranean to the second century BC were also lower. The late Republic saw a large rise in the price of wheat at Rome, while in Sicily prices varied between the traditional western lower level up to the Greek civic range. Through the first to third centuries AD, despite the slight initial drop in prices in early Roman Egypt, there was an increasing correlation of wheat prices throughout the Roman Empire. Out of the monetary inflation of the fourth century AD there emerged a new stable monetary system based on the gold *solidus*, and a new ratio between the value of wheat and precious metals, especially gold, to the advantage of those with money salaries and disadvantage of wheat producers.

The long-term trend over the third century BC to the third century AD to a more unified Mediterranean grain market was patently a result of increasing political and cultural unity, and hence monetary and general economic convergence, although it would take a book to argue the case properly. Of course the extent and depth of unification was conditioned by the three fundamental factors of transport links, agricultural productivity and consumer demand. The core zone was the coastal areas of the Mediterranean which were linked by shipping, the most efficient transport means of the time, although within this zone there will have been regional differences. Rome and its surroundings, to take the clearest example, where there was the greatest concentration of consumer demand and disposable wealth, always had higher than usual prices. Prices in inland areas will have depended on the balance between productivity and transport possibilities. For instance, it might seem surprising that wheat prices in inland Asia Minor should have been as low in Egypt where yields were at least double, but two ancient comments about prices in inland cities of Asia Minor point to the answer. In a speech in the AD 70s criticizing his fellow citizens at Prusa for a riot about the high price of wheat, Dio noted that the current price (no figure is given) was high but not disastrous and was the norm in cities elsewhere (i.e. on the coast); this recalls Cicero's observation in the 70s BC that Roman governors of Asia can profit legitimately from allowing Philomelium to commute levies of wheat due for delivery at the great coastal city of Ephesus to cash payments at the higher price that is normal at Ephesus.[102] Cicero claims that this is a general phenomenon in provinces like Asia and Spain which have extensive inland areas, in contrast to Sicily where no city is more than a day from the coast and the province therefore has a unified wheat market and price. In Egypt, conversely, the wheat price was driven down by the high yields but pushed up by the ease of shipping it down the Nile to Alexandria: hence, perhaps, the relatively high price variability in Ptolemaic and Roman Middle Egypt, oscillating between the opposite pulls of autarky and overseas export. Unfortunately our data leave us largely in the dark about wheat prices in continental European and the inland north African areas of the Empire which probably formed a number of sub-zones linked hierarchically, like Egypt, to the dominant Mediterranean price zone.

In view of the poverty of our data, it is worth noting the belief of Romans of the first to fourth centuries AD, and perhaps beyond, that the economy and markets of their empire were fundamentally unified. A prime example of this is the uniformity of the pay of soldiers and also, apparently, the prices at which their grain rations and other supplies were deducted from their pay. From Augustus to Domitian HS 240 was deducted from each legionary's annual salary, wherever he was stationed, to cover his monthly ration of five *modii* of wheat, – the iconic price of one *denarius* per *modius* which emerged in the Principate; when legionary pay was increased by a third in AD 85, so too, roughly, was the charge for wheat to HS 328 a year, a curious sum in that it implies a price of HS 5.47 per *modius*, which was probably a ploy to claw back some of the rise rather reflecting abandonment of the iconic price.[103] Another indicator of a general perception that the Roman Empire had an integrated market for wheat is that all the inscriptions and other sources from the Greek-speaking provinces outside Egypt cite prices in *denarii* although they used local measures and regional drachma-based coinages were still minted and widely used (Table A8.11 nos. 20–6). The most striking case, however, is the belief of

Diocletian and his officials in AD 301 that they could legislate maximum prices and wages for the whole Empire, or at least the eastern provinces. Whether or not this was sensible, I note only that they may have had empirical data on which to base their prices: in fourth-century AD Egypt we have evidence that the state collected and compiled monthly market prices of a set of goods from civic associations of traders (e.g. Table A8.15 nos. 20, 24; Table A8.16 nos. 35, 37), a practice which may have older roots. A hint of the same mentality in late antiquity is that the official commutation price for wheat publicized with reference to Africa in AD 445 is also attested in Egypt in AD 541 (Table A8.10 no. 21; Table A8.17 no. 1n).

As a coda to this section, the price ratio between wheat and barley deserves a moment's attention. A first point to note is the rarity of attested barley rices in the Roman world excluding Egypt: only three from Rome and the west (Table A8.10 nos. 10, 15b, 23), all in provincial contexts and cited alongside wheat, and only four from the Greek east under Roman rule (Table A8.11 nos. 18, 23, 27, 30), three along with wheat and one for barley alone. In the Hellenistic world, including Egypt, the most common official ratio between the prices of wheat and barley had been 5:3 (or 1.7:1), which is also the ratio used in Diocletian's Price Edict (Table A8.11 no. 27). In the Roman world lower ratios are attested only for Spain in the 150s BC and Edessa around AD 500 (Table A8.10 no. 10; Table A8.11. no. 30), both exceptional cases, and a couple of times in Egypt, although the most striking case of around AD 216/7 (Table A8.16 no. 20) may relate to exceptional state requisitions of fodder (see later in this chapter). Otherwise, through to the end of the fourth century AD the attested ratios range from 1.8 to 2.3:1 (Table A8.10 nos. 15b. 23; Table A8.11 nos. 18, cf. 21; Table A8.16). Conversely in later Egypt, the ratio for the fifth to sixth centuries AD is 1.5 to 1.6:1 and for the seventh to eighth centuries AD 1.4:1. The paucity of price attestations of barley compared to their frequency in the earlier Greek world and the low value of barley in relation to wheat imply that by the second century BC wheat had become the staple grain of the Roman world, and that supplies were normally adequate and reliable, so where once barley had been valued as a back-up if not alternative to wheat, its main function now, including in Egypt, was as a fodder crop (perhaps too because there were more horses in the Roman world). It is interesting, however, to note that after the socio-economic and monetary changes of the fourth century AD, barley gradually regained its relative value in Byzantine Egypt, which implies a return to barley as an alternative staple for human consumption.

Towards a re-assessment II: the causes and limits of variability

A major factor in the variability of wheat prices in the Roman world must have been the quality of the harvest. Ancient literature has many references to good and bad harvests, but specific examples with price data are few. The sources which do cite peak prices in shortages very rarely specify the cause (apart from the exceptional cases of cities under siege and armies in dire straits, which I am ignoring), which was not necessarily a poor harvest, and often we may suspect self-interested or sensationalist exaggeration of the peak price. In the Hellenistic and Roman worlds, excluding Egypt and leaving until later a few high prices caused only, it seems, by state action, four levels of unusually high prices can be distinguished. There are four extraordinary peak prices in the equivalent range of 390 to 650 g/hl, some eight to ten times the top of the normal range: at Erythrai c. 270–265 BC (perhaps in wartime), in Judaea in 65 BC (after a hurricane), at Thuburnica in the second century AD, and in Asia Minor around 312 AD (Table A8.11 nos. 4, 15; Table A8.10 no. 26; Table A8.11 no. 28). Then there is a group of six peak prices mostly in the equivalent range of 220 to 270 g/hl (but also 536 g/hl at Rome, and less at Edessa), around five to six times the normal highest price: at Olbia c. 225–175 BC (second phase of second shortage, probably exaggerated), at Arsinoe c. 125–75 BC, at Rome c. 130–70 (but price and context are dubious), across Sicily in 74 BC (due also to state intervention), in Greece in AD 49, and at Edessa c. AD 490–500 (Table A8.11 nos. 6b, 12; Table A8.10 nos. 13, 15a; Table A8.11 nos. 19, 30). Third comes a group of five peak prices in the equivalent range of 75 to 170 g/hl (and 246 g/hl at Rome in AD 6), around three times the normal highest price: on Andros c. 290–240 BC, at Olbia c. 225–175 BC (first phase of second shortage), at Rome in 211/0 BC (but also with warfare in Italy), at Rome in AD 6 (with big military preparations), and at Carthage in AD 366–8 (Table A8.11 nos. 3, 6b; Table A8.10 nos. 4, 17, 27). Lastly there is a group of three 'shortage' prices in the equivalent range of 30 to 50 g/hl which barely, if at all, exceed the normal highest price range: at Ephesus c. 300–275 BC, at Olbia c. 225–175 (first shortage), and at Sebastopolis c. AD 175–200 (Table A8.11 nos. 2, 6a, 25).

Only three cases give both the peak and the normal (or reduced) prices. In Olbia around 200 BC a high price of 97.8 g/hl later rose to 271 g/hl (probably exaggerated), which may represent the outcome of two poor harvests in a row (Table A8.11 no. 6b). In wheat-producing Sicily the poor harvest of 75 BC saw wheat soar to an amazing 223 g/hl, after which it took two decent harvests for prices to return to normal levels, but this was in the context of heavy supplementary levies by Rome, perhaps partly themselves a response to a poor harvest in Italy, which turned a local problem into a crisis (Table A8.10 nos. 15a–c, cf. 14).[104] Lastly at Edessa c. AD 490–500, in a more precarious natural environment, it took at least two harvests for prices to fall to the norm again after a severe shortage (Table A8.11 no. 30). Poor harvests could and did cause very sharp spikes in the price of wheat, typically of three to six times the normal top price, exceptionally (if these cases are not rhetorical exaggerations) of eight to ten times the normal price. However in almost every attested case the shortage was fairly swiftly resolved by the intervention of the state or an individual, and cases of a succession of poor harvests causing real hardship are very rare. Conversely some claimed 'peak' prices are so low that they must represent imagined or feared shortages, or even the dumping by 'benefactors' of surplus wheat stocks.

Documents from Roman Egypt also provide some price data for the effects of poor harvests, although with the local peculiarity that a poor or excessive Nile inundation around September gave clear warning of a poor harvest to follow in May. For example the doubling of the wheat price in an Arsinoite village over a few days in September AD 45 must reflect market reaction to a bad inundation in anticipation of a poor harvest in May AD 46; the price was still or again at a high level in December 46, but seems to have fallen in AD 47 (Table A8.12 nos. 4a–b, 5). A poor inundation in autumn AD 99 caused an anticipatory doubling to 16 dr. of the state purchase price for wheat in December AD 99, but this was only 25 per cent over the normal highest price, and by January AD 100 the state was again paying the usual 8 dr. (Table A8.14 nos. 10–11); the problem was known at Rome (a testimony to the diffusion of information) and lies behind the hyperbole in the younger Pliny's consular oration of summer AD 100 that Rome was feeding Egypt, in reality perhaps drawing less wheat from Egypt than usual.[105] Expectation of a poor harvest is again implied in a governor's edict of 18 December AD 191 that all private surpluses of wheat throughout Egypt should be registered and put on the market on pain of confiscation, and that 'nobody is to hide it away banking on opportunist prices'.[106] However the prices attested in January and February of AD 192 of 18 and 20 dr. are at the top of, but not above, the normal range for the period (Table A8.12 no. 18). An apparent run of poor inundations in the later 240s had more serious effects. An edict of 17 March AD 246, probably originating from the governor and affecting all Egypt, ordered the declaration of all private stocks of grain for compulsory purchase by the state at the price of 24 dr. per *artaba*, presumably for re-sale at that price or lower (Table A8.14 no. 29). This was an exceptionally heavy intervention: in AD 191, as at Antioch in 93/4 (though with a maximum price), sales had been left to the market. High private prices of wheat recur in AD 249 to 252 on a large estate in the Arsinoite nome before returning to more normal levels by June AD 253 (Table A8.12 nos. 30–4). The situation implies that a disastrous flood in September AD 245 followed an unusual run of poor floods, which meant that it took time to restore the reserves depleted in AD 246–7. This is the worst grain shortage attested in Roman Egypt, but it is worth noting that it was a period of slightly higher than average prices and that the highest price of 24 dr. was only 20 per cent greater than the top of the normal range. The relatively low spikes in crisis prices in Egypt compared to the Mediterranean world is striking. In part this may be because we are dealing with documents, not records which may have exaggerated shortages and their prices; in part it must be because considerable stocks, both private and public, were constantly held in the network of state granaries (there were private granaries too), and the early warning of a poor harvest given by the inundation allowed the state and private individuals to plan management of their grain stocks before the shortfall occurred.

Another factor which we would expect to have caused variability in wheat prices even in years of regular harvests is the seasonal cycle of lower prices after the harvest, when stocks were high and some producers needed to raise cash to pay taxes or rents or repay loans, with prices then rising through the year as stocks ran down before the next harvest. Occasional literary and documentary references to this phenomenon can be found, such as a July (early second-century AD) letter from an agent to a landowner in Egypt reporting that he could not sell wheat for more than 7 dr. per *artaba* (Table A8.12 no. 9).[107] For most of the Roman world, unlike Hellenistic Babylon, we have no month-by-month price data, and very little even from Egypt. For the AD 40s to 160s we have 14 wheat prices dated by month (four months do not occur), and for the AD 190s to 270 we have 42 prices covering all twelve months. Bar-charts of the average price per month in these two periods show no meaningful pattern – the highest average prices in the later period occur in November and the harvest month of May. If the charts were printed here, they would only illustrate the statistical inadequacy of the data. However there are clues that if we had more data we would see a seasonal pattern: for instance the lowest prices in the early third-century AD Pakysis archive do fall around the wheat harvest (Table A8.12 nos. 24a–b).

Some price variability might also be expected according to type of sale, but even in the Egyptian data this is hard to discern because most of our prices come from the documents of medium to large estates and represent the 'farmgate' prices at which they sold smallish quantities of wheat to outsiders and their own staff. Large wholesale deals and petty retailing are both underrepresented. There are two relatively large sales, of 77.7 *artaba* in 5 BC and over 350 *artaba* in AD 138/9, where the fractional unit price implies a bulk discount (Table A8.12 nos. 3, 11). The private accounts of Kronion at the village of Tebtunis in AD 45–6 show that in retail sales of wheat, minor price adjustments were neatly achieved by varying the amount of wheat sold per silver tetradrachm (Table A8.12 nos. 4a–b), as in Hellenistic Babylon. Otherwise the Egyptian wheat prices display a curious roundness. In the AD 70s to 160s all but two of the prices across the range of 6 to 12 dr. are in round drachmas, and the state mostly paid 8 dr. (two tetradrachms) per *artaba*. In the AD 190s to 270 almost all wheat prices, apart from a couple of cases at 18 dr., are stepped at tetradrachm intervals, so that the normal range comprised only three prices: 12, 16 and 20 dr., extending to a shortage price of 24 dr. The extent of variability had declined too: whereas in the AD 70s to 160s it had been plus/minus 33 per cent around the median price, in the AD 190s to 270 it was 25 per cent. My guess is that this crude price-stepping may have benefitted consumers rather than producers (by pressure to round down rather than up), but that the ability to maintain it does imply a stable wheat market limited by broad consensus and with good information about other areas. Overall the wheat prices from Roman Egypt imply an integrated and increasingly stable provincial market, with distinct wholesale and retail levels, in which the state was an important but largely reactive participant, where public and private systems of distribution (taking advantage of the Nile) and storage (the network of state granaries) to a considerable extent were able to even out variations in production, and more so in the third than in the second century AD.

Price variability in the Roman world was also affected for worse or better by the Roman state. The violent imperial expansion of the Roman Republic, with enforced diversions of food supplies to its armies and the city of Rome, must have often disrupted local wheat markets although documented cases are sporadic.[108] The relatively high grain prices on Delos from 190 to 169 BC (Table A8.4 nos. 8–13; Table A8.5 nos. 16–19) presumably reflect that it was a major base for the contractors (*publicani*) who supplied the Roman armies then operating in the eastern Mediterranean. In 74 BC the wintering of a Roman fleet at Epidaurus exacerbated a mild local shortage (Table A8.11 no. 14). In the same year supplementary

Roman levies in Sicily turned a local shortage into a crisis; however, the imposition of a second tithe to supply the revival of public grain distributions at Rome in 73 BC does not seem to have caused particular problems, even if grain prices might have been lower without it (Table A8.10 no. 15a–c). In the Principate such ad hoc exactions were replaced by a more regular system of taxation and purchases to supply the now capped grain distributions at Rome and the now standing army, but occasional imperial tours and major campaigns still caused disruption. One factor behind the high prices in Rome in AD 6 must have been the diversion of supplies to Tiberius' grand army in the Balkans (Table A8.10 no. 17). One of the peacetime visits of Hadrian and his entourage to Sparta in either spring AD 125 or autumn 128 was probably the cause of a serious spike in the local price of wheat (Table A8.11 no. 22). The extraordinarily high wheat and barley prices in a set of early third-century AD accounts from Egypt similarly must reflect Caracalla's visit to Alexandria in December AD 215 to March 216, followed in 216/7 by special levies of supplies, including barley for fodder, for the invasion of Parthia on which he died in April AD 217 (Table A8.12 nos. 24a–b; Table A8.16 nos. 20a–b). Lastly, there is the emperor Julian's own account of the surge in the local price of wheat when he was wintering at Antioch in AD 362/3 prior to his own fatal Parthian campaign, in which he rails indignantly at local profiteering despite his specially organized extra imports (Table A8.11 no. 29).

In the more regular system of the Principate there was an imperial food supply administration (*annona*) whose basic aim was to supply an annual ration of 60 *modii* of wheat, somewhat more than an adult male needed, to 200,000 ticketholders at Rome and some 350,000 to 400,000 soldiers. The *annona* dealt also in other goods, such as wine, olive oil and fodder for the imperial court, provincial officials and their staffs and the armies. Much of this was purchased at set, but not unfair, prices in the provinces.[109] The *annona* had no transport division but contracted private shippers who were given various status and fiscal inducements to commit to five-year contracts with the state. In theory these needs were to be supplied by the annual tax on arable land in the provinces which was normally assessed in wheat. However, it could be (assessed and) paid in other crops or even cash at a price set by the state – as attested, for instance, in Sicily in the 70s BC (Table A8.10 no. 15a–b) and in Egypt (Table A8.14 *passim*).[110] The frequent use of compulsory purchase of wheat, best attested in Egypt but also known in other provinces, implies that the state often failed to meet its target for wheat to be acquired by taxation. Conversely, the overall target of the *annona* apparently included a generous safety margin, for there is evidence that its centralized stores at Rome and Alexandria, for instance, had surplus wheat to sell on the market, including to cities in the Greek east suffering shortages and to individual citizens at Rome.[111] In effect state taxation in grain and storage of stocks and the system of the *annona* provided a safety blanket in wheat supplies across the Empire, reinforcing in a practical way the government belief in a unified market and a fair universal price level, and also subsidized private shipping on the main Mediterranean supply routes and land transport to the frontier garrisons, thereby encouraging cross-Empire trade in other goods.

State intervention also occurred at civic level. The common concern of imperial and local officials in a highly urbanized and civilian society with a strong civic ideology was that their cities, the embodiment of their regime, should appear prosperous and happy, and that meant avoiding severe food shortages which might provoke unsettling riots by aggrieved citizens. In the Greek east, in the 'democratic' tradition modelled on Athens, cities appointed special officials (*sitōnai*), sometimes backed by earmarked funds, to resolve bad shortages.[112] In the Roman-style municipalities of the Latin-speaking centre and west, a more oligarchic tradition instead empowered town councils to punish any attempt to force up prices (and clearly this primarily meant grain prices) by heavy fines: this clause, which almost certainly derived from Augustus' law about the food-supply (*annona*) of 18 BC, is found in the standard constitution granted to the towns of Spain by the Flavian emperors, and was probably in every western municipal charter.[113] The two different approaches share a common presupposition that normally the free market should work and that when it did not, this was often caused or exacerbated by large landowners and merchants trying to profiteer. They also share the same fundamental weakness that the civic officials were drawn from the very landowners and investors in commerce who were seeking to profit from grain sales. Hence sometimes, as at Pisidian Antioch in AD 93/4, the local elite was unable to achieve a solution by internal consensus and had to take the embarrassing step of calling in the Roman provincial governor to enforce one (Table A8.11 no. 20). This and the two attested cases from Egypt of intervention by the governor in AD 191 and 246 (see above) reveal that the imperial administration had devised a standard play-book for the situation: make all large landowners declare their wheat stocks immediately and put their surpluses on sale by a set date; if necessary, set a maximum price, and even buy stocks at it.

It is worth noting the ideological limits to state intervention. The political elite of the Roman Empire, to a man large landowners and investors in commerce, were perfectly aware of the economic downside of over-intervention. At Antioch in AD 93/4 and Egypt in 246 the governor took pains to fix a price which would still give landowners a reasonable profit. So too the emperor Tiberius, when obliged to set a maximum price for wheat at Rome in AD 19, paid compensation to merchants (Table A8.10 no. 18). The founder of the Principate, Augustus, is cited approvingly by Suetonius, writing under Hadrian in the earlier second century AD, for his attitude: Augustus apparently recorded that he had only retained the *frumentatio* at Rome for political peace, and tried to manage it with farmers and merchants in mind, presumably referring to his strict restriction of the number of entitled recipients; he also once flatly refused a demand to subsidize wine, telling the protestors that Rome's aqueducts supplied plenty of water.[114] In contrast, Commodus is criticized for the so-called Golden Age he proclaimed following the grain shortage at Rome in AD 189: 'he ordered low prices, by which he created a greater shortage'.[115] Only in the late third century AD, after his failed coinage reform, did the emperor Aurelian start providing subsidized wine and meat to the populace of Rome. The farmers' lobby is neatly represented to us by an epigram written around AD 102/3, under the populist emperor Trajan, by Martial, himself a modest landowner: 'Wine sells for twenty *asses* and wheat for four: drunk and stuffed, the farmer is broke' (Table A8.10 no. 24).[116] The Romans knew full well that golden age iconic prices were good politics and poor economics.

Some conclusions

My analysis of the attested prices of wheat in the Roman world, thinly grounded and speculative as it is, raises doubts about some previous views of the grain market in the Roman world. The thesis of Kessler and Temin (2008) just does not fit the Roman data as a whole (while the selective figures it uses are seriously flawed), at least in the simplistic form in which it is presented. Like the thesis of Hopkins (1980; 1995/6), it attributes too much influence to the market of the city of Rome, and ignores the regional pull of other great cities such as Carthage, Alexandria and Syrian Antioch. The Von Freyberg (1998) thesis works well as an explanation for the rise in prices in Italy in the second to first centuries BC, when we know that huge quantities of booty and indemnities were drained from the east to Rome, although it ignores the economic dislocation that Roman aggression caused in the east. Both Hopkins and Von Freyberg exaggerate the fiscal suction of Rome in the Principate, granted the empire-wide dispersal of Roman troops and officialdom, and the probability that well over half of Roman taxation (which did not in fact increase) was recycled in the provinces rather than flowing to Rome, so that there was much less capital transfer than Von Freyberg imagines. Archaeological evidence, incidentally, now suggests that Italy did not stagnate, while the provinces which did demonstrably benefit from the comparative cost advantage were the western ones of Africa, Spain and southern Gaul. The regularized Roman taxation of the eastern provinces in the Principate was much less draining than the arbitrary levies which had been made in the Republican period of conquest, and these provinces had enough urbanization and internal capital transfer of their own not to need the stimulus of the city of Rome. Conversely, the thesis of Erdkamp (2005) and others that a restricted market in grain is indicated by the high variability of wheat prices in the Roman world (which Erdkamp asserts without demonstration) raises questions as to how we judge 'high' both across time and across space. Where we do have some evidence, we find fairly compact normal ranges of wheat prices, perhaps increasingly so in the third century AD. The short-term crisis prices which dominate our data precisely because they were abnormal and hence worth recording, and even exaggerating, are exceptions to and not part of normal variability. The probability that the Roman world had distinct zones, and even sub-zones, of different normal price ranges is not incompatible with an overarching integrated market, once production and transport costs are taken into consideration.

We also need to put Roman wheat prices in their wider economic context, as do scholars such as Erdkamp and Bang, who use broad considerations to create their arguments that the free market in wheat – or indeed any other good they discuss – in the Roman Empire was small and unintegrated. Erdkamp, for example, asserts that wheat was the main staple crop and food of the Roman Empire. Many farms were small and from partially to near fully autarkic. Much of the wheat surplus of the Empire was managed by the state, which acquired it through taxation to supply its armies, officials and capital city. In the Greek east, and perhaps the Latin west too, the actions of cities and individuals to acquire wheat for their urban populations further limited the market. Land transport was very slow and costly, which inhibited inland movement of bulky low-value goods like wheat. However, while these points are all to some extent true, they are all also open to qualification. Here I can only outline some salient points that a counter-argument might make. By pre-industrial standards, agriculture in the Roman Empire was relatively productive: yields were quite high, and many farms were large enough to produce regular surpluses. Agriculture was diversified, with important cash crops such as wine and olive oil and fodder crops to feed the probably historically high number of draught animals. The impact of the imperial *annona*, although significant because of its ubiquity, was restricted: it supplied regularly at most 25 per cent of the total wheat demand of the city of Rome, assuming one million inhabitants, and, adding in the armies, no more than 2 per cent of the Empire's total population of, say, fifty million. The number and capability of civic grain funds in the Greek east should not be exaggerated, and we know of no civic scheme with the regularity and scope of the *frumentatio* at Rome.[117] It should also give pause for thought that not a single grain fund or civic intervention has as yet been attested in the cities of Italy or the central and western Latin-speaking provinces.[118] While land transport was not easy, its costs have been exaggerated, and much of this Mediterranean-centred empire was within practicable carrying distance by cart or donkey to a navigable river or the sea.

In conclusion, various factors made the Roman world and economy of the first to third centuries AD different from ancient Babylonia on the one hand and early modern Europe on the other. The market in wheat in the Roman world was essentially a free market, which in the imperial period comprised and was influenced by the administered market of the imperial *annona* and civic interventions. Rome's achievement deserves recognition. For several centuries an urban population of around 30 per cent of the total – say some 15 million people, and more if we include the non-farming element in rural communities – was provided with a reliable supply of wheat at reasonable prices, at least in the main urban centres. It is striking that no serious food shortage at Rome is attested after AD 6 until the Antonine plague in the late AD 160s. That the wheat market was not entirely free is not surprising. Even in modern free-market economies prices of food and petrol are affected by political considerations. More positively, as Hopkins (1978; 74) once suggested, if urban consumers in the Roman world benefitted from state-influenced lowish grain prices, that increased their spending power on other agricultural and manufactured goods. Of course it might instead have depressed wages, but we know that urban and also rural consumption of wine, olive oil, clothes, jewellery and so on was relatively high, and indeed it was through viticulture, oleiculture and pastoralism, as well as investment in craft production and commerce, that the elite made and increased their wealth.

In my Roman world the structural problems common to pre-modern (or 'under-developed') economies which cause variability in wheat prices were all present: natural disasters, limited agricultural techniques, poor transport and rudimentary economic structures. They were exacerbated, at least potentially, by the particular socio-political feature of the conflict of interest within the civic elites of the Roman world who were both the main grain producers, and financers of its commerce, and the officials responsible for civic food supplies, a contradiction normally ignored by the central imperial government because of its reluctance to intervene, except when pushed, in the affairs of those local elites on whom it depended for everyday running of the Empire. However the emergence of a relatively integrated and effective grain market in the Roman world, compared to other pre-industrial economies, was due to distinct factors which stemmed from its political, cultural and economic unification of the Mediterranean and inland Europe. First, commerce over long and hence short distances was encouraged and facilitated and, connected to this, agriculture, transport and economic institutions were atypically developed and sophisticated. Second, the imperial government promoted and underwrote the dominance of a civic culture of entitlement which, despite the conflict of interest within the elite, in effect limited excessive profiteering, that is, profiteering which risked causing serious socio-economic disruption. The price inflation of the fourth century AD in the silver-bronze token coinage, never experienced before or after in antiquity, is one sign of a crisis in the traditional civic ideology and its essentially free-market economy. Out of this crisis emerged the much more differentiated social and economic order of late Antiquity, which privileged those who drew their revenues in gold coins – the state, the church, large landowners and the agents of this triad – and replaced the ideology of entitlement with one of charity.[119]

Overall observations

Sitta von Reden and Dominic Rathbone

Our chapter necessarily stresses the fragility of the ancient data, such as our lack of price data from the megalopolis capital of the Roman Empire, and the need to locate their interpretation within a wider socio-economic context (institutions and mentalities), because we wish to expose the dangers of a decontextualized simple quantitative approach. On the other hand, we have tried, with some success, to extrapolate from the data broad long-term patterns of grain prices in and across our worlds, and also to analyse variability in the few cases we have of rich local data. Attentive readers will note a certain difference of approach and tone between the sections on the Greek and Roman worlds. This does reflect some difference of attitude and emphasis between the authors, but also, we think, a real economic difference between the Greek and Hellenistic worlds (fifth to second/first centuries BC) and the Roman Empire of the Principate (first to third centuries AD). To some extent this was the result of a long-term process of market integration, roughly – and unsurprisingly – in step with political unification from the Greek city-states and Hellenistic kingdoms to the Roman Empire. It started before the Principate with Rome's imperial expansion under the Republic: for instance, while earlier second-century BC prices on Delos in general may reflect a fairly local market, the high wheat prices do show the growing impact of Rome and its market. Even in the Principate some regional diversity persisted: for instance, the continuity of price levels of wheat (in silver bullion) and of their range of variation from later Ptolemaic to earlier Roman Middle Egypt implies that this grain-rich zone managed to meet new Roman demands while maintaining its traditional price levels, in part because Roman demands were less than often imagined, and in part, we suspect, by increased productivity. However, some regional diversity is a feature of modern integrated economies too, and the apparent existence of price zones within the Roman Empire does not detract from its overarching integration, evident in the apparently universal doubling of prices after the Antonine plague.

Scholars have often criticized Moses Finley for lumping Greece and Rome together into a single 'ancient' economy, and this criticism is largely justified, especially from a quantitative and practical institutional standpoint: the institutional facilities of the Roman world, including production, transport, finance, security, and so on, were significantly more developed than the norm for pre-industrial societies. However, Finley's idea of the 'civic' nature of his ancient economy still has value: in our view it was the common Graeco-Roman civic ideology of entitlement which drove the limited but essential state support of and intervention in the mainly free market in wheat. The result was a level of market performance which made serious food shortage a very rare experience in peacetime, at least in urban centres – and by the Roman imperial age had made the supply of wheat so reliable that barley was reduced to a cheap fodder crop. The strongly normative feature of many of our attested grain prices, including the curious stepping of free-market prices in third-century AD Egypt, symbolizes the success of this market performance as well as the ideology which nurtured it. The contrast with subsequent developments – the extraordinary fourth-century price inflation in silver/bronze coin and the new price stability in gold coin which emerged from it as centralising institutions replaced civic culture – underlines the point. However, if the picture drawn here of market performance in the Roman Empire of the Principate is broadly correct, it is not really plausible, as the Persson (1999) thesis would invite us to consider, that Rome, at least, missed an industrial revolution for want of a sufficient agricultural surplus and a sufficient stability of food prices to facilitate industrial investment.

Appendix: Tables of data

Table A8.1 Multipliers for converting ancient grain prices into grams of silver per hectolitre

Region and period	Measures	× unit price	Multiplier
Athens and Greek world V–I BC (Tables A8.2, A8.3; A8.4, A8.5; Table A8.11 nos.1–17)	*medimnos* 53.0 l drachma 4.32 g	dr./*med.*	8.151
Ptolemaic Egypt 306 BC–I BC (Tables A8.6, A8.7, A8.8)	*artaba* 40 l drachma 3.56 g	dr./*art.*	8.900
Rome and Italy c. 211 to 157 BC (Table A8.10 nos. 4–8)	*modius* 8.62 l *as* 0.45 g (1/10 den. @ 4.49 g)	*as/mod.*	5.220
Rome and west 156–141 BC (Table A8.10 nos. 9–10)	*modius* 8.62 l *as* 0.39 g (1/10 den. @ 3.85 g)	*as/mod.*	4.524
Rome and empire 140 BC–AD 64 (Table A8.10 nos. 11–20; Table A8.11 no. 19)	*modius* 8.62 l HS 0.9625 g (1/4 den. @ 3.85 g)	HS/*mod.*	11.166
Rome and empire AD 64–c. 270 (Tables A8.10 nos. 21–26; Table 13 nos. 20, 24, 26)	*modius* 8.62 l HS 0.84 g (1/4 den. @ 3.36 g)	HS/*mod.*	9.745
Roman Empire in east AD 64–c. 270 (Table A8.11 nos. 21–23, 25)	*medimnos* 51.72 l drachma 3.36 g	dr./*med.*	6.497

Roman Egypt 30 BC–AD 64
 (Table A8.12 nos. 1–5;
   Table A8.13 nos. 1–4;
   Table A8.14 nos. 1–7)
	artaba 38.78 l
	 drachma 0.9625 g
	 (1/4 den. @ 3.85 g)
		dr./*art.*	2.482

Roman Egypt AD 64–274
 (Table A8.12 nos. 6–43;
   Table A8.13 nos. 5–7;
   Table A8.14 nos. 8–30)
	artaba 38.78 l
	 drachma 0.84 g
	 (1/4 den. @ 3.36 g)
		dr./*art.*	2.166

Roman Egypt AD 275–290s (Table A8.12 no. 44; Table A8.14 nos. 31–33)	*artaba* 38.78 l drachma 0.042 g (1/4 den. @ 20 to 3.36 g)	dr./*art.*	0.1083

Late Roman and early
 Byzantine Empire
 IV–VII AD
 (Table A8.10 nos. 27–30;
   Table A8.11 nos. 29–30;
   Table A8.17. no. 1n)
	modius 8.62 l
	 solidus 4.49 g gold,
	 ×14.4 = 64.60 g
	   silver
		sol./*mod.*	749.42

Byzantine Egypt late IV–early VIII AD (Table A8.15 nos. 15, 26; Table A8.17 nos. 1–2)	*artaba* 38.78 l *solidus* 4.49 g gold, ×14.4 = 64.60 g silver	sol./*art.*	166.58

Table A8.2 Wheat prices at Athens, fifth to fourth centuries BC

No.	Date	Price/medimnos or phormos	Price in g silver per hl	Reference	Notes
1	415	6 dr. 3 ob.	53.0	IG I³ 421.137	Public sale of confiscated grain
2	415	6 dr.	48.9	IG I³ 421.138	ditto
3	415	6 dr. 2 ob.	51.6	IG I³ 421.139	ditto
4	392	3 dr.	24.5	Ar. *Ecc.* 547–8; cf. Suidas *s.v. hekteus*	Comic figure?
5	Early IV BC	6 dr.	48.9	IG II² 1356.17, 21	Law concerning price at which wheat offerings were sold by temple
6	335	16 dr.	130.0	Dem. 34.39	Current price during shortage
7	334	5 dr.	40.8	Dem. 34.39	Price referred to as 'normal', 'established' or 'official' price (*kathestēkuia timē*)
8	c. 330	9 dr.	73.3	IG II² 408	Special price of imported wheat during shortage
9	330	5 dr.	40.8	SIG³ 304	Special price of imported grain during shortage
10	329/8	5 dr.	40.8	IG II² 1672.282–6	Account of the sale of wheat by the temple at Eleusis
11	329/8	6 dr.	48.9	IG II² 1672.282–6	ditto
12	324	5 dr.	40.3	IG II² 360	Honouring decree for a benefactor having provided grain at this price during shortage

Table A8.3 Barley prices at Athens (and elsewhere), fifth to fourth centuries BC

No.	Date	Price per medimnos	Price in g silver per hl	Reference	Notes
1	430	2 dr.	16.3	Plut., *Mor* 470F.	Evidence not contemporary
2	410/09	4 dr. and 6 dr. (Attic standard)[a]	35.3	[Arist.], *Oik.* 2.2.7 = 1347a33	Current price of *alphita* at Lampsakos; state orders merchants to sell it at 6 dr. to visiting fleet (state to take the 2 dr.)
3	Late V BC	3 dr.	24.6	*Gnom. Vat.* 495	Evidence not contemporary
4	400	4 dr.	35.3	Stratt fr.13 (Edmonds)	*phormos* used as measure
5	360	1 dr. 5 ob. 4 ch. (Aiginetan standard)	32.9	SIG³ 239B (= FD III 5.3) ii.1–22	*krithē* imported to Delphi sold at this price; 1 Aiginetan med. = 0.37 hl[b]
6	330	5 dr.	40.3	IG II² 408	Special price of imported grain during emergency; *krithas* restored
7	329/8	3 dr.	24.6	IG II²1672.282	Sale price of barley at Eleusis temple (cf. Table A8.2 nos.10 and 11)
8	329/8	3 dr. 5 ob.	31.2	IG II²1672.283	ditto

Notes:
[a] Lampsakos being an ally of Athens at the time, this price may have been expressed in the Attic standard.
[b] Garnsey (1988: 160) for the use of the Aiginetan medimnos here.

Table A8.4 Wheat prices at Delos, third to second centuries BC

No.	Date	Price in silver dr. per medimnos	Price in g per hl	Reference	Notes
1	282 (Jan.)	7 dr.	57.0	ID 158 A 37–38	Wheat for feeding or paying actors. (*technitai*)
2	282 (Feb.)	6 dr. 3 ob.	53.0	ID 158 A 39–40	ditto
3	282 (Mar.)	6 dr.	48.9	ID 158 A 41–42	ditto
4	282 (Apr.)	4 dr. 3 ob.	36.7	ID 158 A 42–43	ditto
5	282 (May)	6 dr. 5 ob.	55.7	ID 158 A 43–44	ditto
6	282 (Aug.)	7 dr.	57.0	ID 158 A 45–46	ditto
7	282 (Sep.)	10 dr.	81.5	ID 158 A 46–7	ditto
8	190 (Dec.)	10 dr.	81.5	ID 401, 22	ditto
9	180/179 (Dec./Jan.)	3 dr.	24.5	ID 442 A 100–106	Reduced price, Numidian donation
10	179 (Mar./Apr.)	4 dr.	32.6	ID 442 A 101	ditto
11	178 (Dec.)	10 dr.	81.5	ID 445, 13	Wheat for feeding or paying *technitai*
12	174 (Dec.)	11 dr.	89.6	ID 440 A 69	ditto
13	169 (Dec.)	10 dr.	81.5	ID 461 Bb 53	ditto

Table A8.5 Barley prices (*krithē* and *alphita*) at Delos, third to second centuries BC

No.	Date	Price in silver per medimnos	Price in g silver per hl	Reference	Note
1	282 (Oct.)	4 dr.	32.6	ID 158A 48	*alphita* for feeding *technitai*
2	282 (Nov.)	5 dr.	40.8	ID 158A 48–49	ditto
3	282 (Dec.)	5 dr.	41.3	ID 158A 49–50	ditto
4	258 (Feb.)	3 dr.	24.5	ID 224A 29	*krithai* for geese
5	250 (Jan.)	3 dr. 2 ob.	27.2	ID 287A 45	ditto
6	250 (May)	3 dr. 1 ob.	25.8	ID 287A 59–60	ditto
7	250 (June)	3 dr.	24.5	ID 287A 64	ditto
8	250 (July)	2 dr. 4 ob.	21.7	ID 287A 66	ditto
9	250 (Aug.)	2 dr. 2 ob.	19.2	ID 287A 67–68	ditto
10	250 (Sept.)	2 dr.	16.5	ID 287A 71	ditto
11	247 (Aug.)	2 dr. 3 ob.	20.3	ID 291b +55	ditto
12	247 (Nov.)	2 dr. 1.5 ob.	18.3	ID 291b +82	ditto
13	246 (July)	4 dr.	32.6	ID 290.82	ditto
14	246 (Oct.)	4 dr.	32.6	ID 290.97–98	ditto
15	224 (May)	2 dr.	16.5	ID 338Aa35	ditto
16	179 (Dec.)	4 dr.	32.6	ID 442A220	(*alphita?*) for feast
17	178 (Dec.)	3 dr. 5 ob.	31.2	ID 445.4–5	ditto
18	177 (Dec.)	4 dr.	32.6	ID 452.9	ditto
19	174 (Dec.)	4 dr.	32.6	ID 440A 62–63	ditto

Table A8.6 'Market' prices of wheat in Egypt, 330–30 BC

No.	Date	Price listed	Price in silver standard	Price in g silver per hl	Reference	Notes
1	320s	10 dr. (Attic standard)	10 dr.	107	[Arist.], *Oik.* II 1352b	Current price at which grain (*sitos*) was sold to exporters in the *chōra*
2	270	4 dr. 5 ob.	4 dr. 5 ob.	43.0	P. Hib. I 110.11	Market price of wheat in Alexandria
3	267	2 dr.	2 dr.	17.8	P. Hib. I 100.6	Receipt of wheat valued at this price
4	256 (Mar.)	2 dr. 5 ob.	2 dr. 5 ob.	25.2	P. Mich. Zen. 28	Bulk sales price of wheat in local harbour
5	254	1 dr. 1 ob.	1 dr. 1 ob.	10.3	P. Lond. VII 1974.38	Payment for *sitometria* grain[a]
6	c. 250	3 dr.	3 dr.	26.7	P. Lond. VII 1996.41	Price paid for wheat
7	c. 249	2 dr. 5 ob.	2 dr. 5 ob.	25.2	P. Lond. VII 2002.28	Payment for wheat
8	249	5 dr. 2 ob.	5 dr. 2 ob.	47.4	P. Cair. Zen. 59320	Price of grain (*sitos*) in Alexandria
9	Mid-III BC	3 dr.	3 dr.	26.7	P. Sorb. 33.15	Market price of wheat (letter)
10	Mid-III BC	1 dr. 3 ob.	1 dr. 3 ob.	13.4	P. Petr. III 47 (a).3	Payment for *sitometria* grain
11	Mid-III BC	1 dr. 3 ob.	1 dr. 3 ob.	13.4	P. Cair. Zen. 59698.5	ditto
12	III BC	2 dr.	2 dr.	17.8	P. Petr. III 80 (a) ii.15 f., 22	Wheat valued at this price paid into store
13	c. 220–204	7 dr. 3 ob.	?23 dr. 4.5 ob.	66.8/33.4	UPZ 149.24	Payment for fine bread (*kakis*) made from bread wheat[b]
14	?195	170 dr.	2 dr. 5 ob.	25.2	P. Köln V 217.6 ff.	Price of wheat sold
15	193/87	160 dr.	2 dr. 4 ob.	23.7	BGU VII 1536.3	ditto
16	193/87	155 dr.	2 dr. 3.5 ob.	23.0	BGU VII 1532.12	ditto
17	193/87	180 dr.	3 dr.	26.7	BGU VII 1532.13	ditto
18	158	400 dr.	1 dr. 5 ob.	16.3	SB V 7617.98	Payment for grain in Serapeion
19	131	400 dr.	1 dr. 5 ob.	16.3	SB VI 9420.6	Price of wheat in 'sale with deferred delivery'
20	118 (Mar.)[c]	1,200 dr.	2 dr.	17.8	P. Grenf. I 22.11	Price for wheat paid by local tax office

Table A8.6 Continued

No.	Date	Price listed	Price in silver standard	Price in g silver per hl	Reference	Notes
21	112 (Mar.)	1,200 dr.	2 dr.	17.8	P. Tebt. I 112.113	Price for wheat paid by local tax office
22	111	1,560 dr.	2 dr. 4 ob.	23.7	Botti, Test. Dem. 4 *r*	Price of wheat (Thebes)
23	?100	1,080 dr.	1 dr. 4 ob.	14.8	SB XVI 12675.16	Payment for wheat
24	99	1,680 dr.	2 dr. 5 ob.	25.2	P. Tebt. I 117.10	Payment for wheat
25	99	1,500 dr.	2 dr. 3 ob.	22.3	P. Tebt. I 117.18 n.	Payment for wheat
26	99	1,689 dr.	2 dr. 5 ob.	25.2	P. Tebt. I 117.47	Payment for wheat
27	97 or 64	1,800 dr.	3 dr.	26.7	P. Tebt. I 120.72	Payment for wheat
28	94 or 61	1,500 dr.	2 dr. 3 ob.	22.3	P. Tebt. I 121.140	Payment for wheat
29	I BC	800 dr.	1 dr. 2 ob.	11.8	PSI VIII 968.3	Price of wheat; reading of price uncertain
30	I BC	2,200 dr.	3 dr. 4 ob.	32.6	P. Oxy. IV 784 *descr.*	Price of wheat

Notes:

[a] Depending on their status, workers could receive *aleuron katharon* or *aleuron autopyros* (milled or whole meal wheat), the latter being of lesser quality and bulkier, thus of lesser value per unit.

[b] For a discussion of this figure (which may have still been reckoned in the silver standard of period 1) and the type of bread referred to; see Lanciers (1990).

[c] The following calculations are based on a price of the silver drachma at 600 dr.

Table A8.7 Variation of *olyra* prices in Egypt in 159/8 BC

No.	Date	Price per artaba as listed	Price in silver per artaba	Price in g silver per hl	Reference	Notes
1	1 Pharmouthi (May)	250 dr.	1 dr. 1 ob.	10.3	UPZ I 91.7	
2	1 Pharmouthi	300 dr.	1 dr. 2.5 ob.	12.6	UPZ I 91.9	Purchase on the same day from a different seller
3	13 Pharmouthi	320 dr.	1 dr. 3 ob.	13.4	UPZ I 91.9	
4	17 Pharmouthi	290 dr.	1 dr. 1.5 ob.	11.1	UPZ I 91.9	
5	27 Pharmouthi	320 dr.	1 dr. 3 ob.	13.4	UPZ I 92.iii.12	
6	29 Pharmouthi	320 dr.	1 dr. 3 ob.	13.4	UPZ I 91.10 with Wilcken *ad loc.*	
7	1 Pachon (June)	290 dr.	1 dr. 1.5 ob.	11.1	UPZ I 91.15 (June)	
8	1 Pachon	300 dr.	1 dr. 1.5 ob.	11.1	UPZ I 91.18	Purchase on the same day as no. 7, but from a different seller
9	1 Pachon	300 dr.	1 dr. 1.5 ob.	11.1	UPZ I 91.19 with Wilcken *ad loc.*	ditto
10	Pauni (July)	315 dr.	c. 1 dr. 3 ob.	c. 13.4	UPZ I 93.6	
11	Pauni	300 dr.	1 dr. 1 ob. 4 ch.	11.1	UPZ I 93.7	Purchase on the same day as no. 10, but from a different seller
12	Hathyr (Dec.)	360 dr.	1 dr. 4 ob.	14.8	UPZ I 96.8	

Table A8.8 Conversion rates of wheat into cash and *vice versa* in Egypt, 330–30 BC

No.	Date	Price as listed	Price in silver standard per artaba	Price in g silver per hl	Reference	Notes
1	270	2 dr. 1 ob.	2 dr. 1 ob.	19.3	P. Hib. I 99.14	Conversion of wheat rent into cash value
2	256	1 dr. 1 ob.	1 dr. 1 ob.	10.3	SB XIV 11659.4	Conversion of cash loan (*katerga*) into wheat rent (tenancy contract)
3	254 (Jan. and Feb.)	1 dr. 3 ob.	1 dr. 3 ob.	13.4	P. Cair. Zen. III 59499 *recto*.4, 5	Conversion of wheat payment into cash value
4	254 (Mar.)	1 dr. 2 ob.	1 dr. 2 ob.	11.8	P. Cair. Zen. III 59499.7	ditto
5	Mid-III BC	2 dr.	2 dr.	17.8	P. Col. I 54	Official conversion rate of wheat obligations into cash value
6	250	1 dr. 2 ob.	1 dr. 2 ob.	11.8	P. Col. I 54.16	Conversion of cash loans (*katerga*) into wheat (tenancy contract)
7	209	6 dr.	3 dr.	26.7	P. Heid. VI 383.20	Conversion of cash loan into rent in wheat (prodomatic tenancy contract – interest of 50% included?)
8	112 (Mar.)	1,000 dr.	1 dr. 4 ob.	14.8	P. Tebt. I 112.58	Conversion of wage in kind into wheat (by local tax office)
9	112 (Mar.)	800 dr.	1 dr. 2 ob.	11.8	P. Tebt. I 112.118	ditto
10	110/9	1,200 dr.	2 dr.	17.8	P. I. Bat. XIX 6.33	Conversion of purchase price of land into wheat equivalent (Pathyris)
11	108	720 dr.	1 dr. 1 ob.	10.3	P. Tebt. I 224 *verso.*	Conversion of wage in wheat into cash
12	Late II BC	1,000 dr.	1 dr. 4 ob.	14.8	P. Tebt. I 116.2	Conversion of wage in wheat into cash(?)
13	Late II BC	1,100 dr.	1 dr. 5 ob.	16.3	P. Tebt. I 116.32	ditto
14	94 or 61	840 dr.	1 dr. 1.5 ob.	11.1	P. Tebt. I 208 *descr.*	Conversion of cash into wheat equivalent
15	93	2,000 dr.	3 dr. 2 ob.	29.6	P. Tebt. I 109.15	Conversion of cash loan into rent in wheat (prodomatic tenancy contract – interest of 50% included?)

Table A8.9 Penalty prices in Egypt, 330–30 BC

No.	Date	Penalty price listed	Penalty price in silver standard per artaba	Price in g silver per hl	Reference
1	306	4 dr.	4 dr.	35.6	P. Loeb dem. 3.18 (Hermopolite nome)
2	301/300	4 dr.	4 dr.	35.6	P. Hib. I 84a.8–9
3	c. 265	4 dr.	4 dr.	35.6	P. Hib. I 65.24
4	260/59	4 dr.	4 dr.	35.6	BGU VI 1226.13
5	258/7	4 dr.	4 dr.	35.6	BGU 1228.13
6	257	4 dr.	4 dr.	35.6	P. Sorb. 17a.15, b.16
7	244/3 or 218/7	?4 dr.	?4 dr.	35.6	P. Hib. I 91.11
8	III BC	4 dr.	4 dr.	35.6	BGU VI 1267.13
9	223/2	4 dr. (silver)	4 dr.	35.6	P. Tebt. III 1.815. fr.3 ii.14
10	222	5 dr. (silver)	5 dr.	44.5	P. Hib. I 90.15
11	216/5	10 dr. (bronze)	5 dr.	44.5	BGU VI 1262.13
12	215/4	10 dr.	5 dr.	44.5	BGU VI 1264.22 f.
13	215/4	10 dr.	5 dr.	44.5	BGU X 1969.8
14	215/4	10 dr.	5 dr.	44.5	BGU XIV 2383.12
15	215/4	10 dr.	5 dr.	44.5	BGU X 1943.12–14
16	214/3	10 dr.	5 dr.	44.5	BGU VI 1265.20
17	214/3	10 dr.	5 dr.	44.5	BGU X 1944.12
18	214/3	10 dr.	5 dr.	44.5	P. Frankf. I 23
19	214/3	12 dr.	6 dr.	53.4	BGU XIV 2397.10, 11, 29
20	213/2	10 dr.	5 dr.	44.5	BGU X 1946.12
21	173	500 dr.	4 dr. 1 ob.	37.0	P. Amh. II 43.12
22	160/59	400 dr.	3 dr. 2 ob. (1:120)	30.0	BGU XIV 2390.34 (Herakleopolite nome)
23	before 145	1,000 dr.	4 dr. 1 ob.	37.0	BGU VI 1271.8
24	128/7[a]	2,000 dr.	3 dr. 2 ob.	29.6	P. Loeb dem. 55.13 (Hermopolite nome?)
25	119	2,000 dr.	3 dr. 2 ob.	29.6	P. Tebt I 11.17
26	116	2,000 dr.	3 dr. 2 ob.	39.6	P. Dion. 34.11 (Hermopolite nome)

Table A8.9 Continued

No.	Date	Penalty price listed	Penalty price in silver standard per artaba	Price in g silver per hl	Reference
27	116	3,000 dr.	5 dr.	44.5	P. Dion. 26.18
28	c. 115	3,000 dr.	5 dr.	44.5	P. Fay. 11.17
29	113	3,000 dr.	5 dr.	44.5	P. Dion. 21.22
30	113/2	3,000 dr.	5 dr.	44.5	P. Dion. 27.19
31	112	3,000 dr.	5 dr.	44.5	P. Dion. 13.24
32	111	3,000 dr.	5 dr.	44.5	P. Dion. 22.21
33	110	3,000 dr.	5 dr.	44.5	P. Dion. 14.25
34	110	3,000 dr.	5 dr.	44.5	P. Dion. 1.16
35	110?	3,000 dr.	5 dr.	44.5	P. Dion. 28.27
36	109	3,000 dr.	5 dr.	44.5	P. Dion. 2.11
37	109	3,000 dr.	5 dr.	44.5	P. Dion. 15.23
38	109	3,000 dr.	5 dr.	44.5	P. Dion. 16.28
39	109	1,200 dr.	4 dr. (1:300)	35.6	P. Chicago Field Mus. dem. 31323.14 (Thebes)
40	108	1,200 dr.	4 dr. (1:300)	35.6	P. Turin dem. Suppl. 6086 .16 (Thebes)
41	108	3,000 dr.	5 dr.	44.5	P. Dion. 3.15
42	108	3,000 dr.	5 dr.	44.5	P. Dion. 4.16
43	108	3,000 dr.	5 dr.	44.5	P. Dion. 23.22
44	Late II BC	2,000 dr.	3 dr. 2 ob.	29.6	P. Dion. 32.17
45	106	1,500 dr.	5 dr. (1:300)	44.5	P. l. Bat dem. XX II 5.20
46	105	3,000 dr.	5 dr.	44.5	P. Dion. 19.21
47	104	3,000 dr.	5 dr.	44.5	P. l. Bat XX II 25.28
48	104/3 or 102/1	3,000 dr.	5 dr.	44.5	P. Köln VI 275.11
49	103	2,000 dr.	3 dr. 2 ob.	29.6	P. Louvre. dem. 2436b
50	100	2,400 dr.	4 dr.	35.6	P. Adler 15.9
51	92 or 59	3,000 dr.	5 dr.	44.5	P. Tebt. I 110.9
52	73 or 44	4,000 dr.	6 dr. 4 ob.	59.2	P. Oxy. XIV 1639.13
53	77	3,000 dr.	5 dr.	44.5	P. Merton I 6.24 f.
54	51	3,000 dr.	5 dr.	44.5	PSI X 1098.28

Note:
[a] The rate of 1:600 is used for conversion, unless indicated otherwise.

Table A8.10 Grain prices in Rome, Italy and the west, third century BC to fifth century AD

No.	Date BC	Silver g/hl	Place	Reference	Details and notes
1	c. 440?		Rome	Livy 4.16.2; Pliny, *NH* 18.15	Shortage(s), officials distribute emmer wheat (*far*) at 1 *as*/*mod*. (Story current by later II BC; cf. no. 13 below.)
2	250		Rome	Pliny, *NH* 18.17 (citing Varro)	Emmer wheat (*far*) normally 1 *as*/*mod*.
3	216		Casilinum	Strabo 5.4.10	During siege a *medimnos* of grain is sold for 200 dr. But Val.Max. 7.6.3; Pliny, *NH* 8.222; Frontin.. *Strat*. 4.5.20: the item sold was a rat!
4	211/0	131.0	Rome	Polybius 9.11a.3	Shortage, wheat reaches 15 dr. per Sicilian *medimnos*, i.e. 25 *asses*/*mod*.
5	203	20.9	Rome	Livy 30.26.5–6	Grain cheap, aediles distribute wheat from Spain at 4 *asses*/*mod*.
6	201	20.9	Rome	Livy 31.4.6	Aediles distribute wheat from Africa at 4 *asses*/*mod*.
7	200	10.4	Rome	Livy 31.50.1	Grain very cheap, aediles distribute wheat from Africa at 2 *asses*/*mod*.
8	196	10.4	Rome	Livy 33.42.8	Aediles distribute wheat from Sicily at 2 *asses*/*mod*.
9	c. 150	4.5	Gallia Cisalpina (Po valley)	Polybius 2.15.1	So fertile that wheat could cost only 4 obols per Sicilian *medimnos* (nearest Greek equivalent for 1 *as*/*mod*.)
10	c. 150	11.3	Lusitania (Spain)	Polybius 34.8.7 (from Athenaeus 8.330c)	So fertile that wheat costs 9 obols 'of Alexander' (added by Athenaeus?) per Sicilian *medimnos*, i.e. 2.5 *asses*/*mod*., and barley 1 dr./*med*.. i.e. 2.5(?) *asses*/*mod*.
11	122 –c.105, 100–83 and 73–59	17.9	Rome	Livy, *Epit*. 60: *Scholia Bob*. 2.135 St.; Cicero, *pro Sestio* 55 (cf. *Rhet. ad Herenn*. 1.21)	Subsidized price of Gracchan *frumentatio* (wheat distribution) is 6 1/3 *asses*/*mod*., presumably from 5 *modii* (monthly ration) for 2 *denarii*, i.e. HS 1.6/*mod*. (100 BC Saturninus passes grain law '*de semissibus et trientibus*' (5/6), probably scribal error for '*de senis et trientibus*' (6 1/3), i.e. re-instating Gracchan price.)

Table A8.10 Continued

No.	Date BC	Place	Reference	Silver g/hl	Details and notes
12	c. 120–110	Rome	Lucilius, *Sat.* 15.538–9 (Warmington)	?	Except as regards the price: the first (*modius?*) for a *semis* (0.5 *as*), the second for a *nummus* (HS 1, or 1 *as?*), the third for more even than a whole *medimnus*
13	c. 130–70?	Rome	Dionysius Halic. 12.1.12	536.0 89.3	In shortage (439 BC; cf. no. 1 above) price reaches 12 dr. (HS 48)/*mod.*; Maelius sells grain at 2 dr. (HS 8)/*mod.* (Prices probably imagined by annalistic historian of c. 130–70 BC.)
14	74	Rome	Pliny, *NH* 18.16; Cicero, *De Off.* 2.58	2.8	Bad shortage, aedile sells wheat at 1 *as* (HS 0.25)/*mod.*
15a	74, pre-harvest post-harvest	Sicily	Cicero, *In Verrem* 2.3.213–6	223.0 <134.0	Wheat cheap in 76, but expensive in 75 because taken to meet shortage at Rome. In 74 (shortage at Rome again; cf. no. 14 above) pre-harvest price reached 5 *denarii* (HS 20)/*mod.*: Verres' commutation of *frumentum in cellam* (supplies) at 3 *denarii* (HS 12)/*mod.* is fair pre-harvest, but unfair after it, i.e. price now below HS 12
15b	73–71	Sicily	Cicero, *In Verrem* 2.3.163, 173–4, 188–97, 201–2	33.5	To supply revived *frumentatio* at Rome (cf. no.11 above), senate tells Verres to purchase a second tithe (3 million *modii*) at HS 3/*mod.*,
				39.1	and also 800,000 *modii frumentum emptum* (extra compulsory purchase) at HS 3.5/*mod.*:
				28.0	Verres commutes Halaesa's contribution at HS 15/*med.*, i.e. HS 2.5/*mod.*, when the average price was HS 2 to 2.5/*mod.*;
				44.7	senate authorizes Verres to buy supplies at HS 4/*mod.*, and HS 2 for barley;

(*Continued*)

Table A8.10 Continued

No.	Date BC	Silver g/hl	Place	Reference	Details and notes
15c		89.3 / 22.3 to 33.5			he commutes it all at HS 8/*mod.* (pocketing HS 12/*mod.*): the normal market price across all Sicily was then HS 2 to 3/*mod.*
16	49	2,233.0	Spain	Caesar, *BC*1.52.2	Caesar's army starving, wheat sells at 50 *denarii* (HS 200)/*mod.*
	Date AD				
17	6	246.0	Rome	Eusebius, *Chron.* (Schoene) II 146–7	Bad shortage (cf. Garnsey 1988: 220–2), wheat reaches 5.5 den. (HS 22)/*mod.*
18	19	?	Rome	Tacitus, *Ann.* 2.87	Shortage, Tiberius sets maximum price, and pays merchants compensation of 2 *nummi* (HS)/*mod.*
19	40s	4,466.0	Africa	Suetonius, *Galba* 7.2	Soldier on desert expedition sells his *modius* of wheat for 100 *denarii*
20	64	33.5	Rome	Tacitus, *Ann.* 15.39.2	Fear of shortage, Nero reduces the price of wheat to 3 *nummi* per unit, i.e. HS 3/*mod.*
21	70s?	29.2 and 73.1?	Pompeii	Graffiti (Duncan-Jones 1982: 145–6)	Prices equivalent to HS 3 and, probably, HS 7.5/*mod.*
22	c. 75–100	39.0	Forum Sempronii (Italy)	CIL XI 6117 (+ p.1397)	Shortage, benefactor (see PIR² V.2 no. 79 for date) provides wheat at 1 den. (HS 4)/*mod.*
23	c. 100	51.2	Northern Britain	T.Vindol. II 185.19, 27–8 (+ III p.156)	Officer's expenses: 60 *mod.* wheat bought for 78.75 den. (HS 5.25/*mod.*), and 1 *mod.* barley for 9 *asses* (HS 2.25)
24	c. 102/3	9.7	Italy?	Martial 12.76	'Wine sells for twenty *asses* and wheat for four: drunk and stuffed, the farmer is broke'

Table A8.10 Continued

No.	Date AD	Silver g/hl	Place	Reference	Details and notes
25	c. 100–200?	39.0?	Histonium (Italy)	CIL IX 2861	Shortage, benefactor provides wheat, perhaps at 1 den./mod. (reading 'xxx]L modios sin[gulis den.')
26	c. 100–200?	390.0 [78 to 234]	Thuburnica (Africa)	CIL VIII 25703 and 25704	Shortage, when price of wheat had reached 10 den. (HS 40/mod.), benefactor sells at [2 to 6?] den. (/mod.)
27	366–8 pre-harvest	74.9	Carthage (Africa)	Ammianus Marcellinus 28.1.17–18	Shortage pre-harvest, proconsul sells wheat at 10 mod. (italici?) per solidus;
	post-harvest	25.0			later buys back at 30 mod. per solidus, so both locals and annona gain
28	445	18.7	Numidia and Mauretania	Valentinian III, Nov. 13.4	Commutation of military requisitions set at 40 mod. (italici?) per solidus
29	491–3	4,497.0	Ravenna	Anonymus Valesianus 11.53	Three-year siege, wheat reaches 6 solidi per mod. (italicus?)
30	493–526	12.5	Italy	Anonymus Valesianus 12.73	Italy prosperous under Theodoric, wheat normally 60 mod. (italici?) per solidus

Table A8.11 Grain prices in the Greek east (excluding Delos and Egypt), third century BC to sixth century AD

No.	Date BC	Silver g/hl	Place	Reference	Details and notes
1	295	2,445?	Athens	Plutarch, *Demetr.* 33.3	During siege wheat (*pyroi*) sells for 300 dr./*mod.* (i.e., *med.*?)
2	c. 300–275	>48.9	Ephesos	I.Eph. V 1455	When wheat (*pyroi*) selling at over 6 dr./(*med.*), honorand sells 14,000 *hekteis* (2,333 *med.*) at below market price
3	c. 290–240	40.8	Andros	SEG XLIV 669 (cf. III 799)	Royal general acts in shortage: normal or honorand's price of wheat (*sitos*) is 5 dr./*med.*;
		>163.0			possibly he pays 20+ dr./*med.* for foreign wheat. (Text lacunose and uncertain.)
4	c. 270–265	489.0	Erythrai	I.Erythr. I 18 (Migeotte, *Emprunt* 85)	Serious shortage, price of wheat (*pyroi*) reaches 60 dr./*med.*, honorand helps
5	c. 250	32.6	Pergamon	I.Perg. I 13 (OGIS 266)	Royal edict: generals to pay 4 dr./*med.* (presumably low) for requisitioned wheat (*sitos*)
6a	c. 225–175	32.6	Olbia (Scythia)	IosPE II² 32 (Migeotte, *Emprunt* 44)	a. Shortage, wheat (*sitos*) selling at 1 *chrysous* (20 dr.) per 5 *med.* (4 dr./*med.*),
		16.3			honorand promises 2,000 *med.* at 1 *chrysous* per 10 *med.* (2 dr./*med.*)
6b		97.8			b. Another year: serious shortage, wheat selling for 1 *chrysous* per 1 2/3 *med.* (12 dr./*med.*),
		271.0			rises to 1 *med.* for 1 2/3 *chrysous* (33.3 dr./*med.*, or just a rhetorical inversion?).
		39.1			honorand provides 500 *med.* at 1 *chrysous* per 4 1/6 *med.* (4.8 dr./*med.*),
		62.8			and 2,000 *med.* at 1 *chrysous* per 2 7/12 *med.* (7.7 dr./*med.*)
7	216?/ 174?	21.8	Gazoros (Macedon)	I.Philippi 543	In shortage honorand promises to sell wheat (*pyroi*) at 2 dr. 4 ob./*med.* and barley at 1 dr. 4 ob.

Table A8.11 Continued

No.	Date BC	Silver g/hl	Place	Reference	Details and notes
8	c. 200–175	>43.5	Samos	Ditt., Syll.[3] 976 (Pouilloux, Choix 34)	Civic regulation that grain officials to pay the goddess not less than the previous 5 dr. 2 ob./med. for wheat (*sitos*) bought from sacred land
9	129	44.8	Thessaly	SEG XXXIV 558	Penalty of 2 staters 9 ob. per *kophinos* on cities for non-delivery of their shares of 430,000 *kophinoi* of wheat (*sitos*) for Rome. Most plausible fit is that *kophinos* is half a *med.* and this is the base price again (i.e. a 100% penalty) of 5 dr. 3 ob./med. (cf. no. 11 below)
10	c. 129–100	32.6	Priene	I.Priene 108	In shortage honorand provides 206(?) *med.* wheat (*sitos*?) at 4 dr./med.
11	c. 125–100	44.8	Megalopolis	IG V.2 437	In shortage honorand sells wheat (*pyroi*) at [2] staters 9 ob./med., i.e. 5 dr. 3 ob. (Staters in plural, more than 2 implausible.)
12	c. 125–75	245.0	Arsinoe (Cyrene)	SEG XXVI 1817	Shortage, honorand acquires wheat (*sitos*) at 30 dr./metron (i.e. *med.*?)
13	86	8,151.0	Athens	Plutarch, *Sulla* 13.2	During siege wheat (*pyroi*) reaches 1,000 dr./med.
14	74	81.5 40.8 32.6	Epidauros	SEG XI 397 (IG IV².1 66)	Shortage exacerbated by presence of Roman fleet, wheat (*pyros*) sells at 10 dr./med.; honorand keeps price down through year to 5 and 4 dr.
15	65	538.0	Judaea	Josephus, *AJ* 14.28	Hurricane destroys crops, wheat (*sitos*) reaches 11 dr./mod., i.e. say 66 dr./med. (Conversion from local measures by Josephus, may be approximate.)
16	43, June	587.0	Laodicea (Syria)	Cicero (Cassius Parmensis), *Ad Fam.* 12.13.4	In blockade wheat (*triticum*) reaches 3 tetradrachms, i.e. probably 12 den./mod. (rather than 12 dr./med.), i.e. say 72 dr./med.

(*Continued*)

Table A8.11 Continued

No.	Date BC	Date AD	Silver g/hl	Place	Reference	Details and notes
17	36		19,562.0	Mesopotamia	Plutarch, M. Antonius 45.4	Supply problems in army, wheat (pyroi) reaches 50 dr./Attic choinix, i.e. 2,400 dr./med.
18		c. 1–50	29.8?	Chaironeia (Greece)	SEG XXXVIII 380	Temple accounts, wheat sold at 6 kophinoi for a tetradrachm; also barley at 11(?) kophinoi per tetradrachm. If kophinos is half a med. (cf. no. 9 above), wheat price equals 1.33 dr./med.; if it is a hekteus, price more plausibly equals 4 dr./med. (@ 3.85 g/51.72 l)
19		49	268.0	Greece	Eusebius, Chron. (Schoene) II 152–3	Severe shortage, wheat reaches 6 den. (HS 24)/mod.
20		93/4	39.0 — 19.5 to 21.9	Antioch (Pisidia)	AE 1925, 126b	Winter shortage, governor orders surplus stocks to be sold at not more than one (den.: = HS 4)/mod. Before shortage had been 8 or 9 asses (HS 2 to 2.25)/mod. (presumably 3 dr. to 3 dr. 2 ob./med.)
21		c. 90–100	312.0	Asia Minor	St John, Revelation 6.6	Prediction: 'a choinix of wheat for a denarius, and three choinikes of barley for a denarius', but wine and oil prices the same; i.e. wheat at 48 dr./med.
22		c. 125 or 128	260.0 — 78.0	Sparta	SEG XI 492 (AE 1929, 20)	Shortage, when price had reached 40 den. (= dr.)/med., sitōnes distributes wheat at one hemiekton (1/12 med.)/den., i.e. 12 dr./med.
23		c. 100–200		Tenos	IG XII.5 947	When price of barley had reached 5 den. (= dr.)/med., benefactor sells at 5 asses (0.2 ob./med.).
24		c. 50–250	39.0 to 156.0	Judaea (and beyond)	Rabbinic texts (Sperber 1991: 102, 107–8)	Wheat normally costs between 1 den./se'ah (cheap) and 4 den./se'ah (expensive). (Assuming se'ah stands for modius.)
25		c. 175–200	52.0 — 26.0	Sebastopolis (Caria)	Robert, La Carie II no. 172	When price of wheat had reached 4 den./kypros (= 0.5 med.: cf. Hesychius d1955, k4655 Latte), benefactor sells 2,000 kyproi at 2 den., i.e. 4 dr./med.

Table A8.11 Continued

No.	Date AD	Silver g/hl	Place	Reference	Details and notes
26	c. 230–270?	975.0 19.5?	(Cilicia/Syria)	*Historia Apollonii regis Tyri* 10	Bad harvest, famine in Tarsus, wheat at a gold coin (HS 100)/*mod.*; Apollonius sells at market price at Tyre of 8 bronze units – if *asses*, HS 2/*mod.* (Story: this episode probably reflects Caracalla at Tarsus in 215.)
27	301	26.0	(Eastern provinces?)	Diocletian, *MPE* 1.1a-2 (Giacchero)	Diocletian sets maximum price for wheat at 100 den./*mod. castr.*; also for barley at 60 den.
28	312?	650.0?	Asia Minor	Eusebius, *Hist.Eccl.* 9.8.4	Shortage. wheat reaches 2,500 Attic dr./*metron*, i.e. den./*mod.castr.*? (Attic dr. = Diocletian's new den.)
29	362/3	? 33.3? 50.0? 99.9?	Antioch (Syria)	Julian, *Misopōgōn* 368e-370a	Julian and army arrive, prices rise. First he fixes prices; then imports *modii* of wheat; then sells Egyptian wheat at 15 *metra* per *argyrion* He says summer price was 10 *metra* per *argyrion* /*nomisma*, so winter price of 5 *metra* not bad: no-one can recall a price as good as 15 *metra* per *chryson*. Probably *mod.castr.* per *sol.* meant
30	c. 490–500	25.0 187.0 ? 150.0	Edessa (Mesopot-amia)	Joshua Stylites (Garnsey 1988: 3–6)	To 495, normal price 30 *mod.* per *dinar* (= *solidus*); in 500 severe shortage, wheat reaches 4 *mod.* per *dinar* (and barley 6 *mod.*); in February 500 wheat peaked at 13 *kabs* per *dinar* (and barley at 18 *kabs*); by July 500, after harvest, wheat back to 5 *mod.* per *dinar*

Table A8.12 Private wheat prices in Egypt, 30 BC to third century AD

No.	Date BC	Silver g/hl	dr./art.	Area	Reference	Details and notes
1	c. 20–15, Jun.–Jul.	8.3?	3 dr. 2 ob.?	Arsin.	P.Fay. 101 *recto*.ii.2–3, cf. *verso*.i.10	If 60 *art.* wheat = 50 *art.* safflower at 4 dr. (so Johnson 1936: 174; contra Duncan-Jones 1990: 154)
2	10, Dec.		0.4??	Herakl.	BGU XVI 2611.7	Estate letter. Merchant offers 200 dr. for 500 *art.* wheat (nature of transaction unclear)
3	5, Dec.	4.7?	1.90?	Arsin.	P.Tebt. II 459 descr.	148 dr. received for 77.7 *art.*
	Date AD					
4a	45, Sep.	10.8 14.2 19.9 18.0 18.9 19.9	4.36 5.71 8 7.27 7.62 8	Arsin.	P.Mich. II 127. i.8 i.12 i.13–16 i.17 i.37 i.38	Private account (Kronion *grapheion* archive) Prices expressed as *art.* per tetradrachm
	Oct					
4b	46, Dec.	21.7	8.73	Arsin.	P.Mich. II 123 *verso*.xi.26–7	Private account (As above)
5	46/7	14.9	6	Arsin.	SB XX 14576.34	Account of expenditure (Nemesion archive)
6	78, Oct. 79, Jan. Feb.	21.7 23.8 23.8	10 11 11	Hermop.	SB VIII 9699. 177–8, 181 360–2 454–5	Estate account
7	c. 75–125	10.8	5	Arsin.?	P.Louvre II 103.5, 12, 17	Conversion of private(?) rent payments. General price
8	124, Apr.	19.5	9	Hermop.	P.Sarap. 60.10	Estate account (Sarapion archive)
9	c. 100–130, Jul.	15.2	7	Hermop.	P.Sarap. 92.18–19	Estate letter (Sarapion archive) General price
10	c. 128?, Dec./Jan.	26.0	12	Hermop.	P.Sarap. (p. 292) 79b.i.13 (SB VIII 9729)	Estate account (Sarapion archive)

Table *A8.12* Continued

No.	Date AD	Silver g/hl	dr./art.	Area	Reference	Details and notes
11	138/9	12.1?	5.60?	Oxy.	PSI IV 281.7–9	Estate letter. 'Grain' sold at 560 dr. per 100 *art.*: discount?
12	c. 100–200	13.0	6	Hermop.	P.Berl.Zill. 10.12–14	Estate letter (year 4) General price (post-harvest?)
13	c. 100–200	17.3	8	?	P.Erl. 92.6–9	Private(?) account
14	c. 100–200	17.3	8	Arsin.	SPP XXII 110.1	Estate(?) account
15	c. 100–200?	19.5	9	Upper Egypt	O.Ashm. 91	Private(?) receipt
16	160, Oct.	8.0 or 12.0?	5.52? (or 3.68)	Arsin.	P.Berl.Leihg. II 39 recto.64	Private account 0.2 or 0.3 *art.* for 8 ob., at 29 to the tetradrachm
17	c. 160, Aug.	23.8	11	Arsin.	P.Stras. IX 847.42	Private account (probably same author as item 16)
18	192, Jan.	39.0	18	Arsin.	P.Cair.Goodsp. 30.xiii.10–13	Estate account
		43.3	20		xv.24	
	Feb.	39.0	18		xx.22–3	
19	c. 175–250	26.0	12	Arsin.	SB XVI 12607.6–7	Estate letter; general, refers to 'the low price of crops' (1.3)
20	c. 175–250	39.0	18	Arsin.?	P.Iand. VI 94.5–6	Estate letter
21	c. 175–250	43.3	20	Arsin.?	SB XVI 12981.6–8	Estate(?) letter
22	202 or 231?, Jul.	43.3	20	Arsin.	P.Lund IV 11.i.25–6 (SB VI 9348)	Temple account (Bacchias archive)
23	202/3 or 231/2?	34.7	16	Oxy.?	P.NYU II 8.9	Estate account Price suggests III AD

(*Continued*)

Table A8.12 Continued

No.	Date AD	Silver g/hl	dr./art.	Area	Reference	Details and notes
24a	215?, Nov.– Dec.	60.6	28	Arsin.	P.Louvre I 51. 5, 10*	Estate account
	216?, Jan.– Jun.	60.6	28		17*, 23, 34, 42–3, 46, 47*, 51	(Pakysis archive)
	217?, Jan.– Mar.	21.7	10		90, 94, 104	Correcting scribal slips in asterisked
	Apr.	<17.3?	<8?		118–9	entries. Years not given, but close to,
	Jun.	17.3	8		126, 128–9	probably before, P.Louvre I 50 which
						post-dates 216 (see text for probable
						historical context)
24b	217?, Jun.	21.7	10	Arsin.	P.Louvre I 54. 8	Estate account
	Jul.	21.7	10		11	(Pakysis archive)
		26.0	12		12	Probably same period as item 24a
	218?, Jan.	43.3	20		29	
	Mar.	39.0	18		34	
	Jun.	34.7	16		42	
	Aug.	34.7	16		45	
25	226 or 242, Feb.	26.0	12	Arsin.	P.Laur. I 11.A10–11	Estate account
						(linked to Heroninos archive)
26	c. 200–300, Mar.	42.2	19 dr. 3 ob.	Arsin.	P.Grenf. I 51.10	Private account
27	c. 200–300	43.3	20	Arsin.	BGU VII 1717.11	Temple(?) account
28	c. 200–300	52.0	24	Middle Egypt?	P.Princ. III 175 descr.	Estate account
29	c. 200–300	69.3	32	Middle Egypt?	P.Brook. 18	Estate letter
						General price

Table A8.12 Continued

No.	Date AD	Silver g/hl	dr./art.	Area	Reference	Details and notes
30	249, Jun.	52.0	24	Arsin.	P.Flor. I (p.27) 9b	Estate account (Heroninos archive)
31	250, Sep.–Dec.	43.3	20	Arsin.	P.Prag.Varcl II 2.12 (SB VI 9408.1) and P.Prag. III 240.29, 31, 33, 57, 78, 81, 99–100, 122	Estate accounts (Heroninos archive)
32	251, Nov.	43.3	20	Arsin.	SB XX 14645.10	Estate account (Heroninos archive)
33	252, Apr.	52.0	24	Arsin.	P.Prag.Varcl II 4.8 (SB VI 9409.1)	Estate account (Heroninos archive)
34	253, Jun.	34.7	16	Arsin.	SB XX 14197 recto.9	Estate account (Heroninos archive)
35	254, Sep.	26.0	12	Arsin.	P.Lond. III (p.103) 1226.10	Estate account (Heroninos archive)
36	255, Aug.	34.7	16	Memph.	BGU I 14.ii.14	Estate account
37	c. 255–9, Mar.	26.0	12	Arsin.	P.Flor. III 321.9	Estate account (Heroninos archive)
38	c. 255–60	34.7	16	Arsin.	P.Sorb. inv. 2186 ined.	Estate account (Heroninos archive)
39	259, Oct.	34.7	16	Arsin.	P.Prag. III 236.11	Estate account (Heroninos archive)
40	260, May	34.7	16	Oxy.	P.Oxy. XLIX 3513, 3516, 3518–19	Estate letters
41	260, Dec.	26.0	12	Arsin.	P.Prag.Varcl II 6.10 (SB VI 9409.3)	Estate account (Heroninos archive)
42	263, Jan.	26.0	12	Arsin.	P.Prag. III 238.85	Estate account (Heroninos archive)
43	270, (Jun.–Aug.)	52.0	24	Oxy.	P.Erl. 101.30–1	Estate account
44	c. 275–290?	26.0?	240?	Oxy.	P.Oxy. LXXXV 5063.2	Private letter; Name of crop in lacuna

Table A8.13 Private penalty prices for wheat in Egypt, 30 BC to second century AD

No.	Date BC	Silver g/hl	dr./art.	Area	Reference	Details and notes
1	6/5			Oxy.	PSI X 1099	4,000 bronze dr./*art.*
2	4, Oct.			Oxy.	SB XII 10942	4,000 bronze dr./*art.*
	Date AD					
3	15, Oct.	22.3	9	Arsin.	PSI IX 1028	Or 'the highest price then current in the village'
4	22, Oct.	12.4	5	Arsin.	P.Athen. 14.26–8 (+ BL III 216)	Double?; or 'the highest price then current in the market (*agora*)'
5	68, Mar.			Oxy.	P.Oxy. XLVII 3352	6,000 bronze dr./*art.*
6	70/71			Oxy.	P.Oxy. XLIX 3488	4,000(?) bronze dr./*art.*
7	112, Oct.	13.0	6	Oxy.	P.Oxy. XXII 2351	Rent on land under fodder due in wheat or cash equivalent

Table A8.14 Wheat prices set by the state in Egypt, first to third centuries AD

No.	Date BC	Silver g/hl	dr./art.	Area	Reference	Details and notes
1	c. 15–5	7.4	3	Thebes	O.Med.Habu dem. 98	*adaeratio*
2	13, Sep.	9.9	4	Thebes	O.Stras. I 46	*adaeratio*
3	10	6.2	2 dr. 3 ob.	Thebes	O.Stras. I 48	*adaeratio*
4	9, Jul.	6.2	2 dr. 3 ob.	Thebes	O.Stras. I 51	*adaeratio*
5	4, Jan.	8.7	3 dr. 3 ob.	Koptos	O.Petr. 195–201	*adaeratio*
	Date AD					
6	33, Aug.	7.4	3	Thebes	O.Wilck. 1372	*adaeratio*
7	56, Feb.	10.2?	4 dr. 3.5 ob.?	Thebes	O.Wilck. 1558	*adaeratio*. Reading 1.5 *art.* by heaped *art.* at 6 dr. 5 ob. (contra Johnson 1936: 311; Duncan-Jones 1990: 155; DDbDP.)
8	65, Mar.	5.4	2 dr. 1 ob.	Koptos	O.Petr. 210	Probably *adaeratio*.
9	79, Feb.	17.3	8	Hermop.	SB VIII 9699.456–7	Compulsory(?) purchase for *euthēnia*, i.e. *annona*
10	99, Dec.	34.7	16	Oxy.	P.Oxy. XLI 2958 and XLVII 3335?	*pyros synagoristikos*
11	100, Jan.	17.3	8	Oxy.	P.Oxy. XLI 2960	*pyros synagoristikos*

No.	Date AD	Silver g/hl	dr./art.	Area	Reference	Details and notes
12	125, Aug.	15.5	7 dr. 1 ob.	Arsin.	BGU III 834.22–3	Cash equivalent for wheat allowance to liturgists
13	c. 100–150	17.3	8	Arsin.	P.Iand. VII 138	*pyros synagoristikos*
14	128, Feb.–May	17.3	8	Hermop.	P.Sarap. (p. 297) 793.iii–vii (SB VIII 9732)	Probably *pyros synagoristikos*
15	137, Oct.	17.3	8	Oxy.	PSI XII 1262	*pyros synagoristikos*
16	149, Mar.	15.2	7	Arsin.	P.Tebt. II 394	*pyros synagoristikos*
17	c. 100–200	17.3	8	Thebes	O.Stras. I 283 (+ BL II.2 150)	*adaeratio*
18	c. 100–200	17.3	8	Thebes	SB I 2088	*adaeratio*. (Taking L as 'art.', not '1/2'.)
19	c. 100–200	26.0	12	Arsin.	SB XIV 12128	Cash equivalent for wheat allowance to liturgists
20	153, Sep.	13.0?	6?	Thebes	O.Wilck. 1587	Payment of bath-tax by 1 dr. and 1/24 *art.* wheat, for 1.5 ob.?
21	154, Mar.	17.3	8	Oxy.	P.Oxy. XLI 2961–67	*pyros synagoristikos*
22	154/5	17.3	8	Prosopite	P.Oxy. IX 4056	*pyros synagoristikos*
23	154/5	17.3	8	Arsin.	SB XVI 13060	Cash equivalent for wheat allowance to liturgists
24	155, Feb.	17.3	8	Arsin.	P.Berl.Frisk 1 + P.Col. II 1 *recto* 4 + P.Graux IV 30 (and other fragms.)	ditto
25	162, Nov.	18.1	8 dr. 2 ob.	Arsin.	P.Ryl. II 197a	3 dr. paid for 3% customs duty on 12 *art.* wheat

(*Continued*)

Table A8.14 Continued

No.	Date AD	Silver g/hl	dr./art.	Area	Reference	Details and notes
26	183, Dec.	17.3	8	Arsin.	BGU I 200	Cash equivalent for wheat allowance to liturgists
27	198, Sep.	17.3	8	Arsin.	SB X 10293	Conversion of wheat paid for tax due in cash
28	216, Jul.	17.3	8	Koptos?	O.Amst. 58	*adaeratio*
29	246, Mar.	52.0	24	all Egypt?	P.Oxy. XLII 3048.5–6	Shortage, prefect orders compulsory purchase of all private stocks at 6 den./*art.*
30	c. 270–280?, Jun.	86.7	40	Arsin.	P.Stras. IV 295.14, 17	*adaeratio*, or allowance to liturgists
31	276	21.7	200	Arsin.	O.Mich. I 57, cf. *TAPhA* 76 (1945) 144–6	*adaeratio*
32	293?, Sep.?	32.5	300	Oxy.	P.Oxy. XVII 2142	Compulsory(?) purchase for *annona* (date probably same as for 2143; ignore BL III 141)
33	294, Dec.			Oxy.?	P.Harr. I (p.109)	Cash equivalent for wheat allowance to liturgists
		23.4	216		93 *verso*.5	
		23.8	220		*verso*.3-4	
		22.5?	208?		*verso*.2	
		25.1	232		*recto*.ii.13	

Table A8.15 Wheat prices in Egypt, fourth century AD

No.	Date AD	Silver g/hl	dr./art. (or art./sol.)	Area	Reference	Details and notes
1	301, Feb.		640	Hermop.	CPR VI 75	Private receipt
2	c. 300–310		852	Hermop.	SB XX 14657.18	Official(?) account
3	304/5	31.2	1,200	Oxy.	P.Oxy. XXXVI 2798	Private receipt (standard *art.*) 1 lb silver worth 32,000 dr. (SB VI 9253.2–3, SB XIV 11345.13)
4	c. 305–310?, Jun.		1,200	Middle Egypt	SB XVI 12666	Private notice of payment
5	311, Apr.	(26.0)	(1,200)	Arsin.	P.Cair.Isid. 11.50	Wheat tax assessed by value at 100 den./*mod.castr.*: for 65 tal. 297.9 *art.* paid, apparently using heaped *artaba* (= 5 *mod. Ital.*)
6	312/3		2,000	Arsin.	P.NYU I 18.4–5, cf. 9–10	Private account
7	314, Jul.		6,000? 8,000	Hermop.	CPR VIII 22. 16 18, 27–9	Private account
8	315, Sep.		3,000	Arsin.	SB V 7621.157 (P.Princ.Roll)	*adaeratio*
9	c. 310–330		(2,000 or 5,000?)	Hermop.	P.Ryl. IV 706 *verso*.9, cf. 12	Estate account 2,000 given for wheat, 5,000 for barley: wrong round?
10	c. 296–300 or 312–323?		3,936	Oxy.	P.Oxy. XXIV 2421.2, 4–8	Official account (*adaeratio?*). Bagnall (1985: 57) dates to c. 312–323 because of prices. It post-dates 290 (text on *recto*), but perhaps not long after since some people named here appear in texts of AD 271 to 279

(Continued)

Table A8.15 Continued

No.	Date AD	Silver g/hl	dr./art. (or art./sol.)	Area	Reference	Details and notes
11	c. 310–330		6,000	Arsin.	P.Cair.Isid. 28	Fiscal account (*adaeratio*?)
12	c. 310–330, Apr.		7,000	Arsin.?	P.Stras. VI 559.7–9	Private account
13	c. 323–330?, May		1,640.5 or 6,640.5?	Hermop.	P.Worp 25.11–13	Private order to pay Price uncertainly read
14	327. Feb.		17,333	Oxy.	PSI IV 309	State compulsory purchase
15	325–345 or 370s?	30.3–33.3 12.8	5 to 5.5 *art./sol.* 13 *art./sol.*	Tentyrite	*Vita Pachomii* 33 (*Patr.Or.* IV 5)	Shortage: grain selling at 5 *art./sol.*: monks bought at 5.5 after Pachomius refused tax-collector's offer to sell to them at 13 *art./sol.* Prices may reflect author's time (370s on?)
16	335, May	20.6	84 k (14 tal.)	Alex.?	P.Lond. VI 1914.51	Private letter 1 lb silver worth 3.4 million dr. (PSI XIV 11345.13)
17	338, Nov.		144 k (24 tal.)	Oxy.	SB XVI 12648.64–5 (P.Oxy. I 85)	Price declaration by traders
18	c. 340		156 k (26 tal.)	Hermop.	SB XIV 11593.14, 21	Account of official expenditure
19	c. 340, Aug.		180 k (30 tal.)	Hermop.	SPP XX 75.ii.23	Military account

Table A8.15 Continued

No.	Date AD	Silver g/hl	dr./art. (or art./sol.)	Area	Reference	Details and notes
20	c. 340,			Oxy.	P.Oxy. IIV 3773	Collated prices from declarations by traders. In same record, 1 lb of silver worth:
	Oct.	39.5?	270 k (45 tal.)			5.7. million dr.? ([9]50 tal.)
	Nov.–Jan.	36.3	270 k			6.2 million dr.
	Feb.	33.3	277 k (46 tal.)			7 million dr.
	Mar.	35.7	300 k (50 tal.)			7 million dr.
	May	35.1	300 k			7.12 million dr.
	Jun.–Aug.	31.6	270 k (45 tal.)			7.12 million dr.
	Sep.–Oct.	27.5	240 k (40 tal.)			7.28 million dr.
21	c. 340–350		300 k (50 tal.)	Arsin.	P.Abinn. 68 *recto*.38	Private(?) account
22	c. 350–355		2,004 k (334 tal.)	Middle Egypt?	P.Princ. III 183 *verso* descr.	Private(?) account
23	357/8		5,076 k (846 tal.)	Middle Egypt?	SB XIV 12154.6 (P.Stras. VI 595)	Private(?) account
24	359, Jan.	25.1	8,202 k (1,367 tal.)	Oxy.	P.Oxy. II 3625.16	Price declaration by traders. 1 lb silver worth 272 million dr. (P.Oxy. II 3624.17)
25	c. 366		6,000 k (1,000 tal.) 4,200 k (700 tal.)	Dakhla Oasis	P.Bingen 120 *verso*.15, 26	Estate account
26	362/3 or 377/8	16.7 22.2?	10 art./sol. 7.5 art./sol.?	Dakhla Oasis	P.Kellis IV 96. 766 872	Estate account

Table A8.16 Barley prices in Egypt, first to fourth centuries AD

No.	Date BC / Date AD	Wheat: barley price ratio	dr./art.	Area	Reference	Details and notes
1	10 BC	1.67:1	1 dr. 3 ob.	Thebes	O.Stras. I 47	*adaeratio* Penalty price in loan
2	3		3	Arsin.	SB IV 7341	
3	45, Nov.	2.4:1 2:1	3.33 4	Arsin.	P.Mich. II 127.ii.1 ii.44	Account of personal expenditure (Kronion *grapheion* archive). Prices as *art.* per tetradrachm
4	c. 75–125	1.4:1	3 dr. 3 ob.	Arsin.?	P.Louvre II 103.16	Conversion of private(?) rent payments. General price
5	c. 75–125?		16	Wadi Fawakhir	SB VI 9017.8	Private letter between soldiers
6	c. 128?, Dec./Jan.	1.5:1	8	Hermop.	P.Sarap. (p. 292) 79b.ii.12 (SB VIII 9729)	Estate account (Sarapion archive) Reading 2 *art.* for [1]6 dr.
7	138/9		5.60?	Oxy.	PSI IV 281.7–9	Estate letter. 'Grain' sold at 560 dr. per 100 *art.*; or cheap wheat?
8	c. 138–161		5	Arsin.	P.Fay. 333 *verso descr.*	Private account
9	155, Feb.	1.8:1 1.7:1	4 dr. 2 ob./ 3 ob. 4.80	Arsin.	P.Berl.Frisk 1.i, iv + P.Col. II 1 *recto* 4 + P.Graux IV 30.ii–iii, x	Cash equivalents for barley allowance to liturgists
10	c. 100–200		7	Oxy.	SB XVI 12764.ii.12	Estate account
11	c. 100–200, Apr.–May		4 dr. 2 ob.	Middle Egypt?	SPP XXII 59.12	Private account. One *sakkos* (= 3 *art.*) sold for 10 dr. 20 ob. (at 28 ob./tetradr.?)
12	157, Jan.		5.96	Oxy.	P.Wisc. II 82	Private note of payment. 100 *art.* sold to merchants for 596 dr.; with discount?

Table A8.16 Continued

No.	Date AD	Wheat: barley price ratio	dr./art.	Area	Reference	Details and notes
13	160, Oct.	1.8:1	3.03	Arsin.	P.Berl.Leihg. II 39 recto.58	Private account. 1 *art.* for 22 ob., at 29 ob. to the tetradrachm
14	c. 160, Jul.–Aug.			Arsin.	P.Stras. IX 847.1, 4, 5, 6,	Private account (probably same author as item 13)
					17, 26	At 29 ob./tetradr
	Aug.	2.6:1	4.83		11, 12	
		2.8:1	4.21		30, 31	
			4			
15	162/3		6	Arsin.	P.Mil.Vogl. I 28.68	Estate account (Patron archive)
16	168, Sep.		6	Arsin.	P.Mil.Vogl. IV 215.8–9	Estate account (Patron archive)
17	192, Mar.?	1.8:1	10+	Arsin.	P.Cair.Goodsp. 30.xxxiii.21	Estate account 3 *art.* sold for 30 dr. 2 ob. 1 *ch*
18	200, Apr.		4	Arsin.	P.Prag. III 242.14	Estate account (linked to Heroninos archive)
19	209, Mar.	1.6:1	5	Arsin.	P.Bingen 106.11	State compulsory purchase
20a	216?, Mar.	1.8:1	15 dr. 5 ob.	Arsin.	P.Louvre I 51.37	Estate account (Pakysis archive) Years not given, but close to, probably before, P.Louvre I 50 which post-dates 216 (see text for probable historical context)
	217?, Apr.	1.2:1	6 dr. 5 ob.		110	
	Jun.	0.8:1	9 dr. 4 ob.		127	
20b	217?, May	1.5:1	6 dr. 6 ob.	Arsin.	P.Louvre I 54. 6–7	Estate account (Pakysis archive).
	Jul.	1.2:1	8 dr. 4 ob.		14	Probably same period as item 20a
	218?, Jan.	1.9:1	10 dr. 2 ob.		26	
	Feb.	c. 1.7:1	11 dr. 3 ob.		31	
	Jun.	1.3:1	12 dr.		43	
21	c. 150 –250?	1.8:1	6 dr. 4 ob.	Arsin.	P.Flor. III 366	Estate letter. General (high?) price

(Continued)

Table A8.16 Continued

No.	Date AD	Wheat: barley price ratio	dr./art.	Area	Reference	Details and notes
22	c. 190–225		8	Middle Egypt?	P.Münch. III 121	Estate letter. Agent told to sell if price reaches 8 dr. (general)
23	c. 200–300		14	Arsin.	P.Fay. 131.5	Estate letter
24	c. 200–300		16?	Arsin.	SPP XXII 56.20	Temple account / Quantity not given (1 art.?)
25	c. 250–270		16	Arsin.	P.Gron. 16.19–20	Estate letter (Heroninos archive)
26	c. 265–275?		20	Kharga Oasis	P.Grenf. II 77.26 (+ BL IV 35)	Private account / Dated by use of 'old dr.'
27	c. 275–295?		160 / 140	Oxy.	P.Oxy. XIV 1733.1, 7 13	Estate account
28	c. 300–310	1.6:1	54[0]	Hermop.	SB XX 14657.19	Official(?) account
29	304, Feb.		–	Arsin.	BGU XIII 2334	Private purchase on credit of a 'basket'(?) of barley-meal'(?) for 5 tal. 1.500 dr.
30	315, Sep.		1,000	Arsin.	P.Cair.Isid. 58	State compulsory purchase
31	316, Feb.	3:1	1,000	Arsin.	SB V 7621.114 (P.Princ.Roll)	adaeratio
32	c. 310–330	2.5:1?	2,000 / 2,100 (5,000?)	Hermop.	P.Ryl. IV 706 verso.6, 8, 12	Estate account / If the 5,000 given for barley should be for wheat
33	c. 296–300 or 312–323?	1.5:1	2,620	Oxy.	P.Oxy. XXIV 2421.1, 3–6, 8	Official account (adaeratio?). Bagnall 1985: 57 dates to c. 312–323 because of prices. It post-dates 290 (text on recto), but perhaps not long after since some people named here appear in texts of AD 271 to 279

Table A8.16 Continued

No.	Date AD	Wheat: barley price ratio	dr./art.	Area	Reference	Details and notes
34	c. 330 (or 315)		70 k (11.67 tal.)	Arsin.	P.Bodl. I 143.7–8 with BL XI 48	Private(?) account
35	338, Nov.	1.8:1	80 k (13.33 tal.)	Oxy.	SB XVI 12648.96 (P.Oxy. I 85)	Price declaration by traders
36	c. 340, Aug.	2:1?	90 k (15 tal.?)	Hermop.	SPP XX 75.ii.21–2	Military account. [.]5 art. cost 375 tal.: probably 25 art.
37	c. 340, Sep.–Nov.	2.25:1	120 k (20 tal.)	Oxy.	P.Oxy. IIV 3773	Collated prices from declarations by traders
	Jan.	1.8:1	150 k (25 tal.)			
	Feb.	2.3:1	120 k			
	Mar.	2:1	150 k			
	May	3.3:1	90 k (15 tal.)			
	Jun.	3:1	90 k			
	Jul.–Sep.	2.25:1	120 k (20 tal.)			
	Oct.	1.8:1	132 k (22 tal.)			
38	c. 350	1.7:1?	180 k (30 tal.)	Arsin.	P.Abinn. 43.13–15	Private(?) account Comparing P.Abinn. 68
39	c. 366	2:1 and 1.4:1	3,000 k (500 tal.)	Dakhla Oasis	P.Bingen 120 verso.16, 28	Estate account
40	372, Dec.		2,400 k (400 tal.)	Arsin.	P.Col. VII 184	Private sale in advance (for 600 tal., inc. 50% interest)
41	373 (or 372), Feb.		2,000 k (333 tal.)	Arsin.	P.Col. VII 182	Private sale in advance (for 500 tal., inc. 50% interest)

(Continued)

Table A8.16 Continued

No.	Date AD	Wheat: barley price ratio	dr./art.	Area	Reference	Details and notes
42	362/3 or 377/8		6,000 k? ([1,000 tal.])	Dakhla Oasis	P.Kellis IV 96.1071–4	Estate account Price reconstructed from equivalence to price of chickling
43	368/9 or 383/4?		4,800 k (800 tal.)	Dakhla Oasis	P.Kellis I 10.	Private letter
44	c. 370–385?		12,000 k (2,000 tal.)	Dakhla Oasis	P.Kellis I 11.	Private letter Probably similar date to P.Kellis I 10
45	c. 375–385		9,000 k (1,500 tal.)	Oxy.	P.Oxy. XLVIII 3410.15–17	Private letter re-state compulsory purchase?
46	388/9		30 *mod./sol.*	Thebaid	P.Lips. I 63.9–11	Tax credit (reverse *adaeratio*). Probably *mod.castr.*

Table A8.17 Grain prices in Egypt, fifth to early eighth centuries AD

No.	Date AD	Silver g/hl	Price range Wheat	Sources and notes
1	V–VI	13.9–20.8	normal (c. 50%): 12 to 8 *art./sol.* cheaper (c. 30%):	F. Morelli, research in progress; cf. Carrié (1997: 123–6)
		>6.9	down to 24 *art./sol.* more expensive (c. 20%)	
		<41.6	up to 4 *art./sol.*	
1n	541	18.7	Wheat commuted at 40 *mod./sol.*	P.Cair.Masp. III 67320.10: order for military supplies (*annona*) (Dioskoros archive, Antinoopolis)
2	VII–early VIII	12.8–18.5	normal (c. 75%): 13 to 9 *art./sol.* cheaper (c. 20%):	F. Morelli, research in progress; cf. Carrié (1997: 123–6)
		>6.0	down to 28 *art./sol.* more expensive (one case)	
		<20.8	8 *art./sol.*	
		Wheat: barley price ratio	*Barley*	
3	V–VI	1.5–1.6:1	normal (c. 55%): 18 to 13 *art./sol.* cheaper (c. 35%): down to 24 *art./sol.* more expensive (c. 10%) up to 7 *art./sol.*	F. Morelli, research in progress
4	VII and early VIII	1.4:1	(as in V–VI)	F. Morelli, research in progress

Notes

1 The main previous collections of grain prices we have used are: Markle (1985: 293–7); Reger (1994: 289–308); Maresch (1996: 181–94); Heichelheim (1930, 1935); Szaivert and Wolters (2005: 331–3); Duncan-Jones (1990: 143–55); Drexhage (1991: 13–18, 25–6); Ermatinger (1996: 117–20); Bagnall (1985: 64–5 with P. Kellis IV p. 226). We also build on our own previous studies, such as: Rathbone (1997, 2009, forthcoming a–b) and Von Reden (2007b, 2010, forthcoming). We thank G. Husson, S. Kovarik, B. Palme and M. B. Trapp for help with specific items. Prices cited in previous studies which do not appear here, or seem not to, have been rejected, re-read or had their form of citation updated.

2 Judaea: Sperber (1991: 102–3, 107–8). Dr Federico Morelli is engaged on a grand project to make an up-to-date collection of all prices and earnings from Byzantine Egypt; we are very grateful to him for putting his preliminary grain price data at our disposal.

3 For example Reger (1994) emphasizes, against Rostovtzeff (1935/6) and Bresson (2008: 118–26), institutional and political impediments to the development of

price-setting markets in the Hellenistic world, while Eich (2006) discusses various aspects of price formation, but does not argue for a particular pattern. For the Roman world contrast the approaches, for instance, of Erdkamp (2005) and of Kessler and Temin (2008) and Temin (2013).

4 Heichelheim (1930: 74, cf. 1954/5: 501 n.1). For instance, Heichelheim's use of the extremely low state price of wheat in the Gracchan *frumentatio* at Rome and a contemporary price in Egypt as a pair of base-points artificially inflated other Roman prices.

5 Hultsch (1882) is still very useful for his collation of ancient written evidence, but his penchant for creating hypothetical metrological systems makes many of his conclusions unacceptable.

6 Elsen (2002); in practice, coins were minted *al marco*, depending on the amount of silver available; but weight studies show an extremely accurate minting to the target weight throughout the fifth and fourth centuries BC; see also Hultsch (1882: 146–9), who set the target weight at 4.36 g.

7 Lang and Crosby (1964: 39–55), at 47–8. The *medimnos* held 48 *choinikes* and 192 *kotylai*. Seven officially labelled measures imply a *kotylē* of from 252 to 300 ml; their median value, and also the mean of the five central cases, is 276 ml, which we use. The commonly used value of 52 l for the *medimnos* (in fact 51.72 l, with a *kotylē* of 269 ml) is the adjusted size of the Roman period.

8 Reger (1994: 13); Hackens (1983).

9 Athens: Elsen (2002). Other states: Howgego (1995: 114).

10 Noeske (2000: 21); Von Reden (2007b: 39–40); Lorber (2012: 211–13).

11 Von Reden (2007b: 112); Lorber (2012).

12 The currency changes of the late third and second centuries BC are highly controversial and not fully understood. We use here a combination of the models proposed by Reekmans (1948) and Maresch (1996), discussed in more detail in Von Reden (2007b: 75–83). See now also Lorber (2012) in the light of the numismatic evidence. Against the view of a merely nominal increase of prices due to monetary changes see Cadell and Le Rider (1997), who argue for real price inflation due to economic problems and an over-supply of coinage.

13 Possibly because in 183 BC the weight of the bronze coins was doubled while their value was halved, but light-weight bronze coins reappear; see Maresch (1996: 61).

14 Maresch (1996: 70–88).

15 Maresch (1996: 25).

16 We ignore here that the 10 per cent agio continued to be added to payments of taxes and rents to the state during the period of the bronze standard (see Maresch 1996: 19). We need to emphasize, moreover, that the model suggested here might not be uncontroversial and further research into the Ptolemaic monetary systems of the second and first centuries BC might lead to greater clarity on the issue.

17 Ptolemaic *artabas* could contain different numbers of *choinikes*. Whether this was the standard Attic *choinix* of 1.1 l or a smaller one of c. 0.808 l cannot be ascertained from the papyrological evidence, but extant measuring containers of the late Pharaonic period may argue for the latter (Pommerening 2005: 172–3). It seems that different sizes of Persian *artabai* were adapted to Egyptian measures of the *hin*, and that the *artaba* of different *choinikes* was the Ptolemaic adaptation to different sizes of *artabai* in use before the Ptolemaic period. Further discussion of this issue can be found in Duncan-Jones (1979), Shelton (1977), Vleeming (1979), and Pommerening (2005: 164–173).

18 The Ptolemaic standard *artaba* used for measuring grain, at least in the Fayyum, may be derived from the Persian 'big' *artaba* of 80 *hin* = 37.84 l; see Pommerening (2005: 170–1).

19 For example the quadrantal ($= 3$ *modii*) was one cubic foot (29.57 cm^3 $= 25.86$ l) and held 80 lbs of water or wine (80×323 g $= 25.84$ kg or l). For the empirical evidence see Duncan-Jones (1982: 369–71). The still commonly used values of 324 g or 327 g for the Roman pound are inexact.

20 Rathbone (1983); Sperber (1991): implicit in discussions. Other sizes of *artaba*, such as the 'heaped' *artaba* (1/9 larger) sometimes used for official recording of receipts, were similarly adjusted.

21 Summarized by Crawford (1975: 575–85); Howgego (1995: 126–33).

22 Crawford (1975: 575–7, 581) argues from its silver content for a face value of 4 *denarii*, but also accepts that the later billon coin of Diocletian similarly marked 20:1 was tariffed at 20 *denarii*. This complex issue requires further discussion elsewhere.

23 Diocletian's new silver coin, the *argenteus*, was minted at 96 to the pound (3.36 g) like the previous *denarius*, but prices, as in his Edict on Maximum Prices, were set in *denarii* tariffed at 100 to the *argenteus*. The Edict (28.1a, 9 Giacchero) priced 1 lb gold bullion or coins at 72,000 *den.*, and 1 lb silver bullion at 6,000 *den.*, which implies that the *argenteus* was overvalued by 60 per cent, but we use the implied face value of 0.0336 g. Actual *argentei*, of which very few were minted, in fact weighed around AD 3.15 g.

24 Diocletian: see n. 23 above. Bagnall (1977: 327, 336) shows that receipts for bullion levies at the Egyptian village of Karanis around AD 307/8 imply a 1:12 ratio between gold and silver.

25 *CTh* 13.2.1 (397) $= CJ$ 10.78.1: for all payments to the imperial treasuries 1 lb silver may be commuted to 5 *solidi*. In *P.Oxy.* LI 3628–36 (fifth century AD), official collations of current prices of goods in middle Egypt, 1 lb silver bullion is always worth 5 *solidi*, and 1 lb 'idle', i.e. unrefined(?), silver worth 4.75 *solidi*. *CTh* 8.4.27 (AD 422) allows staff to commute the 'presents' they owe to *duces* at 4 *solidi* per 1 lb silver, which was clearly a special concession to the staff. The new ratio may have been introduced c. AD 355–360 when the *argenteus* was reduced to 144 to the pound (King 1993: 13).

26 For details see Rathbone (forthcoming b).

27 Bresson (2008: 219), and below.

28 Much of the following seems to be uncontroversial among historians of the Greek economy. For more detail, see Bresson (2008: II 177–210, 226) explicitly on the demand-and-supply mechanism in local markets; Möller (2007: esp. 363 f., 371–75); Eich (2006: 183 ff.); and still fundamental, Garnsey (1988). The much-debated issues of how much surplus was produced at Athens, consumption levels and the relative importance of home produced against imported cereals, and the behaviour of peasant households in relation to local markets (for which see esp. Gallant (1991: 99–110)) are beyond the scope of this chapter. I have suggested in Von Reden (2007a: 403–5) that – consumption levels in, and carrying capacity of, Attica apart – much of the Athenian need of imported grain in the fourth century BC was due to a growing preference for wheat varieties that could be baked into bread, rather than having to be consumed as porridge.

29 See White (1984: 145) and Parker (1992) for the archaeological evidence of the size of ships, and White (1984: 127–133), Casson (1994: 101–40) and Möller (2007: 367 f.) for the relative advantages and costs of water against land transport.

30 See Morley (2007: 26) for these figures.

31 Reger (2003): 333 f., cf. 1994: 90. The basic study for the argument of micro-climates, the prevalence of geographical micro-regions and their economic impact is Horden and Purcell (2000: esp. 123–43).

32 On storage as part of other household strategies, see Gallant (1991: 94–8); the figures about the size of regular storage vary: Forbes (1982: 234) suggested on the basis of the modern peninsula Methana that quantities sufficing to feed a family for two full

years were typical; Gallant (1991) questions these figures on the basis of a variety of comparative figures and archaeological evidence for storage facilities.

33   The question is intimately linked to the question of agricultural strategies of ancient peasants vis-à-vis landowners systematically producing cash-crops; some comments can be found in Möller (2007: 371 f.), Eich (2006: 194–97), Horden and Purcell (2000: 206) and Gallant (1989).

34   Möller (2007: 364); Bresson (2008: II 102–4).

35   See, for example, Olbia late third/early second century BC (Table A8.11 nos. 6a–b).

36   See Millett (1991: 188–97); Von Reden (2010: 101 f.) for some of the extensive literature on maritime finance.

37   Persuasively argued by Cohen (1992: 136–60); although his linkage of maritime finance and the development of banking is speculative and poorly attested.

38   For the following, see esp. Bresson (2008: II 178–98).

39   Garnsey (1988: 73, 155) and Bresson (2008: II 127–30).

40   Migeotte (1990; 1991); Fantasia (1984); Robert (1969: 26–7).

41   Garnsey (1988: 137–68).

42   For the following, Von Reden (2010: 118–34) and Schaps (2004).

43   Eich (2006: 197).

44   See Kim (2001) for the importance of silver fractions in the sixth and fifth centuries BC and Von Reden (2010: 32 f.) for their replacement by bronze coinage as an indication of increasing monetization in the fourth century BC.

45   For the important issue of coin circulation and their dependence on weight standards, often buried in the details of numismatic analyses, see Figueira (1998), Meadows (unpublished) and Von Reden (2010: 65–91). For a list of major weight standards in classical Greece, see Kraay (1976).

46   Scheidel (2008: 268–70); see also Schaps (2004: 16).

47   See Von Reden (2007b: 79 ff.) with reference to earlier literature.

48   Gold, silver and bronze, too, had both a metrological relationship and a relative market value that were at times adjusted to each other: Maresch (1996: 17). A customary relationship of value between wheat, barley and *olyra* (Egyptian wheat/emmer) was 2:3:5, see Maresch (1996: 183) with some pieces of demotic evidence.

49   Thus first Pringsheim (1961), and still Gallo (1997).

50   [Aristotle], *Athēnaiōn Politeia* 47.2 with Rhodes (1981 *ad loc.*); Hallof (1990).

51   See above, and Migeotte (1997).

52   Thus Migeotte (1997) argues correctly that there is an element of 'fixing' involved in the term, although he goes too far in regarding it as a term for 'official' price; thus also Bresson (2008: II 120).

53   Unfortunately, the evidence for barley does not add to our picture, as references are either late, or derived from the same texts as those of wheat.

54   For price formation and the economy of Delos, see the authoritative study by Reger (1994); his argument is set deliberately in contrast to the modernizing interpretations of Delian price development by Heichelheim (1930) and Rostovtzeff (1935/6); cf. Reger (1997: 53–55) and Chankowski (1997: 76–80) in relation to commodities other than grain.

55   Reger (1994: 10 f).

56   Thus the argument by Heichelheim (1930) on that series.

57   Manning (2003; 2007).

58   For different qualities of wheat given to, and consumed by, different kinds of people, see Reekmans (1966; 1996: 16–18).

59   Von Reden (2007b: 122 f.), and esp. the register of contracts P. Tebt. III 815.

60   *Ibid.*

61   For all these forms of commuting cash into kind, and vice versa, see Von Reden (2007b: 79–152;181–226).

62 On the role of *epitima* in Egyptian contracts, see still Berger (1911: 4 ff.).
63 See Von Reden (2007b: 153) with note for discussion of the controversial meaning of this clause.
64 For example Duncan-Jones (1976: 243).
65 *Katerga* were loans of cash made to tenants of a plot of land for financing agrarian work during the rental period. Such loans were repayable at the end of the agrarian year together with the rent.
66 See Horden and Purcell (2000: esp. 123 ff.), Parkins (1998) and Bresson (2008: II 219 ff.).
67 Reger (1994; cf. 1997).
68 See Von Reden (2010: 72–9) and Figueira (1998 *passim*).
69 *Ibid.*
70 Eich (2006: 137–42); see also Bresson (1993: 209 f.) and now Mackil (2013: 237–325), which appeared after this chapter was written.
71 Figueira (1998).
72 See Meadows (unpublished); summarized in Von Reden (2010: 80). Further examples of this pattern are given in Meadows (2001).
73 Meadows (2001: 56 f.).
74 Bresson (2008: II 220) with Loomis (1998).
75 De Callataÿ (1989).
76 Bresson (2008 II: 221 f.).
77 Hopkins (1980); but see also the critical comments by Howgego (1995).
78 Reger (1994: 220–30), for example, suggests that it was specific changes in contractual patterns of tenancy contracts during 300 to 290 BC that could explain the changes in prices on Delos during the post 290s BC.
79 Cadell and Le Rider (1997).
80 See Bagnall (1999) and Maresch (1996). Only the increase of penalty prices of wheat from 4 dr. to 5 dr., and possibly some variation in penalty prices during the second century BC, may be regarded as effects of real price increase.
81 Von Reden (2007b: 76 ff.).
82 See Eich (2006: 225 f.; 232 f.). The point has been made influentially by Amartya Sen (Sen 1999: 164–88).
83 Prag (2010).
84 In draft form this chapter has been available online since 2005; the reworked version in Temin (2013: 29–52) includes responses to some criticisms (cf. n.88 below).
85 Hopkins (1995/6: 220).
86 Heichelheim (1930: *passim*). For his earlier studies of prices which underlie this, see Rathbone (forthcoming b).
87 See Bang (2008: 153–66) on the trade in grain.
88 I am grateful to the author for showing me his chapter before publication. Temin (2013: 29–52) responds, but does not entirely rebut.
89 The actual range may have been more like 5 to 7.5 dr., with a variation around the median price of 20 per cent.
90 In the monetary system before 141/0 BC, 20 *asses* (5 modii at 4 *asses*) were equivalent to 2 *denarii*. Livy's record of events in any year is not necessarily full, and his narrative for 166 BC on is lost.
91 Frank (1933: 192), with many followers.
92 Cf. Meijer (1993).
93 Possibly the prices are specifically those of 104 BC when the senate first appointed a special supervisor of the grain supply, one of the models for the story of 439 BC.
94 The coinage reform of 141/0 BC may have been a reaction to rising monetary values; it was accompanied by a reform of the minimum census levels for Roman citizens

which substantially raised those of the top four *classes* but reduced the level for the fifth *classis*.

95 It is possible that the *se'ah* was equivalent to the *modius castrensis* (not, as Sperber assumes, the *modius italicus*), in which case the silver equivalent for 1 to 2 *den.* would be 26–52 g/hl. For an explanation of the high prices at Sparta (no. 22) see below.

96 Rathbone (1996); Scheidel (2002).

97 Rathbone (2007: 159–60, 165).

98 *Pap.Agon.* 6; 4; *P.Oxy.* LXXIX forthcoming; *Pap.Agon.* 1; 3.

99 The fundamental study remains Bagnall (1985), with reactions in Camilli and Sorda (1993). He argues that prices rose in steps in response to successive debasements of the coinage, but not all are convinced.

100 On the artificially low prices for some goods in Diocletian's Edict see Rathbone (2009: 317–21), also doubting that it can have been intended to apply to the western provinces.

101 See further Rathbone (2009: 309–10, 313, 323–4).

102 Dio Chrysostom, *Oration* 46.10; Cicero, *In Verrem* 2.2.191–2.

103 See Rathbone (2009), with some other examples of state and private allowances which seem to suppose that a modius of wheat was typically worth 1 *denarius*.

104 The shortage at Rome probably also reflected the culmination of supply problems (and civic unrest) caused by Sulla's abolition of the Gracchan distribution scheme which the senate was about to restore in 73 BC.

105 Pliny, *Panegyricus* 30–2.

106 *P.Oxy.* XLVII 3339.

107 Cf. Table A8.12 no. 19, an undated third-century AD letter which mentions a general reluctance to pay taxes because of 'the low price of crops'.

108 The grain demands and resources of the Republican state are explored in Rathbone (forthcoming a).

109 The assertion of Kessler and Temin (2008: 157) that there is no evidence to contradict their assumption that the *annona* purchased its supplies in Rome at market rates is simply wrong.

110 In March 200 AD Septimius Severus banned *adaeratio* in Egypt (*P.Col.* VI 123.43–4 = Oliver, *Greek Constitutions* no. 235), perhaps because of problems of supplies during his long stay in Egypt; it is attested again later, although compulsory purchases (*pyros synagoristikos*) disappear.

111 Erdkamp (2005: 232–4) lists eastern cases, albeit trying to minimize them to support his thesis, which I find implausible, that Rome consumed almost all Egypt's grain. Rome: Tacitus, *Annals* 14.51 (AD 62): a prefect of the *annona* popular for not profiteering; Dio 72.13.1–6, Herodian 1.12.3–5 and *HA Commodus* 14.1–3, cf. 7.1–2 (AD 189): senior officials profiteer from the *annona* by exploiting a feared shortage (after a plague) to charge high prices for sales of grain surplus to the free distributions.

112 Concisely surveyed by Erdkamp (2005: 271–9).

113 *Lex Irnitana* Chapter 75; cf. *Digest* 48.12.2 pr, from Ulpian's commentary on the Augustan law.

114 Suetonius, *Augustus* 42.

115 *HA Commodus* 14.3, written in the fourth century AD but probably taken from the early third-century AD biography by Marius Maximus; cf. Dio 72.15.6, and n.111 above.

116 The prices are rhetorical, not real, a poetic barb about the excessive subsidy of urban consumers to which populist emperors tended.

117 Erdkamp (2005: 276) lists some perhaps analogous civic schemes, but only the Oxyrhynchus one of the AD 260s is clearly based on the *frumentatio*, and none seems to have lasted long.

118 Only a handful of individual benefactions and some imperial support are known: e.g. Table A8.10 nos. 22, 25, 26; also Erdkamp (2005: 280–1).

119 Cf. Banaji (2001) and Brown (2002), both provocative and controversial.

Abbreviations for ancient sources

Generally as in *The Oxford Classical Dictionary* (Fourth edition 2012).
For papyrus texts see: http://scriptorium.lib.duke.edu/papyrus/texts/clist.html

Bibliography

Bagnall, R. S. 1977. 'Bullion Purchases and Landholding in the Fourth Century', *Chronique d'Egypte*, 52: 322–36.
—— 1985. *Currency and Inflation in Fourth Century Egypt*, Chico: Scholars Press.
—— 1999. Review of Cadell and Le Rider 1997, *Schweizerische Numismatische Rundschau*, 78: 97–103.
Banaji, J. 2001. *Agrarian Change in Late Antiquity. Gold, Labour and Aristocratic Dominance*, Oxford: Oxford University Press.
Bang, P. F. 2008. *The Roman Bazaar: a Comparative Study of Trade and Markets in a Tributary Empire*, Cambridge: Cambridge University Press.
Berger, A. 1911. *Die Strafklauseln in den Papyrus Urkunden*, Berlin and Leipzig: Teubner.
Bransbourg, G. 2012. 'Rome and the Economic Integration of Empire', ISAW Papers 3: http://dlib.nyu.edu/awdl/isaw/isaw-papers/3/.
Bresson, A. 1993. 'Les cités grecques et leurs emporia', in *L'Emporion*, edited by A. Bresson and P. Rouillard, Paris: De Boccard: 163–226
—— 2008. *L'économie de La Grèce des cités*, vol. II, Paris: Armand Colin.
Brown, P. 2002. *Poverty and Leadership in the Later Roman Empire*, Hanover NH: University Press of New England.
Cadell, H. and Le Rider, G. 1997. *Prix du blé et numéraire dans l'égypte lagide de 305–173*, Brussels: Fondation Égyptologique Reine Élisabeth.
Camilli, L. and Sorda, S., eds. 1993. *L'<inflazione> nel quarto secolo d.C.*, Rome: Istituto Italiano di Numismatica.
Carrié, J.-M. 1997. 'L'arithmétique sociale de l'économie agraire: prix de la terre, rente foncière et prix des céréales dans l'Égypte Romano-Byzantine', in *Économie antique. Prix et formation des prix dans les économies antiques*, edited by J. Andreau, P. Briant, and R. Descat, Saint-Bertrand-de-Comminges: Musée archéologique départemental: 121–46.
Casson, L. 1994. *Ships and Seafaring in Ancient Times*, London: British Museum Press.
Chankowski, V. 1997. 'Le sanctuaire d'Apollon et le marché délien', in *Economie antique. Prix et formation des prix dans les economies antiques*, edited by J. Andreau, P. Briant, and R. Descat, Saint-Bertrand-de-Comminges: Musée archéologique départemental: 73–90.
Cohen, E. E. 1992. *Athenian Economy and Society. A Banking Perspective*, Princeton: Princeton University Press.
Crawford, M. H. 1975. 'Finance, Coinage and Money from the Severans to Constantine', in *Aufstieg und Niedergang der römischen Welt* II.2, edited by H. Temporini and W. Haase, Berlin: Walter de Gruyter: 560–93.
De Callataÿ, F. 1989. 'Les trésors achéménides et les monnayages d'Alexandre: espèces immobilisées et espèces circulantes', *Revue des Études Anciennes*, 91: 259–74.
Drexhage, H.-J. 1991. *Preise, Mieten/Pachten, Kosten und Löhne im römischen Ägypten bis zum Regierungsantritt Diokletians*, St Katharinen: Scripta Mercaturae.
Duncan-Jones, R. P. 1976. 'The Price of Wheat in Roman Egypt under the Principate', *Chiron*, 6: 241–62; revised in Duncan-Jones 1990: 143–55.
—— 1979. 'Variation in Egyptian Grain Measure', *Chiron*, 9: 347–75.
—— 1982. *The Economy of the Roman Empire. Quantitative Studies*, 2nd edition, Cambridge: Cambridge University Press. 1st edition 1974.
—— 1990. *Structure and Scale in the Roman Economy*, Cambridge: Cambridge University Press.

Eich, A. 2006. *Die politische Ökonomie des antiken Griechenland (6.–3. Jh. v. Chr.)*, Cologne: Böhlau.

Elsen, J. J. 2002. 'La stabilité du système pondéral et monétaire attique', *Revue Belge de Numismatique*, 148: 1–32.

Erdkamp, P. 2005. *The Grain Market in the Roman Empire*, Cambridge: Cambridge University Press.

Ermatinger, J. W. 1996. *The Economic Reforms of Diocletian*, St Katharinen: Scripta Mercaturae.

Fantasia, U. 1984. 'Mercanti et sitonia nelle città greche. In margine a tre documenti epigrafici della prima età ellenistica', *Civiltà classica e cristiana*, 5: 283–311.

Figueira, T. 1998. *The Power of Money*, Pennsylvania: University of Pennsylvania Press.

Forbes, H. 1982. *Strategies and Soils: Technology, Production and Environment in the Peninsula of Methana*, PhD thesis, University of Pennsylvania.

Frank, T. 1933. *Rome and Italy of the Republic*, in *Economic Survey of Ancient Rome*, edited by T. Frank, vol. I, Baltimore: Johns Hopkins Press.

Gallant, T. 1989. 'Crisis and Response: Risk-buffering Behaviour in Hellenistic Greek Communities', *Journal of Interdisciplinary History*, 19: 393–413.

—— 1991. *Risk and Survival in Ancient Greece*, Stanford: Stanford University Press.

Gallo, L. 1997. 'I prezzi nelle stele attiche: un'indagine campione', in *Économie antique. Prix et formation des prix dans les économies antiques*, edited by J. Andreau, P. Briant, and R. Descat, Saint-Bertrand-de-Comminges: Musée archéologique départemental: 21–32.

Garnsey, P. 1988. *Famine and Food Supply in the Graeco-Roman World: Responses to Risk and Crisis*, Cambridge: Cambridge University Press.

Hackens, T. 1983. 'Les Monnaies', in *Guide de Délos*, edited by P. Bruneau and J. Ducat, 3rd edition, Paris: Boccard: 107–11.

Hallof, K. 1990. 'Der Verkauf konfiszierten Vermögens vor den Poleten in Athen', *Klio*, 72: 422–36.

Heichelheim, F. 1930. *Wirtschaftliche Schwankungen der Zeit von Alexander bis Augustus. Beiträge zur Erforschung der wirtschaftlichen Wechsellagen. Aufschwung, Krise, Stockung*, vol. 3, Jena: G. Fischer; repr. New York 1979.

—— 1935. 'Sitos', in Pauly-Wissowa, *Real-Encyclopädie*, suppl. VI: 819–92.

—— 1954/5. 'On Ancient Price Trends from the Early First Millennium B.C. to Heraclius I', *Finanzarchiv*, 15: 498–511.

—— 1970. *An Ancient Economic History: from the Palaeolithic Age to the Migrations of the Germanic, Slavic and Arabic Nations*, Leiden: A. W. Sijthoff 1958, 1964, 1970; originally: *Wirtschaftsgeschichte des Altertums: vom Paläolithikum bis zur Völkerwanderung der Germanen, Slaven und Araber*, Leiden: A. W. Sijthoff, 2nd edition, 1969.

Hopkins, K. 1978. *Conquerors and Slaves. Sociological Studies in Roman History, Volume I*, Cambridge: Cambridge University Press.

—— 1980. 'Taxes and Trade in the Roman Empire, 200 BC–AD 400', *Journal of Roman Studies*, 70: 101–25.

—— 1995/6. 'Rome, Taxes, Rents and Trade', *Kodai*, 6/7: 41–75; reprinted in *The Ancient Economy*, edited by W. Scheidel and S. von Reden, 2002, Edinburgh: Edinburgh University Press: 190–230.

Horden, P. and Purcell, N. 2000. *The Corrupting Sea. A Study of Mediterranean History*, Oxford: Blackwell.

Howgego, C. 1992. 'The Supply and Use of Money in the Roman World: 200 BC to AD 300', *Journal of Roman Studies*, 82: 1–31.

—— 1995. *Ancient History from Coins*, London: Routledge.

Hultsch, F. 1882. *Griechische und römische Metrologie*, 2nd edition, Berlin: Weidmann; reprinted Graz 1971. 1st edition 1862.

Johnson, A. C. 1936. *Roman Egypt to the Reign of Diocletian*, in *Economic Survey of Ancient Rome*, edited by T. Frank, vol. II, Baltimore: Johns Hopkins Press.

Kessler, D. and Temin, P. 2008. 'Money and Prices in the Early Roman Empire', in *The Monetary Systems of the Greeks and Romans*, edited by W. V. Harris, Oxford: Oxford University Press: 137–59.

Kim, H. 2001. 'Small Change and the Moneyed Economy', in *Money, Labour and Land. Approaches to the Economics of Ancient Greece*, edited by P. Cartledge, E. E. Cohen and L. Foxhall, London: Routledge: 44–51.

King, C. 1993. 'The Fourth Century Coinage', in *L'<inflazione> nel quarto secolo d.C.*, edited by L. Camilli and S. Sorda, Rome: Istituto Italiano di Numismatica: 1–87.

Kraay, C. 1976. *Archaic and Classical Greek Coins*, London: Methuen.

Lanciers, E. 1990. 'Ägyptisches Brot (k′k′) in UPZ I 149 und die wirtschaftliche Lage zur Zeit Ptolemaios IV Philopator', *Zeitschrift für Papyrologie und Epigraphik*, 82: 89–92.

Lang, M. and Crosby, M. 1964. *The Athenian Agora*, X. *Weights, Measures and Tokens*, Princeton: American School of Classical Studies at Athens.

Loomis, W. T. 1998. *Wages, Welfare Costs and Inflation in Classical Athens*, Ann Arbor: Michigan University Press.

Lorber, C. 2012. 'The Coinage of the Ptolemies', in *The Oxford Handbook of Greek and Roman Coinage*, edited by W. E. Metcalf, Oxford: Oxford University Press: 211–34.

Mackil, E. 2013. *Creating a Common Polity. Religion, Economy and Politics in the Making of the Greek Koinon*, Berkeley and Los Angeles: University of California Press.

Manning, J. 2003. *Land and Power in Ptolemaic Egypt*, Cambridge: Cambridge University Press.

—— 2007. 'Hellenistic Egypt', in *The Cambridge Economic History of the Greco-Roman World*, edited by W. Scheidel, I. Morris and R. Saller, Cambridge: Cambridge University Press: 434–59.

Maresch, K. 1996. *Bronze und Silber. Papyrologische Beiträge zur Geschichte der Währung im ptolemäischen und römischen Ägypten bis zum 2. Jh. n. Chr.*, Köln: Westdeutscher Verlag.

Markle, M. M. 1985. 'Jury Pay and Assembly Pay at Athens', in *Crux. Essays Presented to G. E.M. de Ste Croix on his 75th Birthday*, edited by P. Cartledge and D. Harvey, Exeter: Imprint Academic: 265–97.

Meadows, A. 2001. 'Money, Freedom, and Empire in the Hellenistic World', in *Money and its Uses in the Ancient Greek World*, edited by A. Meadows and K. Shipton, Oxford, Oxford University Press: 53–65.

—— Unpublished. 'Ptolemaic Financial Policy and the Chronology of the Second Syrian War', Unpublished conference paper, Hellenistic Economies, Liverpool, June 1998.

Meijer, F. 1993. 'Cicero and the Costs of the Republican Grain Laws', in *De Agricultura: In Memoriam Pieter Willem de Neeve*, edited by H. Sancisi-Weerdenburg, R. J. Van der Spek, H. C. Teitler and H. T. Wallinga, Amsterdam: Gieben: 153–63.

Migeotte, L. 1984. *L'emprunt public dans les cités grecques*, Paris and Quebec: Editions du Sphinx.

—— 1990. 'Le pain quotidien dans les cités hellénistiques: une affaire d'état?' *Hommage à La memoire La mémoire d'Ernest Pascal*, Cahiers des études anciennes: 291–300.

—— 1991. 'Le pain quotidien dans les cités hellénistiques. À propos des fonds permanents pour l'approvisionnement en grain', *Cahiers du Centre G. Glotz*, 2: 19–41.

—— 1997. 'Le contrôle des prix dans les cités grecques', in *Économie antique. Prix et formation des prix dans les economies antiques*, edited by J. Andreau, P. Briant, and R. Descat, Saint-Bertrand-de-Comminges: Musée archéologique départemental: 33–52.

Millett, P. 1991. *Lending and Borrowing in Classical Athens*, Cambridge: Cambridge University Press.

Möller, A. 2007. 'Classical Greece: Distribution', in *The Cambridge Economic History of the Greco-Roman World*, edited by W. Scheidel, I. Morris and R. Saller, Cambridge: Cambridge University Press: 362–84.

Morley, N. 2007. *Trade in Classical Antiquity*, Cambridge: Cambridge University Press.

Noeske, H.-C. 2000. *Die Münzen der Ptolemäer*, Frankfurt: Historisches Museum Frankfurt.

Parker, A. 1992. *Ancient Shipwrecks of the Mediterranean and Roman Provinces*, Oxford: Tempus Reparatum.

Parkins, H. 1998. 'Time for Change? Shaping the Future of the Ancient Economy', in *Trade, Traders and the Ancient City*, edited by H. Parkins and C. Smith, London: Routledge: 1–16.

Persson, K. G. 1999. *Grain Markets in Europe 1500–1900*, Cambridge: Cambridge University Press.

Pommerening, T. 2005. *Die altägyptischen Hohlmaße*, in *Studien zur altägyptischen Kultur*, Bd. 10, Hamburg: Buske.

Prag, J. 2010. 'Siculo-Punic Coinage and Siculo-Punic Interactions', in *Meetings between Cultures in the Ancient Mediterranean. Proceedings of the 17th International Congress of Classical Archaeology, Rome 22–26 Sept. 2008, Bollettino di Archeologia*, edited by M. Dalla Riva, Online 1, Volume Speciale: http://151.12.58.75/archeologia/bao_document/articoli/2_PRAG.pdf

Pringsheim, F. 1961. 'Der griechische Versteigerungskauf', in *Gesammelte Abhandlungen*, edited by F. Pringsheim, Heidelberg:Winter: 262–329.

Rathbone, D. W. 1983. 'The Weight and Measurement of Egyptian Grains', *Zeitschrift für Papyrologie und Epigraphik*, 53: 265–75.

—— 1996. 'Monetisation, not Price-inflation, in Third-century A.D. Egypt?', in *Coin Finds and Coin Use in the Roman World, Studien zu Fundmünzen der Antike* 10, edited by C. E. King and D. Wigg, Berlin: Mann: 321–39.

—— 1997. 'Prices and Price-formation in Roman Egypt', in *Économie antique. Prix et formation des prix dans les économies antiques*, edited by J. Andreau, P. Briant, and R. Descat, Saint-Bertrand-de-Comminges: Musée archéologique départemental: 183–244.

—— 2007. 'Military Finance and Supply', in *The Cambridge History of Greek and Roman Warfare*, II, edited by P. Sabin, H. Van Wees and M. Whitby, Cambridge: Cambridge University Press: 158–76.

—— 2009. 'Earnings and Costs: Living Standards and the Roman Economy (First to Third Centuries AD),' in *Quantifying the Roman Economy. Methods and Problems*, edited by A. Bowman and A. Wilson, Oxford: Oxford University Press: 299–326.

—— Forthcoming a. 'Mediterranean Grain Prices c. 300 to 31 BC: the Impact of Rome', in Baker and Jursa (forthcoming).

—— Forthcoming b. 'Mediterranean and Near Eastern Grain Prices c. 300 to 31 BC: Some Preliminary Conclusions', in Baker and Jursa (forthcoming).

Reekmans, T. 1948. 'Monetary History and the Dating of Ptolemaic Papyri', *Studia Hellenistica*, 5: 15–43.

—— 1951. 'The Ptolemaic Copper Inflation', *Studia Hellenistica*, 7: 61–119.

—— 1966. *La sitométrie dans les archives de Zénon*, Brussels: Fondation Égyptologique Reine Élisabeth.

—— 1996. *La consommation dans les archives de Zénon*, Brussels: Fondation Égyptologique Reine Élisabeth.

Reger, G. 1994. *Regionalism and Change in the Economy of Independent Delos*, Berkeley: University of California Press.

—— 1997. 'The Price Histories of Some Imported Goods on Independent Delos', in *Économie antique. Prix et formation des prix dans les économies antiques*, edited by J. Andreau, P. Briant, and R. Descat, Saint-Bertrand-de-Comminges: Musée archéologique départemental: 52–71.

—— 2003. 'The Economy', in *A Companion to the Hellenistic World*, edited by A. Erskine, Oxford: Blackwell: 331–53.

Rhodes, P. J. 1981. A Commentary on the Aristotelian Athenaion Politeia. Oxford: Oxford University Press.

Robert, L. 1969. 'Inscriptions d'Athènes et de la Grèce centrale', *Archaiologikê Ephêmeris*, 1969: 1–58.

Rostovtzeff, M. 1935/6. 'The Hellenistic World and its Economic Development', *Ancient History Review*, 41: 231–52.

Schaps, D. 2004. *The Invention of Coinage and the Monetization of Ancient Greece*, Ann Arbor: Michigan University Press.

Scheidel, W. 2002. 'A Model of Demographic and Economic Change in Egypt after the Antonine Plague', *Journal of Roman Archaeology*, 15: 97–114.

—— 2008. 'The Divergent Evolution of Coinage in Eastern and Western Eurasia', in *The Monetary System of the Greeks and Romans*, edited by W. V. Harris, Oxford: Oxford University Press: 267–86.

Sen, A. 1999. *Development as Freedom*, Oxford: Oxford University Press.

Shelton, C. 1977. 'Artabs and choinikes', *Zeitschrift für Papyrologie und Epigraphik*, 24: 55–67.

Silver, M. 2007. 'Grain Funds in the Roman Near East: Market Failure or Murder of the Market?', *Ancient History Bulletin*, 21: 95–104.

Sperber, D. 1991. *Roman Palestine, 200–400: Money and Prices*, 2nd edition, Ramat-Gan: Bar-Ilan University Press. 1st edition 1974.

Szaivert, W. and Wolters, R. 2005. *Löhne, Preise, Werte. Quellen zur römischen Geldwirtschaft*, Darmstadt: Wissenschaftliche Buchgesellschaft.

Temin, P. 2001. 'A Market Economy in the Early Roman Empire', *Journal of Roman Studies*, 91: 169–177.

—— 2013. *The Roman Market Economy*, Princeton: Princeton University Press.

Vial, C. 1985. 'Les sources de revenue des Déliens à l'époque hellénistique', in *L'origine des richesses dépensées dans La ville antique*, edited by P. Leveau, Aix-en-Provence: Université de Provence: 47–53.

Vleeming, S. P. 1979. 'Some Notes on the Artaba in Pathyris', *Enchoria*, 9: 93–100.

Von Freyberg, H.-U. 1998. *Kapitalverkehr und Handel im römischen Kaiserreich (27 v. Chr. – 235 n. Chr.)*, Freiburg im Breisgau: R. Haufe.

Von Reden, S. 2007a. 'Classical Greece: consumption', in *The Cambridge Economic History of the Greco-Roman World*, edited by W. Scheidel, I. Morris and R. Saller, Cambridge: Cambridge University Press: 385–408.

—— 2007b. *Money in Ptolemaic Egypt*, Cambridge: Cambridge University Press.

—— 2010. *Money in Classical Antiquity*, Cambridge: Cambridge University Press.

—— Forthcoming. 'Wheat Prices in Ptolemaic Egypt', in *Documentary Sources in Ancient Near Eastern and Greco-Roman History: Methodology and Practice*, edited by H. D. Baker and M. Jursa, Oxford: Oxbow Books, forthcoming.

White, K. D. 1984. *Greek and Roman Technology*, London: Thames and Hudson.

9 Soldiers and booze

The rise and decline of a Roman market economy in north-western Europe

Eltjo Buringh and Maarten Bosker

Introduction

Two millennia ago Rome had a large economy based on market institutions and a stable government.[1] In Italy, the Middle East and in Egypt the Roman Empire (RE) was highly urbanized, containing cities of 100,000 inhabitants and more, despite being a pre-industrial society. In a seminal article Hopkins (1980) argued that it was the taxes in the form of money that greatly contributed to the development of a market economy in the RE, as people now had to produce a surplus that could be sold on a market to generate the money with which to pay their taxes.[2] This chapter aims to study what happened in north-western Europe in this respect. An important and, in our opinion, as yet inadequately answered question is how the Romans got a market economy to flourish in the backward part of the empire that then was newly conquered. In considerably less than a century the Romans produced an effective and successful local economic system largely based on market exchange. This is a surprising result: European colonizers in Africa, for example, were later to experience that just imposing a tax in money on the native inhabitants does not automatically lead to the establishment of a local market economy, not even with military presence as a backup. How did the Romans succeed? The short answer is that the Roman military delivered this feat.[3]

However, for us this answer is too simple, as the role of the Roman army has up to now only been presented in very general terms, while its more specific local influence has not been unravelled and differences in regional economic consequences of the army's presence have never been properly quantified. Intriguing questions have not yet been answered, such as why did the military *limes* (fortified frontier) along the River Rhine produce the large Roman towns of Cologne and Xanten, while along similar military establishments of equal size at a very comparable *limes* in the German Taunus and along Hadrian's Wall in Britain such large Roman towns did not develop? And why do we see such a huge difference in economic development between, for example, the Roman settlements along the rivers Scheldt and the Thames, while both are seemingly similar local river systems in north-western Europe and both are located well outside the frontier zones of the RE?

The first aim of this chapter is to study the regional development of a Roman market economy. For this we use local coin finds as a proxy. The idea is that the proportion of small change in these coin finds can be used as an index of the degree to which processes of commercialization have occurred; large denomination (gold or silver) coins will mainly have been used in long-distance trade, but the appearance of small (copper or bronze) coins points to the existence of small, local transactions.[4] Our contribution is that we collected information on the fraction of precious metals in stray coin finds in various zones and time periods inside and outside the RE, which can supply additional evidence about the rise and decline, and the spatial structure, of the monetization.

The second aim of this chapter is to study how the Roman market economy in north-western Europe was spatially distributed and which were its main drivers. Our main contribution is that we have estimated the regional settlement density in various fluvial catchment areas by quantifying the sizes of over 2,000 Roman settlements at the height of the empire around AD 150.[5] We will use this regional settlement density along waterways as a proxy for economic development and consider the differing distribution of the Roman military over the larger fluvial areas in north-western Europe as a natural historical experiment that can be used to quantify the influence of the military on the development of the local economy.[6] We will also be looking at and trying to quantify the other potential factors that could have driven the local economy in Roman times. With the help of a specific statistical technique (multivariate analysis) we can eventually determine which of these potential drivers were the most important and quantify their regional influence.

This chapter is composed as follows: in the next section we describe the methodical approach, indicating how we defined the study area, period, and concepts such as settlement densities, fluvial catchments and how we used the coin finds in various zones to assess local monetization. In the following section we give some overall geographical results of the study area and describe the checks we made on the obtained results. On the basis of coin finds we then go on to describe the rise and decline of a market economy in north-western Europe before, during and after the local Roman presence. We then devote a section to presenting the Roman settlement densities in the various fluvial catchments as a proxy for the development of the Roman economy. Finally we describe the various potential drivers of the local settlement density and statistically assess their influence on the economy.

Methodical approach

Study area and period

The study area we concentrate on is the former Roman territory in current day France, Switzerland, Belgium and Luxembourg, England and Wales as well as parts of Holland and Germany. Our study on urbanization concentrates on the situation around the year AD 150, at the height of the RE. In AD 150, our study area and its originally 'barbaric' population had been exposed to nearly one-and-a-half centuries of Roman civilization, after the original conquests by Julius Caesar and his successors around the start of the common era.

Settlement density

In accordance with regular practice in economic history we will use the levels of urbanization as a proxy for economic success.[7] The term urbanization needs somewhat more qualification here, as it nowadays usually indicates the proportion of the population living in towns with more than 10,000 inhabitants. For our north-westerly fringe areas and this very early period such a criterion is definitively too stringent, as fewer than two dozen towns would be large enough to qualify. There-fore we have used the population housed in Roman settlements[8] as an alternative indicator for the 'urbanization' around the year AD 150 in the study area. Also the numbers of the population living in Roman settlements have in their turn been estimated indirectly, as there is a lack of accurate and detailed population censuses for this time and place. Here archaeological evidence comes to the rescue, and we have used excavation reports of the surface area (in hectares (ha)) of habited Roman settlements as a direct indicator of the numbers of the Roman population.[9] The names and locations of the more than 2,000 Roman settlements, forts or mines in our study area can be found in the *Barrington Atlas of the Greek and Roman World* edited by Talbert (2000). The inhabited surface area of a settlement in ha can be directly translated into the numbers of its inhabitants.[10] Such an indica-tor allows us to geographically visualize the working of the Roman economy and quantify its effects in the various regions.

We scanned the archaeological literature to find the inhabited surface area (in ha) around the year AD 150 of all Roman settlements from the *Barrington Atlas*. For walled cities we looked further than just to the value of its walled surface area in ha, as sometimes the surface occupied by the extramural population may have been adding substantially to the inhabited surface area of a walled town. For some other cities the opposite was true, as their walls had been built to surround an area considerably larger than the surface that was in fact actually inhabited by its population. The methods we used to fill in missing values of surface areas for which we could not find archaeological information and the whole process of data handling have been described extensively in a separate Data Appendix on the Internet.[11]

The geographical unit of analysis

We could have used the current 1990-countries (see *study area* above) as a geo-graphical subdivision on which to report our findings and carry out our analyses, but we thought such a subdivision not appropriate, as current national boundaries were completely artificial 2,000 years ago. Instead we opted for a subdivision of the study area that incorporates the most important form of transport of bulk goods in Roman times. Buringh *et al.* (forthcoming) have shown that transport on inland waterways was the cheapest and most widely preferred way to transport bulk goods in antiquity. Therefore we concentrated on fluvial catchment areas as our geographical unit of analysis for this chapter. To find the settlements that are interconnected to one another by riverine transport without the necessity of transhipment we grouped all settlements along waterways located on one and the same fluvial system. By using fluvial catchment areas as our unit of analysis we follow the more or less natural boundaries that limited waterborne commerce in history. In principle the various settlements along such a fluvial system could be reached by boat or barge and their mutual trade would have profited from the relatively lower cost of riverine transport compared to transport overland. We discerned twelve important fluvial systems in the study area (cf. Figure 9.1).

A fluvial system is defined as comprising all Roman settlements located along a river in the water catchment area of a river flowing from its source(s) to the sea; this also includes the various settlements along all of its different tributaries right up to the last before their various sources. The sum of the actual length of all riverine waterways up to the sea (including all of its bends and curves) connecting the Roman settlements in a catchment area has been called the length of the fluvial system.[12] To estimate the relative economic importance of a fluvial system we summed the total inhabited area in ha of all settlements along waterways of that fluvial system and divided that by the total length of the fluvial system to get a relative measure (in ha/km) that can readily be used for comparative purposes.[13]

Figure 9.1 Fluvial catchment areas in NW Europe.

The seven main catchment areas are: the Thames, Seine, Loire, Garonne, Meuse, Rhone and Rhine. The Rhine catchment area is of course limited to the actual area within the confines of the Roman *limes*, and we have subdivided it further into three smaller areas: that of the Moselle entering the Rhine at Koblenz (*Confluentes*), that of the Lower Rhine from Remagen (*Rigomagus*) to the sea and that of the Upper Rhine from Remagen inland up to the Alps. The catchment area of the Garonne also incudes that of the Dordogne, lying in the northern part of the basin. Just above that of the Seine we can find the (rather minor) catchment area of the Somme, a river of local importance. The basin of the Scheldt can be found just north-west between the Meuse and the sea.

Monetization

As explained in the introduction, we use data on coin finds to document the rise and decline of local market economies. We focus on coin finds in the Netherlands, because of the ready availability of this information.[14] Data on coins have been collected from the NUMIS-database that was located at the Netherlands Geldmuseum in Utrecht, which can be accessed on the Internet.[15] It shows all coin finds in the Netherlands (currently some 260,000 coins) on 10×10 km^2 grids or in the respective municipalities where they were found. NUMIS can be freely searched for different aspects of each individual coin (e.g. was it part of a hoard or a stray find? its minting date and place; find date and place; what ruler was depicted; metal composition, etc.). Additional Roman coin finds outside the Netherlands have been collected from various specific archaeological reports on excavations, but were unfortunately less comprehensive than NUMIS. We have mainly used the stray finds of coins and neglected hoards, because we think stray finds are probably a better representation of the coin that was actually in circulation. The choice to use the information from stray finds of course also has a drawback, as obviously the distribution of such coin finds generally will be biased toward the lower values in circulation.[16] Therefore one should not mistake the proportions found in NUMIS and elsewhere for those that were in actual circulation.[17] However, for this chapter this is not a real problem, as we just use coin finds as a relative measure and calculate the proportions of precious metals to show relative differences in coin use in various periods and zones.

Geographical results

Figure 9.2 shows a map of the actual study area and the distribution of the settlements from Roman times found in the *Barrington Atlas*.[18]

Using an average value of 100 inhabitants/ha we estimated that the various Roman settlements in the study area of nearly 1 million km^2 probably contained 1.7 million inhabitants in this period, while there were some ten million inhabitants in total.[19] The two biggest Roman cities, Lyon and Cologne, each had some 20,000 inhabitants, which certainly was large for this north-westerly area but not very large compared to Rome or some cities in the east of the empire which could exceed 100,000 or a multiple thereof. In France, in decreasing order,

Figure 9.2 Settlements around AD 150 in three Gauls, Britannia, Belgica and the Germanias.

Source: see Data Appendix, Section 2.

Bordeaux, Amiens, Autun, Vienne, Besancon, Reims, Poitiers, Sens, Saintes, Cahors, Limoges, Metz and Nimes probably contained between 20,000 and 10,000 inhabitants. Mainz and Trier in Germany and Cirencester, St Albans and Wroxeter in London belong to this size category too. Except for Nimes all of the towns in this largest category were located along a river, indicating that only 5 per cent of this size class was not directly connected to a waterway. In the study area we estimate that some 50 Roman towns had a population of between 5,000 and 10,000 inhabitants, while 131 towns may have harboured between 2,000 and 5,000 persons around the year AD150. Of the towns of the intermediate class only 18 per cent were not lying on a river, while of those in the smallest size class 23 per cent were not directly connected to a riverine waterway.

Before coming to an analysis and interpretation of the collected material we think it is appropriate to first perform a few simple checks on the collected settlement sizes. We would expect, for instance, to find a relationship between the dimensions of a settlement and the size of its commercial activities. A way to test this is to analyse whether there is a relationship between the size of a forum in a Roman town and the dimensions of a town's surface area. Of course a forum then also had religious, administrative, judicial and symbolic functions as well as its commercial role. We would also expect to find a relationship between the size of a town and the amount of cash that was used locally, assuming that the sizes of towns are a measure of their economic success. For this aspect we will study the relationship between the total amount of stray Roman coins found in a town and its size around AD 150.

For north-western Europe data it turns out that there is a considerable relationship between the excavated surface area of a forum in a town and its size (correlation: 0.79, *p*-value <0.01). Market transactions need coins and therefore we will explore to see if we can find a relationship between local coin circulation (with total numbers of stray finds of all Roman coins minted before AD 402 as a proxy for this) and the size of the various settlements; see Figure 9.3. There is

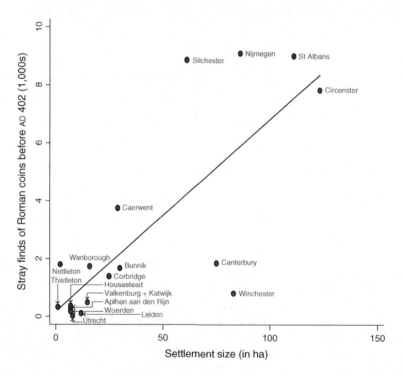

Figure 9.3 Total stray finds of Roman coins (in 1,000s of coins, *y*-axis) minted before AD 402 and settlement size in hectares (*x*-axis).

Sources: Casey (1974), Reece (1973), NUMIS and Data Appendix, Section 2.

Note:
The correlation between settlement size and stray coin finds is 0.78 [*p*-value < 0.01].

noise in the data in the figure due to the fact that the various find totals have not been corrected for the fraction of the Roman town that was actually excavated. Some settlements have been nearly totally excavated, while others have only been partially excavated because, for example, the current habitation prevents such a total excavation.

We conclude from these checks that there is a considerable relationship between the Roman town size in north-western Europe around AD 150 and the dimensions of its forum, and we also find a fair relationship between town sizes and the amount of coin in local circulation. These results are a reassuring check for the quality of the data collected. Now we continue with the question of whether a Roman market economy developed in the study area.

Rise and decline of a Roman market economy

As explained in the previous section, we use the proportion of coins composed of precious metal as a proxy for the development of a market economy. For this we will look at three different periods – the pre-Roman, Roman and of course the post-Roman period – to find out if the coin finds point to a local market economy with quite some use of small change or on the contrary that they indicate that long-distance trade was the more usual pattern of local commerce.

The pre-Roman period

Compared to the period 330 to 30 BC directly preceding the Roman period, in most of our study area the *Barrington Atlas* indicates a more than tenfold rise in the numbers of settlements in the northerly area (above 47 degrees latitude). Of course there were Celtic or Germanic settlements pre-dating the Roman conquest, but their geographical locations were often quite different from those of the later Roman towns. The larger native settlements in Britain and on the Continent mostly comprised extensive hill forts not directly connected to navigable water, such as Bibracte in France: people who lived there were concentrated up to a point when compared with the adjoining countryside, but were considerably less concentrated than was customary in Roman towns later on.[20] The Celts also knew coins. But generally such Celtic coins, which were sometimes large and beautifully decorated gold pieces, were too valuable to use in daily commercial exchange. The role of Celtic coins was rather limited. It did not include regular circulation or monetization.[21] Their purpose was probably either to allow a comfortable way of wealth accumulation, or to be used for social or political reasons, for instance to pay a tribute. In the Netherlands there are no stray coin finds in NUMIS of Celtic coins predating 58 BC.[22] Because of a lack of coins and small change in our study area we cannot speak of a market economy in this period. This conclusion is corroborated by hoard finds elsewhere, e.g. in the pre-Roman coinage in Britain.

The Roman period

Over a period of three centuries the Roman silver coinage gradually lost nearly all of its precious metal as a result of inflation, with the higher inflation occurring in the last part of the third century. To get figures that are not too heavily influenced by this phenomenon and to get a picture close to the period around our time window of circa AD 150 we have concentrated our data collecting on stray coin finds from the period AD 96 to 192, essentially capturing the Roman coins minted in the second century (from Nerva to Commodus and all emperors in between).[23] For this period we collected the total numbers of stray coins and those that were composed of precious metals (either gold or silver, for coins classified in NUMIS as *aureus* or *denarius*). With this we calculated the proportion of precious metals within the stray coin finds. A fortunate coincidence is that part of the Netherlands belonged to the RE while a different part has always remained non-Roman. Therefore the finding spots of coins in the Netherlands are either at various distances from the Roman *limes* within the RE or lying at various distances outside of it, allowing us to gauge its spatial influence, up to at most circa 200 km from the *limes*, as the Netherlands is a rather small country geographically.

In Table 9.1 we can see a clear gradient of precious metals in the coins in general use in the second century. Deep within the RE coins of low denominations are by far in the majority. The precious metal content is only 0.08, such a low fraction indicating that mainly small denominations were in circulation, and may be indicative of coin use in a local market economy. Closer to the *limes* the precious

Table 9.1 Stray finds of Roman coins in the Netherlands minted between AD 96 and AD 192 and the precious metal fraction with its standard deviation

Zone	No. of gold and silver coins	Total no. of coins	Fraction precious metals	Standard deviation	No. of coins per square kilometre
Within the RE[a]					
>75 km from *limes*	6	80	0.08	±0.03	0.045
0–75 km to *limes*	421	2,291	0.18	±0.01	0.209
On the *limes*	508	1,550	0.33	±0.01	1.448
Outside the RE					
0–75 km to *limes*	104	242	0.43	±0.03	0.023
75–150 km to *limes*	292	637	0.46	±0.02	0.084
>150 km from *limes*	100	196	0.51	±0.04	0.092

Source: NUMIS.

Note:

[a] All the municipalities along the Rhine and its old course between the line Rijnwaarden to Katwijk have been classified as lying on the *limes* (in the RE) with a total surface of 1,071 km². The whole of Zeeland has been classified as lying on average more than 75 km from the *limes* in the RE, with a surface of 1,787 km². All municipalities south of the *limes* (and not in Zeeland) were classified as a part of the RE lying between 0 and 75 km from the *limes* with a total surface of 10,960 km². The municipalities south of the line Den Helder to Hardenberg and north of the *limes* were classified as non-Roman and lying between 0 and 75 km from the *limes*, with a total surface of 10,374 km². All municipalities north of this line and south of the line Ameland to Veendam were classified as lying between 75 and 150 km from the *limes* with a total surface of 7,570 km², while all municipalities lying north and east of it were classified as further than 150 km from the *limes* with a total surface of 2,212 km².

metal fraction gradually rises to 0.33, suggesting that at least part of the money brought into circulation there was passed out in the form of silver.[24] Outside the *limes* the precious metal content rises further, but not terribly quickly, suggesting that Roman coins were used to some extent. Geographically we can see such use more in the Frisian knolls in particular, which were often relatively easily accessible by small boats. When we look at coin finds from archaeological excavations at a distance of some 350 km outside the *limes*, in the Thorsbergermoor in Schleswig-Holstein, we find that the fraction of precious metals of ($N = 29$) Roman coins minted between AD 96 and 192 has risen to unity.[25] Because these Roman coins were locally used as jewellery or as decoration on clothing they were not in regular use for market purposes there.

The number of coins lost (and in circulation) increased considerably in the RE period, compared to the pre-Roman period. On the *limes* in the RE the average coin density is the highest (which in our opinion should be no surprise).[26] In the area outside the empire directly bordering the *limes* we find relatively the lowest coin density, suggesting that Romans did not stimulate barbarian occupation of this frontier zone, and may even have deliberately kept it more or less uninhabited.[27] At a distance of a few hundred kilometres outside the *limes* in barbarian land (such as in Germany), the stray Roman coin density drops again to virtually zero.[28]

There are data on coin finds from outside the Netherlands that can corroborate the picture from Table 9.1: in fact they show that we may probably generalize it to north-western Europe. Unfortunately these data are not organized in a similar all-covering and easily accessible electronic way as in NUMIS and we have to carry out quite some tedious counting by hand to obtain results. From the data reported by Johan van Heesch (1998: 119) we can determine the second-century fraction of precious metals in the stray coin finds in north-western Belgian Gaul. There we find on average a precious metal fraction of 0.06 ± 0.01 for the *vici*, 0.06 ± 0.03 for the villas and 0.07 ± 0.02 for a temple site in Belgium. These fractions are quite similar to what we found at more than 75 km outside the *limes* in the RE in the Netherlands.

A sample of eight (of the 55) stations on the Germania Superior-*Raetia* (GSR) *limes* from *Die Fundmünzen der Römische Zeit in Deutschland* (Komnick and Alföldi 1994) leads to a fraction of precious metal of 0.18 ± 0.02, while the zone in the RE between 0 to 50 km had a fraction of 0.10 ± 0.01 and the precious metal fraction in the Roman zone at more than 50 km distance had a value of 0.07 ± 0.01.[29] The pattern of coin use that emerges for Germany is more or less comparable to what we found in NUMIS: the fraction of precious metal being the highest at the *limes* and dropping off at increasing distances, to a low value that is quite similar to the one found in Belgium and the Netherlands far from the *limes*. Doyen (2007) gives information on coin finds in 70 emergency excavations in Reims executed between 1972 and 2005; in this important Roman town (*Durocortorum*), far from the *limes*, we find a fraction of 0.07 ± 0.02, while he also gives comparative information on other towns, such as Cologne (0.07 ± 0.01). The fact that in larger Roman towns such as Reims and Cologne as well as in villas and *vici* in rural Belgium and in parts of the Netherlands far from the *limes* we find rather similar (low) fractions of precious metal in the second-century stray coin finds is quite remarkable, and we see this as a corroboration of a more or less widely dispersed and developed Roman market economy in north-western Europe.

Though the generally low fraction of precious metals in the stray coin finds in north-western Europe supports the hypothesis of a developing Roman market economy, a few spots and areas in the RE show somewhat deviant patterns. Such a pattern does not mean that we do not have a market economy there – it merely indicates that within a market economy there may have been locations with a higher fraction of silver due to a larger local circulation of such coins. We can give some examples. Along the *limes* we generally find a higher fraction of precious metals than further away in the RE. This we think points in the direction of the Roman military, who could have spent part of their silver in this *limes* area, leading to a higher fraction of precious metals in the local stray coins. The other hotspots we think suggest the influence of the silver resulting from local medium- and long-distance commercial and industrial activities. Reece (1973) gives us some data to corroborate such a hypothesis. Rheinzabern (*Tabernae*), a town over 75 km from the *limes* along the Upper Rhine, did not yet have a large pottery industry in the first century and at that time had a fraction of 0.08 ± 0.02 of precious metal in its coins. In the second century it had a flourishing ceramic industry with a yearly production of half a million to one million pieces of Samian ware which were sold throughout the north-western area, and that time the local fraction precious metal in its stray coins had risen to 0.16 ± 0.02. In nearby Speyer (*Spira*), also on the Upper Rhine but without such a flourishing commercial industry, these fractions were 0.03 ± 0.01 and 0.05 ± 0.02 for the first and second centuries respectively. These examples corroborate the theory that occurrence of commercial silver may be a plausible reason why we may locally find a higher fraction of precious metal in stray coins. For an important commercial and legionary centre as Mainz (*Mogontiacum*), the data of Reece produce a fraction of 0.15 ± 0.02 in the second century, and we find a fraction of 0.17 ± 0.05 for the Rhine Valley. Reece's data from Britain show more or less similar fractions: for the averages of the excavations in St Albans (*Verulamium*) 0.12 ± 0.01 and Cirencester (*Corinium Dobunnorum*) 0.15 ± 0.02.

Though we have not been able to explicitly cover the whole of our study area with data on local coin finds we may assume that the areas not covered would probably not have been fundamentally different, as only geographical data availability was behind the limited sample presented (but see for local deviations Aarts, Chapter 15, this volume). Our conclusion from the Roman coin finds is that they corroborate the idea of a developing market economy after the Roman arrival in these north-westerly fringes of the empire.

The post-Roman period

In the period AD 240 to 275 most of the forts in the Netherlands that were part of the Lower Rhine *limes* were gradually abandoned and the Roman military departed. We have only looked at two 10 × 10 km grids, as the process of correcting for double counts in this late period of time is crucial (because of the relatively small numbers involved), and the way NUMIS is accessible makes this correction a rather time-consuming exercise.

For the 10 × 10 km grid in Bunnik (*Fectio* = Vechten, between Utrecht and Bunnik), NUMIS contains 29 coins minted in the fourth century, all of them of non-precious metals (down from 775 coins minted in the first, 281 in the second and 134 in the third century). In Katwijk (*Lugdunum*) there are nine coins minted in the fourth century, also all from non-precious metals. In Valkenburg (*Praetorium Agrippinae*) we find no fourth-century coins at all in NUMIS.[30] Nevertheless there was still some use of local money in small denominations, though also at a much lower level compared to the first few centuries AD. Johan van Heesch (1998: 174) indicates that in *Gallia Belgica* during the fourth century the economy was still largely monetized with coins of low denominations, which in the fifth century gradually diminished.

Table 9.2 presents data on stray coin finds in the Netherlands that were minted in the sixth and seventh centuries (well after the Roman period). These show that the market economy substantiated by the low fraction of precious metals in the coin finds in Roman times seemed to have disappeared by that time, as the fraction of precious metals was close to unity again. A value close to one indicates an inclination to long-distance trade, if we want to speak of commercial activity at all. The low absolute numbers of coins compared to those in Roman times also points in a direction of less trade. The differences in coin use between Roman and non-Roman territories within the Netherlands that had been clearly visible in the second century (Table 9.1) had disappeared as well in the sixth to seventh century.

If for the zone previously outside the RE we limit the analysis of Table 9.2 to a sub-zone, that of the Frisian knolls, we find a similar precious metal fraction of 0.90 ± 0.02. The local coin density for this sub-zone rises by 0.067 (per century),

Table 9.2 Stray finds in the Netherlands of coins minted between AD 500 and 700 and the precious metal fraction with its standard deviation

Zone	No. of gold + silver coins	Total coins	Fraction precious metals	Standard deviation	No. of coins per square kilometre per century
Previously within the RE[a]	1,267	1,311	0.97	±0.01	0.047
Previously outside the RE	412	451	0.91	±0.01	0.011

Source: NUMIS.

Note:
[a] In NUMIS for this analysis we used the geographical classification of the find place based on the municipalities. All the municipalities along the Rhine and its old course between the line Rijnwaarden to Katwijk have been classified as lying on the *limes* (in the RE). All municipalities south of this line were later part of the RE, while all that were lying to the north of it never were part of the RE. The Roman area in the Netherlands was roughly 13,800 km², while the non-Roman part was approximately 20,100 km².

making it similar to the zone that previously was Roman and which in this period contained a developing commercial centre at Dorestad.

Table 9.2 suggests that the previously existing market economy during Roman times, with low fractions of precious metals in the local coins and a somewhat higher coin density, had been succeeded by one of long-distance trade, operating at a considerably lower level of intensity.[31] This is the form of commercial activity usually found in the North Sea world in these centuries; see for example Barrie Cook and Gareth Williams (2006). Peter Spufford (1988: 15) states that sixth-century France lacked the necessary coinage to foster its local economy: though the pages of *History of the Franks* by Gregory of Tours drip with blood and gold, it was gold not in circulation and use, but a fortune that was clotted and hoarded. A different indicator of long-term economic output can be found in the numbers of manuscripts that were produced locally. For north-western Europe this production also shows a minimum in the sixth century.[32] In the sixth century the Franks did not pay their soldiers with gold; the loyalty of the vassals was bought with land.[33] This process later led to the emergence of a feudal system in Europe, which in turn formed a break with the more market-based economies of the Roman period.

Our conclusions from this section are that in pre-Roman times there was no market economy in the north-westerly parts of Europe to speak of. The situation totally reversed in the Roman period when we can find a large use of small-denomination coins virtually everywhere. After the demise of the RE this picture completely changes again; we now find a considerably higher fraction of precious metal in the coin finds at a few hot spots, pointing in the direction of long-range commerce at those specific locations.

The distribution of Roman settlement densities

Because of their pivotal role in the transport of commercial goods over inland waterways in north-western Europe, we have concentrated our analysis on the different fluvial systems, by quantifying their average economic relevance. As previously explained, the relative urbanization of a fluvial system has been calculated as the sum of all inhabited surfaces of settlements along a waterway in AD 150 located in the catchment area of river in hectares, divided by the total length in kilometres of the waterway connections in the fluvial system (see Table 9.3 for the results).

The Lower Rhine and the Thames are the two fluvial systems that pop up in Table 9.3 as the most densely urbanized in north-western Europe. First we try to find out if we can find some corroboration for the pattern of relative urbanization that seems to emerge from Table 9.3. We looked at reports on the archaeological remains of non-perishable Roman goods imported from outside the study area that described the finding places of such goods, which were commercially transported into the study area. These concern the so-called Dressel 30 amphorae (Peacock 1978) and oil amphorae and fine pottery from southern Spain (Greene 1986). Both finds are shown in Table 9.4 and eventually lead to a combined amphorae index.[34]

Table 9.3 Settlement density (in ha/km) of the fluvial systems at about AD 150

Fluvial system	Current basin (1,000 km²)	Current length (km)	Total Roman fluvial connections (km)	Absolute Roman urbanized area (ha)	Settlement density (ha/km)
Gironde			**1,960**	**976**	**0.50**
Dordogne	23.8	483	610	131	0.21
Garonne	84.8	602	1,350	845	0.63
Loire	117.0	1,013	2,800	1,219	0.44
Rhone	98.0	813	2,270	1,647	0.73
Rhine	**170.0**	**1,233**	**2,765**	**2,688**	**0.97**
Lower Rhine			460	809	1.76
Moselle	28.3	545	610	471	0.77
Upper Rhine			1,695	1,408	0.83
Seine	78.7	776	2,085	1,141	0.55
Somme	6.0	245	215	207	0.96
Scheldt	21.9	350	615	208	0.34
Meuse	36.0	925	955	284	0.30
Thames	12.9	346	470	585	1.24

Source: see Data Appendix, Sections 1.2 and 2.

Table 9.4 Archaeological remains of non-local amphorae per fluvial system

Fluvial system	Peacock Dressel 30 amphorae	Amph/ 1,000 km	Greene Spanish wares (amph)	Amph/ 1,000 km	Combined amph index
Gironde					
Dordogne	0	0.0	0	0.0	0.0
Garonne	0	0.0	2.4	1.8	1.8
Loire	3	1.1	3.6	1.3	2.4
Rhone	6	2.6	11.9	5.2	7.9
Rhine					
Lower Rhine	4	8.7	2.4	5.2	13.9
Moselle	0	0.0	0	0.0	0.0
Upper Rhine	10	5.9	8.9	5.3	11.2
Seine	5	2.4	0	0.0	2.4
Somme	1	4.7	0	0.0	4.7
Scheldt	0	0.0	0	0.0	0.0
Meuse	0	0.0	0	0.0	0.0
Thames	3	6.4	3	6.4	12.8

Sources: Peacock (1978) and Greene (1986).

The combined amphorae index from Table 9.4, as an indicator of Roman trade intensity, has a correlation of 0.85 with the settlement density of the various fluvial systems presented in the last column of Table 9.3.[35] This correlation corroborates the theory that settlement density and commercial transport go hand in glove.[36]

Table 9.5 Potential drivers (indexed per 1,000 km fluvial system) of Roman urbanization

Fluvial system	Military demand	Town councils	Casks	Mines	Viticulture (preliminary)	Loess (preliminary)
Gironde						
Dordogne	0.8	1.6	0.0	0.7	19.7	0
Garonne	0.7	3.0	0.7	1.2	12.6	0
Loire	0.3	3.9	2.9	0.9	no data	0
Rhone	0.4	9.3	4.4	2.6	14.5	5
Rhine						
Lower Rhine	77.0	8.7	82.6	1.1	0.0	0
Moselle	0.0	3.3	0.0	0.3	27.9	5
Upper Rhine	29.5	4.7	18.9	0.2	0.6	10
Seine	0.7	4.3	1.9	0.0	no data	10
Somme	7.0	4.7	0.0	0.0	0.0	70
Scheldt	1.6	1.6	8.1	0.2	0.0	10
Meuse	3.1	2.1	4.2	0.0	no data	5
Thames	29.5	8.5	23.4	1.1	2.1	0
Correlation with settlement density	0.87***	0.78***	0.82***	0.26	−0.44	0.10

Sources: see Data Appendix, Section 1.2 and text.

Note:
*** = p values < 0.01, implying statistically significant correlations.

Factors potentially driving a Roman market economy

In this section we describe various variables that can potentially influence the process of market development we are interested in. We also strive to come to a quantification of those factors because we want to tease out statistically which of them were the most important in this respect, as well as how important they actually are in explaining the found distribution of urbanization and monetization in north-western Europe. We have managed to find quantitative information on a number of potential drivers in the various fluvial areas in Roman times: the military demand, the numbers of town councils, the numbers of excavated casks (as a proxy for the wine trade), the density of Roman mines, the density of remains of Roman viticulture and the fraction of loess soils as a proxy for the production of grain in Roman times. In Table 9.5 we show the various potential drivers of Roman urbanization per fluvial area. In this table only the indexed values are reported, and not the absolute values as they can be found in the archaeological references (all values have been divided by the total length in kilometres of the waterborne connections per specific fluvial system and multiplied by one thousand in order to get a relative measure). Later on all these data will be used for a multivariate analysis, which then can tell us something about their relative importance.

The Roman military

After the Roman conquests with its temporary campaigns, which started in 58 BC and continued until around the first decades AD, the Roman army was in western Europe to stay for centuries. Once a legion was stationed somewhere in the empire it mostly stayed put for at least a number of decades and sometimes even longer, as Roman military transport facilities were a strain on state resources.

The average pay of a soldier was 300 silver *denarii* which is equal to 1,200 bronze sesterces (HS) per year in AD 100, rising to 1,800 HS in AD 200.[37] Generally three times a year a soldier received part of his pay as a form of pocket money; deductions were made for his cost of living, his kit and for his savings.[38] It has been estimated that he paid some 32 per cent of his salary on food and approximately 40 per cent of his salary on his kit and its upkeep.[39]

The commercial importance of the Roman military can be substantiated by the fact that a legionary fort was generally accompanied by a considerably more extensive civilian settlement (*canabae*), where smiths, tailors, weavers, leather workers and other commercial artisans made the products and services they sold to the military.[40] Even for a smaller Roman fort there was nearly always a civilian village (*vicus*) lying right next to it, where a bathhouse could be found, for instance. This decentralized Roman way of conducting military business led to a huge demand for such commercial goods and services on the fringes of the empire, which previously had in no way been accustomed to a market economy.[41] The parallel that can be drawn between the military in the RE and those of the early Islamic state (c. AD 650 to 900) is quite straightforward. Kennedy (2002: 155) examined the military payment in cash of the early Islamic state, which put a massive amount of coinage into circulation that was spent locally by the soldiers. He concluded that military payments played an important part in creating the urban, cash-based market economy of the early Islamic world, which contrasts so sharply with land- and kind-based economies of the then contemporary Christian states in the east and in the Latin West.

The first column of Table 9.5 is an index of the local military demand, estimated in millions of HS per year. This has been done by multiplying the numbers of military per kilometre of fluvial length[42] times 1,800 HS times 0.72 to find what the Roman army generally spent on to keep itself alive and equipped. We have taken this value times 0.8 because we assumed that a certain fraction of the necessary military materials by its very nature (such as for instance olive oil, wine, *garum* (fish sauce), etc.), say 20 per cent in value, had to come from outside the local fluvial area.[43] For the fluvial area of the Thames we have therefore added 20 per cent of the total British military expenditure to the military demand of this fluvial area because London was the main point of entry and distribution for the military in the British Isles for goods arriving from the Continent.

Roman town councils

Recent economic literature shows that local town councils were an important element in the economic take-off of cities in Europe in the Middle Ages and early modern period.[44] To study whether these institutions, for whose membership a certain amount of personal wealth was a criterion, were influential in the Roman era too we indexed the numbers of town councils per kilometre of fluvial length in the second column of Table 9.5. Urbanization in western provinces led to the emergence of a wide variety of nucleated settlements. As a simple index of urbanization for our purposes we count those nucleated settlements which had a council and magistrates who administered a civic territory – i.e. the so-called *civitas*-capitals and the *coloniae*.[45]

A proxy for the wine trade

The third column of Table 9.5 contains the numbers of casks found in excavations, as presented by Élise Marlière (2001: 194–201). As such they signal the end product of the life cycle of a barrel, which was often reused at local wells, and these archaeological artefacts probably are an indicator of previous commerce in alcoholic beverages.[46] The high correlation (0.97) in Table 9.5 between casks and military demand is striking, indicating that booze and soldiers are an ancient combination of which the Romans already were well aware.

Roman mines

The fourth column of Table 9.5 contains the index per 1,000 km of fluvial system of the total number of mines (whether for certain stones or metals) as indicated in the *Barrington Atlas*.

Regional Roman viticulture

The fifth column of Table 9.5 is an index of the Roman viticulture. Due to a lack of data this does not include the Loire, Upper Rhine and Seine basins, but the other areas probably have been adequately covered.[47] It is based on the numbers of different places where immobile artefacts in connection with viticulture, such as a vine press, vine yard or wine making establishments, have been excavated. For Aquitaine this is based on Balmelle *et al.* (2001), for the Moselle area on Brun and Gilles (2001), for the Tricastin on Jung *et al.* (2001), for the Languedoc-Roussillon on Buffat and Pellecuer (2001), for the Provence on Brun (2001), for the south of Gaul on Boissinot (2001) and for the British Isles on Brown *et al.* (2001: 755).

Regional Roman grain production

The sixth column of Table 9.5 contains an index of the loess soils per fluvial area. It is preliminary and based on an analysis of a soil map available on the Internet from which the relative surface areas in per cent have been deduced, as indicated in Table 9.5.[48]

In a simple multivariate analysis (leading to expression (9.1)) the first two columns of Table 9.5 already explain 86 per cent of the variance in the settlement density (the last column of Table 9.3):

$$\text{Settlement density} = \underset{|\pm 0.003|^a}{0.0117} \times \text{Military demand} + \underset{|\pm 0.0246|^b}{0.0668}$$

$$\times \text{ town c. } + 0.27 \tag{9.1}$$

(Note: [a] = the calculated standard deviation for military demand and [b] = the calculated standard deviation for town c.)

In itself the military demand in monetary terms explains some 75 per cent of the variation in the urbanization around the year AD 150 in north-western Europe, and adding into the regression the effect of town councils explains another 11 per cent points. The fact that none of the other variables concerning mining or agriculture have any significant additional contribution to the explained variance indicates that they have probably not driven the urbanization in this part of the RE. This urbanization has been driven by the military demand and the presence of local town councils. By itself the associations determined with a multivariate analysis of course do not imply causation. However, the historical narrative that points at the important role of the military presence for the local economy makes causation plausible. There are many examples that show that when the Roman army departed somewhere the local economy declined, as well as examples of their arrival giving it a boost. Wierschowski (1984: 140–1) gives the example of *Vindonissia*, whose legion departed in AD 101 and the local finds of coins minted before and after this date changed considerably in volume. When Roman soldiers returned to *Vindonissia* in AD 260–268 coin numbers rose too. A different example he gives is for Strasbourg (*Argentorate*) where after the departure of the *Legio II Augusta* to Britain the local coin numbers declined. These rose again after the new arrival in AD 71 of *Legio VIII Augusta* into the legionary camp at Strasbourg. In Cannstadt there was a military camp between AD 90 and 150–160, and economically this town managed to prosper for another two decades after the Roman troops had left. However, after that, local prosperity declined markedly. Oberstimm is an example of a town where 'with the departure of the troops the market economy stopped de facto' (Wierschowski 1984: 143). Wierschowski continues with more examples on 'the Roman army and the economy'. In the multivariate analysis above we found a high correlation between military requirements and the settlement density in the various fluvial areas. Though a formal econometric proof has not been given for causation we nevertheless think that the historical narrative on individual towns and settlements developed by Lothar Wierschowski and others supports our interpretation of the Roman military as the most important driver of the local economy in the study area.

If we take a different geographical unit of analysis (grids of 1×1 degrees squared, in north-westerly Europe an area of approximately 110×75 km^2) we arrive at 135 observations in our study area instead of only the twelve fluvial catchments used above.[49] However, with a similar multivariate analysis as previously employed, this larger number of observations does not lead to a higher explained variance; quite the contrary. The explained variance reduces to a value of 41 per cent (was 86 per cent), the effect of town councils now becoming the more important factor and explaining 32 per cent points of the variance, while the military demand now only explains a mere 9 per cent points. We think that differences in the geographical scale of operation of the various driving factors are responsible for this very different outcome compared to that of the previous analysis based on the considerably larger fluvial areas. Bosker and Buringh (forthcoming) have shown that urban interaction and development is hampered at close range (by an 'urban shadow') and at far ranges (by transaction costs becoming too high) while at intermediate distances of some 20 to 100 km a different nearby town (for which the town council effect may be seen as a proxy here) stimulates urban growth. This stimulating effect falls exactly in the range of our 1×1 degree squared unit of analysis. On the other hand Wierschowski (1984: 140) indicates that provisioning the army was not only a regional affair but even supra regional, as general purchasing agents were sent out by the army (*seplasiarii*) far afield, and he indicates that the direct economic effect of the military demand would have been visible much further away than at a distance of 1 degree (for example grain and wine coming from Gallia, olive oil from the Mediterranean, etc.).[50] We can see a similar distance effect in the fraction of precious metals in Table 9.1, visible in the coin distribution outside the *limes* over a range of 2 or 3 degrees. The reduction of our unit of analysis to a smaller geographical scale than that of the economic influence of the military seems to reduce its significance considerably. This very different analysis thus strengthens our view that the use of a fluvial catchment area as the preferred analytical unit for the analysis of the economic effects of the military demand.

Local Roman economic growth along inland waterways

The three different Roman *limes* systems can be considered a kind of natural historical experiment, allowing us to delve somewhat deeper into factors influencing economic growth in Roman times, thereby unravelling the influence of the military and other variables. A Roman system of manned forts and watchtowers was in operation along the north-western borders, possibly to collect taxes on passing commerce in and out of the RE and to prevent marauding gangs of barbarians from plundering the more wealthy – and therefore to them attractive – countryside of the empire. These forts were interconnected by walls or were located along a river, where the water formed a natural border. In the year AD 200 Hadrian's Wall (HW), 100 km long and containing sixteen forts, was operational at the border between the Scottish territories and Roman Britain, lying between South Shields (*Arbeia*) and Burgh by Sands (*Aballava*). In the Lower Rhine area from Bonn (*Bonna*) up to the now disappeared fort of Brittenburg at the North Sea (*Lugdunum*, close to Katwijk) we have discerned the Lower Rhine *limes*, or LR-*limes*. This LR-*limes* without any walls had the Rhine as the natural border and had a length of 325 km and contained 35 forts. The third *limes* was the Germania Superior-Raetia-*limes* (GSR-*limes*, in the German literature it is also known by the acronym of ORL, the *Obergermanischen Raetischen Limes*). It ran from Heddesdorf on the Rhine to

Table 9.6 Military strength in 'ha of fort' per 'km of *limes*'

Limes	Military strength (ha/km)
Hadrian's Wall	0.30
Lower Rhine	0.36
GSR	0.25

Eining (*Abusina*) near Regensburg on the Donau. This specific *limes* was formed partly by a wall through the Taunus Mountains and for a larger part by a wall through southern Germany; and for a small distance it also was fluvial with the River Main as a natural border. Overall it had a total length of some 500 km and contained 55 forts.[51]

On the basis of the surface areas we collected from the archaeological record we can easily calculate the military strength in 'ha of fort' per 'km of *limes*', by summing all by the military inhabited surfaces (in ha) and dividing this value by the length (in km) of the *limes* in question.

Despite the geographical differences in location and terrain these values seem remarkably similar in their sizes; one could say that we find on average some 0.30 ± 0.06 ha/km for the strength of the Roman *limes* in north-western Europe. For one of the values we even have an independent check. Baatz (1982: 140) indicates that he estimates the strength of the GSR-*limes* to have been approximately 50 men per km.[52] When we multiply our value of 0.25 ha/km with the average value of the military density of 200 men/ha, we also arrive at exactly the same figure.

Around the year AD 200 there were three legions in Britannia[53] and four legions along the Rhine, not only at the *limes* itself but also more strategically located somewhat behind the actual *limes*, such as in York, Nijmegen, Mainz or Strasbourg. All the legionary forts in north-western Europe were located on rivers and could be reached easily by inland water transport.

In Table 9.7 we model the expected settlement density in ha/km (using expression (1)) based on the military demand in millions of HS per year for the three different *limes* systems in north-western Europe. Table 9.7 also contains the residuals, a statistical concept used to quantify the differences between realized and modelled values.

Though the differences between the realized settlement density and the modelled values in the three *limes* systems are within a reasonable band width of ± 30 per cent, the residuals nevertheless show a distinct pattern. Both *limes* systems without a waterway had negative residuals, indicating that they actually had a smaller settlement density than expression (1) would expect them to have had, while along the Lower Rhine the *limes* had realized a somewhat higher urbanization than might have been expected. This actually points at the important role of the rivers themselves in fostering economic growth, which does not follow from our analyses because we have analysed the influence of various factors (such as military demand or town councils) on a fluvial system. The actual settlement density along the whole of 460 km of fluvial connections on the Lower Rhine was considerably higher (1.76 ha/km) than what was actually the case along the military camps and their *vici* (1.31 ha/km) along the 325 km of the LR-*limes*.

Along the *limes* there are also two civilian settlements – Cologne (*Colonia Claudia Ara Agrippinensium*) and Xanten (*Colonia Ulpia Traiana*). Data on their inhabited areas have not been included into that of the *limes*, because strictly speaking they were no part of it. If we include these two towns, which originally were indigenous towns (*Ara Ubiorum* and *Vetera*) later reorganized as colonies of veterans, we model a value of 1.55 ha/km in Table 9.7, while the actual realization is 1.99 ha/km, indicating a residual of 0.44, or an influence of some 28 per cent extra urbanization because of a navigable waterway. Assuming a Roman presence of some 140 years then leads to an average extra economic growth rate of 0.18 per cent per year because of the local connection to an inland waterway.[54] Mokyr (1990: 4) distinguishes four distinct processes that, roughly speaking, can lead to economic growth: investment, commercial expansion, scale effects and increase in human capital. These four processes seem to have been more or less similar in their impact and consequences for the three different *limes* systems. However, the main difference between HW and GSR (the two landlocked *limes* systems), and the LR *limes* located strategically along a river are the lower transaction costs at the LR-*limes* because of the reduced cost of transport due to the riverine character of the traffic. Table 9.7 suggests that this lower transport cost has led to some 25 to 30 per cent extra economic growth for locations along a river under otherwise more or less similar circumstances.

Although the Roman military presence was crucial for a market economy to develop in north-western Europe, an additional local economic growth was only observed where Roman military demand and fluvial transport met (Table 9.7). This new finding explains why the *limes* in the German Taunus and along HW, in spite of similar numbers of locally billeted military, did not lead to a similar level of urbanization as found along the River Rhine.

Despite the fact that it was a boon to be situated on a river in Roman times, our conclusion is that the various fluvial systems in Roman times differed considerably in their economic significance. The Lower Rhine in particular stands out as a major

Table 9.7 Modelled (with expression 1) and actual urbanization around AD 200 and their residuals for the three *limes* systems

Limes system	Modelled value	Realized density (ha/km)	Residuals	Transport mode
Hadrian's Wall	1.00	0.88	−0.12	land
GSR	0.88	0.78	−0.10	land
Lower Rhine	1.14	1.31	0.17	river
LR + Cologne, Xanten	1.55	1.99	0.44	river

Sources: see Data Appendix, Section 2, text and expression (1).

Table 9.8 Settlement density in the Roman Empire and the medieval relative urbanization in AD 1200 and AD 1400 per fluvial area

Fluvial system	Settlement density in the RE × 100	AD 1200 Inhabitants 1,000s	Relative urb	AD 1400 Inhabitants 1,000s	Relative urb
Dordogne	21	0	0	6	10
Garonne	63	35	26	71	52
Loire	44	101	36	139	50
Rhone	73	74	33	140	62
Lower Rhine	176	64	139	101	220
Moselle	77	52	85	36	59
Upper Rhine	83	103	61	157	93
Seine	55	225	108	312	150
Somme	96	12	56	10	47
Scheldt	34	84	137	278	452
Meuse	30	41	42	102	107
Thames	124	40	85	50	106

Sources: Bosker and Buringh (forthcoming) and Data Appendix, Section 2.

artery of transport of goods to the local military and probably farther afield to and from Britain.[55] In Britannia, London is the major hub in the distribution of goods for the local legions and therefore economically the role of the Thames is considerably larger than that of the nearby Scheldt. The fluvial systems of the Thames, Seine and Somme seem to be relatively important economically. The Rhone and Upper Rhine come out as not unimportant too: this is logical when their intermediate function in the transport routes to the Mediterranean is taken into account.

Spatial differences in Roman and medieval market economies

In the Latin West market economies started to function again somewhere around or after the twelfth century. In Table 9.8 we explore whether the patterns of relative urbanization in AD 1200 and in AD 1400 are similar to those of the RE (as presented in Table 9.3). The relative urbanization in AD 1200 and AD 1400 is calculated as the total number of medieval town dwellers in thousands in a specific fluvial catchment area divided by the same fluvial length we used for the RE.

Table 9.8 and the scatter plot in Figure 9.4 show that, in the study area, the pattern of relative urbanization at the restart of a market economy after the twelfth century has become quite different from that in the RE. The correlation between Roman times and the year AD 1200 is 0.49; and when comparing with the later date of AD 1400 the correlation of this drops to 0.05. In AD 1400 especially the Scheldt area stands out as the undisputed centre of urbanization. Note that this area does not contain the inhabitants of the important medieval town of Bruges (because geographically this town does not belong to the Scheldt's fluvial catchment area). Including Bruges would have made the difference even larger.

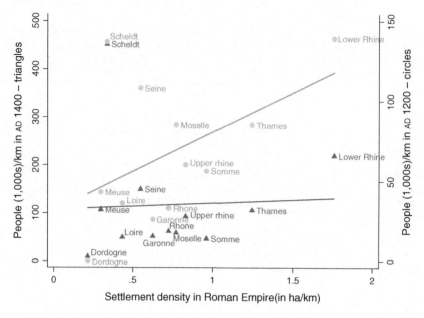

Figure 9.4 Scatterplot of relative urban density in the Roman Empire and in AD 1200 (circles, right-hand axis) and in the Roman Empire and in AD 1400 (triangles, left-hand axis).

Source: Table 9.8.

A comparison of the relative urbanization in AD 1200 and 1400 in the study area leads to a correlation of 0.79, which indicates a fair continuity in medieval commercial development. The differences between the RE and the medieval pattern are obviously related to the disappearance of military demand and the *limes* as factors driving the urban system, and to the rise of the Flanders cities as the typical 'producer cities' of the Middle Ages. But some similarities can be found as well: the south-west of France is not very urban (the Dordogne, the Garonne and the Loire are only weakly urbanized), and the Lower Rhine continues to be strongly urbanized. Seen in this light, the high level of urbanization of the Netherlands, though not on the same locations, has very old – even Roman – roots.

Conclusions

We have studied the kick-start of the process of urbanization and the development of a market economy in Roman times in two different ways: via coin finds and in particular the share of coins composed of precious metals, and via the size and place of Roman settlements in the region. Both approaches tell a similar story of urbanization and monetization, directly linked to the Roman military presence in the region. Roman military presence and its huge demand for goods and services can explain to a large extent (75 per cent) the differences in the economic development of the various fluvial systems in north-western Europe around AD 150. The local finds of large numbers of coins and the low fraction of coins consisting of precious metals suggest a functioning market economy in the region. The high correlation between the Roman military demand in monetary terms and the local distribution of archaeologically recovered casks (probably once containing alcoholic beverages) is striking – it suggests a strong impact of the combination of soldiers and booze.

Although the Roman military presence was crucial for a market economy to develop in north-western Europe, an additional local economic growth was only observed where Roman military demand and fluvial transport met. This new finding explains why the *limes* in the German Taunus and along HW, in spite of similar numbers of locally billeted military, did not lead to a similar level of urbanization as found along the River Rhine.

After the Roman military had left the study area its market economy faded away (as coin finds show) and only a few centres of long-distance trade remained active. The much later medieval market economy that started somewhere during the eleventh and twelfth century in north-western Europe had a geographical pattern that differed considerably from that found during the RE, which is quite logical because the medieval market economy was the result of local or regional bottom-up commercial processes and not of a market economy that was mainly driven by the military demand of some large army.

Notes

1 See Rathbone and Von Reden, Chapter 8, this volume. Temin (2006: 133), Bowman and Wilson (2009: 28) argue that the actual extent and the precise nature of the economic growth at the time continue to provoke debate among scholars.
2 Hopkins (1980: 101) and later in (2002: 229). This, however, does not preclude the possibility that taxes could still be paid in kind as well, as Duncan-Jones (1990: 30 ff) argued.
3 Hitchner (2003: 4, 398). Some decades earlier Wierschowski (1984) had made a similar point in his study of the Roman army and the economy. And before him Jones (1974: 127) had indicated that the expenditure of the army had stimulated development, in particular the growth of towns, in backward areas of the RE such as Britain and the Rhineland.
4 The remark that the use of coins of low denominations can be used as an index for the extent of a market economy has already been made by Liebeschuetz (2001: 24). Lucassen (2007) describes how the end of the Roman rule meant the end of small change, with the consequence that without a reliable and abundant coinage wage labour (a labour market) could no longer exist.
5 The year AD 150 is some decades before the Antonine plague decimated part of the population in the RE. In accordance with Talbert (2000) we use the time limit from circa 30 BC to AD 300 as the dates to characterize the Roman period, and use the term Late Antique for the next period from c. AD 300 to 640.
6 Rather similar to the natural experiments of history described by Diamond and Robinson (2010).
7 Lo Cascio (2009) wrote on urbanization as a proxy of demographic and economic growth in the RE; for more general examples see Acemoglu *et al.* (2005) and Bosker *et al.* (2013).

8 A settlement is hereby defined as one that is indicated as such on the *Barrington Atlas* (Talbert 2000).

9 Of course, when a surface area in ha is multiplied by the population density as presented by Woolf (2000) or others we arrive at the total population of a settlement. However, in practice we do not have to execute such a multiplication as we only use urbanization in this chapter as a relative measure and therefore without any problems can stick to the numbers of ha of surface area of Roman settlements as reported in the archaeological references.

10 The actual numbers of inhabitants per ha have, however, been heavily debated. Woolf (2000: 137 n. 103) indicates that a figure of 100 inhabitants per hectare seems to be preferred for many towns in our study area and period. We will follow Woolf in this respect. For a more densely inhabited Italian city, for example Pompeii, covering 65 ha, and sheltering a population of 8,000 to 12,000, Greg Woolf reports that a figure of 123–87 inhabitants/ha has been used.

11 In this appendix we present a thorough description of the data collection of the Roman settlements in north-western Europe. This can be accessed on the Internet: www.cgeh.nl/soldiers-and-booze-rise-and-decline-roman-market-economy-north-western-europe (accessed 29 May 2013).

12 Of course we do not know for sure if all the settlements lying on a waterway in the *Barrington Atlas* could in the year AD 150 actually be reached by boats or barges. However, we use the fluvial length as a relative measure to compare the various fluvial systems, and as long as we treat all fluvial systems uniformly the resulting figures can be used for comparative purposes.

13 In fact this measure in ha/km is quite similar to a local settlement density per surface area (or an indicator of the urbanization/km^2), as there is a large explained variance ($R^2 = 0.8$) in north-western Europe between the surface of the water basin in 1,000s km^2 of a fluvial system and the direct river length (km). The main outlier here is the River Meuse; if this river is excluded the explained variance rises to a value of 0.9, indicating that generally we are in fact also making some estimate of local settlement density by dividing the habited surfaces in a specific riverine catchment area by its river length (with the Meuse being somewhat less well covered, but we will show that for our later arguments this possible fluvial exception is not relevant).

14 Because the Netherlands was partly in and partly out of the RE, this sample gives us information on the monetary situation in various zones in both areas.

15 See http://numis.geldmuseum.nl/en/introduction (accessed 13 May 2014). Note that the Geldmuseum has been closed and that the collection has been transferred to the Nederlandsche Bank.

16 Another drawback of lost coins outside a specific archaeological stratification is that the date of loss often will be difficult to determine with any certainty. However, using coin hoards has even larger limitations: the relation between numbers of coins in hoards and those in actual circulation is even more remote, the chance aspect associated with a hoard find also leads to larger statistical uncertainties and, finally, the composition of coins in hoards is often quite different from those in circulation.

17 To get a better glimpse of the Roman coins that were in actual circulation we should probably look at the stray coins found at battlefields or other sudden disasters. Van Heesch (2007: 91) gives an example of finds on the battlefield of general Varus (which the Romans lost) at Kalkriese in Germany, where the fraction of precious metals was 0.45 ± 0.02 for the (901) stray coins that were found there, while at Oberaden (which was a nearby legionary camp in *Germania* in a similar period) the fraction of precious metals was only 0.09 ± 0.02 (364 coins).

18 The actual results of some 2,300 settlements are available upon request.

19 This has been estimated from McEvedy and Jones (1979). For Germany and the Netherlands we have only included in our calculation the area contained within the

limes that we estimated at 150,000 and 14,000 km^2 respectively. For the German *limes* area we also assumed a similar population density as in Belgium, some 12.0/km^2, which is slightly higher than that derived for the German total of 9.8/km^2, based on McEvedy and Jones.

20 Bakels (2009: 155) describes how there were lowland and hilltop *oppida* in pre-Roman times in the north-western European loess areas. The hilltop *oppida* were more common, and were strongly fortified settlements generally occupying strategic higher points in the landscape.

21 Van Heesch (1998: 40).

22 There is, however, a Celtic hoard found in the south of the country with 116 coins completely composed of precious metal. After he had won the Gallic wars, which started in 58 BC, Caesar had most of the Gallic gold transported to Rome as spoils of war (there leading to a fall in the price of gold) and the lack of precious metals then forced the Celts to use bronze instead to make their coins later on. Therefore 58 BC is a natural cut-off to use when looking at the local precious metal fraction in the stray coins of the pre-Roman period (Roymans *et al.*, 2012, esp. p.171–214).

23 Of course we do not know for certain that the coins were actually lost during this period, we can only be sure that they were minted then. In the Netherlands, Roman coins have been found dating from two centuries before the Romans arrived in the country, suggesting an actual coin use over quite some time in the early empire. Later, with the inflation and the strongly reduced silver content in especially the third century, the more valuable old coins will have been withdrawn from circulation sooner rather than later and the actual period of coin use will have been considerably reduced.

24 The existence of a local market economy in this part of the RE has been corroborated by data collected during a combination of botanical, zoological and settlement archaeology in the Dutch River Area. These data show that it was possible for the local rural communities in the non-villa landscape to produce a surplus of animals as well as cereals for a market, see de Groot *et al.* (2009).

25 Komnick and Alföldi (1994).

26 Kellner *et al.* (1975: 8) estimate that some 150,000 to 200,000 Roman coins have been found in Germany, which would lead to a coin density there of some 0.25 to 0.33/km^2 per century in Roman Germany if we assume a Roman stay of some four centuries. These numbers are not completely comparable to those in Table 9.1, as the German coin finds are more than just stray coins and include hoards too.

27 Whittaker (1983: 110) mentions the expulsion, reported by Tacitus, by the Romans of two Frisian tribes in AD 58 that had newly arrived and had attempted to settle in unoccupied military territory.

28 As can be deduced from the few Roman coins excavated at the Thorsbergermoor in Schleswig-Holstein.

29 For the *limes* we collected data on stray coins minted between AD 96 and 192 from Stockstadt, Niedernberg, Obernburg, Miltenberg, Dambach, Ruffenhofen, Gnotzheim-Gunzenhausen and Theilenhofen (406 coins). For the zone 0–50 km: Regensburg, Nassenfels, Pfünz and Weissenburg (685 coins), while for the zone >50 km we sampled Günzburg and Kempten (354 coins). As these data are not available electronically they have to be counted by hand, so we only did a limited sample.

30 Wierschowski (1984: 140/1) gives the example of *Vindonissa*, from where the Roman legion departed in AD 101: the local coin finds of coins minted before and after this date changed considerably in volume. When Roman soldiers came back to *Vindonissa* again in AD 260–68 coin numbers rose too. Other such examples can be found on pages 142–7.

31 A similar result was found for South Germany located, just as for the Netherlands, partly in and partly out of the RE. Drauschke (2009: 279) describes how after the time of the

RE, no money-based economy existed in the eastern Merovingian areas in Germany between the late fifth and eighth centuries.

32 Buringh and Van Zanden (2009: 416); the production for Europe as a whole shows a minimum in the seventh century, but this is caused by the specific local situation in Italy, where the Lombard invasions and Byzantine wars reduced the local manuscript production in Europe's largest producer of manuscripts in that period.

33 Van Heesch (1998: 174). This was quite different from how in the Middle East the Muslim armies were compensated after AD 650, as we will show later.

34 In Table 9.4 we first show the actual numbers of finds of the various amphorae per fluvial system and then standardize these to an index per 1,000 km fluvial system to facilitate mutual comparison. To arrive at a combined index of the 32 finds of Dressel 30 amphorae indicated by Peacock and the 54 finds of Spanish wares by Greene we have standardized Greene's figures to those of Peacock by first dividing his absolute numbers by 54 and then multiplying them by 32. The combined amph(ora) index is simply the sum of both individual indexes and is shown in the last column of Table 9.4.

35 Combining the Moselle and the rest of the Upper Rhine into one category, Upper Rhine proper, leads to a correlation of 0.92. The current correlation is lower because no amphorae finds were reported in the Moselle area by either Peacock or Greene. However, taking into account how important Trier was economically in the RE it seems hard to believe that the Romans would not have transported such amphorae to Trier or the Moselle area.

36 A similar general indicator of commerce is the number of casks shown in Table 9.5 (third column); this indicator also has a correlation of 0.82 with the settlement density. However, a word of caution may be appropriate. Loughton (2003: 199) warns that it may be easy to fall into the trap of believing that maps showing the distribution of Republican amphorae provide an unbiased picture of trade and exchange, when for example ritual and cult activity may seriously complicate this picture. His report on find spots of Republican amphorae is limited to France (and covers only six of our twelve fluvial catchments). The Republican amphorae date from the third century BC to the Roman period and thereby predate our settlement density data, and they turn out to have no correlation with them at all.

37 In this chapter we will give all prices in sesterces (HS).

38 Wierschowski (1984: 5).

39 A slightly different estimate comes from Wierschowski (1984: 203). He estimated that a Roman soldier had some 20 per cent of his salary, or 50 to 60 *denarii* per year, to spend freely. Because we use the pay of Roman soldiers as a relative measure, the exact fraction that he actually had available to spend for himself is not relevant for our analysis, and a different choice of numbers would not have altered the influence of the military eventually found in expression (9.1).

40 Wierschowski (1984: 123/5) indicates that the neighbourhood of camps was very attractive for artisans and commerce, that traders from further afield were attracted to the camps to fill in gaps in the market, and smaller local farmers also had a regular outlet for the sale of their agricultural products at the nearby forts.

41 Even nowadays, when the direct local demand of goods by the military is considerably less (as modern transport facilities have become very much more efficient and cheaper than in classical times), the positive economic influence of a military base on the local economy can still be a strong incentive to tolerate such a presence, as can be seen from a report by Cooley and Marten (2006) on a large US base in Okinawa, Japan. During the Second World War, in Iceland, a force of 20 to 30 thousand Allied military personnel (on some 140 thousand inhabitants in 1950) upset the small local labour market, leading to an increasing demand for a wide range of products and services (Jónsson 2004). In these war years the local military demand caused an unprecedented growth of the Icelandic economy with on average 8 per cent per year (expressed as GDP per

capita), showing a contemporary version of the Roman military influence on relatively backward economies.

42 This has been found from the database by selecting all summed fort areas in ha and multiplying the summed value by 200 soldiers/ha, giving an indicator of the numbers of Roman soldiers.

43 For the later multivariate analysis the exact realization of this choice of 20 per cent is not very critical, as different values such as 10 per cent or 30 per cent lead to rather similar results. Also the exact numerical value of the 72 per cent used to estimate what a 'soldier' spent on food and his kit is not critical at all in this respect, as it just leads to a relative measure, which is only used to obtain a relative picture in the different fluvial areas. Using any other fraction that was spent on his upkeep and kit will eventually lead to a similar correlation.

44 Bosker *et al.* (2013).

45 Sources: Bedon (2001); Millett (1992) (Table 4.4).

46 Bakels (2009: 160) indicates that casks may have been used for transporting other items too in the RE, and gives pomegranates as an archaeological example, although on page 179 she indicates that their main purpose was the transport of alcoholic beverages.

47 The low correlation (−0.44) between viticulture and settlement density implies that even if these missing data could have been found after an extensive search the correlation would remain low, therefore for our purpose of comparison these preliminary data are sufficient. A similar remark can be made of the preliminary character of the data on loess in the next column of Table 9.5; a further refinement there would also not lead to a significantly higher correlation. As potential drivers of Roman settlement density both factors are out of the picture.

48 Source: www.ufz.de/data/European_Loess_Map_hires7613.jpg (accessed: 10 January 2011).

49 An implicit assumption with such a smaller unit of analysis is that the effect of the different potential drivers of the economy is geographically restricted to such a smaller unit.

50 Middleton (1983: 82) also makes the point that army garrisons of necessity drew their bulked supplies from regions far beyond their *territoria*.

51 One has to realize that the habitation density of military settlements (legionary, cohort or auxiliary forts and road stations) was approximately a factor of two higher than the 100 inhabitants per ha of a typical urban civilian settlement in the Gauls and Germanias. Thus military settlements as a rule comprised some 200 men per ha.

52 Baatz (1982) reports the length of the *limes* to be 375 km and at the same time postulates that 17,000 to 19,000 soldiers were at some time involved with it.

53 These legions in Britannia were located at the borders of fertile agrarian areas to allow an easy provisioning of the military (Wierschowski 1984: 66).

54 Simply calculated as $(1 + \text{growth rate})^{140} = 1.28$, implying that growth rate is 0.18 per cent per year. As a matter of comparison, based on Buringh and Van Zanden (2009), we come to a yearly average growth rate of 0.23 per cent for the urbanization in the Latin West in the period from the sixth to fifteenth centuries, which is a very reasonable growth rate for pre-industrial societies.

55 See for example Duncan-Jones (1990: 35).

Bibliography

Acemoglu, D., Johnson, S. and Robinson, J. 2005. 'The Rise of Europe: Atlantic Trade, Institutional Change and Economic Growth', *American Economic Review*, 95: 546–79.

Baatz, D. 1982. 'Das Leben in Grenzland des römisches Reich', in *Die Römer in Hessen*, edited by D. Baatz and F.-R. Herrmann, Stuttgart: Theiss: 84–156.

Bakels, C. C. 2009. *The Western European Loess Belt, Agrarian History, 5300 BC–AD 1000*, Dordrecht: Springer.

Balmelle, C., Barraud, D., Brun, J.-P., Duprat, P., Gaillard, H., Jacques, P., Maurin, L., Petit-Aupert, C., Regal, D., Robin, K., Roudié, P., Sillières P. and Vernou, C. 2001. 'La viticulture antique en Aquitaine', *Gallia*, 58: 129–64.

Bedon, R. 2001. *Atlas des villes, bourgs, villages de France au passé romain*. Paris: Editions A. & J. Picard.

Boissinot, P. 2001. 'Archéologie des vignobles antiques du sud de la Gaule', *Gallia*, 58: 45–68.

Bosker, M. and Buringh, E. Forthcoming. 'City Seeds, Geography and the Origins of the European City System', *CEPR discussion paper 8066*.

Bosker, M., Buringh, E. and Van Zanden, J. L. 2013. 'From Baghdad to London, Unraveling Urban Development in Europe, North Africa and the Middle East, 800–1800', *The Review of Economics and Statistics*, 95/4: 1418–37.

Bowman, A. and Wilson, A., eds. 2009. *Quantifying the Roman Economy, Methods and Problems*, Oxford: Oxford University Press.

Brown, A. G., Meadows, I., Turner S. D. and Mattingly, D. J. 2001. 'Roman Vineyards in Britain: Stratigraphic and Palynological Data from Wollaston in the Nene Valley, England', *Antiquity*, 75: 745–57.

Brun, J.-P. 2001. 'La viticulture antique en Provence', *Gallia*, 58: 69–89.

Brun J.-P. and Gilles, K. G. 2001. 'La viticulture antique en Rhénanie', *Gallia*: 165–79.

Buffat, L. and Pellecuer, C. 2001. 'La viticulture antique en Languedoc-Roussillon', *Gallia*: 91–111.

Buringh, E. and Van Zanden, J. L. 2009. 'Charting the "Rise of the West": Manuscripts and Printed Books in Europe, a Long-term Perspective from the Sixth Through Eighteenth Centuries', *Journal of Economic History*, 69: 409–45.

Buringh, E., Bosker, M. and Van Zanden, J. L. Forthcoming. 'A New Look at Roman Sea Freight Rates', (under review).

Casey, J. 1974. 'The Interpretation of Romano-british Site Finds.' in *Coinage and the Archaeologist,* edited by John Casey and Richard Reece, Cambridge: BAR: 37–51.

Cook, B. and Williams, G., eds. 2006. *Coinage and History in the North Sea World, c. AD 500–1250: Essays in Honour of Marion Archiebald*, Leiden: Brill.

Cooley, A. and Marten, K. 2006. 'Base Motives, the Political Economy of Okinawa's Antimilitarism', *Armed Forces & Society*, 32: 566–83.

de Groot, M., Heeren, S., Kooistra, L. I. and Vos, W. K. 2009. 'Surplus Production for the Market? The Agrarian Economy in the Non-villa Landscapes of *Germania Inferior*', *Journal of Roman Archaeology*, 22: 231–52.

Diamond, J. and Robinson, J. A., eds. 2010. *Natural Experiments of History*, Cambridge, Mass: Belknap Press.

Doyen, J.-M. 2007. *Économie, monnaie et société à Reims sous l'Empire romain*, Reims: Bulletin de la Société archéologique champenoise.

Drauschke, J. 2009. 'Byzantinische Münzen des ausgehenden 5. bis beginnenden 8. Jahrhunderts in östlichen Regionen des Merovingerreiches', in *Byzantine Coins in Central Europe between the 5th and 10th Century*, edited by M. Woloszyn, Krakow: Polish Academy of Arts and Sciences: 278–323.

Drinkwater, J. F. 1983. *Roman Gaul: The Three Provinces, 58 BC–AD 260*, Ithaca NY: Cornell University Press.

Duncan-Jones, R. P. 1990. *Structure and Scale in the Roman Economy*, Cambridge: Cambridge University Press.

Greene, K. 1986. *The Archaeology of the Roman Economy*, London: Batsford.

Hitchner, R. B. 2003. 'Roman Empire', in *The Oxford Encyclopedia of Economic History*, edited by J. Mokyr, Oxford, Oxford University Press: 4: 397–400.

Hopkins, K. 1980. 'Taxes and Trade in the Roman Empire (200 BC–AD 400)', *The Journal of Roman Studies*, 70: 101–25.

—— 2002. 'Rome, Taxes, Rents and Trade', in *The Ancient Economy*, edited by W. Scheidel and S. von Reden, Edinburgh: Edinburgh University Press: 190–230.

Jones, A. H. M. 1974. *The Roman Economy: Studies in Ancient Economic and Administrative History*, Oxford: Blackwell.

Jónsson, G. 2004. 'The Transformation of the Icelandic Economy: Industrialisation and Economic Growth, 1870–1950', in *Explorations in Economic Growth*, edited by S. Heikkinen and J. L. van Zanden, Amsterdam: Aksant: 131–66.

Jung, C., Odiot, T., Berger J.-F. and Seris, D. 2001. 'La viticulture antique dans le Tricastin (moyenne vallée du Rhône)', *Gallia*, 58: 114–28.

Kellner, H.-J., Overbeck, B. and Overbeck, M. 1975. *Die Fundmünzen der Römische Zeit in Deutschland.* Abt. I. *Bayern*, Band 1, *Oberbayern*, Berlin: Mann.

Kennedy, H. 2002. 'Military Pay and the Economy of the Early Islamic State', *Historical Research*, 75: 155–69.

Komnick, H. and Alföldi, M. R. 1994. *Die Fundmünzen der Römische Zeit in Deutschland. Abt VIII. Schleswig-Holstein und Hamburg*, Berlin: Mann.

Liebeschuetz, J. H. W. G. 2001. *Decline and Fall of the Roman City*, Oxford: Oxford University Press.

Lo Cascio, E. 2009. 'Urbanization As a Proxy of Demographic and Economic Growth', in *Quantifying the Roman Economy, methods and problems*, edited by A. Bowman and A. Wilson, Oxford: Oxford University Press: 87–106.

Loughton, M. E. 2003. 'The Distribution of Republican Amphorae in France', *Oxford Journal of Archaeology*, 22: 177–207.

Lucassen, J. 2007. 'Wage Payments and Currency Circulation in the Netherlands from 1200 to 2000', in *Wages and currency*, edited by J. Lucassen, Bern: Lang: 221–63.

McEvedy, C. and Jones, R. 1979. *Atlas of World Population History*, London: Allen Lane.

Marlière, E. 2001. 'Le tonneau en Gaule Romaine', *Gallia*, 58: 181–201.

Middleton, P. 1983. 'The Roman Army and Long Distance Trade', in *Trade and famine in classical antiquity*, edited by P. Garnsey and C. R. Whittaker, Cambridge: Cambridge Philogical Society: 75–83.

Millett, M. 1992. *The Romanization of Britain: An Essay in Archaeological Interpretation*, Cambridge: Cambridge University Press.

Mokyr, J. 1990. *The Lever of Riches: Technological Creativity and Economic Progress*, New York: Oxford University Press.

Peacock, D. P. S. 1978. 'The Rhine and the Problem of Gaulish Wine in Roman Britain', in *Roman shipping and trade: Britain and the Rhine provinces*, edited by J. du Plat Taylor and H. Cleere, London: Council for British Archaeology: 49–51.

Reece, R. 1973. 'Roman Coinage in the Western Empire', *Britannia*, 4: 227–51.

Roymans, N., Creemers, G., Scheers, S., eds. 2012. *Late Iron Age Gold Hoards from the Low Countries and the Caesarian Conquest of Northern Gaul*, Amsterdam: Amsterdam University Press.

Spufford, P. 1988. *Money and its Use in Medieval Europe*, Cambridge: Cambridge University Press.

Talbert, R. J. A., ed. 2000. *Barrington Atlas of the Greek and Roman World*, Princeton: Princeton University Press.

Temin, P. 2006. 'The Economy of the Early Roman Empire', *Journal of Economic Perspectives*, 20: 133–51.

Van Heesch, J. 1998. *De Muntcirculatie tijdens de Romeinse tijd in het noordwesten Van Gallia Begica, de civitates Van de Nerviërs en de Menapiërs (ca. 50 V.C.–450 N.C)*, Brussels: Koninklijke Musea voor Kunst en Geschiedenis.

—— 2007. 'Some Aspects of Wage Payments and Coinage in Ancient Rome, First to Third Centuries CE', in *Wages and Currency*, edited by J. Lucassen, Bern: Lang: 77–96.

Whittaker, C. R. 1983. 'Trade and Frontiers of the Roman Empire', in *Trade and famine in classical antiquity*, edited by P. Garnsey and C. R. Whittaker, Cambridge: Cambridge Philogical Society: 110–27.

Wierschowski, L. 1984. *Heer und Wirtschaft, das römische Heer der Prinzipatszeit als Wirtschaftsfaktor*, Bonn: Habelt.

Woolf, G. 2000. *Becoming Roman, the Origins of Provincial Civilization in Gaul*, Cambridge: Cambridge University Press.

Part III

Market performance from the Middle Ages to the nineteenth century

10 Price volatility and markets in late medieval and early modern Europe

Victoria N. Bateman

Introduction

Until relatively recently, economic history was simple. Students were commonly taught that nothing much happened until the modern period of continuous technological change that was ushered in by the British Industrial Revolution. The West was seen as the first part of the world to economically develop and the East as, in general, backward. Economic historians focused their efforts on explaining the Industrial Revolution in an attempt to draw lessons that might enable the rest of the world to follow suit. However, the scholarship of the last two decades has in many ways completely overturned this story. It has now become clear that for much of history, from the times of ancient Babylonia and continuing through to Byzantium, economic life centred on the Near and Far East.[1] It is only in relatively recent times that the West has become economically dominant. In late medieval times, European wealth depended on trading the silks, chinaware and spices of the East. This all changed around 1800 when the British Industrial Revolution was under way and Britannia came to rule the world seas. As we stand today, the world economy is on the cusp of reorienting itself back to the East, bringing history full circle.

At the same time that the Euro-centric vision of history has been being demolished, economic historians have been in the process of pushing backwards the frontiers of economic development. The origins of today's world, which were once found in the Industrial Revolution, are now found in the early-modern or medieval period, or even earlier.[2] It is perhaps unsurprising that alongside these new interpretations of the past we are also finding markets both well before the Industrial Revolution and in parts of the world other than Europe. Traditionally, the market was viewed as a recent phenomenon, with origins in the eighteenth and nineteenth centuries, and in many ways seen as an 'invention' of the West.[3] However, recent work has identified markets much earlier in European history, noting a significant commercialization process in the medieval period.[4] Furthermore, as this book attests, markets have been found as far back as ancient times and in parts of the world outside of Europe.[5]

Having seen that markets are ubiquitous in time and place, the new research agenda on the table involves comparing the precise level of market development in different parts of the world and in different time periods. After all, as Van der Spek and Mandemakers write, 'That market mechanisms played their part in the Babylonian economy seems now to be unquestionable... This conclusion, however, does not entail that markets had the same significance in ancient Babylon as in modern times'.[6] Only by striking exact comparisons is it possible to fully chart the evolution of markets in history from ancient times to the present day and so ultimately to gauge the contribution of markets to economic development.

As this chapter argues, price volatility represents the most foolproof method for comparing markets over long spans of time, as it allows us to examine market development in ancient as well as more recent times (as well as across countries) (see Foldvari and Van Leeuwen, Chapter 2, this volume). As a result, it would be useful to have reliable volatility estimates for medieval and early-modern Europe with which to make comparisons with the ancient world. However, much of the literature on European markets has focused on other methods of measuring market development, such as price gaps and speeds of market adjustment, and, perhaps in part for this reason, has failed to knit itself together in a way that builds a long-run picture of market development from the ancient period onwards. In what follows, the first section attempts to pull together this existing literature, presenting a preliminary picture of market development in Europe from Roman times to the twentieth century. In an effort to help complete the picture, the second section goes on to measure market development in late medieval and early-modern Europe by examining price volatility, whilst the third section makes volatility comparisons with the ancient world, using evidence from Babylonia. The results suggest that early-modern European markets were two to three times as well developed as those in the ancient world. In other words, markets made significant strides earlier in history than is traditionally thought.

Markets in Europe from Roman times to the twentieth century: a brief summary of the literature

Until very recently, economies of the past were viewed as backward and non-market using. Polanyi (1944) typifies this view, and describes how a 'great transformation' to a market-using economy took place around the time of the Industrial Revolution. Beforehand, custom and regulation supposedly suffocated markets. The work on ancient economies by authors such as Finley, with its use of evocative words such as 'primitive', appeared to confirm the idea that markets are a recent invention. Influenced by this vision of the past, empirical studies of European market integration initially focused on the early-modern period, attempting to establish a significant improvement in the eighteenth century. However, cracks soon began to form. Research on the Roman economy indicated that markets existed in the distant past.[7] The work of medievalists uncovered evidence suggesting a commercialization boom in their area of study.[8] At the same time, economic historians of the modern period argued that globalization was a product of the Industrial Revolution, rather than an initiator.[9] Hence, in contrast to Polanyi, it now seems plausible to suggest that the most significant periods of market development occurred at either side of the early-modern period (for more on this see Van der Spek *et al.*, Chapter 1, this volume). Hence, our survey begins centuries ago, in Roman times.[10]

Trade and markets played a much more important role in Roman Europe than is traditionally thought.[11] In addition to the well-known evidence of Temin (2001), archaeological evidence on ceramics has demonstrated that 'fine-wares' were 'distributed very widely' and that 'the percentage of imported pottery, as opposed to local wares, is impressively high'.[12] Indeed, in terms of the degree of institutional unity and the lack of jurisdictional fragmentation, Roman times provided fertile ground for the development of markets (see also Rathbone and Von Reden, Chapter 8, this volume). However, markets could and did unravel. With the end of the Roman Empire in Western Europe came a process of de-specialization, de-urbanization and a general collapse in standards of living. During that time, Western Europe became highly fragmented, something which rarely favours the reformation and further development of markets. By medieval times, the well-known institution which is commonly thought to have resulted from this fragmentation and which arguably limited market participation and productivity improvements – serfdom – was in decline. Law and order also improved with the re-discovery of Roman law and a move to 'written-down' law, together with limitations on property right abuses of monarchs through, for example, the Magna Carta.[13] Furthermore, as individual states increasingly began to form, jurisdictional fragmentation declined once again, eliminating some of the coordination failures which had plagued market development for some centuries.[14] Where states were still too fragmented to provide institutions to support markets, it is argued that the private sector took on the role through merchant guilds, city 'communes' and craft guilds.[15] Further to these developments, the late fourteenth and fifteenth centuries saw the establishment of the first chartered public banks in Genoa and Barcelona, the invention of printing, the spread of bills of exchange, the 'multinational' merchant company, maritime insurance and double-entry book-keeping, further lowering the transaction costs of market exchange.[16]

In the light of all of these changes, it is perhaps unsurprising that whether one looks at labour markets, capital markets or goods markets, evidence increasingly suggests that markets in medieval times were experiencing a development boom. In the capital markets, market improvement is evident in falling interest rates across Europe. According to Epstein (2000), between the thirteenth and sixteenth centuries, interest rates in Western Europe (including England, Switzerland, West Germany, France and Flanders) fell from around 10 per cent to 5–6 per cent. Labour market development was enhanced as labour mobility increased, increasing the diffusion of skills, knowledge and ideas.[17] In the goods market, falling price volatility, evident for cities such as Douai, Milan, Saragossa, Utrecht and Exeter, suggests increasing trade and exchange, which smoothed prices in the wake of local shocks.[18] Whilst Söderberg (2004) is not able to confirm the finding of falling volatility, he does conclude that price volatility in medieval Europe was considerably below that in the Near East at the time and that north-west Europe witnessed high and increasing integration. According to Bateman (2011), markets in late medieval Europe were on average as well developed as those in the eighteenth century. This picture of reasonably well-developed medieval markets is supported by more specialized studies of England and the Low Countries.[19] According to Studer (2009), the advantages of coastal and lowland geography in north-western Europe may have naturally given birth to an earlier market-based economy than that seen elsewhere in Europe.

Markets in early-modern times have been even more extensively studied in empirical terms than those of medieval times, not only as a result of the long shadow cast by Polanyi but also because of the relative abundance of price data which originate in the historical accounting records. When applied to this data, econometric techniques have enabled the consistent and extensive measurement of price convergence, speeds of market adjustment and price volatility, with a particular focus in the literature on the first two of these. The conclusions arrived at differ according to the level of analysis. At the inter-continental level, the investigation of O'Rourke and Williamson (2002a, b) suggests that despite colonization and growing trade volumes between Asia, the Americas and Europe, there is little evidence that global markets were becoming better integrated in the sense of falling price gaps. They argue that whilst inter-continental trade was expanding, it was not being driven by falling transaction costs or greater market efficiency, but by expanding demand from Europe. Global integration had to wait for the nineteenth century. For the European continent alone, it has also proved difficult to argue that markets were becoming better integrated from early-modern times to the eve of the Industrial Revolution. Using monthly data Persson (1999) calculates speeds of market adjustment and finds a rise from one and a half to three years in early-modern times to three to four months by the mid-nineteenth century, although most of the improvement appears to be concentrated in the nineteenth century.[20] Persson also considers the evidence relating to price volatility, finding a reduction in price volatility between the sixteenth and seventeenth centuries for Brussels, Siena, Pisa, Toulouse and London but increases for Cologne, Ruremonde and Vienna.[21] Only in the nineteenth century do we find reductions across the board. Using a broader set of European cities for the period 1350–1800, Bateman (2007, 2011) looks for evidence of price convergence, rising speeds of market adjustment and falling volatility using monthly and annual wheat price data, but fails to find consistent and clear evidence on any of these three counts. Using a set of price data covering not just wheat but also other products, Özmucur and Pamuk (2007) find it similarly difficult to make a case for European market development on the run up to the Industrial Revolution. Only studies conducted at shorter- or medium-range have more successfully identified integration in early-modern times. Jacks (2004) finds evidence of rising integration in the North and Baltic Seas in the period 1500–1800, although not without setbacks. It is, of course, important to note that the North-West was already relatively well integrated in medieval times, as the studies referred to previously have revealed. Integration has also been noted for France and Italy, and within each of the lowland and landlocked zones of Europe.[22] However, given the evidence for Europe more generally, such localized integration may not have been strong enough to drive Europe as a whole to sig-nificantly higher average levels of integration than were present at the start of the early-modern period.

Moving to the nineteenth century we once again find evidence pointing in the direction of improving markets. In contrast to the standard approach of studying price gaps, speeds of adjustment and volatility, Studer (2009) applies Princi-pal Components Analysis to the European price series. The results suggest that before the nineteenth century, European markets were divided into landlocked and lowland zones. By the nineteenth century, however, this division is absent and the whole of Europe forms a single market. Furthermore, whether one looks at the cities located in landlocked or lowland Europe, prices were much more highly correlated in the nineteenth century than the eighteenth century. Work at the inter-continental level also indicates integration in the nineteenth cen-tury.[23] However, calculating the coefficient of variation across forty cities in six countries (Austria-Hungary, Belgium, France, Norway, UK and USA), Fed-erico and Persson (2007) demonstrate that whilst price convergence between these (mostly Atlantic) economies was taking place until the 1870s, thereafter it receded such that by the eve of the First World War it was at the levels of the 1830s.[24] Nevertheless, a decomposition of the finding reveals that within themselves, most countries witnessed convergence. Between free-trade economies convergence was also taking place. Hence, the reversal was a result of what was going on between protectionist countries in the late nineteenth-century backlash against free trade.[25] Whilst the technologies of the Industrial Revolution (steam and metallurgy enabling the railways and the steamship) aided integration, protec-tionism could act in the opposite direction between economies. Both technology and policy affected the path of integration – and sometimes the latter more than the former, as the events of the 1930s also clearly reveal.

Taking together the extensive empirical work on medieval, early-modern and modern times, the medieval period and the nineteenth century – rather than the early-modern era – increasingly stand out as periods of action on the market devel-opment front. If this is correct, it leads to some interesting inferences regarding the relationship between markets and growth. In particular, markets may take some time to culminate in economic growth, and may be as much of a consequence as cause of such growth. However, even more powerful inferences could be made if we could make accurate comparisons as to the precise level of market devel-opment in ancient as well as medieval, early-modern and modern times. Hence, in the following section, we will seek to measure European market development between medieval and modern times in a way that best facilitates such a compari-son, using the price-volatility approach which has been relatively neglected in the existing literature.

An examination of price volatility in Europe

Market integration is commonly measured by taking two or more price series and looking for evidence of price convergence, using simple price-gap calculations and co-integration techniques. Furthermore, to investigate the behaviour of markets in the short-run, speeds of adjustment in response to shocks can be calculated using prices from a pair of cities. However, given that data for ancient economies are only available for single locations, it is not possible to measure and compare market development over long spans of history in this way. Consequently this chapter attempts to measure European market development by examining price volatility, a method which can be applied to single price series and which therefore better supports comparisons across place and time.

Volatile prices are the result of shocks to the economy. Given the dominance of agriculture in history, harvest failures were a prominent source of shocks, the consequence being that food prices regularly peaked above their more 'normal' levels. However, where trade and markets were well developed, supplies of agricultural produce from outside the local area were able to help dampen the price rise, resulting in smoother prices. Hence, using price volatility as a measure of market integration seems theoretically well justified and, whilst less utilized than other measures, it is certainly not uncommon. Wheat prices are commonly used in studies of European market integration, and are available on a monthly and annual basis. Annual prices for Madrid, Valencia, Naples, Tuscany, Toulouse, Amsterdam, Leiden, Arnhem, Utrecht, Chester, Edinburgh, London, Exeter, Antwerp, Louvain, Lier, Bruges and Brussels are used in the present study, and span the period 1300–1899.[26] Monthly prices for Toulouse, Paris, Cologne, Munich, Siena, Pisa, Vienna, Antwerp, Brussels, London, Utrecht and Ruremonde are also used, to capture seasonal fluctuations, although coverage is limited to the sixteenth century onwards.[27]

At the most basic of levels, volatility can be measured by looking at the standard deviation of prices across a particular period of time relative to the mean price. However, when prices are trending, such as in sixteenth-century Europe, this is subject to serious upward bias. To help alleviate the problem, we calculate coefficients of variation on a rolling basis using short intervals of time (five years for monthly and ten years for annual data) and then take averages of these values to provide figures for longer periods. Table 10.1 reports the results of calculating coefficients of variation using the annual wheat price series. The values are calculated on a rolling ten-yearly basis and then averaged for each fifty-yearly period.

Beginning with the Mediterranean price series, we find a significant reduction in volatility by the early seventeenth century for most of the cities. In Naples, volatility falls from 0.29 to 0.22 between the early sixteenth and early seventeenth centuries, and in Tuscany from 0.32 in the fourteenth century to 0.20 by the early seventeenth century. Whilst volatility continues to fall up to the end of the early-modern period in each of these two Italian regions, the fall is relatively minor compared with that achieved in earlier centuries. In France, markets also appear to witness improvement, with volatility in Toulouse declining from 0.29–0.34 in the late fifteenth and early sixteenth centuries to 0.21 by the late seventeenth century and 0.15 by the end of the eighteenth century, although with a setback in the first half of the eighteenth century. As with France and Italy, Istanbul also witnesses a reduction in volatility towards the end of the seventeenth century. Unlike the rest of

Table 10.1 Coefficients of variation: annual wheat prices (averages of rolling ten-year coefficient of variation by period)

	1300	1350	1400	1450	1500	1550	1600	1650	1700	1750	1800	1850
Naples	0.32		0.33		0.29	0.24	0.22	0.21	0.18	0.18	0.20	
Tuscany		0.34		0.34	0.37	0.25	0.20	0.18	0.15	0.17		0.27
Toulouse				0.29	0.34	0.29	0.32	0.21	0.26	0.15		
Istanbul						0.33	0.22	0.19				
Madrid					0.33	0.23	0.26	0.34	0.27	0.23		
Valencia			0.13	0.15	0.22	0.17	0.13	0.10	0.16	0.13		
Amsterdam				0.35	0.22	0.21		0.23	0.21	0.17		
Leiden			0.26	0.41	0.24	0.15	0.17	0.29	0.46	0.16	0.25	0.14
Arnhem						0.18	0.19	0.29	0.25	0.19	0.28	0.16
Utrecht				0.35	0.22	0.21		0.23	0.21	0.14		
Chester		0.23	0.25	0.27								
Edinburgh							0.22	0.25	0.17	0.13		
London	0.32	0.25	0.30	0.22	0.32	0.33	0.23	0.25	0.25	0.22	0.19	0.14
Winchester							0.26	0.27	0.25	0.22	0.24	
Windsor									0.25	0.17		
Eton						0.26	0.23	0.26	0.25	0.21	0.22	
Exeter	0.27	0.27	0.24	0.20	0.40	0.37	0.16	0.22	0.21	0.17	0.22	
Antwerp										0.12	0.25	0.17
Louvain			0.22	0.29			0.19					
Lier			0.28	0.33	0.26	0.30						
Bruges		0.21	0.30	0.36	0.23	0.30	0.20	0.25	0.30	0.11		
Brussels			0.26	0.34								

Source: Allen-Unger grain price dataset.

the Mediterranean, the results suggest that volatility at the end of the early-modern period was no lower than that achieved in 1400–49 in the case of Valencia and 1550–99 in the case of Madrid. As may be expected, the overall level of volatility was significantly lower in Valencia than in Madrid, suggesting that markets in coastal Valencia were better integrated than those of inland Madrid.

Moving from the Mediterranean to the North-West, we find a significant reduction in volatility in the Netherlands by the late sixteenth century, from 0.35 to 0.21 in Amsterdam, from 0.26 to 0.15 in Leiden and from 0.35 to 0.21 in Utrecht. In the late seventeenth and early eighteenth centuries, as the Dutch Golden Age was coming to an end, volatility increases before recovering and achieving levels of volatility below those achieved earlier. In Britain, volatility falls significantly by the late fifteenth century, from 0.32 to 0.22 in London and from 0.27 to 0.20 in Exeter. Of these two cities, only in late nineteenth-century London do we find levels of volatility well below those achieved centuries before. In Edinburgh, volatility falls significantly in the eighteenth century, commensurate with the process of unification with England. In contrast with the rest of the north-western region, Belgium stands out for its significant rise in volatility by the late fifteenth century, as is clear in the results from Louvain, Lier, Bruges and Brussels. Only in the late eighteenth century does volatility appear to achieve levels significantly below those in the fourteenth and fifteenth centuries.

Whilst available for shorter periods of time, the monthly price series allow us to calculate volatility in a way that picks up higher frequency price movements associated with the seasons. This provides a useful cross-check to the annual results, as well as an extra level of detail. Detailed results are reported in Bateman (2012), and are in many ways consistent with those arrived at using the annual data. Initially, we find high levels of volatility in the French and Italian cities, with subsequent improvement. In Italy, the most significant fall in volatility occurs by around 1600, from 0.35 in Pisa and 0.39 in Siena (1550–9) to around 0.16 by the early seventeenth century (1600–09). Thereafter, volatility is subject to some temporary setbacks, particularly in the 1670s and 1680s, but manages to fall further to around 0.1–0.13 in the eighteenth century. In Paris, volatility also falls significantly from 0.24 (1550–9) to 0.14 (1600–09), although high volatility later returns in the seventeenth century. In Toulouse, volatility declines throughout the era, from 0.34 in 1560–9 to 0.13 in 1780–9, although with setbacks along the way. In the north-western cities of Cologne, Antwerp, Brussels and Utrecht, we find relatively low levels of volatility by the late sixteenth and early seventeenth centuries, indicating a higher level of market development. Volatility is 0.19 in Brussels (1560–9), 0.14 in Antwerp (1600–9), 0.18 in Cologne (1550–9) and 0.15 in Utrecht (1570–9). In the cities for which monthly data are only available for the latter half of the period (Munich, Vienna, Ruremonde and London), it is not clear that volatility ends the period significantly below where it began. Overall, the monthly and annual coefficient of variation calculations are consistent with the idea that markets in much of Europe significantly improved and developed relatively early on, at some point between 1300 and 1600 (Epstein 2000). For a number of cities, this period of improvement appears to be much stronger than that seen in the later period 1600–1850. Furthermore, this improvement in this later period was far from smooth, with volatility rising in some cities. As in the recent work of Van Zanden (2009) and Allen (2009), and in line with the work of medievalists, emphasis deserves to be shifted from the later early-modern period to the earlier era.

Whilst useful and easy to understand, the coefficient of variation measure of volatility is not always an ideal measure. Not only is it subject to error if prices trend over time, but it can also capture aspects unrelated to market integration, such as agricultural structure and the structure of demand.[28] For example, an economy with two harvests in the course of a year might be expected to have lower volatility than an economy with a single harvest. In addition, if the good for which volatility is measured has few substitutes in one region or period of time, its prices will be more volatile in the presence of shocks compared with a place or time in which the good has many substitutes (as consumers can easily substitute away from the good). Hence, differences across time and place and the nature of agriculture and demand can disrupt the extent to which we can make comparisons on the level of market development using a coefficient of variation measure of volatility. The way to overcome this problem is to estimate a structural model of prices or, in other words, to model the factors which *predictably* affect prices, such as lagged prices, seasonality and time trends. After doing so, one can find the residuals and examine how the variance of the residuals changes over time. Given that the residual captures unexpected (i.e. unpredictable) changes to prices (changes that cannot be predicted on the basis of lagged prices, time trends or seasonality), the variance of the residual can be thought of as a way of capturing the volatility of (unexpected) price movements. Two key methods have been used in the literature which relate to this approach. Persson (1999) models prices as a random walk and looks at the standard deviation of the associated residuals, finding (as previously discussed) a reduction in price volatility between the sixteenth and seventeenth centuries for Brussels, Siena, Pisa, Toulouse and London but increases in volatility for Cologne, Ruremonde and Vienna.[29] However, as prices do not always follow a random walk, the model is not always well specified (suffering from auto correlation). Söderberg (2004) uses a less restrictive autoregressive (AR) model of prices (which models prices as a function of lagged prices) for the medieval period, and similarly looks at the standard deviation of residuals from the model. However, an even more sophisticated approach can be borrowed from empirical finance, the generalized autoregressive conditional heteroskedasticity (GARCH) model, as recently recommended to economic historians in the measurement of volatility by Foldvari and Van Leeuwen.[30] Using the GARCH model, one can also flexibly model prices as a function of lagged prices, seasonal dummies and time trends, and then obtain the residuals from the model as a proxy for unexpected price shocks. However, a key difference compared with the approaches of Persson and Söderberg is that the variance of the residuals is explicitly modelled as a function of lagged residual variance. This allows us to control for what appears to be a well-established fact when examining volatility – periods of high volatility alternating with periods of low volatility, or, in other words, a degree of persistence in volatility behaviour. To correctly measure volatility it is necessary to control for this behaviour by modelling the variance of price residuals as a function of lagged squared residuals. A time trend can be added to the variance model allowing us to test to see whether volatility is declining over time. Using the results of the model one can calculate and compare the steady state variance of (unexpected) price shocks across time and place. Given the advantages of this approach, we applied GARCH models to the annual wheat prices of Europe. We modelled prices (the 'price equation') as a function of lagged prices and time trends, and added lagged prices to the point that any serial correlation in the residuals was eliminated. We modelled the resultant variance of the residuals (the 'variance equation') as a standard GARCH model, including lagged squared residuals to help capture the persistent behaviour of volatility, together with a time trend to capture any potential downward trend in volatility over time. The results tend to confirm the findings based on the coefficient of variation measure of volatility. For early-modern Madrid, we find no downward trend to volatility. In the case of Tuscany, for which prices span the long period from the thirteenth to the mid-nineteenth century, we find a significant downward trend to volatility. The steady state variance falls from 0.21 in 1286 to 0.017 in 1859, indicating an exceptional reduction in the unpredictable element of price movements. Volatility also shows a significant downward trend in Toulouse, with the steady state variance falling from 0.1 in 1490 to 0.024 in 1792. Moving to north-western Europe, we find no significant downward trend to volatility in Amsterdam between 1462 and 1900, with a steady state variance of 0.088. This arguably captures the idea that markets in the Netherlands had already become well developed early on, and in fact even earlier than the coefficient of variation results suggest (by the late fifteenth century at the latest, rather than the late sixteenth century). For London, we find no reduction in volatility from the late thirteenth century to the end of the eighteenth century, with a steady state variance of 0.063, again arguably indicating that markets had developed early on. In the case of Bruges, the GARCH model applied to the period 1370–1499 indicates a trend of rising volatility, as was the case with the coefficient of variation measure. Only when the model is extended to include the eighteenth century does volatility witness a downward trend in Bruges.

The volatility calculations based on the coefficient of variation measure and the GARCH model are reassuringly consistent both with each other and with the broader picture of market development in Europe which has recently been emerging. This adds credence to using a volatility measure for making market comparisons over long spans of history, including between ancient and more modern day economies. It is on this basis that the next section compares the level of market development in Europe with that in ancient Babylonia by applying the volatility approach to barley prices.

Volatility: Europe and ancient Babylon compared

Whilst wheat price data are not available for Babylon, Babylonian barley prices are available for the period 385–61 BC as a result of the careful work of assyriologists

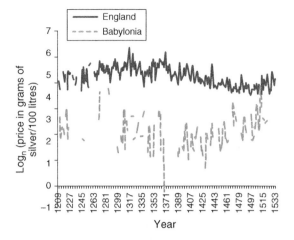

Figure 10.1 Barley prices: England compared with Babylonia (385–61 BC).

Source: The Appendix of Babylonian prices (this volume); Clark (2004).

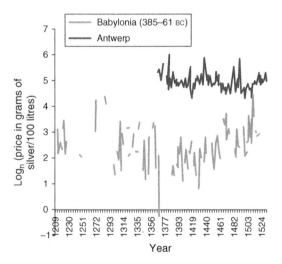

Figure 10.2 Barley prices: Antwerp compared with Babylonia.

Source: The Appendix of Babylonian prices (this volume); Allen and Unger, online database.

and historians (cf. Van der Spek *et al.*, Chapter 1, this volume). Annual barley prices for Europe are also available and for the purposes of this chapter are selected to enable coverage from late medieval times through to the modern period: England 1209–1914, Antwerp 1366–1600, Vienna 1469–1800 and Paris 1520–1788.[31] By way of a comparison, Figure 10.1 and Figure 10.2 show the natural logarithm of annual barley prices (in grams of silver per 100 litres) for

Table 10.2 Coefficients of variation on the basis of barley price data for Europe and Babylon (averages of rolling ten-year coefficient of variation by period)

	385–86 BC	*1200–1499*	*1500–1799*	*1800–1914*
Babylonia	0.48			
England		0.24	0.21	0.14
Antwerp		0.27	0.26	
Vienna		0.31	0.28	
Paris			0.34	

Sources: See text.

England and Antwerp, overlaid with prices from Babylonia. Volatility is clearly higher in the case of Babylonia. Whilst the graphical comparison is incisive, a more formal comparison needs to be made using the method discussed above.

Table 10.2 records the results of calculating the coefficient of variation on the basis of barley price data for Europe and Babylon.

Dickey-Fuller tests are applied to the rolling barley coefficients of variation to test whether there is evidence of a decline in volatility over time. The test for the Babylonian coefficient of variation rejects the null hypothesis of non-stationarity, suggesting that volatility was unchanged in the period 385–86 BC (a similar conclusion is reached by Foldvari and Van Leeuwen, Chapter 2, this volume). As reported in Table 10.2, Babylonian volatility was around double that of late medieval and early-modern Europe (see also Van Leeuwen *et al.*, Chapter 20). In Europe, the average coefficients of variation for barley are similar to those arrived at using wheat. They also suggest that volatility falls only very slightly between the late medieval and early-modern period. Furthermore, Dickey-Fuller tests for the stationarity of the rolling ten-year coefficients of variation in the early modern period reject the null hypothesis of non-stationarity for England, Vienna and Paris, implying that volatility in these areas was not subject to significant change in the period 1500–1799, consistent with the earlier results. The only exception is Antwerp where volatility appears to have risen up to 1600, again consistent with earlier results. It is only when we move into the nineteenth century that volatility falls significantly below that at the start of the early-modern period, to around one-quarter of that in ancient Babylonia.

Table 10.3 (based on the complete results of the GARCH methodology shown in Table 10.4) reports the results of applying the GARCH model to the barley price data.

Monthly dummies are included in the Babylonian price equation to control for any variation in prices caused by the patchy nature of the data (prices for some years were formed on the basis of a December price, others on the basis of a July price, and others on the basis of an average of two, three or four monthly prices). The dummies are used to capture which months have contributed to the annual average price, and have the effect of making the results more comparable with those of Europe for which the data are much less patchy.[32] The time trend in the Babylonian variance equation was insignificant, suggesting, as with the coefficient

Table 10.3 GARCH volatility estimates (annual barley prices)

	Long-run steady state variance
Babylonia (385–86 BC)	0.34
England (1255–1914)	0.092 (to 0.012 by the end)
Antwerp (1383–1600)	0.066
Vienna (1470–1753)	0.11 (to 0.05 by the end)
Paris (1527–1788)	0.11

Sources: See text. See Table 10.4 for complete results.

of variation, that volatility was subject to little change in ancient Babylonia. In other words, markets were at a stable level of development. The associated steady state variance is 0.34. It should be noted that the residual variance equation suffers from serial correlation, which has proved difficult to eliminate given the patchiness of the data. However, the steady state variance is robust to various specifications that were tried.

Moving to the European results, the time trend in the variance equation for England was found to be significant, indicating a declining in volatility over the long period 1255–1914 for the barley market. Assuming volatility was reasonably stable before and after this period, we can calculate the initial and final steady state variances, which are 0.092 and 0.012 respectively. This initial value for medieval England is between one-quarter and one-third of the value for Babylonia.

Moving on to restrict ourselves to the consideration of Europe before the nineteenth century, an insignificant time trend in the variance equation implies an unchanging level of steady state volatility in Antwerp and Paris, with steady state variances of 0.066 and 0.11 respectively (falling within the range of the initial English value). Only in the case of Vienna does volatility show a significant downward trend. However, if we focus on the period 1500–1753 (excluding the late fifteenth-century observations), this downward trend disappears. Consistent with the previous findings, it is certainly not clear that volatility was falling consistently everywhere in the early-modern period, although falls before and after this seem consistent with these GARCH results. Comparing Europe with ancient Babylonia on the basis of the estimates, we find that volatility in Babylonia was around three to four times that in medieval Europe.

As with the coefficient of variation measure, the levels of volatility arrived at using the GARCH model for barley are reassuringly similar to those arrived at using the wheat price data. Whilst we are fortunate to have prices for a common good (barley) in this particular comparison of Babylonia and Europe, when making comparisons across long spans of time and very different locations this may not always be the case. We could be comparing, so to speak, the volatility of apples with the volatility of pears. This could be seen as a significant stumbling block for the research agenda of comparing markets. However, the similarity of our barley and wheat price volatility estimates suggests that the comparison of volatility of different products (where it is necessary) will not always cause problems. The

Table 10.4 GARCH estimates: price and variance equation

	Babylonia 385–86 BC	England 1255–1914	Vienna 1470–1753	Paris 1526–1788	Antwerp 1383–1600
Price equation[a]					
L1	0.45	0.88	0.67	0.59	0.52
	(2.26)	(21.35)	(13.09)	(9.41)	(6.8)
L2	0.24	−0.33			−0.073
	(0.80)	(−6.29)			(−1.07)
L3	−0.35	0.12			
	(−1.43)	(2.18)			
L4		0.11		0.13	
		(2.80)		(2.37)	
L5					
L6				0.089	
				(1.86)	
L7		0.12			0.072
		(3.87)			(1.23)
TREND	−0.12	−0.0018	−0.0026		−0.089
	(−2.01)	(−1.96)	(−1.99)		(−4.29)
TREND-squared	0.000039	0.00000066			0.0000307
	(2.36)	(2.21)			(4.36)
Constant	1.98	1.31	−0.75	1.12	67
		(1.81)	(−1.9)	(3.54)	(4.28)
Variance equation (with trend)					
ARCH	0.73	0.070	0.11	0.24	0.45
	(3.23)	(2.57)	(1.49)	(2.53)	(2.91)
GARCH		0.86	−0.73	0.47	0.00036
		(13.07)	(−2.24)	(2.48)	(0.0)
TREND	−0.0006	−0.0030	−0.0026	−0.000065	0.0016
	(−0.93)	(−6.06)	(−1.99)	(−0.04)	(0.77)
Constant	0.22	−1.2	2.1	−3.3	−5.7
		(−1.34)	(0.98)	(−1.18)	(−1.83)
Variance equation (no trend)					
ARCH	0.78			0.24	0.43
	(3.54)			(2.53)	(2.94)
GARCH				0.47	0.0053
				(2.51)	(0.03)
Constant	0.076			0.032	0.037
	(1.36)			(2.21)	(3.65)

Note:
[a] *t*-statistics are in brackets. Price equations were subjected to a general to specific procedure in order to eliminate insignificant terms. For Babylonia, the price equation included monthly dummies (unreported). The insignificant lagged terms remained in the Babylonian and Antwerp price equation in an effort to eliminate serial correlation. Except for Babylonia, the GARCH models were estimated using STATA. STATA includes the trend in the variance equation as follows: ARCH term + GARCH term + exp (constant + beta × trend). For Babylonia, the price and variance equations were estimated separately using ordinary least squares (OLS). Residuals from the price equation were squared and used as the dependent variable in the variance equation. Steady state variances were calculated as standard by setting equal the ARCH, GARCH and dependent in the variance equation, and then solving.

research agenda of measuring and comparing markets across the world and across history – even when data are quite limited – is full of possibilities.

Conclusion

Since Adam Smith, economists have placed markets at the heart of economic development. It is argued that by enabling specialization and incentivizing capital accumulation and technological change, markets support modern economic growth. However, as a survey of the literature on European market integration suggests, markets are much older than modern economic growth. This indicates that more precise comparisons of markets over time still need to be made if we are to fully understand the course of markets in history and their relationship with economic development. In making such comparisons, it is useful to employ a price volatility measure. Given that this measure has been relatively neglected in favour of price gaps and speeds of adjustment, this chapter has examined price volatility in Europe using two different approaches, coefficients of variation and GARCH models. The results are reassuringly consistent with the existing literature, appearing to confirm the suggestion that a significant improvement in market development had already taken place by 1600. Further reductions in price volatility came in the seventeenth and eighteenth centuries, but were both smaller and often temporarily undone. The comparison of volatility in Europe and Babylon further supports the notion that markets developed earlier in history than is typically thought: markets in ancient Babylonia were developed to around one-third of the level of early-modern Europe, suggesting that a significant advance took place between these two periods. That markets existed so long ago and made such significant strides confirms that they indeed have a long heritage. Markets are far from 'modern'.

Notes

1 Blaut (1993); Frank (1998); Frank and Gills (1993); Hobson (2004).
2 Allen (2009); Epstein (2000); Van Zanden (2008, 2009).
3 Finley (1965); Polanyi (1944).
4 See, for example: Bateman (2011, 2012), Britnell (1981, 1993), Britnell and Campbell (1995) and Epstein (2000).
5 Keller and Shiue (2007); Temin (2001).
6 Van der Spek and Mandemakers (2003).
7 Temin (2001).
8 See, for example, Britnell (1981, 1993), Britnell and Campbell (1995) and Epstein (2000).
9 Harley (1988).
10 For a more extensive history of markets in Europe, see Bateman (2012, Chapter 1).
11 Temin (2001); Silver (2007).
12 Howgego (1994), cited in Silver (2007: 211).
13 Mann (1986); Berman (1983). For a summary, see Van Zanden (2008).
14 Epstein (2000: Chapter 7).
15 Grief *et al.* (1994); Grief (2006); De Moor (2008).
16 Epstein (2000: 66).
17 Epstein (2000: 67).

18 Epstein (2000: 158–60).
19 On England, see for example Clark (2002), Britnell and Campbell (1995) and Mass-chaele (1993). On the Low Countries, see for example Unger (1999), Zuijderduijn *et al.* (2012) and Van Bavel *et al.* (2012).
20 Persson (1999: 98–105).
21 Persson (1999: 112).
22 Bateman (2011); Epstein (2000: Chapter 5). On the latter point, see Studer (2009: 37–8.)
23 O'Rourke and Williamson (2002a, b); Findlay and O'Rourke (2003); Jacks (2005).
24 p. 91.
25 p. 93–7.
26 Kindly supplied by Robert C. Allen, and also available online from the Allen-Unger grain price dataset: www.gcpdb.info/about.html.
27 See Bateman (2011) for details and sources of the data.
28 Foldvari and Van Leeuwen (2011).
29 Persson (1999: 112).
30 Foldvari and Van Leeuwen (2011).
31 The data are accessible at the IISH website (www.iisg.nl/hpw/data.php#united), following the work of the Global Price and Income History Group.
32 Steady state variances are calculated using the method detailed in Table 10.4.

Bibliography

Allen, R. C. 2009. *The British Industrial Revolution in Global Perspective*, Cambridge: Cambridge University Press.
Allen, R.C. and Unger, R.W. *Allen – Unger Global Commodity Prices Database.* www.gcpdb.info/, accessed April 2012.
Bateman, V. N. 2007. 'The Evolution of Markets in Early Modern Europe, 1350–1800: a Study of Grain Prices', *Economics Series Working Paper*, University of Oxford.
—— 2011. 'The Evolution of Markets in Early Modern Europe, 1350–1800: a Study of Wheat Prices', *Economic History Review*, 64: 447–71.
—— 2012. *Markets and Growth in Early Modern Europe*, London: Pickering and Chatto.
Berman, H. 1983. *Law and Revolution: The Formation of the Western Legal Tradition*, Cambridge, MA: Harvard University Press.
Blaut, J. M. 1993. *The Colonizer's Model of the World*, New York: Guilford Press.
Britnell, R. H. 1981. 'The Proliferation of Markets in England, 1200–1349', *Economic History Review*, 34: 209–21.
—— 1993. *Commercialisation of English Society*, Cambridge: Cambridge University Press.
Britnell, R. and Campbell, B. M. S, eds. 1995. *A Commercialising Economy: England 1086 to c.1300*, Manchester: Manchester University Press.
Clark, G. 2002. 'Markets and Economic Growth: Grain Markets in Medieval England', *Mimeograph*, Department of Economics, U.C. Davis.
—— 2004. 'The Price History of English Agriculture, 1209–1914', *Research in Economic History*, 22: 41–124.
De Moor, T. 2008. 'The Silent Revolution: the Emergence of Commons, Guilds and Other Forms of Corporate Collective Action in Western Europe from a New Perspective', *International Review of Social History*, 53 (Supplement): 179–212.
Epstein, S. R. 2000. *Freedom and Growth: The Rise of States and Markets in Europe*, London: Routledge.
Federico, G. and Persson, K. G. 2007. 'Market Integration and Convergence in the World Wheat Market, 1800–2000', *Discussion Papers 06-10*, Department of Economics, University of Copenhagen.

Findlay, R. and O'Rourke, K. 2003. 'Commodity Market Integration, 1500–2000', in *Globalisation in Historical Perspective*, edited by M. Bordo, A. Taylor and J. Williamson, Chicago: University of Chicago Press: 113–64.

Finley, M. I. 1965. 'Technical Innovation and Economic Progress in the Ancient World', *Economic History Review*, 18: 29–45.

Foldvari, P. and Van Leeuwen, B. 2011. 'What Can Price Volatility Tell Us About Market Related Institutions? Conditional Heteroscedasticity in Historical Commodity Price Series', *Cliometrica*, 5: 165–86.

Frank, A. G. 1998. *Re-Orient*, Berkeley: University of California Press.

Frank, A. G. and Gills, B. K. 1993. *The World System*, London: Routledge.

Grief, A. 2006. *Institutions and the Path to the Modern Economy: Lessons from Medieval Trade*, Cambridge: Cambridge University Press.

Grief, A., Milgrom, P. and Weingast, B. R. 1994. 'Coordination, Commitment and Enforcement: the Case of the Merchant Guild', *Journal of Political Economy*, 102: 745–76.

Harley, C. K. 1988. 'Ocean Freight Rates and Productivity, 1740–1913: The Primacy of Mechanical Innovation Reaffirmed,' *Journal of Economic History*, 48: 851–76.

Hobson, J. M. 2004. *The Eastern Origins of Western Civilization*, Cambridge: Cambridge University Press.

Howgego, C. 1994. 'Coin Circulation and the Integration of the Roman Economy', *Journal of Roman Archaeology*, 7: 5–21.

Jacks, D. 2004. 'Market Integration in the North and Baltic Seas, 1500–1800', *Journal of European Economic History*, 33: 285–329.

—— 2005. 'Intra- and International Commodity Market Integration in the Atlantic Economy, 1800–1913', *Explorations in Economic History*, 42: 381–413.

Keller, W. and Shiue, C. H. 2007. 'Markets in China and Europe on the Eve of the Industrial Revolution', *The American Economic Review*, 97: 1189–1216.

Mann, M. 1986. *The Sources of Social Power*, volume 1: *A History of Power from the Beginning to AD 1760*, Cambridge: Cambridge University Press.

Masschaele, J. 1993. 'Transport Costs in Medieval England', *Economic History Review*, 46: 266–79.

O'Rourke, K. and Williamson, J. (2002a) 'When did Globalisation Begin? The Evolution of a Nineteenth Century Atlantic Economy', *European Review of Economic History*, 6: 23–50.

—— (2002b) 'After Columbus: Explaining Europe's Overseas Trade Boom, 1500–1800', *Journal of Economic History*, 62: 417–56.

Özmucur, S. and Pamuk, Ş. 2007. 'Did European Commodity Prices Converge During 1500–1800?', in *New Comparative Economic History*, edited by T. J. Hatton, K. O'Rourke and A. M. Taylor, Cambridge MA: The MIT Press: 59–85.

Persson, K. G. 1999. *Grain Markets in Europe, 1500–1900: Integration and Deregulation*, Cambridge: Cambridge University Press.

Polanyi, K. 1944. *The Great Transformation: The Political and Economic Origins of our Time*, Boston: Beacon Press.

Silver, M. 2007. 'Roman Economic Growth and Living Standards: Perceptions Versus Evidence', *Ancient Society*, 37: 191–252.

Söderberg, J. 2004. 'Prices in the Medieval and Near East and Europe', paper for 'Towards a Global History of Prices and Wages' conference, Utrecht. Available at www.iisg.nl/hpw/papers/soderberg.pdf (accessed 1 August 2011).

Studer, R. 2009. 'Does Trade Explain Europe's Rise? Geography, Market Size and Economic Development', *London School of Economics Working Paper*, Department of Economic History, 129/09.

Temin, P. 2001. 'A Market Economy in the Early Roman Empire', *Journal of Roman Studies*, 91: 169–81.

Unger, R. 1999. 'Feeding Low Countries Towns: the Grain Trade in the Fifteenth Century', *Revue Belge de Philolgie et d'Histoire*, 77: 329–58.

Van Bavel, B., Dijkman, J., Kuijpers, E. and Zuijderduijn, J. 2012. 'The Organisation of Markets As a Key Factor in the Rise of Holland, Fourteenth-sixteenth Centuries: a Test Case for an Institutional Approach', *Continuity and Change*, 27: 347–78.

Van der Spek, R. J. and Mandemakers, C. A. 2003. 'Sense and Nonsense in the Statistical Approach of Babylonian Prices', *Bibliotheca Orientalis*, 60: 521–37.

Van Zanden, J. L. 2008. 'The Medieval Origins of the European Miracle', *Journal of Global History*, 3: 337–59.

—— 2009. *The Long Road to the Industrial Revolution*, Leiden: Brill.

Zuijderduijn, J., De Moor, T. and Van Zanden, J. L. 2012. 'Small is Beautiful: the Efficiency of Credit Markets in Late Medieval Holland', *European Review of Economic History*, 16: 3–22.

11 Markets and price fluctuations in England and Ireland, 1785–1913[1]

Liam Kennedy and Peter Solar

Introduction

The contours of the English economy at the end of the eighteenth century are reasonably well known. The agrarian sector was still the largest employer of labour but this highly commercialized society was also experiencing the first stages of the Industrial Revolution. The economy was on a war footing, prosecuting a hugely expensive war against France, but with the Peace of 1815 its manufactured products began to flood onto markets in continental Europe and the New World. Population was growing rapidly, with young workers migrating to the industrializing towns and thereby accelerating the process of urbanization. The agrarian social order was organized, with some regional variation, into three broad social categories comprising landlords, tenant farmers and agricultural labourers. Proto-industrial workers also peopled the countryside, but were being gradually superseded by the new, factory-based production. Industrialization and urbanization increased the demand for marketed foodstuffs. London emerged as the great metropolitan food market of the nineteenth century, drawing in supplies from overseas, including produce from Ireland. London is therefore a particularly good reference point when discussing prices, and changes in price volatility as they affected markets in the British and Irish economies in the modern period.

How to characterize the Irish economy at the end of the eighteenth century is perhaps a less straightforward task. This was a predominantly rural economy and society in which property rights were well established though not always readily enforced, market relationships were widely diffused, and the rent nexus structured social relationships in the countryside. Land was the primary means of production and urbanization was limited. While there was a varied range of occupations in trades, food processing, petty manufacturing and distribution, the bulk of the population drew its livelihood from owning, renting or working the land. Access to land was vital to the existence of landlords, middlemen, tenant farmers, cottiers and labourers – the various strata that constituted the rural social hierarchy. Proto-industry was firmly established, particularly in relation to the production of linen textiles in the northern counties of the island, linking rurally-based handicraft industry to regional and overseas markets. Indeed, at the close of the eighteenth century, the value of linen goods exported exceeded that of agricultural produce

(Cullen 1972). The older-established and more urban-based woollen industry, located in the southern counties of the island, catered mainly for the home market. It provided thousands of households with the means of making a living, and had done so for generations (Bielenberg 1991, 2009). The spectre of the Industrial Revolution, in the form of low-cost mechanized production of textiles, and all the competitive pressures this implied for the handicraft industry on the Irish side of the Irish Sea, was only beginning to take shape. So, when the Union of Britain and Ireland was being hammered out in 1800, it is fair to say that this was a society in which production for the market was extensive and in which the foreign trade sector was highly developed and increasingly focused on Britain (Cullen 1968).

This picture of a society suffused in market relationships, caught in the force field of urban, industrializing Britain, needs to be heavily qualified. In fact in the 1960s two economists, Patrick Lynch and John Vaizey, proposed a radically different image of the Irish economy. Ireland was a country 'with two economies, one capitalist and the other subsistence' (Lynch and Vaizey 1960: 17). The modern or capitalist sector had these properties: production for the market, often for export; monetized exchanges; and more advanced techniques, including the use of capital goods in production. The subsistence sector, by contrast, engaged in little production for the market – household or neighbourhood self-sufficiency was the norm; techniques of production were primitive; and money transactions were virtually unknown. Few economic ties linked these two types of economy. They also inhabited different spaces, not only metaphorically but literally. The modern economy, in the main, was situated in the principal towns scattered along the eastern coastline. Included with these were their hinterlands, though it was supposed that only 'a day's cart-journey from any town the use of money was rare' (Lynch and Vaizey 1960: 25). The subsistence sector occupied most of the land area of Ireland and was particularly deeply entrenched in the western half of the island.

This resonated with treatments of dualism in contemporary developing countries. Thirlwall (1999: 176), for instance, is of the view that 'it is not unusual for geographical, social and technological dualism to occur together, with each type of dualism tending to reinforce the other.' But few if any historians nowadays subscribe to this simple dichotomy of economic conditions on the island of Ireland.[2] Yet the stark formulation directs us to important and distinctive features of the Irish rural economy that have major implications for the functioning of markets, the impact of harvest failures and the economic welfare of social groups occupying different levels within the class structure. For one thing, progression toward market involvement was not a unidirectional process in the localities. In the second quarter of the nineteenth century there was a retreat from market activity on the part of tens of thousands of women in the west and the north-west of Ireland, as earnings from hand-spinning flax went into steep decline (Collins 1982). The collapse of woollen textiles, located in town and countryside, also involved an extensive withdrawal from handicraft production for the market.[3] Of more general significance, at the base of agricultural society relatively little money changed hands. Cottiers and agricultural labourers bartered labour services with local farmers in exchange for a cabin and access to a piece of land on which to produce subsistence, mainly

Table 11.1 The social class structure in rural Ireland, c. 1845

	Number of households
Landlords	10,000
Rich farmers	50,000
Comfortable farmers	100,000
Middling & smaller farmers	250,000
Poor peasants	300,000
Cottiers, labourers	1,000,000

Source: Ó Gráda (1994).

potatoes. These exchanges were calculated by reference to market rates and at the end of the season the labourer, including possibly other members of the household, might have accumulated a small cash surplus which was then paid by the farmer, who in turn was a tenant producing a food surplus for the market and paying rent to his landlord in cash. Thus, although not much money changed hands, the transactions were conditioned by market experiences of rents and wages. The million or so poor households, accounting for half or more of the population, inhabited what might be termed a world of semi-subsistence production. As one ascended the social hierarchy (see Table 11.1), the use of money was increasingly common and the web of market transactions more dense. Thus, as Mokyr (1983) has pointed out, there is more than residual validity in the notion of a dual economy but it needs to be reformulated more carefully, taking account of social class and regional variations.

Markets, prices and vulnerability

In addition to the ubiquitous potato, Ireland produced three major cereal foods: in descending order of acreage, oats, wheat and barley. In terms of human food, oats and oatmeal were by far the most important of the cereals. This was particularly so in the northern counties of Ireland where oats and potatoes, with the addition of some milk, formed the backbone of the popular diet.[4] This two-crop system of provisioning suggests a high degree of insurance against food failure, as poor potato and grain harvests were unlikely to go hand-in-hand.[5] This spreading of risk probably operated effectively enough for the second half of the eighteenth century, but by the early nineteenth century the rural poor in the south of Ireland, already massively swollen by rapid population growth, were largely or almost exclusively dependent on the potato crop. One of the commissioners of the *Poor Inquiry* into the conditions of the poorer classes in Ireland, J.E. Bicheno, put the point succinctly:

> We find that they [peasants] have sunk by degrees from the potato, with milk and oatmeal, to the potato alone; and that in most districts a further deterioration has taken place by the use of a potato of an inferior quality.[6]

This process of immiseration served to undermine the food security of millions of cottiers and labourers. Thus, the rapid population growth experienced between 1750 and the eve of the Great Famine of 1846–50 pushed the poorer classes in the countryside in the direction of monoculture or an increasingly heavy dependence on the miracle food of the potato. The potato blight of the 1840s would reveal that the risk associated with potato cultivation had been underpriced. But rather like medical insurance and the AIDS epidemic of the later twentieth century, there are no obvious ways whereby markets can price the risk of an as yet unknown risk factor. In the case of the Irish catastrophe, in which 15 per cent or so of the population was swept away by hunger- and famine-related diseases, ringing the alarm bells would have required an omniscient market regulator, armed with perfect foresight (or twentieth-century historiographic writings).

The next section of this chapter considers the volatility of Irish and English agricultural prices, and how patterns of price fluctuations evolved between 1785 and 1913. Twelve different commodities are considered, extending from the cheap, carbohydrate end of the spectrum, represented by potatoes, to the expensive, protein-rich foods in the form of processed beef and mutton. The three markets used in this exploration are London, Belfast and Waterford.

At first sight, price volatility might seem like a merely technical aspect of the functioning of markets, largely divorced from the everyday experience of life. This impression could not be more wrong-headed. The implications of severe price fluctuations, signifying in turn surpluses and deficits in the public availability of produce, can be profound. To take the Irish case, and focusing on the semi-subsistence sector, the surges in potato prices could be harbingers of life or death. With no cheaper provisions available to which the rural poor might trade down, and no minimum welfare net before 1840, years of dearth were times of absolute deprivation. Price volatility and food insecurity were two sides of the same coin.

More generally, as Persson has pointed out, there are welfare losses associated with poorly functioning markets and high degrees of price volatility (Persson 1999 and Chapter 4, this volume). This is the case both for producers and consumers. Conversely, other things being equal, increases in market performance as manifested by more muted price variations, result in welfare gains at an individual and at a societal level.[7] Nor are the effects necessarily confined to the economic sphere – the very bedrock of survival – as sharp price fluctuations may have knock-on effects for social and political order, varying in scope from agrarian agitations to food riots and possible revolution (Scholliers and Zamagni 1995: xvi).

Price volatility

There are various ways to measure the volatility of prices. Two approaches are presented in this chapter. The first, and the one preferred here, is to calculate the standard deviation of the natural logarithm of the ratio of the price of the commodity in year $t + 1$ to the price in year t, over the time span in question.[8] Thus, for the first sub-period, for wheat for example, we are speaking of the standard deviation of the natural logs of the price ratio of wheat in successive years, starting in 1785 and ending in 1815. This index of price volatility for different food commodities in each of five time periods is presented in Table 11.2. Prices are for harvest or production years rather than calendar years. A second, alternative measure is to use the coefficient of variation and to compare changes in the value of the coefficient over time. We make use of this measure also and the results, relating to the period 1785–1914, divided into the same five sub-periods, are presented in the Appendix to this chapter (see Tables A11.1–A11.3).

So far as possible, we have endeavoured to capture the price of a single *quality* of foodstuff through time. On the whole we are confident we have achieved this goal but of course where we have not succeeded this will introduce artificial price volatility into the price data. It is important, therefore, to examine a range of foodstuffs to view the consistency of the findings across different commodities and time periods. It should be noted also that climatic and environmental shocks may vary between time periods, thereby introducing non-comparable price variations between time periods. The supreme example in the Irish case is the Great Famine of the later 1840s, which was precipitated by massive and repeated destructions of the potato crop due to the intrusion of a new potato disease, *phytophora infestans*.

The price data are collected from newspaper reports relating to the Belfast market in the north-east of Ireland and the Waterford market in the south-east of the island. These are both port towns and there is a distance of some 270 kilometres between the two.[9] The London prices are from recent work by Solar and Klovland (2011), and were collected and turned into annual prices. The bulk of Irish agricultural trade was with Britain, even before the Act of Union, hence the relevance of the British connection in economic as in other matters (Cullen 1968).

The results on price volatility for the English market (London), the north of Ireland market (Belfast) and the south of Ireland market (Waterford) are presented in Table 11.2.

The findings show a remarkable degree of consistency both in the direction of change over time and in the experience of different commodities. As economic theory and economic history would suggest, price variance tends to be smaller on a large metropolitan market, in view of its diverse sources of supply. Thus the price variance on the London market tended to be lower than that experienced in the Irish regional markets of Belfast and Waterford, though of course there were a few exceptions in particular time periods (oats for example in the periods 1851–73 and again in 1896–1913). Even in the final time period, when price convergence was most pronounced and when the first phase of globalization was reaching its apogee during the Kondratiev upswing of 1896–1913, price fluctuations on the London market were still generally on a lower plane than they were in the Irish regional markets.

What was happening to price variance over time is of special interest. Had much of Ireland been a large, marketless backwater at the end of the eighteenth century, one might well expect severe fluctuations in food prices from time to time. As Lynch and Vaizey (1960: 12) put it (though the point is of more relevance to

Table 11.2 An index of price volatility on the London, Belfast and Waterford markets, 1785–1913

		1785–1815	1815–44	1851–73	1873–96	1896–1913
Wheat	London	0.3054	0.1798	0.2138	0.1610	0.1060
Wheat	Waterford	0.2337	0.2055	0.1854	0.1390	0.1162
Wheat	Belfast	0.2718	0.2240	0.1983	0.1223	0.1431
Flour	London					
Flour	Waterford	0.2939	0.1874	0.1667	0.1422	0.1537
Flour	Belfast	0.2423	0.2030	0.1794	0.1458	0.1613
Oats	London	0.2551	0.1613	0.1494	0.1041	0.1236
Oats	Waterford	0.2648	0.2497	0.1318	0.1514	0.1033
Oats	Belfast	0.2822	0.2603	0.1269	0.1002	0.0811
Oatmeal	London					
Oatmeal	Waterford	0.3255	0.2262	0.1197		
Oatmeal	Belfast	0.3066	0.2790	0.1354	0.1028	0.0747
Barley	London	0.2668	0.1952	0.1259	0.0884	0.0854
Barley	Waterford	0.2835	0.2374	0.1359	0.0993	
Barley	Belfast	0.3004	0.2178	0.1435	0.0680	
Potato	London		0.2392	0.3151	0.2751	0.2910
Potato	Waterford	0.5018	0.3986	0.2738	0.3596	0.3154
Potato	Belfast	0.5103	0.5080	0.2844	0.4496	0.3951
Butter	London	0.1298	0.1466	0.0865	0.1056	0.0829
Butter	Waterford	0.1304	0.1290	0.0687	0.0741	0.0675
Butter	Belfast	0.1250	0.1281	0.0752	0.0902	0.0505
Beef	London	0.0899	0.0857	0.059	0.047	0.038
Beef	Waterford	0.1269	0.1308	0.072	0.101	
Beef	Belfast	0.1232	0.1076	0.067	0.069	0.088
Mutton	London	0.1011	0.1136	0.0786	0.0685	0.0393
Mutton	Waterford	0.1170	0.1388	0.0740	0.1164	
Mutton	Belfast	0.0678	0.0816	0.0625	0.0553	0.0697
Pigmeat	London	0.1416	0.1345	0.1019	0.0932	0.1342
Pigmeat	Waterford	0.2559	0.2021	0.1018	0.1005	0.1160
Pigmeat	Belfast	0.2330	0.2199	0.1394	0.0885	0.1011
Eggs	London					
Eggs	Waterford			0.0813	0.1027	0.0751
Eggs	Belfast		0.1101	0.1446	0.0808	0.0626
Maize	London					
Maize	Waterford			0.1465	0.1334	0.1125
Maize	Belfast			0.1303	0.1449	

Source: calculated from data contained in Kennedy and Solar (2007) and Solar and Klovland (2011).

genuinely subsistence economies with tiny market sectors): 'These subsistence conditions were always threatened by the risk of bad harvests: when famines occurred the precariousness of a non-monetary economy which was normally unnoticed became apparent with startling rapidity'.

Starting with the opening period, which was dominated by the French wars and wartime inflation, three points may be made with reference to Table 11.2. First, to echo an earlier observation: with the significant exception of wheat prices, price volatility was greater in the Irish as compared to the London markets. Second, price fluctuations in the Belfast and Waterford markets were broadly similar, suggesting at least indirectly that markets along the eastern coastline of Ireland were fairly well integrated, even in this early time period. Third, the levels of price volatility were not radically different between all three centres (at least as measured by our index of price volatility). Again this suggests a high degree of market integration, not just between the north and south of Ireland but between eastern Ireland and Britain as well. In other words, even before the Union of 1801 created a common trading area, the prices for Irish export commodities were being driven by British prices and British consumer demand. Situated next door to the industrializing and urbanizing society that was Britain at the end of the eighteenth century, Ireland served as a subsidiary granary for its larger neighbour, as well as a source of livestock products.

The early to mid-nineteenth century saw important developments in transport, which should have had the effect of eroding price differentials between different markets within Ireland, and between Ireland and Britain. The canal system, particularly the Royal and Grand canals and their offshoots which served central and southern Ireland, brought geographically disparate markets into closer contact. It is more difficult to speak of productivity improvements to the road system, though there must have been some improvements as networks of horse-drawn coaches, the famous Bianconi coaches being the exemplar, criss-crossed the countryside (Nowlan 1973). The impact of railways was primarily in the next or the mid-Victorian period, though the origins of the Irish rail system go back to the 1830s. But steam power already mattered greatly in one area of transport, as steam-ships linked Irish to British ports from the 1820s onwards (Solar 2006). Transport improvements overland within Britain complemented these developments, serving to deepen market integration within the British and Irish isles (see Gourvish 1980).

Are these various reductions in transaction costs reflected in the measures of price volatility? Reassuringly, they are. The majority of changes to the index as between the first (1785–1815) and second (1815–44) periods – 23 out of the 30 possible changes noted in Table 11.3 – shows a diminution in the value of the index. Where the index has increased in value, as for butter and mutton, the change was slight.

One might well expect a continuing trend towards a compression in price variation in the third time period, that of 1851–73. Railways were now coming into their own, while market and transport facilities were improving. The repeal of the Corn Laws by the Westminster Parliament in 1846 exposed British and Irish farmers more fully to international competition. Falling transport costs, on European and trans-Atlantic routes, produced evermore competitive market conditions over wider trading areas (Foreman-Peck 1995). It is, therefore, a shade embarrassing to find that *that* most internationally traded of commodities, wheat, does not fit this

Table 11.3 Number of commodities for which price volatility increases or decreases in a given period at London, Waterford and Belfast[a]

	Between 1785–1815 and 1815–44	Between 1815–44 and 1851–73	Between 1851–73 and 1873–96	Between 1873–96 and 1896–1913
Decline	21	26	20	16
Increase	6	3	11	10
Total	27	29	31	26

Source: derived from Table 11.2.

Note:
[a] The number of products (such as wheat, butter etc.) that either increase or decrease their volatility in a given period. The final row indicates the total number of products.

picture (see row one of Table 11.2). Further compounding the sense of surprise is the fact that this is so in relation to the London market, one of Europe's great wheat markets. The reason for this contrary finding is not obvious, though it may have to do with quality differences that are invisible to later historians of wheat prices. It is all the more anomalous in that the variability of wheat prices, at least as captured by our measure, moves in the expected direction in the two regional centres of Belfast and Waterford. This anomaly, and some others notwithstanding, the broad direction of change was as expected for the period 1851–73.

In the final two periods, those of 1873–96 and 1896–1913, the trend in values of the index was broadly downwards. Inevitably there were some contrary observations, though not of any great magnitude. Looking across the period as a whole, from the later eighteenth century to the eve of the First World War, the general conclusion must be that price volatility decreased for all commodities, in all markets, over this long time span. As between the opening period of 1785–1815 and the closing period of 1896–1913, the median decline in the value of the index of volatility across all the price series was a striking 51 per cent. (The number of price series for which this could be computed was 22, drawing on all three market locations.) The more muted behaviour of prices in the final period was especially pronounced for livestock as compared to cereal products, in part presumably because transport by railway and steamboat favoured the animal trade.

The decline in the index for the different price series was virtually the same for the two regional markets, with Waterford experiencing a median decline of 49 per cent and Belfast a median decline of 47 per cent. The decline in the index over time for London was higher still at 58 per cent but it is the similarity in the course of change in the three markets, rather than any small differences, that impresses. Placing these findings in economic historical context, we conclude that the British market largely shaped Irish prices for traded commodities well before the repeal of the Corn Laws and the dismantling of agricultural protectionism. Thereafter, the international economy was the primary determinant as an increasingly globalized world economy serving the UK market. These changes enlarged the geographical boundaries of the various commodity markets and increased the diversity of climatic conditions within the supplying regions. This process of market integration, along with declines in transaction costs (insurance, communication, transport and related costs), served to constrain (though not eliminate) price fluctuations arising from initial supply shocks affecting some but not all parts of the system. The fact that the UK remained a free-trading area, despite a retreat into protectionism on the part of some European countries in the face of the American 'grain invasion' of the 1870s, left the British, and hence the Irish markets facing world prices.

Price volatility along other dimensions: grouped data

We might take these arguments a stage further and consider the likely behaviour of prices under the contrasting conditions of market-oriented production and subsistence-oriented production. While continuing to abjure the heresy of a dual economy for Ireland, at least in our period,[10] the Irish price materials offer useful clues as to likely outcomes. In the Irish case we have two quintessential subsistence products; potatoes (discussed earlier), and peat (turf), which may be introduced at this point. To these might be added an intermediate good, hay, which was also only weakly marketed. All three share the unfavourable characteristic of being bulky and of relatively low value, and hence were used primarily in self-provisioning. On theoretical grounds one might expect subsistence products, defined as those for which only a small proportion of output is ever sold, to exhibit greater price volatility than heavily marketed goods. The demand for food,[11] and possibly fuel as well, is usually held to be inelastic; hence supply shocks produce disproportionate impacts on prices, making for price instability even under conditions of unchanging population. As most food crops are affected by variations in climate and disease, and typically are produced only once or twice in the year rather than continuously under controlled conditions, supply shocks are inevitable (cf. Persson, Chapter 4, this volume).

In the case of subsistence goods, however, there are additional forces making for price instability. To take one scenario, after a bad harvest the overall deficiency in the subsistence good gives rise to a disproportionate decline in the *marketed* surplus. This is because the small-scale producers of subsistence goods, in an attempt to maintain habitual levels of consumption, are likely to retain more of their now reduced harvest for self-provisioning (Gould 1963; see also 1962). A much diminished supply reaching the market inevitably drives up prices. After a bumper harvest, by contrast, the disproportionately large *market* supply – what is available after the usual subsistence needs have been met – serves to heavily depress prices. On top of that, subsistence goods with a large volume to value ratio, such as potatoes and peat, have limited market areas, thus the possibility of averaging supplies over surplus and deficit areas is less readily available. The experiences of an internationally traded commodity, such as wheat, stand in stark contrast.

Perhaps we can attempt to predict price volatility, not only by reference to the subsistence-oriented and the market-oriented distinction but also by reference to other economic properties. The following typology is based on *a priori* reasoning:

- Subsistence goods
- Unprocessed cereals
- Processed cereals
- Processed livestock products
- Manufactured goods.

Of course there will be all kinds of individual exceptions. This hierarchy simply attempts to capture distinctive clusters of price behaviour that may be broadly observable. In terms of this hierarchy, subsistence goods should show the greatest price volatility (unless there are possibilities of low-cost storage, which is usually not the case), while basic manufactured goods should show the least. Processed cereals such as oatmeal and flour occupy an intermediate position because the cost structure of the final product includes not only the cost of raw cereals but also returns to labour and capital which tend to be fairly stable in the short and medium term. Indeed in the case of labour, nominal wages can remain constant over long periods of time.[12] Similarly, processed livestock products such as butter, beef and mutton also have a more complicated cost structure than potatoes or cereals, and thus more muted price variations are to be expected. Finally, manufactured goods are likely to exhibit the least price volatility because the production process is continuous, so allowing production adjustments to take place in line with market demand. The cost structure is also complex, with some stable or relatively stable elements contained therein. Needless to say, there will be exceptions, for example industrial goods subject to the whims of fashion are not likely to fit this general picture. In addition, the labour element may not be all that stable in some sub-periods, as for instance in the case of prolonged strikes that radically disturb supply.

We can test these propositions by reference to the price data. In Table 11.4 we present the evidence on price volatility, arranged according to the typology outlined above, for southern Irish prices. The summary measure on the right hand side of the table is the average of the price volatility indices for the particular *group* of commodities. The average chosen is the median, so as to minimize the impact of extreme values. Each row shows the index of volatility for the commodities making up each of the five groups within a specified time period. As in Table 11.2 earlier, the long time span is divided into five sub-periods, beginning with the years 1785–1815.

What of the findings? There is little doubt that the subsistence category of goods (Group 1 in Table 11.4) shows high levels of price instability until the late nineteenth century and there is indeed a strong contrast with the price behaviour of heavily market-oriented goods, as originally supposed. Potatoes are the outstanding example of this. The internal differences within the subsistence category are worthy of some note also. Hay is not perhaps the best example of a subsistence crop, being more of an intermediate product in farming (though an end product in urban markets), but peat is undeniably a subsistence crop, enjoying only limited local markets.[13] That

Table 11.4 The index of price volatility, arranged by five commodity groups, Southern Ireland, 1785–1913

Group 1: subsistence crops

	Potatoes	Hay	Peat	Median
1785–1815	0.5018		0.3319	0.4168
1815–1844	0.3986	0.3142	0.2675	0.3142
1851–1873	0.2738	0.2885	0.2850	0.2850
1873–1896	0.3596	0.3101	0.1732	0.3101
1896–1913	0.3154	0.1830	0.0794	0.1830

Group 2: cereals

	Wheat	Oats	Barley	Maize	Median
1785–1815	0.2337	0.2648	0.2835		0.2648
1815–1844	0.2055	0.2497	0.2374		0.2374
1851–1873	0.1854	0.1318	0.1359	0.1465	0.1412
1873–1896	0.1390	0.1514	0.0993	0.1334	0.1362
1896–1913	0.1162	0.1033		0.1125	0.1125

Group 3: processed cereals

	Flour	Oatmeal	Median
1785–1815	0.2939	0.3255	0.3097
1815–1844	0.1874	0.2262	0.2068
1851–1873	0.1667	0.1197	0.1432
1873–1896	0.1422		0.1422
1896–1913	0.1537		0.1537

Group 4: processed livestock products

	Butter	Beef	Mutton	Pig meat	Median
1785–1815	0.1304	0.127	0.1170	0.2559	0.1286
1815–1844	0.1290	0.131	0.1388	0.2021	0.1348
1851–1873	0.0687	0.072	0.0740	0.1018	0.0729
1873–1896	0.0741	0.101	0.1164	0.1005	0.1006
1896–1913	0.0675			0.1160	0.0918

Group 5: industrial products

	Coal	Median
1785–1815	0.1361	0.1361
1815–1844	0.1025	0.1025
1851–1873	0.2000	0.2000
1873–1896	0.1695	0.1695
1896–1913	0.1310	0.1310

Sources: the food prices are from Kennedy and Solar (2007); the peat prices are from the Franciscan Account Books, Galway and the *Belfast Newsletter*. The Franciscan manuscript records are housed at Dún Mhuire, Killiney, Co. Dublin.

it displays less price volatility than potatoes may be down to a number of factors. Unlike potatoes, which could not be carried over from one season to the next, the storage of turf was possible, even if only practised to a limited extent as storage carries its own costs. Peat is not a crop, and hence a store of seeds does not have to be carried over from one season to the next. But most importantly perhaps, by the later nineteenth century, coal had penetrated all but the most remote areas of Ireland. One might expect the presence of an industrial substitute to moderate fluctuations in the price of a non-marketed or weakly marketed good. If so, the later behaviour of peat prices seems to be a case in point. In the final sub-period the price volatility of potatoes was still high – there was no close market substitute – whereas the volatility of peat prices was remarkably low.[14]

It is somewhat surprising that the price behaviour of cereals is apparently not very different from that of processed cereals. To some extent the two categories are not directly comparable, as we have evidence for four types of cereals but only two types of processed cereals. If we confine the comparison to wheat and oats on the one hand, and flour and oatmeal on the other, then the expected result comes through, though hardly very decisively. We have yet to include bread in the processed cereals category, which should add an interesting dimension, though it has to be borne in mind also that bread prices were controlled in the early years of our period.

As anticipated, processed livestock products, in this case butter, beef, mutton, pig meat, all show low levels of price volatility. Our one industrial product in Table 11.4, coal prices in Belfast, is at the lower end of the price volatility spectrum but not as low as for the Group Four products. While the coal price series is suggestive, a wider range of manufactured and industrial goods is needed to test the proposed typology more closely. The trouble is that it is not easy to identify manufactured goods that are of the same quality over long periods of time, as such goods tend to be subject to product as well as process innovation. Even in the case of small adaptations – perhaps the typical case – these are cumulative and result in significantly different products in the medium and longer term (Rosenberg 1971). A possible candidate is nails, a simple industrial product for which price series exist, though in this case for the United States. In Table 11.5 the volatility of Philadelphia nails is contrasted with the price behaviour of Philadelphia wheat, and the results are as predicted earlier, with the differences being particularly pronounced for the periods before the 1840s.

Covariance of the prices of staple foodstuffs

Although by the early nineteenth century a large and growing proportion of the Irish population had come to depend almost exclusively on potatoes, many in Ireland still ate both potatoes and cereals (Cullen 1981). In the north of Ireland oats and potatoes were the two pillars of the diet, and oats were also eaten by farmers and others in social layers above the cottiers and landless labourers. In Irish towns both oats and wheaten bread were consumed along with potatoes. Even among the well-to-do, who in England would have eaten only bread, visitors to

Table 11.5 Comparing the price volatility of nails and wheat, Philadelphia, 1785–1914

	Nails	*Wheat*
1785–1815	0.0788	0.2209
1815–1844	0.0856	0.2072
1851–1873	0.1953	0.2029
1873–1896	0.1437	
1896–1913		0.1428
1785–1913	**0.1275**	**0.1915**

Source: Carter *et al.* (2006, vol. 3: 202–5, 212–15).

Ireland from the early eighteenth century onward remarked on the widespread taste for potatoes. Of course, after the Famine of the later 1840s, when the introduction of blight reduced the average yield and increased the variance of the potato crop and when the class of landless labourers had declined heavily through death or emigration, cereals again became a more prominent element in the diet. Viewed chronologically, the two-crop system of subsistence followed a U-shaped curve.

So how were the prices of these two staples related? Table 11.6 shows the correlation coefficients among potatoes and oats on each of the three markets. First differences were used in order to remove the complicating effect of trends in prices. There are a number of striking features. One is the persistently higher correlations of potato and oats prices in the north of Ireland. This presumably is the counterpart of the greater importance of a two-crop diet in that part of Ireland, as already noted. Oats and potatoes were close substitutes. The continued use of oats in the north shows up as well in the still relatively high correlations between potato and oats prices on the Belfast market in the mid-Victorian period.

On the Waterford and London markets, however, the close association between oats and potato prices does not survive into the second half of the nineteenth century. The late 1840s marked a sharp break in price behaviour. What could have caused this sharp break? One possibility is the repeal of protection, which changed the UK from a closed to an open economy as regards agricultural products. Against

Table 11.6 Price correlations for the two staple foodstuffs, oats and potatoes, London, Waterford and Belfast, 1785–1913

	London	*Waterford*	*Belfast*
1785–1815		0.68	0.86
1815–1844	0.30	0.75	0.80
1851–1873	0.04	−0.08	0.44
1873–1896	0.05	−0.14	0.53
1896–1913	−0.13	−0.03	0.06
1785–1913	0.41	0.49	0.61

Source: as for Table 11.2. The time period for London in the final row is 1808–1913.

this interpretation might be set the somewhat different behaviour of cereal prices. The correlations of wheat and oats prices (not shown) remained high through the 1850s and 1860s in all three places. If the opening of the UK economy detached movements of potato prices from those of cereal prices, it is not clear why the same would not have been true of wheat and oats also. That said, it could be argued that it was not until the 'grain invasion' after 1870 that supplies of wheat and oats were sufficiently independent of each other as to diminish the co-movement in their prices.

Another possible explanation is that consumption patterns among the potato-eating population of Ireland changed after the Famine (Clarkson and Crawford 2001: 95–101). During and after the Famine, Ireland imported large quantities of Indian corn and meal. Some was fed to pigs and chickens, but much entered human consumption, particularly in years of poor potato harvests. Oats and wheat may no longer have been the main substitutes in consumption. However, some things tell against this explanation. One is the simultaneous drop in the correlations between potato and cereal prices in London. Another is the relatively low correlation between potato and Indian corn prices in Ireland: it was only about 0.3. Finally, in post-Famine Ireland there were also large imports of wheat and flour and there is a good deal of evidence that bread was more widely consumed.

A third possibility is that the introduction of blight increased the variance of potato crops to such a degree that substitution in consumption was insufficient to keep potato prices in line with those of cereals. The blight, once introduced in 1845, remained present thereafter. Its effects on the yields depended on weather conditions and could, as shown in the late 1840s, be devastating. It is unfortunate that this last possibility cannot really be tested since there exist no annual series for Irish potato output or potato yields (or, for that matter, for any crop yields) before 1847.

This last observation, as well as the mention above of the importance of substitution in consumption, is a reminder that the price movements being analysed here are the market outcomes of both supply and demand factors. What may have been more immediately relevant to many in Ireland were harvest outcomes. If they grew both potatoes and oats, as was the case in the both the north and south of Ireland, their subsistence would have been determined in the first instance by yields. Here the use of two food crops may have helped to smooth consumption. An analysis of newspaper reports on harvests in the north-east and south-east of Ireland from the late 1810s to the early 1840s suggests that there was only very weak covariation between the crop yields of potatoes and oats, with a slight tendency for yields to be positively correlated in the north-east and negatively correlated in the south-east (Solar 1989: 163–4).

The Famine years: the exception?

The years of the Great Famine in Ireland, 1845–51, were exceptional and tragic in almost all respects. The potato blight, imported from America via Europe, wiped out the staple diet of the mass of the population. As Table 11.1 reminds us, more than

Table 11.7 An index of price volatility on the London, Belfast and Waterford markets during the years of the Great Famine in Ireland

	London	*Waterford*	*Belfast*
Wheat	0.1777	0.2122	0.2429
Oats	0.2026	0.2468	0.2628
Oatmeal	0.2551	0.2625	0.2551
Barley	0.2272	0.2234	0.2284
Maize		0.1910	0.1816
Potatoes	0.4594	0.4014	0.4385
Hay	0.1195	0.1719	0.1886
Butter	0.1033	0.0905	0.0888
Beef	0.0620	0.1740	0.0790
Mutton	0.1059	0.1308	0.0691
Pig meat	0.0970	0.1651	0.1428
Eggs		0.1428	0.2682

Source: as for Table 11.2.

half the population was vulnerable by virtue of extreme poverty. How food markets behaved under conditions of scarcity, social dislocation and uncertainty, was hugely important for the very survival of millions of the rural and urban poor. Turning to the metropolitan market first, it seems that the famine in Ireland, despite its scale, seems to have exercised little influence on food price fluctuations on the London market. This is the view formed if we compare measures of price volatility in the preceding period of 1815–44 (Table 11.2) with the years of crisis after 1844 (Table 11.7).

The index of price volatility for livestock products, it transpires, was actually on a lower plane in London during the Famine years. For wheat there was barely any change. In the case of oats, but not oatmeal curiously, the index increased in value. The most noticeable increase, by far, was in the case of potatoes, suggesting price fluctuations became more violent due to supply-side shocks occasioned by the potato blight which of course affected England and Scotland as well as Ireland. Viewed across the range of commodities, the long-run tendency towards a decline in price volatility on the London market was maintained during the mid- and later 1840s.

It is when we look at the Irish markets during the Famine that we begin to entertain some doubts. On the face of it, the variation in Irish livestock prices declined during the Famine period, whereas for cereals the results varied as between the two Irish markets.[15] The most anomalous outcome relates to potatoes – the staff of life before potato blight struck. The price variance of potatoes on the Waterford market increased, as one might perhaps predict, but on the Belfast market it actually declined by comparison with the preceding period (1815–44). At this point, some methodological reflection, if not outright scepticism, is called for. First, potatoes had virtually disappeared from markets in Ireland during phases of the Famine years. Second, it should be noted that in making comparisons between the findings in Tables 11.2 and 11.7 – the pre-Famine and the Famine periods – the duration of the two time periods is very different. Thus the results are averaged over a number of years, and unweighted or even weighted averages can sometimes be mislead-ing. A methodology that is appropriate for broad historical brush strokes, such as detecting long-run trends, may not be sufficiently nuanced to capture radical changes in prices that happened to be compressed within a short envelope of time. There is no doubt, as is clear from the raw data, that the prices of potatoes, oats and oatmeal surged forward between 1845 and 1846, at the start of the Famine, but prices moderated in the later years of hunger as massive imports of Indian meal reached Ireland, thereby serving to dilute the earlier changes. Third, there is the issue of the time unit for the individual prices. The raw data are in annual form (harvest years) and these in turn are averages of bi-monthly market prices (Kennedy and Solar 2007). A month is a long time in the struggle for life of a malnourished man or woman. In times of famine prices often move with dizzying rapidity, and more finely-grained time units are needed to capture the full tragedy of events. There is no doubt from the raw data that further, more detailed research would illuminate these kinds of issues, and not just for the Famine period.

Conclusion

It is assumed on the basis of earlier work by the authors (Kennedy and Solar 2007), that Irish markets, at least in eastern Ireland, were well-integrated from the end of the eighteenth century onwards, and the evidence on price volatility at Waterford and Belfast serves to reinforce this conviction. In the first half of the nineteenth century it is apparent that the British market for foodstuffs drove prices in the neighbouring Irish economy. Good sea-links, duty-free access to the much larger British food market, and the relatively closed agricultural economy of the United Kingdom of Britain and Ireland, ensured this outcome. The dismantling of agricultural protectionism, with the repeal of the UK's Corn Laws in 1846, served to change the conditions facing Irish food producers. Over time, the international economy came to exercise the decisive influence on Irish prices and hence on the prosperity, or otherwise, of Irish farmers.

One way of tracing changing market conditions and the changing trading envi-ronment is to look at changes in price volatility over time. While there are exceptions in particular sub-periods that might repay further study, there is no doubt about the direction of change across a range of price series. The direction was unmistakably downwards. Price instability, and all the negative welfare impli-cations that flowed from that, was considerably less on the eve of World War One than it had been in the years before the battle of Waterloo. One historian, look-ing at the secular trends apparent in Table 11.2, has commented to us on the Whiggish feel to the findings.[16] The world of food prices, in terms of gains in market performance and reductions in welfare losses, just seemed to get better and better.[17] Could this really be the case?

A further objection might draw on contemporary economic experience. The behaviour of globalized financial markets in the early twenty-first century shows that market integration, for example, does not necessarily result in reduced price variance. Market integration may be a necessary condition but it is certainly not a sufficient condition, as was painfully demonstrated towards the end of the first decade of the new millennium. So one is pressed to understand why the outcomes in food markets should have been so benign between the later eighteenth century and the beginning of the twentieth. Why was there, apparently, so little market failure? A large part of the answer must be that characteristic features making for market inefficiencies or market failure were largely absent from the particular markets we have been examining. First, asymmetric access to information was unlikely to have been a problem either for purchasers or sellers, at least for any length of time. Second, these were not markets characterized by principal-agent problems. Third, market participants were in a position to make informed judgements about the nature and quality of the goods they were dealing in (unlike some complex financial packages, for example, whose true value may be difficult to assess). Fourth, there is no reason to suspect any serious misalignment of incentives facing merchants engaged in the food trade. These were straightforward acts of buying and selling, largely in wholesale markets, involving skilled market operators. In effect, competitive forces were given free rein in well-supplied markets with large numbers of participants, where frictions were being progressively eroded.

This raises questions about the determinants of price volatility. Various influences – by no means comprehensively listed – are suggested in this chapter, including market type, economic policy (protectionism versus free trade), the effectiveness of competition and the possibility of securing substitute goods. As also indicated, certain kinds of innovation, as seen for example in the introduction of an effective antidote to potato blight, served to reduce variance in crop yields and hence in prices. An innovation such as the development of low-cost methods of storage would also work in the direction of reducing intertemporal price instability. Though not considered here, the influence of varying price levels, as between inflationary and deflationary periods, would also repay attention.

An attempt was also made in this chapter to create a typology of products by reference to price volatility. This requires further development and a wider range of commodities but the preliminary findings are suggestive. The apparent distinction between marketed goods and subsistence goods – price volatility being much more pronounced for the latter – comes through clearly, at least for this sample of goods, in this time period, using this particular methodology.

Finally, there is the issue of the covariance of prices. The key interest is in the major food sources, in the Irish case the two staples of potatoes and oats. In the half century or more before the repeal of the Corn Laws, potato prices and oat prices were strongly correlated. This does not necessarily mean that poor potato harvests and poor oats harvests coincided but rather that one foodstuff was substituted for the other, in the event of a significant deficiency in one or other of these staples. The relationship broke down after mid-century, however, (though Belfast was an exception for some decades thereafter). In the southern Irish case the break with the past may have been due in part to the advent of a relatively new, low-cost food alternative in the form of maize or Indian meal. Indian meal was mainly fed to animals but there is no doubt it was also consumed by humans, particularly in years of dearth. But we also suggest other possibilities because the reasons behind declining covariance, as between the price of oats and potatoes, are still obscure. On a more general note, it is perhaps worth noting the obvious: that prices, and price variation, were the outcome of *demand* as well as of supply conditions, in view of the tendency of some writers to focus on the more dramatic supply-side stories in the study of food prices.

Appendix: Coefficient of variation for the prices of foodstuffs on the London, Belfast and Waterford markets, 1785–1913

Table A11.1 Coefficient of variation for the prices of foodstuffs on the London market

	1785–1815	1815–44	1851–73	1873–96	1896–1913
Wheat	0.36	0.20	0.19	0.23	0.10
Oats	0.32	0.16	0.15	0.15	0.11
Oatmeal	0.34	0.26	0.13	0.15	0.08
Barley	0.34	0.21	0.12	0.11	0.07
Potatoes	0.26	0.18	0.25	0.31	0.19
Hay	0.27	0.16	0.20	0.17	0.15
Butter	0.27	0.14	0.12	0.16	0.10
Beef	0.26	0.10	0.13	0.11	0.06
Mutton	0.25	0.12	0.13	0.09	0.05
Pigmeat	0.30	0.14	0.10	0.10	0.11

Source: Solar and Klovland (2011).

Table A11.2 Coefficient of variation for the prices of foodstuffs on the Waterford (southern) market

	1785–1815	1815–44	1851–73	1873–96	1896–1913
Wheat	0.26	0.24	0.19	0.27	0.10
Flour	0.21	0.26	0.18	0.22	0.22
Oats	0.30	0.24	0.13	0.20	0.11
Oatmeal	0.33	0.21	0.12		
Barley	0.32	0.25	0.17	0.14	0.08
Maize			0.17	0.21	0.16
Potatoes	0.59	0.35	0.22	0.33	0.21
Hay		0.25	0.25	0.23	0.17
Butter	0.29	0.13	0.12	0.16	0.06
Beef	0.17	0.15	0.21	0.16	
Mutton	0.24	0.15	0.16	0.10	
Pigmeat	0.32	0.21	0.10	0.14	0.14
Offal		0.21	0.22	0.06	
Eggs			0.17	0.09	0.10

Source: Kennedy and Solar (2007).

Table A11.3 Coefficient of variation for the prices of foodstuffs on the Belfast (northern) market

	1785–1815	1815–44	1851–73	1873–96	1896–1913
Wheat	0.31	0.22	0.19	0.22	0.10
Oats	0.34	0.24	0.13	0.13	0.10
Oatmeal	0.33	0.26	0.13	0.15	0.08
Barley	0.38	0.20	0.13	0.07	
Maize			0.14	0.18	
Potatoes	0.48	0.34	0.24	0.36	0.24
Hay		0.23	0.28	0.24	0.13
Butter	0.28	0.14	0.12	0.14	0.08
Beef	0.23	0.09	0.16	0.10	0.07
Mutton	0.24	0.11	0.13	0.06	0.08
Pigmeat	0.32	0.22	0.12	0.13	0.14
Bacon		0.16	0.11	0.10	
Eggs		0.09	0.19	0.07	0.13

Source: Kennedy and Solar (2007).

Notes

1 This chapter was presented at a workshop in Trinity College, Dublin in September 2011, to celebrate the lifetime achievement of the historian and economist, Cormac Ó Gráda.
2 For an early and effective critique see Lee (1971).
3 This view is critically examined by Geary (1998).
4 *Poor Law Inquiry (Ireland)*, British Parliamentary Papers, XXXV (1836), Appendix D; Connell (1950).
5 For some qualitative evidence on this issue, translated into quantitative form, see Solar (1989).
6 *Remarks on the Evidence taken in the Poor Inquiry (Ireland), contained in the Appendices D, E, F by one of the commissioners*, British Parliamentary Papers, XXXIV (1836): 697.
7 Other things may not necessarily be equal of course, as some social groups may be disadvantaged in the process of commercialization, but those are issues lying outside the scope of this chapter.
8 In general terms, it is the standard deviation of $\mathrm{Ln}(P_{t+1}/P_t)$ from year $t = 1$ to year n at the end of a sub-period.
9 For a discussion of the source materials and the methodology see Kennedy and Solar (2007).
10 The qualification as to time period is important. There is at least a *prima facie* case for arguing for a dual economy in Ireland in the seventeenth century, though multiple or fragmented economies might be a more appropriate image.
11 On the inelasticity of demand for food products see Ritson (1977) and Persson (1999).
12 The stickiness of wages was pointed out by Adam Smith in the *Wealth of Nations*. For evidence of this effect on Irish wages see Kennedy and Dowling (1997). Even in the New World, the same phenomenon was evident. See Carter *et al.* (2006).
13 Naturally the physiochemical properties of commodities matter. Potatoes are susceptible not only to weather conditions but to disease as well. The yield of hay, or dried grass, by contrast, is primarily determined by weather conditions and grassland management (within human control), and is not affected by animal and plant diseases to any extent.

14 It would be interesting to explore price variation on a continuous basis, rather than between extensive sub-periods, because the case of potatoes offers a good test case for the impact of innovation on price instability, in this case the discovery of the Bordeaux Mixture as an antidote to potato blight and its use from the 1880s onwards in Irish and British agriculture.

15 Using the time frame of 1815–44 or 1815–45 makes only a marginal difference to the results.

16 Comment by Gregory Clark at the Ó Gráda workshop, Dublin, September 2011.

17 It might be added that the index of volatility does not fall for all commodities, in all succeeding time intervals. There are exceptions, as was pointed out earlier, and these might repay further investigation.

Bibliography

Bielenberg, A. 1991. *Cork's Industrial Revolution 1780–1880*, Cork: Cork University Press.

—— 2009. *Ireland and the Industrial Revolution: The Impact of the Industrial Revolution on Irish Industry, 1801–1921*, London: Routledge.

Carter, S. B., Gartner, S. S., Hanes M. R., Olmstead, A. L., Sutch, R. and Wright, G., eds. 2006. *Historical Statistics of the United States*, 5 volumes, Cambridge: Cambridge University Press.

Clarkson, L. A. and Crawford, E. M. 2001. *Feast and Famine: A History of Food and Nutrition in Ireland, 1500–1920*, Oxford: Oxford University Press.

Collins, B. 1982. 'Proto-industrialization and Pre-famine Emigration', *Social History*, 7: 127–46.

Connell, K. H. 1950. *The Population of Ireland*, Oxford: Clarendon Press.

Cullen, L. M. 1968. *Anglo-Irish Trade, 1660–1800*, Manchester: Manchester University Press.

—— 1972. *An Economic History of Ireland since 1660*, London: Batsford (2nd edition 1987).

—— 1981. *The Emergence of Modern Ireland, 1600–1900*, London: Batsford.

Geary, F. 1998. 'Deindustrialization in Ireland before 1851: Some Evidence from the Census', *Economic History Review*, 51: 512–41.

Foreman-Peck, J. 1995. *A History of the World Economy: International Economic Relations since 1850*, 2nd edition, Harlow: Pearson Higher Education.

Gould, J. D. 1962. 'Agricultural Fluctuations and the English Economy in the Eighteenth Century', *Journal of Economic History*, 22: 313–33.

—— 1963. 'Y. S. Brenner on Prices: A Comment', *Economic History Review*, New Series, 16: 351–3.

Gourvish, T. R. 1980. *Railways and the British Economy, 1830–1914*, London: Macmillan.

Kennedy, L. and Dowling, M. 1997. 'Prices and Wages in Ireland, 1700–1850', *Irish Economic & Social History*, 24: 62–104.

Kennedy, L. and Solar, P. M. 2007. *Irish Agriculture: A Price History from the mid-18th century to the eve of the First World War*, Dublin: Royal Irish Academy.

Lee, J. J. 1971. 'The dual economy in Ireland, 1800–50', in *Historical studies VIII*, edited by T. D. Williams, Dublin: Gill & Macmillan: 191–201.

Lynch, P. and Vaizey, J. 1960. *Guinness's Brewery in the Irish Economy, 1759–1876*, Cambridge: Cambridge University Press.

Mokyr, J. 1983. *Why Ireland Starved*, London: George Allen & Unwin.

Nowlan, K. B., ed. 1973. *Travel and Transport in Ireland*, Dublin: Gill & Macmillan.

Ó Gráda, C. 1994. *Ireland: A New Economic History, 1780–1939*, New York: Oxford University Press.

Persson, K. G. 1999. *Grain Markets in Europe, 1500–1900: Integration and Deregulation*, Cambridge: Cambridge University Press.

Poor Law Inquiry (Ireland), British Parliamentary Papers, XXXV 1836, Appendix D.

Remarks on the Evidence taken in the Poor Inquiry (Ireland), Contained in the Appendices D, E, F by One of the Commissioners, British Parliamentary Papers, XXXIV 1836.

Ritson, C. 1977. *Agricultural Economics: Principles and Policy*, London: Crosby Lockwood Staples.

Rosenberg, N., ed. 1971. *The Economics of Technological Change: Selected Readings*, London: Penguin.

Scholliers, P. and Zamagni, Z. 1995. 'Introduction', in *Labour's Reward: Real Wages and Economic Change in 19th and 20th Century Europe*, edited by P. Scholliers and Z. Zamagni, Aldershot: Edward Elgar Publishing.

Solar, P. M. 1989. 'Harvest Fluctuations in Pre-Famine Ireland: Evidence from Belfast and Waterford Newspapers', *Agricultural History Review*, 37: 157–65.

—— 2006. 'Shipping and Irish Economic Development in the Nineteenth Century', *Economic History Review*, 61: 717–42.

Solar, P. M. and Klovland, J. T. 2011. 'London Agricultural Prices, 1770–1913', *Economic History Review*, 64: 72–87.

Thirlwall, A. P. 1999. *Growth and Development, with Special Reference to Developing Countries*, sixth edition, Basingstoke: Palgrave Macmillan (7th edition 2003).

12 Market integration in China, AD 960–1644

Liu Guanglin

Introduction

This chapter explores the market performance in pre-industrial China by comparing food prices and per capita money stocks in the Song (AD 960–1279) and Ming dynasties (AD 1368–1644). As recent economic research seems to show, macro-level stability based on increasing market performance is a necessary, although not sufficient, condition for pre-industrial growth. This increase in a pre-industrial economy would reduce the price volatility caused by harvest failures and promote specialization of production. All this advances agricultural productivity and improves the living standard of farmers and consumers alike.[1] Other studies in this book have already identified a few contributing factors that help to explain market performance (i.e. lower conditional price volatility): trade, farming technology (increasing output), storage, consumption (if people started to diversify their consumption), institutions/government and monetary developments (which affect income and prices). However, in this chapter, because of the large monetary changes that occurred in China in the period under study, I focus my analysis on long-term changes in money stocks from the Song to the Ming dynasties to define and explain the performance of food markets in these nearly seven centuries.

In the following, I first present a survey of long-term changes in grain prices in late imperial China. The survey clearly indicates the existence of two different price regimes, separated by the Mongol conquest of China in the late thirteenth century and the establishment of the Ming dynasty in 1368. The average level of food prices measured in silver remained much lower during the sixteenth century when the population grew and the market expanded. However, documenting rises and/or declines in prices does not itself explain increasing or decreasing market integration. To explain the century-long deflation and its impact on trade, I further compare the money supply between the Song and Ming eras. This comparison points to a huge decline in money stocks between the eleventh and sixteenth centuries at both aggregate and per capita levels, and it was this decline that was chiefly responsible for the lower price level in the sixteenth century.

The contraction or expansion of the market in the traditional Chinese economy essentially determines the monetary needs. This chapter challenges the current wisdom about the transition towards a silver economy in the Ming era, which often assumes a deepening in the monetization of the economy and an enormous increase in the money supply during the transition, by providing a comprehensive measurement of the sharp decline in the money stock after the Ming dynasty was founded. The paucity of hard currencies was still felt even when China began to import silver from overseas trade. I argue that it was the anti-market policies implemented by the early Ming court (1368–1450) that substantially converted the whole economy into a barter economy and thus diminished the volume of hard currencies in circulation. The prevalence of payment-in-kind and counterfeit coins increased transaction costs and produced difficulties for long-distance trade. To test how currency affects market performance, I examine in detail the economic instability in the economy of the fifteenth and sixteenth centuries, an instability caused by the insufficient supply of hard currencies. Although this is the first time in the literature of Chinese economic history that an attempt has been made to explicitly relate long-term price movements to the quantity of money, the following analysis does successfully demonstrate the important role that the money supply performed. In sum, the comparison reveals a regression in market integration from the collapse of the Song dynasty in AD 1279 through the Ming period.

Long-term changes in food prices of late imperial China

The historical study of grain prices in China is a difficult task because there were substantial variances in units of measurements when sales and purchases took place. Leaving aside the question of the difference between the basic volumes of grains across regions, the consistency of price records was also influenced by differences in the medium of exchanges, especially between silver and bronze coins.[2] The monetary system in the Song dynasty comprised multiple forms: bronze coins, precious metals such as silver, and credit instruments.[3] Bronze coins were recognized by the state and widely accepted by the commoners at marketplaces. However, by 1450, silver began to take the dominant position in the circulation of hard currencies.[4] The available records of food prices from that time were thus on most occasions measured by *taels* of silver. The changing ratio between the values of silver and bronze coins certainly increases the difficulty of making a cross-dynastic comparison of food prices.

Although a few scholars have studied the prices in specific dynasties, such as those of the Song (960–1279), Ming (1368–1644) or Qing (1644–1912) periods, the only comprehensive study that covers all the periods of later imperial China is the work by Peng Xinwei, *A Monetary History of China*.[5] Peng (1965) reported average rice prices measured both in silver and bronze coins for the last millennium of Chinese history. The former is particularly convenient for observing long-term changes in prices, as silver-based prices of rice are likely to reduce the short-term fluctuations produced by temporary shocks such as harvest failures. Yet even Peng failed to make an explicit cross-dynastic comparison that would allow us to view changes in the different price levels from the tenth to the twentieth century through a single index, thereby enabling a link to be made between price changes and changes in the real economy (such as growth in population, trade and urbanization). To provide such an index, I have tabulated a series of Peng's indexes of rice prices into a single index – the Peng index – as presented in Table 12.1.

The Peng index has obvious limits. Most records of food purchases and sales were found in reports made by local agencies to central administrations and thus were not all produced by a same institute. Food prices at rural or local markets could vary considerably. Chen Xiang, for example, reported in 1051 when the local official purchased wheat in Henan, that the price usually ranged between 90 and 120 *wen* per *dou* (900–1200 per Song *shi*); in contrast, the private market price was about 60 *wen* per *dou* at the harvest season.[6] The data series by Peng and others cannot give us a detailed account of the short-term fluctuations (such as seasonal changes and regional variances) in food prices, because for every three to four years, one will find only one record, which was often not at the same site, but only in close proximity. Nonetheless, the prices at private markets and public purchases were not very different and shared the same trend. The general trend described by Peng's observations of long term changes in prices (such as those of food and textile goods) is least contentious as many researchers have drawn the same conclusion in their price surveys on a specific dynasty.[7]

In the Peng index (Table 12.1) the price of rice in 961–70 is set at 100 points. It gradually increased to 200 points over a period of nearly one hundred years. After 1126, the rice price in Southern China increased 50 per cent during the twelfth century. By the beginning of the thirteenth century, it had risen to three-and-a-half to four times the price in the early Song period. During the three centuries, the price of rice rose continuously, reaching a level of four to five times the prices in the pre-Song periods. However, the lengthy upward trend in prices came to an end in the late fourteenth century.

During the Ming period, grain prices moved in the opposite direction. The Peng index demonstrates that, by early in the Ming dynasty, prices had almost returned to the original levels of the mid-tenth century.[8] Yet they did not hit the lowest point – grain prices bottomed out in the first half of the fifteenth century. The most noticeable phenomenon in the Ming price history is the century-long deflation that prevailed in the years from 1381 to 1500. Ming historians often identify the first century from 1381 to 1450 as the period of economic recovery, during which the Chinese economy steadily regained the wealth and population that were lost in the century before the founding of the Ming dynasty, mostly caused by the Mongol conquest and civil wars.[9] Yet the low price level continued in the century after this recovery period. Although the sixteenth century is usually identified as a period of prosperity and for noticeable developments in trade, not until the 1580s did grain prices reach 200 points. In addition, it was only in the second quarter of the eighteenth century that grain prices reached the maximum found during the Song era. The two peaks were five hundred years apart.

What the underlying forces were behind the long-term price movements is a major concern for historians of prices. As well as the quantity and velocity of money in circulation, one must also consider non-monetary factors – such as

Table 12.1 Peng's index of rice prices, 960–1910

Period	Index[a]	Price[b]	Period	Index[a]	Price[b]
961–70	100	12.39	1481–90	148	18.39
971–80	153	31.12	1491–1500	180	22.31
981–90	95	11.76	1501–10	172	21.3
991–1000	119	14.73	1511–20	144	17.83
1001–10	184	22.76	1521–30	162	20.14
1011–20	95	11.79	1531–40	172	21.3
1021–30	98	12.21	1541–50	165	20.48
1031–40	159	19.67	1551–60	184	22.75
1041–50	382	47.33	1561–70	182	22.6
1051–60	136	16.81	1571–80	159	19.66
1061–70	207	25.7	1581–90	203	25.18
1071–80	444	55.1	1591–1600	203	25.22
1081–90	260	32.25	1601–10	215	26.6
1091–1100	283	35.04	1611–20	182	22.57
1101–10	481	59.61	1621–30	293	36.37
1111–20	366	45.37	1631–40	271	33.57
1121–30	2,141	265.42	1641–50	380	47.11
1131–40	1,960	243	1651–60	361	44.81
1141–50	243	30.18	1661–70	258	31.94
1151–60	346	42.84	1671–80	196	24.31
1161–70	355	44.05	1681–90	260	32.22
1171–80	297	36.81	1691–1700	223	27.5
1181–90	359	44.5	1701–10	290	36.01
1191–1200	510	63.19	1711–20	279	34.53
1201–10	775	96.08	1721–30	265	32.84
1211–20	367	45.56	1731–40	301	37.37
1221–30	401	49.66	1741–50	344	42.69
1231–40	306	37.9	1751–60	493	61.06
1241–50	306	37.9	1761–70	518	64.22
1251–60	305	37.83	1771–80	458	56.75
			1781–90	484	60.01
1361–70	89.7	11.12	1791–1800	591	73.28
1371–80	280	34.73	1801–10	654	81.13
1381–90	140	17.35	1811–20	647	80.19
1391–1400	105	13.02	1821–30	584	72.44
1401–10	85.4	10.59	1831–40	728	90.19
1411–20	a	a	1841–50	679	84.13
1421–30	104	12.87	1851–60	514	63.72
1431–40	78	9.63	1861–70	789	97.84
1441–50	84	10.41	1871–80	523	64.88
1451–60	100	12.38	1881–90	468	58.04
1461–70	122	15.07	1891–1900	724	89.72
1471–80	124	15.33	1901–10	1,172	145.28

Sources: Peng (1965: 505, 705, 498; 850).

Notes:
[a] Index: 961–70 = 100.
[b] The price is rice per hectolitre in grams of silver in silver value. The rice prices in the Song period are reported by Peng in silver-*taels*, and I converted them into silver-grams at the rate of 1 *tael* equal to 37.68 g.

changes in population growth, agricultural productivity and real wages – that would contribute to such changes. Yet the prevailing arguments focus only on the shift from bronze coins to silver as the dominant medium of exchange in the sixteenth century and largely fail to capture this divergence in average price level.[10] A market economy is initially a money economy. A monetary perspective is thus required as a starting point in a study of price history. In the following I attempt to provide a tentative explanation, based on the Fisher equation, for the two different price regimes in the Song and Ming eras.

To seek a monetary explanation, it is necessary to look into changes in both money supply and population at the aggregate level. The Fisher equation considers four variables: money supply, velocity of money in circulation, prices and aggregate outputs. Assuming that velocity of money in circulation and per capita income/outputs remain constant, changes in prices are expected to be accounted for by changes in two contributing variables: money supply and population. Therefore, per capita money stock is the best indicator that addresses changes in these two variables. Table 12.2 compares changes in China's money stocks and tabulates per capita money stock over the millennium from 750 to 1750. The basic

Table 12.2 Money stock in China, 750–1750

	Tang (750)	Song (1120)	Ming (1550)	Ming (1600)	Qing (1750)
Bronze coin (000,000 string)	21.3–42.6[a]	193.4–262	36–54[c]	36–54	122.8–146.8
Coins per capita[d] (in strings)	0.31–0.61	1.53	0.18–0.45	0.18–0.45	0.4–0.48
Silver (in millions of *tael*s)	–	–	15–25	125.8–130.6	317
Money supply (in millions of strings)	21.3–42.6	193.4–262[b]	46.5–71.5	124–145[e]	376–400[f]
Money supply per capita (in strings)	0.31–0.61	1.53	0.23–0.6	0.62–1.21	1.25–1.33

Sources: for Tang China in 750, see Peng (1994: 781). For a rough estimation of the money stocks in Song and Ming China, see Sections 2 and 3 of this paper; see also Liu (2011a). For an estimate of coins and silver in the Qing, see Lin Man-hung (1991).

Notes:
[a] Peng assumed that the quantity of private coins was probably not different from the total of official coins, and thus doubles the number of the officially minted coins to get this figure. I decided to use the amount of officially minted coins as a low bound value for my estimate of the Tang money supply and Peng's figure as the high bound value.
[b] I included only coinage as the Song money supply. It would be larger if we take into account precious metals (gold and silver) and commercial bills.
[c] The Ming coinage accounts for only 1/9 of coins in stock. The majority are Song coins; see Liu (2012a, b).
[d] The aggregate population for each period is assumed to be: Tang (750)–69 million; Song (1120) – 126 million; Ming (1550, 1600) – 120~200 million; Qing (1750) – 300 million.
[e] 1 *tael* of silver is equal to 0.7 string of coins.
[f] 1 *tael* of silver is equal to 0.8 string of coins.

unit of copper coins in late imperial China is a string of cash, which comprises nominally 1,000 coins and is normally equivalent to 1 *tael* of silver around AD 1080.

The comparison of long-term changes in per capita money stocks not only shows the severe decline in the Ming era, but also points to the two economic booms in monetary terms. The money supply remarkably expanded to a total value of 400 million strings of coins around 1750, the height of Chinese monetary history. Song China maintains the record for money stock per capita, and is second only to the Qing period in total value. The Ming story shows a substantial difference between the money supply in 1550 and 1600, which calls for further explanation if such radical change ever occurred. However, for most of the Ming period, money supply per capita seems to have been very low. Such a trend perfectly matches what is reflected in the Peng Index. Obviously changes in money stocks and populations are likely to be chiefly responsible for long-term changes in prices, including the changes that resulted in the different price regimes in the Song and Ming eras.

Although the result of the tabulation is even better than expected, it also raises more important questions for researchers of price history. Contrary to common wisdom about the process of monetization, the transition towards a silver economy in the Ming dynasty was associated with a sharp decline in the money stock. Why China's money stocks dwindled so severely after the Mongol conquest of China (1206–79) shall concern us here. It must be noted that this millennium-long survey is made possible on the basis of the comparison of only five benchmark years. To test this generalization, it is necessary to examine the relationship between the quantity of money and price movements within each dynasty. Furthermore, the above assumptions of both a constant velocity of money in circulation and a stable level of per capita outputs/incomes are also subject to question. Given the huge gap in per capita money stock between the Song and Ming eras, the impact of insufficient money supply on the performance of the market must be examined. A general interpretation needs to be drawn from this comparison, and further examined in historical context.

I next examine market performance in the Song and Ming eras.

Market performance in Song dynasty China

Our study of the market performance in the Song era is made possible because of reliable macroeconomic data on changes in population, money stocks and commercial taxes. The Song dynasty was the only state power in pre-modern China that drew the majority of state revenues from indirect taxes.[11] To tax the market, the administration knew how to cooperate with merchants and collect information that covered the different aspects of trade, urban consumption and population growth. The preserved data allow us to study market expansion in the centuries from 960 to 1279 and to examine the relationship between prices, the money supply and trade, a rare opportunity for researchers studying market performance in late imperial China.

The general trend in long-term changes of grain prices was upwards, as reflected in the Peng index. Nonetheless, there were three spikes over the three centuries: the 1040s, 1121–40, and the 1200s. The extremely high food prices at these times were undoubtedly the result of hyperinflation caused by wartime financial crises. The border wars with the Tangut in the 1040s produced heavy costs; to wage wars, the court adopted expansive/inflationary policies in public finance. In the years between 1125 and 1141, the northern Song court was defeated by the Jurchen nomadic power and lost half of its territory. The court fled to Hangzhou and managed to survive in an area to the south of the Huai River. The financial crisis in the decade 1200 to 1210 was a direct result of the failure of the military campaign against the Jurchen Jin dynasty launched by the Song court in 1206.[12]

One can use, for instance, the Song dynasty indirect tax data to test the reliability of the Peng index. The 1040s case deserves special attention because changes in prices significantly increased the nominal value of marketed goods and, in turn, caused the boom in taxes. Indeed, inflation was the most likely explanation for the fluctuation of the domestic market and commercial taxes.[13] In the mid-eleventh century, state expenditure spiralled out of control due to the war against the Tanguts, and caused severe inflation nationwide. According to the index of rice prices measured in bronze coins, grain prices rose more than threefold between 1031 and 1050 (see Table 12.3). This is a rise in prices even more steep than that measured in silver (see Table 12.2). Consequently, long-term changes in Song state revenues from the liquor monopoly form a similar pattern and if graphed would present an A-shape curve (Table 12.4).

The peak value in 1041–8 presented in Table 12.4 was about ten times greater that of the first half of that century, but one can account for this enormous increase in revenue by a similar boost in price: the sale price of liquor increased sixfold at the same time. As bronze coins were being widely used at the market, the coin-measured index presented in Table 12.3 would be more realistic than the silver-based one in Table 12.1 as an indication of this dramatic fluctuation in food prices. Meanwhile, liquor sales were also paid for in coin. Therefore, it is not surprising

Table 12.3 The Peng index of rice prices measured in coins, China, 960–1120

Year	Index[a]	Year	Index
960–70	100	1041–50	1,527
971–80	164	1051–60	544
981–90	101	1061–70	276
991–1000	127	1071–80	592
1001–10	221	1081–90	416
1011–20	203	1091–1100	452
1021–30	210	1101–1110	962
1031–40	423	1111–1120	732

Source: Peng (1965: 505). Grain prices were measured in bronze coins.

Note:
[a] Year 960 = index 100.

Table 12.4 Liquor monopoly revenues, China, 995–1100

Year	Tax amount (000s string)	Index (995–7 = 100)	Index of liquor prices (995–7 = 100)
995–7	1,850	100	100
1004–7	4,280	231	Y/N
1021	8,959	484	164
1041–8	19,750	1,068	Y/N
1049–53	14,986	810	670
1055–7	12,863	695	Y/N
1077	13,109	709	67
1086	12,870	696	67
1100	11,560	625	670

Source: Li Huarui (1995: 305–6, 352–4).

that the fluctuation of liquor monopoly revenues shown in Table 12.4 was much closer to that shown in the coin-measured index.

The corresponding relationship between grain prices and the aggregate value of liquor production testifies to the market integration in the Song era. As the major materials for liquor production were grain, inflation affected foodstuffs, liquor and industrial goods, in descending order of degree.[14] Meanwhile, the liquor monopoly relied heavily on urban consumption. The 1,861 outlets of liquor sales were all located in cities and towns.[15] Because the Song brewery industry was more urban-centred and monetized than most sectors, it was more susceptible to price shocks.[16] In other words, underneath the urban consumption and long-distance trade, a genuine market mechanism was at work: even the collection of excise and commercial taxes are not exempt from the effects of market risks. It is for this very reason that long-term changes in the liquor monopoly revenues indicate changes in urban consumption and, furthermore, in the development in urbanization. A comparison of the two indexes in Table 12.3 and Table 12.4 indicates that in the three decades after the mid-century price shock, the liquor monopoly revenues increased at a pace much faster than the rise in grain prices.

Monetization is a significant contributor to the performance of a market economy. Market expansion in a pre-industrial economy that was previously dominated by a self-sufficient mode of production would greatly increase the demands for money and thus lead to the augmentation of hard currencies. No doubt the size of the money stocks in eleventh-century China did increase enormously. The imperial mints produced a large number of bronze coins – actually the largest number in imperial China – over the one and a half centuries of the Song dynasty.

Increases in the outputs of imperial mints can demonstrate the expansion of money stocks in the Song era. There were 19 Song imperial mints that produced bronze coins in the late eleventh century. According to Hino's data on Song imperial coinage, the average yearly output increased from 0.8 million strings in AD 995 to 5.06 million strings in the 1080s, a sixfold increase (see Table 12.5).

Table 12.5 Average amount of minted coins per year, China, 995–1119

Year	Number[a]	Year	Number[a]	Year	Number[a]
995	0.80	1021	1.05	1077	3.73
1000	1.25	1030	1.00	1080	5.06
1007	1.83	1050	1.46	1105	2.89
1015	1.25	1065	1.70	1119	3.00

Source: Hino (1936), in *HKTSR*, 6: 345.
Note:
[a] Numbers shown in million strings.

Table 12.6 Per capita money stocks in China, 995–1125

Year	Total number of bronze coins (million strings)	Aggregate households	Per capita string of bronze coins	Index (982 = 100)
982	0.49	6,418,500	0.01–0.02	100
1015	25.84	8,422,403	0.51–0.61	4,037
1048	58.84	10,723,695	0.91–1.10	7,219
1073	98.84	15,091,560	1.09–1.31	8,617
1085	152.84	17,957,092	1.42–1.7	11,148
1125	262.04	20,882,258	2.09–2.51	16,511

Sources: The estimates of the total bronze coins in circulation are made by Gao Congming (Gao 2000: 103). For aggregate households, see Wu Songdi (2000: 346–8). I follow Wu Songdi and assume 5–6 people for the average family size in the Song era.

The production of the imperial mints in fact depended on a sufficient supply of metals, especially copper and tin. Hino also surveyed the yearly output of copper controlled by the Song state, and found that there is a very small margin between the reported copper output and average number of coins minted yearly.[17] This means that the imperial mints could maintain their production at full scale. Based on Hino's estimates of the average number of coins minted yearly, Gao calculated the numbers made for different periods of time. In the following calculations, I use Gao's estimate to reach the value of per capita money stock. Note that Gao's estimate can be taken as the real output of Song bronze coins, which should be smaller than the quantity of money in circulation. In considering other means of exchange in circulation (paper notes, silver and gold, and iron coins), the Song money supply at the dawn of the twelfth century would at least approximate Peng's estimates; the amount is therefore about 250–260 million strings.[18]

Per capita money stock is the most important indicator of the degree of monetization in a pre-industrial economy. Reliable aggregate figures of populations and money stocks are needed to make this calculation. Fortunately we can obtain all relevant information to set a series of benchmark years from 982 to 1125 and just cover the northern Song period.

The calculation of per capita money stock in Table 12.6 is confined to changes in the supply of bronze coins. In 1015, less than half a century after the establishment of the Song dynasty, the money supply from imperial mints had already dramatically increased to about 26 million strings. In the succeeding century, the supply increased an astonishing tenfold. This result also shows that the supply of hard currencies far outpaced population growth. In one and a half centuries from 982 to 1125, aggregate households increased from 6.4 million to 20.9 million, an over threefold increase. At the same time the supply of bronze coins expanded by more than five hundred times.

The diminution of the money economy in the early Ming period

As we turn to the price movements and per capita money stocks in the Ming era, the comparison as presented in Table 12.1 and Table 12.2 reveals the huge gap in the money economies during the Song and Ming periods. The price level remains very low in the early Ming period and takes a long time to regain the high level of the thirteenth century. The money supply went down as well. Even by the mid-sixteenth century, estimated per capita money stock was roughly 15–40 per cent of that in 1120. A sharp decline in the money supply is likely the first and most important reason for the low, motionless behaviour of early Ming prices. Theoretically, deflation (a low level of prices for a long period), means either a shrinking of the money supply or an extraordinary expansion in the marketing share of aggregate outputs, possibly driven by both population growth and technical improvements. If we turn to quantitative monetary theory, we might calculate from either side of the equation to see if the results are compatible. Obviously the second possibility can be ruled out because the early Ming population declined and technological innovation was also lacking. The first possibility, the shrinking of the money supply, is more plausible: scholars tend to attribute the low price level to the Ming money supply, especially to the dearth of coinage from Ming imperial mints, which was negligible in comparison to the large money supply in the Song era.[19] According to this monetarist argument both the lack of bronze coins and consumer preference for silver led to the higher purchasing power of silver. However, this argument does not tell us how and why the money stock declined sharply after the Ming dynasty was established. It also ignores whether such a decline had an impact upon the real working of the Ming economy, or vice versa.[20]

In the remainder of this section, I first provide a rough estimation of the money stocks in Ming China prior to 1550. This estimation explains how I am able to reach a conclusion that the money stock declined sharply in the two centuries after the collapse of the Song dynasty in 1279. Second, I attribute this huge loss of the money supply to early Ming anti-market policies, which demonetized the entire economy and made it unnecessary to maintain a large number of hard currencies in circulation. The decline in the money stocks and price level in Ming China cannot be taken as a change in the nominal senses but a consequence of the market contraction.

A reconstruction of the money supply in Ming China refers to estimating not only the aggregate value of precious metals such as silver, but also the number of bronze coins. The estimation of the number of bronze coins in circulation during this period is an extremely complicated task because one has to find a ratio between the coins produced by the Ming dynasty and the coins that were produced by the Song dynasty and were still circulating in the fourteenth and fifteenth centuries. Ming imperial minting is usually thought to have produced only a small number of coins in the last millennium of Chinese history.[21] The government was neither willing nor able to produce a large amount of coinage. The peak number of coins annually produced in the early Ming period was about 0.22 million strings in 1372, which was only 4.3 per cent of the Song annual production in the 1070s. It is estimated that for the first 174 years, the average Ming annual output was less than 35,000 strings of coins.[22] Although 'monetary contraction' became apparent, the Ming governments made no serious attempt to resolve coin shortages in the economy. In the century after 1430 there was only a little official minting, if any at all. The Jiajing reign (1522–66) launched new attempts to regulate the circulation of coins, which had been then dominated by counterfeiting and coins from previous dynasties, by opening new mints in Beijing, Yunnan and other provinces. This resulted in a minimal increase in coin output. If the average annual output for the first 174 years was indeed less than 35,000 strings, this adds up to 4 to 6 million strings in total for the aggregate output of Ming imperial minting from 1368 through to 1572, a figure that roughly matches the annual output of the Song state in the 1080s.

The majority of coins in circulation were in fact Song coins that were preserved in the day. Song bronze coins continued to serve as one of the major currencies in the Ming period, and were necessary for small-scale transactions at local markets.[23] Without exception, Ming hoards discovered today contain large quantities of Song coins.[24] In comparison, the proportion of excavated Ming coins is much lower. As monetary historians usually focus on the rise of silver as the medium of exchange in the Ming dynasty, they fail to recognize changes in the size of money stocks during the fourteenth and fifteenth centuries. For the purpose of this chapter, we need to know how many Song coins were preserved and used again in the Ming period. This might be found by examining the proportional amount of Song coins in the excavation sites of Ming hoards. Based on the hoarding sites found in Japan, I have estimated the quantity of qualified bronze coins, produced in both Song and Ming eras, that were circulated in the fifteenth-century Chinese markets.[25] This exercise leads to an estimate of 36–54 million strings of coins, an amount roughly 15–27 per cent of that in the money supply exclusive to coins in China before 1125. We need to keep in mind that, before significant imports of silver into China began in the late sixteenth century – quite late in Ming history – the money supply from the domestic side was limited. Elsewhere I have estimated the total of the money supply around 1500: 15–25 million *taels* of silver plus 36–54 million strings of coins, adding up to 46.5–71.5 million strings of coins in total value.[26] This figure is only half of the money supply of the Song state prior to 1043.[27] In the succeeding New Policies era (1069–85) the output of coinage outstripped all that had ever been produced previously by the Song imperial mints. By all the monetary measures, the Ming money stock prior to 1550 was only one-sixth to one-third of the total output of bronze coins from the Song imperial mints until the 1220s, not to mention other kinds of money in circulation during the Song era. Largely due to the inflow of silver from overseas trade, the estimated per capita money stocks rose from 0.23–0.6 *tael* of silver in 1550 to 0.62–1.21 *tael* of silver in 1600. Until the final decades of the sixteenth century, the money supply from the imports of silver was in limited quantities.

But an insufficient money supply alone does not explain the initial decline and later rise within the Ming price regime. An examination of the available data challenges such a purely nominal monetary explanation. The money stock in late eleventh-century China, as shown in Table 12.1, was in fact about three to six times as large as that of the Ming period 1550s. If we assume the early Ming phase stops at around 1450, we can roughly estimate the money supply then as only two-thirds of the Ming money stock in the 1550s. The imperial mints closed after the early Ming phase, and we believe that many Song coins still remained in circulation, thus giving more weight to the money supply in the early Ming period. We can then estimate that the money supply in the early Ming period was only 11–22 per cent of that in the 1120s. We know that the early Ming population in 1394 was 60 million, and that it would reach 80–100 million by around 1450 after a half century of peace and recovery. This would imply a moderate decline in China's aggregate population, less than 10–20 per cent, between 1450 and 1120. If we follow the Fisher Equation $P = MV/T$, and assume V constant and that T just exactly follows population change – a decline of less than 10–20 per cent without decline in real income per capita – then we can predict that the price level in the early Ming period would be 4–8 per cent of that in the 1120s. The Peng index shows the average price in 1450 as 27 per cent of that in 1120, much higher than our conjecture from the purely nominal monetary perspective. In other words, neither per capita real income nor the velocity of money (V) remained constant during these three hundred years.

Evidence on changes in relative prices suggests that not only did the money supply decline in an unexpected way but the marketing share of production outputs also shrank substantially. As shown in Table 12.7, changes in relative prices show a wide range of variance. What is striking is the relative price between silver and coinage, which declined sharply from an exchange rate of 50 grams of silver equal to 2,000–3,000 *wen* (the minimum monetary unit for Chinese bronze coins) to 750 *wen*. This change is in stark contrast to the ratios of other items. The exchange ratio between textile and grain also changed between Song and Ming: as shown in Table 12.7, 1 bolt of silk cloth in the eleventh century was worth 507 litres of rice, while in the sixteenth century it had risen to 634 litres. The increase in silk–rice ratio, which means that the price of Ming silk cloth became even more expensive in comparison to the Song, implies a decline in the marketed amount of silk textile production in the late Ming period.

In addition to changes in relative prices between the Song and Ming periods, the price movement in the Ming era itself also contradicts the nominal monetary interpretation. At first sight it seems that the great gap between the Song and Ming money supply should account for the price divergence. However, the price in the Ming era showed a deeper decline in the first half of the fifteenth century, and remained at a low level for most of the century. It was not until the end of the

Table 12.7 Relative prices of 50 grams of silver in the Song and Ming eras

Era	Gold (gram)	Silk cloth (bolt)	Rice (litre)	Coin (wen)
Song	1.0	0.67	340	2,000–3,000
Ming	7.5 (1:7.5)[a]	1.67 (1:2.5)	1,060 (1:3.1)	750 (1:0.32)

Sources: Quan (1967); Wang Wencheng (2001: 175, 198).

Note:
[a] Figures in parentheses indicate the ratio between the Song and Ming prices of the same item purchased with silver.

fifteenth century that the price level moved toward a level higher than earlier in the history of Ming prices. Such a trend implies no linear relationship between the price level and the Ming money supply, since the latter had not changed profoundly since the end of the fourteenth century. Most of the imperial mints were closed in the 1390s, and the silver output from state-controlled domestic mining reached a relatively high output in the first decade of the fifteenth century.[28] When grain prices began to decline again from 1400 on, the money supply during the period (1400–35) was larger than before or after. There is no reason from the money supply side to explain why the price level declined during most of the fifteenth century and began to rise at the end of that century.

It is the demonetization of the economy that caused a decline in total demand and marketed outputs, and hence the sluggishness of transactions between people who held the money.[29] Researchers in the last decade have paid attention to institutional changes during the Song–Yuan–Ming transition that had a direct impact upon the economic structure and rural communities. Many discussions point to the rise of a command economy in the late fourteenth century that was based on an unusually large scale of government-organized immigration and on strict control over the populace. Common people were forced to move from rich, densely settled areas to devastated areas in northern and south-west China. The total number of immigrants, according to Cao Shuji, may have reached 11 million, over one-sixth of the early Ming population.[30] In addition to involuntary immigration, the Ming government enforced strict control over the Ming populace in professions and residential places through household registration. All the households under jurisdiction were identified by profession (peasants, artisans, soldiers, and so on). Those who were registered could not freely change their professions or move to a new place.[31] The categories covered all kinds of military and administrative services, ranging from soldiers, mining labourers and artisans, to sedan carriers, trumpeters and even graveyard keepers. The majority of the households in the registration were farmers, who were called upon for three months every three years to labour at places where certain state needs, such as building city walls or conveying grain taxes to the capital, had to be fulfilled.

An institutional analysis of the Song dynasty demonstrates contrasting differences between Song and Ming population administration and immigration policies. The growth of the population in Song times accompanied the rise of a market economy and urbanization. The literature on Song institutional and legal history points to the fact that labour migrated from countryside to cities or from one profession to another by choice, usually depending on the opportunities provided by the market economy. To maintain its capacity to negotiate with society in a market economy, the Song government was consistently sensitive to information on labour and wealth. The official registration of the local population and households, carried out once every three years, took particular care over revaluating property and recording male adults.[32] Consequently, a very distinctive feature presented in the Song official records of the population and households is the basic division between taxable people (*zhuhu*) and non-taxable people (*kehu*).[33] For the individual falling into the former category, all of his and his family's mobile and immobile properties (cash, estate, farm, incomes, etc.) were precisely assessed.[34] This concept of wealth enabled Song officials to tax people in accordance with the amount of family property and income, regardless of where they lived (urban or rural), or what they were doing (farmers, merchants, owners of transport vehicles, or landlords). However, there was no national standard for property gradations; local officials graded all taxable farmer families (*xiangcun-zhuhu*) invariably into five income levels from the high to low, and urban residents (*fangguohu*) into ten income levels. By comparison, *kehu* such as tenants on a farm, or urban labourers were defined as employed labourers without any other major income.[35] In the 1260s, the urban *kehu* population at Fuzhou, a middle-level city in the mid-Yangtze River, was about 65,000, nearly one half of the registered urban population.[36]

The ideology of the early Ming government promoted a self-sufficient mode in rural communities. Neither the market nor the bureaucracy was favoured as the means for state building, because they both brought out corruption in government and local communities.[37] Thus, the early Ming state relied solely upon its direct control of individuals and resources. The early Ming military organization comprised 2.76 million soldiers, and if one takes into account their immediate families, their extended families in their hometowns, and the reserves, the number of households connected to the military services was in the region of 2.19 million,[38] about 20 per cent of the total households.[39] Yet the early Ming state spent very little to sustain such a large number of soldiers and staff. The military troops, for instance, whether stationed in the hinterland or frontier, had to use more than half of their staff to cultivate and farm, to maintain themselves in a self-sufficient way. In 1403 the grain output from military farms was reported to be 23 million *shi*, which was not far below the annual agricultural tax the Ming government could collect from rural peasant households.[40]

These policies reduced cash payments in public finance and private sectors to a minimum. Even officials and generals were paid in grain instead of money. The early Ming regime obtained grain and other products through taxation. As for its impact on society, people were requested to provide services according to status, which the state assigned to them, and their duties would be transferred to the succeeding generation when the seniors passed away. Soldiers in the military, for instance, were enrolled from the households identified in the registration as 'military households'. Once a family was chosen to be a military household, it was obliged to remain as such over generations. People had to request permission from the government when migrating, changing professions, or travelling.[41] The entire empire had in fact been organized as a workshop in which the intra-regional flow of personnel and goods was shifted away from the market to central government demand. Such a command system had severe impacts upon the economy in Ming China, including a decrease in monetary transactions and a very low price level, both of which we will discuss in the following part of this chapter.

There are a few pieces of evidence for the diminution of hard currency in transactions in the early Ming period. Li Ruoyu reports about 1,062 Huizhou contracts collected in the Anhui History Museum, dating from 1368 to 1644.[42] He finds 226 cases for the first century (1368–1457) in the Ming history, among which payments in kind (cloth and grain) were 72, about 32 per cent of the total contracts. Especially for the early and middle fifteenth century, cloth and grain became the means for land purchases.[43] In the early Ming period it was not permitted to use silver as currency; however, payments in silver represented another one-third of land purchases. Units and quality of these silver payments varied tremendously, and were described with particular attention in the contracts. Some cases even indicated that they were from personal ornaments. In later times, these variances disappeared from the contracts as silver became widely accepted in circulation.

The Huizhou cases reported by Li Ruoyu explicitly points to the rising of a barter economy in local communities in the Lower Yangtze Delta, the leading region in the Ming economy. Cloth and grain were widely used in purchases in the fifteenth century. These non-standard payments were unlikely to encourage people to make more transactions beyond the necessities. In addition to the cases of land purchases and sales in Huizhou, we know from many (but incomplete) accounts that coins were rare and that silver was not yet popularly used. The conclusion is that if the role of Ming paper currency in money circulation is not considered important, then the early Ming economy would have done little with monetary exchange, and was instead run on a basis of a barter economy and 'unilateral payments', in which farmers and artisans paid taxes in kinds to the state.[44]

The early Ming regime left almost no precise information on market prices. Except for the official exchange rates between money, grain and cloth in unilateral payments recorded by the government, which were kept unchanged over years, scholars have found little information available on early Ming prices and markets. Merchants and craftsmen were, according to official records, sent for administrative and military services to the capital and frontier garrisons mostly from the Lower Yangtze Delta. They were paid very low wages, if any, and had to make a living from other resources.[45]

In addition to grain transportation and military services, the early Ming state used more than a hundred thousand craftsmen and labourers in construction projects; these workers were classified as artisans in the Yellow Registers (*Huangce* 黃冊). In 1393, more than 230,000 artisans across the country were recorded in the Yellow Registers for the building of the city wall of Nanjing, then the capital.[46] They were called on once every three years from their rural

Table 12.8 Land purchase in Huizhou, 1393–1430

Period	(a) Baochao	(b) Coin	(c) Kind	(d) Silver	(e) Record	(f) c/e (percentage)	(g) a/e (percentage)
1393–98	6	–	4	–	10	40	6
1399–1402	3	–	8	5	16	50	18.8
1403–13	0	0	6	0	6	100	0
1414–24	–	–	–	–	0	0	0
1425–30	0	0	5	0	5	100	0
Total 1393–1430	9	0	23	5	37	62.2	24.3

Source: Anhuisheng bowuguan (1988), Vol. 1: 1–15, 24–26; Vol. 2: 19–23, 28.

residences and worked at the assigned place for three months. However, there is no evidence indicating that they were able to do business there, or that a commercial network spread out along the migration area. As noted before, the early Ming policies tended to reduce the size of bureaucracy as well as the amount of money in circulation to a minimum. Many projects, including grain transportation and military defence, were enforced on the basis of unilateral payments. The early Ming state's three capitals (Fengyang, Nanjing and Beijing), for instance, were built by corvée labour enlisted from rural communities, soldiers and prisoners. Labourers exceeded one million people for each project.[47] Except for reimbursements made on rare occasions, most of the seasonal labourers such as peasants were supposed to feed themselves, and soldiers and artisans working yearly were paid in grain, by an amount that was less than that required to support a family.

If the diminishing long-distance trade produced weak demands for money, did local markets draw much money? Many early Ming records suggest that this was not the case either. In Ming gazetteers, scholars find only a few towns and periodic markets dating back to the early Ming period, while the majority of local markets and towns appeared in the sixteenth century.[48] Before that, one can hardly expect the ongoing transactions on a trivial scale at rural markets to absorb much currency. The early Ming land sale contracts from the Huizhou archives also demonstrate the dominant pattern of land transactions: most parcels of land were small in size and sold at low prices.[49]

In a mountain village situated in Huizhou, a region at the far western part of the Lower Yangtze delta, The Wang brothers, Wang Qiugan and Wang Qiuguan, left 37 contracts of land purchases.[50] These land purchases mostly occurred in early Ming, with the first case recorded in 1393, just seven years after the establishment of the Ming dynasty, and the last case in 1430. These contracts, as displayed in Table 12.8, show the withdrawal of currency, especially paper currency, in the first decade of the fifteenth century. From the late fourteenth century until the mid-fifteenth century, people had to use cloth, grain and silver to complete transactions. In total, payment-in-kind accounted for nearly two-thirds of land transactions recorded here.

The anti-market policies implemented by the early Ming court, together with a severe loss of population, weakened the fourteenth-century economy significantly. The weak demand from domestic markets was a direct cause of the enduring low-level prices in the fifteenth century. The anti-market policies of the early Ming government certainly appears to have shattered the society and delayed the recovery of a market economy because, for the first hundred years, one can find little evidence of the resurgence of markets and consumption in local society.[51]

A silver economy in the sixteenth century: an unprecedented phase of the money economy?

It is common for scholars in the study of the Ming–Qing transition to emphasize the monetary transition from using bronze coins to silver, and view it as a milestone development in Chinese monetary history, arguing that the silver transition relates the Chinese economy to the emergence of the sixteenth-century world economy.[52] The monetarist historian Miyazawa puts forward a significant argument that this transition was an important aspect of the social and economic transformation of China from Song through Ming–Qing times. The different uses of these two kinds of metal currencies, according to him, can be identified as a sequence of temporal stages in which each of them, either coins or silver, was predominant in response to the needs of the Chinese economy and society at different times.[53]

Miyazawa's argument reiterates the bullionist view that a nation's prosperity depends on its means of payments, especially the role of precious metals. Yet, by focusing solely on the transition between metallic currencies, such an argument has to a great extent misinterpreted the evolution of Chinese monetary economy. The rapid expansion of the Song market economy was made possible by an unprecedented increase in means of payment, one of the most striking features in the economic history of this period. In addition to bronze coins, a variety of monetary tools such as currency reserve (gold and silver), promissory notes (including *yanyin, jiaoyin, chayin*) backed by precious metals (gold and silver) and expensive goods (tea, salt, spice and alum), and paper notes (*huizi*) were widely used.[54] Nor did the absence of large-scale silver imports in the eleventh century deter Song China from attaining a very complicated and efficient monetary economy. With the help of these innovative instruments of credit, Song merchants could easily save on the costs of transferring low-value, heavy coins in long-distance trade by using bills of exchange issued or guaranteed by the imperial ministry of the treasury.[55] By the mid-twelfth century, paper money known as *huizi* had become the principal kind of currency, successfully maintaining their nominal value for over sixty years.[56] However, during the transition from Song to Ming, the state lost sovereignty in issuing money. It was the rejection of paper currency by society and the inability of the government to provide large amounts of coinage that gave rise to the prevalence of silver as the standard value.

From a viewpoint of Song monetary history, doubt can be cast on the story of the silver economy: how could the late Ming economy, if it was as advanced as Miyazawa has suggested, rest on a single medium of exchange such as silver? But after all, it is not the *kind of* but the *amount of* money available to the needs of a developing market economy that should concern us. Bronze coins are not necessarily inferior to silver as long as the former is maintained in sufficient quantity and supported by other monetary means.[57] The monetarist argument of the silver economy pays no attention to the money stock, namely, how much money – regardless of its form; bronze coins, or silver, or negotiable instruments – was put into circulation, and it is far less clear whether the size of the late Ming monetary economy could really exceed that of the eleventh century. The silver influx into sixteenth-century China undoubtedly stimulated a market economy, but the peak years of silver imports from America and Japan took place in the first half of the seventeenth century (see Table 12.9); how, then, could the Ming market economy have sustained itself prior to that date?

The early Ming policies lasted one and a half centuries. Beginning in the late fifteenth century, one sees the recovery of the market economy and the prosperity of local society in many parts of Ming China, especially in the Lower Yangtze Delta. Many scholars describe the Ming economy at that time as so vibrant that it was entering an economic and cultural boom that lasted into the eighteenth century. However, the collapse of the early Ming system also terminated any effective state intervention into the private economy, so that the sixteenth-century economic boom brought no significant expansion in the Ming state revenues.[58] As a result little information is contained in official documents on the wealth and population. Estimates of growth in sixteenth- and seventeenth-century China's economy and population should therefore be made with great caution and is sometimes at best guesswork in nature.

The import of silver in late Ming times has been used to argue that the Ming monetary economy developed to an unprecedented size, pumped up by its strong connection to an emerging world economy. However, because of the lack of data in Chinese sources pertaining to this issue, much of this assertion is not tested in a quantitative way. To solve the problem, one has to rely on the records documented by officials and merchants in Japan, Manila, Macao and Europe, countries that did not necessarily distinguish their exports to China from those to other countries in East Asia and South East Asia. Researchers take quite different views on the aggregate value of silver imported in exchange for Chinese goods such as silk and tea in late Ming China. The estimates, for instance, vary from 100 million to over 300 million *taels* for the inflow of silver by the end of the Ming history (see Table 12.9).

Although the estimates in Table 12.9 show obvious variances in the estimated total values of silver imports, they reveal a similar trend: silver imports grew rapidly in the first half of the seventeenth century. The significance of silver imports, rendered by these estimates, should not be underestimated. One may calculate, following Von Glahn's opinion, that:

> during the second half of the sixteenth century silver imports were adding at least eight times more bullion to China's stock of money than domestic mines; in the first half of the seventeenth century, imports exceeded domestic production by perhaps twenty-fold.[59]

Table 12.9 Ming China: estimates[a] of imports of foreign silver, 1550–1645

	Von Glahn	Wu Chengming	Yamamura and Kamiki	Chuan
1550–1600	57.7–62.5	41.27–51.77	47.4–63.5	–
1601–1645	134.2	44.4–59.4	184.9–225.1	–
Total 1550–1645	191.9–196.7	85.7–111.2	232.4–288.9	45.8

Sources: Von Glahn (1996: 140); Wu Chengming (1995: 170–173); Yamamura and Kamiki (1983); for Japan, Chuan (1974: 644); for Spain, Chuan (1976a, b, c, d) and also see Lin Man-houng (1991: 303–4).
Note:
[a] All figures in millions of *taels* (1 ton = 27,000 *taels*).

One can also conclude, merely by recalling that the Ming money supply (coins plus silver) before 1550 was estimated to be 40–63 million strings of coins, that this would mean that the money stock had swelled by 100 per cent by around 1600, and by more than 250 per cent around 1650.[60] This was an extraordinary increase in the money supply by silver imports within about one century; the Ming empire had no rival in the world when it came to absorbing precious metals from an emerging global economy. After the discovery of the New World, the bullion flow from America into Europe has been emphasized as playing a vital role in causing the collapse of the European feudal system. However, imports between 1500 and 1650 increased Europe's stock of silver bullion by only 26.7 per cent. For gold, the increase was even lower: 3.6 per cent.[61] The bullion flow triggered by the European colonialism caused a much more radical change to the money stock in Ming China compared to what it did to early modern Europe.

In sum, the size of the Ming monetary economy could probably be as large as 174–201 million strings of coins, an amount that already approximates that of the Song money supply in the early twelfth century. Contrary to the Song case, however, the increase in the Ming money supply was secured through marine trade: the volume of about 200 million *taels* would indicate a similar size of exports from China, of commodities such as silk and tea. If these speculations can be proved, they reveal an export-leading economy in the late Ming period. This pattern, though emphasizing the significance of foreign trade, contradicts the current paradigm of the Ming domestic-based market economy. Economic historians usually argue that the development of the market economy was largely determined by domestic needs. And, in fact, until 1550, there is no sign of a strong connection between domestic output and foreign markets.

How large, then, was China's domestic trade, and what was its share of foreign trade in China's overall trade? Wu Chengming suggests an annual volume of long-distance trade in domestic markets of 12.1 million *taels* of silver.[62] Multiplying this figure by five (because long-distance trade probably represented no more than 20 per cent of the aggregate value of domestic trade), results in an annual value of 121 million *taels* of silver for domestic trade in China.[63]

Table 12.10 Estimated annual volumes[a] of domestic trade and overseas trade in Ming China, 1550–1645

Period	Domestic trade	Overseas trade[b]	Total trade	O/T[c]
1550–60	121	1.2	122	0.98%
1601–45	121	2.98	124	2.4%
Total				
1550–1645	121	2	123	1.6%

Notes:
[a] All figures in million *taels* silver.
[b] To get the annual volume of overseas trade, I divide the total silver imports (Von Glahn's figures in Table 12.9) by the years from respective periods. Annual average amount of silver imports were 1.2 million for 1550–1600, 2.98 million for 1601–45, and about 2 million for the entire period of late Ming.
[c] The ratio between overseas trade and trade in total.

The estimates of domestic and overseas trade are shown in Table 12.10. The figures are best viewed as an order of magnitude rather than as a precise measure of quantity. Nonetheless, they demonstrate the very minor percentage of overseas trade in the total trade, supporting Wu's argument. However, these two narratives of the Ming economy, one of a gradual process driven by domestic markets, the other a spurt in foreign trade and silver imports in the late sixteenth and early seventeenth centuries, cannot both be true at the same time. Either might be possible, but neither supports the other.

Estimates of coins in circulation and silver imports suggest an obvious delay in the reaction of the Ming money supply to monetary demands from a market economy. In the first narrative, the development of domestic markets in the sixteenth and seventeenth centuries was achieved on the basis of specialization in agriculture and handicraft industries, a specialization that led to increasing exchanges between agricultural products and non-agricultural goods across regions as well as a growth in productivity on both sides. This pattern has been recognized as a successful way to a high-level market economy, and named the *Jiangnan* (the Lower Yangtze Delta) *Path*.[64] Such a theory reserves little space for the argument of foreign trade and silver imports as an engine for development in the Ming economy, because regional specialization in agriculture and industry was a gradual process starting from the late fifteenth century, and was thus independent of foreign trade, which was still negligible until the late sixteenth century. Silver imports only began to influence the trend of the economy almost a century later. As such, one must ask how the Ming market economy could maintain expansion with such a small money stock before 1600.[65]

In the second narrative, one cannot find a corresponding relationship between silver imports and price movements. Silver imports began to surpass the domestic part of the money supply, which I estimate to be 36–54 million strings of coins, prior to 1600. However, the prices still remained stable around 1600.[66] How to explain the expansion of the market economy in late Ming at an aggregate level still remains a puzzle. In sum, there is no direct evidence either to support or to deny the existence of a market economy of such size. The very backward nature of the Ming fiscal administration made its tax revenues irrelevant as a measure of growth in the market economy, and thus the Ming official documents recount few changes in trade or industry at the aggregate level. Neither do we have a clear idea of the size of the population around 1600.[67] Any estimate of the size of the monetary economy in late Ming China, therefore, is no more than a speculative effort.[68]

Conclusion

In this chapter I have attempted to explore the market performance in pre-industrial China from a monetary perspective. As addressed in the introduction to this book, market performance is defined as the ability of a market to adapt to exogenous shocks. This means: the lower price volatility, the higher market performance. Monetary developments can contribute to market integration (i.e. lower price volatility) as sufficient money supply certainly promotes trade by decreasing transaction costs. The comparison between the Song and Ming periods is a perfect illustration of how the market performance in a traditional economy could vary greatly due to dramatic changes in economic or monetary policies. The survey of long-term changes in grain prices in late imperial China highlights two different kinds of price movements that were separated in time by the establishment of the Ming dynasty. By adopting per capita money stocks as a key criterion, I show a close but not identical connection between the trend of price movements and the amount of hard currency in circulation. The shift towards a silver economy in China from the Song to Ming periods was accompanied with and triggered by a huge loss of hard currencies in circulation. The money supply in the Ming era remained disappointingly low until the 1580s when a massive amount of silver began to be imported into China via a global trade network chiefly organized by European colonialists. Furthermore, this extremely low level of per capita money stocks highlighted by the comparison clearly demonstrates that market integration was worsening in the Ming era.

The tentative yet important conclusion drawn from this monetary perspective casts light on the ongoing debate on the expansion and contraction of the market economy in pre-industrial China. While Mark Elvin proposes the 'medieval (Song China) commercial revolution' thesis, many other researchers maintain that commercial development in sixteenth-century China marks a turning point in Chinese history.[69] Yet neither side can provide important quantitative evidence on the size of domestic markets in the Song and Ming eras and thus fail to find the great contraction of the market in China around 1400. I have elsewhere conducted a survey on long-term changes in China's water transportation in the centuries between 1000 and 1600 and the survey points to the same conclusion: that long-distance trade in Ming China was in a radical decline because water transportation was deteriorating.[70] There is no doubt that the demonetized economy caused by anti-market policies features strongly in the first century of Ming China. From this point of view, China was monetarily backward and financially vulnerable as it came to approach the emerging global trade network in the sixteenth century.

Notes

1 Persson (1999) and Chapter 4, this volume.
2 For instance, 1 *shi* of rice in the Song dynasty was equivalent to 0.67 *shi* in the Ming dynasty.
3 For the latest research on the monetary history of the Song dynasty, see Wang Shengduo (2003).
4 Von Glahn (1996: 76–7).
5 I am using the third version of *Zhongguo huobishi* (published in 1965); the English translation, *A monetary History of China*, is provided by Edward H. Kaplan (1994).
6 Chen Xiang (1988), *Guling xiansheng wenji, juan* 16.
7 For researches on the prices in the Song dynasty, see Chuan (1944; 1948), Long (1993), Wang Shengduo (2004); for researches on the prices in the Ming dynasty, see Chuan (1967d), Terada (1972), Ichiko (1977), Huang Miantang (1985).
8 See Ikeda (1968).
9 Wei (1961: 79–87); Brook (1999: 69).
10 Heijdra acknowledges this deficiency in the monetary history of the Ming dynasty but attributes it to the lack of economic data: 'Because there are no comparable figures for earlier periods, there is no way of knowing whether the supply of money kept up with the population growth or the price level' (Heijdra 1998: 457).
11 Liu (2008: 265–80).
12 Peng (1965: 325–6, 344–9, 356–9).
13 This point was first made by Chuan and Song (Chuan 1944; Song 1947; Li Xiao 2000: 193–9). In fact, Miyazawa also acknowledged that the price of rice in the 1040s was 150 to 300 *wen* per *dou* (thus 1,500 to 3,000 *wen* per Song *shi*), dropping to several tens in the 1070s (Miyazawa 1993, 2). One should not underestimate the impact of this extraordinary inflation upon the escalation of social conflicts in the mid-thirteenth century. The concurrence of social and political conflicts and the fiscal crisis during the Renzong reign (1023–63) was not a coincidence, as already noted by a few scholars (Chuan 1944; Qi 1987: 1092; Peng 1965: 443–5; Li Huarui 1995: 303–5).
14 Among all of the non-agricultural tax revenues, salt monopoly revenues increased at the slowest rate (at most, threefold). This is likely because changes in salt demand had much less to do with foodstuffs.
15 Li Huarui (1995: 146).
16 According to Li Huarui's study of a Song local brewery in 1162, the cost of grain alone accounted for 75 per cent of the production costs, with items such as salaries, management, etc. comprising 22 per cent (Li Huarui 1995: 317–8).
17 Hino (1936: 357–666).
18 Peng (1965: 451).
19 The Ming money stock (including all the monetary means) prior to 1550, as I will discuss later, was only one-sixth–one-third of the total output of bronze coins from Song imperial mints until the 1220s, not to mention other kinds of money in circulation during the Song period.
20 Peng (1965: 706–12); Chuan (1967a).
21 Peng (1965: 468); Atwell (1998: 385).
22 Wang Wencheng (2001: 3).
23 Peng (1965: 646); Von Glahn (1996: 98–102). Because of the sharp change in the silver-coin ratio, the silver-based Peng index has disguised the Ming deflation; using bronze coins as the value unit, the gap between Song and Ming price levels might be magnified

at least three times. The rice price in the early thirteenth-century Lower Yangtze Delta, for instance, was, in fact, about ten times that in the 1430s.

24 A special report on the hoarding in Henan, for instance, revealed that there have been more than ten thousands of kilograms of Song coins excavated in 3,000 sites across the whole province (*Xinyang Zhumadian qian bi faxian yu yanjiu*, 2001, 10).

25 For this estimated ratio, see Liu (2011a).

26 See Table 12.2. I estimate 1 *tael* of silver as being equal to 0.7 string of coins according to the contemporary price of coins in silver. For the details about the estimation, see Liu (2011a).

27 I have dismissed the preservation of silver from previous dynasties into the Ming circulation. Certainly, the Ming economy inherited certain precious metals from previous dynasties, but contrary to the case of Song coins, precious metals such as gold and silver, because of their precious value in relatively small volumes, were more likely to have been transferred outside China or disappeared over nearly three centuries of wars before the establishment of the Ming state. To make the estimate convenient, I also dismissed silver from the Song money supply, and further dismissed the potential inheritance of silver by the Ming dynasty. These will more severely underestimate the Song money supply as opposed to that of Ming.

28 Chuan (1967b).

29 For the latter case, the Fisher equation $MV = PT$ indicates that the price (P) may descend or rise in direct proportion with the change of the money supply (M), only when the velocity of circulation (V) and quantity of transaction (T) remain constant. Thus the change of the money supply may only influence the price level, without interfering with the working of the real economy.

30 Cao (1997: 472–3).

31 Wang Yuquan (1991).

32 For the institutional aspect of Song household registration, see So (1982); Wu Songdi (2000, Chapter 2).

33 Qi (1987: 329).

34 For the property classification in household registration, see Liang (1998: 19–36, 37–68); Wang Zengyu (1996: 8–27). For the household registration in rural areas, see Yanagida (1986: 102–131).

35 See Yanagida on the rural *kehu* households (Yanagida 1986: 240–83, 284–323). It is undeniable that a large number of urban *kehu* households lived in Song cities, but due to scanty documentation, scholars still debate whether the ten-level urban household registration should include the urban *kehu* households (Yanagida 1995: 198).

36 Fuzhou's population reached 247,000 households (*hu*), including 17,000 urban households and 15,300 rural households (Wang Zengyu 1996: 13–14).

37 For a discussion on the early Ming state, see the next section.

38 The maximum estimate was made by Wu Han, who estimated 2.8 million Ming soldiers in the early Ming by citing a high official's report made in 1501 (Wu Han 1937: 101).

39 The number of soldiers in 1392 was 1,198,434 (Wu Han 1937: 101; 2000: 236). Wu Han also estimated 2.8 million soldiers for the Ming army in the Yongle reign (Wu Han 1937: 101). Cao Shuji reports three aggregate figures of the soldiers in the Hongwu and Yongle reigns: 1.91 million, 2.06 million, and 2.19 million. He estimates the total number of the military households in the Yongle reign would have reached 2.19 million (Cao 2000: 379).

40 Wang Yuquan (1965: 209).

41 Yu (1988: 47–76); Hucker (1998: 62–5).

42 Li Ruoyu (1988: 40–1).

43 Li Ruoyu (1988: 43). Also see Von Glahn (1996: 78).

44 The term 'unilateral payments' is borrowed from a study of medieval European economy which indicates the revenues due to landlords and settled in kind or in labour

(Cipolla 1956: 7–8). I use it in the Chinese case to indicate that the early Ming state extracted revenues from local societies almost exclusively in kind or in labour. Not until the mid-sixteenth century did local governments gradually convert these 'unilateral payments' into cash income. This was not accomplished nationally until as late as in the mid-eighteenth century.

45 In the Wang brothers' contracts, I have found six cases of land sales made as a result of the cost of grain transportation taxes: in the summer of 1401, six farmers from the same place sold their lands in small lots to Wang in order to accumulate money for travelling expenses incurred in delivering grain taxes to state depots (Anhuisheng bowuguan 1988: Vol. 1: 10–11; Vol. 2: 20–1).

46 *Ming Taizu shilu*, Vol. 230; *Ming Huidian*, Vol. 189, Ministry of Works.

47 Yang Guoqing gives estimates of the corvée in the construction of Nanjing's city wall; he points out that the potential human resources for building works included 200,000 soldiers, probably fewer than 200,000 artisans, 1 million peasants and several hundred thousand prisoners. The total work required 7 million individual workdays. (Yang 2002: 37–44).

48 For North China, see Yamane (1995). The early Ming economy just saw the beginnings of rural market development following the long-lasting civil wars that had destroyed the local economy and society.

49 Most early Ming contracts, such as those of the Wang brothers, dealt with tracts of land less than 1 acre in size. The price, if paid in grain, often doubled the annual rent of the land. Although in terms of *baochao*, the land value inflated much in the Yongle reign, the prices of Huizhou land in the early Ming period remained as low as less than 1 *tael* of silver per *mu* (1 *mu* = 0.16441 acre) until the 1440s. It then jumped up to about 10 *tael*s in the Hongzhi reign (1488–1505), then lowered somewhat in late sixteenth and mid-seventeenth centuries. In the late seventeenth and the first decade of the eighteenth century, it rose slowly, but seemed to accelerate in the second decade, and came to a peak in the Qianlong reign (1736–95), with an average price of something over 20 *tael*s per *mu*. The high price in land markets in the Qianlong reign can find a parallel in Suzhou (see the contracts of land sales collected by Hong Huanchun (1988: 87–177)). For a long-term survey of changes in land prices over the five centuries 1400–1900, see Chao (1986: 130); Kishimoto (1990: 755).

50 Wang's contracts are preserved at Anhui Provincial Museum and History Institute, China Academy of Social Sciences. These contracts, along with many other land documents have been published in *Ming-Qing Huizhou shehui jingji ziliao congbian*, Vol. 1–2, 1988, 1990. For Wang's contracts, see ibid., Vol. 1, 1–15, 24–26, 388; Vol. 2, 19–23, 28.

51 In the next section I will continue to discuss the early Ming state and economy.

52 Atwell (1998); Von Glahn (1996: 113–41); Miyazawa (1998).

53 Miyazawa (1993: 213–6).

54 Gernet (1962: 78). For silver functioning as the medium of exchange in the Song, see Wang Wencheng (2001).

55 The Song financial market is discussed later in this chapter.

56 Gernet (1982: 325–6).

57 Von Glahn doubts if the existence of a unified monetary system can be applied as a standard to judge the development of the Chinese monetary economy, and acknowledges that 'the manifold currencies of late imperial China reflected the increasing diversity of market demand for monetary media as the range of money-use broadened'. Tokugawa Japan even reverted from coins back to rice as the standard for its payment; yet, this 'regression' was particularly related to economic growth occurring then in Japan (Von Glahn 1996: 8–9, 11; Yamamura 1988). Sweden is another example of a country that used low-value metal coins and introduced paper banknotes. Stockholms Banco (Bank of Sweden) issued the first paper money in Europe in 1661. To sustain a steady growth

in money supply and to resolve the problems of using *daler* (a currency minted by copper) for making large payments, which required transferring large amounts by horse and cart, Sweden resorted to issuing paper banknotes.

58 The state after 1500 was inactive due to diminished revenue. This situation remained unchanged even up to the twentieth century. According to Rawski, at this period the taxes and public spending remained below ten per cent of gross domestic product. With such a low share of state revenue, only two countries in the post-war world, Afghanistan and Ethiopia, were able to stay alive (Rawski 1989: 25–6). For a discussion of the very limited role of the state in Ming-Qing China, see Eastman (1988: 103–7, 130–4).

59 Von Glahn (1996: 140–1). Wu Chengming also suggests that the silver import before the eighteenth century would triple the Ming silver stock (Wu Chengming 1995: 173, 249).

60 I estimate that the contemporary rate between silver and bronze coins is: 1 *tael* of silver = 0.7 string of coins.

61 Braudel (1974: 28).

62 This figure was calculated by using Wu's estimates of several major goods in late Ming long-distance trade: grain (8.5 million *taels*), cloth (3.3 million *taels*), silk (0.3 million *taels*). See Wu (1983). The size of long-distance trade, according to Wu's estimates, was no more than 20 per cent of the aggregate value of domestic trade in the eighteenth century. Perkins' study indicates that the ratio between the size of long-distance trade and that of rural markets prior to 1900 was about 1:3–4 (Perkins 1969: 114–5). When applying this ratio to estimating the late Ming's trade, I assumed that the gross value of goods at the rural markets was about ten times the long-distance trade, and that because of the underdevelopment of the long-distance trade in late Ming, late Ming domestic trade did not exceed 121 million *taels*.

63 Wu's estimate is closely related to his Marxist view of the market economy in a pre-industrial society. He focuses his demonstrations on the supply side instead of the demand side. This supply-centred approach makes his estimates particularly indecisive because of the difficulty in measuring aggregate farm output.

64 For the recent theories of the market economy in the Lower Yangtze Delta, see Li Bozhong (1998).

65 The Single Whip reform, for instance, was first launched in Jiangxi in the 1560s. This reform allowed farmers to replace labour services by money payments and consequently increased the demand for silver. Scholars usually agree that the undertaking of the Single Whip reform became nationwide no later than 1592; some favour an earlier date such as 1581 (Kuroki 1993: 599).

66 According to Braudel and Spooner, the total amount of metal money in circulation in Europe and the Mediterranean before the discovery of America was approximately 5,000 tons of gold and 60,000 tons of silver. The arrivals of bullion from America during the century and a half between 1500 and 1650 amounted to 1,600 tons of silver and 180 of gold (Braudel 1974: 28). The amount of silver imported into Europe in the sixteenth century now looks less significant than it used to. In contrast, late Ming's silver imports would be an extremely unusual case, indicated by the dominant size of silver imports over the domestic stock of money.

67 It is currently recognized that the Ming population peaked in 1600. However, there is no reliable data on mid- and late Ming population. Estimates of the aggregate population vary between 120 and 200 million. A few examples are: Ho, 150 million (Ho 1959: 264); Perkins, 120–200 million (Perkins 1969: 216); Wu Chengming, 120 million (Wu Chengming 1995: 148); Cao, 200 million in 1590 (Cao 2000: 201).

68 Despite the fact that most of China's socioeconomic historians, especially those engaged in the study of the Lower Yangtze Delta and south-east coastal areas, often acknowledge the late Ming and early Qing as an integral part of economic development, the study of economic performance in pre-industrial China encounters two different cases in regard to aggregate data.

69 Elvin (1973: 131–78).
70 Liu (2011a, 2011b, 2012, 2013).

Bibliography

Anhuisheng bowuguan (安徽省博物馆). 1988. *Ming-Qing Huizhou shehuijingji ziliao congbian* (明清徽州社会经济资料丛编), Vol. 1–2, Beijing: Zhongguo shehuikexue chubanshe.

Atwell, William S. 1998. 'Ming China and the Emerging World Economy, c.1470–1650', in *The Cambridge History of China*, edited by D. C. Twitchet and F. W. Mote, Cambridge: Cambridge University Press: 376–417.

—— 2002. 'Time, Money, and the Weather: Ming China and the "Great Depression" of the Mid-fifteenth Century', *Journal of Asian Studies*, 61: 83–113.

Braudel, F. 1974. 'The Mediterranean Economy in the Sixteenth Century', in *Essays in European Economic History, 1500–1800*, edited by P. Earle, Oxford: Clarendon Press: 1–44.

Brook, Timothy. 1999. *The Confusions of Pleasure, Commerce and Culture in Ming China*, Berkeley: University of California Press.

Brown, R. M. 2005. 'Ming ban-Ming Gap: Southeast Asian Shipwreck Evidence for Shortage of Chinese Trade Ceramics', in *Proceedings: Chinese Export Ceramics and Maritime Trade 12th–15th Centuries*, edited by Pei-kai Cheng, Guo Li and Chui Ki Wan, Hong Kong: Chinese Civilisation Centre, City University of Hong Kong and City University of Hong Kong Interdisciplinary Research Project: 78–104.

Cao Shuji (曹树基). 1997. *Zhongguo Yiminshi* (中国移民史), Vol. 4, *Ming shiqi* (明时期), Fuzhou: Fujian renmin.

—— 2000. *Zhongguo Renkoushi* (中国人口史), Vol. 4, *Ming shiqi* (明时期), Shanghai: Fudan Daxue.

Carus-Wilson, E. M. 1962. *Essays in Economic History, Reprints edited for The Economic History Society*. 3 vols, London: St. Martin's Press.

Chao Kang [see also Zhao Gang (趙岡)]. 1986. *Man and Land in Chinese History: An Economic Analysis*, Stanford: Stanford University Press, 1986.

Chen Xiang (陈襄, 1017–1080). 1988. *Guling xiansheng wenji* (古靈先生文集), Beijing: Shumu wenxian chubanshe.

Chuan Han-sheng [also spelled as Quan Hansheng, (全漢昇)]. 1944. 'Bei Song wujia de biandong (北宋物價的變動)', *Zhongyang Yanjiuyuan Lishiyuyan Yanjiusuo Jikan* (中央研究院历史语言研究所集刊), Vol. 11: 201–30. Later reprinted in *Zhongguo jingji shi luncong* (中國經濟史論叢), Hong Kong: Xianggang zhongwen daxue xinyashuyuan xinya yanjiusuo, 1972: 29–86.

—— 1948. 'Songmo de tonghuopengzhang jiqi duiyu wujia de yingxiang (宋末的通貨膨脹及其對於物價的影響)', in *Zhongyang Yanjiuyuan Lishiyuyan Yanjiusuo Jikan* (中央研究院历史语言研究所集刊), Vol. 10: 201–30. Later reprinted in *Zhongguo jingji shi luncong* (中國經濟史論叢), Hong Kong: Xianggang zhongwen daxue xinyashuyuan xinya yanjiusuo, 1972: 325–54.

—— 1967a. 'Song-Ming jian baiyin goumaili de biandong jiqi yuanyin (宋明间白银购买力的变动及其原因)', in *Xin Ya xuebao* (新亚学报), Hong Kong: Xinya yanjiusuo, 8 (1): 157–86; reprinted in *Zhongguo jingjishi yanjiu*, Vol. 2, 179–208.

—— 1967b. 'Mingdai de yinke yu yinchane (明代的银课与银产额)', in *Xinya shuyuan xueshu niankan* (新亚书院学术年刊), Vol. 9: 245–67. Reprinted in *Zhongguo jingjishi yanjiu*, Vol. 2: 209–32.

—— 1967c. 'Ming-Qing jian meizhou baiyin de shuru zhongguo (明清间美洲白银的输入中国)', in *Zhongguo Wenhua Yanjiusuo Xuebao* (中国文化研究所学报) 1: 27–49; reprinted in *Zhongguo jingji shi luncong* (中國經濟史論叢), Hong Kong: Xianggang zhongwen daxue xinyashuyuan xinya yanjiusuo, 1972: 435–50.

—— 1967d. 'Mingdai beibian miliang jiage de biandong (明代北边米粮价格的变动)', *Xin Ya xuebao* (新亚学报), 9 (2): 49–96. Reprinted in *Zhongguo jingjishi yanjiu*, Vol. 2: 261–308.

—— 1974. 'Ming-Qing shidai yunnan de yinke yu yinchane (明清时代云南的银课与银产额)', in *Xinya xuebao* (新亚学报), Hong Kong: Xinya yanjiusuo, Vol. 11: 61–88.

—— 1976. *Zhongguo jingjishi yanjiu* (中国经济史研究), Vols. 1–3, Hong Kong: Xinya yanjiusuo.

Cipolla, C. M. 1956. *Money, Prices and Civilization in the Mediterranean World, Fifth to Seventeenth Centuries*, Princeton: Princeton University Press.

Earle, P. 1974. *Essays in European Economic History, 1500–1800*, Oxford: Clarendon Press.

Eastman, L. E. 1988. *Family, Fields, and Ancestors, Constancy and Change in China's Social and Economic History, 1550–1949*, Oxford: Oxford University Press.

Elvin, M. 1973. *The Pattern of the Chinese Past*, Stanford: Stanford University Press.

Gao Congming (高聪明). 2000. *Songdai Huobi yu Huobi Liutong Yanjiu* (宋代货币与货币流通研究), Baoding: Hebei daxue chubanshe.

Gernet, J. 1962. *Daily Life in China, On the Eve of the Mongol Invasion, 1250–1276*; translated by H. M. Wright, New York: Macmillan.

——1982. *A History of Chinese Civilization*; translated by J. R. Foster. Cambridge: Cambridge University Press.

Goetzmann, W. N. and Rouwenhorst, K. G., eds. 2005. *The Origins of Value, the Financial Innovations that Created Modern Capital Markets*, Oxford: Oxford University Press.

Heijdra, M. 1998. 'The Socio-economic Development of Rural China During the Ming', in *The Cambridge History of China*, edited by D. C. Twitchet and F. W. Mote, Cambridge: Cambridge University Press: 417–578.

Hino Kaisaburo (日野開三郎). 1935. 'Hoku-So jidai ni okeru dotetsusen no chu-zogaku ni tsuite (北宋時代における銅鐵の鑄造額に就いて)', *Shigaku zasshi* (史學雜志), 46 (1): 46–105; later collected in *Hino Kaisaburo toyo shigaku ronshu* (日野開三郎東洋史学論集), 1983, Vol. 6: 239–80. Tokyo: Sanichi shobo.

——1936. 'Hoku-So jidai ni okeru dotetsusen no jukyu ni tsuite (北宋時代における銅鐵錢の需給に就いて)', in *Rekisjigaku kinky u* (歷史學研究), Vol. 6: 482–510, 663–85, 791–98; later collected in *Hino Kaisaburo toyo shigaku ronshu* (日野開三郎東洋史学論集), 1983, Vol. 6: 341–99, Tokyo: Sanichi shobo.

Ho Ping-ti. 1959. *Studies on the Population of China, 1368–1953*, Cambridge, MA: Harvard University Press.

Hong Huanchun (洪煥椿). 1988. *Mingqing Suzhou nongcun jingji ziliao* (明清蘇州農村經濟資料), Nanjing: Jingsu guji.

Huang Miantang (黄冕堂). 1985. 'Mingdai wujia kaolue (明代物价考略)', in *Mingshi Guanjian* (明史管见), Jinan: Qilu shushe: 347–72.

Hucker, C. O. 1998. 'Ming Government', in *The Cambridge History of China*, edited by D. C. Twitchet and F. W. Mote, Cambridge: Cambridge University Press: 9–105.

Ichiko Shozo (市古尚三). 1977. *Mindai Kahei Shiko* (明代貨幣史), Tokyo: Otori shobo.

Ikeda On (池田温). 1968. 中國古代物價の一考察(1)(2)—天寶元年交河郡市估案斷片お中心として (Price Levels in Ancient China: Fragments on Market Price Documents in the Jiaohe District Dated the 1st Year of the Tianbao Era), *Shigaku zasshi* (史學雜志), 77 (2): 1–64.

Kishimoto Mio (岸本美緒). 1990. 明末の田土市場に関する一考察', in *Yamane Yukio kyōju taikyū kinen Mindaishi ronsō* (山根幸夫教授退休記念明代史論叢), Mindaishi Kenkyūkai, Mindaishi Ronsō Henshū Iinkai (明代史研究会, 明代史論叢編集委員会), Tōkyō: Kyūko Shoin: 751–70.

Kuroki Kuniyasu (黑木國泰). 1993. '一条鞭法研究の課題と展望', in *Minshin jidai no ho to shakai* (明清时代の法と社会), Tokyo: Kyoto shoin: 593–608.

Li Bozhong. 1998. *Agricultural Development in Jiangnan, 1620–1850*, New York: St. Martin's Press.

Li Huarui (李华瑞). 1995. *Songdai jiu di shengchan he zhengque* (宋代酒的生产和征榷), Baoding: Hebei daxue chubanshe.

Li Longsheng (李隆生). 2005. 'Mingmo baiyin cunliang de guji (明末白银存量的估计)', *China Numismatics* (中国钱币), 22: 3–8.

Li Ruoyu (李若愚). 1988. 'Cong Mingdai de qiyue kan Mingdai de bizhi (从明代的契约看明代的币制)', *Zhongguo Jingjishi Yanjiu* (中国经济史研究), 3 (3): 39–43.

Li Xiao (李晓). 2000. *Songdai gongshangye jingji yu zhengfu ganyu yanjiu* (宋代工商业经济与政府干预), Beijing: Zhongguo qingnian.

Liang Taiji (梁太济). 1998. *Nan-Song jieji guanxi de ruogan wenti* (南宋阶级关系的若干问题), Hebei: Hebei Daxue.

Lin Man-hung (林滿紅). 1989. 'Shijie jingji yu jindai zhongguo nongyeshi (世界經濟與近代中國農業)', in *Jindai Zhongguo nongcun jingji shi lunwenji* (近代中國農村經濟史論文集), Taipei: Institute of Modern History, Academia Sinica: 291–325.

—— 1991. 'Zhongguo de bayin wanliu yu shijie de jinyin jianchan (中國的白銀外流與世界的金銀減產)', *Essays in Chinese Maritime History* (中國海洋發展史論文集) 1, Taipei: Sun Yat-sen Institute for Social Sciences and Philosophy, Academia Sinica: 1–44.

Lindert, P. H. 1980. 'English Occupations, 1670–1811', *Journal of Economic History*, 40: 685–712.

—— 1985. 'English Population, Wages, and Prices: 1541–1913', *Journal of Interdisciplinary History*, 15: 609–34.

Liu, William Guanglin. 2005. *Wrestling for Power, the Changing Relationship between the State and the Economy in Late imperial China, 1000–1770*. Cambridge MA: Harvard University, PhD thesis.

—— 2008. 'Shichang, zhanzheng he ciahzengguojia (市場、戰爭和財政國家): dui Nan-Song fushui wenti de zai sikao (對南宋財政問題的再思考)', *Historical Inquiry* (臺大歷史學報), 42: 221–85.

—— 2011a. 'Mingdai tonghuo wenti yanjiu (明代通货问题研究—对明代货币经济规模和结构的初步估计)', *Zhongguo jingjishi yanjiu* (中国经济史研究), 26 (1): 72–83.

—— 2011b. 'Yinjin qiantui yu Mingdai huobi liutongtizhi (银进钱退与明代货币流通体制)', *Journal of Hebei University, Philosophy & Social Sciences* (河北大学学学报人文社会科学版), 36 (2): 24–32.

—— 2012. 'Song China's Water Transport Revolution Revisited: A Study of the 1077 Commercial Tax Data', *Pacific Economic Review*, 17: 57–85.

—— 2013. 'Long-distance Trade and Water Transports in China, 1000–1800', in *Feudalism in Multiple Perspectives, A Collection of Papers in Celebration for Professor Keyao Ma's 80th Anniversary*, 多元視角下的封建主義：慶賀馬克垚先生80華誕學術論文集, Beijing: Zhongguo shehuikexue wenxian chubanshe: 446–85.

Long Denggao (龙登高). 1993. 'Songdai liangjia fenxi (宋代粮价分析)', *Zhongguo jingjishi yanjiu*, 29 (1): 152–60.

Maeda Naonori (前田直典). 1973. 'Gencho jidai ni okeru shihei no kachi hendo (元朝時代における紙帀の價值変动)', Maeda Naonori, *Gencho shi no kenkyu* (元朝史の研究), Tokyo: Tokyo Daigaku Shuppankai: 107–43.

Mayhew, N. J. 1995. 'Population, Money Supply and the Velocity of Circulation in England, 1300–1700', *Economic History Review*, New Series, 48: 238–57.

Ming Huidian (明會典), Xu Pu (徐溥, 1428–1499) zhuan, Li Dongyang (李東陽, 1447–1516) chong xiu. Shanghai: Shanghai guji chubanshe, 1987.

Ming Taizu shilu (明太祖實錄), Li Jinglong (李景隆, ?–1424) zhuan, preserved in *Ming shilu* (明實錄), Vol. 1–8, Taipei: Institute of History and Philology, Academic Sinica, 1961–66.

Miyazawa Tomoyuki (宮澤知之). 1993. 'Tou yori Min ni itaru kaheikeizai no tenkai (唐より明にいたる貨幣経済の展開)', in *Higashi Ajia sensei kokka to shakai, keizai* (東アジア専制国家と社会·経済), edited by Nakamura, Satoru (中村哲), Tokyo: Aoki Shoten, 185–220.

—— 1998. *Sōdai Chūgoku no kokka to keizai: zaisei, shijō, kahei* (宋代中国の国家と経済), Tokyo: Sobunsha.

—— 2007. *Chūgoku dōsen no sekai: senka kara keizaishie* (中国銅銭の世界: 銭貨から経済史へ), Kyōto: Shibunkaku.

Momose Hiromu (百瀬弘). 1935a. '明代中国外国貿易'; reprinted in Momose 1980: 3–21.

—— 1935b. '明代の銀産と外国銀に就いて'; reprinted in Momose 1980: 22–70.

—— 1980. *Min Shin shakai keizaishi kenkyu* (明清社会経済史研究), Tokyo: Kenbun Shuppan.

Mote, F. W. and Twitchett, D. C., eds. 1988. *The Cambridge History of China*, Vol. 7, *The Ming Dynasty, 1368–1644, Part 1*, Cambridge: Cambridge University Press.

Ni Laien [(倪来恩), Brian Moloughney] and Xia Weizhong (夏维中). 1990. 'Waiguo baiyin yu Ming diguo de Bengkui: Guanyu Mingmo waiguo baiyin shuru jiqi zuoyongde xin jiantao (外国白银与明帝国的崩溃：明末外国白银输入及其作用的新检讨)', *Zhongguo shehui jingjishi yanjiu* (中國社會經濟史研究), 9 (3): 46–56.

Otagi Matsuo (愛宕松男). 1973. 'Atsudatsusen to sono haikei: Jusan-seki Mongoru Gen-cho niokeru gin no doko (斡脱銭とその背景–13世紀モンゴル=元朝における銀の動向)', *The Journal of Oriental Researches* (東洋史研究) 32(1): 1–27; 32(2): 23–61; reprinted in Otagi 1989.

—— 1989. *Tozai koshoshi* (東西交渉史). *Otagi Matsuo Tōyō shigaku ronshū* (愛宕松男東洋史學論集), Vol. 5. Tokyo: San'ichi Shobo.

Peng Xinwei (彭信威). 1965. *Zhongguo Huobi Shi* (中国货币史), third edition, Shanghai: Renmin chubanshe.

—— 1994. *A Monetary History of China (Zhongguo Huobi Shi)*, Vol. 1–2, translated by Edward H. Kaplan, Bellingham: Western Washington University Press.

Perkins, D. H. 1969. *Agricultural Development in China, 1368–1968*, Chicago: Aldine Publishing Company.

Persson, Karl Gunnar. 1999. *Grain Markets in Europe, 1500–1900*. Cambridge: Cambridge University Press.

Qi Xia (漆侠). 1987. *Songdai Jingjishi* (宋代经济史), Shanghai: Shanahai renmin.

Quan Hansheng 1967. 'Song-Ming jian baiyin goumaili de biandong jiqi yuanyin 宋明间白银购买力的变动及其原因', *Xinya xuebao* 新亚学报, 8 (1): 157–86. Reprinted in *Zhongguo jingjishi yanjiu*. Hong Kong: Xinya yanjiusuo, 1976, Vol. 2: 179–208.

Rawski, Th.G. 1989. *Economic Growth in Prewar China*, Berkeley: University of California Press.

So, Billy K. L. 1982. 'The System for Registration of Households and Population in the Sung Dynasty: An Institutional Analysis', *Papers on Far Eastern History*, 25: 1–30.

Song Xi (宋晞). 1947. 'The Position of Commercial Tax in National Income and Tax-Supervisors in the Northern Sung Dynasty (北宋商税在國計中的地位與監税官)', in *Shihuo, Zhongyang ribao* (中央日報食貨周刊), 61 (17 Feb. 1947); later reprinted in *Essay on the History of the Sung Dynasty* (宋史研究论叢), Vol. 1, Taipei: Zhongguo wenhua yanjiusuo: 65–72.

Terada Takanobu (寺田隆信). 1972. *Sansei shonin no kenkyu; Min-dai ni okeru shonin oyobi shogyo shihon* (山西商人の研究: 明代における商人および商業资本), Kyoto: Toyoshi kenkyukai.

Twitchet, D. C. and F. W. Mote, eds. 1998. *The Cambridge History of China*, Vol. 8, *The Ming Dynasty, 1368–1644, Part 2*, Cambridge: Cambridge University Press.

Von Glahn, Richard. 1996. *Fountain of Fortune: Money and Monetary Policy in China, 1000–1700*. Berkeley: University of California Press.

Wang Shengduo (汪圣铎). 1985. 'Nansong liangjia xibiao (南宋粮价细表)', *Zhongguo shehui jingjishi yanjiu* (中國社會經濟史研究), 4 (3): 38–52.

—— 1989. 'Beinan Song wujia bijiao yanjiu (北南宋物价比较研究)', in *Songshi yanjiu lunwenji* (宋史研究论文集), edited by Deng Guangming (鄧廣銘) and Qi Xia (漆侠), Shijiazhuang: Hebei jiaoyu: 238–54.

—— 2003. *Liang-song huobi shi* (两宋货币史), Vol. 1–2. Beijing: Shehuikexue chubanshe.

—— 2004. *Liang-song huobi shiluo huibian* (两宋货币史料汇编), Beijing: Zhonghua shuju.

Wang Wencheng (王文成). 2001. *Songdai Baiyin Huobihua Yanjiu* (宋代白银货币化研究), Kunming: Yunnan University Press.

Wang, Yeh-chien. 1973. *The Land Taxation in Imperial China, 1750–911*, Cambridge MA: Harvard University Press.

Wang Yuquan (王毓铨). 1965. *Mingdai de juntun* (明代的军屯), Beijing: Zhonghua shuju.

—— 1991. 'Mingchao de peihudangchai zhi (明朝的配户当差制)', *Zhongguoshi Yanjiu* (中国史研究), 13(1): 24–43.

Wang Yuxun (王裕巽). 1998. 'Mingdai baiyin guonei kaicai yu guowai liuru shu'e shikao (明代白银国内开采与国外流入数额试考)', *China Numismatics* (中国钱币), 16 (3): 18–25.

—— 2001. 'Shilun Ming Zhong-hou qi de shizhu yu wujia (试论明中、后期的私铸与物价)', *China Numismatics* (中国钱币), 19 (3): 18–25.

Wang Zengyu (王曾瑜). 1996. *Songchao Jieji Jiegou* (宋朝阶级结构), Shijiazhuang: Hebei jiaoyu.

Wei Qingyuan (韋庆远) 1961. *Mingdai huangce zhidu* (明代黄冊制度), Beijing: Zhonghua shuju.

—— 1983. 'Lun Mingdai guonei shichang he shangrenziben (论明代国内市场和商人资本)', in Zhongguo shehui kexueyuan jingjiyanjiusuojikan (中国社会科学院经济研究所集刊), Vol. 5. Later reprinted with revisions in Zhongguo de xiandaihua, shichangyushehui, Beijing: Sanlianshudian: 2001: 111–43.

Wu Chengming (吳承明). 1995. 'Shiliu yu shiqi shiji de zhongguo shichang (16 与 17 世纪的中国市场)', in Zhongguo shangyeshi xuehui, ed *Huozhi: Shangye yu shichangyanjiu* (货殖: 商业与市场研究), Vol. 1, Beijing: Zhongguo caizheng chubanshe; reprinted in *Wu Chengming Ji* (吴承明集) 2002. Beijing: Zhongguo shehuikexue: 140–76.

Wu Han (吳晗). 1937. 'Mingdai de junbing (明代的军兵)', in *Zhongguo shehui jingjishi jikan* (中國社會經濟史集刊), 2(2); reprinted in *Dushi zhaji* (读史札记), Beijing: Sanlain shudian 1955: 92–141.

——2000. *Zhu Yuanzhang zhuan* (朱元璋传), Beijing: Sanlian shudian.

Wu Songdi (吳松弟). 2000. *Zhongguo Renkoushi* (中国人口史), Vol. 4, *Liao Song Jin Yuan Shiqi* (辽宋金元时期), Shanghai: Fudan daxue.

Xinyang Zhumadian qian bi faxian yu yanjiu (信阳驻马店钱币发现与研究). 2001. Beijing: Zhonghua shuju.

Yamamura Kozo. 1988. 'From Coins to Rice: Hypothesis on the Kandaka and Kokudaka Systems', in *Journal of Japanese Studies*, 14: 341–67.

Yamamura Kozo and Kamiki Tetsuo. 1983. 'Silver Mines and Sung Coins: a Monetary History of Medieval and Modern Japan in International Perspective', in *Precious Metals in the Late Medieval and Early Modern Worlds*, edited by J. F. Richards, Durham NC: Carolina Academic press. 329–62.

Yamane Yukio (山根幸夫). 1995. *Min Shi Kahoku teikishi no kenkyu* (明清華北定期市の研究), Tokyo: Kyuko shoin.

Yanagida Setsuko (柳田節子) 1986. *So Gen Gosonsei no Kenkyu* (宋元鄕村制の研究), Tokyo: Sobunsha.

——1995. *So-Gen Shakai Keizaishi Kenkyu* (宋元社會経済史研究), Tokyo: Sobunsha.

Yang Guoqing (杨国庆). 2002. 'Ming Nanjing chengqiang zhucheng renyuan goucheng ji yonggongliang chutan (明南京城墙筑城人员及用工量初探)', *Dongnan Wenhua* (东南文化), 153 (1): 37–44.

Yang Lien-sheng 1952. *Money and Credit in China, a Short History*, Cambridge: Harvard University Press.

Yu Zhijia (于志嘉). 1988. *Mingdai jinhu shixi zhidu* (明代军户世袭制度), Taipei: Xuesheng shuju.

Zhou Shaoquan (周绍泉) and Zhao Yagaung (赵亚光), eds. 1993. *Doushan gong jiayi jiaozhu* (窦山公家议校注), Hefei: Huangshan chubanshe, 1993.

13 The organization and scope of grain markets in Qing China, 1644–1911

Carol H. Shiue

Introduction

The existence of markets and the performance of markets depend upon a multitude of factors, including trade, storage, consumption diversification and technology (see Foldvari and Van Leeuwen, Chapter 2, this volume). Analogous to the discussion on the factors of economic growth in economics, these factors can be considered 'proximate' causes of market performance. They are proximate since they directly affect price setting and, hence, the working of markets. In addition, economic and political institutions as well as geographic characteristics may affect market performance. Using again the analogy with economic growth, these may be considered 'ultimate' causes since they only indirectly influence market performance.

Perhaps one of the most important proximate determinants of market performance in early economies is trade. Trade, however, is not only a contributor to market performance, but is also a composite of the joint contribution of potential ultimate factors which may affect price gaps between markets. In many settings, price development is the first and most important feature of the marketplace that we want to know about. The availability of price data allows us to compare changes in market integration over time for an economy, or to make a comparison across different economies, all of which is extremely useful.

But a more detailed outline is needed to understand which factors are responsible for creating the overall market outcomes observed. Different levels of integration may arise from the endowments of the country. Mountain cliffs or rocky terrain between two markets, for example, could result in costs of transport that are so high that they preclude the possibility of profitable arbitrage between the markets. Excessive tolls and tariffs might also preclude gains from trade, as might the chaos of civil war or rampant piracy. Technological progress can explain differences in market efficiency over time in the same country, even if all other contributing factors have not changed. In comparing two pre-industrial economies with similar levels of transport technology, however, differences in market performance must be due to other reasons. Greater overall political stability may influence the possibility of trade, since war or arbitrary taxation may have a detrimental effect on trade. Besides political institutions, economic institutions, such as currency standards and financial instruments, can affect the potential gains of trade and affect the calculation of buyers and sellers in their view of whether the transaction costs are limited and predictable, and thus whether the trade is one that they want to undertake. Thus, an analysis of the institutional innovations of society can usefully reveal not only what is being captured in the measure of market performance, but also, in a comparison across societies, which attributes may be relatively more important in creating higher levels of integration.

In this chapter, I discuss the grain price data available from the Qing Dynasty and issues of the quality of the data. I also highlight what the data say about comparative market integration between Europe and China, and then survey the setting in which markets operated in the domestic economy of the Qing, with a focus on the institutions that allowed trade to take place.[1] European markets of the same period are used as a benchmark for comparison. Europe is the chosen benchmark because more is generally known about the functioning of European prices and markets, and of European institutions, than about their Chinese counterparts. Another reason for making the comparisons with Europe is that the Industrial Revolution began first in England and a handful of European countries, so it is interesting to form a side-by-side comparison of the performance of markets in China and Europe.

Grain market data

This section gives an overview of the grain market data that are available from China. While both foreign and domestic trade existed in China since antiquity, and Chinese records on grain prices date to as early as the Tang Dynasty (618–906), the existence of substantial quantitative information on the economy at the prefectural level across the entire empire begins only during the Qing Dynasty (1644–1911). The original source of these data are the *zhupi yuzhi* (Vermillion endorsements and palace memorials) for each reign periods. The Qing emperor Kangxi (reign 1662–1722) established certain procedures that started to become more widespread over the reign of Yongzheng (1723–35). In particular, records include prices on three different gradations of quality of rice and, depending on the location, the prices of as many as three additional grain products, for example, wheat or millet or soybeans. For each grain, the price records include the midpoint price, as well as the spread between the highest and the lowest prices observed in that prefecture. These extensive price records on grain form the basis of nearly all current findings on Chinese market integration.

There are at least three aspects of the Chinese data that make them exceptional. First, as I will discuss in more detail below, the data are of high quality. Second, they cover the entire empire, which in the case of China is an area of very broad geographic scope and includes a wide variety of climates and indigenous grains. Third, for most provinces, the time span covered is fairly long. Moreover, the frequency is given at regular intervals for every region, at 12 or 13 times per year. Taken together, the price data are available for every major province of China over a period from the early to mid-eighteenth century to the end of the dynasty.

The work for digitizing the entire price series is still ongoing, but a rough esti-mate suggests that with 11–13 prefectures in each province, 18 core provinces, there are at a minimum 200 prefectural locations, each of which reports two prices (the minimum and the maximum) for at least three different grains, at intervals of every lunar month, of every year, for about 170 years. This amounts to well over two million potential price observations. Of course data entries are sometimes missing, but the bulk of the data are undoubtedly present. In the data that I have used over ten provinces (see Figure 13.1) that spanned the years 1742–95, housed in the *First National Archives* of China.[2]

Figure 13.1 Map of China.

Accuracy of reporting is always a concern for any dataset. It is notable, however, that the Qing government had in place various measures to ensure the accuracy of the actual reporting of prices. This system included the standardization of the form and content in the reports and a system of audits and checks on the regular reports. A dual system to check on the accuracy of the regular reporting system seems rather extraordinary, especially for the eighteenth century. That the government did this suggests that accuracy in the information contained in the price reports was important.[3] In fact, the reports on market prices had a practical purpose. While taxes in kind helped in part to support the government's contingency of bureaucrats, officials and army households, the state was also engaged in the purchase of food grain, which could be used to stock government granaries and occasionally even provide for civilian famine relief. The reports on prices in different localities throughout the empire thus not only informed the emperor where there were food crises, but also where and when government purchases would be economical because prices were low. Clearly then, the purpose of the reports would be rather pointless if the prices were not comparable from one province to the next.

The prices are given in standardized units of silver. Prices for the grains are reported in units of *taels* (silver ounces) per *shi* of rice, where 1 *shi* equals about 103.8 litres. At the time, the bimetallic system was used in China, with copper commonly used for smaller transactions. Because local currencies and exchange rates varied from place to place, contemporaries in each locality would have had to be well informed about these rates in order to make an accurate conversion from local currencies to the *tael* unit. Could contemporaries have been able to resolve these complexities in such a way that the overall national price for grain in any one region is a meaningful price? Although the different local standards are confusing to us, contemporaries were likely to have been minutely informed on the value of grain in either local copper or in silver because this price determined whether a seller would be willing to part with a certain quantity of grain for a certain amount of metal coin, and whether a buyer would be willing to take a certain quantity of grain while paying out its equivalent price in coin.

Speculative arguments about the reliability (or not) of some one million numbers, however, are not as convincing as statistical tests. Below, I present the results of three methods I have used to see if the price data of the Qing produce patterns that are internally consistent with what we should expect if they do indeed contain systematic information about real prices, as opposed to random noise. These are strategies that can be implemented in other countries and time periods as well. What is key about all of the approaches is that just looking at the price data alone is not enough to establish whether they contain any useful information. One must also find and obtain a secondary data source and see if the two sets of data produce sensible correlations. Of course, the secondary data source needs to be reasonably accurate as well for the procedure to work. Note that if any of the problems that preclude the possibility of trade are present (including confusing currency standards, inaccurate price accounts, etc.), then we would not find any evidence of price correlations between markets that systematically correspond to expected patterns in transaction costs or in local supply proxies. Conversely, because the data have been independently recorded by individuals at different local places, the finding of a systematic pattern to the price across regions can suggest a correspondence to economic conditions of supply, demand, costs of trade and storage.

First, we can ask whether local prices are sensitive to local weather and harvest fluctuations. Since poor (good) harvests and high (low) local prices generally go hand in hand, data on weather can also serve to confirm the validity of the price data. Price correlations are likely to be higher between two markets if, after controlling for bilateral distance, the correlation between weather shocks in the two locations is also higher. In the case of China, this is generally true. Stronger correlations between prices and weather are more likely to occur in regions which are less integrated to other markets (and this fact offers yet another perspective for examining whether the data behave in line with prior expectations), but even in regions that are reasonably well integrated, we might expect that a series of very bad weather shocks will still affect local prices. Weather data for China are available from the State Meteorological Society (1981), which in turn draws on historical compilations; these data enable the ranking of weather in each year on a scale of 1 through 5 on wetness and dryness. For the purposes of this exercise, the extremes are considered poor weather.

The specific estimate is an Ordinary Least Square (OLS) regression between P_t, the mean price recorded in time t in each prefecture across the years 1742–95, and $Q_{j,t}$, the current year t weather in prefecture j, and $Q_{j,t-1}$, last year's weather, and $Q*_{j,t-1}$ is a fixed effect for the worst years of weather. If either the price data or the weather data are composed of random noise, there will be no significant relationship. Examining this relationship over the 121 prefectures of ten provinces, one can establish that prices are indeed affected by weather shocks in the current as well as the previous year, and the worse weather shocks are also significant (Shiue 2002). This relationship is robust to the inclusion of a time trend.

Second, note that the prices were collected by officials in different localities who were supposed to observe prices in their own market. If it were not possible to convert local copper values into a systematic standard unit, such as the *tael*, then we would not be able to detect any correlations across market samples that are systematically related to the costs of transport between markets. Distance is the most sensible variable that captures the cost of transportation. This is because in a relationship of the price correlation between two markets and bilateral distance, if there were nothing but noise from currency conversion problems, then we would find no relationship, even among markets that are very close to each other. However, there is a clear systematic relationship.

For example, consider European market locations (Figure 13.2) and Figure 13.3, which plots the wheat price correlation on distance in kilometres for market pairs, for which we have data in the seventeenth century. A separate line in the same figure plots the same for the eighteenth century. The downward sloping regression line shows that correlations are higher between pairs of markets that are closer

1. Aalst
2. Antwerp
3. Boizenburg
4. Brussels
5. Cologne
6. London
7. Luxemburg
8. Munich
9. Nijmegen
10. Rostock
11. Ruremonde
12. Schwerin
13. Toulouse
14. Utrecht
15. Vienna

0	337.5	675	1,350

Kilometres

Figure 13.2 Map of Europe.

in distance, and this correlation declines as distance increases, precisely what we would expect.

For comparison, Figure 13.4 plots the relationship using the Chinese rice prices for the Yangzi Delta, historically the most commercialized region of China and

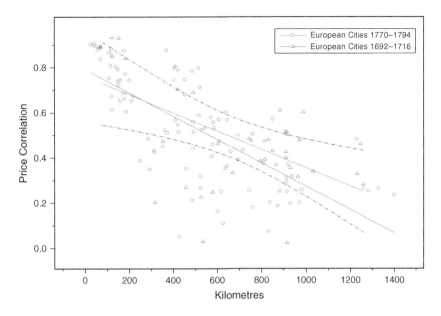

Figure 13.3 European samples, wheat price correlation on distance: seventeenth and
eighteenth centuries compared.

the neighbourhood of modern-day Shanghai. Wheat price correlations are plotted
for central France for comparison. The 95 per cent confidence interval for France
is provided by the dotted lines. The reason for using only the data from within
one country in Europe is because we would expect that transaction costs across
national borders may contribute to lower correlations. In addition, it is worth noting that although rice is used for China and wheat is used for Europe, separate
analyses performed elsewhere, in which we have been able to examine wheat-
producing regions of China, show that in comparisons of this sort it makes little
difference whether rice or wheat is used. What Figure 13.4 shows is that there
is a systematic relationship that depends on distance within the Yangzi Delta –
bilateral price correlations fall as the distance increases between markets because
evidence of trade declines. For historians of China, it will be no surprise that trade
is present – however, this is clear statistical evidence. Moreover, the regression line
for China lies within the confidence interval given for France, demonstrating that
the degrees of market integration in the Yangzi Delta and in central France were
quite comparable in the late eighteenth century.[4] This then is a second empirical
relationship that increases our confidence in the reliability of the Chinese price
data.

A third test makes use of the implied consequence of differences in natural geography. This test is based on the observation that between certain pairs
of markets, costs of transport may be lower than between other pairs of markets. If the data are high quality, then independent records of prices in different

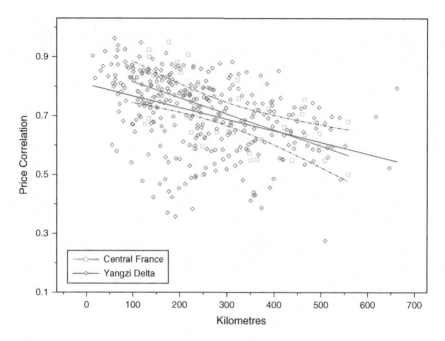

Figure 13.4 Yangzi Delta and France, wheat price correlation on distance, 1770–94.

locations should reveal systematic patterns based on transport costs between markets. Between all market pairs where we would forecast lower transport costs (e.g. such as along a river or canal) we should find a systematic relationship where there are higher bilateral correlations than among market pairs located in high transport cost regions (e.g. such as land-locked provinces). This is because the costs of transport drives a wedge between the price of grain in two markets, and the higher the cost of transport, the larger the price wedge.

Figure 13.5 shows the result of dividing the available Chinese data into two groups, ranked by their relative accessibility to water transport routes. As is well known, prior to steam ships, water transport cut costs of moving commodities dramatically. However, unless there was a river, canal, or navigable coast nearby, land transport was the only option. The two dotted lines show the estimates for China from 1770–94. The upper dotted line depicts the relationship for markets in China located near a river, while the lower dotted line depicts the relationship for provincial capitals. As expected, the estimated relationship produces a higher price correlation for every distance among market pairs located near to a river, compared to the provincial capitals, which were administrative cities, but not necessarily located close to low-cost waterway transport.

I turn now to the question of what the measures of market integration capture in the case of China.

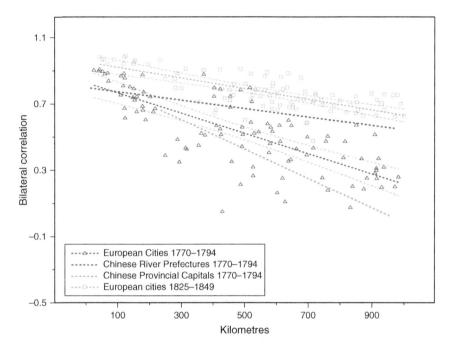

Figure 13.5 China and Europe: bilateral correlation on distance for selected markets over the eighteenth and nineteenth centuries.

Market integration in China

The price data show that market integration in China was higher in areas that were close to natural waterways and transport routes. They also show that markets in China were operating pretty well – not as efficiently as in England, but as well as in central France, a region that was an early industrializer. What is the historical evidence that supports the claim that high degrees of market integration existed in China? What institutions served to create the degree of market integration observed? The bulk of grain circulating in the domestic market likely passed through private hands – peasants, local merchants and long-distance traders. There nevertheless existed a complicated interaction of interests among public and private agents that contributed to the whole set of market supporting institutions. This part of the chapter surveys both the public and private institutions that influenced overall market integration. There are six main aspects of the organization of the grain market of China, which I discuss below:

1 The nature of the buyers and sellers (or the actors) engaged in the grain trade.
2 The manner in which information about prices and quantity was transmitted.
3 Regulation of the marketplace by the government and merchant groups.
4 The maintenance of public roads and other transport routes.

5 The security of property rights.
6 The nature of financial instruments.

Each of these six aspects was critical to the operation of the grain market.

Actors

Most of the direct accounts of trade in eighteenth-century China deal with government officials transporting rice. Far fewer records exist on the role of private merchant trade. In reality, the official shipments were only a minor component of total trade (Chuan and Kraus 1975: 56–8). In the mid-Qing period, official shipments – primarily tribute grain to Beijing and food for soldiers – were about 16.7 per cent of China's total long-distance trade (Xing *et al.*, 2000: 170). Even on the Grand Canal, which was constructed, first and foremost, for the transport of tribute grain and other goods to the capital, the volume of private shipping probably outnumbered the official tonnage (Feuerwerker 1995: 31). If anything, the government was a participant in the private market, rather than a force that controlled the flows of commodities.

Prices were not, as a rule, fixed by official decree. They were allowed to fluctuate according to supply and demand. The most likely scenario in which the government might act to influence grain prices was when grain stocks were shifted from one region to another, or from one period to another in the form of storage. Because the government was a large holder of grain stocks, it had the potential ability to affect prices. However, this statement needs to be qualified. Overall, the government spent as much as 7 per cent of its revenues on famine relief (Shiue 2005a). In areas close to Beijing, where the government was most concerned with riots at its doorstep, and where there were larger holdings of granary stocks from accumulated in-kind taxes and grain tribute across the empire, the supply of grain could well have lowered general grain prices. The supplies may also have kept the price of grain relatively stable. Government grain holdings per capita for other provinces across the empire, however, on average was fairly small even at the peak of the system's operations in the mid-eighteenth century, at around 3 per cent of consumption, or 11 days (see Shiue 2005a). Thus, by the late eighteenth century, outside of the immediate vicinity of the capital, it is at best questionable whether the government had strong influences on the market and the private trade of grain being produced and consumed for most areas of the empire. In addition, as documented by Will *et al.* (1991), after the initial push by the early Qing emperor to build up granary reserves in local places, the system started to deteriorate from the mid-eighteenth century on, so that by the end of the century, shortfalls to the official granary stocking quota were quite commonplace. The reasons for this are many, but one possibility is that local granary managers preferred to hold granary equivalents in cash rather than in grain, so that grain could be purchased on the market in periods of poor local harvest (Shiue 2004). Holding cash would have been a cost-saving alternative to stocking grain if the costs of storage were higher than the costs of trade – which we would expect to be the case in a prefecture relatively well-integrated with surrounding markets.

Who were the main actors in this trade? In China, trade was a relatively specialized activity involving local (petty) traders, brokers, wholesale dealers and itinerant (travelling) merchants. Petty traders worked on a small scale, usually with little capital, and were engaged in retail sales as well as carrying goods between urban centres and rural markets. Brokers (*yahang*) were middlemen engaged in a variety of roles, including supervising payment between buyers and sellers, overseeing delivery, providing information, inspecting for quality and quantity, and serving as guarantor on the exchange (Rowe 1984: 188–9; Mann 1987: 63–5). The broker was also responsible to the merchant for the safety of his goods during shipment, so that if the merchant was swindled, or incurred losses, the broker or shipping agent was obligated to pay compensation (Jing 1994: 59). In return, the brokers earned commission and rental fees for warehousing. Wholesale dealers typically specialized in a single item or a line of items and in some cases partially processed the merchandise.

Merchants varied greatly in their scale of operation, and grain was not a special product that was only traded by certain merchants. Small amounts of grain must have been transacted by small-scale peddlers within the market town, while larger deliveries were made by traders that operated on a larger scale. Some merchants formed networks, typically identified by their common place of origin, such as the merchant networks from Huizhou or Shanxi. A particular merchant network was typically known for its trade in one commodity, such as the Fujian merchants' paper trade (Xing *et al.*, 2000: 180) or the Yangzhou merchants' trade in salt (Ho 1954). Nevertheless, even these merchants frequently carried grain on the return trip. For instance, a large percentage of the rice shipped downriver on the Yangzi River travelled on the ships of the salt merchants of Hankou, who would bring back salt from Yangzhou in Jiangsu (Rowe 1984: 55). What this suggests is that the development of long-distance grain trade was directly linked to the development of long-distance trade overall. Thus, the grain trade cannot be separated from trades in other commodities.

Thus, even though the grain prices were collected by officials for purposes of the government, the government did not transact on a separate market form the rest of the population. Moreover, the distinction between merchants, gentry and officials was blurred, at least by the early eighteenth century. The largest fortunes in Ming–Qing times were as a rule built on domestic and international trade. Although formal Qing laws took a relatively hands-off approach to the daily affairs of trade, this did not mean that there was little interaction between merchants and the state. Many merchants purchased low level official titles or became officials of the state, and officials not only accepted but regularly solicited financial contributions from merchants for government projects. The value of rich merchants to the government was enhanced by their large monetary contributions to the central treasury. The Liang-huai salt merchants contributed more than 36 million *tael*s of silver to the government between 1738 and 1804, not counting the 4.6 million *tael*s spent on the Qianlong emperor's southern tours and the numerous smaller contributions of salt officials (1 *tael* of silver is about 37 grams). Although the merchant guilds authorized to trade out of Canton contributed only 3.95 million *tael*s between 1773 and 1832, the Wu family alone contributed at least 10 million *taels* in three generations. For their contributions merchants were awarded with official titles and ranks, some as high as that of financial commissioner (Ho 1964: 82).

Information

Information about prices, market conditions and travel routes were transmitted in several key ways. First, teahouses and lodges formed meeting points at which merchants, gentry and other members of the marketing community exchanged information, built up relationships, extended credit, coordinated actions and negotiated over deals (Skinner 1964: 37). Second, merchant networks were an important means by which geographically dispersed groups cooperated and shared information about conditions in distant markets. Such groups were well-coordinated internally, and their spread over China amounted to networks of 'commercial intelligence' sharing information on possible production and marketing opportunities. Merchant route books were practical manuals that laid out roads between market towns, giving distances that can be covered in a day, suggestions on where to stay overnight, as well as advice pertaining to commercial transactions (Brook 2002: 3). Third, the Qing state gathered information about agricultural practices, harvest outcomes and market prices. In the case of agricultural technology, written treatises distributed among officials helped to spread information about agricultural techniques that could help to increase land productivity among farmers (Myers and Wang 2002: 599).

Although information on harvests and prices was not widely distributed, local agents nevertheless knew official Qing harvest ratings; tenants, for instance, used the rating to reduce the amount of rent they expected to pay landlords (Marks 1998: 208). It is likely that merchants were aware of this information as well, and it probably spread through market towns and networks quickly. The information flow between merchants and officials occurred in both directions – Qing government officials both imitated merchant trade practices and followed trade routes long established by merchants. As Chuan and Kraus (1975: 66) note, if government officials thought about going to Shandong, for example, to buy grain, it was because they knew merchants frequently did it.

Regulation, trade taxes, measurements and standards

At the local market town or community, itinerant merchants relied both on government-licensed brokers and on guilds (*huiguan*) to assess market prices (Mann 1987: 63–5; Xing *et al.*, 2000: 180, respectively). The brokerage system allowed the state to have an official presence in certain wholesale transactions. The list of commodities subject to brokerage involvement varied from place to place, but in most central market towns it included grain. In Hankou in the mid-Qing period, for instance, there were licensed brokers for 14 agricultural commodities, as well as cotton and silk cloth (Rowe 1984: 186). Although it was illegal to conduct any wholesale transaction without a licensed broker, the requirement was not fully enforced, resulting in a proliferation of unlicensed brokers and eventual protests calling for the removal of the brokerage system altogether in the name of free trade.

Local guilds in China were corporate, self-governing organizations. They provided lodging and services for merchants, helped to calculate profit and loss, and they taught merchants bargaining techniques. Guilds also had discretionary powers to deal with a broad range of functions (Mann 1987: 23), including the establishment of dates that the market was open as well as regulations for sales, deliveries and business conduct more generally (Xing *et al.*, 2000: 180–3; Rowe 1984: 295–6). Unlike the guilds of Europe, where membership was based on residence, Chinese guild organizations were dominated by interregional merchant networks. Thus, while European guilds would often pitch residents (potential importers) against non-residents (potential exporters) and created a barrier to entry for new members, Chinese guilds typically did not keep out arriving merchants from membership (Rowe 1984: 297). One reason for this was that guilds operated on membership dues. Membership in the Hankou rice guild, for instance, cost 15 *tael*s up front and 0.8 per cent of a member's annual gross receipts (Rowe 1984: 301–2).

It appears that neither government brokers nor guilds ever came to dominate the marketplace. Whereas the Qing state saw monopolization and collusive behaviour as a key reason for intervention in the marketplace, the guilds worked to oppose the state brokers and their high commissions (Xing *et al.*, 2000: 180–2). If anything, the state relinquished the task of market regulation to the guilds, as the latter were delegated the unusual privilege of assessing and collecting trade taxes for the state (Mann 1987: 23–4).

The Chinese state also regulated the market directly. In addition to the brokerage tax, the state levied domestic customs, the Imperial maritime customs and later, in the nineteenth century, the *likin* transit tax (Rowe 1984: 181). However, not only was the degree to which guilds restricted competition relatively low in China, but the amount of revenue the Chinese state received from trade taxes appears to have been lower than in Western Europe as well. With the notable exception of England, in Europe there were significant trade taxes within many countries at least through the eighteenth century, in addition to the tariffs between countries. For example, the trade of grain was highly regulated and restricted in eighteenth-century France, and there were also many tolls in the German areas.[5] Revenues from trade taxes were a higher fraction of total revenues in Europe even though over time, the Qing state came to rely relatively more on trade taxes. One reason for this was that the state-licensed brokerage system was increasingly abolished in the nineteenth century (see above). At the same time, the Qing state's relatively stronger reliance on trade taxes during the nineteenth century may just have brought China to where the European countries already were. Consistent with this, the relative importance of land taxation in eighteenth-century China was much higher than in England: by the year 1753, about three-quarters of the total state revenue came from the land tax, declining to 35 per cent by 1908 (Wang Yeh-chien's estimate, reported in Rowe 1984: 181), whereas by 1750 in England, land, income and property taxation accounted for only 29 per cent (Mitchell 1988: 825).

Relative to a situation where measures and monies are standardized, the different currencies and units of measurement used across Europe likely led to higher transaction costs and greater trade barriers. Even within countries, there were persistent variations in measurements. In England, for example, the final demise of local weights and measures did not occur until after 1850 (Mingay 1989: 226–7). Conversion rates into other units and currencies of (local) importance are occasionally available, but they tend to be subject to considerable uncertainties.

In the case of China, there was a consistent effort to ensure that the official unit of accounting for rice prices in terms of *taels* of silver per *shi* was comparable across regions (Chuan and Kraus 1975: 12–14). Nevertheless, there were numerous local weights and measures in use. In addition, local exchange rates between copper cash and silver also varied across regions.[6] Variation in local exchange rates may not have been as large as the variation in totally different currencies in Europe, but they may nevertheless have been an important trade barrier.

Overall, is difficult to say for certain whether the variations in the level of standardization presented a greater problem in China or in Europe since the issues were different. Merchants and other market participants were likely to be aware of and sensitive to variations in measurements and the value of the currency, so that the lack of standardization *per se* would not necessarily make trade impossible, but still, the variations had to be sorted out by local buyers and sellers. For example, the 1678 Rice Market Guild of Hankou stated that

> when any [guild member] acts as a wholesale rice broker for an itinerant merchant in the transactions of his business, the weights and measures employed in the transaction much first be submitted to the guild for approval, rather than adoption on an individual basis.
>
> (Rowe 1984: 295)

In this regard, guilds may have reduced the transaction costs since common local units of measurement were chosen and partly enforced by the guilds.

Maintenance

The maintenance of transport routes was critical for the transport of grain. The Qing state devoted some 10 per cent of its total revenues to public projects, and also effectively supplied the necessary technology, especially for large-scale projects such as flood control and maintenance of the navigability of the Yellow River and the Grand Canal. The state was also active in organizing local communities in the upkeep of transport routes, dykes, bridges and roads (Naquin and Rawski 1987: 23; Myers and Wang 2002: 597). When provincial officials received an order to undertake a project, they called on local leaders to help finance the work. The costs of the repairs would usually come mainly from cash contributions of local landowners, gentry and merchants, and labour contributions of tenant households. These efforts probably benefited the economies nearby to some extent, although it remains unclear whether public goods were still undersupplied.

Also in Europe, local authorities were initially responsible for maintaining transport infrastructure. In France, the central government finally assumed control over new investments along the major roads leading into Paris, but it did not improve secondary roads, leaving instead local governments responsible for them. After 1700 in England, however, the transport infrastructure was improved because maintenance was entrusted to private organizations created by Acts of Parliament (turnpike trusts and river navigation companies).[7]

Security and property rights

Predation and extortion by bandits, pirates and governments alike threatened the trade of merchants both in China and in Europe. Some Chinese merchant route books note the locations of not only police stations but also bandit hideouts (Tong 1991: 146). In England, farmers, millers and corn dealers at times of bad harvests in the late eighteenth century were often stopped and had their loads seized, in spite of significant penalties (Mingay 1989: 234–5), and arbitrary tolls imposed by local rulers in continental Europe were effectively another form of extortion. It is difficult, however, to assess how the overall security risks for traders in China compared with those in Europe. Qing laws sanctioned bandit activity with capital punishment, while predation and extortion of merchants by Qing officials or by local gentry was illegal and also subject to severe punishment. Nevertheless, capturing the bandits could be difficult, especially in harsh terrain. Complementing the Qing state, a variety of private activities emerged to provide security. For example, civilians joined forces with local military commanders, and local communities raised bounties to reward soldiers (Tong 1991: 85). Large-scale merchants were also known to commission a merchant-militia for protection while travelling.

The Qing Code, the formal legal framework of Qing China, contains many articles related to property, such as on theft, sale of property belonging to others and trespassing (Jing 1994: 43–4). Legal protection from acts of government officials as well as private agents was afforded to all privately owned property, regardless of whether it was held by individuals or lineages. The laws applied also to disputes among family members, so that intra-familial property disputes were not off-limits to the laws of the empire. Other laws forbade monopolization and price collusion, especially by government brokers, and prohibited counterfeiting and the use of fraudulent weights and measures in trade. It appears that the court system was widely used and that official arbitration of property disputes was available for poor people as well as for the better off. For instance, civil cases accounted for about a third of the total case load of local courts in a study by Huang (1996: 11).[8]

Fundamentally, however, the Qing Code was not designed for the reconciliation of conflicting private economic interests. Rather, the emphasis was on maintaining public order by providing incentives for lawful behaviour through the threat of punishment (Huang 1996, 107). For instance, the law on bridge maintenance simply states the following: 'If there is injury to the bridges and roads, and there is neglect in repairing them, hindering traffic along the routes, then the supervisory official and clerk will receive 30 strokes of the light bamboo.'[9] In contrast with the written laws of the British Commonwealth, there is little in Qing laws on what evidence is needed before judgement on guilt is passed, and how the punishment is to be enforced.

With respect to the legal framework for trade, merchant guilds probably played a greater role than the Qing Code. They established rules for business conduct and means of contractual documentation (Rowe 1984: 295). Merchant guilds were also involved in adjudicating disputes (Mann 1987: 23). In short, the guilds supplied a wide range of legal functions – sometimes called 'customary' or informal – both independently of the state and in parallel to official notions of justice. Private (white) contracts were legally valid and eventually outnumbered official (red) contracts, which were stamped official versions registered for a fee with the local government headquarters. There does not appear to have been much of a contradiction or competition between the official and the customary laws since customary practice was judged within the official code, and conversely, private written contracts were enforced in the ruling of the Qing official's court when disputes arose. The system allowed legally recognized and enforced written commercial agreements to be routinely circulated, from shipping orders to bills of loading to promissory notes to contracts of sale (Rowe 1984: 75 and Chapter 5, this volume). In this sense, the legal framework for trade was present in China (see Naquin and Rawski 1987: 102 and Jing 1994: 42).

Financial instruments

The involvement of the Qing state in financial institutions was relatively limited, but the state was not inactive: state-controlled customs banks issued certain notes and stored customs revenue collected by the government. There were also government-owned pawnshops. Another important area controlled by the state was the bimetallic monetary system of the Qing period, based on silver and copper cash, which produced some seigniorage revenue. There was, however, no formal regulatory agency responsible for overseeing financial administration and banking.

Many innovations in the area of credit and banking in the Qing period can be traced to private merchant activity. From the early Qing period, merchants purchased peasants' agricultural products and handiworks by paying money in advance, and this became an important method for purchasing commodities in rural areas. Financial institutions of various types often took deposits and made loans. Among the most important were the so-called *yinhao* ('native banks') and *piaohao* ('currency stores') (Zurndorfer 2004). During the Qianlong era (1736–95), native banks conducted local money exchanges, accepted deposits, issued private banknotes, and lent money to partnerships in the local market (Zhou 2000, Rowe 1984: 161). There exist some similarities with early deposit banks in Europe (Mann Jones 1972: 47). In contrast to the local focus of the native banks, the currency stores dealt with interregional transactions, often having several branches all over the empire, and were related to the merchant networks. The *piaohao* were closer than the *yinhao* to being a state institution in banking, since the government used these banks for deposits and required that companies desiring to found similar institutions be endorsed by the members of the established banks (Mann Jones 1972: 50). These financial institutions issued promissory notes payable in the future, and facilitated the movement of goods and money over long distances through innovations in credit.

It appears that some merchants entered the banking business as a means of capitalizing their commercial projects (Rowe 1984: 162). The private paper money issued by these banks may have constituted as much as one-third of total money in circulation in the mid-Qing period (see also Kaixiang Peng, Chapter 17, this volume). Thus, even though the Qing state did not issue paper notes, it permitted merchants to transform the monetary economy into one where paper notes circulated widely (Naquin and Rawski 1987: 101; 104–5).

That these banks developed relatively free from government involvement meant both little obstructionism and little constructive support. The establishment of ties and contract enforcement between creditors and debtors was mostly informal, and often based on kinship, common origin, or otherwise established through the merchant networks. This was especially true of the Shanxi merchants, for example, who relied on network connections to facilitate transactions between their operations in North China and the Yangzi Delta (Wong 2002). There were also Hunanese merchants that operated through an interlocked chain of banks at various points of their trade route (Rowe 1984: 162), and merchants from neighbouring provinces to the north who dominated Sichuan's financial institutions for most of the Qing period (Zelin 1993: 88). While we know that the interregional transactions were served by the *piaohao*, there is still the question of what extent of access to credit was available for non-members of the interregional networks.

There is suggestive evidence that China's financial institutions were multifaceted and extensive, but to date there is little quantitative evidence on the size and the performance of China's banking and credit sector during the eighteenth and nineteenth centuries in comparison to those in Europe. The most pronounced difference between Europe and China, at least from the point of view of the secondary literature, revolves around the notion of the predatory state (North and Weingast 1989). National monarchs of Europe emerged from the chaos and instability of the Middle Ages as a force of unity and power. However, as the power to tax and raise emergency revenue to fight wars evolved and became synonymous with an arbitrary and unchecked power to expropriate, the government itself and the unchecked power that it brokered became the central problem. Thus institutional innovations that had the effect of constraining the arbitrary power of the crown occupy a central place in the history of Europe. In China, tax revenues as a percentage of national income was on the whole less than in Europe, partly due to the fact that expensive international warfare was not the main preoccupation of the early Qing emperors, but also because emperors were effectively constrained by precedents set by their ancestors. Tax quotas were rolled over from one year to the next, and it would have been impossible to arbitrarily raise them. In fact, shortages of revenue did become problematic towards the end of the dynasty, and even then, the lack of effective instruments to allow for government borrowing and for the raising of tax revenue limited the ability of the state carry out its functions.

Conclusion

This chapter has examined grain price data from the Qing period. The rice prices produce consistent implications when examined in the light of separate series on supply shocks, trade costs between markets and geographic location. The fact that we can establish these systematic patterns suggests not only that the data are of high quality, but that institutions existed that allowed such trades to take place.

The second section of the chapter provided an overview of the specific institutions in China that allowed trade to be possible. These aspects are important because marketplace activity requires the presence of contracts or agreements, laws, and an authority (such as the government or the local community) to enforce agreed-upon rules of engagement between buyers and sellers. There are different institutional forms that can serve this purpose. In contemporary, developed countries, formal, legal recourse in court under a set of predefined laws allows markets to operate smoothly. Prior to formal, enforceable, national laws, the city-based trades of Europe relied on the market power of the group in enforcing contractual agreements.

Since better-enforced laws and institutions should give rise to better-performing markets, we can indirectly measure and compare the level of institutional strength across countries by measuring the degree of market integration. This approach is attractive since directly quantifying the quality of institutions is exceedingly difficult and rarely leads to uniform opinion, while quantifying the function of markets with available price data are a much more straightforward task. With the exception of England, where markets were more efficient at shorter distances, up until the eighteenth century, Chinese markets functioned as well as markets in Western Europe. The comparison of eighteenth century European market integration to nineteenth century levels of integration is given in Figure 13.5. The line which lies between the dotted lines is the estimate of price correlations on distance for European cities from 1770–94. Clearly, it lies below the level of integration of the well-connected Chinese markets, but above the Chinese administrative capital cities. This suggests that whatever advantages Europe had in terms of institutional efficiencies, once we aggregate everything that contributed to market performance, markets in continental Europe were not performing better than Chinese markets. However, this situation changes dramatically by the early nineteenth century, 1825–49. The upper regression line captures the level of bilateral price correlation among European markets in the early nineteenth century, and shows that there was a significant improvement over the level of integration in Europe only fifty years earlier.

A frequent point of emphasis in the history of Europe is the constraint of power of the predatory state (North and Weingast 1989). In the Qing period, the emperor was always constrained by the precedents of tax quotas set by previous emperors, so this issue does not have the same traction. However, in China, the emphasis of the Great Qing Code on maintaining public order, through the threat of corporal punishment, rather than judicial process, may explain why customary laws originating from merchant guilds created a wide range of legal functions that operated in parallel to formal laws, although not necessarily independently from them. Instead, public and private institutions evolved endogenously, each influencing the other.

Merchant guilds of China occupied a more important role than formal laws in enforcing the framework for trade, compared to the European context, which had to do with the inability of the government to provide certain types of public goods. Part of the reason was that, for the most part, tax revenues that went to the central government during the Qing period were relatively low. Instead, the government tended to delegate certain tasks of maintaining public goods to local leaders and merchant groups. Thus, China did have institutions to support markets, but they looked very different from their European counterparts. Merchants groups, typically identified by a common place of origin and kinship, used their social capital to help build a coordinating framework for trade that relied on social enforcements, establishing trust within a network of traders with a shared lineage of certain merchant rights. There are limits, in theory, to the scope of private merchant networks. If new networks cannot form, and membership in the existing network increases, it can become increasingly difficult for a large group to rely on social capital to enforce honesty. However, since historical evidence suggests that markets in advanced areas of China were as integrated as those in continental Western Europe up to the first quarter of the nineteenth century, it is debatable whether those limits had yet been reached. Future work that provides a more detailed comparison with Western legal frameworks will prove useful for understanding different notions of property rights, how the rules of marketplace transactions were enforced and who enforced these rules.

Notes

1 This discussion draws on background material from Shiue and Keller (2007).
2 These data can be downloaded via the links to Shiue and Keller (2007) at www.aeaweb.org. Additional price data are available through a database initiated by Wang Yeh-chien at https://140.209.152.38.
3 For more details on the origin, functions, purposes and reliability of the grain price reporting system in the Qing Dynasty, see Wilkinson (1969) and Chuan and Kraus (1975).
4 This qualifies Ken Pomeranz's claim that markets in China were comparable to those in Europe – we find that they were comparable only to those in continental Europe, but not England. Markets in England were clearly more integrated. See Shiue and Keller (2007).
5 For example, see Kaplan (1984) on France, and Henderson (1939) on the pre-*Zollverein* situation in Germany. An analysis of the economic effects of the *Zollverein* can be found Shiue (2005b).
6 Vogel (1987: 30–1) reports some local copper exchange rates for Jiangsu and Zhejiang provinces.
7 Jackman (1962) is the classic reference for England; see also Bogart (2005) for recent work on these issues.
8 Also see Buxbaum (1971: 268) and Bernhardt and Huang (1994: 5).
9 Board of Works Article 436 Repairing Bridges and Roads; in Qing (1994: 412).

Bibliography

Bernhardt, K. and Huang, Ph. C. C., eds. 1994. 'Civil Law in Qing and Republican China: The Issues', in *Civil Law in Qing and Republican China*, edited by K. Bernhardt and Ph. C. C Huang, Stanford: Stanford University Press: 1–12.

Bogart, D. 2005. 'Did Turnpike Trusts Increase Transportation Investment in Eighteenth-Century England?', *Journal of Economic History* 65: 439–68.

Brook, T. 2002. *Geographical Sources of Ming-Qing History*, 2nd edition, Ann Arbor: Center for Chinese Studies, University of Michigan.

Buxbaum, D. C. 1971. 'Some Aspects of Civil Procedure and Practice at the Trial Level in Tanshui and Hsinchu from 1789 to 1895', *Journal of Asian Studies*, 30: 255–79.

Chuan Han-sheng, and Kraus, R. A. 1975. *Mid-Ch'ing Rice Markets and Trade: An Essay in Price History*, Cambrdige MA: Harvard University Press.

Feuerwerker, A. 1995. *Studies in the Economic History of Late Imperial China*, Ann Arbor MI: University of Michigan Press.

Henderson, W. O. 1939. *The Zollverein*, Cambridge: Cambridge University Press.

Ho Ping-ti. 1954. 'The Salt Merchants of Yang-chou', *Harvard Journal of Asiatic Studies*, 17: 130–68.

—— 1964. *The Ladder of Success in Imperial China: Aspects of Social Mobility*, Cambridge MA: Harvard University Press.

Huang, Ph. C. C. 1996. *Civil Justice in China. Representation and Practice in the Qing*, Stanford: Stanford University Press.

Jackman, W. T. 1962. *The Development of Transportation in Modern England*, 2nd edition, London: Frank Cass & Company Ltd.

Jing Junjian. 1994. 'Legislation Related to the Civil Economy in the Qing', in *Civil Law in Qing and Republican China*, edited by K. Bernhardt and Ph. C. C Huang, Stanford: Stanford University Press: 42–84.

Kaplan, S. L. 1984. *Provisioning Paris*, Ithaca: Cornell University Press.

Mann, S. 1987. *Local Merchants and the Chinese Bureaucracy, 1750–1950*, Stanford: Stanford University Press.

Mann Jones, Susan. 1972. 'Finance in Ningpo: The "Ch'ien Chuang", 1750–1850', in *Economic Organization in Chinese Society*, edited by W. E. Willmott, Stanford: Stanford University Press: 47–77.

Marks, R. B. 1998. *Tigers, Rice, Silk, and Silt*, Cambridge: Cambridge University Press.

Mingay, G., ed. 1989. *The Agrarian History of England and Wales*, Volume VI, *1750–1850*, Cambridge: Cambridge University Press.

Mitchell, B. R. 1988. *British Historical Statistics*, Cambridge: Cambridge University Press.

Myers, R. H. and Wang Yeh-Chien. 2002. 'Economic Developments, 1644–1800', in *The Cambridge History of China*, edited by W. J. Peterson, Volume 9, Part 1, Cambridge: Cambridge University Press: 563–645.

Naquin, S. and Rawski, E. S. 1987. *Chinese Society in the Eighteenth Century*, New Haven: Yale University Press.

North, D. C. and Weingast, B. 1989. 'Constitutions and Commitment: Evolution of Institutions Governing Public Choice in Seventeenth Century England', *Journal of Economic History*, 51: 23–46.

Qing Code. 1994. *The Great Qing Code*, translated by William C. Jones, Oxford: Oxford University Press.

Rowe, W. T. 1984. *Hankow. Commerce and Society in a Chinese City, 1796–1889*, Stanford: Stanford University Press.

Shiue, C. H. 2002. 'Transport Costs and the Geography of Arbitrage in Eighteenth Century China', *The American Economic Review*, 92: 1406–19.

—— 2004. 'Local Granaries and Central Government Disaster Relief: Moral Hazard and Intergovernmental Finance in 18th and 19th Century China', *Journal of Economic History*, 64: 101–25.

—— 2005a. 'The Political Economy of Famine Relief in China, 1740–1820', *Journal of Interdisciplinary History*, 36: 33–55.

—— 2005b. 'From Political Fragmentation towards the Nation State: Border Effects of the German Zollverein, 1815 to 1855', *European Review of Economic History*, 9: 129–62.

Shiue, C. H. and Keller, W. 2007. 'Markets in China and Europe on the Eve of the Industrial Revolution', *The American Economic Review*, 97: 1189–216.

Skinner, G. W. 1964. 'Marketing and Social Structure in Rural China: Part I,' *Journal of Asian Studies*, 24: 3–43.

State Meteorological Society. 1981. *Zhongguo jin wubai nien hanloa fenbu tuji* [Collected maps of droughts and floods in China in the past five hundred years], Beijing: *Ditu chuban she*.

Tong, J. W. 1991. *Disorder under Heaven*, Stanford: Stanford University Press.

Vogel, H. U. 1987. 'Chinese Central Monetary Policy, 1644–1800', *Late Imperial China*, 8 (2): 1–52.

Wilkinson, E. 1969. 'The Nature of Chinese Grain Price Quotations, 1600–1900', *Transactions of the International Conference of Orientalists in Japan/Kokusai Toho Gakusha Kaigi Kiyo*, 14: 54–65.

Will, P.-E., Wong, R. Bin, Lee, James, Oi, Jean and Perdue, P. 1991. *Nourish the People*, Ann Arbor: University of Michigan Press.

Wong, R. Bin. 2002. 'The Search for European Differences and Domination in the Early Modern World: A View from Asia', *American Historical Review*, 107: 447–69

Xing Fang, Shi Qi, Jian Rui and Wang Shixin. 2000. 'The Growth of Commodity Circulation and the Rise of Merchant Organisations', in *Chinese Capitalism, 1522–1840*, edited by Xu Dixin and Wu Cheng-Ming, New York: St Martin's Press: 165–83 (first published in Chinese in 1985:165–83).

Zelin, Madeleine. 1993. 'The Rise and Fall of the Fu-Rong Salt-Yard Elite: Merchant Dominance in Late Qing China', in *Chinese Local Elites and Patterns of Dominance*, edited by J. W. Esherick and M. B. Rankin, Berkeley: University of California Press: 82–109.

Zhou Yumin. 2000. *Wan Qing caizhen yu shebui bianqian*, Shanghai: Shanghai renmin chubanshe.

Zurndorfer, H. T. 2004. 'Imperialism, Globalization, and Public Finance: The Case of Late Qing China', *Global Economic History Network Working Paper* No. 06/04, London: London School of Economics.

Part IV
Markets and money

14   The circulation of coins in Syria and Mesopotamia in the sixth to first centuries BC[1]

Frédérique Duyrat

Introduction

According to the last studies of our best archaeological source, the invention of coinage dates back to the end of the seventh century BC: the foundations of the temple of Artemis in Ephesos. From the very beginning of the fifth century BC, more than one hundred mints are known to have operated in the Mediterranean region.[2] The wide circulation of the Athenian owl coinage since the mid-fifth century BC till the end of the fourth century BC is followed by the wider success of the silver coins and gold staters of Alexander the Great struck by the conqueror and his successors almost everywhere in the Empire.[3] During that time, hundreds of mints were opened in the Greek world, for both huge and tiny outputs.

The role of money is crucial in every economy, but money is not necessarily coined. This is the first point to remember: studying coinage is not studying money; the economy can use means of payment other than coins. The production of coinage during Greek times never covered the whole economic activity. F. de Callataÿ gave a clear demonstration of that phenomenon in his study of the Mithridatic wars. In spite of the large output of many mints in the name of Mithridates VI or his allies and enemies during the wars against Rome, the coins issued couldn't cover even the expenses of Mithridates' armies. A large part remained paid in kind.[4] This leads to the conclusion that coinage attests only a part of the economic activities, others, quite hard to evaluate, being covered by other means of exchange.

The second point to remember is that our knowledge of ancient coinage is partial: coins are scattered in museums, archaeological depositories and on the market of antiquities. These impediments explain why corpora are so rare compared with the number and variety of mints and coinages to be studied.

Can numismatic studies improve our knowledge of the integration of the market? Or of the general frame of the economy? To answer such questions, we need to give a view as complete as possible of our source. It is not an easy task and a complete overview can't be done. This is the reason why it is an absolute necessity to consider the whole material available if we want to shed light on the role of struck money in ancient economies. For now, a complete view on that subject remains a *pium desiderium*. But it is possible to propose a case study for one region, an exercise that would allow us to build a method and emphasize the limits of such a study. I tried it on Syria, in the most general sense: from the Mediterranean to the Euphrates and from the southern limit of the Taurus Mountains to Gaza. This area is a margin of Mesopotamia, the starting point of the present volume, but it is also an interface with the Mediterranean world and one of the cores of the polycentric empires of the Achaemenids and the Seleucids.

I start my enquiry at the very end of the sixth century BC[5] and go on till the last years of the first century BC. Such an elongated period is necessitated by the material I study: the coin hoards and the excavation coins found in Syria. To have a complete view of those specific sources, we must consider their whole evolution, from the very beginning till the end of the Hellenistic period.

During these five centuries, Syria was ruled by the Achaemenids and the Seleucids, with several usurpations and invasions (Armenian, Parthian, Roman) at the end of the period. The sources for economic history in Syria during this period are rather scarce compared with those for Babylonia.[6]

There is no hope to have a view, even partial, on prices. But our knowledge of the monetary situation of the area is better than ever and allows us to have a long-term overview of monetary supplies. It cannot be complete and we have to take precautions in our interpretations, but the role of coinage in ancient economies cannot be ignored. Therefore, the aim of this chapter is to propose a case study on coinage in Syria – its circulation and some conclusions on the information it gives us on the regional economy and its integration.

The first part of this chapter details the features of the 356 hoards and 58 publications of coins from legal excavations I gathered. It is far from complete, especially because to go through the Israeli archaeological data are an endless task. The following sections will propose some interpretations of the data.

Numismatic sources

The provenance of coins is of two kinds: hoards and excavations. Both sources are not regular in time and space. The archaeological activity is not the same in all the countries of the Near East. Israel developed a remarkably active service and has a large staff of numismatists of international rank. Thus our archaeological information is denser in the southern Levant. I selected 58 sites in the whole area, some giving large amounts of coins, others being only small towns or villages and having provided less than ten bronzes.

Hoards give a different view: most are found in an illegal context and their distribution is closely linked with the ancient history of the area. I tried to gather all the hoards attributed to the Syrian area in the available literature.

Hoards

The complete catalogue of the 356 Syrian hoards is beyond the scope of this article but should be published soon with an accompanying bibliography. Most of the data are conveniently found in the *Inventory of Greek Coin Hoards* (*IGCH*)[7] and the *Coin Hoards* series (*CH*). The aim of these inventories is 'to record new hoards as they enter museums or as they pass through the coin trade' and 'to compile a bibliography on hoards published or discussed during the previous year'.[8]

These series only give short descriptions of the lots and bibliographical references when they exist. Most of them have been published in scientific articles and books whose conclusions are integrated in my commentary. The data are growing quickly and it is now extremely difficult to give an accurate catalogue since new hoards regularly appear on the market of antiquities. Unfortunatly, most of the hoards have been discovered in illegal circumstances. Only 12 per cent of the 356 in our catalogue come from legal excavations. But the comparison between the data from scientific provenance and that from trade hoards show that, most of the time, results of both sources are consistent.[9]

Excavations

There is a contrast between the origin of silver and bronze coins. Silver coins are almost never found isolated in excavations. Of the 58 excavations I gathered, 20 had between one and six silver coins. A more striking example is the agora of Athens: of the 14,600 coins dated from the sixth to the first century BC, less than 1 per cent were made of precious metal, that is electrum,[10] gold and silver.[11]

The 356 hoards found in Syria between the sixth and the first centuries BC give a total of about 60,000 coins, mostly in silver: 313 hoards of the 356 contain silver (87.9 per cent). The silver coins isolated in excavations number about 120 (i.e. only 120 silver coins in total were discovered as stray finds). Clearly, excavations are our best source on bronze coins, but we need the hoards to know the silver.

Corpora

The best medium to pinpoint ancient coin production is to publish die corpora of mints or rulers. The dies are the two tools used to punch a plain metal blank with the obverse and reverse types carved on it. A large series of coins giving a good sample allows the numismatist to recognize the original dies. Then a statistical study can say if the sample is representative of the original production and what extent it had.

To gather a corpus means visiting public coin collections, going through numismatic auctions (today mostly electronic), and as far as possible knowing the results of the excavations within the territory of the city or kingdom studied. Once the coins are gathered, the die study allows the numismatist to calculate how many dies were used and evaluate the original output. Each corpus is a huge work and very few are available for ancient Syria.

During the Achaemenid period, the mints are concentrated on the Mediterranean shore. Only two have received a complete die study (by J. and A.G. Elayi): Sidon and Tyre. Studies of Arwad and Byblos are in progress by the same authors.[12] Our knowledge of coinage of the Hellenistic period is not much better than that of the preceding period and the main publications also focus on the Phoenician shore: Arados (Arwad)[13] and Berytos[14] are now published, and

G. Le Rider wrote the catalogue of the Seleucid mint of Antioch on the Orontes, but excluding the bronze coinage.[15] Some die studies of isolated series exist for other mints, but they are quite hard to compare without the background of the whole output.

The scholarship is far from illustrating the variety and rich output of the Syrian mints during the Achaemenid and Hellenistic periods. So, no synthesis of the whole production exists. To publish die studies of mints remains the principal task to improve our knowledge of the role of coinage in ancient economies. For instance, during the sole reign of Antiochos III (222–187 BC), one of the most powerful Seleucid kings whose empire extended from the Hellespont to India, twenty-one royal mints are firmly identified and several others are suspected.[16] A complete study of their output would be a remarkable improvement of our knowledge of the economic frame of his reign.

Coins were produced by royal mints but also by civic ones during the Achaemenid and Hellenistic periods. An interesting study by L. Mildenberg gives an overview of the origin of coins in the Persian Empire; synthesis for the Achaemenid and Hellenistic times by G. Le Rider and C. Augé are also available.[17] During the Hellenistic period, dozens of mints were operating.

Conclusion

Coins are an archaeological source, as incomplete as are all the data we obtain from earth. But excavations inform us on bronze, and hoards on silver, gold remaining scarce in both cases. Moreover, a large majority of our silver coins come from the black market of art: they have been unearthed illegally and we are totally incapable of giving them an archaeological context. To add to this disappointing conclusion, our knowledge of ancient coinages is weakened by the lack of corpora.

But despite these faults, coins shed some light on ancient economies. At this point, it is only a partial drawing of what they were, a basic information that can only be improved as more corpora, publications of excavations and other numismatic studies are published.

Geography of circulation

Coins are not everywhere in ancient Syria. For instance, maps of eastern hoards allowed me to show, several years ago, that silver coins were hoarded only along the Mediterranean shore (broadly conceived) including the Beqa'a Valley and the west bank of the Tiberias Lake and the Dead Sea. East of this area, hoards are well represented along the road leading from Aleppo/Beroia to the foot of the Taurus range, then running southward along the Tigris River to Babylon, crossing Babylonia to the Euphrates River and following its bank to Elam and the Persian Gulf. Eastward, hoards are scarce and only found in the 'silk road' oases.[18] The excavations confirm the geography of coin finds: they are scarce or non-existent in excavations eastward of the Anti-Lebanon, the Jordan Valley and the Dead Sea.[19]

The concentration of hoards and archaeological coins in the Mediterranean area and their scarcity in the hinterland lead to a first conclusion: the role of coinage in the economy is limited to this area. Eastward, exchanges and accumulation of wealth were done in kind: crops, raw metal, etc. But the use of coinage is a subtle matter. In the eastern zone, some places deliver many coins. For instance, Jebel Khalid, a fortress on the Euphrates in an area without a mint, delivered 267 coins dated from Alexander the Great to the first century BC. C.E.V. Nixon, the editor of the coins, linked this particularity with the important Seleucid garrison that occupied the fortress during the whole period. Coins disappeared from the site at the same time as the royal soldiers. During their presence, the fortress had a monetary economy in an area without coins. In these desert regions, only cities and some military camps used coins, creating coinage zones in non-coinage ones. The Seleucid administration centres and the garrisons probably increased the coin needs for they were paid and met their own expenses in coins rather than in kind.

The contrasts between the east and west areas of Syria are probably not only regional. N. Cahill's careful study of Olynthus emphasized strong differences of means of payments inside a single city. Olynthus, in the Chalcidic Peninsula, in northern Greece, is a most interesting site: the settlement is narrowly dated between 432 and 348 BC. In 348 BC Philip II, king of Macedonia, captured the city and sold its inhabitants as slaves. The city was abandoned till the twentieth century AD. Large excavations between AD 1928 and 1938 revealed over 100 houses and provided much information on the daily life and economic activities of the city. It also shed light on the use of coinage:

> It is immediately clear from the distribution plan that coins are particularly concentrated in the area around the agora at the south end of the North Hill. On average, the houses at Olynthus contain about 20 coins per house. The houses within a block or so of the agora, however, average more than four times as many coins. Considered another way, ten of the fifteen houses at Olynthus with the greatest number of coins adjoin the square, and two more are a block away.[20]

Of 4,638 coins found at Olynthos, 4,237 were bronze. They were lost by their owners and never recovered. Their concentration in the agora area emphasizes a larger use of coins in daily transactions. Many other shops and workshops are well-attested in the city, but nowhere is there such a concentration of small change. Coins are especially scarce in the 'villa area', in the south-east borough of Olynthos. From these data we may conclude that the use of coins is not the same in the different areas of a city, even when there are shops everywhere. The agora is the principal place where coins are needed in daily transactions.

We have no comparable studies in Syria: no large city has been totally excavated, none has been abandoned without being settled again later. Antioch, Seleucia, Apamea, Jerusalem and the Phoenician cities are still inhabited or only partially excavated. But it is highly probable that within the same town, some exchanges demanded coins and others not.

History of circulation

The first hoards in Syria are exclusively made of foreign coinages since c. 625 BC till the mid-fifth century BC. The Athenian owls enjoyed an obvious popularity: they are found in 63.2 per cent of the hoards dated to the fifth century BC. The Phoenician mints started issuing around the 450s BC. The increase of their output during the fourth century BC gives them a leading place in the hoards: they are represented in 71.8 per cent of the hoards.

The big change dates back to the Macedonian conquest. In 333 BC, Alexander the Great entered Phoenicia with his armies. They camped in the continental area of Arados on the Syrian coast during the 333/332 BC winter. But deep monetary modifications can be noticed only after 325 BC, when the Asia Minor mints began a coin production with Alexander-types and the output of the Eastern mints increased.[21] The real increase of the output of Alexander tetradrachms in Syria and drachmas in western Asia Minor is due to the Diadochi after the death of Alexander, around 320 BC. These noticeable changes are visible in hoarding: between 333 and 325 BC, only three hoards contain Alexander's tetradrachms. The first hoard exclusively made of Alexander coins dates back to 325–324 BC.[22] After 325 BC, and for the next twenty years, Alexander tetradrachms are virtually the only currency in Syrian hoards.

From Alexander to the Roman conquest, during the first century BC, the monetary history of Syria is particularly rich. To give a detailed overview of the output and rulers is beyond the scope of this volume chapter, but a general frame is necessary. Political changes obviously have a strong influence on coinage. From 301 to 200 BC, Syria is separated between the Seleucid kingdom, north of the Eleutheros River, and the Ptolemaic possessions to the south. Ptolemy I conquered Koile Syria in 301 BC, restoring the traditional glacis that protected Egypt against Asian invasions during the Pharaonic period. At the same time he imposed his own currency with a light standard and a limited circulation: Ptolemaic coins were not supposed to be in use out of the Ptolemaic possessions and implied a coin change at the border, especially in the harbours (Alexandria and the harbours of Phoenicia and Cyprus). In contrast, the Seleucid accepted every silver coinage of the Attic standard, having their possessions largely provided by foreign currencies.

The main changes happened during the second century BC. First of all, Antiochos III drove the Ptolemies out of Koile Syria during the Fifth Syrian War (202–198 BC). But he maintained his predecessors' monetary system: light silver standard and Ptolemaic coin types continued to be in use in this special area of the Seleucid kingdom (Figure 14.1).[23] This means that Ptolemaic tetradrachms were authorized to cross the border between the two kingdoms and that economic transactions were not cancelled by the new political situation. But during Alexander I Balas' reign (150–145 BC), a new disruption occurred. The royal mints of southern Syria started minting coins of the Ptolemaic standard but with the Seleucid king's portrait (Figure 14.2) and the Ptolemaic silver issues quickly disappeared from the area. The 140s BC mark an important turning point in coin circulation: Ptolemaic coins are not the only ones to vanish; foreign tetradrachms that have been so

Figure 14.1 Tetradrachm, Ptolemy II, BnF MMA Dattari Z 2884,166.

Figure 14.2 Tetradrachm, Alexander I Balas, BnF MMA FG 893.

Figure 14.3 Tetradrachm, Lebedos (Ionia), BnF MMA Henri Seyrig 1973.1.155.

frequently found in hoards of the Attic weight area became scarce. It is particularly noticeable because since the 150s BC, civic tetradrachms issued by cities of Asia Minor were the principal currency buried in Syria,[24] when they were scarce everywhere else, even in Asia Minor. They were easily identified because most of them were adorned with a wreath around the reverse type (Figure 14.3 and Figure 14.4).[25]

The removal of such common issues (i.e. the disappearance of Ptolemaic silver issues and foreign tetradrachms, which were common before) is contemporary with a significant increase in the royal Seleucid output. We lack die and mint studies, but the development of royal coinage is indubitable from the beginning of the second century BC. The tetradrachm issues of Antioch are a good example of this phenomenon (see Figure 14.5), although our figures run only to Antiochus V (164–162/1 BC).[26]

And the increase goes on during the following reigns. A. Houghton's preliminary study gives ten obverse dies a year under Demetrius I's rule in Antioch.[27]

Figure 14.4 Tetradrachm, Myrina (Aeolis), BnF MMA Henri Seyrig R2099.

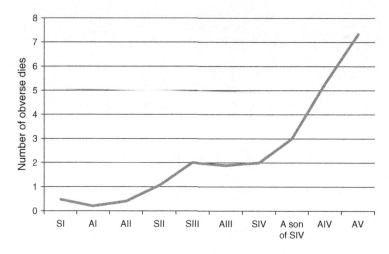

Figure 14.5 Tetradrachms obverse dies per year at Antioch.

Note:
S = Seleucus; A = Antiochus.

Seleucid Coins identifies a probable 37 mints in activity in the reign of Antiochus IV (175–164 BC).[28] The growth of the royal output is illumined by the change in the hoards' composition. From the 140s BC, the share of Seleucid royal coinage increases. They are found in more hoards and their share dominates everywhere (compare Figure A14.12, Figure A14.13 and Figure A14.14 in Appendix 14.C).

Alexander I Balas' reign seems to have been a turning point in Seleucid monetary policy: the removal of the Ptolemaic currency from Koile Syria, the increase of a large output of Ptolemaic weight but with Alexander I's portrait in the southern mints, the decrease of the Asia Minor tetradrachms in hoards and the growth of the Attic standard royal output, all point to a big change in monetary matters during his reign. With Demetrius I, who issued a large range of gold denominations – a metal rarely struck by the Seleucids – Alexander I Balas is probably one of the most innovative kings in the dynasty. The choices of these two rulers were

Table 14.1 The bronze issues of Aradus during the Hellenistic period[29]

	3rd century BC	2nd century BC	1st century BC
Bronze series	5	10	13
Total of obverse dies	75	506	89

Table 14.2 Share of the fractions in the Sidonian Corpus[a], after 450–333 BC[31]

Double shekels	Shekels	Halves	Quarters	1/16	1/32
c. 25.67 g		c. 6.94 g		0.76–0.55 g	
978	1	237	73	882	89

Note:
[a] This table categorizes 2,260 of 2,614 in the corpus.

certainly guided by needs: after the death of Antiochus IV in 164 BC, the Seleucid dynasty started a century of fratricidal wars between two rival branchs. Their military needs led to an increasing demand for coined money.

This chapter is too short to allow a more detailed account of the monetary history of the period. However, it is important to underline the contemporary development of the bronze coinage. During the second century BC, all the Eastern mints' output in this alloy grew significantly. The mint of Aradus, which enjoyed a favourable situation in the Seleucid Empire, is a good example of the increasing role of bronze (Table 14.1).

The number of series struck in bronze increases regularly, but the number of obverse dies in use reaches a peak during the second century BC. It is also the apogee of the city: it went into decline during the first century BC. Other examples would give different figures. For instance, the Hasmonean kingdom reaches its maximum bronze output – which was considerable – during the reign of Alexander Jannaeus (103–76 BC).[30]

Nature of circulation

The nature of circulation is very different according to the period and the area considered. It is absolutely not a regular phenomenon that would lead from times with few denominations, and consequently a low degree of monetization, to more 'modern' times with a lot of fractions and a higher monetization. It is crucial to remember that coins are not everywhere and that the capability of ancient people to have a developed economy without coins is very high and always true during the period studied in this chapter.

It is particularly striking to observe that the end of the fourth century BC, before Alexander's conquest, is characterized by hoards of small change: one-third are made of small silver coins frequently struck by the Phoenician and Philistian mints. Tables 14.2–14.4 give an overview of the most recent corpora.

Table 14.3 Share of the fractions in the Tyrian Corpus[a], c. 450–333 BC[32]

Shekels	Quarters	1/16	1/32	1/160
13.56 g then 8.77 g	3.16 g	0.57 g	0.32 g	
1160	76	285	13	3

Note:
[a] This table categorizes 1,537 of 1,814 in the corpus: 194 silver fractions (around 0.70 g) and the whole bronze series (81 coins in five groups) are excluded from this table as J. and A.G. Elayi were unable to classify them.

Table 14.4 Denominations in use in the Philistian Mints[33]

Tetradrachms	Didrachms	Drachmas	Obols	Hemiobols	Fractions
–	–	–	0.92–0.40 g	0.32–0.17 g	0.15–0.04 g

The number of fractions gathered in these corpora and catalogues is striking, especially if we remember that the smaller the coins are, the more they disappear, being worn more quickly than large denominations and being less easily found by archaeologists (except when the earth is sieved, which does not occur so often).[34] So the figures given in these tables emphasize impressive productions of fractions. These are sometimes tiny. The smallest denominations of the Philistian mints weigh only about 0.15–0.04 g. The Phoenician mint of Arwad (Arados in Greek) gives the same range of tiny coins. The best example of the ordinary use of this very small change is one of the Al Mina hoards.

Al Mina is an ancient town situated at the mouth of the Orontes River. It was abandoned in c. 300 BC, probably as a result of the Macedonian conquest and the foundation of new powerful cities in its neighbourhood. Fifty-five tiny coins were gathered in a very small cylindrical silver purse closed by a silver lid.[35] This purse had a diameter of 2.5 cm. This means that it was not intended to contain double shekels, shekels or tetradrachms whose diameter is always larger.[36] It was a small-change purse. The coins are 51 fractions from the mint of Arwad and four from Sidon. Their weight range runs from 0.04 g to 0.59 g, the last weight being the giant of the lot (Figure 14.6 and Figure 14.7)! In total, the whole hoard weighs only around 6 g![37]

The particular demand for fractions during the fourth century BC is also noticeable in hoards (see Table 14.5).

Figure 14.6 Arwad, coin fraction, BnF MMA L. De Clercq 292.

Figure 14.7 Enlargement ×10 of 14.6, BnF MMA L. De Clercq 292.

Table 14.5 Percentage of hoards containing each type of denomination[38]

Period	Denominations over the drachma %	Drachmas %	Fractions %
Persian	76.47	10.29	44.12
Alexander and the Diadochi (333–280)	76.67	11.67	25
3rd century BC (279–200)	77.78	13.89	5.56
2nd century BC (199–100)	84.92	13.49	1.59
1st century BC (99–1 BC)	66.67	4.55	1.52
Total	**78.81**	**10.96**	**13.2**

Large denominations remain the favourite currency for burial (generally over the two-thirds of a lot). Most of the time drachmas represent around 10 per cent of the hoards, but there is a clear evolution in the fractions. They are frequently hoarded during the Persian period, in fact mostly during the fourth century BC. Their proportion remains high till the 320s BC and drops after this date: from the 320s BC, they are noticed only marginally in hoards. Such a change could be easily explained by the development of bronze issues, more convenient for daily transactions than tiny silver coins of the same value – except that from the 320s BC till the very end of the third century BC, bronze output is scanty in Syria. That means that during one century, this region mainly used Alexander tetradrachms as coinage, and something else, but no coins, for daily transactions.

Even after the increase of the bronze output, Syria never issued many drachmas and bigger silver fractions. Coinage was principally composed of large silver coins (double shekels, shekels and tetradrachms) and very small silver during the Persian period, or bronze since the end of the third century BC.

Therefore, we must conclude that the development of coinage is not such a regular process: more silver small change was available before Alexander than during the third century BC. The large increase of bronze small change dates back to not earlier than the second century BC.

Another phenomenon must be noted: during the fourth century BC, hoards show different contents according to the area where they are buried. Of fourteen hoards containing fractions, eleven are located south of Saida (Figure A14.15 in

Appendix 14.C). This is rather astonishing because we observed that the Phoenician mints, including the northern one, Arwad, struck a large range of small denominations. Thus we can conclude that hoarding emphasized the southern users' partiality to fractions while those in the north preferred large denominations. Large denominations are also found in southern hoards, but fractions are scarce in the north.

This observation can be compared to a later one: after 320 BC, two out of three hoards are bronze in the southern area and the Hasmonean kings started an overwhelming output of bronze at the very beginning of the first century when they increased their possessions from Jerusalem.[39] Samaria, Judea and Philistia seem to have been distinguished during the last four centuries BC by a marked predilection for silver small change and bronze coins, one of the standards for the definition of a high degree of monetization.

Conclusion

Although we lack die studies and need special precautions to study ancient coinages, we can safely conclude that the use of coinage is characterized by heterogeneity. Its increase and its features vary greatly from the fifth to the first century BC as much geographically as in time. These variations are probably also strong inside the areas, and even inside the cities if we follow the example of Olynth.

Therefore, it seems extremely tentative and not relevant to give general and totally theoretical views on the coinage and the Seleucid monetary policy. There were strong regional and even micro-regional features, with varying adaptations in the long trend, not necessarily in the sense of what we consider to be progress. The choice of one area such as Judea to build a model to be extended to the whole empire is not appropriate: according to numismatics, Judea's features make it a very special region, certainly not comparable with others, and it is most probable that each area had strong features that made it different from its neighbours, contra Aperghis (2004).

The evolution of the use of coinage is not steady and seems to be narrowly linked to political and military need for silver. Bronze is less influenced by these events and played probably a role greater than usually thought: this alloy is less studied than silver, quite poorly represented in public collections if compared with silver, yet it seems to have been common, and even abundant, during the second and first centuries BC. Some scholars used to consider that it was so plentiful that large payments could be made in bronze. This could be an explanation for the scarcity of silver small change during the Hellenistic period: payments below the tetradrachm being made in bronze, as suggested by O. Picard for Thasos (North Aegean):

> Dès lors que pour effectuer un paiement, le payeur pouvait utiliser soit des espèces en bronze inutilisables hors de la cité, soit des espèces en argent qui avaient partout une certaine valeur, il était assurément plus avisé de choisir la première solution, ce qui devait amener logiquement une rétention des pièces en argent, et donc une dépréciation des pièces en bronze. [...] Que

le bronze ait chassé l'argent se constate, à Thasos et dans bien des cités, mais pas dans toutes, par l'élimination progressive des espèces d'argent inférieures au tétradrachme.[40]

Coinage can hardly inform us on commercial intercourse: we have no means to distinguish a payment to the state from a soldier's pay, or an inheritance. We have no way to know which part of an exchange was paid in coins and which part in crops or other commodities. But the range of denominations, the abundance of small change or bronze, the geography of hoards and excavation finds, and the output studies give a frame that we will improve progressively. Moreover, if an integrated market is supposed to be an interdependent and unified whole, it is noticeable that Syria, since the end of the fifth century BC, used common coinages (Athenian owls and their Eastern imitations, Alexanders) or local coinages circulating in the whole area (Phoenician silver during the fourth century BC, Attic standard silver during the Seleucid Empire). No unification can be observed, but rather an adaptation to allow the most abundant silver coinage to circulate widely. The 140s BC mark a turn: the Attic standard was no longer the only criterion to allow a silver coinage to be accepted in Syria. From these years, foreign silver coinage decreases in the hoards, progressively replaced by Seleucid silver, in the Attic as in the Ptolemaic zones. Aradus, a powerful northern Phoenician city traditionally allied to the Seleucids, adopted a new light standard unique to itself.[41] At the very end of the century, the development of the young Jewish state leads to the development of the huge bronze issues of the Hasmonean dynasty.[42] The Near East goes from an empire-wide open circulation to a more fragmented one.

Appendix 14.A: Coin circulation in the Seleucid East (Mesopotamia, Babylonia, Iran)

This appendix gives a general account of coin circulation in the Seleucid East, with a focus on Babylonia, which is the core of this volume. Most of the general features given here come from a previous paper published in 2004.[43] A complete study of the hoards buried in Babylonia during the Hellenistic period is currently in progress.[44] My appendix is based on the geography of the hoards found in the area and is therefore a very general overview on circulation. A complete description would include detail on material from the excavations and a detailed analysis of each hoard. They are mostly silver hoards: bronze coins are rarely buried and the gold output of the Eastern mints remains scarce and usually travels westward.

The Hellenistic period marks a major turn in the monetary practices of the Mesopotamian area.[45] During the Achaemenid period, there were no mints in this part of the Persian Empire. The coins circulating in the Empire have long been proved to come from foreign mints, especially Greek ones.[46] Even the Persian darics and *sigloi* came from Asia Minor, probably Sardes. The mints in the Empire were situated in Greek, Phoenician, Jewish and Syrian cities.[47] One of the leading

Figure A14.1 Tetradrachm of Athens with the name of Mazakes in Aramaic, BnF, MMA, collection Henri Seyrig 1973.1.190.

coinages came from Athens or was imitated locally, probably in Syria and Phoenicia. Therefore, the coin hoards buried in the East were scarce compared with the relative abundance of finds in the Mediterranean area.[48]

Another feature of the rare fifth- and fourth-century BC hoards found in Mesopotamia is their contents: some gather cut coins (*CH* 2.47), others precious objects (*CH* 8.90). The coins were probably considered as small ingots of silver, and thus, cut and mixed with pieces of silver (jewels, ingots, dumps, etc.), usually called *hacksilber*.[49] Babylonian texts of the Hellenistic period mention it as *istatirru* (*statēr*) and their value is marked in minas and shekels, the traditional standards. This leads to the conclusion that the coins were weighed instead of being counted:[50] that practice draws the limit between an economy without struck coins, with crops and weighted raw materials as money, and an economy using counted struck coins. During the Achaemenid period, this is not a special feature of the East. The hoards of the Mediterranean shore often show the same devices. But they are far more numerous and many give neither cut coins nor jewels or silver objects. The ones with *hacksilber* are far less frequent during the fourth century BC.[51] In the same time, local mints start striking silver, first in Phoenicia since the mid-fifth century, then in the southern area (Samaria, Judaea, Philistia) during the fourth century. The use of counted coins spreads through the western area, one coinage being especially appreciated: the Athenian tetradrachms with an owl, frequently imitated by local mints. Some of them with the legend AΘE or the name of Mazakes in Aramaic have been attributed to Babylonia, for technical reasons and because most of them come from this region (Figure A14.1).[52]

Before presenting the other coinages of Babylonia at the end of the fourth century BC, it is necessary to note the importance of a single hoard of about 400 coins probably found in 1973 (Babylon, Iraq hoard, *CH* 1.38, 2.49, 3.22, 8.188, 10.248).[53] It contained all the silver coinages issued in that area, even the most singular ones. It has been partially published by M.J. Price in 1991[54] and P.G. van Alfen gave a more detailed account in 2000.[55] G. Le Rider considers that it was buried c. 320 BC.[56]

At the end of the fourth century, between 331 and 328 BC, a mint started issuing staters with a lion following the Attic standard, probably in Babylon.[57] On the obverse, Baaltarz is sitting to left, a scepter in his outstretched right hand. The

Figure A14.2 Lion stater with the name of Mazaios in Aramaic, BnF, MMA, E. Babelon, *Catalogue des monnaies grecques de la Bibliothèque nationale. Les Perses achéménides, les satrapes et les dynastes tributaires de leur empire: Cypre et Phénicie*, Paris, 1893, no 284.

Figure A14.3 Lion stater post-Mazaios, hammer on the obverse, Γ on the reverse, BnF, MMA, 1982.329

name of the god is written in Aramaic in the left field. The reverse carries a lion walking to left, the name of the satrap Mazaios (*MZDY*: Mazdai) is written above, in Aramaic again. Most of these coins have been found in Babylonia.[58] Seven lifetime issues are known with or without control-marks: snake, shell, wreath, club, M, K or no control-mark (Figure A14.2).[59] This satrapal coinage can be considered as a grant by Alexander to the satrap Mazaios who rejoined him after the defeat of Darius III at Gaugameles in 331 BC.[60] Mazaios opened the doors of Babylon to the Conqueror and was confirmed in his position of governor as a loyal supporter of the new power. The famous Babylon hoard gives evidence of the popularity of the lion staters: they have been imitated, probably during a short period.[61] The coinage with the lion continued after Mazaios' death in 328 BC, probably down to c. 280 BC, but without his name on the reverse and with new symbols (Figure A14.3); several are Seleucid as the anchor[62] or the horned horse head.[63] Other Eastern mints have issued short series with the same types.[64] To summarize, the lion staters circulated mostly in Babylonia during fifty years or more. They were an appreciated local coinage at the time the Babylonian mint issued a large output of Alexander type tetradrachms that massively travelled to the West.

Other issues are probably from Babylon. The official coinage of the Persian Empire during the fifth and fourth centuries BC comprised gold darics and silver *sigloi*. Neither of these two were struck in Babylonia – although, probably during the 320s BC, double-darics were issued in Babylonia with some darics carrying the same types. They copy the obverse type of the original darics group 3,[65]

Figure A14.4 Double daric, BnF, MMA, FG 113.

Figure A14.5 Tetradrachm of Alexander, BnF, MMA, FG 678.

Figure A14.6 Gold stater of Alexander, BnF, MMA, FG 374.

but the reverse is no longer an incuse rectangle but a geometric pattern with waves; some Greek letters or monograms appear on the obverse of certain issues (Figure A14.4). Some of the double darics carry an M or a wreath in the field. As these control-marks appear too on the lion staters, it seems probable that the mint was the same and that these issues of the double darics were contemporary with the lion staters.[66]

I noted earlier the wide spread created by the beginning of the output of Alexander the Great tetradrachms. It increased at the end of the 320s BC in several mints, including eastern ones: Babylon seems to have been one of the most active mints of Alexander and moreover of the Diadochi. The bulk of Alexander coinage in the East is divided between silver tetradrachms and gold staters. The silver tetradrachms carry on the obverse the head of Heracles wearing a lion scalp to the right and Zeus seated on a throne to the left, carrying an eagle in his right hand on the reverse (Figure A14.5). On the gold staters, the obverse is struck with a helmeted head of Athena to the right and, on the reverse, a Victory holding a wreath in her right hand and a mast in the left (Figure A14.6).

There is a rare peculiarity in the output of Babylon: the mint struck three different issues of decadrachms with the obverse and reverse types of the tetradrachms (Figure A14.7).[67] It is a unique event in the whole Alexander coinage.

Figure A14.7 Decadrachm of Alexander, BnF, MMA, K1945 FG 664.

The attribution of large series to this mint dates back to the major study of the Demanhur hoard (*IGCH* 1664) by E.T. Newell and has been more recently confirmed by G. Le Rider.[68] However, there is still debate on the attribution of the bulk of the Alexander issues to Babylon. M.J. Price mentions the various payment and gifts to the army in 331 BC and later. As far as we know they took place at Ecbatana and Susa (Arrian, *Anabasis Alexandri* 3.19.5; Plutarch *Alexander* 68,7).[69] Thus 'Ecbatana and Susa would seem to have as good a claim as Babylon to the main eastern mint'.[70] H. Nicolet-Pierre adds that the weddings of Susa in 324 BC were an official event that could explain the issues of such prestigious denominations as decadrachms.[71] Despite these objections, scholars, including M.J. Price and H. Nicolet-Pierre, still continue to give these series to Babylon. The output seems to have been especially wide: we have no complete die study for this mint,[72] but the Babylonian Alexanders are found in many hoards and it points to impressively large issues. The Demanhur hoard gives the second rank to the Babylon mint, behind Amphipolis.[73] After 323 BC, the lion staters, the double darics and the Alexanders carry the same control-marks and are considered to have been struck between 323 and 317 BC.[74]

As regards circulation, the situation differs once more from the Mediterranean shore. Instead of finding the tetradrachms of Alexander in every hoard, often excluding other series,[75] Babylonia – which shows the highest concentration of hoards in the East – goes on with traditional series such as Babylonian staters with a lion and Athenian tetradrachms. So the end of the fourth century BC is characterized by the variety of coin production in Babylonia as well attested by the Babylon hoard 1973: all the silver coins previously described were represented in this hoard and closely related by die links, including the last group, probably the most attractive. These coins have unexpected Indian types and two denominations: 'tetradrachms' and 'decadrachms'.[76] The decadrachms are usually called 'Poros decadrachms', since they bear, on the obverse, a scene depicting a soldier (Alexander?) riding a horned horse (usually considered as Bucephalus) fighting an elephant to right on which a mahout[77] and another man are sitting, the first brandishing a spear in the rider's direction, the second grasping the rider's sarissa (Figure A14.8).

This type is supposed to commemorate the victory of Alexander against the Indian king Poros at the Battle of the Hydaspes. The reverse type is also unusal: Alexander (?) is standing, resting on a sarissa with his left hand and holding a thunderbolt in his right. He wears a headdress with two long feathers. A Nike flying above crowns him. There is a monogram in the left field. There is a debate concerning this representation of Alexander: half-god or only victorious with the help of Zeus?[78] These decadrachms were known from only three examples before 1973. The Babylon hoard contained seven new coins. The tetradrachms with the similar types were unknown before 1973.

On the obverse, that first series of tetradrachms shows the elephant to the right and its two riders, without the horseman. The mahout is holding a goad, the second rider a long standard. On the reverse, an Indian archer draws his large bow in a galloping quadiga driven to the right by a charioteer (Figure A14.9). The second series of tetradrachms carries an Indian archer drawing a bow to the right and, on the reverse, an elephant standing to the right. On both series, the archers and elephant riders share the same features as the decadrachms characters. They wear distinctive Indian clothes and headdresses and draw a very large Indian bow (Figure A14.10).[79] These particulars explain why there is a discussion about the date and the place where the Indian decadrachms and tetradrachms were issued, but there is little doubt that the Babylon hoard has been buried c. 320 BC and it is our best source for these very rare series. None comes from India itself and the hypothesis of an Indian mint seems relatively weak.[80] There is no determining evidence to decide between Susa[81] and Babylon[82] and I prefer to keep the traditional Babylonian attribution.

So the 1973 Babylon hoard is a good witness to the variety of the Babylonian silver coinage at the end of the fourth century BC: Athenian tetradrachms and their

Figure A14.8 Decadrachm of Poros, BnF, MMA, FG 1978.21.

Figure A14.9 Tetradrachm of Poros, BnF, MMA, FG 1975.194.

Figure A14.10 Tetradrachm of Poros, BnF, MMA, FG 1978.22.

Figure A14.11 Tetradrachm of Antiochos II, Seleucia on the Tigris, BnF, MMA, FG 126.

imitations, Alexanders, 'Indian types', silver decadrachms, tetradrachms and staters, local and Attic standards are represented. We must add the gold darics and double darics to have a complete view of the currency of the area.

During the third century BC, Alexanders remain one of the main coinages in use, especially in the region of the Persian Gulf where imitations of this coinage are known. But the Seleucid issues increase at the end of the century and are the majority coinage in the hoards dated to the second century BC, except in Susiana. This marks a noticeable difference with the Mediterranean shore where the Alexanders remained largely in use till the 140s BC. But they are no longer struck and the Mesopotamian area is supplied by the local Seleucid royal mints (Figure A14.11; see also Appendix 14.B to this chapter). The area of Susa is the exception to that rule: the Alexanders and their imitations are frequently found in hoards. Some imitations bear Aramean or Himyarite legends and draw attention on the relations between southern Mesopotamia and Arabia.[83]

A major change took place in 141 BC: the Parthians defeated the Seleucids and this had numismatic consequences. A Parthian mint opened in Susa probably as early as 140 BC according to G. Le Rider[84] and the first hoards of Parthian kings date back to this year.[85] During the first century BC, Alexanders and Seleucid coins are still represented in the Mesopotamian hoards, but they are finally replaced by Parthian drachmas. Bronze hoards are extremely rare, but it is a general feature: bronze is never easily hoarded in the East, except in well-defined areas and periods, such as the Hasmonean kingdom in the Mediterranean region, or some late Hellenistic kingdoms in the East.

During the Hellenistic period, hoarding increases in the same areas as previously. Therefore, the tenuous road drawn by the hoards becomes a continuous line marking the main road from the Mediterranean to Babylonia where there is a higher concentration of deposits.[86] That road is not followed at random: it is determined by the geographical conditions such as mountains and water supply. The distribution of the hoards is consistent with what literary sources tell us about the safest and easiest road from the Mediterranean to the Persian Gulf. Cuneiform texts from Mari, at the beginning of the second millennium BC, shed light on the itinerary favouring the foothills of the Taurus and Zagros Mountains.[87] It is also the road attested in the itinerary from Larsa to Emar, during the first half of the second millennium BC.[88] It is the most direct way as long as merchants are not transporting heavy materials.[89] The road is still mentioned in Herodotus (5.52) who underlines that it is inhabited and safe. It is also the road chosen by Alexander the Great and his army in July 331 BC:

> Thence he continued inland, keeping on his left the Euphrates and the mountains of Armenia, through the country called Mesopotamia. But on leaving the Euphrates he did not lead direct on Babylon, since going by the other road he found everything more convenient for the troops, and it was easy to obtain fodder for the horses and any necessities from the country, and, what is more, the heat did not burn so strongly.
>
> (Arrian, *Anabasis Alexandri*, 3.7.3)[90]

Once in Babylonia, it seems that the lower Euphrates is usually preferred to the lower Tigris.[91] Therefore, during the two millennia BC, the most comfortable road runs along the foothills of the Taurus, then southward along the upper Tigris until Babylon, and there crosses the river and follows the lower Euphrates. It is the exact line along which the Hellenistic hoards are located.

The Mesopotamian region did not use coinage as frequently as did the Mediterranean area during the Hellenistic period, but this does not explain why the hoards are so narrowly concentrated along a single road. It was one of the main reasons, but all the sources emphasize the existence of numerous other itineraries.[92] Moreover, a higher concentration of deposits is noted in northern Mesopotamia, in Babylonia and in Susiana. These areas also contain the highest concentration of cities,[93] some of them being the royal mints of the Seleucids: Carrhae, Edessa and Nisibis in the north, Seleucia on the Tigris and Babylon in the centre, and Susa in the south (Table A14.1).[94] Therefore, the presence of the royal administration could be a convenient explanation for the concentration of deposits. The soldiers' pay and the expenses due to the garrisons, the financial needs of the royal administration, the payment of taxes – all these factors must have made coins more needed there than in the countryside where the Greek usages must have been hardly known, and anyway unnecessary for daily life. In the main corridor of circulation, repeated contacts with the more monetized Mediterranean area probably spread the use of coinage in commercial transactions. We can assume that the use of coinage in Mesopotamia was mostly an urban phenomenon and probably closely related to the state by way of taxes and official payments. The large melting pot of different populations along the road from the Mediterranean to the Persian Gulf certainly favoured the development of the use of coinage among local populations who, in the principal cities, lived with Greek communities. These arguments could explain the confinement of coinage along this road and its absence in the rest of the area. The usually accepted idea of an increasing 'monetization' of Babylonia during the Hellenistic period could have been geographically limited. Traditional means of payment were still in use and coins had probably a role limited to certain parts of the economy, in relation with the state and the Mediterranean world.

Appendix 14.B: The Seleucid mints in Mesopotamia according to Houghton and Lorber (2002) and Houghton *et al.* (2008)

The numerous uncertain mints are not mentioned here. The real output of Babylonian mints under Seleucid rule is richer than this summary. A detailed overview is given in Houghton *et al.* (2008, appendix 12, pp. 343–399).

Table A14.1 The Seleucid mints in Mesopotamia

Kings and usurpers	Carrhae	Edessa	Nisibis	Seleucia on the Tigris	Babylon	Orcha (Uruk)	Susa	'Antioch on the Persian Gulf'	Antioch in Persis	Ecbatana
Seleucus I (311–281 BC)	AV, AR, AE			AV, AR, AE	AV, AR		AV, AR, AE			AV, AR, AE
Antiochus I (281–261 BC)				AR, AE			AV, AR, AE			AR, AE
Antiochus II (261–246 BC)	? AR	? AR	AE	AV, AR, AE			AV, AR, AE			AV, AR, AE
Seleucus II (246–224? BC)			AR, AE	AV, AR, AE			AV, AR, AE			AV, AR, AE
Seleucus III (224?–222 BC)			AR?, AE	AR, AE			AR			AR, AE
Molon (222–220 BC)				AE			AR			AE
Antiochus III (222–187 BC)		? AV, AR, AE	AV, AR	AV, AR, AE			AV, AR, AE			AR, AE
Seleucus IV (187–175 BC)				AR, AE			AR, AE		AR, AE	AR, AE

Table A14.1 Continued

Kings and usurpers	Carrhae	Edessa	Nisibis	Seleucia on the Tigris	Babylon	Orcha (Uruk)	Susa	'Antioch on the Persian Gulf'	Antioch in Persis	Ecbatana
Antiochus son of Seleucus IV (175 BC)									AR	
Antiochus IV (175–164 BC)		AE	AE	AR, AE			AR, AE	AR	AR, AE	AR, AE
Antiochus V (164–162/1 BC)								AR		
Timarchus(162/1)				AR						AR, AE
Demetrius I (162/1 –150 BC)				AV, AR, AE			AR, AE	AR	AR	AV, AR, AE
Alexander I (150–145 BC)				AR, AE		AE	AR, AE	AR		AV, AR, AE
Demetrius II (145–138 BC)			? AE	AR, AE			AR	AR		
Antiochus VII (138–129 BC)				AR, AE		AE	AE			

Note:
AV = gold; AR = silver; AE = bronze.

Appendix 14.C: The locations of hoards shown by period

The following maps were drawn by Th. Faucher, ANR Nomisma (M.-C. Marcellesi dir.), University Paris-Sorbonne.

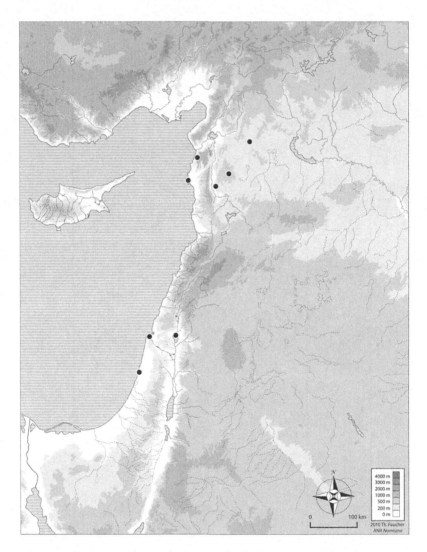

Figure A14.12 Map showing the hoards of coins of Antiochus IV.

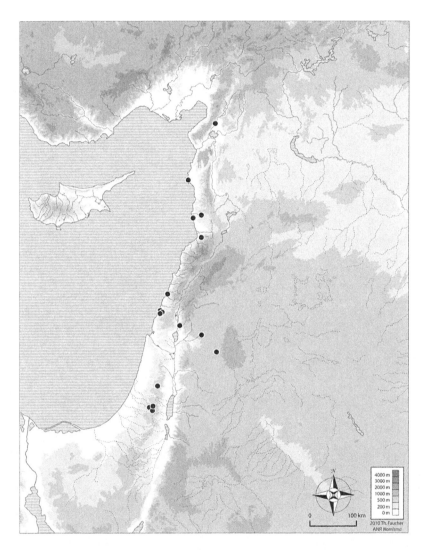

Figure A14.13 Map showing the hoards of coins of Alexander I Balas.

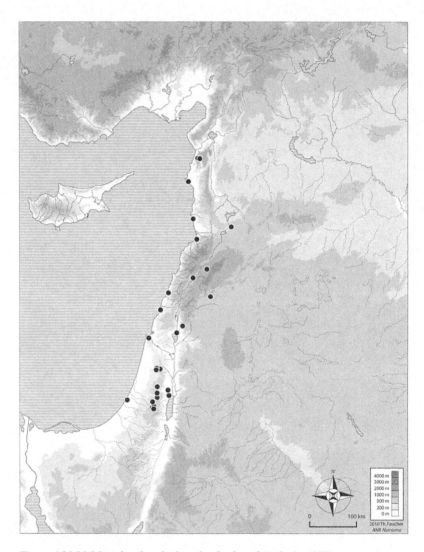

Figure A14.14 Map showing the hoards of coins of Antiochus VII.

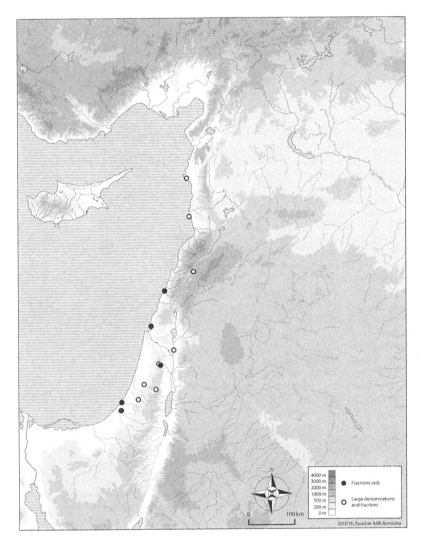

Figure A14.15 Map showing hoards of fractions during the Persian Period.

Notes

1 I am deeply indepted to Cathy Lorber who kindly agreed to read an earlier version
of this text, and to Thomas Faucher who drew the maps. All conclusions are my sole
responsibility.
2 See the maps in Price and Waggoner (1975) and Kim (2001).
3 Price (1991a).
4 De Callataÿ (1997).
5 Ras Shamra hoard, IGCH 1478.
6 Some scattered lists of prices are known in the Zenon papyri devoted to his journey in
Palestine. See Durand (2003).
7 Mapped on nomisma.org.
8 R.A.G. Carson, *CH* 1, p. 1.
9 I give a complete analysis of the differences of information given by hoards from
excavations and from the market in the book in progress.
10 An alloy of gold and silver.
11 Kroll (1993: xvii–xxvi); De Callataÿ (2006): 180 gives similar figures for other
excavations in the Greek world.
12 Elayi and Elayi (2004, 2009).
13 Duyrat (2005a).
14 Sawaya (2009).
15 Le Rider (1999).
16 Houghton and Lorber (2002 1, 1: 362; (map) 364).
17 Mildenberg (1995); Le Rider (1961); Augé (1989).
18 Duyrat (2004) with maps.
19 Lemaire (1995).
20 Cahill (2002: 266). See the map p. 267 and the tables 10 and 11.
21 Le Rider (2003: 124–7; 130–1); Hersh and Troxell (1993/1994).
22 Lebanon hoard, *CH* 8.172.
23 Le Rider (1995).
24 Lorber (2010).
25 See a useful synthesis in Le Rider (1999).
26 Le Rider (1999); see tables of the die study in Duyrat (2002).
27 Houghton (1991: 80), Antioch after Antiochus III; Houghton (2002: 14–15), charts 4A
and 4B for 'the Seleucid Core'.
28 Houghton *et al.* (2008 2, 1: 51–2).
29 Duyrat (2005a: 293).
30 Meshorer (2001).
31 Elayi and Elayi (2004).
32 Elayi and Elayi (2009).
33 Gitler and Tal (2006: 73–5 and 319–320).
34 Butcher (2001/2002: 25) notices that, 'The small coins are difficult to spot, but recovery
is greatly improved if the spoil from each context is sieved'. In the Beirut souks excavations, 'about 48 per cent of the coins found on BEY 006 and 045 were 12 mm or less
in diameter [. . .]. A large proportion of these were recorded during sieving'.
35 Woolley (1938: 166).
36 Elayi and Elayi (1993: 62).
37 Robinson (1937); Elayi and Elayi (1993: 62–7 (no. 6)).
38 Some hoards contain each type of denomination, so the total of each line can be over
100 per cent.
39 Meshorer (1967, 2001).
40 Picard (1994: 41).
41 Duyrat (2005a).

42 Meshorer (2001).
43 Duyrat (2004).
44 By Julien Monerie, Aspects de l'économie de la Babylonie hellénistique et parthe (PhD, F. Joannès supervisor, university Paris 1 – Panthéon Sorbonne, 2013).
45 On the monetary transition between the Achaemenid and Hellenistic periods according to the written sources, see Graslin and Monerie (2012).
46 Schlumberger (1953).
47 Mildenberg (1995).
48 Duyrat (2004: 383–6 and maps 1 and 2, p. 417–18).
49 About the use of silver for payments and prices, see Jursa (2010, Chapter 5). Van Alfen (2004/2005: 47–62); Balmuth (2001).
50 Vargyas (2000: 516–7); Le Rider (2001: 69–70).
51 For a late example see Gitler (2006).
52 See Le Rider (2003: 284–90) for a full discussion.
53 Price (1991b).
54 Price (1991a: 451–7 and 1991b).
55 But his article focuses only on the 165 Athenia-type coins.
56 Le Rider (2003: 332).
57 Le Rider (2003: 274–6).
58 For instance, Le Rider (1972) with two hoards containing Babylonian owls and lion staters: 'les tétradrachmes 'au lion' et ceux de Mazakès aux types d'Athènes circulaient ensemble et servaient au commerce et aux échanges à l'intérieur de la Babylonie', p. 6. Of course also the 1973 Babylon hoard, Price (1991b).
59 See Nicolet-Pierre (1999: 287–8) who provides a catalogue of that series and underlines the strong stylistic links with the lion staters struck by Mazdai at Tarsus.
60 Q. Curtius Rufus, *Historiae Alexandri Magni Macedonis*, 5.1.17.
61 Price (1991b: 70–1, no. 28–133). Lion staters and elephant staters are mentioned in cuneiform tablets of the early Hellenistic period; cf. Boiy (2004: 44–7); Stolper (1993: 22).
62 Houghton and Lorber (2002, no. 88–91).
63 Houghton and Lorber (2002, no. 102–4); Nicolet-Pierre (1999: 287).
64 Seleucia on the Tigris: Houghton and Lorber (2002, no. 144); and Ecbatana: Houghton and Lorber (2002, no. 220–1).
65 According to their classification by Carradice (1987).
66 Nicolet-Pierre (1999: 299, no. 36; 296), she notes that some darics with a barbarous style were probably struck by another mint eastward of Babylonia.
67 Price (1991a: 454 and no. 3598, 3600 and 3618A). That exceptional denomination was represented in the Babylon hoard 1973, Price (1991b: 64–5).
68 Newell (1923: 57–64 and 140–3); Le Rider (2003: 295–7).
69 Only Diodorus, *Bibliotheca Historica*, 17.65.1 mentions Babylon.
70 Price (1991a: 457).
71 Nicolet-Pierre (1999: 303).
72 Newell (1923: 151) counted 172 obverse dies of Babylonian Alexander tetradrachms in the Demanhur hoard. There is an unpublished die study by N.M. Waggoner in the archives of the American Numismatic Society.
73 Duyrat (2005b: 26–7), emphasizing the distortions caused by the Demanhur hoard.
74 Nicolet-Pierre (1999: 303–4).
75 Duyrat (2004: 389–90 and 420 (map 4)).
76 The weights are not easily attached to a standard: they follow a Babylonian standard (1 shekel = *c*. 8.4 g.) according to Price (1991b: 65), a 'light Attic' according to Le Rider (2003: 330).
77 Bernard (1985) showed that the mahout is probably king Poros himself.
78 See the details in Le Rider (2003: 330–1).

79 Bernard (1985).
80 *Contra* Lane Fox (1996). Also see Holt (2003).
81 Bernard (1985); Lane Fox (1996).
82 Le Rider (2003: 332–3).
83 Le Rider (1965: 442).
84 Le Rider (1965: 356).
85 The oldest is *IGCH* 1804, buried *c.* 140.
86 Duyrat (2004: 423–4 (maps 7 and 8)); also published in Van der Spek (2007: 428–9).
87 Joannès (1996: 342–3).
88 Hallo (1964: 86).
89 Graslin-Thomé (2009: 313).
90 Translation by E. Iliff Robson, Loeb Classical Library.
91 Although its upper course is navigable, as several authors testify: Strabo, *Geographica*, 16.1.9–11, 16.3.3; Arrian, *Anabasis*, 7.19.3. But Joannès (1995) underlines the irregularity of the Euphrates, its low waters during the summer and the mighty streams during spring.
92 See, for instance, the map of the first millennium BC roads in Mesopotamia in Graslin-Thomé (2009: 309) and the detailed examinations on the roads in the same area by Joannès (1992, 1996).
93 Joannès (2004: 289–300), who emphasizes the highest urbanization and the concentration of activity in three areas during the Persian and Hellenistic periods: around Nineveh, Seleucia on the Tigris and Alexandria of Characene/Antiochia/Spasinou, which are also the main hoarding areas.
94 See Appendix 14.B.

Abbreviations

BnF Bibliothèque nationale de France.
CH 1 Price, M. J., ed. 1975. *Coin Hoards* 1, London: The Royal Numismatic Society.
CH 2 Price, M. J., ed. 1976. *Coin Hoards* 2, London: The Royal Numismatic Society.
CH 3 Price, M. J., ed. 1977. *Coin Hoards* 3, London: The Royal Numismatic Society.
CH 8 Price, M. J., McGregor, K. and Wartenberg, U., eds. 1994. *Coin Hoards* 8, London: The Royal Numismatic Society.
CH 10 Hoover, O., Meadows, A. and Wartenberg, U., eds. 2010. *Coin Hoards* 10, New York: American Numismatic Society.
IGCH Thompson, M., Mørkholm, O. and Kraay, C. M. 1973. *An Inventory of Greek Coin Hoards*, New York: The American Numismatic Society.
MMA Département des monnaies, médailles et antiques.

Bibliography

Aperghis, G. G. 2004. *The Seleukid Royal Economy. The Finances and Financial Administration of the Seleukid Empire*, Cambridge: Cambridge University Press.
Augé, C. 1989. 'La monnaie en Syrie à l'époque hellénistique et romaine (fin du IVe s. av. J.-C. – fin du Ve s. ap. J.-C.)', in *Archéologie et histoire de la Syrie II. La Syrie de l'époque achéménide à l'avènement de l'Islam*, edited by J.-M. Dentzer, W. Orthmann, Saarbrücken: Saarbrücker Druckerei und Verlag: 149–90.
Balmuth, M. S., ed. 2001. *Hacksilber to Coinage: New Insights into the Monetary History of the Near East and Greece*, New York: The American Numismatic Society.
Bernard, P. 1985. 'Le monnayage d'Eudamos, satrape grec du Pandjab et maître des éléphants', in *Orientalia Josephi Tucci Memoriae Dicata*, edited by G. Gnoli and L. Lanciotti, Rome: Istituto Italiano per il Medio ed Estremo Oriente: 65–94.

Boiy, T. 2004. *Late Achaemenid and Hellenistic Babylon*, Leuven: Uitgeverij Peeters and Departement Oosterse Studies.

Butcher, K. 2001/2002. *Small Change in Ancient Beirut: the Coin Finds from Bey 006 and Bey 045. Persian, Hellenistic, Roman and Byzantine Periods. Archaeology of the Beirut Souks: AUB and ACRE Excavations in Beirut, 1994–1996*, Beirut: The American University of Beirut.

Cahill, N. 2002. *Household and City Organization at Olynthus*, New Haven: Yale University Press.

Carradice, I. 1987. *Coinage and Administration in the Athenian and Persian Empires*, Oxford: B. A. R.

De Callataÿ, F. 1997. *L'histoire des guerres mithridatiques vue par les monnaies*, Louvain-la-Neuve: Département d'archéologie et d'histoire de l'art, Séminaire numismatique Marcel Hoc.

—— 2006. 'Greek Coins from Archaeological Excavations: a Conspectus and a Call for Chronological Table', in *Agoranomia: Studies in Money and Exchange Presented to John H. Kroll*, edited by P. Van Alfen, New York: American Numismatic Society: 177–200.

Durand, X. 2003. *Des Grecs en Palestine au IIIe siècle avant J.-C. Le dossier syrien des archives de Zénon de Caunos (261–252)*, Paris: J. Gabalda et Cie.

Duyrat, F. 2002. 'Review of G. Le Rider, *Antioche de Syrie sous les Séleucides. Corpus des monnaies d'or et d'argent. I. De Séleucos I à Antiochos V, c. 300–161*, Paris, 1999' *Revue numismatique* 158: 408–17.

—— 2004. 'La circulation monétaire dans l'Orient séleucide (Syrie, Phénicie, Mésopotamie, Iran)', in *Le roi et l'économie. Autonomies locales et structures royales dans l'économie de l'empire séleucide*, edited by V. Chankowski and F. Duyrat, Paris: De Boccard: 381–424.

—— 2005a. *Arados hellénistique. Étude historique et monétaire*, Beirut: Institut Français du Proche-Orient.

—— 2005b. 'Le trésor de Damanhour (*IGCH* 1664) et la circulation monétaire en Egypte hellénistique', in *L'exception égyptienne? Production et échanges monétaires en Egypte hellénistique et romaine. Actes du colloque d'Alexandrie, 13–15 avril 2002*, edited by F. Duyrat and O. Picard, Le Caire: Institut français d'archéologie orientale du Caire: 17–51.

Elayi, J. and Elayi, A. G. 1993. *Trésors de monnaies phéniciennes et circulation monétaire (V–IVe s. av. J.-C.)*, Paris: Gabalda.

—— 2004. *Le monnayage de la cité phénicienne de Sidon à l'époque perse (Ve–IVe s. av. J.-C.)*, Paris: Gabalda.

—— 2009. *The Coinage of the Phoenician City of Tyre in the Persian Period (5th–4th century BCE)*, Leuven: Peeters.

Gitler, H. 2006. 'A Hacksilber and Cut Athenian Tetradrachm Hoard from the Environs of Samaria: Late Fourth Century B.C.E.', *Israel Numismatic Research* 1: 5–14, pl. 1–2.

Gitler, H. and Tal, O. 2006. *The Coinage of Philistia of the Fifth and Fourth Centuries B.C.: a Study of the Earliest Coins of Palestine*, Milan: Ed. Ennerre.

Graslin-Thomé, L. 2009. *Les échanges à longue distance en Mésopotamie au Ier millénaire. Une approche économique*, Paris: De Boccard.

Graslin, L. and Monerie, J. 2012. '"Compter, peser, diviser", L'introduction du numéraire en Babylonie, (VIème – IIIème s. av. J.-C.)', in *Monnaie antique, monnaie moderne, monnaies d'ailleurs… Métissages et hybridations*, colloque de l'université Paris-Ouest – Nanterre, 8–9 juin 2011, edited by B. Formoso and P. Pion, Paris: de Boccard: 55–65.

Hallo, W. W. 1964. 'The Road to Emar', *Journal of Cuneiform Studies* 18: 57–88.

Hersh, C. A. and Troxell, H. A. 1993/1994. 'A 1993 Hoard of Alexander Drachms from the Near East', *American Journal of Numismatics* 5–6: 13–43.

Holt, F. L. 2003. *Alexander the Great and the Elephant Medallions*, Berkeley: University of California Press.

Houghton, A. 1991.'The Antioch project', in *Mnemata. Papers in Memory of N. M. Waggoner*, edited by W. E. Metcalf, New York: American Numismatic Society: 73–97.

—— 2002. 'The Production of Money by Mints of the Seleucid Core', in *Les monnayages syriens. Quel apport pour l'histoire du Proche-Orient hellénistique et romain?*, edited by C. Augé, F. Duyrat, Beirut Institut Français du Proche-Orient: 5–19.

Houghton, A. and Lorber, C. 2002. *Seleucid Coins. A Comprehensive Catalogue. With Metrological Tables by Brian Kritt*. Part I. *Seleucus I through Antiochus III*, vol. I. *Introduction, Maps and Catalogue*, vol. II. *Appendices, Indices, and Plates*, New York: American Numismatic Society.

Houghton, A., Lorber, C. C. and Hoover, O. D. 2008. *Seleucid Coins. A Comprehensive Catalogue*. Part II. *Seleucus IV through Antiochus XIII*. Vol. I. *Introduction, Maps, and Catalogue*, Vol. II. *Appendices, Indices, and Plates*, New York: American Numismatic Society.

Joannès, F. 1992. 'L'organisation de l'espace en Irak du nord (région du Sinjar) au début du 2ᵉ millénaire avant J.-C.', *Cahiers du Centre G. Glotz* III, Paris: De Boccard: 1–19.

—— 1994. 'Métaux précieux et moyens de paiement en Babylonie achéménide et hellénistique', *Transeuphratène* 8: 137–44.

—— 1995. 'L'itinéraire des Dix-Mille en Mésopotamie et l'apport des sources cunéiformes', in *Dans les pas des Dix-Mille*, edited by P. Briant, Toulouse: Presses Universitaires du Mirail: 173–200.

—— 1996. 'Routes et voies de communication dans les archives de Mari', *Amurru* 1: 323–61.

—— 2004. 'Quelques traits de l'économie babylonienne, des Achéménides à Séleucos I', in *Le roi et l'économie. Autonomies locales et structures royales dans l'économie de l'empire séleucide*, edited by V. Chankowski and F. Duyrat, Paris: De Boccard: 291–302.

Jursa, M. 2010. *Aspects of the Economic History of Babylonia in the First Millenium BC: Economic Geography, Economic Mentalities, Agriculture, the Use of Money and the Problem of Economic Growth*, Münster: Ugarit Verlag.

Kim, H. S. 2001. 'Archaic Coinage as Evidence for the Use of Coinage', in *Money and its Uses in the Ancient Greek World*, edited by A. Meadows and K. Shipton, Oxford: Oxford University Press: 7–21.

Konuk, K. 2005. 'The Electrum Coinage of Samos in the Light of a Recent Hoard', in *Neue Forschungen zu Ionien*, edited by E. Schwertheim, Bonn: Habelt: 43–56.

Kroll, J. 1993. *The Greek Coins. The Athenian Agora*, vol. 26, Princeton: American School of Classical Studies at Athens.

Lane Fox, R. J. 1996. 'Text and Images: Alexander the Great, Coins and Elephants', *Bulletin of the Institute of Classical Studies* 41: 87–108.

Lemaire, A. 1995. 'La circulation monétaire phénicienne en Palestine à l'époque perse', in *Actes du IIIe congrès international des études phéniciennes et puniques* II, edited by M. H. Fantar and M. Ghaki, Tunis: Institut National du Patrimoine: 192–202.

Le Rider, G. 1961. 'Les ateliers monétaires de la côte syrienne, phénicienne, palestinienne, égyptienne et cyrénéenne', in *VI congresso internazionale di numismatica*, Rome: Istituto Italiano di Numismatica: 67–109.

—— 1965. *Suse sous les Séleucides et les Parthes. Les trouvailles monétaires et l'histoire de la ville*, Paris: Librairie orientaliste Paul Geuthner.

—— 1972. 'Tétradrachmes au lion et imitations d'Athènes en Babylonie', *Schweizer Münzblätter* 22: 1–7.

—— 1995. 'La politique monétaire des Séleucides en Cœlé-Syrie et en Phénicie après 200. Réflexion sur les monnaies d'argent lagides et sur les monnaies d'argent séleucides à l'aigle', *Bulletin de correspondance hellénique* 119: 391–404.

—— 1999. *Antioche de Syrie sous les Séleucides. Corpus des monnaies d'or et d'argent* I. *De Séleucos I à Antiochos V (c. 301–161)*, Paris: Institut de France: 1999.

—— 2001. *La naissance de la monnaie. Pratiques monétaires de l'Orient ancien*, Paris: Presses universitaires de France.

—— 2003. *Alexandre le Grand. Monnaie, finances et politique*, Paris: Presses universitaires de France.

Lorber, C. C. 2010. 'Commerce ("Demetrius I" hoard), 2003 (CH 10.301)', in *Coin Hoards* X, *Greek Hoards*, edited by O. Hoover, A. R. Meadows and U. Warterberg, New York: American Numismatic Society: 153–72.

Meshorer, Y 1967. *Jewish Coins of the Second Temple Period*, Tel Aviv: Am Hassefer.

—— 2001. *A Treasury of Jewish Coins. From the Persian Period to Bar Kokhba*, Jerusalem: Yad Ben-Zvi Press.

Mildenberg, L. 1993 (1995). 'Über das Münzwesen im Reich der Achämeniden', *Archäologische Mitteilungen aus Iran* 26: 55–79.

Monerie, J. Forthcoming. 'Aspects de l'économie de la Babylonie hellénistique et parthe' (unpublished thesis, university Paris 1 – Panthéon Sorbonne, 2013).

Newell, E. T. 1923. *Alexander Hoards. Demanhur 1905*, New York: American Numismatic Society.

Nicolet-Pierre, H. 1999. 'Argent et or frappés en Babylonie entre 331 et 311 ou de Mazdai à Séleucos', in *Travaux de numismatique grecque offerts à Georges Le Rider*, edited by M. Amandry and S. Hurter, London: Spink: 285–305.

Picard, O. 1994. 'Monnaies et commerce à Thasos', in *Économie antique. Les échanges dans l'Antiquité: le rôle de l'Etat*, edited by J. Andreau, P. Briant and R. Descat, Saint-Bertrand-de-Comminges: Musée archéologique départemental: 31–45.

Price, M. J. 1991a. *The Coinage in the Name of Alexander the Great and Philip Arrhidaeus. A British Museum Catalogue*, Zürich/London: The Swiss Numismatic Society/British Museum Press.

—— 1991b. 'Circulation at Babylon', in *Mnemata. Papers in Memory of N. M. Waggoner*, edited by W. E. Metcalf, New York: American Numismatic Society: 63–75.

Price, M. J. and Waggoner, N. M. 1975. *Archaic Greek Coinage. The Asyut Hoard*, London: V. C. Vecchi & Sons.

Robinson, E. S. G. 1937. 'Coins from the Excavations at Al-Mina (1936).', *Numismatic Chronicle*, 5th series, 17: 182–96.

Sawaya, Z. 2009. *Histoire de Bérytos et d'Héliopolis d'après leurs monnaies*, Beirut: Institut français du proche-orient.

Schlumberger, D. 1953. *L'argent grec dans l'empire achéménide*, Paris: Imprimerie Nationale.

Stolper, M. W. 1993. *Late Achaemenid, Early Macedonian, and Early Seleucid Records of Deposit and Related Texts*, Napels: Istituto Universitario Orientale.

Van Alfen, P. G. 2000. 'The "Owls" from the 1973 Iraq Hoard', *American Journal of Numismatics* 12: 9–58.

—— 2004/2005. 'A New Athenian "Owl" and Bullion Hoard from the Near East', *American Journal of Numismatics* 16–17: 47–62.

Van der Spek R. J. 2007. 'The Hellenistic Near East', in *The Cambridge Economic History of the Graeco-Roman World*, edited by W. Scheidel, I. Morris and R. Saller, Cambridge: Cambridge University Press: 409–33.

Vargyas P. 2000. 'Silver and Money in Achaemenid and Hellenistic Babylonia', in *Assyriologica et Semitica. Festschrift für J. Oelsner anlässlich seines 65. Geburtages am 18. Februar 1997*, edited by J. Marzahn and J. Neumann, Munster: Ugarit Verlag: 513–21.

Woolley C. L. 1938. 'The Excavations at al Mina, Sueidia II', *Journal of Hellenic Studies* 58: 133–70.

15 A frog's eye view of the Roman market

The Batavian case

Joris Aarts

Introduction

Since the 1970s, many things have been said about the character of the Roman economy and the extent of its monetary economy. This discussion was led by ancient historians such as Finley, Crawford, Hopkins, Howgego and Duncan-Jones, often using monetary circulation as a measure of economic integration.[1] Both literary and archaeological sources were used to create large-scale models of the Roman economy, concentrating on questions of monetization of the economy: how fast, how wide, how deep. Mostly, coin hoards and museum collections were used as archaeological evidence for monetary circulation: large-scale inventories of stray finds were not yet available, or deemed too time-consuming to analyse. In the last ten years, however, much more work has been done on a regional level, leading to regional inventories and analyses of both hoards and stray finds.[2]

At first, scholarly discussion about the character of the ancient economy was dominated by the of question whether the ancient economy was fundamentally different from modern western economies and if, by extension, modern economic analysis and terminology could, and should, be applied to ancient economies (the formalist–substantivist debate). This ultimately resulted in a tie, and in the last two decades the general agreement seems to be that both substantivist and formalist models and methods can be used, depending on the topic of research. It must be said that recently many ancient historians are inclined to embrace modernist analyses,[3] particularly when dealing with macro-economic analyses. Also, much attention is paid to the extent and nature of credit systems in the (Roman) economy, and how this interacted with the circulation of physical money (coins) and bullion.[4] On the other hand, more cultural approaches to coinage and money appear, although, until now, they tend to stay within the realm of the Greek world.[5]

One returning point in the discussions about the Roman economy is the regionality of economic systems. Although there is some evidence for empire-wide economic integration – in the long-distance trade in luxury items and foodstuffs and chains of credit relations – the circulation of coin suggest that the province or even smaller regional units pressed their mark on coin circulation. Analyses of taxpaying systems show great regional variation in time and place. The strange thing is that Hopkins' model of taxes and trade, which propagates the empire-wide rise of a monetary economy through the interplay between long-distance trade and money taxes, still is accepted by most scholars as explanation for the monetization of the Roman economy. Perhaps it is time to reconcile macro-economic views of the structure of the Roman economy with the interpretation of historical and archaeological data on a regional and local level, and to test the models created by the ancient historians mentioned above. What I propose to do in this chapter is to approach the Roman economy from the bottom up, not from the top down, to see if we can connect the macro-economic models with archaeological and historical data on the level of a *civitas*. I will try to do this thematically, taking the *Civitas Batavorum* as a case study.[6]

The case of the Batavians

A very brief history of the Batavians

The Batavian *civitas* can be located in the eastern half of the Dutch river area (see Figure 15.7 later), although its southern border may have extended to part of the sandy plateaus of the southern half of the Netherlands. Nijmegen (*Ulpia Noviomagus*) was the capital of this *civitas*, which lay on the border of the Roman Empire during the first three centuries AD. The Batavians themselves were probably a construct of the Roman authorities, a group consisting of transrhenane migrants and the local population of the Dutch eastern river area, which may have been a remnant of the tribe of the *Eburones*. The *civitas* and the Batavians can be followed historically into the first half of the third century AD, after which they were likely replaced by Frankish migrants from across the Rhine border. We may assume that this also meant the end of the Batavian *civitas*. We know much about their early history in particular through the narrative of Tacitus, in which they play an important role in a native (Batavian) revolt during the years AD 69–70. Before this uprising, the Batavians were, according to Tacitus, a *gens foederata*: a people with a special treaty with the Romans, the only known – but apparently the main – point of which is the exemption from paying regular taxes to the Roman government. In exchange, the Batavians were enlisted in the Roman army on a grand scale.[7] Vossen has calculated a minimum average of 1.3 young men per household (!) who were serving in the Roman auxiliaries.[8] Also, in the pre-Flavian period these troops seem to have been led by officers who were recruited from the same tribe. This probably all changed after the Batavian revolt, although the treaty was continued, probably along other lines (which we do not know from historical sources).

The Batavian *civitas* was a densely settled area, consisting of a string of auxiliary forts along the Rhine, a city (Nijmegen) , some badly known central places (*vici*), a few large rural sanctuaries and a large number of simple and small rural settlements. Some of these have been the object of large-scale excavations in the previous decades, providing us with a few high-quality archaeological datasets.[9] Using these data, contextual analysis of material culture provides us with a detailed picture of the social, political and economic integration of the Batavians in the Roman Empire.

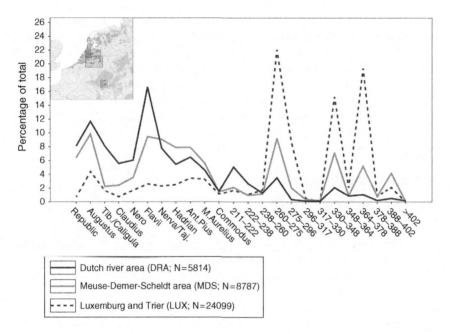

Figure 15.1 Coin supply to the Dutch river area, the Meuse–Demer–Scheldt area and the Luxemburg–Trier region, in percentages of the total.

Money supply

The coin finds of the Batavian area were part of a recent large-scale inventory of Roman and late Iron Age coins in *Germania inferior* and *Gallia Belgica*.[10] Figure 15.1 shows the chronological distribution of these finds in three areas of study: the Dutch river area, encompassing the *Civitates Batavorum* and *Cananefatium*; the area between the rivers Meuse, Demer and Scheldt (part of the *Civitas Tungrorum*), and the area of Luxemburg and Trier (part of the *Civitas Treverorum*). A grand total of 62,518 coins was recorded for all three areas.[11] Because we are dealing with large numbers of coin finds, I propose that they are representative of the (physical) money supply to these areas during the Roman period.

The main difference between the three areas is clear. In the Dutch river area, we see high levels of coin supply in the first century AD (peaks in the Augustan and Flavian periods); from the beginning of the second century AD, a downward trend is visible, from which this area will never recover. In contrast, the curve of coin supply in Luxemburg and Trier stays stable but low until the late third century AD, after which it soars. Even when one takes into account the changes in the character of late Roman money, the proportional differences between these areas remain the same. The Meuse, Demer and Scheldt area lies not only in geographical sense between the two others, but also in terms of coin supply.

The reason for the high supply levels in the Dutch river area in the first century AD lies in all probability in the fact that it was a military zone. The presence of large numbers of troops in the first century AD, and the building (and maintenance) of forts and other infrastructure cost a lot of money. After the army was greatly reduced in numbers at the start of the second century AD, coin supply decreases and never reaches first-century AD levels again. This implies that the army played a key role in the monetary economy of this area, in the sense that it represented its main monetized market.

In the area of Luxemburg and Trier we see a different picture. Here, admittedly after a modest peak in the Augustan period, levels of coin supply stay low, until the end of the third century AD. Also in this case, there seems to be an evident explanation, because Trier became an imperial residence in the fourth century AD and host to one of the mints. This does not mean, however, that the actual coin mass which reached this area was insignificant: as can be seen, the Luxemburg–Trier area shows the largest numbers of coin finds of all three areas (Figure 15.1), although the actual coin numbers in Figure 15.2 show that this is an effect of the late Roman period only.

The main incentive for coin supply to all regions which emerges here is governmental costs, and in particular military expenditure. And indeed, most authors seem to agree that the Roman government was not interested in maintaining a steady flow of fresh coin for the sake of regional markets.[12] But the coin supply to these areas cannot be explained by governmental spending alone. The presence of the Roman army in the Treverian area is too low to account for the high numbers of coin finds there, and Figure 15.2 suggests that coin supply started not much later than in the Dutch river area. It is clear that there must have been other

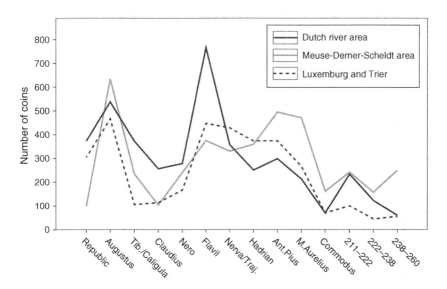

Figure 15.2 Coin supply to the three regions until AD 260.

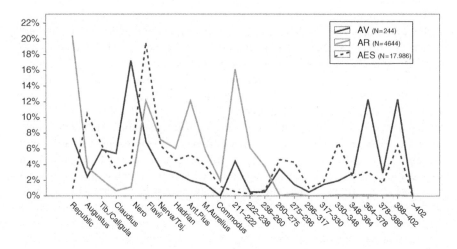

Figure 15.3 Percentages of gold (AV), silver (AL) and bronze (AES) coins in the Dutch river area and Meuse, Demer and Scheldt area (data from NUMIS).

mechanisms of coin supply in play. In the case of Trier, we may assume that the intensive building program in the first century AD has had a monetizing effect on the economy of the city. At the same time, the development of villas producing for the urban market may have profited from this monetized market.

One of the disadvantages of using coin finds to analyse the money supply is that they are heavily biased towards bronze coin.[13] Silver and gold in particular were less regularly lost, and more often recovered. Also, the chance of gold coin finds being reported is many times less than that of bronze.

Still, comparing the chronological distribution of gold, silver and bronze coins shows some interesting points (Figure 15.3).[14] The Augustan peak we saw above in the Dutch river area is absent in the silver and gold. Instead, only from the Flavian period onwards silver and gold appear in large numbers. Furthermore, the Antonine peak in silver coins, that at the beginning of the third century AD and the two peaks in the supply of gold coin in the second half of the fourth century AD spring into view.

The Flavian increase in gold and silver may be linked with a change in the structure of the tax system, accompanied by an increase in (monetized?) exchange in regional pottery and metalware. I will return to this later.

Coin circulation

Once Roman coin reached the Dutch river area, what became of it? Did it linger in the Roman army camps and the city of Nijmegen, never to reach the widely scattered rural villages of the hinterland? The geographical distribution of coin finds in Figure 15.4 shows clearly that this is not the case. The coin finds are not only concentrated in the forts along the Rhine and the cities of Nijmegen and *Forum*

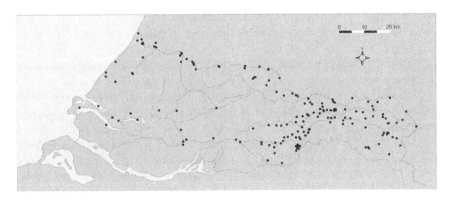

Figure 15.4 Coins finds in the Dutch river area before AD 70.

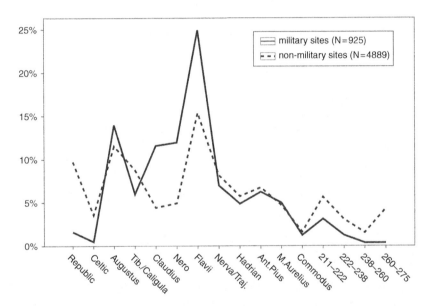

Figure 15.5 Percentages of coins from military and non-military sites in the Dutch river area.

Hadriani (capital of the *Civitas Cananefatium*), but are strewn across the countryside as well, particularly in the *Civitas Batavorum* (eastern half). Moreover, there seems to exist virtually no time lag between the coin supply to the forts and coins reaching the rural settlements. This becomes evident when one compares the chronological distribution of coins from forts and from rural settlements: they are virtually identical (Figure 15.5).[15] A second indication for the quick spread of Roman money over the countryside is the frequent occurrence of coins with pre-Flavian countermarks on rural sites.[16]

The next question, of course, is what were the mechanisms by which these coins flowed so easily from the prime target of Roman money supply (the forts) to these villages? Does this say anything about the speed of monetization of the Batavian economy?

Earlier, I made the point that a large part of the Batavian male population served in the Roman army in the early Roman period. The effect of this was that not only were they paid in Roman coin, but also that they quickly learned how to use it in a 'Roman' way. Part of their wages were probably spent in the forts themselves and the adjacent camp villages, but since they were able to visit their home villages on a regular basis during leave, it is certainly not impossible that they brought the money with them, along with their acquired knowledge of monetary ways. Although this did not mean that exchange *within these villages* became monetized, the people who lived there possessed money and the knowledge of how to use it. The monetary markets in this area were located in, and just outside, of the forts and in the city, and this is where monetary exchange took place (Figure 15.6).

In the pre-Flavian period, there is little evidence for a lively economic inter-action between rural settlements and urban and military markets: percentages of local pottery wares remain high in the rural world. There is no surplus production of grain and other crops that could be sold on the market. We have evidence for surplus production of cattle and horses, but this seems to have started around the middle of the first century AD.[17] The possibilities for the conversion of agricul-tural surplus into money seem limited, in any case for the pre-Flavian period. Also, the tax system did not invite people to use money on a substantial scale. Batavian taxes were paid in manpower, not in money, nor in agricultural produce.

This all changed in the Flavian period. Although the ethnic recruitment of Bata-vians did not stop, it is not likely that it remained the basis of the taxation in the Batavian civitas. The Batavian revolt came as an extremely unpleasant surprise to Roman authorities, and they would have looked very critically at the recruit-ment of Batavian soldiers and where they were based.[18] The re-evaluation of the terms of the treaty after the Batavian revolt and the creation of a formal *civi-tas* organization under Domitian imply that the rules of taxation may well have changed. Archaeological indicators for this change are the increased production of meat, hides and horses for the military and possibly urban markets. Also, the inner structure of rural settlements changed: in the Flavian period, field systems appear which re-structured both the internal space of the settlements themselves and the surrounding fields. Vos has made a plausible case for the field systems of the settlements at Wijk-bij-Duurstede De Geer and De Horden having been based on the Roman *actus* (surface measure of c. 1260 m^2).[19] In the settlements them-selves, larger structures appeared for the storage of agricultural produce. All these changes imply a different approach to the ownership of land and its yield. Perhaps this can be linked to a shift in the taxation system to payments in agricultural pro-duce and/or money; if this is the case, the area would have been subjected to a new *census*.

At the same time, percentages of regional pottery and metalwares increased in the material culture of rural settlements.[20] Coin supply reached another high in the

Flavian period, and this time silver and gold coin joined the bronze (Figure 15.3). The latter could have been an effect of the alteration in taxation, but may also have been a consequence of the increased building in the area. The city of Nijmegen grew steadily, although it stayed essentially a backward town compared to others. In the countryside there is evidence for monumental architecture in the temples of Kessel-Lith and Elst. The military infrastructure continued to grow during the Flavian period. The civilian architecture would have been paid for by elite members of the *Civitas Batavorum*. To do this, they must have lent sums of money (from *patroni* outside of the *civitas*), because this would not have been available (yet) through the workings of a monetary economy on the *civitas* level. This argument for the role of credit in the monetary economy is not backed up by archaeological evidence. There is no complementary flow between supply of credit and physical money. That is, not in the sense that credit took over when money supply was low: if anything, the coin evidence seems to imply that an increase in credit meant an increase in the physical money supply as well.

The drastic reduction in the numbers of Roman troops in the Dutch river area at the beginning of the second century AD took its toll. After this, the general trend in the coin supply is a downward one (Figure 15.1). In any case, a substantially smaller amount of money flowed to the area in the form of army wages. This must also have had repercussions for the exchange between the rural settlements and the army markets, whether or not through urban channels or the tax system (direct army supply contracts?). Both the official supply of money and the income from surplus production dwindled as a result of the shrinkage of the military market. At the same time, debts had to be paid back. This must have put some economic pressure on the urban elite. Perhaps in recognizance of this, Trajan extended municipal rights to the city of Nijmegen (*Ulpia Noviomagus*). However, for the Batavian population there was no real alternative market to turn to. No economic interactive exchange system between the urban settlements and the countryside developed, as it did in the case of the *Civitas Treverorum*. In this light, the Antonine peaks in silver coins and in both gold and silver during the Severan period seem unexpected. The Antonine increase in the supply of silver may have had some connection to the construction of a city wall in Nijmegen, but it is harder to explain the increase in gold and silver coin under the Severans. However, the same Severan increase in silver coin is visible in the coin finds from Luxemburg, and perhaps we must look for an explanation in the changing money system and higher price levels.

The lowest levels of occupation: the coin finds of two rural settlements

Descending from a regional level of analysis to a local one, what can the coin finds of two average rural settlements in the Batavian area contribute to a discussion of the Roman economy? In the manner of research, the settlements of Tiel-Passewaaij and Geldermalsen-Hondsgemet are far from average. Both were thoroughly excavated, Tiel-Passewaaij completely and Geldermalsen-Hondsgemet almost completely; also, they were excavated by the same team of

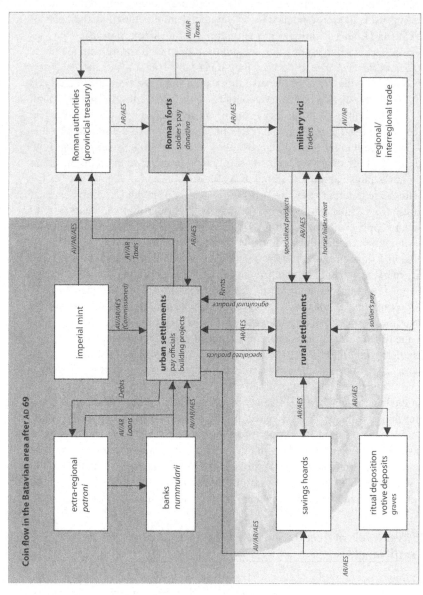

Figure 15.6 Model of the coin circulation in the Batavian *civitas* before and after AD 69. The shaded box, top left, shows added mechanisms after AD 69.

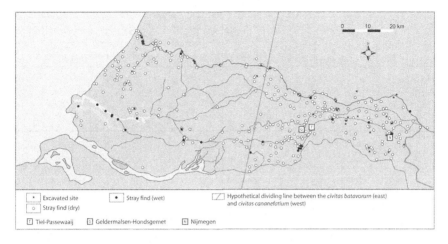

Figure 15.7 Coin finds in the Dutch river area, 50 BC–AD 402.

archaeologists, which used a system of intensive metal detection. In this way, large numbers of coins were retrieved from both sites: 347 coins at Tiel and 320 coins at Geldermalsen. Considering that these were simple rural villages consisting of only a few farmsteads per phase, the number of coins is impressive.

It is even more impressive when one extrapolates these numbers to the other rural villages plotted on the map in Figure 15.7; we have no reason not to, since the rural villages of Tiel and Geldermalsen are representative for the majority of rural settlements in the Batavian *civitas*.

During large-scale excavations at Tiel-Passewaaij, a rural settlement and a large cemetery (400 graves) came to light, lying in the heart of the Batavian *civitas*. Its occupation starts in the late Iron Age and ends in the first half of the fourth century AD. The village itself consisted of five to seven farms which were occupied at the same time. In the last few decades of the third century AD, the population of the settlement changed dramatically, as attested by changes in the material culture. It is thought that new groups of Franks settled here, who had little or nothing in common with their Batavian predecessors. We do not know where these Frankish people buried their dead. This group continued to live there until around AD 350, after which date the settlement was abandoned. The settlement at Geldermalsen is very similar to that of Tiel, but we do not know where they buried their dead.

Almost a third of the coins of Tiel came from three hoards: two (or possibly one) Severan silver hoards buried inside a house, and a hoard of 60+ barbarous radiates recovered from the cemetery, buried there at a moment when it was no longer in use (Table 15.1, showing that 105 coins came from hoards, almost one-third of the total 347 coins found). The only hoard from Geldermalsen is more modest in size: a hoard of 30 barbarous radiates found in the corner of a ditch surrounding the late Roman settlement. The chronological distribution of the coin

Table 15.1 The coin finds of Tiel-Passewaaij and Geldermalsen-Hondsgemet

	Tiel-Passewaaij	*Geldermalsen-Hondsgemet*
	No. of coins	*No. of coins*
Hoards	105	30
Settlement finds	221	290
Cemetery finds	21	–
Total	347	320

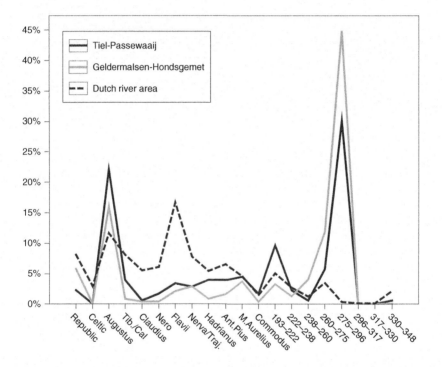

Figure 15.8 Percentage of coins from Tiel-Passewaaij, Geldermalsen-Hondsgemet and the Dutch river area.

finds of both settlements are displayed in Figure 15.8, set off against the general coin supply to the Dutch river area.

I will not present an exhaustive discussion of all aspects of the coin finds of these two settlements, but rather select two points which are pertinent to our theme.[21]

The first point is that the spatial distribution of coins does not imply that they were lost during monetary transactions. They were found in or nearby the houses of the village. There is no indication whatsoever of local marketplaces at which periodically monetary exchange took place. In fact, the only probable monetary

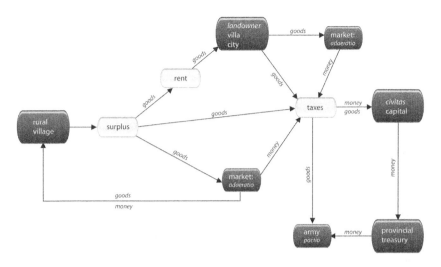

Figure 15.9 The various possibilities for the flow of money, goods and taxes in the Batavian civitas.

exchange taking place that I can think of is with outsiders. The people of the village were closely related, and it is hard to imagine people of such communities exchanging things through the intermediation of Roman money. Most settlements consisted only of three to six houses/families at the most. Even today, in such small communities where families are closely related, money is rarely used to facilitate exchange. In addition, it would be hard to get enough small change to use for the mostly small transactions which we can expect to have taken place. Reciprocal gifts or credit would have been sufficient to manage affairs.

In consequence, the population would not have run around daily carrying money purses. This leaves us with two options for the interpretation of the stray finds: either they were used in a ritual context, as we can clearly see in the case of the cemetery finds, or they were part of (small) hoards waiting to be used again in a monetary context (outside market). This does not mean, of course, that the rural population was not monetized. As I have shown, Batavian communities learned quickly how to use money in market exchange and did so, albeit in monetary market centres.

The second point is related to the spatial distribution of coins: contextual analysis reveals that from the second century AD onwards, there was a large percentage of 'old money' in circulation. This phenomenon was already known from funerary finds, but many second-century AD coins could be assigned to third-century AD structures. Thus, the seemingly continuous supply of coins emerging from the chronological distribution from the settlement finds (Figure 15.8), is misleading. A more likely scenario is that, particularly from the second century AD onwards, money reached the settlement in periodical spurts. Again, this perceived slowness in the circulation of rural money (or periodicity in coin supply) does not imply that the Batavians living inside the villages were not involved in the monetary economy. It simply means that they did not always have the means (surplus) or need to participate in monetary exchange.

Conclusion

I hope I have demonstrated how analysis of coin finds on a regional and local level can be tied to the general discussion of the Roman economy. The comparison of trends in the coin supply to different regions supports the view that the particular historical setting of a region leaves its marks on the chronological distribution of coins, not only of bronze coin which is believed to remain where it ended up, but also silver and gold coin, which display chronological patterns that are characteristic of the region. In the Batavian *civitas*, there are clear indications that the presence of the Roman army was an important influence on the levels of coin supply, at the same time serving as a monetary market for surplus products. This market function started to play a significant role in the regional economy from the second half of the first century AD, and seems to have had a monetizing effect. However, through the extensive enlistment of Batavian soldiers in the Roman army, Roman money and ideas about its use had already spread across the countryside. As a result of the Batavian revolt, the tax system probably underwent rigorous change in the Flavian period, from a tax based on supply of manpower to the Roman army to a regular land tax. The revolt was only an immediate cause for this change, but the foundation for the new tax system was perhaps already laid down by the monetization of the Batavian mind in the pre-Flavian period and by the increasing surplus production for a monetary military market. The flexibility of the Roman tax system would leave enough room for periodical local shortage of cash money, as is shown in Figure 15.9.

The dependence on the military market was also the cause of a severe blow to the monetary economy at the beginning of the second century AD, with the drastic withdrawal of Roman troops from the area. However, the monetary market was not limited to the army alone: there is evidence for monumental building both in Nijmegen and the countryside, which was paid for by the urban Batavian elite, at first using loans from extra-regional *patroni*. These building projects must have had a further monetizing effect on the Batavian economy, although in itself it was not enough to replace the vacuum left by the army. Non-military large-scale spending may be linked to the peaks in gold and silver coins in the second half of the first century and the second century AD. If this assumption is correct, it implies that the extension of credit (most clearly in the Flavian period but also possibly in later periods) had a multiplying effect on the supply and circulation of physical money as well.

The analysis of coin finds of individual settlements shows that a lot of old money was around, particularly from the second century AD onwards. It seems that one of the effects of the reduction of troops was a decrease in the velocity of circulation of money in the rural world. The connection of rural sites with the monetary economy was continuous, but clearly periodical: periods of money flow seem to alternate with periods of less activity. However, it would be wrong to think that the countryside was less monetized than the cities and military sites: the same people moved in different circles and whether people participated in the monetary economy was determined not so much by where they lived, but by the context in which they found themselves. Most coins found on rural sites are by consequence either used in a ritual way (in graves and other ritual depositions) or were part of small hoards which were disturbed in later periods.

Notes

1 Finley (1999) (reprint 1973); Crawford (1970); Hopkins (1980) (and 2002); Howgego (1992) (and 1994); Duncan-Jones 2002 (1990 first edition).
2 See, for instance, Aarts (2000), Katsari (2008).
3 Temin (2001); Temin (2004); Harris (2006).
4 Harris (2008); Lo Cascio (2003); Verboven (2009).
5 I mean the work of Von Reden, Schapps, Kurke and others discussed in Aarts (2005).
6 The Batavians were chosen as an example because they are relatively well known, both historically and archaeologically (see Roymans 2004; Derks and Roymans 2002; Nicolay 2007; Groot 2008; Heeren 2009; Vos 2009).
7 One might argue against Tacitus that the Roman authorities in all probability considered this recruitment as a form of *tributa* (see, for instance, Aarts 2000, 16–17).
8 Vossen (2003: 421). See also Vos (2009: 216–25).
9 Tiel-Passewaaij (Heeren 2009 and Aarts and Heeren 2010); Geldermalsen-Hondsgemet (Van Renswoude and Van Kerckhove 2009); Wijk-bij-Duurstede-De Horden (Vos 2009).
10 Aarts (2000).
11 Only some of these coins could be dated well enough to fit one of the issue periods. The missing coins and late Iron Age coins were omitted from the graph. Also, the coins of the fort of Nijmegen-Kops Plateau were excluded, because they would cause a grotesque distortion of the data of the Dutch river area.
12 However, cf. Heinrichs (2000).
13 This becomes eminently clear when the bronze : silver/gold ratio is compared with the finds of Pompeii (Duncan-Jones 2003, the critique of Andreau notwithstanding, Andreau (2008)) or the coin finds of the battlefield of Kalkriese (Berger 1996).
14 The data of Figure 15.3 are not exactly the same as in Figures 15.1 and 15.2; here, the coin finds of the Dutch river area and the Meuse-Demer-Scheldt area are grouped together, hence the different coin totals. The data are taken from the database of the Geld-en Bankmuseum in Utrecht (NUMIS), including the coin finds after 1997 which are not part of the earlier mentioned survey.
15 The only difference seems to occur in the Claudian period: the military sites show an increase here, but this is probably an effect of the fact that most of the forts in the western zone of the Dutch river area were established somewhat later than those in the east.
16 See Aarts (2003).
17 Vos (2009: 253).
18 See also Van Driel-Murray (1994: 93) for the probability of a restriction on the possession of weapons by citizens after the Batavian revolt; this is corroborated by the change in the finds of *militaria* in rural contexts (see Nicolay 2007; Vos 2009: 197).
19 Vos (2009: 109–216).
20 Van Kerckhove (2009: 189).
21 For a more elaborate account, see Aarts (2007), Aarts (2009) and Aarts and Heeren (2010).

Bibliography

Aarts, J. G. 2000. *Coins or money? Exploring the Monetization and Functions of Roman Coinage in Belgic Gaul and Lower Germany 50 BC–AD 450*, PhD Thesis Vrije Universiteit (VU University) Amsterdam.

—— 2003. 'Monetization and Army Recruitment in the Dutch River Area in the Early 1st Century AD', in *Kontinuität und Diskontinuität. Germania Inferior am Beginn und am Ende der römischen Herrschafft*, edited by Grünewald and Seibel, Berlin: 03: 145–61.

—— 2005. 'Coins, Money and Exchange in the Roman World. A Cultural-economic Perspective', *Archaeological dialogues: Dutch perspectives on current issues in archaeology*, 12: 1–27.

—— 2007. 'Romeins geld: ritueel en de markt in een Bataafse gemeenschap, in *Een Bataafse gemeenschap in de wereld Van het Romeinse rijk. Opgravingen te Tiel-Passewaaij*, edited by Roymans, Derks and Heeren, Amersfoort: Matrijs: 115–30.

—— 2009. 'Romeins geld in Geldermalsen-Hondsgemet', in *Opgravingen in Geldermalsen-Hondsgemet: een inheemse nederzetting uit de Late IJzertijd en Romeinse tijd*, edited by Van Renswoude and Van Kerckhove, Amsterdam: Archeologisch Centrum Vrije Universiteit, Hendrik Brunsting Stichting: 287–99.

Aarts, J. and Heeren, S. 2010. *Het grafveld aan de Passewaaijse Hogeweg. Opgravingen in Tiel-Passewaaij 2*, Amsterdam: Archeologisch Centrum Vrije Universiteit, Hendrik Brunsting Stichting.

Andreau, J. 2008. 'The Use and Survival of Coins and of Gold and Silver in the Vesuvian Cities', in *The monetary systems of the Greeks and Romans*, edited by W. V. Harris, Oxford: Oxford University Press: 208–26.

Berger, F. 1996. *Kalkriese 1. Die römischen Fundmünzen*, Mainz: P. von Zabern.

Crawford, M. 1970. 'Money and Exchange in the Roman World', *The Journal of Roman Studies* 60: 40–8.

Derks, T. and Roymans, N. 2002. 'Seal-boxes and the Spread of Latin Literacy in the Rhine Delta', *Journal of Roman Studies, Supplementary series*, 48: 87–134.

Duncan-Jones, R. 2002. *Structure and Scale in the Roman economy*, Cambridge: Cambridge University Press.

—— 2003. 'Roman Coin Circulation and the Cities of Vesuvius', in *Credito e moneta nel mondo romano*, edited by E. Lo Cascio, Bari: Edipuglia: 161–80.

Finley, M. I. 1999. *The Ancient Economy*, expanded edition with a foreword by I. Morris, Berkeley: University of California Press.

Groot, M. 2008. *Animals in Ritual and Economy in a Roman Frontier Community: Excavations in Tiel-Passewaaij*, Amsterdam: Amsterdam University Press.

Grünewald, Th. and Seibel, S., eds. 2003. *Kontinuität und Diskontinuität. Germania Inferior am Beginn und am Ende der römischen Herrschafft*, Berlin: De Gruyter.

Harris, W. V. 2006. 'A Revisionist View of Roman Money', *Journal of Roman Studies*, 96: 1–24.

—— 2008. 'The Nature of Roman Money', in *The Monetary Systems of the Greeks and Romans*, edited by W. V. Harris, Oxford: Oxford University Press: 174–207.

Heeren, S. 2009. *Romanisering Van rurale gemeenschappen in de civitas Batavorum: de casus Tiel-Passewaaij*, Amersfoort: Rijksdienst voor het Cultureel Erfgoed.

Heinrichs, J. 2000. 'Überlegungen zur Versorgung augusteischer Truppen mit Münzgeld. Ein neues Modell und daraus ableitbare Indizien für einen Wandel in der Konzeption des Germanenkrieg nach Drusus', in *Politics, Administration and Society in the Hellenistic and Roman World*, edited by L. Mooren, Leuven: Peeters: 155–213.

Hopkins, K. 1980. 'Taxes and Trade in the Roman Empire (200 BC–AD 400)', *Journal of Roman Studies*, 70: 101–25.

—— 2002. 'Rome, Taxes, Rents and Trade', in *The Ancient Economy*, edited by W. Scheidel and S. Von Reden, Edinburgh: Edinburgh University Press: 190–230.

Howgego, C. 1992. 'The Supply and Use of Money in the Roman World 200 BC to AD 300', *Journal of Roman Studies*, 82: 1–31.

—— 1994. 'Coin Circulation and the Integration of the Roman Economy', *Journal of Roman Archaeology*, 7: 5–21.

Katsari, C. 2008. 'The Monetization of the Roman Frontier Provinces', in *The Monetary Systems of the Greeks and Romans*, edited by W. V. Harris, Oxford: Oxford University Press: 242–66.

Lo Cascio, E. ed. 2003. *Credito e moneta nel mondo romano*, Bari: Edipuglia.

—— 2008. 'The Function of Gold Coinage in the Monetary Economy of the Roman Empire', in *The Monetary Systems of the Greeks and Romans*, edited by W. V. Harris, Oxford: Oxford University Press: 160–73.

Nicolay, J. 2007. *Armed Batavians: Use and Significance of Weaponry and Horse Gear from Non-military Contexts in the Rhine Delta (50 BC to AD 450)*, Amsterdam: Amsterdam University Press.

Roymans, N. 2004. *Ethnic Identity and Imperial Power. The Batavians in the Early Roman Empire*, Amsterdam: Amsterdam University Press.

Roymans, N, Derks, T. and Heeren, S., eds. 2007. *Een Bataafse gemeenschap in de wereld Van het Romeinse rijk. Opgravingen te Tiel-Passewaaij*, Amersfoort: Matrijs.

Scheidel, W. and Von Reden, S., eds. 2002. *The Ancient Economy*, Edinburgh: Edinburgh University Press.

Temin, P. 2001. 'A Market Economy in the Early Roman Empire', *Journal of Roman Studies*, 91: 169–81.

—— 2004. 'Financial Intermediation in the Early Roman Empire', *Journal of Economic History*, 64: 705–33.

Van Driel-Murray, C. 1994. 'Wapentuig voor Hercules', in *De tempel Van Empel*, edited by N. Roymans and T. Derks, Amsterdam: Amsterdam University Press: 92–107.

Van Kerckhove, J. 2009. 'Aardewerk', in *Opgravingen in Geldermalsen-Hondsgemet: een inheemse nederzetting uit de Late IJzertijd en Romeinse tijd*, edited by Van Renswoude and Van Kerckhove, Amsterdam: Archeologisch Centrum Vrije Universiteit, Hendrik Brunsting Stichting: 115–92.

Van Renswoude, J. and Van Kerckhove, J., eds. 2009. *Opgravingen in Geldermalsen-Hondsgemet: een inheemse nederzetting uit de Late IJzertijd en Romeinse tijd*, Amsterdam: Archeologisch Centrum Vrije Universiteit, Hendrik Brunsting Stichting.

Verboven, K. 2009. 'Currency, Bullion and Accounts. Monetary Modes in the Roman World', *Belgisch Tijdschrift voor Numismatiek en Zegelkunde/Revue Belge de Numismatique et de Sigillographie*, 155: 91–121.

Vos, W. 2009. *Bataafs platteland: Het Romeinse nederzettingslandschap in het Nederlandse Kromme-Rijngebied*, Amersfoort: Rijksdienst voor het Cultureel Erfgoed.

Vossen, I. 2003. 'The Possibilities and Limitations of Demographic Calculations in the Batavian Area', in *Kontinuität und Diskontinuität. Germania Inferior am Beginn und am Ende der römischen Herrschaft*, edited by Grünewald and Seibel, Berlin: De Gruyter: 414–35.

16 The circulation of money and the behaviour of prices in medieval and early modern England

Nick Mayhew

Introduction

The surviving data on English money and prices are extremely rich, and so provide material for a comparative case study, which may be of interest to those studying the interaction of money and prices in other regions and periods.

English currency and the money supply

The circulation of the English currency can be observed from plentiful surviving hoards and single finds. Looking at the distances between mints of origin and find spot, Metcalf found the late Anglo-Saxon currency thoroughly mixed, by commerce even more than by taxation.[1] When hoards are plentiful, above all in the fourteenth century, the London mint consistently contributed some 50 per cent of the currency in both England and Scotland, while Canterbury normally accounted for about 25 per cent, and the other provincial mints, continental imitations and Scottish and Irish issues together usually made up the remaining 25 per cent. The hoards do sometimes show a little minor variation favouring the issues of a more local mint, but this local bias only raises local representation by a few per cent and is only evident for a few years after the operation of the local mint. The medieval English currency was truly national. It is also worth noting that unlike medieval currencies on mainland Europe, the English circulation was not significantly penetrated by foreign issues. The Crown successfully forbade the circulation of foreign coins, which are only rarely found.[2] The maritime coast and the concentration of international trade in the major ports allowed English kings to exclude foreign coin far more effectively than was possible for continental sovereigns. It is thus possible to regard the English money supply as a discrete entity, which can be estimated and compared with prices, and with estimated gross domestic product (GDP).

English mint accounts survive from the early thirteenth century, providing accurate data on the annual mint production of the principal mints in London and Canterbury, together with some other data from provincial mints which were active from time to time.[3] In addition there is some other fragmentary documentary evidence which provides an indication of the general level of mint production from the late twelfth century, when the earliest price data begin, and this mint evidence is supported by die-studies which suggest there was a dramatic increase in the level of coin production in England in the 1170s and 1180s.[4] Coin production was maintained at these new, higher levels from the late twelfth century until the late 1320s. Output revived again in the mid-fourteenth century, when coins were also struck in gold and the mint price for silver was increased, drawing more bullion to the mints to be struck into more plentiful, slightly lighter silver coins. This process of reducing the intrinsic content of the coins in order to strike more of them was repeated with weight reductions to both gold and silver coins in 1411, 1465 and 1526, on each occasion achieving an increase in mint output as a result. These moderate weight reductions reflected the rising international price of bullion which is apparent throughout the later Middle Ages.

However, from 1544 to 1551 a period of much more dramatic debasement of the currency ensued, in which both the weight and the purity of both the gold and the silver coinage was seriously reduced, and the volume of mint output in debased coin was sharply increased. The issue of new debased coins was halted in 1551, but much poor coin remained in circulation at reduced face value until it was entirely demonetized by Elizabeth I's recoinage of 1560. From that point until 1816 the intrinsic content of the coinage was broadly unchanged.

The study of mint output is thus key information for any estimate of the total money supply, but it does not tell the whole story, since it says nothing about the quantities of coin which may have been leaving the circulation, whether carried abroad to pay for imports or war, or hoarded or lost in the ground, or even simply worn away on the fingertips of the population in daily use. To explore these questions, and to understand the size and character of the money supply actually in use, it is necessary to study the coins found as hoards and single finds. Once again England is fortunate to enjoy excellent evidence of coin finds made from all periods over the last two hundred years. It is the combination of all this evidence – the mint output, the die-studies, the hoards and the single finds which underpins the estimates of the size of the currency which have been published over the last forty years. They are set out in Table 16.1.[5]

Even this evidence, for which there is a broad measure of agreement, does not completely represent the money supply, since it is also necessary to make allowance for the role of credit. The extent of medieval credit is increasingly recognized.[6] To a large degree, however, the volume of credit in the form of cash advances or credit sales is closely related to the size of the currency. When coin is relatively plentiful, so is credit; when coin is scarce, credit is much more difficult to find. Nevertheless the development of credit *instruments* – bills and bonds – does create an addition to the money supply to the extent that such instruments began themselves to circulate effectively as money. Although this development did not achieve legally recognized status in England till the early eighteenth century, paper did effectively pass among merchants and bankers in gradually increasing quantities from the fifteenth century onwards.[7] Monetary historians have attempted to estimate the size of this additional element in the currency from the late seventeenth century. Rondo Cameron estimated that in 1688–9 coin supplied 50 per cent of the means of payment, while banknotes and deposits

Table 16.1 Estimates of the size of the English currency from the twelfth to the eighteenth century in millions of £ sterling

Date	Silver (£ million)	Total (£ million)	Comments
1158	0.03–0.08	0.03–0.08	
1180	0.07–0.19	0.07–0.19	
1210	0.2–0.5	0.2–0.5	
1247	0.425–0.45	0.425–0.45	
1279	0.5–0.6	0.5–0.6	
1282	0.8–0.9	0.8–0.9	
1290	1.0	1.0	
1299	1.1	1.1	Plus foreign
1310	1.5	1.5	
1319	1.5	1.5	
1331	1.2	1.2	
1351	0.7–0.9	0.8–1.1	
1422	0.15–0.2	0.95–1.0	Gold biased
1470	0.35–0.45	0.75–0.95	Gold biased
1526		1.4	Gold biased
1546		1.45	March
1548		1.76	September
1549		1.92	Michaelmas
1551		2.66	July
1551		1.38	August
1560		1.71	September
1561		1.45	October
1600		3.5	
1643	7.5	10.0	Inc 2.5 Eliz silver
1670		12.0	
1700		14.5	Plus banknotes, etc.
1750		15.0	Plus banknotes, etc.

constituted 10 per cent and bills, bonds and tallies 40 per cent. By 1750 he estimated the corresponding proportions as 37.5, 12.5 and 50 per cent.[8] But the role of such alternative forms of money was also probably important in the sixteenth century. Eric Kerridge demonstrated the widespread use of credit of various kinds, including inland bills, between 1538 and 1660.[9] Nevertheless, if coin accounted for 50 per cent of the means of payment in 1688, it is hard to think that it accounted for less than 75 per cent a century earlier. Such an assessment would allow us to add some £1,166,666 (i.e. 25 per cent) in 'other means of payment' to the estimate of £3.5 million in coin c. 1600 (see Table 16.2).[10]

English prices

English medieval price data are no less rich, and although the material available for the early modern period is not so plentiful, there is more than enough to occupy the most exacting price historians. In the nineteenth century J. E. Thorold Rogers provided the first rigorously scientific collection of price evidence,[11] which was

Table 16.2 Coin and other means of payment in millions of pound sterling, 1600–1750

Year	Coin (£ million)	Other (£ million)	Total (£ million)
1600	3.50	1.17	4.67
1643	10.00	3.33	13.33
1670	12.00	12.00	24.00
1700	14.50	14.50	29.00
1750	15.00	25.00	40.00

refined and developed by William Beveridge between the wars.[12] In the 1950s Henry Phelps Brown and Sheila Hopkins constructed a cost of living and a wages index,[13] and since then improved price series for individual commodities have been published by David Farmer for the Middle Ages[14] and by Peter Bowden for the early modern period.[15] Most recently Bob Allen and Greg Clark have constructed indexes of their own.[16] This material is capable of much sophisticated manipulation and analysis, and can be presented in various ways. While annual and often almost monthly quotations are available, decennial or rolling averages less susceptible to the extremes of harvest variation can also be instructive. Prices can also be presented either in nominal or in constant silver form, or nominal prices deflated by the consumer price index.[17]

Personally I tend to favour nominal prices which more closely reflect the experience of the people of the time, who generally were required to accept the king's money at its proclaimed face value (cf. Rathbone and Von Reden, Chapter 8, this volume). Prices expressed in weight of silver fail to recognize that the value of silver itself fluctuates, and this was certainly the case in later medieval England, when modest weight reductions in the coinage did not raise prices. Nevertheless there is certainly a role for silver and nominal prices at the time of the Tudor debasement when buyers and sellers did try to reflect the reduced quality of the coin in the prices agreed. To simplify comparison with the behaviour of Babylonian prices, I offer here in Table 16.3 and Table 16.4 English decennial index prices for barley from 1200 to 1750, drawn from the work of Farmer and Bowden.[18]

One needs, however, to retain an awareness of the limitations of studying single commodities. The price of English barley was influenced by the price of wheat and of meat, as purchasers substituted products balancing needs, preferences and price. In the later Middle Ages, when wages were historically high and prices low, more meat could be afforded and cereals were correspondingly less in demand, though the situation reversed in the later sixteenth and seventeenth centuries.[19] Similarly, on an annual basis we know that the Babylonian barley price was affected when the date harvest came in. The movement of the price of different commodities relative to one another thus becomes a consideration.

In addition to the decennial indexes given above, Figures 16.1 to 16.4 illustrate the movement of English annual barley prices, and Figures 16.5 to 16.8 wool prices, from 1209 to 1914, as presented by Gregory Clark.[20]

Table 16.3 English barley prices in shillings per quarter by decades, 1190–1347

Decade	Barley price	Decade	Barley price
1190–1200	1.00	1350–60	5.18
1200–10	3.95	1360–70	5.82
1210–20	2.30	1370–80	4.73
1220–30	3.02	1380–90	3.52
1230–40	2.57	1390–1400	4.08
1240–50	2.81	1400–10	4.24
1250–60	3.28	1410–20	3.89
1260–70	3.11	1420–30	3.51
1270–80	4.39	1430–40	3.84
1280–90	3.50	1440–50	2.73
1290–1300	4.68	1450–60	2.97
1300–10	3.94	1460–70	3.39
1310–20	5.67	1470–80	3.01
1320–30	4.68	1480–90	3.60
1330–40	3.92	1490–1500	3.33
1340–47	3.57		

Source: Farmer (1988: 734), and (1991: 444).

Table 16.4 Price of barley and malt in shillings per quarter by decades, 1500–1609

Decade	Index	Shillings/quarter	Decade	(Index) Shillings/quarter
1500–9	108	2.69	1630–9	(876)–21.81
1510–9	112	2.79	1640–9	(796)–19.82
1520–9	136	3.39	1650–9	17.85
1530–9	158	3.93	1660–9	17.50
1540–9	197	4.91	1670–9	16.91
1550–9	450	11.20	1680–9	16.36
1560–9	338	8.42	1690–9	18.73
1570–9	360	8.96	1700–9	17.06
1580–9	482	12.00	1710–9	18.66
1590–9	600	14.94	1720–9	19.84
1600–9	583	14.52	1730–9	17.30
1610–9	665	16.56	1740–9	16.84
1620–9	648	16.13	1750–9	17.90

Source: Bowden (1967: 857), and (1985: 865). Bowden's prices in (1967) are given only as an Index, but these are converted to shillings per quarter in line with (1985).

Figure 16.1 presents the price of barley expressed in grams of silver, while Figure 16.2 presents the same price in shillings per bushel. The two graphs reveal a clear difference in the later Middle Ages, when a series of weight reductions reduced the silver content of the coinage, and this contrast is illustrated more clearly in Figures 16.3 (silver weight) and 16.4 (shillings face value), which focus on the period 1209 to 1600. Expressing these prices in silver weight shows the

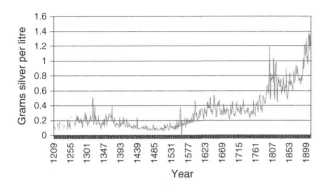

Figure 16.1 Barley prices in grams of silver per litre in England, 1209–1914.
Source: Clark (2006).

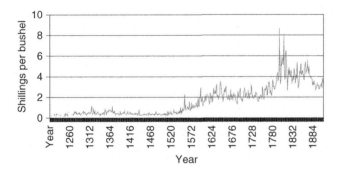

Figure 16.2 Barley prices in shillings per bushel in England, 1209–1914.
Source: Clark (2006).

reduction in the silver content of the coinage between 1351 and 1526 clearly. However, for the people of the time who actually experienced prices in sterling face value the late fourteenth- and fifteenth-century recession was eased somewhat. Reducing the silver content of the coinage acknowledged the rising European price of silver, and stretched the available bullion further. These modest currency devaluations clearly did not generate inflation, but helped to moderate a difficult economic climate by increasing the money supply.

However, the graphs do not reveal a contrast as one would expect in the mid-sixteenth century, when England experienced the worst debasement of its history. This puzzled me until I realized that Clark's silver weight prices do not properly reflect the debasement period. Clark's series needs to be amended at this point.[21] Wool prices are presented in Figures 16.5 to 16.8 in the same way. Again there is close correspondence between silver and shilling prices for wool after 1600, but a marked divergence in the fourteenth and fifteenth centuries (see especially the graphs concentrating on the period 1209 to 1600, Figures 16.7 and 16.8). The

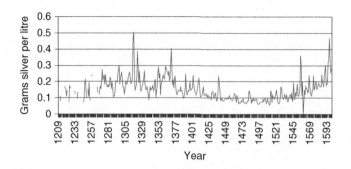

Figure 16.3 Barley prices in grams of silver per litre in England, 1209–1600.
Source: Clark (2006).

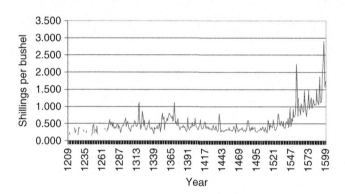

Figure 16.4 Barley prices in shillings per bushel in England, 1209–1600.
Source: Clark (2006).

same flaws in the Clark silver series again obscure the effects of the mid-sixteenth-century debasement.

Although calculating barley and wool prices in grams of silver can provide insights they also distance us from the experience of the people of the time, and they fail to acknowledge the truth that the value of silver was itself liable to fluctuate. It also creates a fertile source of potential error, as Clark's mistakes illustrate.

English and Babylonian prices for wool and barley

Although drawn from centuries and thousands of miles apart, comparison between the English and Babylonian barley and wool series prompts a number of observations.

The Babylonian prices were quoted as the quantity of barley and wool available for 1 shekel, and Van der Spek has explained the implications of this form of price

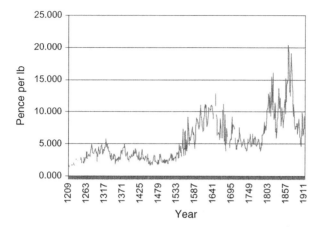

Figure 16.5 Wool prices in pence per pound in England, 1209–1914.
Source: Clark (2006).

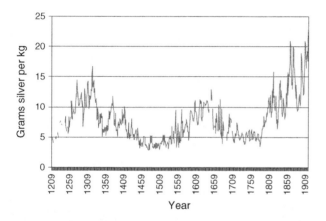

Figure 16.6 Wool prices in grams of silver per kg in England, 1209–1914.
Source: Clark (2006).

quotation, and also derived an alternative series expressed as the price in shekels of 1,000 litres.[22] We may note for example that the Babylonian shekel, like the English pound, was both a unit of weight and a unit of account. In both cases a weight of silver gave its name to a sum of money which was expressed in reality by a number of coins. Two drachma coins made a shekel, weighing about 8.33 grams of silver, but there was no shekel coin. Similarly the pound had no existence as a coin until the time of Henry VII, and coins with the value of a pound were exceedingly rare before the seventeenth century.[23] The correspondence between unit of weight and unit of account prompts the question of how far coins were

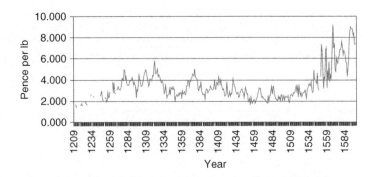

Figure 16.7 Wool prices in pence per pound in England, 1209–1600.
Source: Clark (2006).

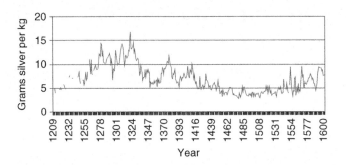

Figure 16.8 Wool prices in grams of silver per kg in England, 1209–1600.
Source: Clark (2006).

taken by weight or by number. The presumption among Babylonian scholars is that coins were weighed,[24] though we can be clear that in medieval England coin payments were sometimes weighed and sometimes taken by number at face value. Domesday Book and the twelfth-century Dialogue of the Exchequer both record payments which are sometimes weighed and sometimes taken by number. On some occasions there was even a requirement that coin be tested for the purity of the metal, though tests for metal fineness and weighing were mostly means by which the Royal Exchequer extracted additional payments from its officials and subjects. For the most part, in ordinary business the Crown required its people to accept coin at the face value it decreed, though very occasionally government did encourage the weighing of coins[25] and often the public weighed coin, especially gold, without any official encouragement.

As we have seen, behind this rather ambivalent attitude to weighing coin in payments or taking them by number lay a fundamental uncertainty about how far the pound was a unit of weight, and how far a unit of account. In the case of medieval England the monetary pound of account, consisting of 240 actual coins

Table 16.5 Pound as unit of account and as measure of weight

Date	Pence struck per pound weight	Weight of penny in grains
1247	242	22.3
1279	243	22.2
1331	Halfpence at 488	No pence struck
1335	Halfpence at 504	83% silver. No pence
1343	243	22.2
1344	266	20.3
1345	268	20.1
1346	270	20
1351	300	18
1413	360	15
1464	450	12
1526	540 (Troy pound)	10.6

(pennies), diverged from the pound weight quite early. It stabilized in the twelfth century at 5,400 grains (349.9 grams) for a monetary pound, compared with 5,760 grains (373.24 grams) for the Troy pound weight, but from the fourteenth century onward the weight of the penny was successively reduced every fifty years or so, so that by 1526 the pound of 5,760 grains was struck into 540 pennies (see Table 16.5).

What is more, on each occasion that the weight of the penny was reduced and more coins accordingly struck from the same weight of silver, there was no apparent impact on commodity prices.[26] This illustrates an important point, which is that the value of silver itself was rising. The idea that payments needed to be weighed or that economic historians should monitor the behaviour of prices in terms of grams of silver rather than in nominal prices are both based on the underlying assumption that metal prices are constant, whereas in truth they fluctuate in accordance with the laws of supply and demand. Nevertheless, if the precious metal content of the coinage were reduced beyond the rising value of the metal, prices certainly would respond, as the English experience during the debasement of Henry VIII and Edward VI makes clear. There seems to be a parallel in the reduction of the silver content of the coinage in the Parthian Empire which also corresponds with a period of rising prices after 141 BC (cf. Huijs *et al.*, Chapter 7, this volume; Appendix of Babylonian Prices, this volume).

Returning to the Babylonian drachma and shekel, we would ask whether it might be possible that payments in coin could on occasion have been made by number rather than always by weight. Much of the point of coin is that it removes the requirement to weigh or even assay payments. If weighing is always required anyway, the distinction between payment in coin and payment in bullion begins to fade away, and the advantages of coin disappear. Yet we need not doubt that those advantages were real, since merchants paid a premium, represented by the mintage and seignorage charges, to have bullion minted into coin. Of course the weight of coin was often checked, but it may be that ancient coin was more often paid by number than has generally been suggested. Nor should the expression of prices in a unit of weight – the shekel – necessarily imply that money payments were all weighed. The English pound shows how a unit of weight could evolve as a money of account without needing to be represented as a single coin. There seems to be some evidence that the shekel sometimes served as a money of account consisting of 2 drachmas. We may also note that both in England and in Babylonia coins were often used as weight standards for measuring other commodities, but this practice does not mean that they might not also pass unweighed as money (cf. Van der Spek *et al.*, Chapter 1 and Chapter 19, this volume).

The custom of presenting prices as the amount of a commodity available for the shekel of 2 drachmas has some similarities with the practice of English towns which recorded the amount of bread and ale available for a penny, thus fixing the unit of money rather than the unit of weight or volume. In England it is clear that this approach allowed for a much finer gradation of price change than the coinage itself permitted (though a loaf could only be priced at 1d, or a halfpenny or farthing, the weight of the loaf could be varied much more, ounce by ounce), and this was especially important for retail trade in towns when purchases were made with the smallest coins available. Whole books have been written about *The Big Problem of Small Change* in medieval Europe.[27] In England even the smallest available silver coins had significant purchasing power, and they were constantly in short supply. Recent research has demonstrated that in sixth-century Babylonia, classical Greece and the Hellenistic Near East small fractions of bullion and coins have been found to have been less exceptional than was once thought.[28] Perhaps it is enough here to note that the English evidence suggests that a pure silver coinage had difficulty providing convenient units for small purchases which were probably an inseparable feature of town life. Surprisingly little has been written about the necessary association of monetization and urbanization, but Jan Lucassen has promoted a comparative study of how far denominational structure may have been geared to the requirements of wage payments.[29]

Another entirely different aspect of the comparison of English and Babylonian money and prices concerns the impact of war. It has been observed that the opening of the Persian treasuries by Alexander in 330 BC made silver abundant and prices high, while after his death the wars of succession had similar effects (cf. Van der Spek *et al.*, Chapter 19, this volume). Although there are some occasions when ransom payments to or from England may have increased or reduced bullion supplies in medieval England, it is noteworthy that trade fluctuations affecting the flow of bullion connected with the wool and cloth trades seem to have been more powerful factors. The outbreak of the Hundred Years War in 1337 saw the effects of war and trade combined, as Edward III diverted the profits of the wool trade directly to funding the war in France, leading to coin shortage in England and a dip in prices. This can be compared to the costs of the war of Antiochus III against the Romans in 189–188 BC, which had similar effects (Van der Spek *et al.*, Chapter 19, this volume).

The wealth of English price and monetary data allows one to explore the relationship between money and prices in some depth. The idea that a rise in the money supply is likely to generate a rise in the level of prices is enshrined in contemporary economic policy of most central banks. In Britain the Monetary Policy Committee of the Bank of England is expected to target an annual inflation rate of 2 per cent by adjusting the rate of interest as the simplest way to influence money supply. Although the accuracy with which the 2 per cent target is achieved may be questioned, the efficacy of the interest rate instrument is widely accepted: raising the interest rate tightens the money supply and tends to lower prices, while cutting the interest rate increases money supply and raises prices. The adoption of these economic principles into an explicitly acknowledged policy is only a feature of the last twenty years, but the core idea that an increasing money supply raises prices and a contracting money supply lowers them can be traced to at least the sixteenth century.[30] In modern times it was codified in Irving Fisher's Quantity Theory, expressed as $MV = PT$, where M stands for the money supply, V for velocity of circulation, P for the price level and T for the level of transactions. Cambridge economists, most famously Maynard Keynes, operated with an alternative version of the same theory, expressed as $M = kY$, in which Y stands for estimated GDP at current prices. This is used as a measure of the size of the economy in place of transactions which are otherwise difficult to quantify; k stands for the demand for money to hold, the inverse of V ($k = 1/V$).[31] After World War II, Keynes' General Theory tended to eclipse his two works on money,[32] and the monetarist argument was propounded above all by Milton Friedman and the Chicago school. Nevertheless it is important to recognize that monetary history need not necessarily be 'monetarist' in the Chicago sense, and an essentially Keynesian monetary history is perfectly feasible.

This point is worth making since for some reason monetary history has encountered vigorous opposition among scholars of medieval and early modern history, who prefer to explain the behaviour of prices – especially the price rises of the thirteenth and the sixteenth–seventeenth centuries – above all in demographic terms. The argument is that rising population increased demand for goods – above all food – faster than could be met by increased supply, and that this shift in the balance of supply and demand caused prices to rise. In fairness it should be admitted that most proponents of the demographic explanation nowadays think of it as the principal determining factor in the movement of prices, but not as the only one. Along with possible environmental factors, monetary influence on the behaviour of prices is accepted, though in a secondary role. Thus Hatcher and Bailey for the Middle Ages, and Wordie[33] and Bowden[34] for the early modern period, together with D. H. Fischer[35] for both periods do accept some monetary influence on prices, while nevertheless reserving the role of 'prime mover' for population change. This school of thought accepts some monetary influence at certain points in the story: for example when prices rise immediately after the Black Death when demand for food fell by one-half to one-third, it is generally accepted that the corresponding rise in coin per capita explains the burst of enhanced prices. The argument that monetary factors influenced prices sometimes but not consistently seems to me difficult to sustain. My own view would be that the monetary effect on prices was constant, though it becomes more or less apparent from time to time.

Nevertheless, several erroneous arguments are still repeatedly proposed to deny money a more permanent role. For example it is often suggested that a price rise occurring for monetary reasons should impact all prices equally.[36] This falsehood has been refuted many times,[37] but it is still being put forward. In fact although money does impact on the general level of prices, there is no reason to expect it to affect all prices equally.[38] Different commodities have varying levels of elasticity of demand. In difficult times of course people economize on luxuries or inessentials, which accordingly rise in price less than necessities.

Money's influence on the behaviour of historic prices has also been questioned on the grounds that the development of credit will have liberated the economy from the constraints of a limited coin supply. It must be readily conceded that the evidence for the role of credit in medieval and early modern England is extensive and powerful. Anglo-Saxon charters show that loans were secured against property, and the evidence of Jewish money-lending is well known.[39] The Jews were excluded from other means of earning a living but found a role where Christians were constrained, lending money. However, much medieval lending did in fact also take place between Christians, for it was usury which was prohibited, while lending at reasonable rates of interest which did no more than compensate for the lender's opportunity cost or for any delayed repayment, was accepted.[40] The twelfth-century lending of William Cade is well known,[41] while in the late thirteenth century Italian bankers assumed an important role financing sovereign debts, and lending to the Church itself. In the 1280s Edward I put in place improved legal machinery for the recovery of debts even before the expulsion of the Jews. This legal machinery has left behind an extensive series of records of credit and debt from all over England, extending into the sixteenth century,[42] and by the fifteenth century the records of bankers involved in international credit reveal the extensive use of international bills.[43] In the sixteenth century such bills were also employed widely in inland trade,[44] even though these merchant obligations could not be enforced in the courts before the eighteenth century.[45] There can be no doubt that lending was extremely widespread throughout English society, as Kowaleski has shown for medieval Exeter and Muldrew for early modern King's Lynn.[46] It is no exaggeration to say that credit was an essential feature of the English economy.[47]

There remains, however, a fundamental dispute between those who believe that these credit networks and legal structures solved the problem of illiquidity on the one hand, and those who argue that universal dependence on credit merely illustrates the size of the problem on the other. Impressive though the legal systems for the prosecution of debt may have been, they were also expensive, and added very significantly to transaction costs. Moreover, it has to be recognized that credit itself was dependent on the extent of the money supply. Historians seem sometimes to have failed to grasp the fundamental point well known to both medieval and modern bankers: when money is tight, so too is credit; when money is plentiful, credit may easily be had. Thus credit grows or contracts with the money supply; it does not compensate for any shortfall. This point can perhaps be most powerfully illustratedby the evidence for the reduction in velocity which is a feature of English economic development from the Norman Conquest to modern times.

The behaviour of velocity has been widely misunderstood, so it is worth taking a little time to explain it. Velocity, the V of Fisher's Quantity Theory (or the inverse of Keynes' k, the demand for money to hold) falls over time from medieval to modern times.[48] Velocity does not measure the frequency of money payments in the economy, which does indeed increase over time, but rather indicates the number of times the money supply (M) needs to turn over in order to accomplish the total amount of required business in the economy (T). V is thus a function of M, P and T. That it can be shown to have risen historically over time demonstrates that it is the rise in M, not V, which is characteristic of growing or modernizing economies. Indeed the historical evidence shows that there are real limits to how large V can become, without impacting seriously on the economy. The eleventh-century V of over 10 in fact required a large amount of business to be carried out by non-monetary expedients, such as labour services or payments in kind instead of money rents and wages.[49] More thorough monetization required a reduction in V and a growth in M.

It is this point which confirms the observation above that credit cannot grow without an increase in the available money supply.[50] If credit itself is dependent on the money supply, the argument that the growth of credit liberated the economy from monetary constraints falls.

A third objection to the monetary explanation for the behaviour of medieval prices is that if the economy suffered from a chronic shortage of currency, bullion would have been diverted from luxury and display functions and made available as coin. In fact there are occasional instances where silver and gold plate was sent to the mints for conversion into coin, but these are exceptional. That it did not happen more often indicates that those who held the plate were not the classes most inconvenienced by the lack of coin. Moreover, the key factor determining the flow of bullion to the mints can be seen to be the price for that bullion offered by the mints. If, as was characteristic of England in the eighteenth century, the mints offered a lower price for silver than the goldsmiths making plate, or the East India Company for export to the East, then bullion would not feed the mints. Thus a shortage of currency might be caused by scarcity of bullion, but plentiful bullion did not guarantee a ready supply of coin if the mint price for metal was uncompetitive.

Of course mints most easily raised the price they offered for bullion by reducing the precious metal content of the coins. Much has been written about the evils of debasement, and there is no shortage of examples of its pernicious effects, but it has perhaps been less widely recognized that maintaining a currency which is too strong could also create difficulties. Strong money keeps prices down, but it can make exports uncompetitive and domestic money scarce, inhibiting growth.[51] Those charged with the control of English monetary policy in the Middle Ages and early modern era generally erred on the side of keeping sterling too strong; or to put it another way, they failed to recognize that other countries were setting a higher price on bullion. Underlying this whole issue, are the conflicting functions of money. Traditionally these are defined as 1) a means of exchange, 2) a store of value and 3) a measure of value, but these functions actually pull in opposite directions. Providing an adequate means of exchange for a growing economy, which often involves an element of inflation, conflicts with the interests of those most concerned to preserve the value of the money they hold. In short, the complexities involved in the valuation of the currency mean that any simplistic assertion that bullion can be found from other sources to supply a monetary shortage is mistaken.

Equally the idea that New World bullion cannot be shown to have reached England can be set aside, as Challis has shown, and in any case the mint accounts prove that money supply was growing.[52] At least £2.7 million must have been present in England in 1603, since that much Elizabethan coin was still in circulation in the 1640s.[53] Thus we may safely discount the suggestion that the money supply was not affected by fluctuations in bullion supply.

Finally, monetary explanations for the movement of prices have also been challenged on the grounds that any change in price should be proportionate to the change in money supply, and demonstrating such proportionality has proved very difficult. In fact the expectation of proportionality originates in Irving Fisher's Quantity Theory, but was effectively dismissed by Keynes and others who have observed that such theoretical proportionality could take a very long time to work through the system. In reality prices and wages do not adjust easily but are often 'sticky', and some adjustments occur faster than others. Generally prices tend to rise faster than wages, but both tend to fall only slowly as sellers and workers are reluctant to accept less than they have come to expect. The Quantity Theory is just that – a theory – which is not borne out precisely by events at any one moment, since the effects unroll at varying speeds. The Fisher *Identity*, however, is constructed as a truism: any disproportionality between money supply and prices is explained by adjustments to velocity (or k in the Cambridge version) or to the level of transactions (or the size of the economy.)

Thus the objections commonly advanced to deny a monetary role in the behaviour of prices can be effectively met. A monetary effect would not impact on all prices equally. Credit follows the money supply, rather than compensating for any shortage (cf. Aarts, Chapter 15, this volume). Both shortages of coin and monetary booms can be related to known mint output, and the estimates of money supply based on them. And finally, there is no need to demonstrate *proportionate* changes to money supply and prices; it is enough to show a broad correspondence, and this can be demonstrated.

Nevertheless, even those convinced of the importance of the monetary role in the economy have recognized the fundamental agency of land and labour. Peter Spufford, who has done more for the cause of monetary factors than any other historian, regarded demographic factors as the motor of the medieval European economy, while monetary growth simply released the brake which allowed the vehicle to move forward. Historians have generally found it easier to accept this elegantly formulated compromise than to swallow the more fully committed monetary theories of scholars like John Day, John Munro and Pamela Nightingale.

I have myself argued for a major but not exclusively monetary role in the determination of prices, and this still seems the most balanced approach, though it should be recognized that monetary and demographic explanations may not always be compatible. Wordie, who places himself in the demographic camp while accepting some role for money, has accepted that a rising population would result in a smaller amount of coin per head of the population, and might therefore very well have a *deflationary* effect on prices.[54] Similarly, other things being equal, a rising population would be expected to lower wage costs. Thus demographic growth would only be inflationary if it could be shown both that money supply grew more than the population, and that population grew faster than the supply of goods.

As we have seen, modern economic policy is founded on the role of money supply as a cause of inflation, while it is also recognized that price rises originating in a shift in the balance of supply and demand can only be reflected in prices if the money supply 'validates' the change. However, there seems to be a fundamental though surprising dislocation between the thinking of twenty-first-century economists on the one hand and economic historians of the medieval and early modern period on the other. While the former generally accept money's influence on prices as a given, the latter resist it doggedly, while neither party even seems to be aware of the existence of the other.[55] However, if as seems to be the case, money supply is nowadays thought to have a major influence on the behaviour of contemporary prices, it seems reasonable to ask why it should not have been equally influential in the past.

Could it be that this distinction between contemporary and medievalist thinking is explained by the much greater role played by money in the modern world? Alfred Marshall, another great Cambridge economist, was always cautious about applying contemporary economic theory to history on the grounds that in many respects the past was different.[56] Such an approach would have obvious implications for the study of Babylonian prices. However, all recent work in medieval economic history has tended to emphasize the fact that commercial factors and the use of money and credit were important much earlier than previous generations (including Marshall's) may have thought. The work of historians such as Dyer, Britnell, Campbell and Kowaleski is vivid testimony to the importance of commercial and monetized transactions in thirteenth-century England. Moreover, Dyer has also argued for much commercial activity as early as the eleventh century, and serious students have long been impressed by the ubiquity of coin in the Domesday Book.[57] The evidence of coin finds also contributes to the impression of widespread use of coin in England in the eleventh century and before.[58] This is not to suggest that there were no differences between ancient, medieval and modern money: self-evidently money has been expressed variously in precious metal, paper, and electronic accounts. The proportion of wage-earners and primary producers has varied. The economy has evolved through all the phases of capital and industrial development.

Nevertheless to the extent that money prices operated in ancient, medieval and modern economies, it would seem to be difficult to argue that monetary factors influenced prices in the twentieth and twenty-first centuries but not in the sixteenth or the thirteenth. Though earlier generations struggled with more or less chronic illiquidity, money has been shown to be central to the conduct of both economic and political business from at least the thirteenth century, and recent interpretations of the Anglo-Saxon, Byzantine, Roman, Iron Age and Babylonian economy all envisage an increasing role for money and the market.

Indeed Peter Temin has argued that the behaviour of Babylonian prices can be shown to be driven by the market in much the same way as medieval, early modern and modern prices.[59] The plentiful English evidence allows us to review the movement of money prices, to establish how far they can be shown to be consistent with the operation of markets and the laws of supply and demand. Of course the efficient operation of markets is always subject to the provision of information and the availability of transport. Moreover those in a position to manipulate markets and exploit inefficiencies have always done so. *Mutatis mutandis*, ancient and medieval markets were no more perfect than modern ones. Yet we can examine the behaviour of prices to see how far they moved in ways capable of rational explanation. I intend to look first at price movements over the course of the harvest, and then to compare prices and yields from year to year to see how far high yields lead to low prices as we would expect, and vice versa. This will be done first as a simple correlation, and then on the basis of a regression analysis. Finally I will examine how far markets appear to be integrated, allowing poor yields to be offset by the movement of grain from higher yielding areas.

Over the course of a single year medieval prices generally did reflect the ebb and flow of supply and demand, typically falling after the harvest when goods were plentiful but rising towards the end of the growing year as the previous year's harvest became exhausted. Temin notes this pattern for barley and date prices in Babylon,[60] and the same trend is clear in thirteenth-century England.[61] However, occasionally the simplicity of this pattern was complicated as farmers and merchants estimated the likely success of the coming harvest. Moreover, some attempts at corn storage or the importing or exporting of corn could have an impact on the 'normal' pattern.[62] Galloway's study of the Exeter data showed that the degree of price variation within the year altered markedly between the 1320s and the 1360s without identifying any clear explanation.[63] In short, the main outlines of the surviving evidence are broadly compatible with modern theoretical expectations but at the detailed level the correspondence is often less than perfect. Yet despite such irregularities, the fundamental underlying features of the growing year are for the most part reflected in the pattern of money prices.

Another approach allows us to observe the consequences of harvest success or failure as they are revealed by the annual price. Medieval English manorial accounts provide a wealth of information that enables us to calculate the harvest yield for most years from the early thirteenth century to the end of the fifteenth. This information on yields of wheat, barley and oat harvests from a host of manors in southern England has been wonderfully made available on the web, as the fruit of Bruce Campbell's ground-breaking research project.[64] Naturally, yields in any one year varied a good deal from place to place, reflecting the character of the soil, the vagaries of the weather, and the efficiency and diligence of the cultivators. These variables resulted in much yield and price variation over the country as a whole. However, Campbell has been able to construct an indication of the national yield for each year to set alongside the notional national price suggested by Farmer and Bowden, and these price series have been adapted by Clark and Allen to permit their continuation into the early modern period. Of course all such abstractions are constructs which can be criticized by other scholars minded to make their calculations and assumptions slightly differently, but although each competing price series differs somewhat from the others, the broad outline pattern they reveal is largely similar.

These data permit us to explore the hypothesis that prices and yields should be inversely correlated, high yields leading to low prices and vice versa. There are many reasons why this correlation might be less than perfect. The national figures for price and yield may imperfectly reflect reality. The medieval markets will have lacked perfect information about yields either locally, regionally, nationally or internationally. Transport networks will have imperfectly connected markets, and if they had worked perfectly the costs of transport would have affected prices as well as the harvest yield. It should also be borne in mind that our yield data come to us entirely from seigniorial accounts, while we know that peasant production contributed very significantly to the market and may have achieved different yields.[65] Nevertheless, despite these distorting factors, Campbell's correlation of these national series of yields and prices is interesting.[66]

Campbell shows how far prices and yields correlate, so that the higher the value of r (the degree of correlation), the stronger the relationship between the two variables.[67] They suggest that the degree of correlation varied over time and from grain to grain. Wheat appears to correlate better than the other grains, perhaps because wheat was more widely bought and sold, while a higher proportion of the barley and oat crop was liable to be consumed by producers rather than sold. The variation in the extent of correlation over time may suggest that prices and yields correlated better in periods of higher prices, and/or times of greater liquidity. Although the evidence taken as a whole confirms the existence of a relationship between prices and yields, it is less clear-cut than we would have expected if markets and money prices were operating perfectly.

An alternative approach also based on the assumption that yields are an important determining factor for prices is a regression analysis of yields and prices. I first attempted this method in 1988, based solely on yields and prices from the estates of the bishop of Winchester.[68] It is now possible to apply the same methods to the additional price and yield data collected by the Campbell project.[69] Taking yield as the independent variable and price as the dependent variable, it is possible to suggest the likely price for any given yield. I have analysed the data in a series of separate periods, since the long-term trend of rising prices through the thirteenth and early fourteenth centuries followed by a falling or flat trend from the late fourteenth underlies the annual variation.

The thirteenth century data appear in Figures 16.9 to 16.11. The *R* squared figures suggest that between 27 and 36 per cent of the price variation observed can be explained by the variations in yield. The *R* squared for the century as a whole is 32 per cent. The slope of the best fit line is negative in all cases, as we would expect, since prices rise as yields fall. The average price in shillings per quarter rises from the 4.3 shillings a quarter in the first half of the century, to 5.7 shillings a quarter in the second half of the century. Only 16 and 26 pairs of data

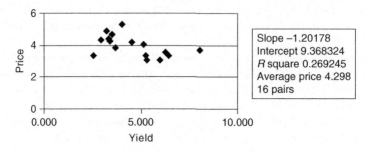

Figure 16.9 Correlation of wheat prices and yields, 1210–57.

Source: Campbell (2007).

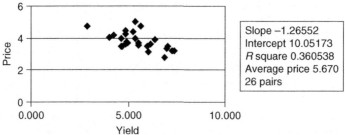

Figure 16.10 Correlation of wheat prices and yields, 1264–1302.

Source: Campbell (2007).

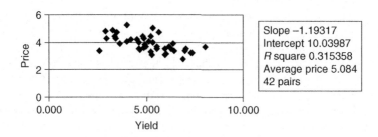

Figure 16.11 Correlation of wheat prices and yields, 1210–1302.

Source: Campbell (2007).

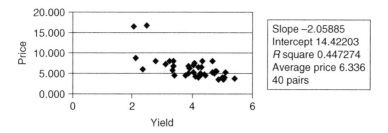

Figure 16.12 Correlation of wheat prices and yields, 1305–50.

Source: Campbell (2007).

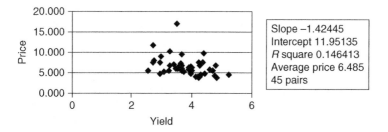

Figure 16.13 Correlation of wheat prices and yields, 1351–1400.

Source: Campbell (2007).

were available for Figures 16.9 and 16.10, which is why the century as a whole was treated in Figure 16.11, which had 42 pairs.

Figure 16.12 shows that prices peaked in the first half of the fourteenth century, when the average price reached 6.34 shillings. The slope of the line was also steepest then, although that and the high intercept point are perhaps unduly skewed by the exceptional famine prices of 1315 and 1316. However, the high R squared number indicates that 44 per cent of the price variation in this period may be explained by the yield variations.

The explanatory power of these regressions falls sharply after the Black Death, as indicated by the R squared numbers for Figure 16.13 (0.15) and Figure 16.14 (0.0820), but the average price remains high, at 6.5 shillings in the second half of the fourteenth century and 6 shillings between 1401 and 1450. In the fifteenth century the slope, at −0.65, though still negative, is alarmingly flat, confirming that in this period prices were much less responsive to changes in yield than previously.

Generally the results confirm the suggestion that the movement of prices is compatible with rational market expectations. The market is, however, far from perfect. In addition to the reasons offered above for such imperfections, one may note here that prices may come from any point in the year, and we know that

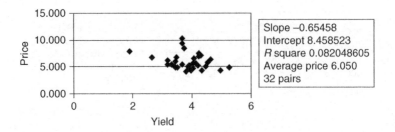

Figure 16.14 Correlation of wheat prices and yields, 1401–50.

Source: Campbell (2007).

they normally varied over the course of the year. A price from the summer of 1251 might reflect either the residue of the previous harvest or be influenced by an awareness of the prospects for the coming harvest, or both. In short, associating any harvest with its subsequent price is not exact. Given all these possible sources of error, the regression of prices and yields is necessarily a somewhat approximate exercise. It does generally confirm their relationship, and demonstrate that market prices were responsive to harvest yields, though more so in the thirteenth and fourteenth centuries than in the fifteenth. However, in a perfect market we might expect prices to be much more closely related to supply, as indicated here by the recorded yields. Transport costs need also to be accounted for if productive areas were to supply areas of shortage, and the possibility of speculative storage could also distort prices. Above all one must recognize that the information at the disposal of medieval price setters can only have been imperfect, and the data available to the historian, though exceptionally rich for historical data, are nevertheless partial.

Conclusion

The plentiful English medieval data also allow us to approach the question of market integration. It has been convincingly demonstrated that London drew its corn supply from its agricultural hinterland to which it was connected by water transport, prices in the capital approximating to those in the hinterland plus the costs of transport.[70] Thus prices to the west of London along the Thames Valley fall gradually as the distance from the capital increases. It can also be shown that farming practice and the prices paid varied from region to region, reflecting the nature of the land and climate. Long ago N. S. B. Gras attempted to map the different regions of medieval England and to demonstrate their different price regimes.[71] This work has been criticized on the grounds that the regions were defined somewhat arbitrarily, that prices were grouped together over long periods, and that the creation of regional price averages lacked statistical sophistication. Importantly it has been pointed out that: 'Rather than regions of price-equality, we should expect to find, if the market were integrated, that prices vary across the country in a logical manner, with differentials reflecting the cost of transport between locations.'[72]

Nevertheless the fundamental observation that different regions were farmed in different ways and experienced different price regimes is sound.[73] For example, Norfolk specialized in barley, which it grew cheaply enough to allow it to bear the transport costs of sending large quantities to London. Generally speaking northern England paid more for corn but less for meat, reflecting the rough grazing which supported cattle and the poorer climate and shorter growing season which discouraged arable. This contrast can be very clearly illustrated by the comparison of prices in England and Scotland.[74] As one goes further north cattle prices fall and grain prices rise, and this difference led to different patterns of consumption and established the basis of longer-distance trade. Scots, unable to successfully grow wheat, ate more oats or imported wheat, which they paid for with the profits of the cattle trade. This was an enduring relationship based on unchanging fundamentals. The drovers' roads that brought cattle south were permanent features of the landscape for centuries. Merchants and farmers knew with certainty that corn was cheaper in the south and meat cheaper further north, and that London would pay good prices for both.

Regional towns had similar relationships with their own hinterlands, but at the very local level the case for market integration may have been less certain. Although corn yields might vary markedly over quite short distances in one year, reflecting better farming practice, unless performance was consistently superior the transport and information networks required were unlikely to develop. In other words the evidence for market integration is confused, and different scholars have reached different conclusions. Gregory Clark found the evidence suggestive of reasonably efficient markets,[75] while James Galloway thought 'it may be that annual prices constitute too coarse-grained a measure to fully reflect changes in integration levels' and 'Clearly, there is as yet no certainty about the long-term course of change in price volatility and integrated levels within the English grain market'.[76]

It is difficult to determine objectively how perfect the correlation of prices and yields or the degree of market integration might reasonably be expected to be. The data from medieval England does provide evidence that prices rose or fell in line with harvest success or failure, and that trade networks were established to allow centres of cheaper production to market their goods where demand was sufficient to justify the transport costs. The market was very far from perfect, but money prices moved broadly in line with expectations, confirming both the commercial nature of medieval society and the fact that monetized transactions were widespread. This is not to deny the existence of labour rents and payments in kind, or of auto-consumption by producers, or uneconomic practice by those wealthy enough to prioritize other religious or social considerations. But it is to assert that the prices and trade patterns we observe are capable of rational explanation consistent with a somewhat imperfect market economy. We concur with Temin's judgement that Babylonian, ancient, medieval and modern prices behave like market-driven prices. In other words, we can see money behaving like money from ancient to modern times.

Appendix

Table A16.1 Corrections to Gregory Clark's calculation of the weight of silver in grams in the pound sterling, 1541–60

Year	GC calculation	NM calculation	% pure silver
1541	153.4	153.4	92.5
1542	143.9	118.0	75.8
1544	143.9	116.6	75.0
1545	143.9	77.8	50.0
1546	143.9	51.8	33.0
1551	143.9	25.9	25.0
1551	115.1	114.5	92.1
1553	115.1	114.1	91.7
1560	115.1	115.1	92.5

Notes

1 Metcalf (1998), for example at p. 279: 'The regional pattern of minting and coin circulation strongly suggest that the predominant uses of coinage were commercial, and involved trade between the east-coast ports and their hinterlands, which overlapped, especially south of the Humber. If coin circulation had been essentially local, the single finds would have consisted mostly of coins of the local mint, which is far from being the case. If the predominant uses of coinage had been fiscal and administrative, one might have expected minting to be more nearly in proportion to the wealth of each shire, and single finds to reveal a tendency towards coin circulation confined within shire boundaries. There are no signs of such a pattern.'

2 Exceptionally Scottish coins were tolerated so far as they were struck on the English sterling standard. Imitation sterling struck in the Low Countries was plentiful in the 1290s, but successfully driven out thereafter. Venetian *soldini* occur in small numbers in the fifteenth century, when they supplied a demand for English halfpennies. Florentine gold enjoyed a very limited circulation among merchants and bankers in the early fourteenth century, but this ceased to be the case once the Crown began to issue its own gold coinage in the 1340s. See especially Cook (1999: 231–84).

3 Challis (1992, Appendix 1). Mint Output, 1220–1985.

4 The use of die-studies to estimate mint output in periods when documentary evidence is not available may be applicable to the ancient world, although some scholars have devoted much energy to the argument that this should not be done. See particularly the work of Ted Buttrey, especially Buttrey (1993). Suffice it to say, on this occasion, that in the medieval period estimates based on die-studies have been confirmed by surviving mint documents and the continuing discovery of stray finds. My own view is that in the absence of such confirmation die-studies need to be interpreted with caution, but they are too important to be rejected altogether.

5 See Allen (2001), which updates and corrects earlier estimates including my own. However, the figures in Table 16.1 for 1290 to 1331 are my own, since I am not persuaded by Allen's estimates for this period. See Mayhew (2004: 81 and 86, n. 41). 1526–1600 estimates are based on Challis (1992). See also Mayhew (1995b) and Cameron (1967).

6 Nightingale (1990) has written extensively on medieval credit, but see also Schofield and Mayhew (2002).

7 Postan (1973). Also Richards (1965: 44–8), where inland and outland bills and promissory notes achieved various stages of assignability and negotiability in the Law Merchant and the Common Law. All types of promissory notes were ultimately declared negotiable by Act of Parliament: Statute of Anne, 1704, 3 and 4 Anne, c.8

8 Cameron (1967: 42).

9 Kerridge (1988: 99), where he observes: 'The volume of inland bills of exchange is unknown, except that it must have been great and increasing.' His attempt to estimate the ratio of money to credit on the basis of 351 inventories is difficult to evaluate.

10 This approach necessarily involves broad estimates and gross simplifications and almost every figure could be discussed at length. Debating and refining these figures is the numismatist's and monetary historian's stock-in-trade. For our present purposes it is perhaps enough to treat them as working hypotheses adequate for methodological comparison with the Babylonian data.

11 Rogers (1866–1902).

12 Beveridge (1939).

13 Phelps Brown and Hopkins (1956).

14 Farmer (1988, 1991).

15 Bowden (1967, 1985).

16 Allen (2001: es p. 419–24). His consumer price indices are available at www.nuffield. ox.ac.uk/users/allen. See also Clark (2009).

17 Allen (2005: 20 and Table 13).

18 The Farmer and Bowden series are not completely compatible, as they reach different prices for the period 1450–1500. See Farmer (1991: 501). Nevertheless Farmer (1991: 497) judged there to be 'a high degree of consistency between the calculations of Thorold Rogers, Lord Beveridge, and P. J. Bowden,' and his own.

19 Dyer (1994: 159f.): 'By the early fifteenth century, harvest workers were allowed a pound of meat for every two pounds of bread, compared with an ounce or two of meat for every two pounds of bread 150 years earlier.' Bowden (1967: 625–9) gives various examples of how the fortunes of the grain harvest could also affect meat and wool sales.

20 Clark (2006) presents annual prices for an extensive series of commodities, essentially based on the work of earlier price historians, but the range of Clark's prices from the thirteenth to the twentieth centuries in both sterling face value and silver weight prices makes this compilation invaluable. It is this series which has principally been used by Bruce Campbell on his website. I am most grateful to Bas van Leeuwen, of Professor Campbell's team, who kindly and swiftly provided me with additional data lying behind Campbell (2007).

21 My corrections to Clark's series are available in the Appendix to this chapter.

22 Van der Spek (2005); cf. Van der Spek *et al.*, Chapter 1, this volume.

23 Actually, although the guinea was initially envisaged as a pound coin, the value of its gold content rose above 20 shillings. It was not until the nineteenth century that the sovereign gave effective expression to the pound of 20 shillings.

24 Powell (1996); Vargyas (2000). Cited by Temin (2002); cf. Van der Spek *et al.* (Chapter 1, this volume).

25 At the time of John's recoinage in 1205.

26 Exceptionally prices do rise after the 1351 currency adjustment, though this is best explained in terms of the sharp rise in money per head of the population resulting from the onset of the Black Death.

27 Sargent and Velde (2003).

28 Kim (1999, 2001); Duyrat, Chapter 14, and Jursa, Chapter 5, this volume.

29 Lucassen (2007).

30 Early writings by Bodin (1568), Smith (1581) and de Malynes (1601) are conveniently summarized by Outhwaite (1969). Volckart (1997) argues that members of the Polish

court discussed the influence of the supply of money on prices in the 1540s (Copernicus in 1517 had observed how the silver content of the coinage influenced prices).

31 Mayhew (1995b).

32 Keynes (1923, 1930).

33 Wordie (1997).

34 Bowden (1967: 595–6).

35 Fischer (1999: 19). Fischer at p. 85 also quotes Hakewill (1630): 'The plenty of coin and multitude of men . . . either of which asunder, but much more together, must needs be a means of raising prices of all things', quoted by Fisher (1965: 120–1).

36 Hatcher and Bailey (2001: 61) describe Postan's use of this mistaken argument. It is repeated by Fischer (1999: 75).

37 For example by Outhwaite (1969: 45–6). He concluded: 'That all prices should have risen, or have risen equally, are the last things we should expect.' Temin (2002: 57) goes even further: 'Only administered [as opposed to market] prices maintain their relative prices over long stretches of time.'

38 Volckart (1997: 447) argues that a change in the general level of prices is to be explained by a change in the supply of money or the velocity of its circulation, while a change in relative prices may result from changes in the structure of demand. Of course such a change in the structure of demand may also be brought about by changes in the money supply (M).

39 On Jewish lending see Stacey (1995) and Mundill (2002). On Anglo-Saxon lending see the paragraphs contributed by Susie Mayhew to Mayhew (2013: 197–213), especially at 199–201.

40 The Christian order of the Knights Templar, who financed the ransom of Louis IX, were prominent lenders. See Joinville (1874), cited by Metcalf (1980: 1).

41 DNB (2004), under William Cade.

42 Nightingale (1990).

43 Bolton (2007).

44 Kerridge (1988).

45 Postan (1973).

46 Kowaleski (1995), especially Chapter 5, and Muldrew (1993, 1998) present a picture in which whole towns seem to be involved in borrowing and/or lending to one another.

47 England was not exceptional. See Smail (2010).

48 Mayhew (1995b), Cameron (1967).

49 Mayhew (1995a: 72) for the suggestion of velocity greater than 10 in 1086.

50 Credit of course contributes to V, so far as it concerns cash loans, credit sales or deferred payments, but once credit instruments begin to circulate themselves they become Money. The exception to the observation that V falls over time is in the sixteenth century, when the calculated figures for V rise before falling again in the seventeenth century and thereafter. The explanation for this may lie in the absence of any allowance in the money supply for the role of Bills, which Kerridge believes was extensive and growing in the sixteenth century. An alternative view, famously propounded by Wordie, is that Elizabethan England actually suffered monetary deflation, i.e. that the price rise would have been even greater if the money supply had grown more. See Wordie (1997) and Kerridge (1988).

51 The effects of debasement are those of a modern devaluation, or of a reduction in the interest level. Debasements include the reduction of the weight of a coinage, as well as the reduction of the purity of the alloy.

52 Challis (1975: 392) reads: 'On the basis of manuscripts hitherto neglected [this brief analysis] has concluded that where documentation does survive [in the Mint ledgers and melting books] there is clear evidence of Spanish bullion not only influencing but actually dominating mint supply, and that this inflow of bullion was certainly connected with the seizures of treasure made by English seamen, and possibly also with both

a favourable balance of trade and a bi-metallic flow.' For France and Spain, metallic analyses confirm the arrival of New World silver in quantity from the 1570s. See Le Roy Ladurie *et al.* (1990).

53 Contrary to Wordie (1997: 60), where he argues that the currency may have been as small as £1.5 million to £2 million in 1603, see Besly (1987: 56), estimating that the silver currency in 1643 stood at £7.5 million made up of £3.5 million of Charles I (1625–49), £1.2 million of James I (1603–25), and £2.7 million of Elizabeth I (1558–1603), based on an analysis of 1640s hoards. If so much Elizabethan silver was still in circulation in 1643, at least as much, and probably significantly more, was present in 1603.

54 One might ponder whether the fall of prices of barley and dates (we have no evidence of wages) in second-century BC Babylon has something to do with a growth of population, perhaps as a result of the arrival of new Greek immigrants. The general idea of Babylon is a city in decline, but there may have been temporal increases. Unfortunately we have no demographic evidence for Hellenistic Babylon; cf. Huijs *et al.* (Chapter 7, this volume), for different explanations [note supplied by R. J. van der Spek].

55 For recent economic historians of modern times who assume monetary explanations of sixteenth- and seventeenth-century inflation, see for example MacDonald (2006: 119–20), and Reinhart and Rogoff (2009: 71). Reinhart and Rogoff (2009: 174) also apply monetary theory to ancient history. For Keynes, the fundamentals of monetary theory applied for the last four thousand years; cf. Keynes (1930, 1971 vol. 1: 4). I am grateful to Randall Wray for this reference.

56 Poynder (1999: 4–5) quotes Marshall thus: 'if we are dealing with the facts of remote times we must allow for the changes that have meanwhile come over the whole character of economic life: however closely a problem of today may resemble in its outward incidents another of recorded history, it is probable that a closer examination will detect a fundamental difference between their real characters.' (Marshall 1920: 774).

57 Douglas (1924: 90–100) and Lennard (1966: 115, 120, 176–80) saw this long ago, but it also informs the current thinking of Sally Harvey.

58 Databases of English coin finds may be found at PAS (2011) and at Fitzwilliam (2011).

59 Temin (2002: 53): 'The ancient prices behave like medieval and early modern prices, which in turn share the time-series properties of prices today.'

60 Temin (2002: 57). See also Jursa, Chapter 5, this volume, n. 8 and after n. 13; Huijs *et al.*, Chapter 7, this volume, AD n. 21.

61 Farmer (1988: 739). Campbell *et al.* (1993: 97) describe the seasonal movement of wheat prices in southern England thus: 'The general pattern was for prices to rise gradually from November to a peak in March, April, May, or June, which was often followed by a slight fall.'

62 Poynder (1999) summarizes the attempts of various historians to calculate the cost of grain storage in accordance with modern theory. However, the difficulty of reconciling the historical evidence with the theory may tell us as much about the quality of our evidence as about the soundness of the theory. Bowden (1967: 619) notes that in 1619 Robert Loder stored wheat after a good harvest for three years to sell it at three times its original value, but storage was not generally well organized; cf. the study of storage and risk aversion by Foldvari and Van Leeuwen, Chapter 18, this volume, arguing for the lack of interannual storage (apart from convenient yield storage) in most societies, including Babylonia. But China was possibly different; cf. Van der Spek *et al.*, Chapter 1, this volume.

63 Galloway (2000: 32 and 27 n. 17) for details on the Exeter sources. Bowden also noted unusual price movement within the year at Exeter (Bowden 1967: 620).

64 Campbell (2007).

65 While it used to be assumed that seigniorial yields exceeded peasant yields as a result of monopolizing manure supplies and maximizing capital inputs, recent work has argued

that peasant labour on smaller acreages may have done better than hired or exploited labour. Demesne estates may also have suffered from pilfering or fraud by accounting officials. Stone (1997) reveals the lower productivity of forced labour, and p. 655 suggests peasants worked harder for themselves. Campbell (1983: esp. at 30–41) suggests that contrary to Postan's view, peasants might have wrung better yields from their own land. It has long been recognized that peasant flocks contributed more to the national wool clip than the demesnes. See Power (1941: 29–31) and Bridbury (1977: 398).

66 Campbell (2007). For wheat see www.cropyields.ac.uk/images/chronologies_graph _05.png, for barley see www.cropyields.ac.uk/images/chronologies_graph_20.png and for oats see www.cropyields.ac.uk/images/chronologies_graph_25.png.

67 Campbell inverts the yield so that the correlation should be positive. The closer the result is to 1, the more perfect the correlation. 0 indicates the absence of any linear correlation.

68 Mayhew (1987).

69 Adding data from, for example, the Westminster Abbey estates.

70 Campbell *et al.* (1993). Also Galloway (2000).

71 Gras (1915).

72 Galloway (2000: 24) for this quotation and the other criticisms.

73 Bowden (1967: 857–75) provides a regional analysis of the 1640 to 1749 prices.

74 Gemmill and Mayhew (1995).

75 Clark (n.d.).

76 Galloway (2000: 41–2).

Bibliography

Allen, M. 2001. 'The Volume of the English Currency, 1158–1470', *Economic History Review*, 54: 595–611.

Allen, R. C. 2001. 'The Great Divergence in European Wages and Prices from the Middle Ages to the First World War', *Explorations in Economic History*, 38: 411–47.

—— 2005. 'English and Welsh Agriculture, 1300–1850: Output, Inputs, and Income', www.nuffield.ox.ac.uk/users/allen/unpublished/AllenE&W.pdf, (accessed on 18 March 2011).

Besly, E. 1987. *English Civil War Coin Hoards*, British Museum Occasional paper No 51, London: British Museum Press.

Beveridge, W. 1939. *Prices and Wages in England from the Twelfth to the Nineteenth Century*, London: Frank Cass & Co.

Bodin, Jean. 1568. *Paradoxes de M. de Malestroit touchant le fait des monnaies et l'enrichissement de toutes choses*, Paris: Jacques du Puys.

Bolton, J. 2007. 'The Borromei Bank Research Project', in *Money, Markets and Trade in Late Medieval Europe. Essays in Honour of John H. A. Munro*, edited by L. Armstrong, I. Elbl and M. M. Elbl, Leiden: Brill: 460–88.

Bowden, P. 1967. 'Agricultural Prices, Farm profits and Rents', in *Agrarian History of England and Wales*, IV, edited by Joan Thirsk, Cambridge: Cambridge University Press: 593–695 and 814–70.

—— 1985. 'Agricultural Prices, Wages, Farm Profits, and Rents', in *Agrarian History of England and Wales*, V, edited by Joan Thirsk, Cambridge: Cambridge University Press: 1–118.

Bridbury, A. R. 1977. 'Before the Black Death', *Economic History Review*, 30: 393–410.

Buttrey, T. 1993. 'Calculating Ancient Coin Production: Facts and Fantasies', *Numismatic Chronicle*, 153: 355–51.

Cameron R. 1967. 'England 1750–1844', in *Banking in the Early Stages of Industrialization*, edited by R. Cameron, Oxford: Oxford University Press: 15–59.

Campbell, B. M. S. 1983. 'Agricultural Progress in Medieval England: Some Evidence from Eastern Norfolk', *Economic History Review*, 36: 26–46.

—— 2007. *Three Centuries of English Crops Yields, 1211–1491*. www.cropyields.ac.uk (accessed on 2 September 2011).

Campbell, B. M. S., Galloway, J. A., Keene, D. and Murphy, M., eds. 1993. *A Medieval Capital and its Grain Supply: Agrarian Production and Distribution in the London Region c.1300*, London: Institute of British Geographers.

Challis, C. E. 1975. 'Spanish Bullion and Monetary Inflation in England in the Later Sixteenth Century', *Journal of European Economic History*, 4: 381–92.

—— ed. 1992. *A New History of the Royal Mint*, Cambridge: Cambridge University Press.

Clark, Gregory. 2006. www.iisg.nl.hpw/data.php#united (English Prices and Wages 1209–1914) links conveniently to the Global Price and Income Group at gpih.ucdavis.edu/files/England_1209–1914_(Clark).xls.

—— 2009. 'The Macroeconomic Aggregates for England, 1209–2008', UC Davis, Economics WP 09–19, revised October 2009.

—— n.d. 'Markets and Economic Growth: The Grain Market of Medieval England', www.econ.ucdavis.edu/faculty/gclark/210a/readings/market99.pdf (accessed on 18 March 2011).

Cook, B. J. 1999. 'Foreign Coins in Medieval England', in *Local Coins, Foreign Coins: Italy and Europe 11th–15th Centuries: The Second Cambridge Numismatic Symposium*, edited by L. Travaini, Milan: Società Numismatica Italiana: 231–84.

De Malynes, G. 1601. *Saint George for England, Allegorically Described*, London: Richard Field.

DNB. 2004. *Oxford Dictionary of National Biography*. Oxford: Oxford University Press.

Douglas, D. C. 1974. *The Social Structure of Medieval East Anglia*, Oxford: Clarendon Press 1927; reprint New York: Octagon.

Dyer, Chr. 1994. *Standards of Living in the Later Middle Ages: Social change in England c.1200–1520*, Cambridge: Cambridge University Press.

Farmer, D. L. 1988. 'Prices and Wages', in *Agrarian History of England and Wales*, II, edited by H. E. Hallam, Cambridge: Cambridge University Press: 716–817.

—— 1991. 'Prices and Wages, 1350–1500', in *Agrarian History of England and Wales*, III, edited by Edward Miller, Cambridge: Cambridge University Press: 431–525.

Fischer, D. H. 1999. *The Great Wave: Price Revolutions and the Rhythm of History*, Oxford: Oxford University Press.

Fisher, F. J. 1965. 'Influenza and Inflation in Tudor England', *Economic History Review*, 18: 120–9.

Fitzwilliam. 2011. 'Corpus of Early Medieval Coin Finds', www.fitzmuseum.cam.ac.uk/dept/coins/emc/ (accessed on 2 September 2011).

Galloway, J. 2000. 'One Market of Many? London and the Grain Trade of England', in *Trade, Urban Hinterlands and Market Integration c.1300–1600*, edited by J. Galloway, London: Centre for Metropolitan History: 23–42; http://sas-space.sas.ac.uk/42/1/galloway.pdf.

Gemmill, Elizabeth and Mayhew, N. 1995. *Changing Values in Medieval Scotland*, Cambridge: Cambridge University Press.

Gras, N. S. B. 1915 (1926). *The Evolution of the English Corn Market from the Twelfth to the Eighteenth Century*, Cambridge Mass: Harvard University Press.

Hakewill, G. 1630. *An Apologie or Declaration of the Power and Providence of God in the Government of the World*, 2nd edition, Oxford: William Turner.

Hatcher, J. and Bailey, M. 2001. *Modelling the Middle Ages: The History and Theory of England's Economic Development*, Oxford: Oxford University Press.

Joinville, J. de. 1874. *Histoire de St Louis*, edited by N. de Wailly, Paris: Librairie de L. Hachette.

Kerridge, E. 1988. *Trade and Banking in Early Modern England*, Manchester: Manchester University Press.

Keynes, J. M. 1923 (1971). *A Tract on Monetary Reform*, London: MacMillan.

—— 1930 (1971). *A Treatise on Money*. Vol. I–II, New York: Harcourt, Brace and Co. (also in *The Collected Writings of John Maynard Keynes*, Vol. V–VI, edited by D. E. Moggridge, London: Macmillan).

Kim, H. 1999. 'Small Change and the Moneyed Economy', in *Money, Labour and Land in Ancient Greece*, edited by P. Cartledge, E. E. Cohen and L. Foxhall, London: Routledge: 44–51.

—— 2001. 'Archaic Coinage As Evidence for the Use of Money', in *Money and its Uses in the Ancient Greek World*, edited by A. Meadows and K. Shipton, Oxford: Oxford University Press: 7–21.

Kowaleski, Mariane. 1995. *Local Markets and Regional Trade in Medieval Exeter*, Cambridge: Cambridge University Press.

Lennard, R. 1966. *Rural England, 1086–1135*, Oxford: Clarendon Press.

Le Roy Ladurie, E., Barrandon, J.-N., Collin, B., Guerra, M. and Morrisson, C. 1990. 'Sur les trace de "argent de Potosi" ', *Annales E.S.C.*, 45: 483–505.

Lucassen, J., ed. 2007. *Wages and Currency: Global Comparisons from Antiquity to the Twentieth Century*, Bern: Peter Lang AG.

MacDonald, J. 2006. *A Free Nation Deep in Debt: The Financial Roots of Democracy*, Princeton: Princeton University Press.

Marshall, A. 1920. *Principles of economics*, 8th edition, London: Macmillan.

Mayhew, N. J. 1987. 'Money and Prices in England from Henry II to Edward III', *Agricultural History Review*, 35: 121–32.

—— 1995a. 'Modelling Medieval Monetisation', in *A Commercialising Economy: England 1086 to c. 1300*, edited by R. H. Britnell and B. M. S. Campbell, Manchester: Manchester University Press: 55–77 and 195–6.

—— 1995b. 'Population, Money Supply, and the Velocity of Circulation in England, 1300–1700', *Economic History Review*, 47: 238–57.

—— 2004. 'Coinage and Money in England, 1086–c.1500', in *Medieval Money Matters*, edited by Diana Wood, Oxford: Oxbow: 72–86.

—— 2013. 'La richesse de l'Angleterre medieval dans ses rapports à La masse monétaire', in *Objets sous contrainte. Circulation des objets et valeur des choses au Moyen Age*, edited by L. Feller and A. Rodríguez, Paris: Publications de la Sorbonne: 197–213.

Metcalf, D. M. 1980. 'The Templars As Bankers, and Monetary Transfers Between West and East in the Twelfth Century', in *Coinage in the Latin East*, edited by P. W. Edbury and D. M. Metcalf, Oxford: British Archaeological Reports: 1–18.

—— 1998. *An Atlas of Anglo-Saxon and Norman Coin Finds, c. 973–1086*, London: Royal Numismatic Society.

Muldrew, C. 1993. 'Credit and the Courts: Debt Litigation in a Seventeenth-century Urban Community', *Economic History Review*, 46: 23–38.

—— 1998. *The Economy of Obligation*, Basingstoke: Palgrave MacMillan.

Mundill, R. R. 2002. 'Christian and Jewish Lending Patterns and Financial Dealing During the Twelfth and Thirteenth Centuries', in *Credit and Debt in Medieval England c.1180-c.1350*, edited by P. R. Schofield and N. J. Mayhew, Oxford: Oxbow: 42–67.

Nightingale, Pamela. 1990. 'Monetary Contraction and Mercantile Credit in Later Medieval England', *Economic History Review*, 43: 560–75.

Outhwaite, R. B. 1969. *Inflation in Tudor and Early Stuart England*, Studies in Economic History, London: Macmillan: 21–3.

PAS. 2011. 'The Portable Antiquities Scheme', http://finds.org.uk/ (accessed on 2 September 2011).

Phelps Brown, E. H. and Hopkins, S. 1956. 'Seven Centuries of the Prices of Consumables Compared with Builders' Wage-rates', *Economica* NS, 23: 296–314.

Postan, M. M. 1973 (2002). 'Credit in Medieval trade', in *Medieval Trade and Finance*, edited by M. M. Postan, Cambridge: Cambridge University Press: 1–64.

Powell, M. A. 1996. 'Money in Mesopotamia', *Journal of Economic and Social History of the Orient*, 39: 224–42.

Power, E. 1941. *The Wool Trade in Medieval English History*, Oxford: Greenwood Publishing Group.

Poynder, N. 1999. 'Grain Storage in Theory and History', paper presented at the 3rd Conference of the European Historical Economics Society, Lisbon. www.iisg.nl/hpw/poynder.pdf (accessed on 10 November 2011).

Reinhart, Carmen M. and Rogoff, K. S. 2009. *This Time is Different: Eight Centuries of Financial Folly*, Princeton: Princeton University Press.

Richards, R. D. 1965. *The Early History of Banking in England*, New York: Augustus M. Kelley, repr. London: Routledge 2012.

Rogers, J. E. Thorold. 1866–1902. *A History of Agriculture and Prices in England, 1259–1793*, 7 vols, Oxford: Clarendon Press.

Sargent, Th. J. and Velde, F. R. 2003. *The Big Problem of Small Change*, Princeton: Princeton University Press.

Schofield, P. R. and Mayhew, N. J., eds. 2002. *Credit and Debt in Medieval England c.1180–c.1350*, Oxford: Oxbow.

Smail, D. 2010. 'Goods and Debts in Mediterranean Europe', Paper presented at a research seminar at Harvard, May 2010.

Smith, Thomas. 1581. *A Discourse on the Commonwealth of this Realm of England*, repr. Cambridge: Cambridge University Press 1906.

Stacey, R. C. 1995. 'Jewish Lending and the Medieval English Economy', in *A Commercialising Economy: England 1086 to c. 1300*, edited by R. H. Britnell and B. M. S. Campbell, Manchester: Manchester University Press: 78–101.

Stone, D. 1997. 'The Productivity of Hired and Customary Labour: Evidence from Wisbech Barton in the Fourteenth Century', *Economic History Review*, 50: 640–56.

Temin, P. 2002. 'Price Behavior in Ancient Babylon', *Explorations in Economic History*, 39: 46–60.

Van der Spek, R. J. 2005. 'Commodity Prices in Babylon 385–61 BC', www.iisg.nl/hpw/babylon.php (accessed on 2 September 2011).

Vargyas, P. 2000. 'Silver and Money in Achaemenid and Hellenistic Babylonia', in *Assyriologica et Semitica: Festschrift für Joachim Oelsner*, edited by J. Marzahn and H. Neumann, Münster: Ugarit Verlag: 513–22.

Volckart, O. 1997. 'Early Beginnings of the Quantity Theory of Money and their Context in Polish and Prussian Monetary Policies, c.1520–1550', *Economic History Review*, 50: 430–49.

Wordie, J. R. 1997. 'Deflationary Factors in the Tudor Price Rise', *Past & Present*, 154: 32–70.

17 Money supply and the price mechanism

The interaction of money, prices and wages in Beijing in the long nineteenth century[1]

Kaixiang Peng

Introduction

Since the nineteenth century, China's economy has become increasingly integrated into the world market while at the same time experiencing large economic volatility and a lagging development of its institutional structure. Against this background, research into prices and wages has attracted much interest. For example, prices and wages have been used to estimate the economic development of a traditional society (e.g. Allen *et al.* 2011, Yan 2009, Wang Yuru 1997: 146–69), or to measure market integration (e.g. Keller and Shiue 2007).

However, the price mechanisms of traditional China still need more research before methods designed for modern market economies can be applied to them. Beijing provides a meaningful case for this purpose, since there were several changes in the currency in the nineteenth century that provided nominal shocks to prices and wages, affording an opportunity to assess how the market system affected the real economy. This analysis will be performed using materials such as account books and epigraphs as well as data compiled by S.D. Gamble and his collaborators nearly one century ago.

The remainder of the chapter is composed of three sections and a conclusion. In the next section, we introduce the development of the monetary institutions of Beijing, paying special attention to the private money supply. We construct a silver-copper coin ratio and price series which can be used to analyse the inflation caused by the debasement and depreciation of currency. We then turn to labour, where we put together different wage quotations and discuss wage adjustment under inflation. We find that wage adjustments could cope with money and labour market shocks even though wage quotations are often considered to be sticky. This finding is confirmed by a time series analysis of wages and prices. Our results show that there was integration among different markets in the long nineteenth century. However, this came about only partly as a result of inflation or living cost pressure. Hence market performance, including competitive private money supply and information producing mechanisms, is the main source of price integration.

Prices and currency: the monetary side

It is important to understand the monetary institutions of nineteenth-century Beijing before we discuss its price history. As in other parts of the empire, there were mainly two types of currency, the silver *tael* and a copper coin. The copper coin was minted officially and was considered the day-to-day coin. The name of the coin was *zhiqian* and its unit was *wen* – 1,000 *wen* was normally about 1 *liang* of silver in official quotations. On the other hand, silver wasn't minted and was used by weight rather than in coin. Nevertheless, silver was the main accounting currency of taxation and government finance. This situation is often called the 'bimetallism of the Qing dynasty'. But when the central government fell into financial difficulties and copper transportation was hindered by the Taiping Rebellion during the reign of Xianfeng (1851–61), the policy could not be maintained. New coins had to be introduced. In 1853, new big coins (*daqian*), face-valued from 10 to 1,000 *wen*, were minted. One of the most successful was a 10-*wen* coin (*dang shi daqian*), meaning a reduction of more than 50 per cent compared to the weight of one old *wen* coin. In addition, an iron coin was minted and paper money, valued by copper coin or silver *tael*, was issued. All these new currencies contributed to the chaos of the monetary market during the 1850s and 1860s. Even after the Taiping Rebellion was suppressed in 1864, things could not return to the way they had been before. Further dramatic changes in the monetary system happened at the end of the nineteenth century, when traditional forms of currency were replaced by silver and copper dollars minted with Western technology.[2]

Besides currencies issued or accepted officially as indicated above, we must also pay attention to private money, which played an important role in daily and market life. In the eighteenth century, a standard money called Jing Cash (*Jingqian*) came into being, which remained in circulation until the 1920s in a rather large region including several provinces around Beijing. It was not real money, rather a money of account. However, private paper money valued by it was issued extensively. Both native banks and large firms issued their own paper money, while there were also a large number of brokers and shops active in the streets dealing with the exchange between metal currency and paper money. The key question in these transactions is how Jing Cash was related to real money. It is well known that two Jing Cashes equalled one standard coin, but this was just the ratio before the debasement of the Xianfeng period. When the debased coins were issued and had to be accepted under coercion, the value of Jing Cash began to shake as its cash reserve became some mixture of old and new coins. In 1861, Jing Cash became debased to half a *wen* of the 10-*wen* big coin, which means that Jing Cash was debased from half an old standard coin to one tenth of it since one 10-*wen* big coin could be exchanged only by two standard coins from that time onward. When the 10-*wen* copper dollar replaced the 10-*wen* big coin, Jing Cash was again debased, now to 0.01 copper dollars. This did not imply a debasement as such since originally 1 copper dollar was valued at about 10-*wen* old standard coins. However, as the copper dollar depreciated step by step, Jing Cash's value relative to old copper coin started to decline as well.

The most convenient way to view the change of Jing Cash's value is to measure it by its value in silver *tael*s. Although there is no continuous silver-copper ratio available, we can construct it from records in account books and guild quotations, which are described in the Appendix to this chapter. We named this series 'Gamble' as most of the data are drawn from S.D. Gamble and his collaborators. A closely related series for the period 1860 to 1900 can be inferred from the wage rates valued by silver dollar and copper coins published by the Beijing Social Research Department (Lin 1931), which we accordingly named 'BSRD'. To check the representativeness of these series we added two other series for comparison. The series 'Urban Pieces' is derived from the urban exchange ratio applied to all kinds of transactions, including exchanges between families, account books and so on. Account books of two Fire God Associations near the centre of urban Beijing provide another nearly continuous series, which is named 'Fire God' (see the Appendix to this chapter). All four series are plotted together in Figure 17.1.

As the relationship between the Gamble and Social Research Department data are close and they might share the same materials, it is not surprising that the Gamble and BSRD series almost coincide. They show the trend of Jing Cash's value and the effects of monetary transformations clearly. From the start of the nineteenth century, silver flowed out of China and copper coin depreciated accordingly. This depreciation reached its peak as a result of the minting of big coins in the reign of Xianfeng (1851–61), and was ended by the debasement of Jing Cash in 1861, which clearly shows up as a peak in the data. Then the new equilibrium appeared and the exchange ratio remained relatively stable until the end of the nineteenth century, when the issuing of copper dollars by the central government ran out of control.

Figure 17.1 also shows a high level of similarity between the different series. The deviation of Urban Pieces from Gamble never exceeded 5 per cent (except in 1876). Likewise, the trend of Fire God is also quite close to Gamble, though

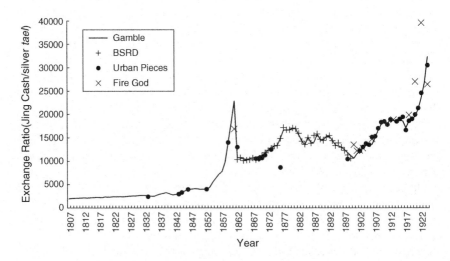

Figure 17.1 Silver-copper cash exchange ratio on Jing Cash basis.

the difference is a little bigger. As Gamble is the annual average data and the other two series are picked from records for special occasions, their differences are acceptable.

The similarity of the series in Figure 17.1 implies that there was not only an exchange ratio integration between urban and rural Beijing, but also between different institutions such as native banks, stores and guilds. This level of integration of exchange rates should be attributed to an open market with freely available information. For example Meng and Gamble (1926: 74) pointed to the daily exchange meeting just outside the Front Gate where the business centre of Beijing was located. Indeed, these standard quotations such as the silver-copper coin exchange ratio and interest rates dated back at least to the reign of Daoguang (1821–50).[3] As soon as market quotations were announced by the guild meeting, they were hung out and broadcasted along the streets or spread by pigeon post.[4] In this way, people whose experience of transactions was too sporadic to get valid information got to know about the total currency demand and supply. This was part of the reason for the relatively integrated money market as reported in Figure 17.1. Given this integrated nature and given the most abundant data, we will regard Gamble as the standard exchange ratio series and use it, in the remainder of the chapter, to convert prices of different monetary units when direct data on such conversions are unavailable from their source.

Some authors have argued that price discrimination and exchange rate fraud were a common phenomenon[5] since in traditional markets the costs of information and arbitrage were simply too high. However, our previous discussion, as well as our finding of relatively consistent exchange series in Figure 17.1, seems to suggest that these problems were quite limited. Further evidence of relatively integrated money markets may be taken from the official regulations of exchange rates. For example, emperor Yongzheng (1723–35) asked the official exchange house to decrease its ratio according to the private price. The reason for this rule was documented more fully by his successor, Qianlong (1736–96), who pointed out that, because the brains of a few persons could not compete with the brains of thousands of persons, transactions should proceed as people like it rather than being regulated by decrees.[6] These regulations showed the difficulties of preventing arbitrage when facing the activities of numerous private individuals or – in Adam Smith's words – the 'invisible hand'.

The above discussion shows not only that the money market integration was profound, but also that, with the rise of the silver Jing Cash exchange ratio, prices valued by Jing Cash increased too. This creates an interesting case study: what happens with price volatility in the Beijing market in the nineteenth century at a time when the Jing Cash exhibited inflation while the same prices expressed in silver (which is what most researchers use) showed deflation?

To analyse the above question, we first have to determine the inflation priced by Jing Cash. To get a picture, we construct several price series and plot them together with the silver Jing Cash exchange ratio in Figure 17.2. The first series is the wheat price, obtained from memoranda to the throne of the Qing dynasty and statistics in the Republic of China. For the living cost index we used Gamble (1943), who

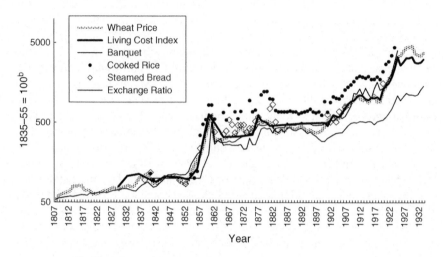

Figure 17.2 Price indexes of Beijing in the long nineteenth century[a].

Notes:
[a] All indexes are based on Jing Cash.
[b] The *y*-axis is in log scale.

calculated it by weighting the prices of grains, wheat flour and condiments from a rural fuel store's account book for 1826–1900. After 1900, similar information was added from the living cost statistics. Both the wheat price and living cost index were originally priced in silver, but we can convert them to Jing Cash basis through the Gamble series as described above. Meanwhile, account books of the Fire God Associations provide price series using Jing Cash as valuation basis. They include prices of dinners, cooked rice and steamed bread. Because records about cooked rice stopped after the 1900s, we combine it with old rice prices in Meng and Gamble (1926: 28) to get a more expanded series named 'cooked rice'. For a more detailed data description refer to the Appendix to this chapter.

Since all price series, except for wheat, were retail, it is likely that some degree of stickiness could be found. It is not strange that this stickiness varied by product, the dinner prices being the stickiest. However, price stickiness does not prevent it becoming clear that the resulting price indices in Figure 17.2 show a common trend of inflation during the long nineteenth century. This is especially true of the period from the end of the nineteenth century, when the increase of prices exceeded the exchange ratio, implying inflation both in Jing Cash and in silver. In addition to a general trend in inflation, we may also observe some changes in relative prices in Figure 17.2. For example, the price of rice tended to be stronger than both that of the cost of living and wheat. This was in accordance with the situation of the national and international grain market discussed by Kaixiang Peng (Peng 2006: 40–1). In addition, an increase in the amount of silver may also have led to changes in the relative prices, as outlined by Foldvari and Van Leeuwen, Chapter 2, this volume.

In the price history discussed so far the rise and fall of prices around 1861 are most dramatic and involved all parts of the economy. They deserve special attention. The government started to issue debased currencies and forced the market to accept them in 1850s. It has been recorded that the government could regulate transactions of native banks more easily and private paper money was even ordered to be replaced by official paper money.[7] However, old coins started to exist side by side with new coins and private notes. As a result, during the period 1854 to 1862 neither bad money drove out good money, nor good money drove out bad money: the market behaved like a seesaw game or 'trotting horse lamp' as Zhang (1981: 251) wrote. However, the main result of this game was the depreciation of big coins and paper money face-valued by Jing Cash, which is what we observe in Figures 17.1 and 17.2.

The money supply expanded greatly in this period as a result of the issue of debased money, but there are no complete statistics about the annual issuance and the money stock. However, from the dramatic reverse of inflation in 1862, we can deduce that depreciation must have exceeded monetary expansion before that point, which was the result of expected inflation. What caused the reverse? The answer lies in the debasement of Jing Cash in 1861. In June 1861, the government finally decided to close the official native bank because of the severe depreciation of the official paper money, but private native banks were allowed to issue paper money separately as before and its value was never required to be linked to the official paper money.[8] The following month, private paper money began again to be issued by native banks and the exchange ratio between paper money and copper cash was set according to market price, which was 1,000 Jing Cashes for 500 *wen* for 10 *wen* big coins or 100 *wen* for old standard coins. This meant the formal debasement of Jing Cash and the relationship that had been in place for more than one hundred years was given up. Although the new quotation was the result of long-term depreciation, the value of Jing Cash not only stopped decreasing, but also began to revert after debasement.

A key point is people's confidence in private paper money, which restored the demand for money and increased its value. Two differences could explain why private paper money gained the confidence of people when official paper did not. First, private money was issued separately by competitive issuers and they had more incentives to keep the value of their money, while both the issue and the withdrawal of official money took place in an ad hoc way.[9] Second, the private money market was efficient. Native banks applied the debased new quotation unitedly and the related information had to be open to the market. Then, as we have observed, all sides of the market adjusted their prices to the new value basis without forcible law or order. In fact, even the price of dinners, which seemed sticky normally, and the wages of servants, whose stickiness will be discussed later, increased their price to five times the old quotations, which matches perfectly with the debasement of Jing Cash. The market restored quickly after 1861, which shows that all these changes were carried out efficiently.

In traditional research, depreciation and inflation were always documented as proof of the inefficiency of monetary institutions – especially inflation, which was regarded as exploitation by feudal government.[10] However, we find price integration facing violent waves caused by political affairs and official intervention. According to the neglect of price integration, the importance of the competitive private money supply is always neglected too, which contributes to the pessimistic estimate of the traditional economy.

Labour market and wage adjustment

In the modern economic debate about the effects of money supply on the market equilibrium or real economy, wage stickiness is a central issue in the arguments of macro-economists. In research on the traditional market, wage stickiness has attracted special attention in different ways. In the Marxist view, one of the crucial characteristics of feudalism is that labour is under the control of employers; this is also the mainstream view of nineteenth-century China, as shown in the classic work of Xu and Wu (2003: 18–24). In this view, wage stickiness is a natural result and the labourers would be the victims of inflation, as researchers on money debasement of the Xianfeng reign have always argued. However, since the decisive debasement of Jing Cash was not applied at the command of the government but according to the self-organization of a competitive market, as discussed above, it is doubtful if the labourers would be weaker than other parts of the market, let alone be exploited by economic force. However, there are different ways to view China's traditional labour market. For example, Zhao and Zhongyi (2006: 245) insisted that employment was free in the Ming and Qing dynasties, especially for short-term labour contracts. Even for those agreeing with classic Marxist students on the lack of freedom to find employment, such as Quan (1934: 197–218), Niida (1950) and Peng (1995: 31), different conclusions can be reached because they give emphasis to the manipulation of guilds which provided protection to the workers. Since such large differences in views exist on the position of the labourers, we will first test their position empirically by analysing how the labour wage rate adjusted and whether there was integration between different wage series.

One often-cited wage series for Beijing is the mason's and carpenter's guild wage rate collected by Gamble and his collaborators. It is derived from the quotation records of guilds during the period 1862–1930 and included two types of wage rates: of skilled workers/craftsmen (*dagong*) and unskilled labourers (*xiaogong*). For both types, wages can be divided into labour costs (*gongqian*), food costs (*fanqian*), and commission, the skill premium being caused solely by labour costs since food costs and commission were the same for both types of labour. The meaning of 'commission' was a bit blurred. It was traditionally called tea or wine cost which had the meaning of 'allowance' or 'reward' and did not have a fixed form. In the quotations of the mason and carpenter's guild, commission included daily rates and a special reward in two parts (daily and irregular);[11] only the regular commission was used by Gamble in calculating his daily wage rate. In this chapter we will follow Gamble's method, as the special reward was minor and difficult to distribute. Furthermore, Meng and Gamble (1926: 95) found that, in contrast to labour or food cost, the commission would be paid to the headmen, and was regarded as a sort of 'squeeze' on workers or repayment for the use of tools. They also noted that commission was more like a profit of the headmen or contractor and was apt to be lowered due to competition, while labour or food costs were set to a minimum by guild regulations (Meng and Gamble 1926: 91–5). For these reasons, we will calculate different wage rate series reflecting the different parts of labour income: labour cost ('net wage'); sum of labour and food cost ('wage'); sum of all the three parts ('total wage'). The calculation of different series is described in the Appendix to this chapter.

However, the publications of Gamble and other authors did not provide many original texts to help us understand the adjustment process of guild quotations. This shortcoming is redressed to some extent by Zeyi Peng (Peng 1997: 5–11), in which nine original epigraphs of the carpenter and mason's guild from 1813 to 1911 are included, and six of them are about wage adjustment. All these epigraphs were located in the Jingzhong temple under the name of Lu Ban who was said to be a great founder of architecture. Here, we also meet the ambiguous usage of the term 'guild'. From presentations in the epigraphs it appears that the guild of masons and carpenters discussed above actually means a meeting (*hui*) of workers. In fact, there were many shrines belonging to Lu Ban in Beijing and meetings of different scale were held in these places for regular sacrifice or on special occasions.[12] Masons and carpenters might also take part in meetings according to non-professional gods and they had meetings in a similar form as those under the name of Lu Ban.[13] So the Lu Ban meetings were not guild meetings in its strict meaning. Nevertheless the Lu Ban meeting at Jingzhong temple was still special as it gathered urban workers of different districts, because wage rate was important to all workers and the quotations could be applied only when it was decided and obeyed by all.

Since guild wage rates functioned as minimum values, only the wage rates in account books exactly conform to market prices. Bearing this is mind, Gamble (1943) calculated wage rates from 1807 to 1900 based on account books of a fuel store located near Beijing. The data included averaged daily wage rates for busy months and the whole year separately, which were all net wages, with piece rates being paid for the harvesting of wheat in the spring. Besides that, we found a regular payment named tea house, tip or wine charge in the account books of the Fire God Associations from 1840 to 1921 (Peng 2010). According to the description of Chang (2003: 81–4), this was a combined payment to the tea house (*chafang*), which consisted of waiters skilled in etiquette. From the records in the account books, the number of servants must be fixed, and therefore the payment could be regarded as a wage rate too.

Because the piece rates in the above series may have been paid in other units, we change them into Jing Cash priced indexes based on 1877 as given in the Appendix to this chapter. Figure 17.3 plots some of the resulting wage series for comparison.

It is clear that all wage rates rose strongly, especially after the middle of the nineteenth century, while skilled wages increased more than unskilled wages and those of fuel store and tea house wages increased least. However, since the

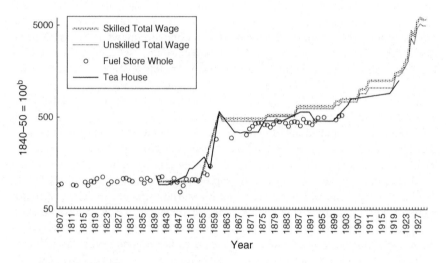

Figure 17.3 Wage indexes of Beijing in the long nineteenth century[a].

Notes:
[a] All indexes are based on Jing Cash.
[b] The *y*-axis is in log scale.

differences are quite minor, the possible bias caused by the calculation method cannot be ignored. If we look at the different items of the guild quotations, we find that in general unskilled labour, costs did not lag behind the skilled labour costs, and that the other two items (food costs and commission) followed the same trend. In fact, skilled wages increased more because labour costs, which represent a greater proportion of skilled wages, increased faster than the other items. So although the totality of the wages of the unskilled labourers seems to lag behind, it was not the intentional arrangement of the guild but rather an overlooked distortion caused by the nature of the quotation method. Tea house and the fuel store wage might also lag behind because their food costs were paid in kind, which reduced their need to increase labour costs because of inflation.

No matter which series lagged, the general trend was similar to that of prices in the long nineteenth century. This implied that the wage rate did increase dramatically when the coin was debased and depreciated in the reign of Xianfeng, contradicting the traditional view that wage rates cannot react to inflation efficiently. One special kind of stickiness was driven by anchoring to the more stable old currency – a form of 'good money driving out bad money'. For example, the mason and carpenter's guild quotation once wanted to maintain 500 *wen* of the old standard coins during the reign of Xianfeng (Peng 1997: 7). Similarly, the monthly wage rate of long-term hired hands in the Jixi guild hall increased to 10 *tiao* in 1873 to keep its value at 0.8 silver *taels*.[14] Given debasements, this meant a strong rise in the new money while wages remained constant in terms of the 'old' money. Since workers could turn to such value stickiness when there were different competitive currencies in supply, it was difficult to exploit them by inflation even when negotiation costs were higher and contract terms were longer for workers. We will test this point formally through the purchasing power of the wages in next section.

As to the variations of the wage rates, even though wages did adapt to prices, it is still clear that, overall, wages were stickier than prices (with the exception of banquet prices which were quite sticky too). Meanwhile, there are some important points to note about wage rate stickiness. First, the stickiness of wage rates was especially apparent in guild quotations, while the true market wages recorded in account books were more flexible. Second, it is important to remember that guild wages represented a bottom limit and there was an obvious downwards rigidity, as Figure 17.3 shows. The role of such rigidity lies in restraining wage competition during deflation and saving transaction costs for wage increases during inflation, which means that the stickiness based on downwards rigidity is more like self-protection than evidence of labourers being powerless.[15] Third, even guild wages were not completely sticky. The intervals between two adjustments might be more than a decade (when inflation was mild from the 1860s to the 1890s), but the wage adjustments followed more quickly when inflation speeded up after the 1890s. This shows the endogenous aspect of the stickiness of wages and supports the above explanation – that combined stickiness and downwards rigidity followed an economic logic.

In the above discussion, we paid much attention to the adjustment of wage quotations. Now, let us turn to differences between wage rates and observe the size of wage rate gaps between different areas and professions. For this purpose, we will use net wage rather than total wage for masons and carpenters, and add some new data to make our comparison broader. One source of data are the wage rate of the Kailuan Mines, a pioneering development in China's modern industry development within 200 km of Beijing. Another source is the account book of the Wansheng Wood Factory, which employed carpenters to work for some big clients. Their detailed description may be found in the Appendix to this chapter. For convenience, the unit of all wage rates are converted to 'cents per day',[16] where 1 cent equals 0.01 silver dollars.

Let us begin by comparing wage rates quoted by the urban mason and carpenter's guild with those of suburban fuel store employees. Obviously, the monthly rate of the workers of the fuel store in the busy months of the year was very close to the net wage of urban unskilled workers (that is to say, it was within about 14 per cent; a little lower since its change lagged behind the guild quotation's increase in 1887).[17] A similar relationship can be found between the wheat harvest rate and wages of skilled urban workers after 1872 but, as there was a dramatic rise of piece-wages in wheat harvesting in 1872, the wheat harvest rate seems close to the net wage of skilled labourers only before 1872. It is impossible that wheat harvest rates really increased so greatly relative to the skilled wage, while the wage rate of fuel store workers remained at former levels. One speculative explanation by Gamble (1943) is that the piece unit of the wheat harvest rate might have changed (i.e. the same wages reflect more work). However, there is little evidence for this. A more reasonable possibility is that most records of the wheat harvest rate after 1872 changed from net wage to wage including food cost.[18] If this is true, we can conclude that both the busy month rate and the wheat harvest rate of suburban or rural Beijing were very close to their urban companions no matter if it was recorded as a net wage or standard wage.[19] When the overall difference of the level between urban and suburban series was small, it is to be expected that there were some differences in their variations, as long as the arbitrage cost existed.

Although the levels of suburban and urban wages were very close, the latter were higher and they were, in addition, not even actual rates, but minimum quotations. What is the gap between the wage rates in actual transactions and in the declarations of the guild? Records of the Jiangxi Guild Hall show that it employed masons and carpenters at the guild wage rate. Although there was additional wine or tea allowance paid in total, its ratio did not exceed 5 per cent of the wage rate on average (*Jiangxi Huiguan Churucun Bu*). But the situation of the Wansheng Wood Factory is quite different. In nineteenth-century Beijing, wood factories were not owned and used by actual wood manufactures, but by contractors and designers of buildings (Wu and Xia 1998: 450–1; Qi 1989: 1). Masons or carpenters would gather in a tea shop waiting for employment, while unskilled labourers had to wait on the street or labour market (*Ren Shi*); consequently contractors, including those from the wood factories, didn't need to keep many workers in regular paid employment, but could hire more when needed (Chang 2003: 122–3). Perhaps for this reason, there was no fixed wage rate in Wansheng Wood Factory payments, which might be adjusted to take account of the distance to the building site and the working requirements. So we can only plot the general range of its wage rate in Figure 17.4.

In the wage rates of the Wansheng Wood Factory, those about the lower boundary are always net wages, while those close to the upper boundary include the cost of food. They both appear to be higher than the corresponding guild wages. However, most of the gap lies in the monetary conversion. Before 1924 guild quotations were priced on the basis of copper coins, but the Wood Factory sometimes paid wages by silver *tael* or silver dollars, and in these situations, the real wages tended to exceed the guild quotations. There was no evidence that such deviation would be punished; on the contrary, the guild quotations increased to catch the wages of the Wood Factory. Meanwhile, the wine costs of the Wood Factory lagged far behind the adjustment of the guild rate; this accords with the observation of Meng and Gamble (1926: 91) that commission was apt to be lowered in competition, and could also meet the 'allowance' or 'reward' meaning in the guild's terminology. In fact, the slack in wage rates meant there was a greater chance of the equilibrium level being reached, pressing the guild quotation to adjust to the market wage levels, or the guild might lose its authority. Thus, shifts of the guild quotation and market wage levels generally coincided.[20]

Let us turn to the modern economic sector, and the Kailuan Mines. In Figure 17.4, 'miner' refers to the average wage rate of all workers and 'underground miner' refers to that of workers down the pit. Both wages include food

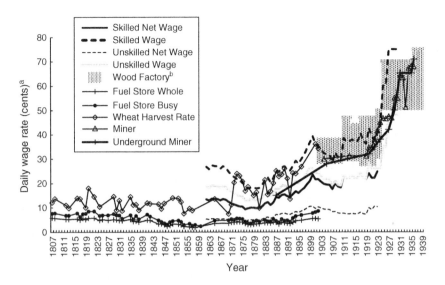

Figure 17.4 Daily wage rates of Beijing in the long nineteenth century.

Notes:
[a] All wage rates are based on silver as 1 cent = 0.01 silver dollars.
[b] 'Wood Factory' shows the variance range of wage rates.

allowances and can be compared to the wage rate of the Beijing masons and carpenters. Figure 17.4 shows that mine wages lay between the Beijing skilled and unskilled wages. They shared a similar trend too: from 1887 to 1905, they rose much more strongly than the cost of living; after that time, their increase almost stopped until the end of 1910s. But some lags also existed between their changes. For example, mining wages rose in Beijing before the 1920s, while the cost of living caught up by great adjustments after 1924. Perhaps demand for labour in the modern economic sector increased after the First World War and this led to tension in the labour supply in Beijing, or, in the usual presentation of epigraphs, 'giving up work and changing profession' took place. This is contradicted by the traditional view that the labour market was fragmented and that labour movement between regions and professions was nearly impossible. However, our finding confirms the observation that most masons and carpenters of Beijing came from nearby Hebei Province, which was also an important source of Kailuan Mines employees.[21]

In sum, the analysis of the wage data will lead to a more positive evaluation of the traditional labour market of Beijing. We find that the guild quotations accorded with wage rates of the market and that quotations of the guild did not distort the market mechanism. Furthermore, there was market integration of wages between urban and suburban or rural areas, and integration between traditional handicraft industry and the modern economic sector. This integration could be observed at least from the middle of the nineteenth century, when different wage series are available, and there was also no significant improvement of integration during the later development of the modern economic sector.

A time series analysis of wages and prices

As discussed above, wage stickiness was not as rigid as is commonly argued and there is no obvious evidence that real wages decreased due to inflation after the middle of the nineteenth century. Nevertheless, other scholars arrive at a pessimistic picture of real wage development, their view based on secondary indicators such increasing population pressure, decreases in agricultural yield and disintegration of the traditional economy. Based on this evidence, they argue that the real income or welfare of labourers was declining or was at least static. Meng and Gamble (1926: 91) and Gamble and Burgess (1921: 170, 184–5) viewed these factors quite differently. They felt that guild relations were close to those of a family relationship and that wage rates were discussed by employers and employees together, so that workers were able to maintain their standard of living or even to improve it. On the other hand, Allen *et al.* (2011), who used the data from Gamble (1943), argue that real wages remained nearly static in China. However, as we have verified the comparability of guild quotations and market rates, their findings might not support the reasoning of Gamble and colleagues, and a further test is needed to show the causality within wage adjustments.

Our methodology is described below. Under the information constraint of a traditional society, expectations should be formed in an adaptive way (that is to say, people base their expectations of the future on past evidence). Thus, if wages increased just to catch up cost of living inflation, as pessimists or Gamble believe, we will observe a breakpoint in the real wage series if adjustments were carried out discontinuously as shown in Figure 17.3. There are two options. One is when an increase takes the form of a sudden jump, as happened in 1862, 1877 or 1887; in these cases, the breakpoint was in the level of the wages. The other is when adjustment is an accumulation of several small increases, as was the situation from 1923 to 1925; in such cases we expect a breakpoint in the growth of real wages. If we find no breakpoint in the real wage series, this implies that there is no serious living cost pressure for wage adjustment. In that case other factors, including the situation of the money or labour market, might play a more important role.

The wage series used in this analysis is constructed by combining guild quotations and wage rates in the fuel store, as we have shown that they are comparable. We append wheat harvest rates to skilled wage rates and fuel store wages from the busy month's rate to unskilled wage rates to get a complete nominal wage series from 1807 to 1934 (see the Appendix to this chapter). To be more robust, we deflated them by both the wheat price and the living cost index in order to calculate two different real wage series. For comparison, the real wage of the tea house is calculated too. The main series are shown in Figure 17.5.

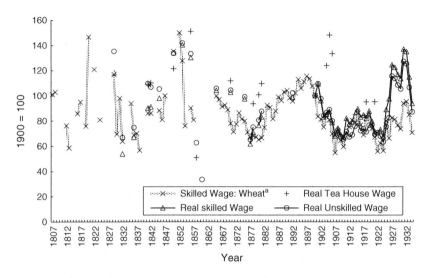

Figure 17.5 Real wage indexes of Beijing in the long nineteenth century.

Note:
[a] Skilled Wage: Wheat is deflated by the wheat price, and other series are deflated by the living cost index.

We can conclude from Figure 17.5 that there were frequent variations of real wages, but wage adjustments didn't cause significant breakpoints in either series. For example, the adjustment in 1877 was too mild to create a breakpoint because, although continual calamities led to a great increase in food prices, many labourers probably moved to Beijing for relief, and this increased the labour supply.[22] In contrast, the wage increase of 1887 was quite strong, but it happened simultaneously with the increase of the wheat price and did not result in an abrupt rise of real wages. To carry out formal tests, a structural time series model (STSM) is set as below:[23]

$$y_t = \mu_t + \psi_t + \varepsilon_t, \quad t = 1, \ldots, T, \varepsilon_t \sim NID(0, \sigma_\varepsilon^2) \tag{17.1}$$

$$\mu_t = \mu_{t-1} + \beta_{t-1} + \eta_t, \quad \eta_t \sim NID(0, \sigma_\eta^2) \tag{17.2}$$

$$\beta_t = \beta_{t-1} + \zeta_t, \quad \zeta_t \sim NID(0, \sigma_\zeta^2) \tag{17.3}$$

$$\psi_t = \rho(L)\psi_{t-1} + k_t, \quad k_t \sim NID(0, \sigma_k^2) \tag{17.4}$$

Here equation (17.1) is the observed function, where y refers to real wage and includes a trend μ, cycle ψ and error ε. The generation of μ is defined by level function (17.2) and slope function (17.3), and its increment comes from innovation in the level function η (17.2) and slope coefficient β. The state transition function ψ is (17.4), where $\rho(L)$ is a stationary lag operator to create a stochastic cycle. If both σ_ζ^2 and σ_η^2 equal zero, there is only a definite trend whose intercept is μ_0

and slope is β_0, or a stochastic trend exists. Moreover, if innovation η or ζ get a non-zero value only for some separate time points; this means a definite trend with an intercept or slope breakpoint.

By estimating the STSM model in this way, we can carry out three tests at the same time. As discussed above, by testing whether the wage adjustment breakpoint is significant, we can detect the role of cost of living pressure. Furthermore, if there is a significant stochastic trend, divergence between wage rates and food prices is a long-term phenomenon, which means that the labour market and the commodity market are not integrated. At the same time, the trend of real wages, as argued in modern publications, can be tested by the significance of the definite trend. The results calculated by OxMetrics4-Stamp are reported in Table 17.1.

As shown in Table 17.1, real wage indexes under different specifications are all stationary processes without significant stochastic or definite trends, except for two breakpoints, each of whose significance is not very robust. One slope breakpoint happened in 1853, when wages were not adjusted, but grain prices varied greatly. However, this does not mean that there was a significant trend of declining real wages; the change of slope was -1.81, and to this should be added 1.31, giving a result of -0.5, which is still not significant. Another problem about the test of the breakpoint of 1853 is that the observations between 1829 and 1853 were incomplete, so the result is, in fact, very weak. Only the breakpoint of 1927 coincided with a wage adjustment, but this is due to the drop of consumer prices when the effect of the Great Depression was transmitted to China, rather than to the wage increase itself. The power of the test about wage variation after 1927 is low in any case, as 1927 is near the end of the sample period and there was a severe problem of missing data before 1900. The rejection of the significant breakpoint in real wages relative to the price of wheat is more dependable and provides passive evidence for the breakpoint of 1927.

Therefore, neither in Figure 17.5 nor in Table 17.1 do we find enough evidence to support cost of living pressure. To understand the wage adjustment motive more

Table 17.1 STSM analysis of real wage rates

Series	Variance ratio		Slope		Level breakpoint		Slope breakpoint	
	Level	Slope	Coef.	S.E.	Time	Coef.[a]	Time	Coef.[b]
Real skilled wage 1829–1934	0	0	1.31	0.89	1927	27.85***	1853	−1.81*
Real skilled wage 1862–1934	0	0	−0.26	0.21	1927	25.19***		
Skilled wage: wheat 1807–1934	0	0	−0.11	0.11				

Notes:
[a] *** = significant at 1%.
[b] * = significant at 10%.

clearly, we next perform a vector auto-regression (VAR) analysis on the silver-copper cash exchange rate, wheat price, skilled total wage rate and tea house wage rate. As before, we convert all series to the Jing Cash standard. It is important to define the simultaneous reaction of the series in the VAR analysis. On the Beijing market, grain was not an important investment object, so the wheat price would not have had a significant effect on the money market directly, but the wheat price valued by the Jing Cash could not escape a great effect of the exchange rate. Meanwhile, wage rates could not have an important direct effect on the money market or grain market as their purchasing power was minor compared with that of merchants, officers, soldiers and the Manchu in Beijing. As to the relationship between the skilled worker, the craftsman and the tea house, it must be weak temporarily because they require different skills. Thus their simultaneous exogeneity order is: exchange rate, wheat price, skilled wage rate and tea house wage rate. The variance decomposition results based on VAR estimate are plotted in Figure 17.6.

Figure 17.6 shows that there is a lag of several years in the effect on the wheat price, but its effect is relatively small and never exceeds the effects of the labour market itself, which is shown by the own-effect of the wage rate and the effect between SKGWAGE and TEAW. At the same time, the effect of the exchange ratio increases greatly in Figure 17.6(a) once the debasement of 1862 is included, which means that an effect of debasement was absorbed in the wage adjustment. That is in accordance with our argument that workers were not exploited by this debasement. Because the guild wages may be too rigid and autocorrelated we use the tea house wages to check our results, and find similar evidence. All in all, since both Table 17.1 and Figure 17.6 show that not all innovations came from the grain prices, more attention should be paid to the money and labour market. This refutes the emphasis placed on pressure of living costs and indicates that we should be more careful in our analyses of the traditional economy, rather than depend on the usual hypothesis of a make-a-living (*Hukou*) economy.

We can also come to some conclusions about the relationship between the different markets: the results in Table 17.1 refute the stochastic trend, which proves that there was market integration between wage rates and consumer prices. Furthermore, since our discussion has shown that their innovations came from different sources (the grain department, the money supply or the labour market), price integration revealed integration between different markets and some form of general equilibrium might have existed. In other words, market institutions played the main role in the distribution of resources, even if it took the form of a guild, which looked more like a family relationship, and the wage adjustments were always expressed as a passive reaction to pressure of the cost of living in the epigraphs.[24] We should also note that the guild was only a special form of labour market, and there are many descriptions about the more natural performance of the market. As noted earlier, both craftsman and unskilled labourers had their regular job markets. Gamble (1943) also suggested that the fuel store might secure labourers from a daily market. Even for long-term employees in the rural Shangdong province, which was an important source of Beijing labourers, Luo Lun and Jing Su (Luo and Jing 1985: 130–59) showed that the most important process in gaining a job

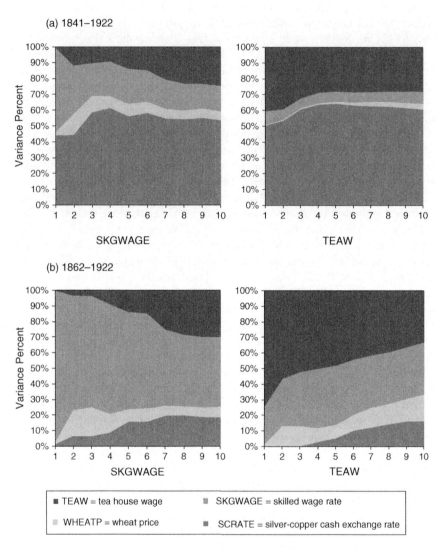

Figure 17.6 Variance decomposition of wage rates by VAR[a,b].

Notes:
[a] Results are estimated by VAR (8), where the lag length is selected by Akaike Information Criterion.
[b] All four variables' relative effects to the variances of SKGWAGE and TEAW from one to ten lag periods are decomposed and shown by cumulated area.

was bargaining. This reflects the normal situation of the labour market in north China. Xianting Fang (Fang 1935: 23, 35) even complained that the employment was so free that the protection of labourers was weak compared with modern Western countries.

Of course, the existence of a free market does not in itself guarantee that price integration or equilibrium was achieved, especially when transactions were sporadic and their costs were high in a traditional society.[25] One factor that perhaps contributed to the strong price integration is that guilds used to declare their quotation publicly, and this provided the standard ghost price for other exchanges, although they were absent in the price deciding process. We have described this possibility for the exchange ratio but, for the labour market, the consequences of overuse of guild quotations may be more severe since the heterogeneity between employees must be greater than it was for currencies. Such distorted integration of information might have played a role in the integration of prices that we found but, if it worked, we also can deduce that guild quotations provided a dependable method to help solve the information problem for individuals of a traditional society. Thus the problem of the integration of information is more likely to provide a new topic rather than change our views on and main estimates about the market performance of Beijing.[26] Or rather, it does not challenge the methodology based on market relationship, but forces scholars to pay more attention to the special characteristics of a market, something also required generally in empirical research about modern market performance.

Once we have reached the conclusion that the variation of wage rate relative to prices was a market phenomenon, real wage series can be used to measure the welfare of workers. Our test on definite trends shown in Table 17.1 supports the conclusion of Allen *et al.* (2011). However, there still exists some gap between wage and welfare that has not yet been sufficiently discussed in current research. For example, working hours and days should not be ignored when we use daily wage rates. Gamble (1929: 13) suggested with hesitation that working hours in the 1920s were lower than those of sixty years previously. Supposing this was not some variant of unemployment, welfare might therefore have improved even if the daily real wage was static. Meanwhile, as there was an urbanization trend from the end of the nineteenth century onwards, the position of suburban and rural labourers would have improved when they got urban employment. Urban wage was a little higher (as shown in Figure 17.4) and, more importantly, the working hours of urban masons and carpenters seemed shorter than that of rural labourers, if the descriptions in Meng and Gamble (1926: 104–5), Chang (2003: 123) and Dai (1995: 65) are correct. On the other hand, because the traffic conditions were better and labour demand was higher in the city, rural labourers would be able to get more working days and a higher annual income. Thus even if the wage rate had a declining trend, the total labour income would most likely have increased.

Besides differences between wage rates and labour income, there is the more substantial gap between income and welfare to consider. The method of Allen *et al.* (2011) is to convert income into calories for international comparison. If we compare the welfare of the labourers of Beijing throughout the long nineteenth century, variation of the consumption space also cannot be ignored. Indeed, as shown by Varian (2005: 133–5), it is very important to take into account how a nominal wage series is deflated. Since our living cost index is constructed similarly to the Laspeyres model, it shows that welfare tended to improve in Beijing when real wages were kept at an approximately constant level. Additionally, the variation of real wages was obvious (as shown in Figure 17.5), and because labourers were always prone to risk aversion, the variation of the general level of interest would affect the welfare of labourers too, if credit was constrained and the cost of smoothing consumption was high.[27] Fortunately, for the series plotted in Figure 17.5, heteroskedasticity tests show that there was a mild decline of variance so, even if we consider the different gaps between wage rate and welfare, we can conclude that the welfare of workers still tended to improve in Beijing during the long nineteenth century.

Conclusion

In this chapter, we have used exchange rates, prices and wage rate series to show that the economy of traditional Beijing was based on market mechanisms. Although infrequent transactions (either in the market or between family members) must have played a big part in a traditional society, the marginal price for them really appeared on the market. For money exchange, prices were set in daily meetings of native banks, while masons and carpenters decided their wage rates in irregular but large-scale meetings under the name of Lu Ban. In the process of price setting, there is little evidence to support a manipulative role of the guild, and we may better regard these meetings as processes of gathering information and detecting an equilibrium price. Quotations declared by the guild were applied generally and became a method to solve the information problem, when private transactions were sporadic. This might lead to the overestimation of price integration when the information source was so limited but, as price integration was long-run and general, the problem of such integration of information is minor and our evidence is still quite positive about the efficiency of the Beijing market.

As for market performance, the monetary sector was mostly related to government policy. This is an important reason for why the price history of the nineteenth century is often described as inflation caused by coin debasements of the government. It is true that debasements caused inflation in most times, but it should be noted that the value standard on the market was Jing Cash, which was private ghost money, while the main currency was paper money issued by private institutions. Although Jing Cash debased too under official intervention in the reign of Xianfeng, information openness and currency competition drove the market back to equilibrium. In this process, the informal guild of native banks played the role of a central bank, while central government had to give up its manipulation. As exchange rate quotations were the most important source of information on the market, the performance of the private money institutions also played a key role in preserving market efficiency, in contrast to the 'exchange rate tricks' they are normally blamed for. Even in the 1930s, when the official or western silver dollar took the role of Jing Cash, the private exchange market still worked. That being said, this chapter does not want to prove that the state policy was all nonsensical, but rather that it was limited to a few aspects, which are not discussed very much here, such as the traditional attitude against disturbing people, mutual guarantee requirement of native banks, punishment of corruption sometimes correlated with private finance, and so on. As a whole, the market institutions were mainly self-organized in the long nineteenth century, and Beijing's experience provides important evidence for understanding how the market adjusted itself to problems of transaction costs and information asymmetry. Of course, we cannot deduce from this evidence that similar institutions were efficient for other parts of traditional China as well, especially for some hinterland areas where market size was very limited and related problems would be much more difficult to solve by self-organization.

We also discussed the dynamic aspect of the long nineteenth century with respect to Beijing. Although we find that the real wage rate seems static in this period, this does not support an image of a make-a-living (*Hukou*) economy where all activities just respond passively to the cost of living pressure. On the contrary, innovations came from different parts of the system and they interacted with each other. From the view of economic development or growth, there might be little in the way of technical innovation, but this cannot hide the fact that the traditional economy was much more active than usually described. As a result, not only is our knowledge of the functioning and performance of the market expanded, but also our estimate of welfare change is more reliable.

Appendix

Silver-copper cash exchange ratio

'Gamble', 1807–1934

Our sources are: 1807–60, rural Beijing exchange ratio from a fuel store's account book (Gamble 1943); 1860–1900, series collected from mercantile account books of urban Beijing (Gamble 1943); 1900–34, exchange ratio quoted by urban financial guilds (Meng and Gamble 1926; *Monthly Publication of Beiping Living Cost Index*, 1928–34). Gamble (1943) did not list the exchange ratio series, but he provided ratios for several key years and listed the wage index both in Jing Cash and silver, data which could be used to deduce the index of exchange ratio. We used them to calculate series from 1807 to 1900. Series after 1900 was silver-copper dollar exchange ratio originally, and copper dollar was converted to Jing Cash as 1 copper dollar to 100 *wen* Jing Cashes.

'BSRD', 1860–1900

Calculated by the silver dollar and copper dollar wage rates listed together in the publication of Beiping Social Research Department (Lin 1931). Copper dollar was converted to Jing Cash as 1 copper dollar to 100 *wen* Jing Cashes.

'Urban pieces', 1833–1925

Combined from urban exchange ratio records scattered in all kinds of documents: 1833, manuscript of imperial kinsmen office (*Zongrenfu Shuotang Gao*, vol. 9);

1843–6, account book of Jiangxi Guild Hall (*Jiangxi Huiguan Churucun Bu*); 1852, letter from Beijing branch of Weitaihou exchange bank (Shanxi Branch of the People's Bank of China, Huang Jianhui 2002: 1209); 1859, diary of an officer in Qing dynasty (Zhang 1981: 267); 1861, diary of a scholar in Qing dynasty (Li 2004, vol. 3: 1861); 1868–71, general cash ledger of Wuxing Guild Hall (*Wuxing Huiguan Churu Zongdeng*); 1873–6, records of Jixi Guild Hall (*Jixi Huiguan Lu*); 1898, diary of a scholar in Qing dynasty (Liu 1990: 79); 1902–25, employee expenditure books and construction cost books of Wansheng Wood Factory (*Huoji Zhishi Zhang*; *Wangzai Yong Gongliao Zhang*).

'Fire God', 1861–1924

Consolidated data from account books of two Fire God Associations near the centre of urban Beijing (*Huoshenhui Bu*; *Gongqing Huo Zhu Hui Zhang Ben*; *Huozhushenghui Yinqian Zongbu*). Peng (2010) provided detailed descriptions for them.

Prices

Wheat prices, 1807–1934

1807–1900: from Shuntian Prefecture's memorials to the throne of Qing Dynasty collected in 'Grain Price Database of Qing Dynasty', edited by Yehchien Wang and supported by Institute of Modern History, Academia Sinica (http://140.109.152.38/); expanded to 1923, using the inflation rate of wheat price calculated from Meng and Gamble (1926: 28); expanded to 1927, using the change rate of first class wheat price calculated from *Quanguo Wujia Tongjibiao* (National Price Statistics); expanded to 1934, using the change rate of wheat price calculated from *Monthly Publication of Beiping Living Cost Index* (1928–34). After constructing the wheat series which was silver valued, we use silver-copper cash exchange ratio series, 'Gamble', to convert its value standard to Jing Cash.

Living cost index, 1826–1934

1826–1900: weighted average index of the prices of grains, wheat flour and condiments from a suburban fuel store's account book (Gamble 1943); 1900–34, linked to the indexes in Meng and Gamble (1926: 72) and *Monthly Publication of Beiping Living Cost Index* (1928–34). This was converted to Jing Cash standard by applying the silver copper cash exchange ratio series, 'Gamble'.

Banquet prices, 1850–1925

See 'Fire God'.

Cooked rice prices, 1850–1925

1840–1909: same source as exchange ratio, 'Fire God'; expanded to 1924, using the change rate of old rice price calculated from Meng and Gamble (1926): 28.

Steamed bread price, 1838–1920

See 'Fire God'.

Wage rate

Skilled total wages, 1841–1934

Daily wage rates of masons and carpenters (*jiang* or *dagong*), i.e. the sum of labour cost (*gongqian*), food cost (*fanqian*) and commission in guild quotations. Gamble (1943) provided data for 1862–1900; Meng and Gamble (1926: 90–8) described the data of 1900–24, and the continued series from 1862 to 1927 and 1930 were listed in Gamble (1929) and Lin (1931) separately. We suppose wage rates from 1930 to 1934 to be unchanged as prices dropped and there was a downward rigidity in wage rates. Data was copper dollar valued before 1924; we convert them back to original Jing Cash basis by multiplying by 100. After 1924, original quotations were priced by silver dollar. We suppose 1 silver dollar valued 0.72 silver *taels*, and use the 'Gamble' exchange ratio to complete the conversion.

For the earlier wage rates, the epigraph of 1862 recalled that the *Gongfanqian* had been 450 copper cash, increased to 500 copper cashes in 1855. While debased copper cashes led to chaos after that time so that any new a quotation was difficult to set, the guild decided to keep the wage rate at 500 *wen*, anchored to original standard coin (Peng 1997: 7). In guild epigraphs collected in Peng (1997: 5–11), the total wage was used to be called *Gongfanqian* (the abbreviation of the first two items), but it also included commission. We can conclude that total wage rate was changed from 450 *wen* to 500 *wen* Jing Cash, and left the Jing Cash basis temporarily from 1855 to 1862. As the silver value and the standard coin were both stable in this period, we convert the standard coin based on 500 *wen* to Jing Cash basis by the silver Jing Cash exchange ratio, 'Gamble'. Another problem occurred when the wage rate of 450 *wen* was set. From the account book of the Jiangxi Guild Hall (*Jiangxi Huiguan Churucun Bu*), we find that labourers were employed at the guild rate exactly, and the earliest record was from 1841 when carpenters were paid 450 *wen* and unskilled labours 350 *wen*. This means that the wage rate of 450 *wen* can be traced back to 1841 at least.

Skilled wages, 1862–1934

Daily wage rates of masons and carpenters (*jiang* or *dagong*), i.e. the sum of labour cost (*gongqian*) and food cost (*fanqian*) in guild quotations: the source and construction method are the same as for total wage. We convert its value basis from Jing Cash to cents by dividing by the 'Gamble' exchange ratio and further dividing 0.0072 (as 0.72 silver *taels* = 1 silver dollar = 100 cents).

Unskilled total wages, 1841–1930

Daily wage rates of unskilled labour (*fu* or *xiaogong*), i.e. the sum of the labour cost (*gongqian*), food cost (*fanqian*) and commission in guild quotations: the source and construction method are the same as for skilled total wage, and the wage rates from 1841–54 were set at 350 *wen*, according to the account book of Jiangxi Guild Hall too.

Unskilled wages, 1862–1930

Daily wage rate of unskilled labour (*fu* or *xiaogong*), i.e. the sum of labour cost (*gongqian*) and food cost (*fanqian*) in guild quotations: the source and construction method are the same as for skilled wage.

Fuel store whole, 1807–1902

Average daily wages for the whole year calculated in Gamble (1943), using records in account books of a suburban fuel store. Because there were no quotations during the off-season, such as winter months, Gamble used the minimum rate of the same year's available data to interpolate the missing months in calculation. For conversion, see *Skilled wages*.

Fuel store busy, 1807–1902

Average daily wages for busy months, from May to August, calculated in Gamble (1943) using records in account books of a suburban fuel store. For conversion, see *Skilled wages*.

Wheat harvest rates, 1807–1902

Gamble (1943) calculated the average wheat harvest rate, i.e. piece-wages paid for the harvesting fields in the spring. In his view, at least part of the wheat harvesting was worked for at unit rates, such as by acreage, rather than on a time basis. However, this supposition cannot explain the different trend between harvest rates and other wage series, and we will put forward another suggestion: that the piece rate was daily wage rate in fact. For conversion, see also *Skilled Wages*.

Tea house, 1840–1921

Culled from a regular payment in the account books of Fire God Associations, under the name of tea house, tip or wine charge. See '*Fire God*' for more.

Mines wages, 1887–1936

The Economic History Room in the Nankai Institute of Economics (1983: 123–31) calculated nominal and real wage rates of workers of different types for some years in the period from 1887 to 1948 using the archive of the Kailuan Mines. The original wage rate was by shift or working day (*ban*), and they calculated monthly wage rates from it by adding allowances and subtracting profit of contractors. To compare this with other daily rate series including food allowances, we divided the monthly wage by working days (average 26.7 days) to calculate the daily wage rate. Their unit was the silver dollar; we converted this to cents by multiplying by 100.

Wood factory, 1902–39

These wage rates were taken from the account books of the Wansheng Wood Factory who employed carpenters to work for some large clients. There were two items in practice, including wages and cost of wine and food. The second item was paid in cash for most records, but its amount was always below 10 per cent of the first item. As discussed in the text, the second item must be similar to commission and the first item was equal to the sum of labour cost and food cost in guild quotations. Original units of records in the Wood Factory changed over time and by occasion. Jing Cash, silver dollar and silver *tael* all appear in the account books. We also find exchange ratio records in the account books, where 1 silver dollar was about 0.72 ~ 0.73 silver *taels* and silver Jing Cash exchange ratios were very close to 'Gamble'. We therefore use 1 silver dollar = 0.72 silver *taels* and exchange ratios in the account books to make the conversion.

Real wages, 1807–1934

We combine mason and carpenter's guild quotations (1862–1934) and wage rates in the suburban fuel store (1807–62) to get complete skilled and unskilled wage series for the whole period. As Figure 17.4 shows, there is a resemblance between 'Skilled Wage' and 'Wheat Harvest Rate', 'Unskilled Wage' and 'Fuel Store Busy' separately. However, in about 1872 the standard of 'Wheat Harvest Rate' changed from net wages to wage rates including food cost, and we double the harvest rate before 1872 to make it comparable, since the labour–food cost ratio of guild quotations remained at about 1:1 during the period from 1862 to 1876. Next, the gap between urban and suburban wage rates should be made up. Using the data in the coinciding period from 1862 to 1902, we estimate that the 'Wheat Harvest Rate' was about 90 per cent of the 'Skilled Wage', and 'Fuel Store Busy' was about 86 per cent of 'Unskilled Wage' on average, and the suburban series were connected to the urban series by dividing by these ratios. Finally, the connected nominal series can be used to calculate real wages of different standards by deflating them with the 'Living Cost Index' or the 'Wheat Price'.

Notes

1 I would like to thank participants of the workshop of Academia Sinica, China's financial history meeting held by Hebei Normal University, and the economic history meeting in Tsinghua University, where preliminary versions of this chapter were presented. In addition, I would like to thank Hanhui Guan for providing some important literature. I also benefitted considerably from discussions with Debin Ma. Finally, I am grateful for the financial support from Hong Kong Institute for the Humanities and Social Sciences of Hong Kong University and the National Natural Science Foundation of China (No. 70928002). However, the author takes sole responsibility for his views.

2 For a more detailed description on the introduction of these coins one may read the Editorial Board of the Beijing Chronicles (2001: 24–43), and Wu and Xia (1998: 35–52).

3 See the discussion of Peng (2010).

4 Related materials in detail were collected in Xi Changgeng, Finance Research Institute of PBC's Beijing Branch (1993: 390, 411).

5 Li (1886: 3–4) paints a vivid picture of those.

6 See *Qinggaozhong Shilu* (2008: 8, 13).

7 Peng (1983: 91–6) described this process in detail.

8 See *Qingwenzhong Shilu* (2008: 10–2).

9 The native banks or merchants were often criticized as manipulators of the silver-copper cash exchange ratio, but there was no monopoly in economic terms. There were many traders in the market and no one could control the price, including the price quoted by the official certified banks; this is proved by different materials collected in Xi Changgeng, Finance Research Institute of PBC's Beijing Branch (1993: 233–432).

10 A related argument can be found in Zhang (1999) and Peng (1983: 111–22).

11 For example, in 1911 the mason and carpenter's guild declared by epigraph that workers should be rewarded 1600 *wen* on the fourth and twenty-sixth day of every month besides 700 *wen* daily commission (tea cost, *chashui qian*). See Peng (1983: 11).

12 Beijing Library (1989) collected seventeen related epigraphs.

13 For example, there were wood factories taking part in the Fire God Associations. See Peng (2010).

14 The monthly wage rate of long-term hired hands in a Jixi guild hall used to be 3 *tiao* old copper cash, which was about 0.8 silver *tael*s. Until 1873, perhaps as a result of the shortage of old copper cash, the wage rate changed to 10 *tiao* new copper cash, whose value was the same as before valued by silver *tael*s (*Jixi Huiguan Lu*).

15 Munro (2005) provides an interesting comparison. He researches the similar phenomenon in late-medieval England and the Low Countries, where wage stickiness was much stronger than in Beijing in the nineteenth century.

16 In fact, we don't know the piece unit of the wheat harvest rate, but, from the wage rates comparison made below, it is very likely that this rate was also paid on a daily basis.

17 Because the whole year rate of fuel store used the minimum rate to interpolate the off-season where there is no data, it would underestimate the daily rate. So the wage rate during the busy months of the year was more comparable to the urban guild rate.

18 Except for 1879 and 1890 when what was recorded was possibly the net wage rate.

19 This is different to the conclusion of Gamble (1943: 66). He compared wheat harvest rate with urban unskilled wages and found the latter was much lower, which he suggested was caused by the problems of distance, difficulties of transportation, lack of information and so on. However, our discussion shows that wheat harvest rate should be compared to skilled wages rather than unskilled wages. The more meaningful question is then how the wage gap could be narrowed so much while there were so many difficulties for arbitrage.

20 Guild quotations seem to rise much more from 1924 to 1927, but this was caused by the wage divergence of masons and carpenters after 1924. In 1924, the total wage rate of masons was 0.65 silver dollars, but that of carpenters was 3 cents lower (Gamble 1929, p. 4). In 1927, the mason's net wage and food allowance was raised to 0.75 silver dollars while that of carpenters was just 0.6 silver dollars (Wang 1928: 595).

21 The epigraph in May 1894 said: 'Members of this profession are seldom residents of Beijing and they mostly come from other regions' (Peng 1997: 8). In the local records of Beijing, it is noted that most masons and carpenters came from the Ji and Nangong counties of the province of Hebei (Wu and Xia 1998: 450).

22 For the effect of calamities on the population during these years, see Cao (2001: 647–89).

23 Koopman *et al.* (1998) provided detailed and technical description for this model.

24 In the epigraphs of Jingzhong Miao, reasons for wage increases were always expressed in terms of rice and fuel having become expensive, costs of living not being cheap any more and so on, which seems to contradict our quantitative result. However, it is not strange that the guild selected such presentations in their public declarations if we think of the comparable appeal of associations in the modern market economy. In fact, some

epigraphs were written by officials, including Zhang Zhidong, one famous statesman, and we could imagine that it was customary to use moral words. So expressions in the epigraphs or related documents should be read bearing in mind their ideological background, and should not be mixed with their economic meanings.

25 Wu (2001: 68) also discussed this problem, but he paid more attention to the manipulation of market in a semi-colonial and semi-feudal society, where he emphasized the monopoly of foreign institutions in particular. However, according to the Beijing market discussed here, the market structure should not be as important as Wu argued.

26 We will not discuss the effect of information integration on dynamic equilibrium here, but leave this question to further research.

27 An extreme example is the welfare loss of modern American consumers because of economic variation, estimated by Lucas (1987: 26–7), of about 1 per cent. But traditional Beijing may be near another extreme of low welfare, with low income and high interest rates.

Bibliography

Allen, R. C., Bassino, J.-P., Ma, D., Moll-Murata, Ch. and Van Zanden, J. L. 2011. 'Wages, Prices, and Living Standards in China, 1738–1925: in Comparison with Europe, Japan, and India', *The Economic History Review*, 64: 8–38.

Beijing Library. 1989. *Beijing Tushuguan Cang Zhongguo Lidao Shike Taben Huibian* (Compilation of Ancient Chinese Epigraph Rubbings Collected in Beijing Library), Beijing: Beijing Library.

Cao Shuji. 2001. *Zhongguo Renkou Shi: Qingdai Juan* (China's Population History: Qing Dynasty), Shanghai, Fudan University Press.

Chang Renchun. 2003. *Jiudu Baihang* (Professions in old Beijing), Beijing: Wenwu Press.

Dai Yusheng. 1995. *Yanshi Jibi* (Frauds in Beijing Markets), Beijing: Beijing Guji Press.

Economic History Room in Nankai Institute of Economics. 1983. *Jiuzhongguo Kailuan Meikuang de Gongzi Zhidu he Baogong Zhidu* (Wage System and Contract System of Kailuan Mines in Old China), Tianjin: Tianjin People's Publishing House.

Editorial Board of the Beijing Chronicles. 2001. *Beijingshi Zhi, Zhonghe Jingji Juan, Jinrong Juan* (Beijing Chronicles, General Economic Administration, Finance), Beijing: Beijing Publishing House.

Fang Xianting. 1935. *Huabei Xiangcun Zhibu Gongye yu Shangren Guzhu Zhidu* (Rural Textile Industry and Commercial Employer System), Tianjin: Economic Institute of Nankai University.

Gamble, S. D. 1929. *Peking Wages*, edited by Maxwell S. Stewart, Peiping: The Department of Sociology and Social work, Yenching University, Series C, No. 21.

—— 1943. 'Daily Wages of Unskilled Chinese Labourers 1807–1902', *Far Eastern Quarterly* 3, No. 1.

Gamble, S. D. and Burgess, J. S. 1921. *Peking: a Social Survey*, New York: George H. Doran Company.

Gongqing Huo Zhu Hui Zhang Ben (Account book of Fire God Association), Beijing: National Library of China.

Huoji Zhishi Zhang (Employee Expenditure Books), Beijing: Beijing Archive.

Huoshenhui Bu (Account Book of Fire God Association), Beijing: National Library of China.

Huozhushenghui Yinqian Zongbu (Cash Account Book of Fire God Association), Beijing: National Library of China.

Jiangxi Huiguan Churucun Bu (Account Book of Jiangxi Guild Hall), Beijing: Beijing Archive.

Jixi Huiguan Lu (Jixi Guild Hall Records), Beijing: Beijing Archive.

Keller, W. and Shiue, C. H. 2007. 'Market Integration and Economic Development: A Long-run Comparison', *Review of Development Economics*, 11: 107–23.

Koopman, S. J. Shephard, N. and Doornik, J. A. 1998. 'Statistical Algorithms for Models in State Space Using Ssfpack 2.2', *Econometrics Journal*, 1: 1–55.

Li Ciming. 2004. *Yuemantang Riji*, Yangzhou: Guangling Publishing House.

Li Ruohong. 1886. 'Shichan'(Market), *Chaoshi Congzhai*, vol. 6, Beijing: Beijing Songzhuzhai.

Lin Songhe. 1931. 'Tongji Shuzi xia de Beiping' (Statistics of Beiping), *Journal of Social Science*, 2(3): 376–419.

Liu Dapeng. 1990. *Tuixiangzai Riji* (The Diary in Tuixiang House) Taiyuan: Shanxi People's Publishing House.

Lucas, R. E. 1987. *Models of Business Cycles*, New York: Basil Blackwell.

Luo Lun and Jing Su. 1985. *Qingdai Shandong Jingying Dizhu Jingji Yanjiu* (Industrial Landlord Economy in Shandong Province During the Qing Dynasty), Jinan: Qilu Publishing House.

Meng, T. P. and Gamble, S. D. 1926. *Prices, Wages, and the Standard of Living in Peking, 1900–1924*, Beijing: Peking Express Press.

Monthly Publication of Beiping Living Cost Index (Beiping Shenghuofei Zhishu Yuebao), Beijing: Social Science Institute of Academia Sinica, 1928–34.

Munro, J. H. 2005. 'Wage-Stickiness, Monetary Changes, and Real Incomes in Late-Medieval England and the Low Countries, 1300–1450: Did Money Really Matter?', *Research in Economic History*, 21: 185–297.

Niida Noboru. 1950. 'The Industrial and Commercial Guilds of Peking and Religion and Fellow-countrymanship as Elements of their Coherence', *Asian Folklore Studies*, 9: 79–206.

Peng Kaixiang. 2006. *Qingdai Yilai de Liangjia: Lishixue de Jieshi yu Zaijieshi* (Grain Prices since Qing Dynasty: Historical Interpretation and Re-interpretation), Shanghai: Shanghai People's Publishing House.

—— 2010. 'A Research on the Currency and Price of Beijing, 1830s–1920s: Focusing on the Account Book of Fire-God Society (1835–1926)', *Researches in Chinese Economic History*, No. 3.

Peng Zeyi. 1983. *Shijiu Shiji Houbanqi de Zhongguo Caizheng yu Jingji* (China's Finance and Economy during the latter half of the Nineteenth Century), Beijing: People's Publishing House.

—— 1995. *Zhongguo Gongshang Hanghui Shiliaoji* (Collection of Materials about China's Guild of Industry and Commerce), Beijing: Zhonghua Book Company.

—— 1997. *Qingdai Gongshang Hangye Beiwen Jicui* (Collection of Industrial and Commercial Epigraphs in Qing dynasty), Zhengzhou: Zhongzhou Guji Press.

Qingshilu. 2008. Vol. 106, Vol. 237 and Vol. 355, Beijing: Zhonghua Publishing House.

Qi Rushan. 1989. *Qingdai Liangjia Ziliao Ku* (Grain Price Database of Qing Dynasty), Beijing: Institute of Modern History, Academia Sinica.

Quan Hansheng. 1934. *Zhonguo Hanghui Zhidu Shi* (History of Chinese Guild System), Shanghai: New Life Press.

Quanguo Wujia Tongjibiao (National Price Statistics), Statistic Section of Agriculture and Commerce Department, 1925–8.

Shanxi Branch of the People's Bank of China, Huang Jianhui. 2002. *Shanxi Piaohao Shiliao* (Materials of Shanxi Exchange Bank), Taiyuan: Shanxi Economic Publishing House.

Varian, H. R. 2005. *Intermediate Microeconomics – A Modern Approach*, New York: W Norton & Company.

Wang Qingbin. 1928. *China Labour Yearbook* (1st), Beijing: Beiping Social Survey Department.

Wang Yehchien, ed. 'Grain Price Database of Qing Dynasty', Institute of Modern History, Academia Sinica (http://140.109.152.38/)

Wang Yuru. 1997. *Jindai Zhongguo Jiage Jiegou Yanjiu* (Research on the Price System of Modern China), Xi'an: Shaan'xi People's Publishing House.

Wangzai Yong Gongliao Zhang (Construction Cost Books of Mr. Wang's House), Beijing: Beijing Archive.

Wu Chengmin. 2001. *Modernization of China: Market and Society* (Zhongguo de Xiandaihua: Shichang yu Shehui), Beijing: Sanlian Press.

Wu Tingxie and Xia Renhu. 1998. *Beijingshi Zhigao* (Beijing Chronicles), vol. 3, Beijing: Beijing Yanshan Publishing House.

Wuxing Huiguan Churu Zongdeng. (General Cash Ledger of Wuxing Guild Hall), Beijing: Beijing Archive.

Xi Changgeng, Finance Research Institute of PBC's Beijing Branch. 1993. *Beijing Jinrong Shiliao-Diandang Qianzhuang Piaohao Zhengquan Pian* (Materials of Beijing Finance History: the Volume about Pawn, Native Banks, Exchange Banks and Securities), Beijing: Finance Research Institute of PBC's Beijing Branch.

Xu Dixin and Wu Chengming. 2003., *Zhonguo Zibenzhuyi Fazhangshi* (History of China's Capitalism), Vol.1, Beijing: People's Publishing House.

Yan Se. 2009. 'Real Wages and Skill Premia in China, 1858–1936', discussion paper presented in the Conference of China's Quantitative Economic History and Economic Institution History, held by Guanghua Management School of Beijing University.

Zhang Guohui. 1999. 'Wanqing Caizheng yu Xianfengcao Tonghuopengzheng' (Finance of Late Qing and the Inflation during Xianfeng Reign), *Modern History Research*, No. 3.

Zhang Jixin. 1981. *Daoxian Huanhai Jianwenlu* (Records about Officialdom Knowledge during the Reigns of Daoguang and Xianfeng), Beijing: Zhonghua Publishing House.

Zhao Gang and Chen Zhongyi. 2006. *Zhonguo Jingji Zhidu Shilun* (History of the Chinese Economic System), Beijing: New Star Press.

Zongrenfu Shuotang Gao (Manuscript of Imperial Kinsmen Office), vol. 9, Taiwan: Collection in Academia Sinica Institute of Modern History.

Part V
Long-term patterns

18 Risk aversion and storage in autarkic societies

From Babylonian times until the era of globalization

Peter Foldvari and Bas van Leeuwen

Introduction

In pre-industrial economies, inter-annual price volatility was much higher due to the uncertainties of next year's production (e.g. McCloskey and Nash 1984; Poynder 1999). Therefore, an important strategy to reduce risks of famines might have been storage. Yet even though much evidence exists of all kinds of storage (government or other) the underlying motives for storage remain unclear. For example, Erdkamp (2005), Will *et al.* (1991) and Claridge and Langdon (2011) stress the role of the government (reducing the chances of unrest, or feeding the army (a similar claim being made by Aperghis (2009) for Babylon)). But the estimates of the size of government storage are generally small and storage turns out to be not commercially profitable. For example Persson (1996: 709) argues that these public granaries were unable to stay solvent for long periods because of the unpredictability of bad harvests. Therefore, McCloskey and Nash (1984), Poynder (1999) and Van Leeuwen *et al.*, (2011) focus on profit maximizing storage of private individuals. They compare the costs of storage (mainly consisting of foregone earnings from alternative investments) and benefits (being equated to the seasonal price increase) and find that the former outweigh the latter. Consequently, they find little evidence of significant levels of storage in such diverse regions as early modern England, France and ancient Babylon.

However, the fact that it was not profitable to store does not mean that no storage took place. Poynder (1999), for example, argues that even when costs outweigh the benefits, a motivation for storage still exists. Based on Kaldor (1939–40) he argues that there might be a convenience yield, because people will store more than is economically profitable in year t since they want to reduce the risk of famine in year $t + 1$ (see also Williams 1994: 39). Following Nielsen (1997), Poynder argues that the first-order autocorrelation of prices (i.e. correlation between the levels of prices in two consecutive periods) conveys information on storage. However, Nielsen only argued for profit maximizing storage, contending that a lower than average price in year t means high levels of storage and a low price in year $t + 1$ while a higher than average price in year t results in low levels of storage and, hence, a high price in year $t + 1$. Poynder, on the other hand, argues that both profit maximizing storage and convenience yield storage existed with low prices, while only convenience yield exists in years with high prices.

This interpretation of the convenience yield suffers from a problem though: almost all series contain autocorrelation of the price levels, even those that cannot be stored, such as butter (Persson 1999: 61). Indeed, if the supply and demand shocks are autocorrelated (for example a bad harvest is followed by another bad harvest because of lack of seed) this will also cause autocorrelation in the prices. Hence, autocorrelation between the levels of prices may have other causes than just storage.

In this chapter we therefore take a closer look at storage as a risk-reducing factor for the individual. We try to model storage in such a way as to incorporate both profit maximizing storage and a convenience yield. The formal model is presented in the next section where we first describe the model in words and then provide its mathematical proof. This model results in some hypotheses which are simple to test, and this is done in the following section. We then describe the results and end with a brief conclusion.

A dynamic model of storage

A brief description

In this subsection we briefly describe the model in words and follow in the next subsections with its formal derivation.

Using an economic model based on individual utility, we try to determine when people will store and how this affects prices (which is basically what we have in the form of data). In the case of profit maximizing agents with the ability to store grain, we would expect, in the case of autarky, that our best guess for current prices is the previous period price.[1] Of course, next year's price may be higher or lower than the price in the current year, but nobody influences the prices in such a way that a price increase or decrease becomes predictable. This implies that price changes are not autocorrelated (the change in price from year 1 to year 2 is not correlated with a price change from year 2 to 3) and not predictable by past prices. In statistical terms: prices follow a random walk (i.e. markets are efficient, as argued by Foldvari and Van Leeuwen, Chapter 2, this volume).

In the model we come to the result that the size of storage depends on past prices. In other words, the choice to store from year t to $t + 1$ depends, among other factors, on the prices in year t. This is the same as is suggested by, for example, Poynder (1999). Here, however, we deviate from the previous literature: instead of explicitly assuming a connection between prices and storage we treat the problem as a dynamic optimization problem. We assume that people derive utility from either selling the grain or storing it. We examine two cases: in the first case agents will gain utility from selling grain on the market, while in the second case they also gain utility from having storage. This latter case represents the existence of a convenience yield.

In the first case, we find that a higher price will reduce storage (Equation (18.21) below). This is the same as argued by Poynder (1999). After all, a higher price makes it unlikely that next year's price will be even higher, hence making storage unprofitable. Since we arrive at the result that the growth rate of storage depends on the growth rate of prices, when these are substituted to the formula for price, we find that the growth of current prices does not depend on the growth of past prices. Consequently, as long as the motive for storage is income maximization (including consumption as well), the price remains non-stationary, and price changes are unpredictable.

But what happens if we add the convenience yield to the model (i.e. storage with the aim of reducing the risk of famine next year)? In this case the price in year $t + 1$ depends differently on that of t. Since the aim of a convenience yield is to reduce the risk of famine next year, more will be stored if the price in year t is higher compared with storage for reasons of profit maximization. Hence, the price in year $t + 1$ will be lower. This means that there is a negative autocorrelation between the price differences from year t to year $t + 1$.

In sum, we argue, together with Persson (1999: 55–64), that autocorrelation in the level of prices may be due to a variety of factors unrelated to storage. As long as agents are motivated by revenue maximization, we find that prices do not deviate from a random walk or random walk with drift process. This means that price changes are not predictable based on previous period prices. Only when convenience yield as an additional motive enters the individual's optimization problem do we find that past prices may help to predict price changes. To find out if empirical evidence confirms the results from the theoretical model we need to turn to a formal testing. This can be done using a unit root test, which we perform later in this chapter.

The model

In this section we offer a simple formalized framework that can later be used to derive the behaviour of agents. As a first step, we define a demand function as follows:

$$Q_t^d = \alpha_0 P_t^{\alpha_1} e^{u_t}, \tag{18.1}$$

where P_t is the price and u_t denotes the random shocks, assumed to be random with zero mean. We assume here a demand function with constant price elasticity ($\alpha_1 < 0$) and no cross-price elasticities since we assume that a single staple food is produced by the economy; hence there is no substitution. There are other factors that could be introduced in the demand equation, such as population and income per capita, but to keep the model simple we choose to omit them. This does not undermine the results from the model since we apply it strictly to pre-industrial economies where change in per capita income and even population are so small that they can be safely included in the demand shocks denoted by u_t.

Supply depends on two factors: the amount of staple produced (Q_t) of which only a portion λ_t is brought to the market, and the price (P_t).

Therefore the supplied amount is:

$$Q_t^s = \lambda_t Q_t. \tag{18.2}$$

The equilibrium price can be obtained by combining (18.1) and (18.2):

$$P_t = \left(\frac{\lambda_t Q_t}{\alpha_0 e^{u_t}} \right)^{\frac{1}{\alpha_1}}. \tag{18.3}$$

To see how prices in different periods are related, we can express the log difference of prices as follows:

$$\Delta \ln P_t = \ln P_t - \ln P_{t-1} = \frac{1}{\alpha_1} [\Delta \ln \lambda_t + \Delta \ln Q_t - \Delta u_t] \tag{18.4}$$

so

$$\ln P_t = \frac{1}{\alpha_1} [\Delta \ln \lambda_t + \Delta \ln Q_t - \Delta u_t] + \ln P_{t-1}. \tag{18.5}$$

This means that unless any factors in the bracket depend on past prices, we can expect that current prices contain a unit root.[2] In other words, prices should be non stationary as long as there is no level effect on the growth rate. The task at hand is to find out which factor(s) might depend on past prices.

In a pre-industrial society it is very unlikely (with the exception of dramatic demand shocks like the Black Death in medieval Europe) that production would depend on prices. It is possible to have substitution among goods, of course, but in this model we have only a single crop (or alternatively some caloric equivalent of all goods produced). Hence we can eliminate Q_t from the candidates. What may depend on prices, however, is the portion of goods supplied to the market (λ_t), which determines the magnitude of storage as well ($1 - \lambda_t$).

Storage with optimizing agents

The key to solving the problem is to understand what factors affect the decision regarding λ (i.e. the proportion of grains supplied to the market).

The representative agent derives utility from two possible actions: it can sell some of its production at price P_t or it can preserve and store it. Storage is subject to a cost (portion τ of the goods is lost in each period as a result) but we also allow for lending which yields an interest rate r.[3] The consumption of goods is expected to yield utility as well, but we assume that in a traditional society per capita consumption is fixed at some level. Our choice of ignoring the choice of consumption reflects our preference for the simplest possible model, but also our belief that in a pre-industrial society, with a very narrow range of consumer goods available, increasing consumption much above the sustenance level would be pointless anyway.[4] Next we formalize the idea.

The utility of the representative agent (the population is set at unit) is a function of the revenue from trading, and the existence of storage (T). We can model the situation without convenience yield by simply omitting storage from the utility function:

$$U_t = f(P_t \lambda_t Q_t, T_t), \tag{18.6}$$

where we assume that:

$$\frac{\partial U_t}{\partial \lambda_t} > 0 \tag{18.7}$$

and

$$\frac{\partial U_t}{\partial T_t} \geq 0. \tag{18.8}$$

Storage accumulates according the following formula:

$$T_t = (1 - \tau)(1 + r)T_{t-1} + (1 - \lambda_t)Q_t. \tag{18.9}$$

The problem for the agent is to choose λ in a way that it maximizes his utility along its lifespan. This can be solved by applying the Bellman principle. The problem can be written with value function V as follows:

$$V_t = \max_\lambda \left[U(\lambda_t, T_t) + \beta V_{t+1}(T_t) \right]. \tag{18.10}$$

The first order condition with respect to the choice variable requires that:

$$\frac{\partial V_t}{\partial \lambda_t} = \frac{\partial U_t}{\partial \lambda_t} - \beta \frac{\partial V_{t+1}}{\partial T_t} Q_t = 0 \tag{18.11}$$

or

$$\frac{\partial U_t}{\partial \lambda_t} = \beta \frac{\partial V_{t+1}}{\partial T_t} Q_t. \tag{18.12}$$

Next we differentiate the value function with respect to T_{t-1}:

$$\frac{\partial V_t}{\partial T_{t-1}} = \left(\frac{\partial U_t}{\partial T_t} + \beta \frac{\partial V_{t+1}}{\partial T_t} \right)(1 - \tau)(1 + r). \tag{18.13}$$

From Equation (18.12) we can express both $\frac{\partial V_t}{\partial T_{t-1}}$ and $\frac{\partial V_{t+1}}{\partial T_t}$:

$$\frac{\partial V_t}{\partial T_{t-1}} = \frac{\partial U_{t-1}}{\partial \lambda_{t-1}} \frac{1}{\beta Q_{t-1}} \tag{18.14}$$

and

$$\frac{\partial V_{t+1}}{\partial T_t} = \frac{\partial U_t}{\partial \lambda_t} \frac{1}{\beta Q_t}, \tag{18.15}$$

which, after substitution into (18.13), yield:

$$\frac{\partial U_{t-1}}{\partial \lambda_{t-1}} = \left(\frac{\partial U_t}{\partial T_t} + \frac{\partial U_t}{\partial \lambda_t} \frac{1}{Q_t} \right) (1 - \tau)(1 + r)\beta Q_{t-1}. \tag{18.16}$$

Let the utility function specify as follows:

$$U_t = \frac{(P_t \lambda_t Q_t)^{1-\theta}}{1 - \theta} + bT_t, \tag{18.17}$$

which is a combination of linear and constant rate of risk aversion (CRRA) utilities, with $\theta \geq 0$. The closer θ gets to zero, the more households are willing to smooth their revenues from selling crop on the market. If $\theta = 1$, the above function would simplify into:

$$U_t = \ln(P_t \lambda_t Q_t) + bT_t. \tag{18.18}$$

In this case derivation with respect to λ would cause prices and production to drop, and λ would not be dependent on price at all. Hence we take the more general case as in (18.17).

First we assume that there is no convenience yield ($b = 0$). Then Equation (18.16) simplifies into:

$$\frac{\partial U_{t-1}}{\partial \lambda_{t-1}} = \frac{\partial U_t}{\partial \lambda_t} \frac{Q_{t-1}}{Q_t}(1 - \tau)(1 + r)\beta. \tag{18.19}$$

Using (18.17) we arrive at:

$$\frac{\lambda_t}{\lambda_{t-1}} = \frac{Q_{t-1}}{Q_t} \left(\frac{P_t}{P_{t-1}} \right)^{\frac{1-\theta}{\theta}} ((1 - \tau)(1 + r)\beta)^{\frac{1}{\theta}}. \tag{18.20}$$

Taking logarithm yields:

$$\ln \left(\frac{\lambda_t}{\lambda_{t-1}} \right) = \Delta \ln \lambda_t = -\Delta \ln Q_t + \frac{1-\theta}{\theta} \Delta \ln P_t + \frac{1}{\theta} \ln ((1 - \tau)(1 + r)\beta). \tag{18.21}$$

Depending on the value of θ, prices can have both negative and positive effects on storage. If we assume $\theta > 1$ (see endnote 4 on possible values of θ), we find that an increase in prices will reduce the portion of goods sold at the market, and so increase storage.

Equation (18.21) can be substituted into (18.5):

$$\ln P_t = \frac{1}{(1+\alpha_1)\theta - 1} \ln ((1 - \tau)(1 + r)\beta) - \frac{\theta}{(1+\alpha_1)\theta - 1} \Delta u_t + \ln P_{t-1}. \tag{18.22}$$

We find in (18.22) that, if there is no convenience yield, λ is cancelled out from the expression, and prices should follow a random walk or random walk with drift process, depending on the parameters in the first term of the right-hand side of the equation. Past prices enter Equation (18.22) with a unit coefficient, which means that the growth rate of prices does not depend on the level of price in the previous period. The reason for this can be found in (18.21) where the growth rate of the portion of production brought to the market (λ) also does not depend on the level of previous period prices but only on their rate of growth. As long as this is the case, we should not expect the prices to behave significantly differently than in (18.22), and we should find log prices to be non-stationary.[5]

What if having a storage increases utility (in other words, if convenience yield exists)? To find it out, we take the derivatives of (18.17) and substitute them into (18.16):

$$\frac{\lambda_t}{\lambda_{t-1}} = \frac{(b(1-\tau)(1+r)\beta)^{\frac{1}{\theta}} \lambda_t Q_{t-1}}{P_{t-1}^{1-\theta}}$$

$$+ \left(\frac{P_t}{P_{t-1}}\right)^{\frac{1-\theta}{\theta}} \frac{Q_{t-1}}{Q_t} ((1-\tau)(1+r)\beta)^{\frac{1}{\theta}}. \tag{18.23}$$

With $b = 0$, this expression simplifies into (18.20). Unfortunately, this time the formula remains much less convenient:

$$\lambda_t = \left[\left(\frac{P_t}{P_{t-1}}\right)^{\frac{1-\theta}{\theta}} \frac{Q_{t-1}}{Q_t} ((1-\tau)(1+r)\beta)^{\frac{1}{\theta}} \right]$$

$$\times \left[\frac{1}{\lambda_{t-1}} - \frac{(b(1-\tau)(1+r)\beta)^{\frac{1}{\theta}} Q_{t-1}}{P_{t-1}^{1-\theta}} \right]^{-1}. \tag{18.24}$$

We do not need to go further, however, to see the major difference between (18.23) and (18.20). While in (18.20) the growth rate of λ depended on the growth rate of prices but not on their level, in (18.23) the price of the previous period enters the expression, with a negative effect (as it is in a denominator). For this reason, we can safely argue that convenience yield (that we modelled by including the stock in the utility function) moves the prices away from unit root and may cause them to become stationary. We can observe that if the price goes up in period t, the portion of grain marketed in period $t+1$ is going to decrease faster than without convenience yield. That is, higher prices in t will (other things being equal) increase the portion of goods stored more than without convenience yield.

We summarize some of the results of this model in Table 18.1.

As may be seen in Table 18.1, the effects of a positive supply shock on the amount stored are not straightforward since they depend on the degree of risk aversion involved as well as the additional utility derived from storage. We can,

Table 18.1 Some outcomes of the dynamic model of storage

Event	Storage	Prices
Cost of storage (τ): i.e. direct losses of grain, rent, opportunity cost of storage increase	increase	increase
Direct gains from storage (interest rate on grain) increase	decrease	decrease
Positive demand shock (effect can only be temporary)	no direct effect	increase
Positive supply shock (only temporary effect)	increase when $b = 0$ (otherwise depends on θ and b)	no effect
Price in previous period was high	decrease	increase

Note:
The effect of convenience yield depends on the value of b (the marginal utility of having storage). At high values of b the reduction in storage is slower than with low or zero b. In case of supply shocks, the effect of b is not straightforward. At low levels storage will increase, at high levels it will decrease, at very high levels it will converge to zero (Figure 18.1(a)). With extreme high risk aversion, the effect is positive on storage (Figure 18.1(b)).

however, model the effect of a supply shock on the amount of marketed products (the inverse of storage) given the rate of risk aversion (convenience yield). The results are reported in Figure 18.1(a) and Figure 18.1(b), where $b = 0$ means no utility is derived from storage and $b > 0$ means increasing utility. If we assume a moderate rate of risk aversion, Figure 18.1(a) shows that a positive supply might decrease the marketed share (i.e. increase the convenience yield) if people derive little utility from storage. If people derive more utility from storage, the marketed share becomes bigger (in other words, the convenience yield becomes smaller). If people derive even more utility from storage, there will be no effect on the share of produce marketed and, hence, the convenience yield will remain the same.

This picture changes if we assume that people are highly risk-averse (see Figure 18.1(b)). In that case, an increasing utility derived from storage simply means a smaller and smaller share being marketed. This implies that a positive supply shock can lead to either more or less storage, depending on the level of risk aversion of the population.

Empirical test

As we could see in the previous section, if there is purely profit maximizing storage, the growth of the share of marketed goods grows in line with the growth of prices (Equation (18.20)). There is no relation between storage and last year's prices. However, if there is a convenience yield, the growth of the share marketed depends negatively on the level of past year's prices (Equation (18.23)). After all, if last year's prices were high, less would be stored and, consequently, less would be sold this year.

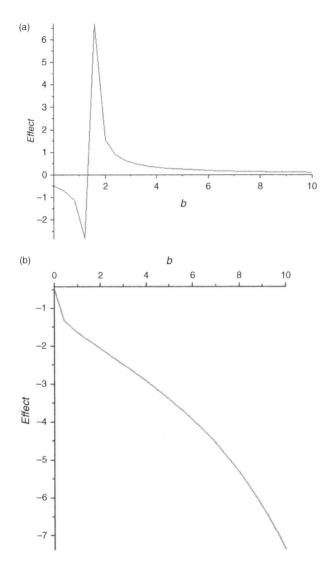

Figure 18.1 The effect of positive supply shock on the portion of marketed products,
(a) with moderate risk aversion and (b) with very high risk aversion.

Note:
For (a) $\theta = 1.1$; $(1 - \tau)(1 + r)\beta = 1$ and for (b) $\theta = 8$; $(1 - \tau)(1 + r)\beta = 1$; prices and quantities
are set to one.

We carry out some empirical tests to find out if historical price data reflect the
working of a convenience yield as suggested in our model. We test if the growth
rate of grain prices (log difference of prices) were indeed negatively dependent
on past prices. If they were, we have an indication that convenience yield was

Table 18.2 Unit root test Near East and Italy, c. 300 BC–AD 1700

	β_1	*t-stat*	*p-value D-F test*	R^2
Babylon, 384–200 BC, barley	−0.358	−2.37	0.388	0.14
Babylon, 200–60 BC, barley	−0.402	−3.96	0.015	0.20
Florence, 1336–1377	−0.492	−3.54	0.049	0.25
Florence, 1521–1615	−0.651	−5.07	0.001	0.32
Istanbul, 1470–1676	−0.470	−5.70	0.000	0.28
Tuscany, 1264–1350	−0.567	−4.17	0.010	0.30
Tuscany, 1350–1500	−0.423	−6.15	0.000	0.21
Tuscany, 1500–1700	−0.294	−5.82	0.000	0.15

working, and agents were engaged in inter-annual (or inter-harvest) storage. The test regressions are basically the same as in the (augmented) Dickey-Fuller unit root test:

$$\Delta \ln p_t = \beta_0 + \beta_1 \ln p_{t-1} + \beta_2 trend_t + e_t. \tag{18.25}$$

The results are reported in Table 18.2 and Table 18.3

In almost all cases we find that the price changes were negatively affected by the previous year; in other words, higher prices in period t led to a reduction in the growth rate of prices from period t to $t + 1$. For Babylon and China we found the coefficients to be insignificant though. Furthermore, whereas all coefficients were around −0.5 until c. 1500, afterwards a divergence took place: countries such as Italy, France and China experienced a downward trending coefficient β_1, while countries such as England, the Netherlands, Poland and Japan experienced a clear upward trend. The reason for this pattern will be discussed in the next section.

Discussion

Although it is difficult to distinguish a pattern in the data at first sight, some do emerge on closer inspection. First, Babylon and China are clear double-crop economies contrary to Indonesia, for example, which was an explicitly single-crop economy. Given the time- and region-specific factors, it looks as though dual crop economies have a lower absolute value of the coefficient; hence the convenience yield is lower. Although not explicitly modelled, this can come into the model by means of potential profit: the dual crop structure removed the need to smooth long-run income. In other words, even if one harvest failed a second harvest could remedy the fallback in one of the staple crops. Hence, nature automatically caused a relatively stable (i.e. smoothed) output of staple crops which made storage to fend off famine less necessary. Second, we find that after c. 1600 there is a divergence: countries like England and the Netherlands experienced an upward trend in convenience yields while Italy and Spain witnessed a downward trend. How can this pattern be explained?

Table 18.3 Unit root test, c. AD 1500–1700

	β_I	t-stat	p-value D-F test	Country
Amsterdam, 1482–1550, wheat	−0.448	−4.69	0.001	Netherlands
Amsterdam, 1669–1758, wheat	−0.628	−4.71	0.001	
Amsterdam, 1828–1867, wheat	−0.779	−4.51	0.001	
England, 1260–1340	−0.503	−5.17	0.000	England
England, 1360–1550	−0.322	−3.09	0.109	
England, 1650–1800	−0.243	−3.87	0.013	
England, 1800–1900	−0.531	−6.85	0.000	
Hiroshima, 1650–1800	−0.309	−5.22	0.000	Japan
Hiroshima, 1800–1858	−0.859	−3.51	0.039	
Douai, 1360–1518, wheat	−0.419	−5.01	0.000	France
Douai, 1650–1789, wheat	−0.331	−4.05	0.007	
Beijing, 1738–1800, rice	−0.411	−3.01	0.130	China
Beijing, 1800–1900, rice	−0.196	−2.93	0.158	
Shandong, Caozhou prefecture, 1744–1800, rice	−0.200	−3.47	0.043	
Shandong, Caozhou prefecture, 1819–1900, rice	−0.127	−1.98	0.613	
Guangxi, Guilin prefecture, 1740–1800, rice	−0.450	−4.70	0.001	
Guangxi, Guilin prefecture, 1828–1900, rice	−0.079	−1.39	0.867	
Krakow, 1706–1728	−0.125	−0.402	0.9875	Poland
Krakow, 1800–1900	−0.411	−2.59	0.283	
Semarang, 1824–1868, rice	−0.615	−4.29	0.008	Indonesia
Louvain, 1423–1494	−0.066	−1.40	0.853	Belgium
Antwerp, 1750–1800	−0.099	−0.31	0.990	
Barcelona, 1501–1550	−0.409	−2.87	0.173	Spain
Madrid, 1650–1744	−0.718	−7.07	0.000	
Pamplona, 1814–1883	−0.327	−3.72	0.028	

As we saw in Equation (18.25), we basically tested whether past prices negatively affect a price change. In other words, if past prices are higher, the growth of prices will be smaller and vice versa: if past prices are low, the growth rate will be higher. This suggests that prices become stationary (they do not have a unit root) because there will not be a permanent increase or decrease in prices. But what does this say about the autocorrelation? A basic formula showing autocorrelation is the following:

$$\ln p_t = \beta_0 + c_1 \ln p_{t-1} + u_t, \tag{18.26}$$

where $c_1 <> 0$. This suggests that past prices are positively or negatively related to current prices. If we rewrite (18.25) in terms of (18.26) we get:

$$\ln p_t = \beta_0 + (1 + \beta_1) \ln p_{t-1} + u_t. \tag{18.27}$$

This suggests that the more negative β_1 is, the closer $1 + \beta_1$ (which is equal to c_1 in Equation (18.26)) gets to 0, i.e. the further from a random walk. In other words, countries like Indonesia and Holland that experience a high (or increasing) β_1 coefficient, actually find declining first-order autocorrelation and move further away from a random walk and, consequently, also move further away from weak market efficiency (Foldvari and Van Leeuwen, Chapter 2, this volume).

This is a peculiar finding: the countries with the highest convenience yields are also the ones with the lowest first-order autocorrelation. Even though not surprising (since a negative coefficient in a unit root test by definition implies that first-order autocorrelation is lower), this does go counter to what Wrigley (1987) and Nielsen (1997) argued when they claimed that more storage results in more autocorrelation. However, they argue about profit maximizing storage which, in our model, is also positively related to first-order autocorrelation.

The question is, therefore, why some countries have a so much higher convenience yield than others. Clear examples of a historical civilization with low convenience yield is Babylon, while in Indonesia, the convenience yield is high. Several explanations may be brought forward. First, autocorrelation was high (and the convenience yield low) for countries with an irrigation agriculture such as China and Babylon. It is indeed well known that, as put by Reger (1994: 90–5), especially in regions where rain agriculture prevails in a climate with precipitation of little more 250 mm p.a. and consequently harvests regularly fail, it is to be expected that wise farmers store grain in case of emergency. Hence the convenience yield is bigger in regions with rain agriculture because the fluctuations in the harvest are bigger there. The same has been argued econometrically for twentieth-century Kansas by Abdulkadri and Langemeier (1999).

Second, China and Babylon are two well-known examples of a dual crop structure, one with rice and wheat and the other with barley and dates. As shown by Temin (2002), Babylon indeed exhibited strong autocorrelation (slightly more than medieval and early modern England), while Van Leeuwen *et al.*, (2011) showed that the dual crop structure smoothed consumption and reduced the risk of famine and, as a consequence, the necessity for a convenience yield.

As far as the divergence in convenience yields after the seventeenth century is concerned – in which Holland and England experienced an increasingly non-stationary series while others such as Italy and Spain find increasing stationarity – an explanation is more difficult. One reason, as pointed out in previous sections, is that our model was designed for autarkic societies and in this period trade and globalization changed the world (e.g. O'Rourke and Williamson 2002). So there may be many reasons for the divergence, unrelated to the convenience yield. However, insofar as one wants to provide an explanation based on the convenience yield anyway, one solution might be an increased agricultural productivity per person, thereby reducing people's dependence on the whims of the weather. Indeed, where Holland, England and Japan continued to increase their output of agricultural products per agricultural labourer (see Allen 1988; Bassino *et al.* 2011), in Italy and France this actually declined (Allen 2000). In Holland, Japan and England average income rose while the share of people working in agriculture declined, which made it necessary to have enough grain, even against higher prices, available from other regions of Europe.

Conclusion

The role of storage as a risk-reducing strategy has always fascinated scholars. From China, to the Inca Empire, to Rome, all societies have a certain level of storage. This was formalized by McCloskey and Nash (1984) on the basis of a cost-benefit analysis. Their seminal study has led to a debate where Wrigley (1987) and Nielsen (1997) argue that autocorrelation is indicative of storage while Persson (1999) denies this on the basis that series without storage (such as butter) also exhibit autocorrelation.

To analyse this question, we divide storage into two categories: profit maximizing storage and the so-called convenience yield (i.e. storage to reduce the risk of famine). We model that people derive utility from income smoothing and profit maximizing storage as well as from reduction in famine risks. We find that in the case of profit maximizing storage, the share of products marketed moves in line with price changes. This means that profit maximizing storage is not affected by past prices but it will increase first-order autocorrelation as assumed by Wrigley (1987) and Nielsen (1997).

But what was driving the convenience yield? Especially in Babylon and China, with regions with a dual crop structure, we find low levels of convenience yields. The same applies to regions dominated by irrigation agriculture and which consequently did not have such high risks of harvest failures. For the post-seventeenth century, however, these simple explanations do not hold ground any more since we witness a divergence: unit root regression coefficients in the more modern countries such as Holland and England increasing, but decreasing in countries such as Spain and Italy. Even though it is impossible to attach too much importance to this since this period is dominated by globalization while our model is intended for largely autarkic societies, if one nevertheless wants to provide a possible explanation it may be that agricultural output rose in the more modern countries. This increased per capita output, and changed their economies in such a way they became more dependent on imports, which in turn acted as an implicit convenience yield.

Notes

1 We would arrive at the same result if no storage was possible, but supply and demand were not autocorrelated.
2 We are aware that this result comes from the functional form of the demand function.

Still, assuming constant price elasticity is not illogical. Price elasticity should not change much once tastes and per capita income are not likely to change either; hence we believe that this functional form is applicable to a pre-industrial economy.

3 An important distinction must be made at this point in relation with the literature on storage and convenience yield. Most authors (see McCloskey and Nash 1984) define interest rate as one of the cost factors of storage. The idea is that by storing grain, agents forfeit the possibility of making some revenue by lending their money. In their approach, interest rate is an important part of opportunity costs of storage, and should be understood as the interest rate on credits in money. In our model, interest rate (r) is introduced as a possible gain from storage. We assume that agents may simply loan some or all of their stored grain, and receive grain in return in the next period. Then r is going to be therefore a real interest rate on grain loans divided by the share of storage loaned. If one seeks to observe the effect of a change in the monetary interest rate instead, it should be seen as an increase in τ.

4 Including consumption in the utility function would not change our results in any significant way. We would receive a second equation as first order condition of maximization, and that would finally lead to the result that there should be some constant ratio between consumption and marketed goods. But the amount of goods sold on the market can also be seen as consumption. We simply assume then that everyone sells a portion of its production, and also that everyone acts as a buyer as well, in other words, there is no direct consumption, all transactions happen in the market.

5 Since we assumed that the demand shocks denoted by u_t are random with zero mean, the (stochastic) trend in prices (if there is any) is finally determined by the discount factor β, the costs of storage τ and the interest rate r. The reaction of prices to demand shocks, and changes in other parameters of the model depends on the θ. If $\theta > (1 + \alpha_1)^{-1}$, we can assume that the price elasticity of demand is between 0 and -1 since the demand for basic foodstuffs is usually inelastic. If, for example, $\alpha_1 = -0.5$, then θ should be larger than 2 in order to have a positive effect of demand shocks on prices. It is usually found in empirical studies on agricultural sectors in developing countries that the constant rate of risk aversion is above 1 (e.g. Elamin and Rogers 1992), meaning that a higher interest rate or a positive demand shock *ceteris paribus* should reduce prices. If $\theta < (1 + \alpha_1)^{-1}$, however, higher interest or a positive demand shock rate leads to higher prices. The prices should have no trend if:

$$\ln((1 - \tau)(1 + r)\beta) = 0 \text{ or } r = \frac{1}{\beta(1 - \tau)} - 1.$$

In words, interest rates should include the cost of storage plus the discount factor (which is the price of postponing revenue from grain trade by one period). Another important finding is that the quantity produced (Q_t) does not affect price changes at all: the portion of harvest marketed grows exactly by the same rate as production reduces, and so the two effects are offset. Interest rates, therefore, should not deviate much from this equilibrium ratio. If some institutional factors cause interest rates to rise above this value, we can expect a reduction in prices as a result. This may be offset, however, by limited access to credit, which would ultimately act as a reduction of the available interest rate of the representative agent. Also, we assumed in this model that money is not a good itself (i.e. has no internal value). In pre-industrial societies, however, where money was usually made of precious metals, debasement would also lead to inflation, even if real interest rates (in this model r denotes real interest rate or interest rate expressed in grain) do not change.

Another, not surprising, finding is that storage reduces conditional price volatility. To see this, let us define Q as follows: $Q_t = Q_0 \cdot e^{v_t}$ where $v_t \sim N(0, \sigma_v^2)$. When lambda is fixed at 1, Equation (18.5) becomes:

$$\ln P_t = \alpha_1^{-1} [\Delta v_t - \Delta u_t] + \ln P_{t-1},$$

and the residual variance is:

$$\mathrm{Var}(\Delta \ln P_t) = 2\alpha_1^{-2} \left[\sigma_v^2 + \sigma_u^2\right].$$

If there is storage, without convenience yield, Equation (18.22) is valid and then the residual variance becomes:

$$\mathrm{Var}(\ln \Delta P_t) = \left[\frac{2\theta}{(1+\alpha_1)\theta - 1}\right]^2 \sigma_u^2.$$

The variance without storage is larger than with storage as long as the inequality $\frac{\theta^2}{(0.5\cdot\theta-1)^2} < 2\left(1 + \frac{\sigma_v^2}{\sigma_u^2}\right)$ holds. With reasonable values of theta (somewhere between 1 and 2) this is the case as long as the magnitude of supply shocks is larger than that of the demand shocks.

Bibliography

Abdulkadri, A. O. and Langemeier, M. R. 1999. 'Estimation of Risk Aversion Coefficients for Dryland Wheat and Irrigated Corn Enterprises in Kansas', Paper presented at the AAEA Annual Meeting, Nashville, Tennessee, August 1999.

Allen, R. C. 1988. 'The Growth of Labor Productivity in Early Modern English Agriculture,' *Explorations in Economic History*, 25: 117–146.

—— 2000. 'Economic Structure and Agriculture Productivity in Europe, 1300–1800,' *European Review of Economic History*, 4: 1–25.

Aperghis, M. 2009. 'ABACUS Historical Modeling System,' Paper presented at the Francqui Conference 'Long-term Quantification in Ancient Mediterranean History', Brussels.

Bassino, J. P., Broadberry, S., Fukao, K., Gupta, B. and Takashima, M. 2011. 'Japan and the Great Divergence, 730–1870', Paper presented at the workshop 'Quantifying Long Run Economic Development in Venice', 22–24 March.

Claridge, J. and Langdon, J. 2011. 'Storage in Medieval England: the Evidence from Purveyance Accounts, 1295–1349', *Economic History Review*, 64: 1242–65.

Elamin, E. M. and Rogers, L. F. 1992. 'Estimation and Use of Risk Aversion Coefficient for Traditional Dryland Agriculture in Western Sudan', *Agricultural Economics*, 7 (2): 155–66.

Erdkamp, P. 2005. *The Grain Market in the Roman Empire: A Social, Political and Economic Study*, Cambridge: Cambridge University Press.

Kaldor, N. 1939–40. 'Speculation and Economic Stability', *Review of Economic Studies*, 7: 1–27.

McCloskey, D. H. and Nash, J. 1984. 'Corn at Interest: The Extent and Cost of Grain Storage in Medieval England', *The American Economic Review*, 74: 174–87.

Nielsen, R. 1997. 'Storage and English Government Intervention in Early Modern Grain Markets', *Journal of Economic History*, 57: 1–33.

O'Rourke, K. and Williamson, J. 2002. 'When Did Globalization Begin?' *European Review of Economic History*, 6: 23–50.

Persson, K. G. 1996. 'The Seven Lean Years, Elasticity Traps, and Intervention in Grain Markets in pre-Industrial Europe', *Economic History Review*, 49: 692–714.

—— 1999. *Grain Markets in Europe, 1500–1900: Integration and Deregulation*, Cambridge: Cambridge University Press.

Poynder, N. 1999. 'Grain Storage in Theory and History', Paper presented at the Third Conference of European Historical Economics Society, Lisbon.

Reger, G. 1994. *Regionalism and Change in the Economy of Independent Delos, 314–167 B.C.*, Berkeley: University of California Press.

Temin, P. 2002. 'Price Behavior in Ancient Babylon', *Explorations in Economic History* 39: 46–60.

Van Leeuwen, B., Foldvari, P. and Pirngruber, R. 2011. 'Markets in Pre-industrial Societies: Storage in Hellenistic Babylonia in the Medieval English Mirror', *Journal of Global History*, 6 (2): 169–93.

Will, P-E., Bin Wong, R. and Lee, J. 1991. *Nourish the People: The State Civilian Granary System in China, 1650–1850*, Ann Arbor: Center for Chinese Studies, The University of Michigan.

Williams, J. 1994. *The Economic Function of Futures Markets*, Cambridge: Cambridge University Press.

Wrigley, E. A. 1987. *People, Cities and Wealth*, Oxford: Basil Blackwell.

19 Growing silver and changing prices

The development of the money stock in ancient Babylonia and medieval England[1]

R.J. van der Spek, Peter Foldvari and Bas van Leeuwen

Introduction

The role of money (and in many ancient economies this is equated with silver) has fascinated people throughout the ages. There has been a lively debate on the role of (coined and uncoined) silver as money in antiquity (Powell 1996; Von Reden 1995, 2007; Le Rider 2001; Jursa 2010: 469–753). We shall not enter into this debate, but it is our contention (following Jursa (2010)) that silver was used as money (means of payment, means of account) already in the ancient Near East and that silver remained the main form of money until the nineteenth century AD.

As explained in Van der Spek *et al.* (Chapter 1, this volume), prices in the Near East were expressed as the purchasing power of silver rather than as prices of products, as we can observe in the following quotation from the Bible. When during a siege of Samaria in Israel by king Ben-Hadad of Aram (840s BC) an extreme famine broke out in the city so that women ate their own children, the prophet Elisha predicted: 'Hear the word of the LORD: thus says the LORD, Tomorrow about this time a seah of fine flour shall be sold for a shekel, and two seahs of barley for a shekel, at the gate of Samaria.'[2] This is apparently a very low price in view of the siege, but it is still high in view of Babylonian parallels.

Many other examples of the use of silver as money and measure of value both in classical antiquity and later can be found. The astronomical diaries (ADs) from Babylon contain a database of the purchasing power of 1 shekel of silver (see Van der Spek *et al.*, Chapter 1, this volume). The recently published commodity price lists for Babylon (also actually lists of exchange values of silver) contain tablets with records concerning every month of a certain year as if to show intra-annual developments and one tablet records the equivalents of dates of month VIII, usually seen as the harvest month of this fruit, over a number of years (Slotsky and Wallenfels 2010).

Clearly people were well aware of the importance of demand and supply factors in the determination of pricing, including the value of silver, since if prices had been set by an authority and not by market forces, people would not have bothered regularly recording them in the hope of being able to make predictions. What is more, this curiosity even led to a primitive formulation of the fundamental idea behind the quantity theory of money in antiquity. We encounter the idea in one of the omen apodoses: KI.LAM *ina* KUR ŠUB *kaspu ul ibašši*, 'the exchange value (of the shekel) will be annihilated, (because) there will be no silver.'[3] We encounter the quantity theory of money even more clearly in an observation made by king Sargon II of Assyria (722–705 BC) in one of his royal inscriptions. In this period copper, bronze and silver were used as money in Assyria, but before 712 BC copper was preponderant. In 712 BC Sargon II conquered Carchemish and brought home a huge amount of silver. After that campaign, silver replaced copper as the main currency and silver is measured in the mina of Carchemish (Postgate 1979: 18; Müller 1997: 120; Radner 1999: 129). Sargon II plundered so much booty in that campaign that he boasted that from that time on the exchange value (*mahīru*) of silver was to equal that of bronze (Annals from Khorsabad 232–4, see Fuchs 1994: 130 ff.).[4]

Later cultures were also aware of the quantity theory of money. For example, Greek and Roman authors give testimony of the effect on an increase of silver in circulation on prices and credit. Cassius Dio and Suetonius assert that Octavian's cash distributions and payments of debts out of his Egyptian booty in 29 BC created such a pool of money at Rome that prices of property rose and interest on loans sank.[5] Conversely, there are two references to property prices at Rome falling because of shortage of coin or credit. In 49 BC, the time of the civil war between Caesar and Pompey, Cicero assumes in a letter to his friend Atticus that landed properties will become cheaper due to a lack of coins[6] and Tacitus has a really impressive discussion of a credit crisis in AD 33, when a scarcity of money arose due to the locking up of money in the imperial treasury and the hoarding of money by rich landowners, till at last the emperor interposed his aid by distributing throughout the banks a hundred million sesterces (95,000 kg of silver).[7]

The lack of direct evidence on the amount of silver in circulation, however, puts a serious limitation on historical research on the monetary development in ancient societies. In this chapter we attempt to remedy this by applying a model to available staple price data from first-millennium BC Babylonia to estimate the changes of the amount of silver in the economy. To do this we introduce a model that establishes a relationship between prices and the quantity of silver in circulation. This establishes the relation between the price level of a staple crop and the growth of the amount of silver in the economy. Using our model, we calculate the amount of silver in circulation. We find that this decreases considerably, which possibly explains the rise in purchasing power of silver observed in the second century BC. We cross-check our model by applying it to medieval and early modern England. We find that our estimates of silver in circulation are close to the independent estimates that exist in the literature. Remarkably, we also find that the influx of Spanish silver in England in the sixteenth century AD was not as large as is often assumed.

A model of the effect of monetary shocks on long-run market performance

As we have seen, there is plenty of evidence of the effect of coins and silver in circulation on price levels. However, there is very little evidence of the amount of money (or silver) in circulation. Therefore, in this chapter, we aim to use the information contained in price data to arrive at an estimate of the trend of silver quantity in circulation in Babylonia between the fourth and first centuries BC and to cross-check this with similar evidence for England between AD 1300 and 1700. It is important to start with the limitations of such an endeavour. First of all, what we attempt here cannot lead to a direct estimate of silver quantity hoarded at some distinct time in Babylonia; hence we only measure coins/silver in circulation.[8] Our method is based on the theoretical and empirical relationship between the movement of prices and the changes in the quantity of money (which reflects the purchasing power of agents in an economy), so we can track changes only. The results will thus be an index rather than an absolute value of silver in circulation. Also, when applied to coins, our results can only be interpreted as an estimation of the quantity of silver, if we believe that the silver content of coins (and their weight) remained the same. Since this was not likely the case, as a gradual debasement might have happened, our results should be interpreted with more caution and it is safer to say that we estimate the number of silver coins in circulation (we attempt to correct for this in the next section). Another limitation stems from the fact that prices can and will be affected by several factors other than the number of silver coins in circulation. Just to mention some: the price of a good will also reflect the price of other goods, changes in tastes, warfare and also policy decisions on taxes or the structure of goods (for example Babylonian kings supported the cultivation of dates at certain points in time (e.g. Van der Spek 1998: 322)). The result is that our estimates will contain an error, which is simply a sum of all these unknown effects and the measurement error. A third limitation is the poor availability of non-staple food prices. What we have are data on the prices of barley, dates, cress, sesame, cuscuta and wool. Obviously, people consumed many other goods as well, but we cannot incorporate information on them into our estimation. It might offer a relief that the goods for which we actually have price data were probably responsible for about 70 per cent of total household expenditure (Jursa 2010: 299), but missing information is never good for estimations. Finally, a problem of latent variables also arises. The standard quantity theory of money on which we rely on in this chapter establishes a relationship between the amount of money (usually dubbed M) in circulation and general price level (often denoted by P). This general price level is a theoretical concept, however, and in practice this is approximated either by the consumer price index (CPI), or gross domestic product (GDP) deflator, both basically being a weighted average of price changes of different products. We could enforce some weighting scheme onto our data, but we would feel uncomfortable speculating on the share of different goods in total consumption. Therefore, the following model should allow for data-driven coefficients of each of the available price series.

In the following we present our theoretical model. Before going into detail, however, we find it important to describe our approach in a heuristic, non-technical manner as well. The existence of a relationship among the amount of silver and prices is straightforward: if the amount of silver increases agents will be able to spend more, which increases the relative supply of silver in the market and consequently reduces its relative value relative to other goods. This is observed as a price increase. The idea of the long run neutrality of money suggests that in the long run all changes in the amount of money should appear in prices and should not affect output expressed in real terms. But it is also logical that not all prices will react the same way to an increase in money supply (see also Mayhew, Chapter 16, this volume). Goods in demand more will likely experience a larger degree of price increase, while some inferior goods may even undergo a price decrease. This means we cannot infer anything of decisive importance about the amount of money by observing the price of a single good: we need to have the price of as many goods as possible. The amount of money in circulation can be estimated as a single common factor behind all observed prices changes. The formal derivation follows.

For the market of goods we assume that there are two goods, a staple food (indexed as F) and the rest (R), which can be seen as a combination of all other goods in the market. In such a market, the demand and supply are defined as follows ($i = F, R$):

$$Q_i^S = a_i e^{u_i},$$
(19.1)

where $u_i \sim NID(0, \sigma_{u_i}^2)$, Q_i^s is the supply shock and a_i is the average production. We assume that all production is offered for sale on the market. For the demand side we get:

$$Q_i^D = b_i Y^{\alpha_i} P_i^{\beta_i} P_j^{\gamma_i} e^{v_i} i = (F, R), \quad j = (R, F),$$
(19.2)

where $v_i \sim NID(0, \sigma_{v_i}^2)$, Q_i^D is the demand shock, b_i is an intercept and Y denotes income (for simplicity we use nominal income, but this should be no problem since α_i is the income elasticity of demand when all prices are fixed). P_i and P_j denote the price of the product expressed in silver for which we define the demand and the price of the alternative good, respectively. The Greek letters are elasticities: α_F is the income elasticity of product F while β_F and γ_F are its price and cross-price elasticities. The price elasticity shows the effect of price change of product F on the demand for F, while the cross-price elasticity shows the effect of price changes of the alternative good on the demand of F.

The equilibrium price is reached when demand and supply satisfy the following equations:

$$P_i = \left(\frac{a_i}{b_i}\right)^{\frac{1}{\beta_i}} Y^{-\frac{\alpha_i}{\beta_i}} P_j^{-\frac{\gamma_i}{\beta_i}} e^{\frac{u_i - v_i}{\beta_i}} \quad (i = F, R \text{ and } j = R, F).$$
(19.3)

Since P_F and P_R are in a simultaneous relationship, to arrive at P_F we need to substitute the equilibrium price P_R into the formula for P_F. This yields two reduced form equations for both products:

$$P_F = \left(\frac{a_F}{b_F}\right)^{\frac{\beta_F}{\beta_F\beta_R-\gamma_F\gamma_R}} \left(\frac{a_R}{b_R}\right)^{-\frac{\gamma_F}{\beta_F\beta_R-\gamma_F\gamma_R}} Y^{\frac{\gamma_F\alpha_R-\alpha_F\beta_R}{\beta_F\beta_R-\gamma_F\gamma_R}}$$

$$\times\, e^{\frac{\beta_R(u_F-v_F)-\gamma_F(u_R-v_R)}{\beta_F\beta_R-\gamma_F\gamma_R}} \tag{19.4}$$

$$P_R = \left(\frac{a_R}{b_R}\right)^{\frac{\beta_R}{\beta_R\beta_F-\gamma_R\gamma_F}} \left(\frac{a_F}{b_F}\right)^{-\frac{\gamma_R}{\beta_R\beta_F-\gamma_R\gamma_F}} Y^{\frac{\gamma_R\alpha_F-\alpha_R\beta_F}{\beta_R\beta_F-\gamma_R\gamma_F}}$$

$$\times\, e^{\frac{\beta_F(u_R-v_R)-\gamma_R(u_F-v_F)}{\beta_R\beta_F-\gamma_R\gamma_F}}. \tag{19.5}$$

As we can observe, the price of the other good is eliminated from the right-hand side of the equations; the price of each product now depends on the production of that product, the production of the other product, the income, an error and the various elasticities.

Now we look at the monetary side of the economy. We start by assuming that the quantity theory of the money holds:

$$Y = M\bar{v}, \tag{19.6}$$

where Y is the nominal value of all goods in the economy that are traded for silver (we assume that this equals total nominal income), M is the amount of silver, and v is the velocity of money, which we take as constant.[9]

Combining the goods and monetary side of the economy, we can substitute (19.6) into (19.4) and (19.5) to obtain a relationship between the quantity of silver and the price of the two goods expressed in silver:

$$P_F = \left(\frac{a_F}{b_F}\right)^{\frac{\beta_F}{\beta_F\beta_R-\gamma_F\gamma_R}} \left(\frac{a_R}{b_R}\right)^{-\frac{\gamma_F}{\beta_F\beta_R-\gamma_F\gamma_R}} \bar{v}^{\frac{\gamma_F\alpha_R-\alpha_F\beta_R}{\beta_F\beta_R-\gamma_F\gamma_R}} M^{\frac{\gamma_F\alpha_R-\alpha_F\beta_R}{\beta_F\beta_R-\gamma_F\gamma_R}}$$

$$\times\, e^{\frac{\beta_R(u_F-v_F)-\gamma_F(u_R-v_R)}{\beta_F\beta_R-\gamma_F\gamma_R}} \tag{19.7}$$

$$P_R = \left(\frac{a_R}{b_R}\right)^{\frac{\beta_R}{\beta_R\beta_F-\gamma_R\gamma_F}} \left(\frac{a_F}{b_F}\right)^{-\frac{\gamma_R}{\beta_R\beta_F-\gamma_R\gamma_F}} \bar{v}^{\frac{\gamma_R\alpha_F-\alpha_R\beta_F}{\beta_R\beta_F-\gamma_R\gamma_F}} M^{\frac{\gamma_R\alpha_F-\alpha_R\beta_F}{\beta_R\beta_F-\gamma_R\gamma_F}}$$

$$\times\, e^{\frac{\beta_F(u_R-v_R)-\gamma_R(u_F-v_F)}{\beta_R\beta_F-\gamma_R\gamma_F}}. \tag{19.8}$$

In this simple model, the price of the two goods will depend only on the amount of silver in circulation in the long run, since the demand and supply shocks have a zero mean. This makes it possible to rewrite (19.7) and (19.8) as:

$$\Delta \ln P_{F,t} = \ln P_{F,t} - \ln P_{F,t-1} = \frac{\gamma_F \alpha_R - \alpha_F \beta_R}{\beta_F \beta_R - \gamma_F \gamma_R} \Delta \ln M_t \qquad (19.9)$$

$$\Delta \ln P_{R,t} = \ln P_{R,t} - \ln P_{R,t-1} = \frac{\gamma_R \alpha_F - \alpha_R \beta_F}{\beta_F \beta_R - \gamma_F \gamma_R} \Delta \ln M_t. \qquad (19.10)$$

We can assume that the income elasticities and cross-price elasticities (the alphas and the gammas) are positive, meaning that both products are normal goods. Similarly, it is safe to assume that they are substitutes and, consequently, their own price elasticities (the betas) are negative. These two assumptions imply that an increase of silver in circulation will have a positive effect on the price of a good, if $\beta_F \beta_R > \gamma_F \gamma_R$. If we assume that both goods are staple crops, we can safely argue, following Allen (2000, 14), that the cross-price elasticity (gamma) is a small but positive number (about 0.1) while the own-price elasticity (beta) is around –0.6. Hence, $\beta_F \beta_R > \gamma_F \gamma_R$ holds and the growth in money supply is positively related with the growth in prices.

Another interesting observation arising from (19.9) and (19.10) is that the effect of the growth of silver does not necessarily have to be the same for all products. This all depends on the elasticities of the products. There are several possible combinations but one might say that, when the own-price and income elasticities are bigger in absolute value than that of the other product, the effect of a change in silver on the price becomes smaller. Since the price of a product is also dependent on the elasticity of other products, if the elasticity of product R goes up, both the effect of the increase in silver on the price of product R and F goes down, but lesser so than for product F. To phrase it differently: if we assume that barley is more a luxury good (with thus a higher income elasticity than dates), an increase in silver will increase the prices of barley less than it would for dates.

Silver in circulation in Babylon, 385–61 BC

In the previous section we established the relationship between price changes and changes in the amount of silver. Now we use the available price data to arrive at an index of the amount of silver in circulation in 385–61 BC in Babylon. However, since we have a lot of missing observations in the price data, we have to rely on an unobserved component model (see for example Commandeur and Koopman 2007) to estimate the underlying long-run trend of price movements which, according to our model, is *ceteris paribus* primarily affected by the amount of money in circulation.

For the available six commodities (barley, dates, cress, sesame, cuscuta and wool) price series in the ADs in Babylon (see Van der Spek *et al.*, Chapter 1, and Foldvari and Van Leeuwen, Chapter 2, this volume) we estimate the amount of silver in circulation as a common factor. That is, we estimate a local-level model for the six commodity prices on the assumption that they have a common factor.

The state-space representation is the following:

$$\mathbf{lnP_t} = \mathbf{c}\mu_t + \boldsymbol{\varepsilon_t}$$
$$\mu_t = \mu_{t-1} + \xi_t$$
$$\mathbf{lnP_t} = (\ln p_t^{barley}, \ln p_t^{dates}, \ln p_t^{cress}, \ln p_t^{cuscuta}, \ln p_t^{sesame}, \ln p_t^{wool})'$$
$$\mathbf{c} = (c^{barley}, c^{dates}, c^{cress}, c^{cuscuta}, c^{sesame}, c^{wool})',$$

$$(19.11)$$

where we have six observations of signal equations (the first row in (19.11)), and a single state equation, describing the unobserved component μ as a random-walk process. Both $\boldsymbol{\varepsilon}$ and ξ are normally and independently distributed random variables (disturbances). Vector $\mathbf{c}$ contains the product specific coefficients or factor loadings, since, as we saw in the previous section, product prices will react differently to an increase in silver.

In state-space methodology, unlike in classical regression analysis, the unknown parameters to estimate are the disturbances. It is possible to find an equivalence between an ARIMA(0,1,1) model and the local-level model described as (19.10), so the stationarity of the price series is not a requirement in state-space modelling. Another great advantage of state-space modelling is that it is not sensitive to missing data. The reason for this lies in the estimation method: the state (μ_t) is estimated by a Kalman-filter based on all past information. If the next observation is not available, the Kalman-filter can fill in the missing value simply by forecasting it from the past observations (more on this: Koopman and Hoogerheide, Chapter 3, this volume). We can also separate the seasonal effects (in all cases deterministic seasonal effects proved sufficient, showing that the relative effect of seasonality remained the same over the whole period).

We report some statistics for the residuals from the six signal equations with the estimated $\mathbf{c}$ coefficients in Table 19.1. Unfortunately, the residuals from the signal equations do not have the hoped-for properties: normality is always rejected at 1 per cent with the sole exception of cress, and we find a serial correlation in all cases.

The obtained coefficients are all positive, showing that all commodities reacted with a price increase to monetary expansion. This is not surprising as we expect that none of the observed commodities were inferior. In other words, with the growth of income the demand for all has increased. The exponential of the smoothed state variable from our model (19.11) can be interpreted as the index of the amount of shekels (irrespective of their silver content) in circulation. We report this as Figure 19.1. For convenience we choose the first observation December 385 BC as base.

The pattern we can observe in Figure 19.1 does not look implausible at all. The most extraordinary finding is the positive peak around the 320s BC. This is attributable to an external shock, namely, the campaign of Alexander the Great, who after the conquest of Persepolis in the autumn of 331 BC opened the Persian treasury and distributed a major share of it among his soldiers, pumping almost 5,000 tonnes of silver into the market. Apparently, the number of coins

Table 19.1 Statistics of the local-level model of the six products in Babylon

	Barley	Dates	Cress	Cuscuta	Sesame	Wool
Number of observations	535	359	484	328	388	335
R-squared[a]	0.839	0.610	0.816	0.261	0.703	0.491
Normality test Jarque–Berra	21.27 ($p=0.000$)	12.25 ($p=0.002$)	7.787 ($p=0.020$)	11.62 ($p=0.003$)	33.83 ($p=0.000$)	19.93 ($p=0.000$)
$Q(1)$ p-value	0.000	0.000	0.000	0.000	0.000	0.000
$Q(5)$ p-value	0.000	0.000	0.000	0.000	0.000	0.000
$Q(12)$ p-value	0.000	0.000	0.000	0.000	0.000	0.000
Coefficient (c_i)	5.736	5.175	6.792	3.919	7.553	1.554

Note:
[a] Calculated as the square of the linear correlation coefficient between the observed prices and the smoothed signal series from the model.

had declined to average levels by the beginning of the third century BC, which lends support to Aperghis' (2004: 29–30) claim that a great quantity of silver left Babylon together with the Macedonian soldiers. This is followed by a remarkable stability, as reflected by prices, for more than a hundred years. It is only after 165 BC that we see a gradual increase in the amount of money in circulation again, which can be explained by either an increase in the economy (requiring more coins) or by a decline in value of the existing coins (either via debasement, i.e. decreasing silver content of coins, or by a reduction of the weight of the coins).

But do we have any reason to believe that there was a debasement (or a weight reduction) in Babylonia after about 165 BC? An important source of confusion may arise from the usage of the unit shekel (denoting either 8.33 grams of silver or approximately 2 drachmas) which is the unit the prices are given in and which we used for Table 19.1. While initially the shekel was used as a weight measure, it is likely that with the increasing importance of silver coins over weighted pieces of silver, similarly to what happened to pound sterling, the term 'shekel' was increasingly used to describe a currency unit (i.e. 1 shekel was 2 drachmas; cf. Van der Spek 1998: 211, 246–7). Hence, whenever the silver content of the drachma fell, as 1 shekel was still equal to 2 drachmas, the silver content of a shekel fell as well. An interesting commodity price list (Slotsky and Wallenfels 2009, text 6 r. 12′– 15′) seems to support the above theory. The text gives two distinct exchange values of barley (for 2 shekels of silver) for month III 175 SEB = 27 May 25 June 137 BC: 2 *pan* 2 *sut* (84 litres) in staters of Demetrius and 2 *pan* (72 litres) in staters of Arsaces.[10] Slotsky and Wallenfels observe (2010: 94, n. 65): 'The increased purchasing power (+6 per cent) of the Demetrius staters is almost identical to the greater average weight of silver tetradrachms minted at Seleucia on the Tigris by Demetrius II (+6.7 per cent) over those of Mithradates.' The document refers to the time shortly after the abortive attempt of the Seleucid king Demetrius II in 138 BC to reconquer Babylonia from the Parthians. In his short reign of a few months he apparently was able to introduce new coins, which had a higher weight

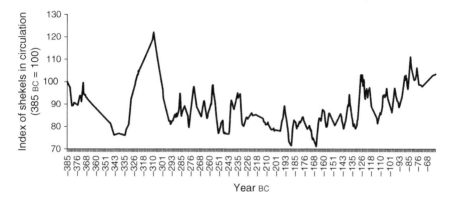

Figure 19.1 Exponential of the smoothed states index, Babylon, 385–61 BC (385 BC = 100).

Table 19.2 Silver content of coins (1 shekel = 2 drachmas) relative to 331 BC

Year BC	% silver in coin
<331	87.5
200	93.0
164	88.0
120	81.6
100	79.0
80	76.5
60	74.2

Sources: http://parthia.com/parthia_stats_gordus.htm; Mørkholm (1991: 5); Le Rider and De Callataÿ (2006: 29–31).

than the Parthian coins. What is of importance for us is that the document distinguishes between two currencies, sharing the same name, by their silver content and/or weight. This gives the impression that by the second century BC the name of currency units did not necessarily refer to their silver content any more, and that governments tried to influence the amount of money by changing the silver content of coins and/or their weight.

Fortunately we do have some information on the size and silver contents of the coins as well (see Table 19.2). We know that until the time of Alexander the Great uncoined silver used in commercial transactions consisted of 87.5 per cent silver. We have little information on coins until c. 200 BC. In the second century BC both the weight of the coins and their silver content began to decline. The weight of the Seleucid coins declined in the period between Seleucus IV (187–175 BC) and Antiochus IV (175–164 BC) from about 17 to 16.8 grams. This process continued after the death of Antiochus IV and even more after the Parthian takeover in 141 BC when the Parthian coins almost linearly declined a further 2 per cent in the period up to 50 BC. More importantly, however, the silver content changed from close to 93 per cent in 200 BC to 75 per cent in 50 BC. The known estimates of the silver content of a shekel (1 shekel = 2 drachmas) are reported in Table 19.2. These numbers refer to the shekel of 331 BC, i.e. they are an index of the total amount of silver that is available in a shekel between 331 and 60 BC.

As we pointed out earlier, our method can only give an estimate of the number of silver *coins* in circulation. If we are interested in the amount of silver instead, our estimates should be corrected for the silver content and the weight of the coins as given in Table 19.2. Unfortunately we only have some point estimates as reported in Table 19.2 so we need to make some assumptions and interpolate the known data points. We use the assumption that the silver content of the coins changed by a constant rate between the years of known data points (a log-linear interpolation).

Hence, dividing the data from Figure 19.1 by the log-linear interpolated data from Table 19.2 gives a result for the amount of silver in circulation, which is plotted in Figure 19.2.

Including the change in the silver content and the weight of coins changes the story profoundly. Based on our estimates from the model at the start of this chapter, we found that after about 165 BC there was an increase in money quantity. Now we find that this was not caused by an influx of silver, but rather by debasement, which was a result of a wilful government policy to increase money supply. In the long run we find the amount of silver constant at best, with only some minor increase during the first century BC.

There are two ways in which we can corroborate or falsify our results. One way is to use the method on the data for England and compare our results with data from the literature, which is what we will turn to in the next section. Another way is to check whether the trend and/or fluctuations we find for Babylon are plausible.

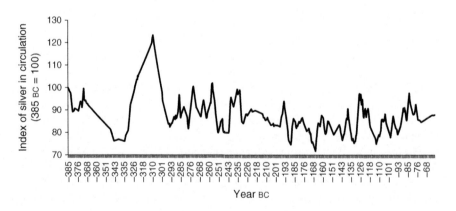

Figure 19.2 Estimates of the quantity of silver in circulation in Babylon, 385–61 BC, corrected for changes in the purity and weight of the coins[a].

Note:

[a] The data in Figure 19.1 divided by an index create from the log-linearly interpolated series reported in Table 19.2.

An extensive long-term die study for Babylon might corroborate or falsify this scheme, but this is far beyond the scope of this chapter. In addition, even when, for example, the mint at Seleucia produced a huge number of tetradrachms, this would not imply an increase of silver in circulation in Babylonia. The money might well have been intended to pay an army that left to another region for campaigns. So we limit ourselves to a few general observations.

We have already mentioned the substantial input of silver by the monetization of the Persian treasures by Alexander the Great and the early successors; this is clearly visible in the graph (Figure 19.2). The peak of about 195 BC may be attributed to a wartime production of coins for the planned campaigns for the conquest of Asia Minor by Antiochus III, who was in Babylon in 205 BC after his successful campaign to the east, and the ensuing drop may be attributed to a drain of money to the west for those very campaigns, the defeat of Antiochus in 189 BC and the Peace of Apamea in 188 BC, when the Seleucid king had to pay 3,000 talents of silver in silver coins to the Romans. The decline at the end of the reign of Antiochus IV (175–164 BC) may attest to the notorious lack of money Antiochus IV had to spend on his sixth Syrian war when he invaded Egypt (169–8 BC), his big parade (*pompē*) in Daphne near Antioch in Syria and his spending of enormous amounts of money in Greece. If this is correct, the huge booty from Egypt did not enter Babylonia. The beginning of the Parthian period (from 141 BC) witnessed an increase of silver in circulation until 138 BC, when the successful conqueror Mithradates I died or was paralysed.[11] The peak in 138 BC may be attributed to the invasion of Babylonia by Demetrius II, which brought two armies into Babylonia that had to be paid. Demetrius brought in his own coins, spent by his troops or robbed from his troops after his defeat (cf. above and Houghton *et al.* 2008: 264). The early Parthian period witnesses the extensive issues of Mithradates I (141–138/2 BC; Sellwood types 7–13) and Mithradates II (123/1– c. 91 BC; Sellwood types 23–29), but also Artabanus I (126–123/2 BC; Sellwood types 19–22) and Hyspaosines of Characene, who briefly ruled Babylonia in 127 BC, issued coins.[12]

Not everything can be explained by contemporary documents and historical events. The ADs (ADART no. −273B) suggest that much silver was brought from Babylonia to Syria in spring 273 BC and that in that year (274/3 BC) purchases were made in Greek copper coins, as noted earlier. This would lead to the assumption of a drop of silver in circulation from 274 BC on, but that is not the case according to the graph in Figure 19.2, which shows a peak in 273 BC. It may be correct nevertheless. We know that just before 274 BC Antiochus I introduced new taxes on the sale of salt, slaves and arable land (and perhaps much more) in order to have resources for his wars against the Galatians and the Ptolemies in the First Syrian war (Doty 1977: 308–35). The drop in circulation of silver that followed may reflect the silver drain to Syria. The low level of silver in circulation in the period 253–242 BC (later reign of Antiochus II, 261–246 BC and early reign of Seleucus II, 246–226 BC) and the sudden high level between 242–232 BC (also Seleucus II) is more difficult to explain. The earlier period witnessed the land grant by Antiochus II to Babylonians with the exemption of taxes (tithes) to the king (251 BC?) and the invasion of Ptolemy III in 246/5 BC (a year for which we have no prices). The later period is a time of unrest in Babylonia due to local warfare and perhaps the war of Seleucus II with his brother Antiochus Hierax (cf. Van der Spek 2006: 296–302).

Cross-checking: England and the Spanish silver

As pointed out in the previous section, our method seems to produce plausible results for Babylonia. Nevertheless, another way to lend credence to our results is to cross-check it using data pertaining to England in the period AD 1300–1700. Not only did this period witness a shock in the amount of silver available, as a result of the influx of Spanish silver from the Americas, but also independent estimates of the amount of silver in circulation are available.

We start with a similar state-space model as outlined in the previous section. Data for England are obviously more extensive and of better quality than that for Babylonia (Clark 2004; 2005a; 2005b) and, since the amount of data increases the computational burden exponentially, we choose the products as given in Table 19.3.

Interestingly, we find some significant negative coefficients, most notably for candle wax, coal (London) and mutton. This suggests that these goods were considered inferior – i.e. that demand for them goes down as soon as income increases – which is not implausible. After all, coal was not a preferred good, because of its polluting nature. Likewise mutton was probably inferior to pork and beef.

Since the data were already given in grams of silver, we can use this information to arrive directly at an estimate of the trend in silver in circulation (see Figure 19.3).

To check the plausibility of these estimates, we also included observations from the literature. For the period up to AD 1600, we used data from Mayhew (1995). His data were corrected for the silver content of the pound to arrive at silver-equivalent value in circulation. Obviously, and especially since the fourteenth century AD, a lot of gold pounds were minted besides silver. Hence it is better to analyse on the basis of a silver-equivalent index.

Table 19.3 Coefficients of different products

Product	Coefficient	Product	Coefficient
Barley	2.181	Coal (London)	−2.362
Beer-strong	2.401[a]	Linen cloth	0.866
Bricks	−0.071[a]	Mutton	−2.147
Butter	0.286	Parchment	0.230
Candles tallow	0.268[a]	Peas	−0.019[a]
Candles wax	−2.465	Saffron	−0.277[a]
Charcoal	0.594	Stockings	0.032
Cheese	1.219	Straw	0.151[a]
Clothing	2.457[a]		

Note:
[a] Not significant at least at 10 per cent level.

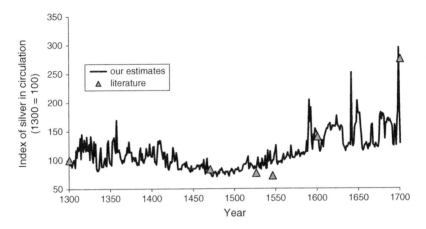

Figure 19.3 The estimated amount of silver in circulation in England, 1300–1700 (1300 = 100).

Source: literature series taken from Mayhew (1995) prior to AD 1600. For AD 1700 data were taken from Pepys, Diary, VI, p. 23.

In the seventeenth century AD Mayhew's estimates trend up quickly. For 1700 Mayhew estimates 14 million pounds in circulation. Even after correction for the silver contents, this boils down to an index value of 550, which is substantially higher than our estimates suggest. But this is different when we look at contemporary estimates. Petty (1695) estimated the number of coins in circulation at six million, while the Mint master told Samuel Pepys in AD 1665 that the best guess was seven million and the House of Commons guessed the amount in AD 1670 not to exceed twelve million (*The Diary of Samuel Pepys* IV: 23, Latham and Matthews 1971; Thirsk and Cooper 1972: 679).

It is difficult to address the reasons behind this big difference. There may be, however, two reasons. First, if we consider Challis (1992: 386), we find that, using the recoinage of AD 1696–8 during which old money was taken out of circulation and replaced with new coins, he arrives at silver in circulation of 6.8 million pounds. The main problem is gold, which, based on the gold output of the mints between AD 1660 and 1700, is set at around 6.6 million pounds. Mayhew thus arrives at his number by assuming that almost no gold left England (basically because he argues that the price of gold in England was higher than elsewhere on the continent). However, for the first half of the century, it is argued that the price of gold was rather higher on the continent (e.g. Besly 1990). If only partially true, a total value of 10 million pounds seems more likely. Secondly, we are looking at silver equivalents in circulation, thus excluding hoarded money. Even if we assume that gold in England was relatively expensive compared to silver, this only suggests that a lot of it must have been hoarded, making the total amount of money in circulation likely to be around 6 to 8 million pounds.

The model thus seems to predict fairly accurately the silver in circulation. In addition, there are two interesting observations to be made. First, we find almost no fluctuations during the Black Death (AD 1347–50). Although this is not surprising (after all silver did not disappear during the Black Death), the fact that we find almost constant silver in circulation lends extra credence to our model. Secondly, we find that, after a small decrease of silver in circulation in the fifteenth century AD, there was a slow increase until AD 1700. Indeed, Figure 19.3 clearly shows the bullion famine which hit Europe in the fifteenth century AD and caused a desperate search for more silver and precious metals in England (e.g. Griffiths 1998: 376–401; Allen 2011: 121). This was caused by a drop in mining, especially in Austria and Germany, as well as by increased hoarding of precious metals after the Black Death and an outflow of silver to pay for the luxury products imported from the Middle East, India and China (e.g. Day 1978). All this changed in the sixteenth century AD when Spanish silver came into the European market. Remarkably, however, the silver equivalents in circulation did not increase as much as might have been expected based on the stories of massive influxes of silver. Speculatively, we may come up with two reasons. First, England around AD 1700 was still a relative economic backwater. Per capita GDP was still 30–40 per cent lower than in Holland (Broadberry *et al.*, 2014; Van Zanden and Van Leeuwen 2012). Combined with the fact that Spain probably sent more silver to neighbouring countries such as the Italian states, England probably did not draw in much silver. Secondly, Braudel and Spooner (1967: 444–5) guesstimated that Spanish bullion imports from the New World amounted to about half the stock which was available in Europe in AD 1500. Yet they assumed that all stocks from ancient and medieval times had accumulated while there is plenty of evidence that substantial parts of these stocks moved abroad (Lane and Mueller 1985: 370–1). We therefore agree with Mayhew (1995) that they probably overestimated the stocks present in Europe and consequently underestimated the share of New World silver. It is important to note that, if we assume that more than half of the European stock assumed by Braudel and Spooner had gone abroad or was otherwise depleted, the share of New World silver made up 100–200 per cent of the existing stocks instead of 50 per cent, i.e. a factor of 2–4 more. So our finding that silver in England more than quadrupled in the seventeenth century AD seems quite plausible if we assume that slightly over 50 per cent of the European silver was exported abroad.

Conclusion

In this chapter we have attempted to estimate the amount of silver in circulation in Babylonia during the period c. 385–60 BC. The lack of direct evidence makes it necessary that we combine available price data with economic theory and statistical methodology to arrive at plausible results. Bearing all the limitations of this approach in mind, our results confirm the historically recorded stories about the inflow of silver into circulation from the treasuries of the Persian Empire after the conquest by Alexander the Great but also that most of this silver left Babylonia. This was followed by a gradual reduction of silver quantity in circulation until about 160 BC, after which we find a constant level or even a small increase during the first century BC.

To verify the model used, we applied the same method to data from medieval and early modern England. We find that our estimates of the silver in circulation match well with those in the literature. Remarkably, we also find that the rise of the stock of silver in the sixteenth and seventeenth centuries AD was not as strong as might have been expected given the well-known stories about the influx of Spanish silver from the New World.

Notes

1 This paper was supported by the Fundamental Research Fund for the Central Universities in China (Jinan University).

2 II Kings 7:1–2. The shekel in Israel weighed about 11 grams and the seah was about 7.3 litres.

3 See Chicago Assyrian Dictionary s.v. *mahīru* 2 c) and Van der Spek's (Chapter 1, this volume) observations on the meaning of the term KI.LAM = *mahiru* = exchange value.

4 In a way one might argue that he boasts here a reversal of Gresham's law that good money drives out bad money, which underscores his achievement. Modern economists would perhaps doubt if a sudden devaluation of the silver is really so good.

5 Cassius Dio 51. 21.5 'So vast an amount of money, in fact, circulated through all parts of the city alike, that the price of (landed) property (*ktēmata*) rose and loans for which the borrower had been glad to pay 12 per cent, could now be had for one third that rate.' Cf. Suetonius, *Life of Augustus* 41: 'When he brought the treasuries of the Ptolemies to Rome at his Alexandrian triumph, so much cash passed into private hands that the interest rate on loans dropped sharply, while real estate (*agri*) soared.'

6 Cicero, *Ad Atticum* 9.9.4 'But in these days I presume all such properties are gone down in value, owing to the lack of coins' (*nummorum caritas*).

7 Tacitus, *Annals* 6. 16–17; cf. Tchernia (2003: 136). We owe the references in nn. 3–6 to Dominic Rathbone.

8 Obviously, we can only estimate the amount of silver in circulation, i.e. silver that has been made available for transactions (paid as income). As hoarded silver is not spent, it will not affect prices and should not appear in our estimates.

9 According to Keynesian theory, the velocity of money should decline with the rise of the money stock. However, some authors, such as Goldstone (1984) and Lindert (1985) have pointed at periods of increasing velocity of money combined with rising numbers of coins in circulation. On average, however, it is safe to assume that the velocity of money did not change dramatically enough to alter our estimates.

10 All Parthian kings had the throne name Arsaces.

11 Cf. Assar (2006: 95). Assar argues (in our view convincingly) that the king became ill and was represented by his brother Bacasis, in the ADs known as Bagayasha. This may have caused a drop in issuing new coins.

12 The years of reign of the Parthian kings are debated. Unfortunately all kings called themselves Arsaces and are so named on coins, cuneiform documents and Greek inscriptions. The personal names are mainly derived from the literary sources. See Assar (2006) and for the coin types Sellwood (1971 (1980)) and www.parthia.com.

Abbreviation

ADART: Sachs, A. and Hunger, H. 1988. *Astronomical Diaries and Related Texts from Babylonia*. Volume 1: *Diaries from 652–262 BC,* Vienna: Verlag der Österreichischen Akademie der Wissenschaften.

Bibliography

Allen, R. C. 2000. 'Economic Structure and Agriculture Productivity in Europe, 1300–1800,' *European Review of Economic History*, 4: 1–25.

Allen, M. 2011. 'Silver Production and the Money Supply in England and Wales, 1086–c. 1500', *Economic History Review*, 64: 114–31.

Aperghis, G. G. 2004. *The Seleukid Royal Economy: The Finances and Financial Administration of the Seleukid Empire*, Cambridge: Cambridge University Press.

Assar, G. R. F. 2006. 'A Revised Parthian Chronology of 165–91 BC', *Electrum* 11: 87–158.

Besly, E. 1990. *Coins and Medals of the English Civil War*, London: Seaby.

Braudel, F. and Spooner, F. C. 1967. 'Prices in Europe from 1450 to 1750', in *The Cambridge Economic History of Europe*, IV, edited by E. E. Rich and C. H. Wilson, Cambridge: Cambridge University Press: 374–486.

Broadberry, S., Campbell, B., Klein, A., Overton, M. and Van Leeuwen, B. 2014. *British GDP ca. 1270–1870*, Cambridge: Cambridge University Press.

Challis, C. E., ed. 1992. *A New History of the Royal Mint*, Cambridge: Cambridge University Press.

Clark, G. 2004. 'The Price History of English Agriculture, 1209–1914', *Research in Economic History*, 22: 41–124.

—— 2005a. 'The Long March of History: Farm Wages, Population and Economic Growth, England 1209–1869', *UC Davis Working paper series*, Paper No. 05–40.

—— 2005b. 'The Condition of the Working Class in England, 1209–2004', *Journal of Political Economy*, 113: 1307–40.

Commandeur, J. F. and Koopman, S. J. 2007. *An Introduction to State Space Time Series Analysis*, Oxford: Oxford University Press.

Day, J. 1978. 'The Great Bullion Famine of the Fifteenth Century', *Past & Present*, 79, 3–54.

Doty, L. T. 1977. *Cuneiform Archives from Hellenistic Uruk*, Ann Arbor: University Microfilms International.

Fuchs, A. 1994. *Die Inschriften Sargons II. aus Khorsabad*, Göttingen: Cuvillier.

Goldstone, J. 1984. 'Urbanization and Inflation: Lessons from the English Price Revolution of the Sixteenth and Seventeenth Centuries', *American Journal of Sociology*, 89: 1122–60.

Griffiths, R. A. 1998. *The Reign of King Henry VI: The Exercise of Royal Authority, 1422–1461*. Berkeley: University of California Press 1981, 2nd edition, Stroud: The History Press.

Hawkins, J. D. 1986. 'Royal Statements About Real Prices: Assyrian, Babylonian and Hittite', in *Ancient Anatolia. Aspects of Change and Cultural development. Essays in Honor of Machteld J. Mellink*, edited by J. V. Canby et al. Madison: University of Wisconsin Press: 93–102.

Houghton, A., Lorber, C. and Hoover, O. 2008. *Seleucid Coins. A Comprehensive Catalogue*. Part 2: *Seleucus IV through Antiochus XIII*. Vol. I: *Introduction, Maps and Catalogue*. New York: The American Numismatic Society.

Jursa, M. 2010. *Aspects of the Economic History of Babylonia in the First Millennium BC: Economic Geography, Economic Mentalities, Agriculture, the Use of Money and the Problem of Economic Growth*, Münster: Ugarit Verlag.

Knudsen, E. E. 1967. 'Fragments of Historical Texts from Nimrud', *Iraq* 29: 29–31.

Lane, F. C. and Mueller, R. C. 1985. *Money and Banking in Medieval and Renaissance Venice*, I, Baltimore: Johns Hopkins Press.

Latham, R. and Matthews, W., eds. 1971. *The Diary of Samuel Pepys*, IV, London: Bell & Hyman; London: HarperCollins Publishers 1995; 2000; Berkeley: University of California Press 1995; 2000.

Le Rider, G. 2001. *La naissance de la monnaie. Pratiques monétaires de l'Orient ancient*, Paris: Presses Universitaires de France.

Le Rider, G. and De Callataÿ, F. 2006. *Les Séleucides et les Ptolémées. L'héritage monétaire et financier d'Alexandre le Grand*. Paris: Éditions du Rocher.

Lindert, P. 1985. 'English Population, Wages, and Prices: 1541–1913', *The Journal of Interdisciplinary History*, 15: 609–34.

Mayhew, N. 1995. 'Population, Money Supply, and the Velocity of Circulation in England, 1300–1700', *Economic History Review*, New Series, 48: 238–57.

Mørkholm, O. 1991. *Early Hellenistic Coinage from the Accession of Alexander to the Peace of Apamea (336–186 B.C.)*, Cambridge: Cambridge University Press.

Müller, G. 1997. 'Gedanken zur neuassyrischen Geldwirtschaft', in *Assyrien im Wandel der Zeiten*, edited by H. Waetzoldt and H. Hauptmann, Heidelberg: Heidelberger Orientverlag: 115–21.

Petty, William. 1682 (1695). *Quantulumcunque Concerning Money*, repr. in *The Economic Writings of Sir William Petty*, II, edited by C. H. Hull, Cambridge: Cambridge University Press 1899: 437–48.

Postgate, J. N. 1979. 'The Economic Structure of the Assyrian Empire', in *Power and Propaganda. A Symposium on Ancient Empires*, edited by M. T. Larsen, Copenhagen: Akademisk Forlag: 193–221.

Powell, M. 1996. 'Money in Mesopotamia', *Journal of the Economic and Social History of the Orient*, 39: 224–42.

Radner, K. 1999. 'Money in the Neo-Assyrian Empire', in *Trade and Finance in Ancient Mesopotamia*, edited by J. G. Dercksen, Istanbul and Leiden: Nederlands Archaeologisch-Historisch Instituut te Istanbul: 127–57.

Schaudig, H. 2001. *Die Inschriften Nabonids von Babylon und Kyros' des Großen*, Münster: Ugarit Verlag.

Sellwood, D. G. 1971 (1980). *An Introduction to the Coinage of Parthia*, London: Spink & Son Limited.

Slotsky, A. L. and Wallenfels, R. 2009. *Tallies and Trends. The Late Babylonian Commodity Price Lists*, Bethesda MD: CDL Press.

—— 2010. *Tallies and Trends. The Late Babylonian Commodity Price lists,* Bethesda MD: CDL Press.

Tchernia, A. 2003. 'Remarques sur la crise de 33', in *Credito e moneta nel mondo romano: atti degli incontri capresi di storia dell'economia antica (Capri 12–14 ottobre 2000)*, edited by Lo Cascio, Elio, Bari: Edipuglia: 131–46.

Thirsk, J. and Cooper, J. P., eds. 1972. *Seventeenth-century Economic Documents*, Oxford: Clarendon Press.

Van der Spek, R. J. 1998. 'Cuneiform Documents on Parthian History: the Rahimesu Archive. Materials for the Study of the Standard of Living', in *Das Partherreich und seine Zeugnisse. The Arsacid empire: sources and documentation*, edited by J. Wiesehöfer, Stuttgart: Franz Steiner Verlag: 205–58.

—— 2004. 'Palace, Temple and Market in Seleucid Babylonia', in *Le Roi et l'Économie: Autonomies Locales et Structures Royales dans l'Économie de l'Empire Séleucide*, edited by V. Chankowski and F. Duyrat, Paris: De Boccard: 303–32.

—— 2006. 'How to Measure Prosperity? the Case of Hellenistic Babylonia', in *Approches de l'économie hellénistique*, edited by R. Descat, Saint-Bertrand-de-Comminges: Musée archéologique de Saint-Bertrand-de-Comminges: 287–310.

Van Zanden, J. L. and van Leeuwen, B. 2012. 'Persistent But Not Consistent: the Growth of National Income in Holland 1347–1807', *Explorations in Economic History,* 49: 119–30.

Von Reden, S. 1995. *Exchange in Ancient Greece*, London: Duckworth.

—— 2007. *Money in Ptolemaic Egypt: From the Macedonian Conquest to the end of the Third Century*, Cambridge: Cambridge University Press.

20 Long-run patterns in market performance in the Near East, the Mediterranean and Europe from antiquity to c. AD 1800

*Bas van Leeuwen, Peter Foldvari and
Jan Luiten van Zanden*

Introduction

Market performance, which we define, following Foldvari and Van Leeuwen (Chapter 2, this volume), as the capacity of the market to absorb unexpected supply or demand shocks[1], is often seen as a driving force in economic development.[2] Whereas some authors emphasize the connection between increasing market performance and growth in the early modern period, others have already found the presence of markets working well in the medieval world (e.g. Masschaele 1993; Galloway 2000; Clark 2002). The view that some of the medieval markets were already functioning well seems to be consistent with recent research showing that per capita income in the late medieval period was already higher than hitherto assumed (e.g. Prados de la Escosura and Álvarez-Nogal 2009; Malanima 2011; Van Zanden and Van Leeuwen 2012; Broadberry *et al.*, 2014).

Recent studies on the classical economies claim that their levels of per capita income were almost comparable with the medieval period.[3] Given the consensus that market performance is connected with economic development (North and Thomas 1973; Studer 2008), this suggests that these economies also experienced an acceptable level of market performance. However, not many studies went into the performance of ancient grain markets. Most studies have so far largely focused on government intervention and trade patterns without actually quantifying their performance (e.g. Erdkamp 2005; Kessler and Temin 2008).

In this chapter we try to construct and explain the development of market performance in the Near East and the Mediterranean world, stretching from the ancient world to the nineteenth century AD. The choice of market performance as indicator, however, needs some consideration. Market performance in general is often measured through the volatility of the price series. The underlying idea is that the more volatile a price series of a good, the less its institutional structure is apparently able to reduce the effect of shocks on the supply (and demand) for that product. Hence, the less well the market performs. Since volatility measures like the variance or the standard deviation are level dependent (the higher a price is, the higher the variance or standard deviation will be), in recent literature it became more common to use the coefficient of variance (CV) (e.g. Persson 1999; Ó Gráda

2005; Söderberg 2006; Jursa 2010). The CV, which is defined as the standard deviation divided by the mean, has as a big advantage in that it can be compared between economies with different absolute price levels. However, its disadvantage is that it is inflated by the presence of a trend, and affected by differences in agricultural structure and other factors that should not be related to market performance.[4] For these reasons, Foldvari and Van Leeuwen (2011) proposed using residual variance for measuring market performance.

This chapter is structured as follows. In the next section we discuss the data. We then move on to the measures of volatility and market performance using a standard CV as well as the conditional volatility measures as proposed by Foldvari and Van Leeuwen (2011). We find that market performance increases in the West and Turkey, but remains remarkably stable in Iraq and Egypt between c. 500 BC and AD 1500. After 1500, market performance increased further in western Europe. We then discuss the possible reasons underlying these deviations, i.e. technological change, changing consumption patterns, trade and storage. In the penultimate section we offer a 'sneak peak' of the period after AD 1500. We end with a brief conclusion.

Data and comparability

To calculate the CV as a measure of market performance between 600 BC and AD 1800, it is necessary to collect time series for periods with sometimes scarce data. In this chapter we limit ourselves to the prices of the main staple crops since these data not only are the most abundant but also capture the most important market in a pre-industrial economy and, as argued by Adam Smith, may also be linked to the value of labour (Smith 1776; repr. 1991: 33).

For the period between 600 and 500 BC the data are taken from Jursa (2010: 443–57). These data refer not only to Babylon, but also to neighbouring Uruk, Sippar, Nippur and Borsippa. Theoretically, it would be preferable to estimate a dummy regression in which we regress the prices on dummies referring to place, year and month, as suggested by Clark (2004). In that way we would be able to correct for regional and monthly variation. Furthermore, this kind of regression improves with the number of observations. Since our sample is small and the price level among the different cities did not strongly deviate, we decided to take the simple annual averages of the prices.

For the period c. 500–50 BC we take the data for the city of Babylon only, as assembled by R.J. van der Spek and his VU University research group on market performance in Babylonia (cf. Preface, Chapter 1, this volume, and Appendix on Babylonian prices).[5] These data are based on the so-called astronomical diaries (ADs), a database of observations compiled by Babylonian scholars containing celestial and terrestrial phenomena. One thing they noted down was the level of the prices of six commodities: barley, dates, cuscuta, water cress, sesame and wool. Theoretically, these prices exist for the period c. 400–50 BC monthly, or even daily (cf. Van der Spek *et al.*, Chapter 1, this volume). However, many observations are missing (for a discussion see Koopman and Hoogerheide, Chapter 3, this volume).

Still, out of a possible 4,079 months, we have observations for 512 months.[6] This allows us to correct the prices for seasonality using a regression with monthly dummies.

For other regions we have far less data. The best dataset outside of Babylon is possibly for Egypt. Von Reden (forthcoming) reports prices for Egypt between c. 300 and 90 BC (see now also Rathbone and Von Reden, Chapter 8, this volume). These data are largely representative for the more densely Greek dominated parts of the country. As Von Reden points out, however, the prices are representative of normal market behaviour in Egypt. In Chapter 8, this volume and in Von Reden (forthcoming) she also presents data for Delos, taken from Reger (1994), and Athens. Further, we use data for the second great empire in this region, Rome, from Rathbone (forthcoming; and Chapter 8, this volume), as shown in Figure 20.1. For the later periods from c. AD 1200 onwards we have data from Iraq, Egypt, Syria and Istanbul (Ashtor 1969; Mortel 1989; Pamuk 2004; Schatzmiller 2011), as shown in Figure 20.2. The earlier estimates are normally taken from contemporary economic historians, often reporting extreme prices, while the Istanbul data refer to retail prices (Pamuk 2004: 452). The data for the period after AD 1500 are more abundant. We included the retail prices for wheat from Istanbul as well as data from Tuscany, Modena and Naples (Coniglio 1952; Romano 1965; Basini 1974; Malanima 1976; Pamuk 2004), as shown in Figure 20.3.

Three problems surround these data. First, some authors, in the Finleyian (Finley 1973) tradition, have doubted whether the prices from antiquity are 'real' market prices.

Yet, as pointed out by Von Reden (forthcoming) and Rathbone and Von Reden (Chapter 8, this volume), the Egyptian, Athenian and Delian prices exhibit relatively strong seasonal variation. At the same time Von Reden argues that imports increased during periods of high prices – all evidence that a working market

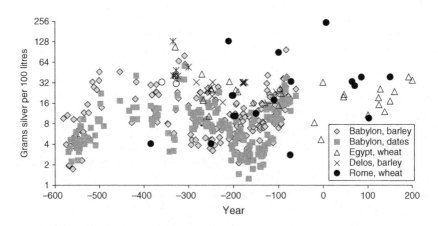

Figure 20.1 Grams of silver per hectolitre (log 2 scale), 600 BC–AD 200.

Sources: Von Reden (forthcoming); Jursa (2010); Rathbone (forthcoming); Rathbone and Von Reden, Chapter 8, this volume; Appendix of Babylonian Prices, this volume.

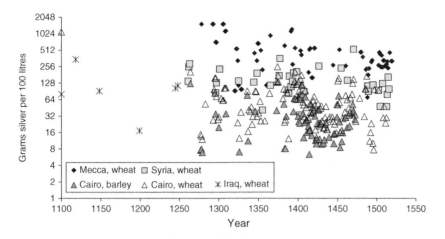

Figure 20.2 Grams of silver per hectolitre (log 2 scale), AD 1250–1550.

Sources: Ashtor (1969); Mortel (1989); Pamuk (2004); Schatzmiller (2011).

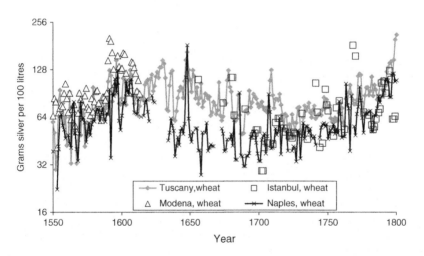

Figure 20.3 Grams of silver per hectolitre (log 2 scale), AD 1550–1800.

Sources: Coniglio (1952); Romano (1965); Basini (1974); Malanima (1976); Pamuk (2004).

existed. The same has also been argued for Babylon by a variety of authors such as Temin (2002), Romero *et al.* (2010), Van der Spek (2000: 295–7; forthcoming), and Foldvari and Van Leeuwen (Chapter 2, this volume). Van der Spek (forthcoming) even explicitly states that '[t]he very fact that prices are recorded in the ADs shows they were regarded as volatile and unpredictable'. The same finding of a working market has been argued for the Roman Empire as well by Rathbone (forthcoming; and Chapter 8, this volume) and, from the perspective of active trade relations, by Kessler and Temin (2008).

The second problem is that not all prices are of the same commodity. Wheat was generally preferred in the eastern Mediterranean and was the main staple in Egypt. However, barley, and to a certain extent dates, dominated food supply in Babylon. This was largely caused by salinization of the soil. Since wheat is less resistant to salt than barley, wheat was slowly replaced by barley in Babylon (Jacobsen and Adams 1958; Artzy and Hillel 1988).[7] In addition, a litre of barley has around 20 per cent less nutritional value than wheat. On the other hand, the Babylonians did not have the opportunity to choose wheat since it was not locally grown and trade was difficult. Furthermore, as argued by Van der Spek and Van Leeuwen (forthcoming), the price difference between wheat and barley was around 60 per cent in Egypt where wheat was the preferred grain, a ratio that we also encounter in present-day Iraq. Also Von Reden (forthcoming) argues that wheat prices in Athens are around 20–30 per cent higher than barley prices, a difference not unlike that found in Egypt. Since barley is the preferred grain in Babylon, however, Van der Spek and Van Leeuwen (forthcoming) argue that its price must be closer to that of wheat. Hence, since barley was the main foodstuff in Babylon and barley did not compete with other grains on an international market, while wheat had that role in the rest of the Mediterranean, we might consider them as identical, as 'grain'. Even if we were not to accept that the prices of barley in Babylon and wheat in litres may be reasonably close, it is still important to stress that we use these prices solely to calculate relative price volatility, which is independent of the level of the prices.

Finally, we have to convert all prices series to a common value, to make them comparable. In this chapter, all price series are converted into grams of silver per 100 litres. Only for the period after AD 1000 does this present a problem, because gold coins entered into circulation and some prices are expressed in terms of gold. Therefore, where necessary, we follow Söderberg (2006) and use the Cairo bimetallic standard for the Near East up to AD 1500. Although this is not necessarily always correct, available evidence shows that this ratio for later periods remained almost constant. Indeed, since this is almost equal to the ratio in Mecca AD 1200, this is an acceptable simplification. For Babylon this question is less relevant since the money was silver-based. For the other series we simply use the silver contents of the coins.

Market performance in the long run

Visual examination yields already a few interesting features of these price series. First, from Figure 20.1 it becomes clear that the average level of prices in Delos is much higher than the other regions. A possible reason, as argued by Reger (1994), is that barley and wheat on Delos were largely imported, increasing prices because of high transportation costs. The same applies to Athens whose economy too was characterized by large-scale grain imports. Second, it is remarkable that Egyptian wheat prices and Babylonian barley prices were almost equal (the Babylonian prices being fractionally lower) since a litre of barley has about 20 per cent less nutritional value than wheat. Third, we can see that in the second half of the sixth century BC barley prices rose faster than date prices. This is explained by Müller by arguing that the price increase is caused by a demographic increase, while the faster increase in the price of barley is caused by 'agricultural stress'; in other words, it is more difficult to increase the output of barley than of dates (Müller 1996/7: 166f.). An alternative explanation is offered by Jursa (2010: 780–3), who argues that most of the price increase is caused by an increasing amount of money in the hands of the ordinary man. The reason why date prices started to increase later than almost all other products, he attributes to land reclamation and a conversion from barley to date production around Sippar. Consequently, the supply of barley, possibly combined with an increased demand due to population growth, declined (Jursa 2010: 465–6). These explanations, however, seem problematic if one considers the whole period up to 50 BC. Whereas barley prices go up around 20 years before dates, the decline of date prices in the fourth century BC is faster than that of barley. Likewise, the increase of date prices around the first century BC is again faster than that of barley. In other words, after c. 550 BC, barley prices almost continuously stay high while date prices go down in the third century BC and up again in the first century BC. Barley prices, however, do not react strongly to the price movement of dates. This seems to contradict an inflation-based argument since it seems inexplicable that dates have such big swings in prices and barley does not (for a discussion of this phenomenon see Huijs *et al.*, Chapter 7, this volume). Likewise, it seems inconceivable that changing population may affect date prices to a much larger extent than barley prices. This decline in prices of barley (unfortunately we do not have comparable material for dates), we also find in Egypt (see Table 20.1). This suggests that whatever happened in Babylon was not a local event: it also took place elsewhere in the Mediterranean world.

How can we analyse these price movements, which took place over a period of no less than 24 centuries? One way, as argued at the start of the chapter, is to look at how markets can cope with external shocks. This is often done using a CV, being a relative measure of volatility. The results are reported in Table 20.1 and Table 20.2.

Tables 20.1 and 20.2 show a great diversity in CVs, ranging from a high 0.96 for barley in Babylon between 581 and 61 BC to as low as 0.25 for barley in Athens between 385 and 300 BC and 0.21 for barley in Delos 282–174 BC. However, for Athens and Delos we have to keep two things in mind. First, the number of observations for both regions is very small, creating a downward bias in volatility. Second, in Delos grain was largely imported (Reger 1994: 83–116) and was furthermore relatively expensive compared to prices in Egypt (Von Reden forthcoming and Chapter 8, this volume). The same applies to Athens, where part of consumption must have been imported. Although it has been argued that intra-annual volatility was large, the few annual observations coupled with a high mean price will have reduced the CV. After all, if all imports come from a region with standard deviation x and mean price y, the CV for that region will be x/y. In Delos and Athens, we have the same standard deviation, but the mean will be inflated by

Table 20.1 Coefficient of variation in the Near East and Rome, c. 581–72 BC

Region	Product	Time	Mean	Std. dev.	CV
Babylon	barley	581–61	13.40	12.91	0.96
		500–220	15.79	14.69	0.93
		200–120	10.11	7.15	0.71
	dates	570–61	9.21	7.38	0.80
		500–220	12.26	8.33	0.68
		200–120	4.65	3.15	0.68
Egypt	wheat	330–200	36.08	30.25	0.84
		200–120	19.86	4.27	0.22
Athens	wheat	385–300	59.15	35.15	0.59
	barley	385–300	37.58	9.39	0.25
Delos	barley	282–174	28.27	5.96	0.21
Rome	wheat	385–72	24.88	21.54	0.87

Table 20.2 Coefficient of variation in the Near East and Italy, c. AD 1000–1800

Region	Product	Time	Mean	Std. dev.	CV
Egypt	wheat	1277–1420	70.09	50.24	0.72
		1420–1500	50.72	39.90	0.79
	barley	1277–1399	40.57	33.25	0.82
		1420–1490	24.90	14.87	0.60
Iraq	wheat	1008–1248	67.46	59.66	0.88
Mecca	wheat	1308–1400	437.84	334.29	0.76
		1400–1520	329.60	128.68	0.39
Syria	wheat	1320–1400	145.78	79.43	0.54
		1400–1515	152.80	124.06	0.81
Istanbul	wheaten flour	1469–1600	0.63[a]	0.31[a]	0.49
	wheat	1656–1800	69.58	29.70	0.43
Tuscany	wheat	1263–1420	45.98	17.45	0.38
		1420–1490	31.64	11.21	0.35
		1550–1800	84.16	26.60	0.32
Modena	wheat	1550–1613	97.55	34.08	0.35
Naples	wheat	1550–1800	60.90	22.30	0.37

Note:
[a] Istanbul data are in grams of silver per kg.

the transport costs (t). Hence, the CV for Delos and Athens will be $x/(y+t)$ and will be lower. Indeed, Table 20.1 shows that the standard deviation in Delos and Athens is not substantially different from the other regions, but the mean prices in both regions are by far the highest for that period.

The second remarkable outlier is the CV of 0.96 for Babylon in Table 20.1. However, on closer inspection, we find that the CV for the overall period in Babylon is actually higher than that of each of the sub-periods. This is strange in view of the fact that the CVs are supposedly indicative of market performance and it is unexplainable that average market performance between 581 and 61 BC is lower than the average of each of the sub-periods. What is also remarkable is that the CV for the later period in Babylon (largely covering the Parthian period) is clearly not higher, perhaps even lower, than the earlier period. This is also surprising since the Parthian period is generally considered to have been a period of great shocks to the economy, shown by hunger and warfare.

More importantly perhaps, we detect a break in the level of the CV after about AD 1300; in particular the European CVs (including Istanbul) are at 0.3 and 0.4; much lower than what seems to be usual in the classical world (with the exception of Delos and Athens, but they are special cases). But the rest of the Middle East – Egypt and Syria – does not share in the decline in the variability of prices. This suggests long-run stability of market performance between c. 600 BC and AD 1300, followed by a strong increase in western Europe, where markets are much more stable than they used to be in antiquity.

Foldvari and Van Leeuwen (2011) argue that to analyse to what extent these factors may reduce the effect of unexpected demand and supply shocks such as wars and plague epidemics, one must first remove all other effects. The appropriate way to measure market performance is thus to look at the residual variance after modelling the movement of prices. The unconditional variance of prices (and the CV) may be very different across countries and time, but does not necessarily reflect differences in market performance. After all, in China there are regions with one, two, or even three rice harvests a year. A failed harvest in a region with only one harvest has of course a massively different effect on price volatility than a harvest failure in a region with three harvests a year, even though this does not say much about market performance. Likewise, Foldvari and Van Leeuwen (2011) showed that a trend in the prices, for example caused by inflation, may inflate the CV. Since the longer the period, the more likely a trend, CVs calculated over longer time periods are almost always higher than over short time periods which is, as we discussed above, what we found in Table 20.1 for Babylon.

To remove this spurious component of volatility (i.e. country- and time-specific demand- and supply-related factors and the trend), Foldvari and Van Leeuwen (2011) use a conditional heteroscedasticity model in which the variance of the residual term (the variance around the conditional expected value of the prices) is modelled, thereby filtering out the effect of the trend. The residual variance therefore captures, in a correctly specified model, only the effect of unexpected shocks. The lower the residual variance, the better markets can cope with shocks.

Unfortunately, since this method requires a lot of data, we can only report these results for a set of regions as in Table 20.3. This table presents some marked changes compared to Tables 20.1 and 20.2. A first interesting finding is that, as one may expect, market performance in Babylon for both barley and dates for the entire period is in between that of each of its sub-periods. This suggests that this measure of market performance is more accurate than simply using CVs. Second, we find a clear increase in market performance, (thus a decrease in conditional volatility) between Babylonian times and the late medieval period for Turkey and Syria and the western part of the Empire. But the same is not true for Egypt, Mecca and Iraq where market performance remained about the same between 500 BC and

Table 20.3 Standard error of the regression on first differences (log prices)

	Barley	Dates	Wheat	Rice
Babylon				
300–60 BC	0.54	0.41		
300–200 BC	0.64	0.32		
199–120 BC	0.45	0.48		
Egypt				
AD 1277–1420	0.61		0.57	
AD 1421–1500	0.52		0.63	
Mecca				
AD 1290–1420			0.50	
Syria				
AD 1300–1500			0.35	
Istanbul				
AD 1469–1650			0.30[a]	0.24
AD 1656–1800			0.19	
Florence				
AD 1338–1377			0.36	
AD 1525–1615			0.58	
Tuscany				
AD 1287–1420			0.32	
AD 1421–1490			0.28	
AD 1491–1650			0.29	
AD 1651–1800			0.21	
Modena				
AD 1550–1613			0.21	
Naples				
AD 1550–1800			0.25	

Note:
[a] Wheat flour.

AD 1500. Indeed, whereas in Babylonian times the average indicator according to Table 20.3 is around 0.48, in the late medieval period it declined in Italy to around 0.32 and around AD 1800 to 0.24. This confirms the results of the 'simple' calculations of the CV presented in Tables 20.1 and 20.2, that market performance increased in the Middle Ages, in particular in western Europe. A similar decrease took place in Syria and Turkey. Yet, in Egypt and Mecca this does not seem to be happening. In sum, after filtering out country-, time- and region-specific factors influencing volatility, we find that conditional price volatility is decreasing in the north-western part of the Near East and the western Empire, and, hence, that market performance is increasing.

Because there are abundant data for Europe after AD 1500, we also tried to find out what happened to market performance between AD 1500 and 1800. Two remarkable phenomena happened. In the first place, most countries and regions show a decline in unexplained volatility; the exceptions are Germany and Poland.

Table 20.4 Unexplained volatility: standard error of the regression of first differences (log prices), AD 1500–1700

	1500	1700
Italy	0.44	0.19
Austria	0.37	0.23
France	0.33	0.23
Belgium	0.31	0.20
Spain	0.30	0.30
Netherlands	0.29	0.22
England	0.29	0.23
Poland	0.22	0.24
Germany	0.19	0.23

Source: Allen and Unger (1990).

There is thus little doubt that market performance increased over time for the western part of the Roman Empire as opposed to Iraq and Egypt. This is also consistent with estimates of national income. Existing estimates show at best a small increase in per capita gross domestic product (GDP) for the area of present-day Iraq between c. 500 BC and AD 1500: for Mesopotamia in or around 500 BC, located in what is nowadays Iraq, Foldvari and Van Leeuwen (2012) calculated about 600 1990 Geary-Khamis (GK) dollars. This can be linked to estimates by Pamuk and Schatzmiller (2011) of 656 GK dollars for southern Iraq around AD 720 and 640 GK dollars around AD 1220. Likewise, for Egypt per capita GDP increased from 580 to 780 GK dollars between AD 300 and AD 1500. This is on the whole lower than the figures for Italy that show an increase to 1,400 GK dollars between c. AD 300 and AD 1400.[8]

The second interesting finding from Table 20.4 is that the relative ranking changed over time. For example, Italy around 1500 had a relatively low level of market performance compared to the other western European regions, but in AD 1700 it topped the list. Likewise Germany, which was top in AD 1500, had dropped almost to the bottom by 1700. If we calculate a correlation coefficient, we find –0.38, suggesting that those countries that had a relatively high level of market performance in AD 1500 ranked at the bottom around 1700.

In sum, the findings thus far seem to suggest that market performance, defined as the capability of the market to handle unexpected shocks, increased significantly during the (High) Middle Ages, and that markets were much more developed after about AD 1300 than in antiquity. Likewise, countries that lagged behind in market performance in AD 1500 seem to have forged ahead around AD 1700. But parts of the Middle East – Egypt and Syria – seem to have missed this transformation of market structures.

Some preliminary explanations

The question that remains is why market performance increased between 500 BC and AD 1800. Given the lack of data and the fact that we cover about 2,000 years for a large area, any answers we provide must necessarily be provisional. Yet, we think it is important to make a first attempt here based on the existing literature.

As pointed out by Foldvari and Van Leeuwen (2011), there are four broad reasons for increasing market performance: temporal spatial risk reduction (trade), change in consumption patterns, technological development and temporal risk reduction (storage). All these broad factors reduce price volatility and thus cause, in terms of Table 20.3, the 'standard error of the regression on first differences' to go down, i.e. market performance to go up. In this section we will focus on the first three explanations since the importance of storage is often considered to be small (McCloskey and Nash 1984; Van Leeuwen et al., 2011). For a longer discussion about storage see Foldvari and Van Leeuwen, Chapter 18, this volume.

The most often quoted factor is technology that increases agricultural output and makes yields more stable. One way of looking at this is to view output per worker, which should rise together with technological change. Looking at per capita GDP, we find at best a marginal increase between Babylonian times and AD 1500 for Iraq (Foldvari and Van Leeuwen 2011; Pamuk and Schatzmiller 2011). This is not true for the western part of the Empire though; here there was a trough around AD 700, but per capita output after AD 1000 was considerably above that of AD 1. This finding of a lack of increase in labour productivity in the Near East (and in the West up to the seventh century AD) is in agreement with the lack of technological development found in both regions (Finley 1965).

It is important though not to treat the Near East as a homogeneous region: in Iraq and Egypt agricultural production took place with the help of irrigation systems while in Turkey and Syria dry-land agriculture dominated. This had a serious effect on technological progress because the irrigation system was complex, difficult to maintain, and required structurally different agricultural technologies. Hence, this system, basically unaltered, continued during the centuries before the fall of the Byzantine Empire. Yet whereas during Byzantine rule (up to about the seventh century AD) old traditions of soil conservation and irrigation were maintained, this changed during the Caliphate. As pointed out by (Ashtor 1976: 46–7), little evidence exists of technological innovations in that period. The Muslim rulers just took over the systems from their predecessors. Many existing inventions, such as the water-wheel, were often badly maintained. It was even stated (Ashtor 1976: 48) that, because of bad dyke maintenance, the area in Iraq under swamps became larger during the Abbasid Caliphate (AD 750–1258). In addition, the tax burden discouraged investment in agriculture. The same applied in Muslim law: a landowner whose estate was not directly threatened by a burst dyke or canal was not obliged to contribute to the repair.

Whereas in ancient Babylonia the arable land was ploughed with iron seeder ploughs, which enabled comparatively low seeding rates (Jursa 2010: 48–9 and Van der Spek 2006: 290 with further evidence), in the early Middle Ages wooden ploughs were used (Samarraie 1972; Ashtor 1976: 49). This contrasts strongly with Europe where there is plenty of evidence of technical developments from the ninth century AD onwards. An example is the introduction of the wheeled plough, introduced around the fifth century AD and largely used on sanded soils:

the introduction of the horse to pull the plough was another great improvement. The latter was possible because improvement in harnessing (a stiff collar over the animals' shoulders that let them breath freely) spread through Europe between the tenth and twelfth centuries AD. In the Near East oxen were used for ploughing, as before. Other developments in Europe were the scythe, which was introduced in the twelfth and thirteenth centuries AD, and the flail for threshing, which remained in use until the nineteenth century AD (Ashtor 1976: 49). In addition, the change from two-course to three-course rotation improved output considerably. This development could not take place in the Near East which had a different crop structure owing to its irrigation agriculture.

That being said, it is clear that in the Near East agriculture remained far more productive per hectare in ancient times than in the West. As pointed out by Van der Spek (2006: 290) and Jursa (2010: 49), output was very high in Babylonian times, largely as a result of the introduction of the seeder plough which deposited the grain seeds in the furrows, the distance between seeds being carefully measured. The seed-yield ratio is estimated to have been as high as 1:24 and even though technological development stagnated afterwards, the remarkable fertility of the earth remained. Ashtor reports a seed-yield ratio of 1:10 whereas in Carolingian times (ninth century AD) in western Europe it was rather lower at 1:2.5 (Ashtor 1976: 50). However, whereas the ratio declined substantially in the Near East, in western Europe it rose from to 1:4 in the fourteenth century, to 1:6 in the sixteenth century AD. Hence, increases in yields in the West were accompanied by declining (or at best stable) yields in the Middle East.

In the Near East agricultural productivity must have declined almost continuously from the sixth century AD onwards, as shown by a continuous decrease in tax revenue. The authorities tried to make up for this by increasing the tax rates, which caused large-scale flight from the land. As pointed out by Ashtor (1976: 67), 'the flight from the land was a major phenomenon of agrarian life in Upper Mesopotamia'. The same thing happened in Egypt. All in all, lower crop yields combined with lower tax incomes suggest in general a deterioration of agricultural output in the Near East. This contrasts sharply with the evidence for the western part of the Mediterranean after c. AD 1000. Before that time, agricultural output most likely had stagnated. However, after that period, there was a considerable growth up to the late fourteenth century AD after which stagnation occurred. Persson (1991: 139) estimated a growth of agricultural productivity of 0.15–0.2 per cent growth per annum between AD 1000 and 1300 in Tuscany. This corresponds to the growth found by Broadberry *et al.* (2014) for the period AD 1270–1700 in England, though this is possibly overestimated given the many changes that took place in England between AD 1300 and 1700 which are not recorded for early medieval Tuscany. Federico and Malanima (2004: 450) arrive at an estimate of 0.05 per cent per capita per annum growth between the tenth and fourteenth centuries AD. This growth was partly caused by the increase of land and capital (particularly livestock) per capita (Federico and Malanima 2004: 451). Only from the mid-fourteenth century AD onwards do we see a declining or at least stagnating trend in agriculture.

These findings clearly suggest that per capita output in the West was higher in the fourteenth century AD, possibly aggravated by the Black Death, than around AD 1. Standard economic theory says that necessity goods such as wheat have an income elasticity between 0 and 1; in other words, when income increases by one unit, the demand for those goods increases by less than one unit (known as Engel's law). This means that with increasing income, the share of that good in the total budget declines. In addition, when income grows, the income elasticity of demand declines (see for example Clark *et al.* (1995) who argue that income elasticity is higher for the poor in nineteenth-century AD England). This means that with increasing incomes an even smaller proportion is spent on that basic product and more on what were previously considered luxury products (i.e. products with a higher income elasticity). For the West this means a shift to goods that produce more expensive calories. Indeed, as shown by Federico and Malanima (2004), consumption of meat products (which provide relatively expensive calories) in Italy started to increase. Equally, in England after the Black Death we note an increase in the consumption of ale, which also provides expensive calories (e.g. Overton and Campbell 1996).[9] For the Near East, with no comparable increase in per capita output, no such consumption change seems to have taken place. This does not, however, mean that there was no change in consumption at all. It is argued that due to soil salinization being lower, wheat became grown in more abundant quantities in Iraq compared to later Babylonian times (Jacobsen and Adams 1958). This can also be deduced from the fact that we actually have wheat prices in the ninth century AD as compared to the first centuries BC when only date and barley prices are reported. This, no doubt, meant that people increased the share of wheat consumed in Iraq. However, since wheat is also a necessity good, and given that this process only took place in Iraq rather than in Syria and Egypt, this will hardly have changed the variability of prices.

Consumption and technological development are not the only factors able to smooth price volatility; a third factor may be trade. According to Wickham (2005: 718), the Mediterranean was full of ships in the twelfth century AD, many of them carrying bulk goods. The same applies for the period around AD 1. The evidence of shipwrecks does indeed show a rise in trade between c. 200 BC and AD 200. For Babylon, being separated from the rest of the Mediterranean, this meant of course that it was largely trade in precious goods rather than bulk products such as grain (Jursa 2010: 224; Van der Spek and Van Leeuwen, forthcoming). However, between AD 200 and 1200 the development in the East was different from that in the West. Whereas the West suffered from a decline in trading activities due to the fall of the western Roman Empire, in the Near East, where the Byzantine Empire lasted several centuries longer, there was a remarkable continuity of trade (Lopez 1987: 307). Or, as argued by Wickham, 'a multiplicity of routes continued to characterize the late empire in the East' (Wickham 2005: 714). This does not mean, however, that there was no trade between the East and the West at all. McCormick, in his famous work on the origins of the European economy, although stating that communications decreased until the mid-eighth century AD, found that after that period communications between the Arab world and the West were on the increase again (McCormick 2002: 436). This increase in communication implies that trade was taking place, but it was probably largely trade in more luxury products and cloth.

Unfortunately, little direct evidence on the relation between transport costs and price volatility exists. One study by Foldvari *et al.* (2011) uses a spatial model to show that an increase in the size of the market contributes to increasing volatility of prices. However, this increasing volatility can be counterbalanced by improving productivity and the reduction of transport costs. Their finding is that, even though market sizes clearly grew in the West (see Figure 20.4) – a factor that, other things being equal, increases price volatility – the increase in output per hectare combined with decreasing transaction and transport costs (and thus increased trade potential) increased market performance substantially. Indeed, whereas during Roman times transport costs were high (McCormick 2002: 307), in the period after c. AD 900 we see that there is an increasing reduction of transaction costs in the Western countries as a result of the introduction of new modes of transport – mainly more efficient ships and improved navigation techniques. McCormick (2002: 473) emphasizes this point forcefully; he shows that, based on the duration of embassies between Constantinople and the West, travel between these places took about two and a half months less in the ninth than in the eighth century AD.

This reduction in transport costs might also explain the difference, noted in the previous section, of leaders in terms of market performance in AD 1500 lagging behind in 1700: whereas first the urban primacy was dominant (i.e. smaller cities were better at market performance), in the later period, with lower transaction costs, this relationship broke down (see Figure 20.5 and Figure 20.6). This means that those regions with a high urban primacy, like Italy, were able to increase their

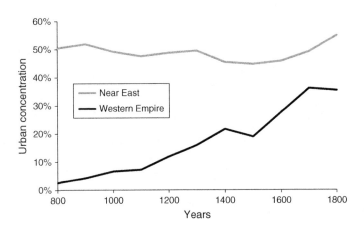

Figure 20.4 Urban primacy of cities in the (former) western Roman Empire and the Near East, c. AD 800–1800.

Source: Bosker *et al.* (2013).

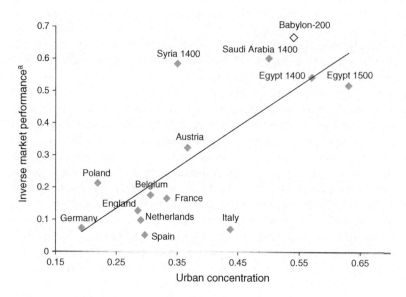

Figure 20.5 Market performance versus urban primacy around AD 1500.

Note:
[a] The lower the value, the higher market performance.

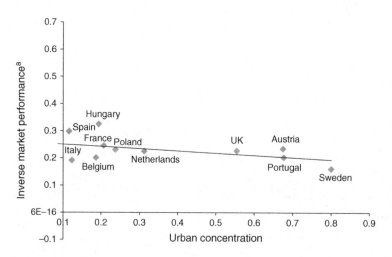

Figure 20.6 Market performance versus urban primacy around AD 1700.

Note:
[a] The lower the value, the higher market performance.

market performance more than those with a relatively low urban primacy, causing a reversal of relative market performance.

In summary, even though this study cannot be very specific, we do find some common trends in factors determining market performance. Clearly, the western part of the Roman Empire was much more dynamic than the Near East. Whereas technology, consumption and trade in the western empire contributed considerably to a decline in price volatility in the long run, the Near East remained almost stable (or perhaps declined a little) during the period of 2,000 years. However, even within the West there were differences. Whereas urban primacy initially worked unfavourably on market performance, i.e. creating a relative disadvantage for countries such as Italy, decreasing transaction and transport costs removed that disadvantage and made it possible for southern European countries to catch up in terms of market performance.

Conclusion

In this chapter we have analysed market performance in ancient Near East empires, the Roman Empire and their successor states, between c. 500 BC and AD 1800. We find that in the long run unexpected volatility decreases over time (i.e. market performance increases) in both the dry-land agricultures of western Europe and the Near East. In regions with irrigation agriculture, such as Egypt and Iraq, no significant increase in market performance took place until c. AD 1500. Consequently, around AD 1500 Italy and Turkey had surpassed Iraq and Egypt, but were still behind countries such as the Netherlands and England. In western Europe the improvement of market performance continued to increase between AD 1500 and 1700.

We have also tried to give a preliminary explanation. Whereas technological change and hence productivity growth was stronger in the dry areas of the Near East and the West, the situation in Iraq and Egypt, which were dominated by irrigation agriculture, remained the same or declined, because the same technologies that were so successful in other parts of the world could not be applied there. Likewise, in the 'developing' parts of the region – mainly western Europe – it seems that consumption diversified as evidence shows that less and less of the household budget was spent on the same staple crops. The same applies to trade, where we find that declining transaction and transport costs worked favourably in the West in increasing market performance. However, even within the Western world there were differences: high levels of urban concentration intensified price volatility for southern Europe up to the sixteenth century AD, but declining transaction and transport costs increasingly offset this effect, enabling southern Europe to catch up with its neighbours in the north-west in terms of market performance.

Notes

1 Foldvari and Van Leeuwen (2011) originally used the term 'market efficiency' but this led to misunderstandings (for example financial economics has the concept of an 'efficient market' which is unrelated to the concept used here); we prefer 'market performance' now.

2 See for example Allen and Unger (1990), Persson (1999), Findlay and O'Rourke (2002) and Jacks (2004).
3 For example Maddison (2007). See also the recent studies from Amemiya (2007) on Athens and from Lo Cascio and Malanima (2009, Table 8) who find a slightly decreasing GDP per capita up to the Middle Ages in Italy, and Foldvari and Van Leeuwen (2012) who find levels of per capita GDP in Mesopotamia (c. AD 400) comparable to those of Iraq in the nineteenth century AD.
4 Actually even in the absence of a trend, CV should not be used for non-stationary series (like random walk). As a general rule: CV is designed for stationary variables (i.e. those with unique, finite mean and variance); with non-stationary price data these conditions are violated.
5 Cf. Van der Spek (2005), now converted into monthly prices by Bas van Leeuwen; see Appendix to this volume. Earlier publications were Slotsky (1997), Vargyas (2001) and Slotsky and Wallenfels (2009).
6 Average of the number of available observations on barley and dates.
7 However, for a critique see Powell (1985).
8 See also Scheidel and Friesen (2009) and Lo Cascio and Malanima (2009). For reasons given in the Scheidel and Friesen paper, we prefer the lower estimates of GDP per capita estimated by them to the much higher estimates by Lo Cascio and Malanima.
9 For an extensive discussion on consumption also see Dyer (1989).

Bibliography

Allen, R. C. and Unger, R. 1990. 'The Depth and Breadth of the Market for Polish Grain 1500–1800', in *Baltic Affairs Relations between the Netherlands and North-Eastern Europe 1500–1800*, edited by J. P. S. Lemmink and J. S. A. M. Van Koningsbrugge, Nijmegen: Institute of Northern and Eastern European Studies: 1–18.

Amemiya, T. 2007. *Economy and Economics of Ancient Greece*, London: Routledge.

Aperghis, G. G. 2004. *The Seleukid Royal Economy. The Finances and Financial Adminis-tration of the Seleukid Economy*, Cambridge: Cambridge University Press.

Artzy, M. and Hillel, D. 1988. 'A Defense of the Theory of Progressive Soil Salinization in Ancient Southern Mesopotamia', *Geoarchaeology: An International Journal*, 3: 235–8.

Ashtor, E. 1969. *Histoire des prix et des salaries dans l'Orient médiéval*, Paris: S.E.V.P.E.N.
—— 1976. *A Social and Economic History of the Near East in the Middle Ages*, London: Collins.

Baker, H. D. and Jursa, M., eds. Forthcoming. *Documentary Sources in Ancient Near Eastern and Greco-Roman History: Methodology and Practice*, Oxford: Oxbow Books.

Basini, G. L. 1974. *Sul Mercato di Modena Tra Cinque e Seicento: Prezzi e Salari*, Milano: Dott. A Giuffré. Downloaded from: www.iisg.nl/hpw/data.php#italy, accessed February 2012.

Bonneau, D. 1971. *Le fisc et le Nil: incidences des irrégularités de la crue du Nil sur la fiscalité foncière dans l'égypte grecque et romaine*, Paris: Cujas.

Bosker, M., Buringh, E. and Van Zanden, J. L. 2013. 'From Baghdad to London: Unrav-elling Urban Development in Europe and the Arab World 800–1800', *Review of Economics and Statistics*, 95(4): 1418–37.

Broadberry, S., Campbell, B., Klein, A., Overton, M. and Van Leeuwen, B. 2014, forthcoming. *British GDB c. 1270–1870*, Cambridge: Cambridge University Press.

Clark, G. 2002. 'Markets and Economic Growth: Grain Markets in Medieval England', *Mimeograph*, Department of Economics, U. C. Davis.
—— 2004. 'The Price History of English Agriculture, 1209–1914', *Research in Economic History*, 22: 41–125.

Clark, G, Huberman, M. and Lindert, P. 1995. 'A British Food Puzzle, 1771–1850', *Economic History Review*, 48: 215–37.

Coniglio, G. 1952. 'La revoluzione dei prezzi nella citta de Napoli nei secoli XVI e XVII', *Spoleta* 1952: 204–40. Downloaded from www.iisg.nl/hpw/data.php#europe, accessed February 2012.

Dyer, Chr. 1989. *Standards of Living in the Later Middle Ages: Social Change in England c.1200–1520*, Cambridge: Cambridge University Press.

Erdkamp, P. 2005. *The Grain Market in the Roman Empire: A Social, Political and Economic Study*, Cambridge: Cambridge University Press.

Federico, G. and Malanima, P. 2004. 'Progress, Decline, Growth: Product and Productivity in Italian Agriculture, 1000–2000', *Economic History Review*, 57: 437–64.

Findlay, R., O'Rourke, K. H. and Centre for Economic Policy Research (Great Britain). 2002. *Commodity Market Integration, 1500–2000*, London: Centre for Economic Policy Research.

Finley, M. I. 1965. 'Technical Innovation and Economic Progress in the Ancient World', *Economic History Review*, 28: 29–45.

—— 1973. *The Ancient Economy*, London: Chatto and Windus.

Foldvari, P. and Van Leeuwen, B. 2011. 'What Can Price Volatility Tell Us About Market Performance? Conditional Heteroscedasticity in Historical Commodity Price Series', *Cliometrica*, 5: 165–86.

—— 2012. 'Comparing Per Capita Income in the Hellenistic World: the Case of Mesopotamia', *Review of Income and Wealth*, 58: 550–68.

Foldvari, P., Van Leeuwen, B. and Van Zanden, J. L. 2011. 'Long-run Patterns in Market Efficiency and the Genesis of the Market Economy: Markets Around the Mediterranean from Nebuchadnezzar to Napoleon (580 BC and 1800 AD)', Centre for Economic Policy Research, Discussion Paper 8521. Available at: www.cepr.org/pubs/dps/DP8521.asp

Galloway, J. A. 2000. 'One Market or Many? London and the Grain Trade of England', in *Trade, Urban Hinterlands and Market Integration c.1300–1600*, edited by J. A. Galloway, London: Centre for Metropolitan History, Working Papers Series, 3: 23–42.

Hunger, H. and Pingree, D. 1999. *Astral Sciences in Mesopotamia*, Leiden: Brill.

Jacks, D. 2004. 'Market Integration in the North and Baltic Seas, 1500–1800', *Journal of European Economic History*, 33: 285–329.

Jacobsen, T. and Adams, R. McC. 1958. 'Salt and Silt in Ancient Mesopotamian Agriculture', *Science* 128: 1251–8.

Jursa, M. 2010. *Aspects of the Economic History of Babylonia in the First Millennium BC: Economic Geography, Economic Mentalities, Agriculture, the Use of Money and the Problem of Economic Growth* (with contributions by J. Hackl, B. Janković, K. Kleber, E. E. Payne, C. Waerzeggers and M. Weszeli), Münster: Ugarit-Verlag.

Kessler, D. and Temin, P. 2008. 'Money and Prices in the Early Roman Empire', in *The Monetary Systems of the Greeks and Romans*, edited by W. V. Harris, Oxford: Oxford University Press: 137–59.

Lo Cascio, E. and Malanima, P. 2009. 'GDP in Pre-Modern Agrarian Economies (1–1820 AD). A Revision of the Estimates', *Rivista di Storia Economica*, 25: 387–415.

Lopez, R. S. 1987. 'The Trade of Medieval Europe: the South', in *The Cambridge Economic History of Europe*, Vol. 2: *Trade and Industry in the Middle Ages*, edited by S. Broadberry and K. I. O'Rourke, Cambridge: Cambridge University Press: 257–354.

Maddison, A. 2003. *The World Economy: Historical Statistics*, Paris: OECD.

—— 2007. *Contours of the World Economy, 1–2030 AD*, Oxford: Oxford University Press.

McCloskey, D. H. and Nash, J. 1984. 'Corn at Interest: The Extent and Cost of Grain Storage in Medieval England', *American Economic Review*, 74: 174–87.

McCormick, M. 2002. *Origins of the European Economy: Communications and Commerce, AD 300–900*, Cambridge: Cambridge University Press.

Malanima, P. 1976. *Aspetti di mercato e prezzi del grano e della segale a Pisa dal 1548 al 1818*, in *Ricerche di storia moderna*, I, Pisa: Pacini: 288–327; downloaded from: www.iisg.nl/hpw/data.php#italy, accessed February 2012.

—— 2011. 'The Long Decline of a Leading Economy: GDP in Central and Northern Italy, 1300–1913', *European Review of Economic History*, 15: 69–219.

Masschaele, J. 1993. 'Transport Costs in Medieval England', *Economic History Review*, 46: 266–79.

Milanovic, B. 2010. 'Income Level and Income Inequality in the Euro-Mediterranean Region: from the Principate to the Islamic Conquest', paper presented at the Angus Maddison memorial Conference, Amsterdam, November 2010.

Mortel, R. T. 1989. 'Prices in Mecca During the Mamluk Period', *Journal of the Economic and Social History of the Orient*, 32: 279–334.

Müller, G. W. 1996/7. 'Die Teuerung in Babylon im 6. Jh. v.Chr.', *Archiv für Orientforschung*, 42/43: 163–75.

Nielsen, R. 1997. 'English Government Intervention in Early Modern Grain Markets', *Journal of Economic History*, 57: 1–33.

North, D. C. and Thomas, R. P. 1973. *The Rise of the Western World: A New Economic History*, Cambridge: Cambridge University Press.

Ó Gráda, C. 2005. 'Markets and Famines in Pre-Industrial Europe', *Journal of Interdisciplinary History*, 36: 143–66.

Overton, M. and Campbell, B. 1996. 'Production et productivité dans l'agriculture anglais, 1086–1871', *Histoire et Mesure*, 11: 255–97, Table XII.

Pamuk, S. 2004. 'Prices in the Ottoman Empire, 1469–1914', *International Journal of Middle East Studies*, 36: 451–68. Data downloaded from www.iisg.nl/hpw/data.php#ottoman, accessed February 2012.

Pamuk, S. and Schatzmiller, M. 2011. 'Real Wages and GDP Per Capita Estimates for Medieval Near East, 700–1500', paper presented at the European Historical Economics Society Conference, Dublin, 2011.

Persson, K. G. 1991. 'Agrarian Productivity in Medieval Agriculture: Tuscany and the "Low Countries"' in *Land labour and livestock: historical studies in European agricultural productivity*, edited by B. M. S. Campbell and M. Overton, Manchester: Manchester University Press: 124–43.

—— 1999. *Grain Markets in Europe, 1500–1900: Integration and Deregulation*, Cambridge: Cambridge University Press.

Pirenne, H. 1957. *Mohammed and Charlemagne*, New York: Meridian books.

Powell, M. A. 1985. 'Salt, Seed and Yields in Sumerian Agriculture: a Critique of the Theory of Progressive Salinization', *Zeitschrift für Assyriologie*, 75: 7–38.

Prados de la Escosura, L. and Álvarez-Nogal, C. 2009. 'The Rise and Decline of Spain (800–1850)', paper presented at the World Economic History Congress, Utrecht, August 2009.

Rathbone, D. Forthcoming. 'Mediterranean grain prices c. 300 to 31 BC: the impact of Rome,' in *Documentary Sources in Ancient Near Eastern and Greco-Roman History: Methodology and Practice*, edited by Baker and Jursa, Oxford: Oxbow Books (forthcoming).

Reger, G. 1994. *Regionalism and Change in the Economy of Independent Delos*, Berkeley: University of California Press.

Romano, R. 1965. *Prezzi, salari e servizi a Napoli nel secolo XVIII*, Milan: Banca Commerciale Italiana. Downloaded from www.iisg.nl/hpw/data.php#europe, accessed February 2012.

Romero, N. E., Ma, Q. D. Y., Liebovitch, L. S., Brown, C. T. and Ivanov, P. Ch. 2010. 'Correlated Walks Down the Babylonian Markets', *Europhysics Letters*, 90 (18004): 1–6.

Samarraie, H. Q. 1972. *Agriculture in Iraq During the 3rd Century A.H.*, Beirut.

Schatzmiller, M. 2011. 'Measuring the Medieval Islamic Economy', http://sites.google. com/site/islamiceconomyuwo/prices/commodities (accessed July 2011).

Scheidel, W. and Friesen, S. 2009. 'The Size of the Economy and the Distribution of Income in the Roman Empire', *Journal of Roman Studies*, 99: 61–91.

Slotsky A. L. 1997. *The Bourse of Babylon. Market Quotations in the Astronomical Diaries of Babylonia*, Bethesda MD: CDL Press.

Slotsky, A. L. and Wallenfels, R. 2009. *Tallies and Trends. The Late Babylonian Commodity Price Lists*, Bethesda MD: CDL Press.

Smith, A. 1776 (1991) *An Inquiry into the Nature and the Causes of the Wealth of Nations*, London: W. Strahan and T. Cadell, reprint: Norwalk, Connecticut: Easton Press.

Söderberg, J. 2006. 'Grain Prices in Cairo and Europe in the Middle Ages', *Research in Economic History*, 24: 193–220.

Studer, R. 2008. 'India and the Great Divergence: Assessing the Performance of Grain Markets in Eighteenth- and Nineteenth-Century India', *Journal of Economic History*, 68: 393–437.

Temin, P. 2002. 'Price Behavior in Ancient Babylon', *Explorations in Economic History*, 39: 46–60.

Van der Spek. 2000. 'The Effect of War on the Prices of Barley and Agricultural Land in Hellenistic Babylonia', in *Economie antique. La guerre dans les économies antiques*, edited by J. Andreau, P. Briant and R. Descat, Saint-Bertrand-de-Comminges: Musée archéologique départemental: 293–313.

—— 2004. 'Palace, Temple and Market in Seleucid Babylonia', in *Le roi et l'économie. Autonomies locales et structures royales dans l'économie de l'empire séleucide*, edited by V. Chankowski and F. Duyrat, Paris: De Boccard: 303–32.

—— 2005. *Commodity Prices from Babylon (385–61 BC)*, www.iisg.nl/hpw/ data.php#babylon

—— 2006. 'How to Measure Prosperity? the Case of Hellenistic Babylonia', in *Approches de l'économie hellénistique*, edited by R. Descat, Paris: De Boccard: 287–310.

—— Forthcoming. 'The Volatility of Prices of Barley and Dates in Babylon in the Third and Second Centuries BC', in *Documentary Sources in Ancient Near Eastern and Greco-Roman History: Methodology and Practice*, edited by Baker and Jursa, Oxford: Oxbow Books (forthcoming).

Van der Spek, R. J. and Van Leeuwen, B. Forthcoming. 'Quantifying the Integration of the Babylonian Economy in the Mediterranean World Using a New Corpus of Price Data, 400–50 BC', in *Long-term Quantification in Ancient History*, edited by F. de Callataÿ and A. Wilson, Bari: Edipuglia.

Van Leeuwen, B., Foldvari, P. and Pirngruber, R. 2011. 'Markets in Pre-industrial Societies: Storage in Hellenistic Babylonia in the Medieval English Mirror', *Journal of Global History*, 6: 169–93.

Van Zanden, J. L. and Van Leeuwen, B. 2012. 'Persistent But Not Consistent: the Growth of National Income in Holland 1347–1807', *Explorations in Economic History*, 49: 119–30.

Vargyas P. 2001. *A History of Babylonian Prices in the First Millennium BC. I. Prices of the Basic Commodities*, Heidelberg: Heidelberger Orientverlag.

Von Reden, S. Forthcoming. 'Price Fluctuations in Babylonia, Egypt and the Mediterranean World, Third to First Centuries BC', in *Documentary Sources in Ancient Near Eastern and Greco-Roman History: Methodology and Practice*, edited by Baker and Jursa, Oxford: Oxbow Books (forthcoming).

Wickham, Chr. 2005. *Framing the Early Middle Ages: Europe and the Mediterranean, 400–800*, Oxford: Oxford University Press.

Wrigley, E. A. 1987. *People, Cities and Wealth*, Oxford: Blackwell.

Part VI

Conclusion

21 Markets from Babylon to Belfast

Some concluding remarks

R.J. van der Spek, Bas van Leeuwen and
Jan Luiten van Zanden

Introduction

From time immemorial people have exchanged goods. Hunters brought home their prey and shared it in the community in exchange for services at home. Friends gave presents to and received presents from each other, mostly in order to get something back: *do ut des*, I give in order that you give. The gift exchange can develop into a sophisticated exchange of necessary goods embedded in all kinds of social customs and values (Mauss 1923–24). In more complex societies people can obtain desired goods by barter, often after a long ritual of bargaining, and barter gets facilitated if there is one commonly valued and accepted means of exchange. In very early times silver took that role and it is stunning that this remained so for about 5,000 years. This acceptance of silver is based on social values and irrational trust: why did people accept silver for any good when it is a commodity that you cannot eat, nor make clothes of, nor live in, and is not suitable for making utensils? Yet it was an important means to get desired goods, to hoard wealth, to provide prestige, to become rich. It helped enormously to fix values and to set what we now call 'prices'. It enables us to write a book on the history of prices.

But is all this exchange of goods evidence of the existence of a market? Is in all these cases a free exchange of goods at stake in which the value is decided on the basis of the relative scarcity of supply and demand?

It is not the place here to give an exposé on the history of the concept of market. That would require another book. For centuries it has not been an issue at all but, especially since the publication of Adam Smith's *Wealth of Nations* (1776), the phenomenon is widely discussed. Adam Smith abstracted the phenomenon and explained how exchanges of goods took place, how the relative value was established by the law of supply and demand, how the seller couldn't ask for prices that were too high as he was restrained by competition from other sellers and the capability and willingness of the buyer to pay a high price. Thus by an invisible hand a 'just price' was established to the benefit of all. The sum of all private interests led to the common interest. This idea contradicted the common opinion on trading in antiquity – which had strong influence on norms and values of later ages until the modern era – that trading is *a priori* bad, that trading necessarily includes cheating, and that honourable people are landowners who can live off their own products (Aristotle, Cicero, Augustine, Thomas Aquinas).

So it is not surprising that not everybody was convinced by Smith's theory. The most influential thinker in this respect was Karl Marx (1818–83). He did not believe in the invisible hand that led to a world of fair prices and harmony. And he had good reasons. The nineteenth century AD was a century that exhibited extreme poverty of growing masses and an accumulation of wealth in a small group of owners of the means of production. Marx took the view that a new system should bring 'just prices' based on the labour that was spent to produce it, and should not be based on the 'anarchic' law of supply and demand. This is in fact a variant on the age-old concept of a 'just price' that represents its commonly established and accepted value. Usury and high prices in times of need were proverbially immoral.

The Hungarian anthropologist Karl Polanyi (1886–1964) went a step further than Marx. He not only distrusted the blessings of the free market, but he denied that it is a common and eternal self-evident aspect of human life and human society. Free markets are a modern phenomenon. In the ancient world an abstract function of human life as 'the economy' did not exist. Goods exchanged hands, but the price was not determined by the law of supply and demand but by social conventions (gift exchange) and reciprocity; it was 'embedded' in society. International trade was conducted by state agents who exchanged goods on the basis of treaties by more or less friendly partners. The profit maximizing individual trader did not exist; the free self-regulating market did not exist.

Presently many economists and especially neo-liberal politicians adhere to the idea that the free market is the motor of the economy and will indeed bring prosperity owing to Smith's invisible hand. The failure of communism has become apparent since 1989 and the official policy of the European Union (EU) is that the state should retreat, that all kind of tasks that the state had acquired (such as public transport, mail services, health care) should be left to the free market, even in branches where competition is hardly possible. Contracting out a railway line is hardly furthering the free market, rather the granting of a monopoly for some years. The customer, however, has no choice. Yet everything is supposed to be better than state control.

On the other hand, economic historians, especially historians of antiquity, have long been under the spell of Polanyi, denying the applicability of modern economic theory to the ancient economy, and arguing that factors of status and tradition played a larger role than laws of supply and demand. We discussed this in Chapter 1.

Who is right and who is wrong? It is our opinion that both are right and both are wrong. The mere fact that through the ages there was discussion about the 'just price' shows that everybody knew that prices were not set by the 'commonly accepted' value, but by the law of supply and demand (cf. the understanding of the value of silver in different circumstances: Duyrat, Chapter 14, Van der Spek *et al.*, Chapter 19, this volume). The traders in the Old Assyrian colony in Kanesh (south-east Asia Minor) were keen on finding ways to maximize their profits in the nineteenth century BC and used remarkably modern instruments, such as the cheque payable to bearer, investment loans and investment companies paying dividends (Veenhof 1997). Traders and people were well aware of the price differences in different regions (cf. nearly all chapters in this volume).

Is then the reasoning of people like Karl Marx and Karl Polanyi (and in their wake historians such as Johannes Renger and Moses Finley) completely wrong? Certainly not. It is true that markets sometimes are not efficient and do not perform very well. In Ancient Babylonia interest rates were for a large part dictated by custom. So it is evident that interest on 1 mina (pound) of silver was ideally 1 shekel per month = 12 shekels per year = 20 per cent. That is a kind of iconic interest and we see it often in the documents. Yet the law of supply and demand did its work. We also encounter deviating interest rates (see for example the price study of Hackl and Pirngruber: Chapter 6, this volume). The same is true for food prices. The Babylonians had a view on a 'just price' of grain and dates: 1 shekel of (8.33 g.) silver is the exchange rate of 1 *kurru* (180 l.) of grain or dates, which corresponds to an iconic salary of 1 shekel of silver per month (see Jursa, Chapter 5, this volume). In Rome a kind of iconic price existed as well: in c. 250 BC a *modius* (about 8.6 l.) of grain was valued ideally as 1 bronze *as*, and this was later changed (c. AD 64) to 1 silver *denarius*. (Rathbone and Von Reden, Chapter 8, this volume n. 95.) Though these prices were sometimes real, the very fact that the Babylonian astronomers daily recorded the exchange rate of the shekel proves that they were well aware of the daily reality and the unpredictability of prices. They even made a study of the prices, as is shown by the commodity price lists.

Yet Polanyi was right in stating that the economy in antiquity was not an abstract formal ubiquitous power monitoring exchange of goods, but that it was embedded in society, was directed by informal rules and conventions. He was not right, however, in setting the modern economy apart. We must accept that in antiquity as well as in modern times the law of supply and demand is valid, but we must also accept that the modern economy cannot be studied ignoring societal forms, rules, values, habits and paradigms that shape the possibilities and limitations of free exchange of goods and services. A rational profit maximizing *homo oeconomicus* did not exist in antiquity, but nor does it in our age – even now, economic decisions are also based on ideas of fairness and reciprocity, as experimental economics has demonstrated.

So what we have done in this book is study the market through the ages, from Ancient Babylonia to twentieth-century AD Belfast. We did not ask *whether* there was a market, but *how* it functioned, *how* it performed. We did this in a fairly formal manner, namely by quantification, by measuring. One of the tools to measure market performance is to look at and analyse price data. Histories of prices are not new. But most of these studies start with the Middle Ages. The innovative aspect of this book is that we are now able to extend the history of prices by one-and-a-half millennia, thanks to the availability of a huge amount of quantitative evidence from Ancient Babylonia, which allows a true statistical approach (see Koopman and Hoogerheide, Chapter 3, this volume). Another feature of this book is that we clearly define what we are doing, what we mean by efficient and well-performing markets (which appear not to be the same).

How did we define these concepts and what did we learn from applying them to price series? A market performs well if it has the ability to cope with unexpected shocks, such as climatic shocks, wars, and human and crop plagues. Factors that directly enhance a market's capability to deal with such shocks are trade (which makes it possible to reduce shortages by imports of foodstuffs), storage (intertemporal risk reduction by storing food from the previous harvest (cf. Foldvari *et al.*, Chapter 18, this volume), technology (increasing output and making production less vulnerable to, for example, natural disasters) and consumption (diversification of consumption means that people have the possibility of consuming other foodstuffs when one harvest fails: see Van der Spek *et al.*, Chapter 1, this volume; Foldvari and Van Leeuwen, Chapter 2, this volume). To this we may add two other factors that indirectly (i.e. via the four previously mentioned factors) affect market performance, namely institutions (for example government actions can reduce risks by the appropriate policy measures, reduce monetary fluctuations) and geography (e.g. having navigable waters increases trade).

Methodologically, many different ways for calculating the working of markets can be distinguished (Federico 2012). Some authors focus on the co-movement of prices in different cities, which is closely related to trade and, as trade is only one of the indicators of market performance, only partially captures market performance. Other researchers focus on the speed of adaptation of prices to a standard price level. This is connected to market performance as, for example, trade may speed up the return of prices to their standard levels. But again this does not capture all aspects of market performance, such as consumption diversification etc.

We therefore used a third method to analyse market performance, i.e. the volatility of prices. We could take back this research into an unprecedentedly long period of time – the history of Babylonia (south Iraq) in the latter part of the first millennium BC – thanks to the recent publication of thousands of prices of food and wool (see Van der Spek *et al.*, Chapter 1, this volume). Point of departure was the study of the grain markets in Europe, 1500–1800, by Persson (1999). Focusing on the long-run factors affecting market performance, he argued that, in terms of institutions, market performance increased over time thanks to a diminishing intervention of the state (state intervention to regulate prices and to store food for times of shortage was hardly of any avail) and consequently a freer market emerged. Another (though not *per se* contradictory) perspective is presented by the work of Douglass North (North and Thomas 1973; North 1990). He stressed that institutions working well may lower transaction costs and, for example, increase trade. From this vantage point it is clear that the state (as the most important institution) may have an essential role in market performance in the form of lowering transaction costs by, for example, providing a good legal framework. In that way it is possible to move from trade-based relationships such as between merchant elites (see for example the chapter for China, Carol Shiue, Chapter 13, this volume) or between kin (see for example Greif 1989) to a much more integrated market.

But the state did not only have an effect (for good or bad) on the legal framework. It could also influence the market via the other factors influencing market performance such as technological development, storage and consumer diversification. For example, markets also improved via increased productivity caused by, for example, the invention of steam power and the building of a railway network, originally by private companies, but later for efficiency reasons taken over by the state in most countries (the present policy of privatization in the EU is in this respect, historically speaking, a step backwards). In the same vein the state has in all times been important as an upholder of justice, builder of roads, provider and protector of a reliable means of exchange (silver, money), defender of safety and security on the roads and so forth. The state has always been important as an investor, even if these investments were not done for the sake of improvement of economic performance. When the state built roads to make transport of armies easier, it also facilitated trade. When the state built harbours and ships to wage war on sea, it also facilitated off-shore trade and provided employment for thousands of people working in the harbours, such as shipwrights, rope-makers and sail makers. When Babylonian kings or Roman emperors built walls, temples and palaces, they provided work for construction workers. When kings issued money to pay armies for some campaigns, they inadvertently promoted the circulation of currency and collateral expenditures. The monetization of the Hellenistic Near East was much furthered by the minting of silver for the payment of the armies (cf. Duyrat, Chapter 14, this volume). Hopkins (1980) argued that the stationing of armies at the borders of the Roman Empire was fundamental to the development of the local economy and trade routes between the centre and the periphery and we see a diminishing market economy as soon as the armies leave (Buringh and Bosker, Chapter 9; Aarts, Chapter 15, this volume).

So it seems that market performance and hence economic activity thrived in states with a strong and active government. The most flourishing economies are those of Babylonia in the Neo-Babylonian Empire (sixth century BC), Athens in the time of the Delian League (fifth century BC), the Roman Empire in the first centuries of the common era, the medieval cities in well-organized city states and developing central states, Venice, the Dutch Republic and England in the early modern period and the United States after its unification and rise to world power. In most of these cases the intervention of the state was not intended to be for the benefit of the economy, but the measures inadvertently facilitated market performance. Of course, the policy of states can be detrimental to the economy as well. The fact that the Neo-Babylonian Empire fell to the Persians in 539 BC, may have been good for Iran, but it was bad for Babylonia, as much of the surpluses now were drained off to Susa and Persepolis, while factor markets were hindered by the allocation of lands to royal princes and other favourites (Jursa 2014). The circulation of coins in the later Hellenistic period in western Asia was fragmented due to the crumbling of the Seleucid Empire (Duyrat, Chapter 14, this volume). And to take an example from contemporary history, George W. Bush II, the president of the United States between 2001 and 2009, whose credo it was that the market should be free and that the state should retreat as much as possible from economic life, had an unheard-of impact on the American economy. The attack on Iraq in 2003 contributed hugely to the vulnerability of the American economy, creating a state deficit of a thousand billion dollars and making China the major creditor; by neglecting to maintain the infrastructure thus raising transaction costs, and by deregulating the supervision of the banks and the stock markets the foundations of the bank crisis of 2008 were laid. Iraq itself is another example. Iraq has the same favourable geographical conditions for (irrigation) agriculture as in antiquity and is even richer thanks to the presence of oil, yet its population is poor, due to a failing state.

One should be wary of trying to find one linear development from poor market performance to better market performance. But there does appear to have been a general trend upwards, although certainly with ups and downs and regional differences, as we shall examine in more detail.

Market performance in the western world

Working markets already existed in sixth-century BC Babylonia. But their function remained limited compared to later periods. Jursa (Chapter 5, this volume) argues that the rise of the market economy is partly due to some sort of commercialization model in which monetization (use of silver as means of exchange), demographic expansion and urbanization all contributed to the increase of a market system. Yet the volatility of prices was fairly high and famines are attested, as in the second year of Cambyses (Kleber 2012). The high volatility of the prices was a major drawback of the Babylonian economy in spite of the advantages of its irrigation agriculture. But even here different trends are detectable. The volatility of prices (combined with a decrease in prices) in the second century BC was reduced, probably thanks to a favourable climate change combined with a fairly stable political situation. In the Parthian period the climate deteriorated again and warfare increased (phenomena which may be related), and this will have had a deteriorative effect on welfare, though strictly speaking market performance did not deteriorate significantly until the first century BC (Foldvari and Van Leeuwen, Chapter 2; Huijs *et al.*, Chapter 7, this volume). This was true for all major products in that society and suggests that factors such as trade, government intervention and technology did not alter significantly over this period to change dramatically the consumption or production structure.

A similar situation existed in the Mediterranean world. Von Reden and Rathbone (Chapter 8, this volume) observe a growing integration of the market over time. While in the Hellenistic period trading in grain and other products was mainly regional, with the growth of the Roman Empire the Mediterranean really became an integrated market with fairly stable prices. This was facilitated by the Roman Empire, which brought unity to the entire Mediterranean in respect of government, legal system, language, coinage, investment in roads, city development and harbours. State intervention saw to it that the city of Rome was fed with preference, which is of course detrimental to market efficiency, but enough was left for the free market in grain to allow a growing market performance in the first two centuries AD.

The importance of institutions even on the fringes of the Roman Empire is clearly exemplified by the studies of Buringh and Bosker (Chapter 9, this volume) and Aarts (Chapter 15, this volume). Buringh and Bosker showed how the presence of the army and Roman city institutions contributed to a well-functioning market economy until the beginning of the third century AD, and from Aarts' study of the circulation of coins we observe a retreat of the market on a regional level (the *civitas Batavorum*) as soon as the army began to withdraw in the beginning of the second century AD. The demise of the Roman Empire brought a long-term regression in market economy, to return later under different conditions and in sometimes different regions.

Van Leeuwen *et al.* (Chapter 20, this volume) demonstrate that market performance was clearly on the rise from the twelfth century AD onwards in the areas of the former Roman Empire. Less evidence for increased market performance is found in the Middle East, which they attribute to increased technological sophistication in the West combined with reducing transaction costs, while the Middle East continued to use its ancient technology. This led to stagnant output per capita in the Middle East compared to significantly rising output in the western countries.

This pattern is confirmed by Bateman (Chapter 10, this volume) who observed relatively well-performing markets in the late medieval period. This is also argued for England by Mayhew (Chapter 16, this volume) who argues that, even though far from perfect, prices and yields moved in line, regional prices showed signs of market integration and the money stock shows signs of a monetized economy. However, after an initial fall back, further improvements in market performance took place around the eighteenth century AD, to about the same degree as happened around the twelfth century AD.

In the eighteenth and nineteenth centuries AD a number of important changes in market performance occurred. However, they were not just driven by trade and government interventions, the two factors that have appeared important in earlier millennia. Kennedy and Solar (Chapter 11, this volume) show that market performance was higher in the urban metropolitan London market than in the semi-subsistence-oriented Irish markets which suggests that, besides trade, also per capita income (thus allowing consumption diversification) may have played a role. In addition, they find evidence for rising market performance over time. A change from previous periods, however, is that the price volatility of subsistence goods differed from that of heavily marketed goods. Although wool in Babylon had a different market performance from dates and barley (Van der Spek *et al.*, Chapter 19, this volume), this difference was less marked than in nineteenth-century AD England and Ireland. This may be partly caused by the higher per capita income in England and Ireland which relaxes the budget constraint (people can actually choose to buy more wool without reducing their consumption of barley or dates).

Market performance and the great divergence

Interestingly, Bateman (Chapter 10, this volume) argues that, in view of the fact that market performance had already increased in the late Middle Ages, increased market performance does not necessarily have to go hand in hand with economic development. On the other hand, several authors have pointed at (pockets of) economic growth already during this period (Broadberry *et al.*, 2014). In any case, most authors seem to suggest that well-performing markets are a necessary (even if not sufficient) condition of economic development.

This is particularly the case in the Great Divergence debate, in which the different economic development paths of China and Europe are compared. Already during the Han dynasty (206 BC–AD 220) value was attached to markets. For example the *Han Shu* (History of the Han) says that:

> 'it is desirable that media of exchange [including money], should be circulated as flows water...' and that 'when [merchandise] is dear, one should get rid of it as if it were [as worthless as] dung or dirt, but when it is cheap, one should gather it as if it were [as valuable as] pearls or jade'.
>
> (Swann 1950: 426–7)

Hence, even though markets were certainly not performing perfectly, the basic principles were definitely adhered to already during Han times.

But what was driving market performance? Much like in Babylonia, trade was of lesser importance, even though some local trade did occur. Long-distance trade took already place during Roman times. Information on Parthian Babylonia we find for the first time in the Hou-Han-Shu, Chapters 86 and 88 (written in the fifth century AD), for AD 25–220. Here they describe the city Hira in T'iao-chih [Babylonia] as situated on a peninsula. It has a circumference of 40 *li* (16.6 kilometres) and borders the Persian Gulf. Only in the north-east can one reach the city via a land route. Little is said about trade. But a little further in the same book it is said that they (i.e. the Romans) always wanted to send an ambassador to Han China, but the Parthians stopped them since they wanted the monopoly on silk trade.[1]

So trade was limited to luxurious silk and perhaps some other products which were unlikely to influence actual market performance. Nevertheless, market performance was influenced in other ways. It was especially the Han government that tried to influence market performance by a variety of measures including storage, tax reduction, expenditure on poor relief and other measures (Lin 2008). But these measures had little effect, resulting in many descriptions of abject poverty and hunger.

The situation was probably a bit better in the Roman Empire where local trade and very limited direct government intervention did go some way to increasing market performance, as we saw in the previous section. However, where market performance in the following centuries at best stagnated, in China it must have increased since Liu (Chapter 12, this volume) shows that market performance was relatively high during the Song period (c. 960–1279). Liu uses increased monetization per capita, coupled with a correlation between grain and liquor output, to show that markets were relatively well integrated and markets must have expanded.

However, this all changed in the Ming dynasty (c. 1368–1644). As pointed out before, in Europe during this period a big step forward had already been made in terms of market performance, largely by increasing trade. Also, per capita output increased substantially in certain parts of Europe (Van Zanden and Van Leeuwen 2012; Broadberry *et al.*, 2014). However, the opposite happened in China where the marketed share of outputs declined considerably (e.g. Broadberry *et al.*, 2012).[2] Part of the explanation is the government's reluctance to advance market economy. For example, almost 20 per cent of the households were directly related to the army (see Liu, Chapter 12, this volume) and even army generals were paid in grain. Also transportation and transactions were not easy. Farmers in the lower Yangtze delta had to carry the grain taxes by themselves on a rotating basis to the state depots in the local capital (Liu, Chapter 12, this volume), at a time when canal, road and sea transport were becoming increasingly common in Europe.

This changed to some extent towards the end of the Ming dynasty with the influx of silver into both Europe and China (see Van der Spek *et al.*, Chapter 20; Liu, Chapter 12, this volume). In the Ming period this seems to have stimulated the markets somewhat, but evidence of wages, prices and urbanization seems to suggest this was the start of stagnation in the Chinese economy (cf. Van der Spek 2011: 413). In Europe, however, the share of consumables that were affordable grew considerably, and now also included coffee and sugar (Fairchilds 1993). In addition, European and world markets became increasingly integrated.

In the nineteenth century AD this shift in goods would finally be towards industrial products (as well as non-subsistence products), which caused a higher market performance. In other words, besides trade and government intervention, people became rich enough to apply consumption diversification. However, in China things worked differently. Even though markets in advanced parts of China could be as integrated as in Europe (Shiue, Chapter 13, this volume), the effects of factors such as government intervention (e.g. the existence of government industries), conflict resolutions and social networks were very much different, mostly organized at a private level. This changed a little in the course of the nineteenth century AD when private money markets became better integrated and the rules of trade were expanded as well as government influence reduced. This led to a better price integration and, consequently, better market performance (Peng, Chapter 17, this volume). Nevertheless, the difference with Europe remained large.

Outlook: markets, market efficiency and market performance in the present

Allow us to make some final remarks on the results of the present study on market performance and prices with an eye to the twentieth century AD and the present.

Market performance increased over the past millennia mainly as a result of increased trade and the greater importance of other factors such as increased consumer diversification and technological change. The question is whether this trend has continued up to the present.

As pointed out before, we used a broad definition of a market as a place where supply and demand meet. How well a market performs is determined by its capability of adapting to unexpected shocks. After all, markets ultimately bring

Table 21.1 Long run conditional volatility (i.e. inverse market performance)

	Babylonia/ Near East		Tuscany	Amsterdam/ Groningen	Thailand	India	Japan
	barley	dates	wheat	wheat/barley	rice	rice	rice
570–539 BC	0.42	0.43					
300–200 BC	0.64	0.32	0.87[c]				
199–120 BC	0.45	0.48					
AD 1287–1420	0.61[a]		0.32				
AD 1421–1490	0.52[a]		0.28	0.33			
AD 1491–1650			0.29	0.23			0.21
AD 1651–1800			0.21	0.19		0.35	0.21
AD 1801–1900			0.19	0.19	0.19	0.23	0.20
AD 1901–1940				0.25	0.26	0.13	0.28
AD 1960–2000	0.23[b]		0.11	0.11	0.14	0.14	0.07

Source: Jursa (Chapter 5, this volume); Van Leeuwen *et al.* (Chapter 20, this volume); Allen and Unger database (accessed 7 June 2013); Faostat (accessed 8 June 2013); Ingram (1964: 102–26); Studer (2008); *Labour Gazette*, Government of Maharastra: Office of the Commissioner of Labour; Iwahashi (1981); *Financial and Economic Annual of Japan* (various years).

Notes:
[a] Egypt.
[b] Iran.
[c] Rome.

together supply and demand. When a market is able, in case of a shortfall in either supply or demand, to sell the surplus elsewhere (or acquire the shortage in supply elsewhere) for example via storage, trade or changes in people's consumption patterns, the supply and demand relations are restored again at price levels not far from the standard levels.

Our measure of market performance is a derivative of the variance (i.e. volatility) of prices. The main difference with direct measures of volatility such as the coefficient of variation (CV) is that we correct for price variation factors that are independent of the working of the market. Examples of these factors may be the existence of a dual crop structure. For example, in large parts of present day China a rice harvest is produced twice a year. This will reduce price volatility since a crop failure in one harvest may partly be compensated by the second harvest. In a country like Indonesia, however, which only has one rice harvest a year, price volatility may be much higher during a crop failure. Since this kind of 'expected' volatility (or lack of volatility) occurs every year, it can be estimated and filtered out of the existing price volatility. This results in the so-called 'conditional' volatility which is, when possible, the measure used in this volume.

Using this measure of market performance (see Foldvari *et al.*, Chapter 2, this volume), we reported estimates (see Table 21.1) for a set of countries: western Europe (Italy, the Netherlands), Middle East (Iraq), fast-developing Japan and developing Thailand and India. The most persistent conclusion is that market performance increased all the way up to the second half of the twentieth century AD, suggesting improvements in the proximate factors of market performance (i.e. trade, storage, technology and consumption diversification) and, more importantly, in the ultimate factors (i.e. geography and institutions). Obviously, this varied by factor. The role of geography in particular became less important over time (Allen 2011). After all, trade in a vast continent such as India was much more difficult before railways made travel much faster and less costly (Bogart and Chaudhary 2012).

The same cannot be said about the role of institutions though. This is especially clear when one gauges the first half of the twentieth century AD. For many of the more developed countries this period is characterized by a deterioration of market performance. This was the period of the emergence of dirigiste communist countries, trade barriers and, more generally, deglobalization (e.g. Williamson 1998; Van Zanden *et al.*, forthcoming).

Another important phenomenon is the fast decline in volatility of price data in developing countries such as India and Thailand in the twentieth century AD, from levels comparable to western countries in the late Middle Ages to levels slightly above what is current in the developed world nowadays. This development, as always, is a combination of many factors such as the increasing focus on free trade and especially the green revolution in which governments, particularly in Asia, have sought to stimulate the introduction of new and high yielding varieties of grains (Hazell 2009).

Another way of looking at this is shown in Figure 21.1, in which we report the CV for the whole world. Even though, as pointed out before, the CV needs to be scaled down for predictable price volatility, if we take a short enough period (in the case of Figure 21.1 we calculated CVs over ten-year periods) we can avoid many of the problems associated with inflation and other forms of non-market-performance related volatility. Hence, even though perhaps slightly overestimated, the CVs reported in Figure 21.1 approximate the conditional variance we used as our measure of market performance. It is clear that, measured in this way, the average level of market performance is slightly below 0.3 while a similarly calculated measure for 91–82 BC Babylon, a period for which we have annual data, would be 0.77. This clearly shows the marked decrease in price volatility and the corresponding increase in marked performance even though this increase in performance seems to slow down in the past century.

If we look at the late twentieth century AD (see Figure 21.1) we may note some remarkable spikes in the development of what is otherwise a relatively stable market performance. The most remarkable peak in the volatility of the world wheat markets is around 1993 when economic turmoil combined with a tight supply, mainly because of failed harvests, created elevated price volatility. This took place mainly because of a reduction of the world stock of wheat, meaning that a failed harvest immediately, and strongly, increased prices while an abundant harvest had a strong price-lowering effect. The following economic growth and increased harvests due to some exceptionally wet years between 1999 and 2002 increased the stock and consequently reduced volatility. After 2001 we witness increased price volatility again. This latter rise, however, is less easy to explain and we cannot

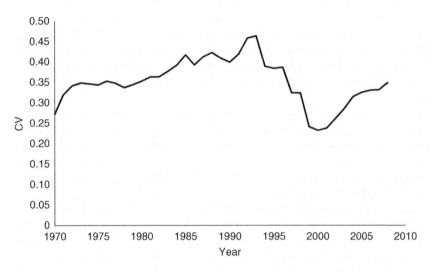

Figure 21.1 Rolling (ten-year) coefficient of variation[a] of average world producer wheat
       prices.

Source: Faostat.

Note:

[a] Calculated for ten-year periods, i.e. the CV for 1970 is calculated over the period 1966–74, for
   1971 over 1967–72, etc.

hope to do more than give a couple of explanations that have been proposed. Some
have argued that silver and gold, being commodities just as grain and oil are commodities, change in value depending on their demand and supply, meaning that
the fluctuations in the grain market, when paid in gold- or silver-based currencies,
may become more erratic during times of monetary instability. A second explanation is that supply or demand shocks resulted from the effects of one or more of
a number of events such as: recurring drought between 2003 and 2006 in major
grain producing regions; an increase in the use of biofuels (e.g. Kazinform 2008);
or an increasing demand from fast-growing countries like India and China (for a
similar line of reasoning see Walker 1982). It is unclear, however, which explanation carries most weight even though most researchers search for the explanation
as a structural change (such as increased consumption by India and China) and,
hence, a permanent increase in prices and low stocks. All this is, no doubt, exacerbated by bad policy. Examples are the indiscriminate lending policy both in
the stock markets and in the mortgage market that existed pre-2008 which chan-
nelled money away from investment in food production. The 2008 crisis caused
a big swing back again, re-channelling trillions of dollars in investment back into
food production, causing instability in the food market (on the big swing see, for
example, Barrows 1990; Weatherspoon *et al.*, 2001).

So far, we have sketched a pattern of market performance in which, even though
there were regional and temporal differences, the general trend was upwards.

Countries became increasingly well integrated, with increasingly more favourable institutional settings even though this was by no means a linear process.

At this point perhaps a brief word of warning is in order. After all, as pointed out by Foldvari and Van Leeuwen (Chapter 2, this volume), market performance is one way in which one may look at markets. There are other ways. For example, among economists, a popular concept of market efficiency is one in which markets are considered efficient when people are unable to outperform the market because all available evidence is commonly known and already incorporated in current prices. In econometric terms, markets are weakly efficient once there is a random walk in the price data, i.e. rising prices do not necessarily predict even more rising prices in the near future, since part of the causes of the present high prices are already apparent in the current prices. Consequently, when a deviation of prices occurs, prices always tend to go back to their initial values. Simply said, this means that the best prediction of current prices is to use past prices. If this happens we speak of 'weakly' efficient markets.[3] If the prices are not established at random, we have an inefficient market, or no market at all, so that commodity prices are driven above or below their true value. In that case we see market crashes or upward spikes, whose existence and magnitude are seemingly incompatible with an efficient market.

The question is whether market performance and market efficiency are in practice related. As shown by Foldvari and Van Leeuwen (Chapter 2, this volume),

Table 21.2 Market efficiency[a]

	Babylon barley	Tuscany barley	Groningen winter barley	Thailand rice
385–200 BC	−0.36 (−2.37)[b]			
199–60 BC	−0.40 (−3.96)			
1264–1350		−0.57 (−4.17)		
1351–1500		−0.42 (−6.15)		
1501–1850		−0.29 (−5.82)		
1851–1900			−0.48 (−5.29)	−0.59 (−3.15)
1901–1940			−0.23 (−1.75)	−0.42 (−2.37)
1950–2000			−0.29 (−2.30)	−0.85 (−4.10)

Source: Van Leeuwen *et al.* (Chapter 20, this volume); Ingram (1964); Tijms (2000).
Notes:
[a] Equation used is $\Delta \ln p_t = \beta_0 + \beta_1 \ln p_{t-1} + \beta_2 trend_t + e_t$.
[b] *t*-values in parentheses (i.e. the error margins of the coefficient, which should not be below −1.67).

the more efficient a market is, the higher unconditional volatility gets (please note that we refer here to total price volatility rather than conditional price volatility which we use as our measure of market performance). This is logical since, with a random walk, price volatility grows to infinity the longer the data series becomes. However, once one calculates conditional volatility, which removes possible trends in the prices and the inflation of variance due to non-stationarity, market performance and market efficiency should be uncorrelated.

The result for a test of market efficiency is provided in Table 21.2. This is measured using a unit root test in which we calculate whether a series is a random walk (i.e. people are unable to outperform the market based on past price evidence).

The results shown in Table 21.2 can be interpreted to mean that a coefficient closer to zero indicates a higher market efficiency, since this implies that next year's prices are not statistically significant different from this year's prices. The important point to stress is that there is no conclusive evidence of improving market efficiency between Babylonian times and the present. In other words, then and now markets have comparable levels of 'weak' efficiency. Apparently, despite all information coming to us via modern communication technology such as the Internet, people are just as unable nowadays to outsmart the market of primary products as they were in Babylonian times 600 BC. One might adduce here a famous dictum by John Kenneth Galbraith: 'The only function of economic forecasting is to make astrology look respectable.' The ancient Babylonians found astrology respectable, as they made their databases of prices and celestial observations exactly with the aim to be able to predict prices.

Conclusion

What can we learn from this historical study that might help our understanding of the present economic situation? The answer must be (as is so often the case in results of scholarship) a little ambiguous. On the one hand we see that at all times market performance, and hence welfare and prosperity, profits from good conditions for marketing products. This can work as a result of the influence of moderately interventionist institutions (such as governments), for example via free trade: this helps market integration and furthers the efficient distribution of goods and satisfying needs (see for this especially Chapter 4, this volume by Karl Gunnar Persson). On the other hand we have had to conclude that markets never function in a void, that they are part of a societal structure which requires active institutions and that, consequently, true free markets do not exist and will not exist. Nor would their existence be a desirable state of affairs.

Markets perform well when they are able to redress exogenous shocks – that is, the effect of unexpected events, such as wars, droughts and plagues (Foldvari and Van Leeuwen 2011). Factors that enhance a market's capability of dealing with such shocks are trade, storage, technology and diversification of consumption. These factors can work well when markets are able to redress these shocks in well-organized societies, with a safe legal system, a stable government, well-maintained public transport, welfare provisions (see for example the corn supply in

Ancient Rome) and well-directed government investments. We have seen that even investments that were not specifically intended for the improvement of economic performance inadvertently did so (as the stationing of Roman armies at the frontiers). Thus the performance of the economy fares well under a well-performing market in a well-organized society. It is the result of a delicate balance between freedom of exchange and formalizing and facilitating institutions.

Notes

1 http://depts.washington.edu/silkroad/texts/hhshu/notes8.html
2 There is some discussion on this topic with the California school headed by Pomeranz arguing for an increase in output and trade until the mid-Qing period. However, urbanization seems to be on the decline from the mid-Ming period, as well as wages going down, and decentralization of markets in small market towns.
3 A distinction can also be made between weakly and strongly efficient. The former is the case when a person only has access to last year's prices and is unable to predict this year's prices. The latter is the case when a person also has additional sources of price information at his or her disposal.

Bibliography

Allen, R. C. 2011. *Global Economic History: A Very Short Introduction*, Oxford: Oxford University Press.

Allen, R. C. and Unger, R. W., *Allen–Unger Global Commodity Prices Database*, www.history.ubc.ca/faculty/unger/ECPdb/index.html (accessed 7 June 2013).

Baker, H. D. and Jursa, M., eds. Forthcoming. *Documentary Sources in Ancient Near Eastern and Greco-Roman History: Methodology and Practice*, Oxford: Oxbow Books.

Barrows, R. 1990. 'Land Tenure and Investment in African Agriculture: Theory and Evidence', *The Journal of Modern African Studies*, 20: 265–97.

Bogart, D. and Chaudhary, L. 2012. 'Railways in Colonial India: An Economic Achievement?', available at SSRN: http://ssrn.com/abstract=2073256 (accessed September 2013).

Broadberry, S., Campbell, B., Klein, A., Overton, M. and Van Leeuwen, B. 2014. Forthcoming. *British GDP c. 1270–1870*, Cambridge: Cambridge University Press.

Broadberry, S., Hanhui Guan and Li, David Daokui. 2012. 'China, Europe and the Great Divergence: a Study in Historical National Accounting', paper presented at the Asian Historical Economics Conference, 13–15 September 2012, Hitotsubashi University Tokyo.

Fairchilds, C. 1993. 'Review: Consumption in Early Modern Europe. A Review Article,' *Comparative Studies in Society and History*, 35: 850–8.

Faostat, *Food and Agricultural Organization, Faostat: prices*; available at http://faostat.fao.org/site/291/default.aspx (accessed 8 June 2013).

Federico, G. 2012. 'How Much Do we Know About Market Integration in Europe?', *Economic History Review*, 65: 470–97.

Financial and Economic Annual of Japan, Tokyo: Dept. of Finance GPO, various years.

Foldvari, P. and Van Leeuwen, B. 2011. 'What Can Price Volatility Tell Us About Market Related Institutions? Conditional Heteroscedasticity in Historical Commodity Price Series,' *Cliometrica*, 5: 165–86.

Greif, A. 1989. 'Reputation and Coalitions in Medieval Trade: Evidence on the Maghribi Traders', *Journal of Economic History*, 49: 857–82.

Hazell, P. B. R. 2009. 'The Asian Green Revolution', *IFPRI Discussion Paper* (Intl Food Policy Res Inst).

Hopkins, K. 1980. 'Taxes and Trade in the Roman Empire (200 B.C.–A.D. 400)', *Journal of Roman Studies*, 70: 101–25.

Ingram, J. C. 1964. 'Thailand's Rice Trade and the Allocation of Resources', in *The Economic Development of Southeast Asia*, edited by C. D. Cowan, London: George Allen and Unwin: 102–26.

Iwahashi, M. 1981. *Kinsei Nippon Bukka-shi no Kenkyu, Tokyo Ohara Shinseisha* (A Study of the History of Price in Early Modern Japan); downloaded from www.iisg.nl/hpw. (Last accessed July 2013.)

Jursa, M. 2014. 'Factor Markets in Babylonia from the Late Seventh to the Third Century BCE', *Journal of the Economic and Social History of the Orient*, 57(2): 173–202.

Kazinform. 2008. 'Biofuels Major Cause of Global Food Riots', *Kazinform* (Kazakhstan National Information Agency), 11 April 2008.

Kleber, K. 2012. 'Famine in Babylonia. a Microhistorical Approach to an Agricultural Crisis in 528–526 BC', *Zeitschrift für Assyriologie*, 102: 219–44.

Labour gazette, Government of Maharastra: Office of the Commissioner of Labour Bombay, vol. I 1921–vol. XVI (1937, no. 10).

Lin Xinglong. 2008. *Some Issues on Social Relief in Han Dynasty*, Xiamen University Doctoral Thesis, August, 2008. (林兴龙 (2008), 关于汉代社会救济的若干问题, 厦门大学博士学位论文).

Mauss, M. 1923–4 'Essai sur le don. Forme et raison de l'échange dans les sociétés archaïques', *L'Année Sociologique* NS 1: 30–180.

North, D. C. 1990. *Institutions, Institutional Change and Economic Performance*, Cambridge: Cambridge University Press.

North, D. C. and Thomas, R. P. 1973. *The Rise of the Western World, A New Economic History*, Cambridge: Cambridge University Press.

Persson, K. G. 1999. *Grain Markets in Europe 1500–1900. Integration and Deregulation*, Cambridge: Cambridge University Press.

Studer, R. 2008. 'India and the Great Divergence: Assessing the Efficiency of Grain Markets in Eighteenth and Nineteenth Century India', *Journal of Economic History*, 68: 393–437.

Swann, N. 1950. *Food & Money in Ancient China: The Earliest Economic History of China to AD 25. Han Shu 24 with related texts, Han Shu 91 and Shih-Chi 129*, Princeton: Princeton University Press.

Tijms, W. 2000. *Groninger graanprijzen*, Groningen/Wageningen: Nederlands Agronomisch Historisch Instituut; available at www.rug.nl/let/onderzoek/onderzoekcentra/nahi/download.(Last accessed July 2013.)

Van der Spek, 2011. 'The "Silverization" of the Economy of the Achaemenid and Seleukid Empires and Early Modern China', in *The Economics of Hellenistic Societies, Third to First Centuries BC*, edited by Z. H. Archibald, J. K. Davies and V. Gabrielsen, Oxford: Oxford University Press: 402–20.

Van Zanden, J. L. and Van Leeuwen, B. 2012. 'Persistent But Not Consistent: the Growth of National Income in Holland 1347–1807', *Explorations in Economic History*, 49:119–30.

Van Zanden, J. L., Baten, J., Foldvari, P. and Van Leeuwen, B. Forthcoming. 'The Changing Shape of Global Inequality 1820–2000; Exploring a New Dataset', *Review of Income and Wealth*, forthcoming.

Veenhof, K. R. 1997. '"Modern" features in Old Assyrian trade', *Journal of the Economic and Social History of the Orient*, 40: 336–66.

Walker, K. R. 1982. 'Interpreting Chinese Grain Consumption Statistics', *The China Quarterly*, 92: 575–88.

Weatherspoon, D., Cacho, J. and Christy, R. 2001. 'Linking Globalization, Economic Growth and Poverty: Impacts of Agribusiness Strategies on Sub-Saharan Africa', *American Journal of Agricultural Economics*, 83: 722–29.

Williamson, J. G. 1998. 'Globalization, Labor Markets, and Policy Backlash in the Past', *Journal of Economic Perspectives*, 12: 51–72.

Appendix: Monthly prices in Babylon (grams of silver per 100 litres and per mina (0.5 kg))

Year BC	Month	Barley Grams silver/ 100 litres	Dates Grams silver/ 100 litres	Cuscuta Grams silver/ 100 litres	Cress Grams silver/ 100 litres	Sesame Grams silver/ 100 litres	Wool Grams silver per mina (0.5 kg)
582	12	5.78					
581	11	4.63					
575	10	4.05					
572	5	10.62					
567	?		3.47				
566	10	4.33					
566	11	4.63					
563	6		2.24				
554	?		2.78				
553	4		3.47				
549	2		2.31				
539	4		4.63				
528	11		3.09				
506	1	25.24					
500	8	46.28					
498	?	29.55					
464	8					138.83	
464	9					138.83	
453	1	48.59	17.35	5.79		104.13	
453	2	50.09	17.35	5.79		104.13	
434	12		9.26				4.17
429	9	8.33					

(Continued)

Year BC	Month	Barley Grams silver/ 100 litres	Dates Grams silver/ 100 litres	Cuscuta Grams silver/ 100 litres	Cress Grams silver/ 100 litres	Sesame Grams silver/ 100 litres	Wool Grams silver per mina (0.5 kg)
429	1						3.79
426	1		9.26				
425	11		13.88				4.17
424	3						
422	9		9.26				
422	10		9.26				
421	10		6.94				
420	2	18.54					
385	12	29.82	14.61				
383	5		9.58	19.83	39.57	111.07	
383	6		8.98	19.83	39.57	111.07	
382	4	25.65					
382	5	23.14					
382	6	18.93	7.79	12.62			4.17
382	7	18.93	7.31	12.62			4.17
382	8					55.53	
382	9	19.83		3.47			
381	12	8.68					4.17
380	1	8.68					4.17
379	2	11.27	9.26				
379	3	10.68					
379	9					55.53	4.17

Year BC	Month	Barley Grams silver/ 100 litres	Dates Grams silver/ 100 litres	Cuscuta Grams silver/ 100 litres	Cress Grams silver/ 100 litres	Sesame Grams silver/ 100 litres	Wool Grams silver per mina (0.5 kg)
379	10	15.87				55.53	4.17
379	11	15.87					4.17
376	9	13.22					
376	10	12.60					
376	12	11.57				55.53	4.17
375	1	10.74				55.53	4.17
375	2	9.92					
374	10		11.90				
374	11		13.88				
373	2		12.62				
373	3		12.62				
373	6			2.78	69.42	46.28	2.78
373	7			2.78	69.42	46.28	2.78
373	8		13.88				
373	9	21.36	13.88			37.02	2.78
373	10					37.02	2.78
373	12	25.24	9.92				
372	1	30.22	9.92				
372	4					11.57	
371	7		13.69				
371	8		13.22				
371	9	23.14	12.62				

(Continued)

Year BC	Month	Barley Grams silver/ 100 litres	Dates Grams silver/ 100 litres	Cuscuta Grams silver/ 100 litres	Cress Grams silver/ 100 litres	Sesame Grams silver/ 100 litres	Wool Grams silver per mina (0.5 kg)
371	10	23.14	13.52	4.63	138.83		
371	11			4.63	138.83		
370	3	8.41					
370	4	8.41					
369	3	13.88	10.68				
369	4	12.83	10.68				
369	5			7.71			
369	6		10.68	7.71	39.67	83.30	
369	7		10.32		39.67	83.30	
368	5				34.71		
367	4		13.88			79.33	
367	5		13.88				
367	7			2.78	39.67	39.67	
367	8	21.36	13.18	2.57	39.67	39.67	
367	9	21.36	13.22	2.70	34.71	46.28	
367	10	21.36		3.09	34.71	46.28	
367	12	8.03		1.16	19.83		1.67
347	1	7.21	5.56	1.09	18.52	23.14	1.67
346	2	7.12	5.71	1.16	17.35	23.14	1.67
346	3	9.26	6.08	0.78	14.00	27.61	1.67
344	12				9.26	19.83	1.04
343	1		2.78		9.26	19.83	1.04

Year BC	Month	Barley Grams silver/ 100 litres	Dates Grams silver/ 100 litres	Cuscuta Grams silver/ 100 litres	Cress Grams silver/ 100 litres	Sesame Grams silver/ 100 litres	Wool Grams silver per mina (0.5 kg)
343	2		2.78				
343	7		3.35				
343	8		3.35				
339	4				11.57		
339	5				10.07		
334	5		3.16				
334	6		3.16				
334	7		3.23	0.85			
334	8		3.23	0.85			
333	8					27.77	1.39
333	9	6.04	4.96				
333	10	5.79			13.88	23.14	1.39
333	11	5.65		1.16	13.88	23.14	1.39
331	9		4.63	1.49		23.14	1.67
331	10		4.63	1.16		23.14	1.67
329	3	11.57					
329	4	11.57					
329	8		13.22	2.31	34.71		
329	9	16.33	14.31	2.31	34.71		
329	10		15.64				
329	12		9.80				
325	4		19.83	1.54			

(Continued)

Year BC	Month	Barley Grams silver/ 100 litres	Dates Grams silver/ 100 litres	Cuscuta Grams silver/ 100 litres	Cress Grams silver/ 100 litres	Sesame Grams silver/ 100 litres	Wool Grams silver per mina (0.5 kg)
325	5	37.49	21.90	1.54	46.28		4.17
325	6	17.92	19.83		46.28		4.17
325	7	18.92	21.36				4.17
325	8	21.42	21.36				
325	9	23.14	20.32	4.11			
323	5	14.61			83.30	238.00	
323	6	26.65			83.30	238.00	
323	7						
323	12				34.71	138.83	8.33
322	1	67.41	32.34	6.31	34.71	138.83	8.33
322	2	64.71	29.84	4.81	87.93	138.83	8.33
322	3	61.70	35.27	4.63	69.42	138.83	8.33
322	4		40.53	4.63	69.42	138.83	
322	5		42.72	4.63	69.42	138.83	
322	7				69.42	138.83	8.33
322	8		34.71	6.94	67.92	138.83	8.33
322	9	69.42	36.96	6.94	46.28	138.83	8.33
310	8		32.04	4.63			8.33
310	9		37.73	4.63			6.54
310	10						8.33
309	4	85.21					8.33
309	5	61.70					8.33

Year BC	Month	Barley Grams silver/ 100 litres	Dates Grams silver/ 100 litres	Cuscuta Grams silver/ 100 litres	Cress Grams silver/ 100 litres	Sesame Grams silver/ 100 litres	Wool Grams silver per mina (0.5 kg)
309	8	92.56	59.81				
309	9	80.99	54.58				
309	10	59.50	49.00				
308	7	57.45					
308	8	60.46					
301	10		13.88	17.35	55.53	69.42	5.55
301	11		13.88	17.35	55.53	69.42	5.55
300	2	14.88				46.28	3.58
300	3					46.28	3.58
295	4	5.55	11.57				
295	5	5.55					
294	4	3.97				104.13	
294	5	3.97				104.13	
294	7	3.86					
294	8	3.98					
292	4				27.77	19.83	5.55
292	5	4.63	6.61	3.47	27.77	19.83	5.55
292	6	4.63	6.62	3.47	27.77	19.83	5.55
292	7	4.63	6.94	3.47	26.42	19.83	4.17
292	8				13.88		4.17
290	5	9.07	10.33				4.17
290	6	8.17	10.68				

(Continued)

Year BC	Month	Barley Grams silver/ 100 litres	Dates Grams silver/ 100 litres	Cuscuta Grams silver/ 100 litres	Cress Grams silver/ 100 litres	Sesame Grams silver/ 100 litres	Wool Grams silver per mina (0.5 kg)
290	7	9.29					3.33
290	8	9.83					3.33
290	9	9.92					
289	3	7.50					
289	4	7.39					
289	5	6.31					
289	6	7.31					
289	7	7.31					
289	9		9.26		23.14	69.42	2.78
289	10		9.26		23.14	69.42	2.78
289	11		8.17				
289	12	7.31	7.81				
288	1	7.05	7.03				
288	2	6.94	6.80				
288	3	6.94	6.61	3.65	12.62	46.28	
288	4	6.94	6.17	3.70	17.53	44.12	
288	5	6.94	6.17	3.75	23.14	41.65	
288	6	6.94	6.25				
288	7	6.94	6.31				
288	8						
287	9	6.94	10.28	2.31	39.67	30.85	
287	10	6.97	10.28	2.31	39.67	30.85	

Year BC	Month	Barley Grams silver/ 100 litres	Dates Grams silver/ 100 litres	Cuscuta Grams silver/ 100 litres	Cress Grams silver/ 100 litres	Sesame Grams silver/ 100 litres	Wool Grams silver per mina (0.5 kg)
287	11	7.75	7.31				
287	12	9.13	7.36				
286	1	11.24	8.31				
286	2	9.12	9.26				
286	3	9.92	9.26				
286	4	10.04	9.26				
286	5	11.40	9.26				
286	6	13.73					
286	7	13.22					
286	10	23.14					
286	11	25.78					
286	12	26.71					
285	1	27.96					
285	2	30.85					
285	10		8.68		23.14	34.71	
285	11				23.14		
284	2	4.63					
284	3	4.63					
284	9		7.71	4.63	23.14	34.71	2.08
284	10		7.71	4.63	23.14	34.71	2.08
282	11	10.68					
282	12	26.11	11.57	3.09	30.85	27.77	

(Continued)

Year BC	Month	Barley Grams silver/ 100 litres	Dates Grams silver/ 100 litres	Cuscuta Grams silver/ 100 litres	Cress Grams silver/ 100 litres	Sesame Grams silver/ 100 litres	Wool Grams silver per mina (0.5 kg)
281	1	12.09	11.57	3.09	34.58	34.48	
279	12			6.19	19.83	69.42	2.78
278	1	5.34	11.57	6.94	19.83		2.78
278	2	5.34	11.57				
278	3	4.21	8.41				
278	4	4.21	8.57				
278	5	4.21	9.58				
278	6				11.57	55.53	
278	7				12.09	50.83	2.78
278	8	3.16	6.94	4.63	13.88	32.92	2.78
278	9	3.14	7.15	4.22	13.55	26.53	2.78
278	10	3.09	7.71	3.09	12.62	23.14	2.78
278	11	3.09	6.94	2.83	12.62		
278	12	3.09	6.94	2.31			
276	2	8.68	12.73				
276	3	8.68					
274	9				55.53		
274	10	23.14	11.57	6.94	94.72	39.67	1.67
274	11	23.14	11.57	6.94	104.13	39.67	1.67
274	12						1.67
273	2				104.13	55.53	2.08
273	3	23.14	9.26	6.94	104.13	55.53	2.08

Year BC	Month	Barley Grams silver/ 100 litres	Dates Grams silver/ 100 litres	Cuscuta Grams silver/ 100 litres	Cress Grams silver/ 100 litres	Sesame Grams silver/ 100 litres	Wool Grams silver per mina (0.5 kg)
273	4	23.14	9.26	6.94	104.13	55.53	
271	10	8.17	11.57				2.78
271	11	8.17	11.57				2.78
270	3	8.41	18.51				
267	7						2.38
267	8						2.38
267	10				15.43	39.67	2.38
267	11				15.43	39.67	2.38
266	10	11.03					
266	11	11.55					
266	12	11.33					
265	1	12.43					
265	4	14.29					
265	5	13.52					
265	6	9.37					
265	8						2.08
265	9				34.71	55.53	2.08
265	10	13.38			34.71	55.53	
265	11	15.68					
265	12	16.83					
264	4	18.51					
264	5	17.55					

(Continued)

Year BC	Month	Barley Grams silver/ 100 litres	Dates Grams silver/ 100 litres	Cuscuta Grams silver/ 100 litres	Cress Grams silver/ 100 litres	Sesame Grams silver/ 100 litres	Wool Grams silver per mina (0.5 kg)
262	9	4.96	10.28				
262	10	4.96	10.28				
262	11		5.55	3.09	25.24	19.83	
262	12		5.55	3.09	25.24	19.83	
261	3				26.03	19.83	2.38
261	4				26.03	19.83	2.38
261	9				34.71	23.14	16.66
261	10				34.71	23.14	16.66
260	12	9.26	7.31	3.69			
259	1	9.26	7.31	3.69			
258	4		15.87	4.17			
258	5		9.42	4.17			
258	6		6.72				
258	7				19.83	46.28	
258	8				19.83	46.28	
257	4						8.33
257	5						8.33
257	6	23.14	16.33	7.71			
257	7	23.14	16.33	7.71			
256	1	34.71	16.33				
256	2	34.71	17.28				
256	3	34.71	18.51	3.70	46.28	46.28	2.08

Year BC	Month	Barley Grams silver/ 100 litres	Dates Grams silver/ 100 litres	Cuscuta Grams silver/ 100 litres	Cress Grams silver/ 100 litres	Sesame Grams silver/ 100 litres	Wool Grams silver per mina (0.5 kg)
256	4	34.71	18.51	3.70	46.28	46.28	2.08
256	5	19.83	18.51	3.70	46.28	46.28	
256	7				46.28		2.08
256	8	19.83	13.88	4.63	46.28	34.71	2.08
256	9	19.83	12.88	4.63	50.29	34.71	2.21
256	10	19.83	11.57	4.63	55.53		2.38
255	12		13.88	3.09	39.67		
254	1		13.88	3.09	39.67	30.85	2.78
254	2			3.09	39.67	30.85	2.78
254	5	11.57	13.88				
254	6	11.57					
254	7	11.42					
254	8	9.18					
254	9	8.45		4.63	17.35	61.70	2.78
254	10	6.94		4.63	17.35	61.70	2.78
254	11	7.71					
254	12	7.71					
253	3			7.71	13.88		
253	4			7.71	12.79		
252	10	3.48	7.71	3.09	9.26	12.62	
252	11	3.52	7.71	3.09	9.26	12.62	

(Continued)

Year BC	Month	Barley Grams silver/ 100 litres	Dates Grams silver/ 100 litres	Cuscuta Grams silver/ 100 litres	Cress Grams silver/ 100 litres	Sesame Grams silver/ 100 litres	Wool Grams silver per mina (0.5 kg)
251	3			2.78	10.68	11.57	3.33
250	6				13.88	27.77	2.78
250	7				13.88	27.77	2.78
250	8	4.63					
250	9	4.63					
250	12						
249	1			2.31	13.88	27.77	2.78
249	2		6.94	2.06	13.88	27.77	2.78
249	3	7.54	7.30	1.88	13.88	27.77	
249	4	7.71	7.93	1.85	13.88	27.77	
248	9	18.51	6.94	1.85			
248	10	18.51	6.94	1.85			
248	12	5.55	6.17	1.54	8.17	23.14	1.67
247	1	5.94	6.17	1.54	8.17	23.14	1.67
247	2	6.31					1.67
247	3	4.09	7.31				
247	4	3.74	6.61				1.67
247	5	3.70	6.61				1.67
247	8					19.83	2.08
247	9	3.97	6.94	1.54	8.68		2.08
247	10	3.97	6.94	1.54	8.68		
246	4				11.57	23.14	1.67

Year BC	Month	Barley Grams silver/ 100 litres	Dates Grams silver/ 100 litres	Cuscuta Grams silver/ 100 litres	Cress Grams silver/ 100 litres	Sesame Grams silver/ 100 litres	Wool Grams silver per mina (0.5 kg)
246	5				11.57	23.14	1.67
246	8	3.23	6.17	2.10	8.68	23.14	
246	9	3.23	6.17	2.10			
242	1	4.08					2.38
242	2	4.08					2.38
242	5	3.70					
242	6	3.70					
241	8	13.88	9.26				
241	9	14.58	9.26				
241	10	18.51	9.92				
241	11		22.61	2.89	39.67	27.77	
241	12	17.35	12.04	2.90	34.71	30.85	
240	1	18.07	11.57	3.09	34.71	30.85	
240	2	20.95	11.57				
240	3	18.51	12.15				
238	6	6.74	11.57	3.47	13.88	104.13	2.08
238	7	6.17	11.57	3.43	13.88	104.13	2.08
238	8			3.10	15.43	92.56	
235	9	23.14	13.22	3.09	79.33	50.49	2.78
235	10	23.14	13.22	3.09	79.33	50.79	2.78
235	11					52.76	2.78
235	12					55.53	2.78

(Continued)

Year BC	Month	Barley Grams silver/ 100 litres	Dates Grams silver/ 100 litres	Cuscuta Grams silver/ 100 litres	Cress Grams silver/ 100 litres	Sesame Grams silver/ 100 litres	Wool Grams silver per mina (0.5 kg)
234	1	27.77					
234	2	27.77					
234	3						3.33
234	4						3.33
233	10	20.44			25.24	69.42	2.38
233	11	23.14	23.14	3.09	25.24	69.42	2.38
233	12	25.38	23.14	3.46	27.77	104.13	2.38
232	1	27.44	23.14		27.77	92.94	2.38
232	2	21.36			27.77	92.56	2.38
232	3			3.97	19.83	138.83	
231	4		7.71	4.63	10.68		
231	5		7.71	4.63	10.68		
231	9	5.05					
231	10	5.05					
229	1	4.21	7.71	4.63	11.57	23.14	
229	2	4.21	7.71	4.63	11.57	23.14	
227	5	8.03	8.68	3.09	17.35	31.05	
227	6	7.71	8.68	3.09	23.14	34.71	
226	6	6.94	8.68	4.63	18.66	34.71	1.67
226	7	6.46	8.68	4.63	11.57	34.71	1.67
226	8	6.17	8.68				1.67
222	1	11.42	6.94				

Year BC	Month	Barley Grams silver/ 100 litres	Dates Grams silver/ 100 litres	Cuscuta Grams silver/ 100 litres	Cress Grams silver/ 100 litres	Sesame Grams silver/ 100 litres	Wool Grams silver per mina (0.5 kg)
222	2	9.92	6.94				
222	12	7.43					
219	9	8.68	8.17				2.08
219	10	8.96	8.17				2.08
219	11						
213	12			2.31	19.83		
212	1			2.31	19.83		
212	9	6.61					
212	10	6.61					
211	6						2.08
211	7						2.08
211	8				11.57	61.70	2.08
210	4				11.57	37.02	2.38
210	5	4.63	7.71		11.57	37.02	2.38
210	6	4.84	7.71		11.57	39.67	2.08
210	7				11.57	39.67	2.08
210	8			1.88	11.57	34.71	2.38
210	9			1.88		34.71	2.38
209	8		5.34	1.98	13.22		
209	9		5.34	1.98	13.22		
208	4	17.35	6.61	2.04		18.51	
208	5	7.01	7.68	2.08		18.51	

(*Continued*)

Year BC	Month	Barley Grams silver/ 100 litres	Dates Grams silver/ 100 litres	Cuscuta Grams silver/ 100 litres	Cress Grams silver/ 100 litres	Sesame Grams silver/ 100 litres	Wool Grams silver per mina (0.5 kg)
208	8		5.34	2.10			
208	9	4.79	5.34	2.10			
205	3	3.86	2.31	1.54	19.83		
205	4	3.86	2.31	1.54	19.83		
204	11	5.34	3.71	1.54	9.92	30.85	2.38
204	12	5.34	4.18	1.54	9.92	30.85	2.38
203	4					30.85	2.08
203	5					30.85	2.08
203	8				9.26	34.71	2.08
203	9				9.26	34.71	2.08
203	10	3.72	3.43				
203	11	3.75	3.43				
202	1				8.68	39.67	2.08
202	2				8.68	39.67	2.08
198	10	5.79	3.09	3.09	8.17	23.14	2.08
198	11	5.79	3.09	3.03	11.00	23.14	2.08
198	12	5.55	3.09	3.02	11.57	23.14	2.08
197	1	5.55	3.09				
197	2	4.79	2.78	3.39	7.71	25.24	2.08
197	3	4.79		3.39	8.61	25.24	2.08
197	4				8.68	25.24	2.08
196	5						2.08

Year BC	Month	Barley Grams silver/ 100 litres	Dates Grams silver/ 100 litres	Cuscuta Grams silver/ 100 litres	Cress Grams silver/ 100 litres	Sesame Grams silver/ 100 litres	Wool Grams silver per mina (0.5 kg)
196	6		4.21	1.85	23.14	25.24	2.08
196	7		4.21	1.85	23.14	25.24	
196	12	11.15	4.08	1.96		27.77	2.08
195	1	9.99	4.08	1.96		27.77	2.08
195	5	7.71	4.63				
195	6	7.71	4.63				
195	7	7.71					
194	9	15.43	8.68	2.31	34.71		2.78
194	10	15.43	8.68	2.31	34.71	50.49	2.78
194	11			2.31	34.71	50.49	
194	12			2.31	34.71	50.49	
193	1	16.33		2.31	34.71	50.49	
193	2	15.89		2.31	13.88	52.06	
193	3			2.31	13.88	52.06	
192	8	6.94	6.04		15.43	39.67	
192	9	6.94	5.79	1.54	15.43	46.06	
192	10	8.17	4.63			27.77	2.78
192	11	8.17	4.63				
191	4	7.31	5.55	1.85	11.57		
191	5	7.31	5.55	1.85	11.37	25.24	
191	6	4.63	5.55	1.85	10.68	25.92	
191	7	4.63	5.55	1.85	13.88	27.77	

(*Continued*)

Year BC	Month	Barley Grams silver/ 100 litres	Dates Grams silver/ 100 litres	Cuscuta Grams silver/ 100 litres	Cress Grams silver/ 100 litres	Sesame Grams silver/ 100 litres	Wool Grams silver per mina (0.5 kg)
191	8		5.55	1.85	13.88		
190	2				15.43		
190	3				15.43		
190	5	2.89					
190	6	2.89					
190	10	3.09					
190	11	3.09					
188	10	2.14	1.46	0.93	6.94	12.62	
188	11	2.14	1.46	0.93	6.94	12.62	
187	3			0.93	7.71		1.67
187	4			0.93	7.71		1.67
187	12					34.71	
186	1		2.31	1.85	13.88	34.71	
186	2	5.34	2.31	2.31	13.88	30.85	1.67
186	3	6.65	2.49	2.31	13.88	30.85	1.67
185	2	9.92	5.14		17.35	34.71	2.08
185	3	9.92	5.14		17.35	34.71	2.08
184	5	6.31					2.08
184	6	6.87	5.55	1.54			2.08
184	7	8.20	7.36	1.54			
184	8	8.68	7.71				
183	1	7.71					

Year BC	Month	Barley Grams silver/ 100 litres	Dates Grams silver/ 100 litres	Cuscuta Grams silver/ 100 litres	Cress Grams silver/ 100 litres	Sesame Grams silver/ 100 litres	Wool Grams silver per mina (0.5 kg)
183	2	7.51					
183	4		3.86				
183	5	4.41	3.86				
183	9	3.86	2.57				
183	10	3.91	2.48	3.31	11.57	33.32	2.08
183	11	4.78	2.31	3.22	13.69	33.32	2.08
183	12		2.26	3.09	17.35	39.67	2.38
182	1	6.31	2.52	3.47	11.57	39.67	2.23
182	2	6.31	2.52	3.47	11.57	39.67	2.08
182	7	3.47	2.10	2.06		50.49	3.33
182	8	3.47	2.10	2.06		50.49	3.33
180	1					34.71	3.33
180	2	12.03	5.06	1.92	11.57	35.12	3.33
180	3	10.07	5.60	1.92	11.57	37.02	3.33
180	6	7.71			11.57		
180	7	8.06	5.79		11.57		
180	8	8.42	5.79				
180	11				13.88		
180	12				13.88		
179	2	8.68					
179	3	8.68					
179	8			1.41			

(Continued)

Year BC	Month	Barley Grams silver/ 100 litres	Dates Grams silver/ 100 litres	Cuscuta Grams silver/ 100 litres	Cress Grams silver/ 100 litres	Sesame Grams silver/ 100 litres	Wool Grams silver per mina (0.5 kg)
179	9			1.41			
178	3	10.46	4.91	1.85	13.88	46.28	
178	4	10.68	4.96	1.85	13.88	46.28	
178	12	13.02				27.77	
177	1	13.55	4.63			27.77	
177	8					39.67	
177	9				15.43		
177	10				15.43		
174	10				6.94		2.78
174	11	9.92	2.78	1.54	11.57	23.14	2.78
174	12	9.92	2.73	1.54	13.88	23.14	
173	1		2.52	1.54	13.88	23.14	
173	3			1.16		21.36	2.38
173	4			1.16		21.36	2.38
172	5						
172	6	9.26	3.86	1.38		29.75	2.08
172	7	9.16	3.86	1.66	11.57	30.85	2.08
172	8	7.05	3.76	1.52	11.57	30.85	2.08
172	9	9.20	3.31	1.85	11.57	31.76	
172	10					33.32	
171	3			1.32	7.71	27.77	
171	4		3.09	1.32	7.71	27.77	

Year BC	Month	Barley Grams silver/ 100 litres	Dates Grams silver/ 100 litres	Cuscuta Grams silver/ 100 litres	Cress Grams silver/ 100 litres	Sesame Grams silver/ 100 litres	Wool Grams silver per mina (0.5 kg)
171	5				9.26	34.71	1.85
171	6				9.65	37.68	1.85
171	7				9.92	31.99	2.08
171	8					32.69	1.79
171	9					34.71	1.67
171	10	5.34				23.14	1.85
171	11				8.68	20.60	1.85
171	12				8.68	19.83	1.85
170	3					34.71	1.85
170	4					34.71	1.85
170	10	4.96	1.71	1.54	9.92	16.33	1.51
170	11	4.71	1.72	1.54	9.92	16.33	1.51
170	12	4.63	1.76	1.54		16.33	1.54
169	1	4.63	1.96	1.73	9.26	15.43	1.67
169	2	3.93	1.90	2.11	9.26	15.43	1.67
169	3	4.06	2.12	1.54	8.97	17.35	1.67
169	4	3.31	2.26	1.16	8.03	17.99	1.58
169	5	3.47	2.31	1.16	7.71	19.15	1.39
169	6		2.31				1.39
169	7						
169	8	3.39	2.52	1.54	8.68	18.51	
169	9	3.35	2.30	1.54	9.30	19.17	1.39

(Continued)

Year BC	Month	Barley Grams silver/ 100 litres	Dates Grams silver/ 100 litres	Cuscuta Grams silver/ 100 litres	Cress Grams silver/ 100 litres	Sesame Grams silver/ 100 litres	Wool Grams silver per mina (0.5 kg)
169	10	3.31	2.20	1.54	9.92	19.83	1.39
169	11	3.97	1.95	1.38	9.92	20.86	1.67
169	12	4.08	1.98	1.38	9.92	21.36	1.67
166	8	2.24	1.24				
166	9	2.24	1.24				
165	5		1.98		13.88		
165	6				13.88		
165	10	2.28	3.97	1.16	19.83	20.85	2.08
164	2					19.83	
164	3				20.83	19.83	
164	4	8.68	5.14			21.36	2.08
164	5	8.68	5.47			24.47	2.08
164	10	12.07	2.67				
164	11	11.81	2.70				
164	12		2.88				
163	1	10.68	2.80	1.42	37.02	18.93	
163	2	9.71	2.75	1.42	37.02		
163	3	9.04	2.83				
162	4	8.68			19.83	37.02	1.67
162	5	5.87			19.83	37.02	1.67
162	8	6.51		1.16	17.35		
162	9			1.16	17.35		

Year BC	Month	Barley Grams silver/ 100 litres	Dates Grams silver/ 100 litres	Cuscuta Grams silver/ 100 litres	Cress Grams silver/ 100 litres	Sesame Grams silver/ 100 litres	Wool Grams silver per mina (0.5 kg)
162	10	6.51					
160	1		11.57	3.09			
160	2		11.57	3.09			
159	7	9.26	8.68	1.54	27.77	55.53	2.78
159	8	8.84	8.40	1.54	27.77	56.91	2.78
159	9	9.26	6.94	1.54	27.77		
158	7					23.14	3.33
158	8		4.27				3.33
157	4	5.61	1.74	3.26			
157	5		1.74	3.86			
157	8			2.31	11.57	23.14	
157	9			2.31	11.57		
157	11	6.76					
157	12	6.31					
156	2	6.31				23.14	3.70
156	3	6.67	2.30			24.66	3.70
156	6		2.31		17.35	32.04	4.17
156	7	8.68	2.31		17.35	32.04	4.17
155	8	15.94					
154	2	8.58	9.26				
154	3	8.96	9.26				
154	8						3.33

(Continued)

Year BC	Month	Barley Grams silver/ 100 litres	Dates Grams silver/ 100 litres	Cuscuta Grams silver/ 100 litres	Cress Grams silver/ 100 litres	Sesame Grams silver/ 100 litres	Wool Grams silver per mina (0.5 kg)
154	9						3.33
150	10				12.62	25.24	3.33
150	11				12.62		3.33
145	8	12.62	3.31				3.33
145	9	12.44	2.86			43.96	3.33
145	10	12.62	2.66	1.16	27.77	51.89	3.33
145	11		2.78	1.16	27.77	55.53	3.33
144	7		3.47		23.90	39.67	
144	8	9.92			23.14		
144	11	6.22					
144	12	6.31					
143	10	7.31					3.70
143	11	7.31					3.70
142	4	5.55					
142	5	4.65					
142	6	4.05					
141	4	5.46	1.78		16.02	34.71	3.33
141	5	6.13			16.02	34.71	3.33
141	7	4.96			16.33	33.32	3.33
141	8					33.32	3.33
141	10	7.94	1.97	3.09	21.36		3.33
141	11		1.93	3.09	21.36		

Year BC	Month	Barley Grams silver/ 100 litres	Dates Grams silver/ 100 litres	Cuscuta Grams silver/ 100 litres	Cress Grams silver/ 100 litres	Sesame Grams silver/ 100 litres	Wool Grams silver per mina (0.5 kg)
141	12	7.04	1.93	1.61	20.83	32.04	3.33
140	1	6.86	1.86	1.61	20.83	31.50	3.33
140	2	7.29	1.85	1.61	20.83	30.85	3.33
140	3	7.31					
139	7				23.14		
139	8	10.68			27.75		
139	9	10.68		1.10	42.19		
139	10	10.54	2.89		32.67	52.56	
139	11	14.07	3.31		41.65	55.53	
139	12	14.82	3.31	1.16	41.65	52.44	
138	1	15.43	2.89	1.16		53.90	
138	2	15.71	2.85		46.28	55.53	3.33
138	3	16.02	2.88		43.14		3.33
138	4	14.22	2.86		44.89	52.06	3.33
138	5	11.45	2.48	1.54	46.28	59.50	3.28
138	6	10.69		1.54		64.97	2.83
138	7	11.57	2.54		46.28	73.84	3.33
138	8	11.11	2.64	1.54	46.28	87.68	
138	9	11.53	2.62				
138	10	13.44					
138	11	15.17	2.69	1.65	18.84	41.65	4.76
138	12	16.65	2.78	1.41	10.41	96.15	4.21
137	1	15.71	2.52		83.30	92.56	3.91

(Continued)

Year BC	Month	Barley Grams silver/ 100 litres	Dates Grams silver/ 100 litres	Cuscuta Grams silver/ 100 litres	Cress Grams silver/ 100 litres	Sesame Grams silver/ 100 litres	Wool Grams silver per mina (0.5 kg)
137	2	16.33	4.03	1.16	119.00		
137	3	16.33	3.97	1.16	115.47		
137	4	19.83		1.16	76.03		4.17
137	5	19.58	4.35	1.54	59.50	104.13	4.17
137	6	19.83	4.22	1.54	56.94	104.13	4.17
137	7	17.43	5.14	1.50	45.23		4.17
137	8	16.67		1.32	41.65		
137	9	19.15			41.65		
137	10	16.02	2.89	2.01	41.65	55.53	
137	11	16.02	2.88	2.01		55.53	
137	12		2.78			49.00	
136	1	15.07	3.31	1.45		49.00	
136	2	16.04		1.16	32.67		
136	3	16.33		1.16	31.85	83.30	4.17
136	4			1.16	30.85	83.30	4.17
135	9	8.41					
135	10	8.50	2.78		13.88	55.53	4.17
134	1						4.17
134	2	8.17	2.03				4.17
134	3	8.17	1.97			52.06	4.17
134	10		2.22			52.06	
134	11		2.38				

Year BC	Month	Barley Grams silver/ 100 litres	Dates Grams silver/ 100 litres	Cuscuta Grams silver/ 100 litres	Cress Grams silver/ 100 litres	Sesame Grams silver/ 100 litres	Wool Grams silver per mina (0.5 kg)
133	1		2.65			34.71	4.99
133	2	7.51	3.22	1.54	10.48	36.20	4.99
133	3		3.23	1.54	10.48		
133	9	6.39	3.47	1.49	10.28	38.74	4.76
133	10	6.69	3.07	1.54	10.28	89.36	4.76
133	11	7.19	2.69	1.54	10.28	65.45	
133	12	7.93	3.09			39.67	
132	1		3.00				
132	2		2.89		10.41	41.65	
132	3	7.44	2.52	1.32	10.41	39.92	4.76
132	4	6.94	2.52	1.32	10.41	39.67	4.76
132	10		2.31				
132	11		2.31				
131	6		4.14				
131	7		3.94				8.33
131	8		3.61				8.33
131	11		2.60				
131	12		2.70				
130	2			0.91			
130	3	8.68	3.31	0.86			
130	4	7.71	3.31			34.71	
130	5	7.31	3.47			34.26	4.17

(Continued)

Year BC	Month	Barley Grams silver/ 100 litres	Dates Grams silver/ 100 litres	Cuscuta Grams silver/ 100 litres	Cress Grams silver/ 100 litres	Sesame Grams silver/ 100 litres	Wool Grams silver per mina (0.5 kg)
130	6	7.31				34.71	4.17
130	7	6.17			27.77	39.67	3.33
130	8					47.14	3.33
130	9	6.94	3.47	1.54			
130	10	6.94	3.47	1.54			
130	11		3.14				
130	12		3.16				
129	11		9.11				
128	11		10.89				
128	12		13.67				
127	5		46.28				
127	6	27.77	46.28				
127	7	27.77					
127	9	34.71					
127	10	34.71					
127	11		12.84			114.90	2.08
127	12		25.24				
126	1		55.53				
126	2		55.53				
126	3	37.79	13.88	1.16			
126	4	32.88	11.39	1.16		39.20	
126	5	31.75	11.48			39.20	

Year BC	Month	Barley Grams silver/ 100 litres	Dates Grams silver/ 100 litres	Cuscuta Grams silver/ 100 litres	Cress Grams silver/ 100 litres	Sesame Grams silver/ 100 litres	Wool Grams silver per mina (0.5 kg)
126	6	24.98	11.81			277.67	
126	7	26.25	11.94			213.07	
126	8	24.81	11.57			238.00	
126	9	30.67	11.57			262.31	
126	10	32.67	7.76			238.00	
126	11	33.42	10.11			222.13	
126	12	35.60	8.67			222.13	
125	1	37.02	6.61				
125	2	28.22	6.61				
125	3	28.63					
125	4		4.63				
125	5	12.65	4.48				
125	6	13.70	4.61				
125	7	19.92	4.85	3.74		208.25	
125	8	22.04	5.37	3.07	83.30	152.72	
125	9	32.34	7.71	2.95	83.30	92.56	
125	10	33.26	7.21			120.74	
125	11	22.61	7.32			208.25	
125	12	36.61	7.80			85.13	
124	1	45.30	11.15	1.34	69.42	93.45	8.33
124	2	55.04	9.64	1.34	69.42	111.12	11.77
124	3	49.00	12.64			125.58	12.43

(Continued)

Year BC	Month	Barley Grams silver/ 100 litres	Dates Grams silver/ 100 litres	Cuscuta Grams silver/ 100 litres	Cress Grams silver/ 100 litres	Sesame Grams silver/ 100 litres	Wool Grams silver per mina (0.5 kg)
124	4	43.84	11.11			107.60	
124	5	78.64					
124	6	28.94	16.02	1.32	39.67	82.17	
124	7	30.29	16.02	1.24	39.67	76.81	
124	8	24.14	16.57	1.54	55.53	74.04	
124	9		17.05	1.54			
124	10		8.41				
124	11	21.36	6.04				
124	12	20.52	6.09				
123	1	15.89	6.31				
123	2	12.07	6.24				
123	3	12.89	6.24				5.55
123	4					77.49	5.55
123	5	16.11	4.07				
123	6	9.26	3.33				
123	9		4.35			138.83	8.33
123	10	18.51	7.02			112.80	8.33
123	11	18.51	9.26				
123	12	19.19	6.17				
122	1	19.83	6.17				
122	3					98.00	
122	4	21.36					

Year BC	Month	Barley Grams silver/ 100 litres	Dates Grams silver/ 100 litres	Cuscuta Grams silver/ 100 litres	Cress Grams silver/ 100 litres	Sesame Grams silver/ 100 litres	Wool Grams silver per mina (0.5 kg)
122	5	21.36					
122	6			2.78			
122	7			2.78			
122	9	29.75					
122	10	29.75					
121	7		9.92	1.16	30.02		
121	8		9.92	1.16	30.02		
120	4	25.93	9.43		52.06	83.30	8.33
120	5	23.14	9.77		52.06	83.30	9.92
120	6	19.90	8.74			81.03	10.65
120	7	19.37	8.41			78.85	8.33
119	4	28.19	12.74	4.63			8.33
119	5	19.08	13.88	4.63			8.33
119	10	14.06	13.76	3.17	41.65	109.00	5.55
119	11	13.44	13.88	3.86		92.56	
118	11		4.87				
117	1		4.87				
117	2		4.98	1.85	35.45	49.00	
117	3		4.87	1.85	35.45	49.00	
113	10					46.28	
112	2						4.17
112	3						4.17

(*Continued*)

Year BC	Month	Barley Grams silver/ 100 litres	Dates Grams silver/ 100 litres	Cuscuta Grams silver/ 100 litres	Cress Grams silver/ 100 litres	Sesame Grams silver/ 100 litres	Wool Grams silver per mina (0.5 kg)
112	4		4.77		13.88	52.35	4.17
112	5	4.34	4.59		11.79	51.26	4.17
112	6	4.14	4.87		11.57		5.55
112	7	4.39				34.71	5.02
112	8					34.71	4.17
111	8			2.31	17.35		
111	9			2.31	20.32		
111	10				20.32		
110	10	10.41			23.14	46.28	4.17
110	11	10.41			23.14	46.28	4.17
109	4	6.94	9.26	2.31	17.35		
109	5		13.02	2.31	17.35	33.32	4.17
109	6					33.32	4.17
109	7	8.17	12.62	3.09			
109	8	8.17	12.62	3.09			
109	10				23.14	37.02	
109	11				23.14		
108	7	12.06			23.14	39.20	
108	8				23.14	39.20	
108	9						
108	10	15.80	10.10	2.31		50.49	4.17
108	11		8.58	2.31			4.17

Year BC	Month	Barley Grams silver/ 100 litres	Dates Grams silver/ 100 litres	Cuscuta Grams silver/ 100 litres	Cress Grams silver/ 100 litres	Sesame Grams silver/ 100 litres	Wool Grams silver per mina (0.5 kg)
108	12	30.85	9.01	2.31			
107	1		8.68				
107	2	22.19	8.67	2.31	49.00		
107	3	20.83	7.94	2.31	49.00		
106	4	16.97	10.41		51.26	116.73	4.17
106	5	13.05	10.41		42.49	107.92	4.17
106	6	10.98		3.56	27.77	88.74	
106	7			3.56	27.77	83.30	
106	8	10.28	14.25	3.70	34.71	103.32	4.76
106	9	10.44	13.02	4.35	42.81	94.63	5.31
106	10	10.28		4.63	38.07	87.68	5.55
106	11				34.71		
105	8	11.11	11.57			87.68	
105	9	11.11	12.62			87.68	
104	4			3.09	92.56		
104	5		10.02	3.09	92.56		
104	11					69.42	
104	12		11.11			69.42	
103	3	14.79					
103	4	14.19					
103	5	13.76					
103	6	13.88					

(Continued)

Year BC	Month	Barley Grams silver/ 100 litres	Dates Grams silver/ 100 litres	Cuscuta Grams silver/ 100 litres	Cress Grams silver/ 100 litres	Sesame Grams silver/ 100 litres	Wool Grams silver per mina (0.5 kg)
100	10		11.57				
100	11		11.57				
100	12	6.94			9.58	43.84	8.33
97	4	27.68					6.66
97	5	29.23					6.66
97	11	18.93		3.86	46.28		
97	12	18.93		3.86	49.71		
96	1					62.87	
96	2	25.15				63.37	
96	3		17.35	4.21	37.02		5.55
96	4		16.53	4.21	37.02		5.55
96	5	12.62				72.85	5.55
96	7	15.43				69.42	8.33
96	8	15.70				69.42	8.33
96	9	15.87				66.41	
95	4		9.26	3.86			
95	5	7.75	9.26	3.86		74.04	5.55
95	6	8.17				74.04	5.55
94	7	7.92	13.91	5.79	37.02	92.56	
94	8		14.82	5.79			
93	2	9.26					
93	3	9.26					

Year BC	Month	Barley Grams silver/ 100 litres	Dates Grams silver/ 100 litres	Cuscuta Grams silver/ 100 litres	Cress Grams silver/ 100 litres	Sesame Grams silver/ 100 litres	Wool Grams silver per mina (0.5 kg)
93	4	9.26					
91	10	12.34	19.51			73.26	5.55
91	11	12.34	20.29			70.30	5.55
91	12	15.90	20.28		34.71	86.02	5.55
90	1	14.67	20.83	2.31	34.71	79.33	
90	2	12.82		2.31			
89	11					111.07	
89	12	37.02		3.86		111.07	
88	1	37.02		3.86			
88	3	34.71	16.18				8.33
88	4	34.71	16.18				8.33
88	8		17.29				
88	9		18.11		34.71	154.54	8.33
88	10				34.71		8.33
87	1					162.73	
87	2	32.35	24.90	4.21		166.60	8.33
87	3	32.43	28.48	4.45			8.33
87	4	32.84	32.35	4.63			
87	5	20.83		4.63	55.53		
87	6			4.63	55.53		
87	10		27.77	4.63			12.43
87	11	24.24		4.63			12.43

(Continued)

Year BC	Month	Barley Grams silver/ 100 litres	Dates Grams silver/ 100 litres	Cuscuta Grams silver/ 100 litres	Cress Grams silver/ 100 litres	Sesame Grams silver/ 100 litres	Wool Grams silver per mina (0.5 kg)
87	12	23.14					12.43
86	5	17.35					
86	8	16.66	14.74			87.68	12.43
86	9	13.07	14.74			87.68	12.43
86	12	12.92	17.87			92.56	
85	1	12.34	16.60			103.98	
85	2	12.48	17.91				
85	3		18.09				
84	6	27.84	24.32				
84	7	28.61	25.02				
84	8		25.24				
83	4	149.13	43.84	3.09			12.43
83	9	69.42			111.07	111.07	8.33
83	10			3.09	111.07	111.07	8.33
83	12	46.28	17.00	3.09			
82	1	45.26	15.60				
82	3		16.18				
82	4	26.56					
80	4						12.43
80	5					98.00	12.43
80	8		18.51	4.63			
80	9		18.51	4.63		83.30	

Year BC	Month	Barley Grams silver/ 100 litres	Dates Grams silver/ 100 litres	Cuscuta Grams silver/ 100 litres	Cress Grams silver/ 100 litres	Sesame Grams silver/ 100 litres	Wool Grams silver per mina (0.5 kg)
79	9	20.04	16.66				
79	10	20.83	16.66				
78	4			2.95	138.83	119.00	12.43
78	5	18.11	16.83	3.06	138.83	114.59	12.43
78	6	18.62	16.75	3.09	92.56	105.48	12.43
78	7	21.07	16.50	4.63	109.87	107.48	12.43
78	8	20.83	16.20	4.63	111.07	107.48	12.43
78	9	20.83	16.18	4.63	143.88	138.83	12.43
78	10		18.01			137.60	12.43
78	11		14.91				12.43
77	1	17.26	17.35	4.63	158.67		
77	2	17.26	18.26	4.63	158.67		
76	12	18.51					
75	1	18.51					
74	6		17.00				11.11
74	7						11.11
73	11		12.34	3.09			
73	12		12.34	3.09			
63	4			4.85			
63	5			4.85			
61	10	25.84					
61	11		20.48				

Index

Printed in Great Britain
by Amazon

44314299R00342